ISSUE LABEL

FIVE HUNDRED YEARS
A HISTORY OF SOUTH AFRICA

A. J. BÖESEKEN
M.A., D.Phil., Editor in Chief, Archives Publications, Cape Town

A. M. DAVEY
M.A., Senior Lecturer in History, University of Cape Town

W. J. DE KOCK
M.A., B.Ed., D.Phil., Editor in Chief, Dictionary of South
African Biography, Cape Town, formerly Professor of History,
University College of the Western Cape

J. S. DU PLESSIS
M.A., D.Litt., Professor of History,
Potchefstroom University for C.H.E.

C. R. KOTZE
M.A., D.Phil., Professor of History,
University College of the Western Cape

B. J. LIEBENBERG
M.A., Drs.Hist., Senior Lecturer in History,
University of South Africa, Pretoria

C. F. J. MULLER
M.A., D.Phil., Professor of History,
University of South Africa, Pretoria

P. L. SCHOLTZ
M.A., D.Litt. et Phil., Senior Lecturer,
Teachers Training College, Graaff-Reinet

S. B. SPIES
M.A., Senior Lecturer in History,
University of South Africa, Pretoria

M. C. E. VAN SCHOOR
M.A., M.Ed., D.Litt., Professor of History,
University of the Orange Free State, Bloemfontein

M. C. VAN ZYL
M.A., D.Phil., Senior Lecturer in History,
University of South Africa, Pretoria

D. ZIERVOGEL
M.A., D.Phil., Professor of Bantu Languages,
University of South Africa, Pretoria

Five Hundred Years
A History of South Africa

EDITED BY

C. F. J. MULLER, M.A., D.PHIL.,

PROFESSOR OF HISTORY,

UNIVERSITY OF SOUTH AFRICA,

PRETORIA

ACADEMICA 1969

PRETORIA AND CAPE TOWN

ERRATA

A few lines of the type on page 101 have been pied during imposition. The following corrections are therefore necessary:

Line 22 : for eaffairs read affairs

    23   ,, action   ,,   reaction

    27   ,, poitics   ,,   politics

    28   ,, cominlg   ,,   coming

Contents

List of Maps

Introduction

During momentous periods of man's history, when each day opens up new prospects before him, he usually experiences an irresistible urge to look back to the past, for the past is apparently the one constant factor in his changing world and its study may enable him to come to terms with his environment. Man looks to the past to provide him with understanding of the present, and the foundations on which his future must rest.

During periods of radical change in South Africa such as 1795 – 1815, 1834 – 1854 and 1881 – 1910, there was a strong tendency to look back to the past. Once again we find ourselves in turbulent times. The task of the professional historian in the late sixties of the 20th century is to reinterpret man's past in the light of the new and more detailed findings of recent research.

The modern South African historian has an advantage over his predecessors in that research has provided him with data which was not previously available; on the other hand, his task has been complicated by the turmoil of the times in which he is living and more particularly, by the possibility of radical changes occurring in his society. As always in times of transition, it is sometimes difficult to view matters objectively. Such times also tend to produce emotional reactions particularly when the changes seem to contain great advantages for some and great disadvantages for others. Major problems create the desire in man to find satisfactory and enduring solutions. Obviously few historians, either in or outside the Republic of South Africa, can detach themselves entirely from the influence of contemporary events. Advocates of positive action are not always the most satisfactory scientific analysers of a past which is inextricably linked with the present. The closer the period under discussion approaches the present the more difficult it is for the historian to write objective history.

This book recounts the activities and experiences, over a period of nearly five hundred years of the White man in South Africa. First he discovered, explored and settled the Cape Peninsula; then he occupied the wide plateaus of the southern African interior, defeating and partially subjugating its non-White indigenous inhabitants and, as a Boer, withdrawing from European control. The English-speaking South African, as trader, entrepreneur, mining magnate and industrialist, developed and marketed South Africa's natural resources. The Second Anglo-Boer War focussed the attention of the world on the republican Boer. Simultaneously he was becoming part of a closely-knit nationalistic unit; this tended to intensify the conflict between the Boer and his English-speaking fellow-citizen of southern Africa. After the formation of the Union of South Africa, the attempts made by the supporters of the republican ideal to withdraw from the British Empire and from the Commonwealth of Nations tended further to estrange the English-speaking minority in South Africa from those who spoke.

Afrikaans. Mainly as a result of its prolonged domestic struggles the white population of South Africa has remained small, especially as compared to that of the non-Whites. As the South African mining and secondary industries developed during the 20th century, it was increasingly the non-Whites of southern Africa, and also of central Africa, who did the unskilled and semi-skilled work of the new white economy: South Africa did not attract white immigrants consistently or in any appreciable numbers. By the sixties South Africa had become a white power in a black continent; she was guided by white intellect and enterprise but for a long time had been dependent on non-white labour.

Whereas South Africa was once preoccupied with the question of white leadership within her borders, her main concern now is whether less than four million white South Africans can maintain their supremacy against the more than 300 million black inhabitants of Africa who are supported by many other nations. How did the few South African Whites acquire their power, and consequently become so important on the continent of Africa and in the international sphere? The concluding chapter of this book attempts to answer these questions.

In Modern History there are few countries which present the historian with such a challenge as does South Africa. Its strategic position in a southern hemisphere poorly endowed with land bases, its mineral wealth, the antiquity of its indigenous inhabitants, the initiative and determination of its white settlers, the conflict and interaction between the many attempts, both domestic and foreign to solve its many problems too tardily and with insufficient zeal in the early period and later too hastily and too ambitiously—all these aspects, and also the increasing world tension concerning South Africa, contribute to an intense and sustained drama. South Africa's history has been by no means fully told: her historians are too few and the field is too large. Too many historians are still busy with specialized studies. This book is an attempt by a group of mainly the younger historians to tell South Africa's story within reasonable limits and in broad outline, in the light of the most recent research to which in most cases they themselves have contributed. In this account of South Africa's history the White man occupies the central position. An anthropologist has described something of the ethnological past of South Africa's non-White tribes in Appendix I, but the almost five centuries of white interest, influence and control in South Africa have received most attention. For the history of these five centuries we have incomparably more reliable sources than for all the centuries before the Portuguese discoveries. Naturally the history of South Africa did not begin with the advent of the White man and the non-Whites have played an extremely significant role in South Africa's development. Nevertheless, reliable factual records in exact chronological focus concerning the Bantu, Hottentots and Bushmen are too scarce for an authoritative history of the non-White to be written at this stage. It must also be recognized that during these centuries, and especially during the 19th and 20th centuries, the White man played, and is still playing a predominant role in the history of southern Africa.

xii

This mainly political history of southern Africa has been written for the student as well as for the general reader. More recent history has received most attention, whereas the history of the pre-nineteenth century period has been presented in broader outline. Considerably more than half the available space has been devoted to the period after the Great Trek, but the early developments which led up to the Great Trek have not been neglected.

I wish to thank all contributors sincerely: their prompt and enthusiastic co-operation, sometimes under difficult conditions, was most heartening. The advice received from many of them is also appreciated. However, I bear sole responsibility for the general presentation of this book. Each contributor is versed in his specific subject through original research or through lecturing in his particular field, or through doing both. I am well aware of the possible defects inherent in a joint undertaking of this nature where production has extended over a number of years. We tried to reduce defects to a minimum by arranging regular discussions with and between contributors, although each writer was allowed to determine his approach and emphasis for himself. I am responsible for the chapter divisions, the general arrangement and the continuity of the book as whole.

To retain an historical atmosphere, monetary units have been given in their contemporary form. In the table in Appendix II I provide modern equivalents.

Except for two chapters, the text presented here is a translation from the Afrikaans; but it is at the same time a revised, more up to date edition. Mr M. Boucher, Senior Lecturer in History at the University of South Africa, Pretoria, and Dr Edwin S. Munger, Professor of Geography at the California Institute of Technology, Pasadena, read a draft of Chapter 21. I am grateful for valuable suggestions, but am solely responsible for the chapter's final form.

Finally I should like to thank Mr P. J. Muller of H. & R. Academica (Pty.) Ltd. particularly for his whole-hearted co-operation over a period of almost five years.

PRETORIA,   C. F. J. MULLER
July, 1968

1. Explorers and Circumnavigators of the Cape

As culture developed in Western Europe and the centres of civilization around the Mediterranean sea, peoples began to trade their goods, in an attempt to get from others what could not be found at home. Some lacked salt or spices for their food, some iron for their weapons, some the ivory, amber, precious and semi-precious stones, gold, tin, bronze or silver, which they had learnt to use and by which they set great store.

Trade was the most important means of contact between the early communities, from Finland to Hellas, and from the Irish island to Egypt and Mesopotamia, the Land of the Two Rivers.

First movements towards the south

More than three thousand years before the first ship from Portugal was to reach the southern tip of the African continent, exploration of this gigantic continent had already begun, but nineteen centuries of the Christian era were to pass before Africa was completely known.

As far as can be determined from the earliest written records, the peoples of the Mediterranean world began to explore Africa, first along the Red Sea and then further southward along the east coast. The first Egyptian expeditions to the Land of Punt during the 15th century B.C. were followed by the expeditions of the Israelite King Solomon and Hiram of Tyre, which penetrated into Ophir, the land of gold, possibly modern Somalia.

It was once again a desire to trade which prompted the Semitic Phoenician people of Tyre and Sidon, the earliest among the seafaring nations, to move westward along the north coast of "Libya", past the great city of Carthage, and even beyond the Pillars of Hercules that guarded the western entrance to the Mediterranean Sea. Five centuries before the start of the Christian era Hanno the Carthaginian made an exceptional voyage: according to fairly convincing evidence, he advanced to approximately the innermost corner of the Gulf of Guinea. After this a silence of many centuries closed round attempts to explore the west coast of Africa.

This was the long twilight of geographical knowledge, when European contact with India, the East and the Land of Silk was sporadic, although the east coast of Africa, where black people lived, was known as far south as modern Dar-es-Salaam. An early outpost of Christendom, the secluded Ethiopian highlands, was well-known, and there were surmises concerning snow-capped Mountains of the Moon at the source of the Nile, in accordance with the theories of the second-century geographer Claudius Ptolemy. His geographical conjectures about unknown Africa were strangely enough still quoted with respect even two centuries after the first seafarers had sailed round the southernmost tip of the continent.

Europe remained ignorant about Africa longer than about the East and the regions around the Indian ocean. The great Arabian authors, Masudi, Idrisi and Ibn-Batuta, stirred imaginations with their descriptions of these distant lands. Marco Polo, the Italian who knew the court of Peking's ruler better than his own Venice, also described them in the book he wrote in 1299. But Africa's vastness was only lightly touched by the ancient caravan routes of its northern deserts, and by the voyages of a few Italian and Catalonian mariners who, before the 14th century, now and again ventured along the west coast into the Sea of Darkness and never returned.

The age during which Venice and other medieval Italian cities proudly increased their power, bringing the riches of the East with difficulty and at great expense through the gateways of Islam, was also the age of conflict between Christianity and Islam. At this time there also developed a picturesque confusion in the European mind concerning certain geographical facts. The legend of a Christian monarch, Prester John, became associated with distant Ethiopia, which mistakenly was thought to be the same as India.

This misconception gave birth to the ideal, held in 1415 by the pious Prince Henry of Portugal, of serving Christianity by sailing around the west coast of Africa to find the "India-in-Africa", land of the Prester King. Thus would be found wealth great as that of the enemies of the Christian faith, and a powerful ally in the struggle against the Sultan of Egypt and the Turkish menace.

The exploration of Africa's west coast as far as Sierra Leone was the life-work of the Infante Dom Henrique (1394 – 1460), third son of the Portuguese King João I. English historians later named him Henry the Navigator.

The Navigator undertook no voyage of discovery himself, but, from Lagos on the Portuguese south coast and later from his home at Sagres, equipped the expeditions that for forty-five years advanced southwards with varying success until the coast of the desert was passed, and the great western curve of Africa with its negro peoples and tropical climate was reached. Thus, at the time of his death, the Infante's ships had come to the beginning of the region south of the Senegal, still known today as Guiné (Guinea), a name probably derived from the ancient inland negro kingdom of Ghana.

The Infante's activity in Africa was essentially an isolated instance of exploration, instigated by an exceptional personality. He was dominated by a fanatical zeal to assist Christendom in its struggle against the infidel, and by a consuming interest in geography. These factors combined in this man of the Renaissance to produce a dedicated organiser of exploration.

After about half a century the Navigator's expeditions had neither reached "India" nor come across any proof of its existence. In the European mind the East was still connected with Ethiopia, and there is plausible contemporary evidence indicating that the advance along the west coast of Africa was still regarded as the search for a sea passage that would lead eastwards from Guinea along a "south coast" to India. There, it was thought, would be found a

Christian king who would be an ally against the Turks and have at his disposal an abundance of the oriental merchandise in which the West was interested.

Africa was pictured as a continent flattened at the south, so that it would be possible to sail from Guinea directly to Abyssinia. Contemporary thought did not recognize the possibility of having to circumnavigate a southern extremity of Africa, even after the return of Dias in 1488 from his first journey round the Cape.

The Prince's caravels had taken many years to cover only about a third of the distance to the Cape. Possibly he was never consciously searching for a route such as that eventually discovered by Da Gama. Whatever the case may be, his work on the theory and art of navigation, which ultimately resulted in the Portuguese becoming the first circumnavigators of Africa, was immensely significant.

What at first had been the work of an individual became, after 1460, the concern of the Portuguese monarchy, which established a valuable royal monopoly in the tropical products and slave trade of the Guinea coast, with its centre at Elmina on the coast of modern Ghana. Until 1481, however, there was little marked royal interest in the exploration of Africa, and during the reign of Alphonso V the Guinea trade was temporarily leased to Fernão Gomes, a businessman, on condition that he continued exploring the coast.

In this way the immense area inside the Gulf of Guinea became known and Gomes's ships advanced to just beyond the Equator, where the voyages of discovery halted.

During his reign João II became personally interested in the expeditions to Africa; at the same time the tropical trade with the coast of Guinea was developed further, and there were sporadic attempts to find the Prester King along an overland route from the Gulf of Guinea.

This interest in a passage through the interior was founded on complete ignorance of the vast distance between Guinea and Ethiopia; it was hoped that such a passage would provide an alternative to the voyages along the African west coast which seemed, discouragingly, to extend endlessly southwards of the equator.

The Portuguese south of the equator

The opening up of Africa's west coast from the equator to north of the present Swakopmund was accomplished between 1482 and 1486 during two voyages in the king's service of Diego Cão, a man of humble birth but of exceptional ability, a mercenary without rank or title, who was made a knight of the royal household after his first voyage. During this voyage Cão discovered the mouth of the mighty river (*Rio Poderoso*) which became known as the *Zaire*, and before long as the Congo River. Here, in April, 1483, he erected an inscribed *padrão* of rough limestone to commemorate the Portuguese visit and as a symbol of Christian contact with Africa. This was the first of four similar stone crosses that he was to erect on his voyages.

Cão did not return from his second voyage; he probably died near Cape

Cross, on the barren coast of the Kaokoveld in South-West Africa, where he left his fourth and last *padrão* early in 1486, nearly five hundred years ago. The information which his expedition brought back to the Tagus was not encouraging: south of the tropics there was another desert coast, and still no sign of the end of the continent. Nevertheless, there are indications that in the royal deliberations the circumnavigation of Africa had for the first time become an immediate objective, with the explicit aim of finding the "India" of Prester John, not necessarily the one of the spices.

The next move, therefore, was to make a double attempt to solve the mysteries of the route around Africa. Cão's work on the west coast was to be continued by an expedition led by Bartolomeu Dias de Novaes, and simultaneously there was to be a secret reconnaissance by two emissaries of João II. These, using Cairo as a base, were to penetrate the colourful world of Islam, and spy, amongst other things, on the sources, nature and extent of the Sultan's trade. While in the East they were to try to learn more about the priest king.

The secret reconnaissance by no means went according to plan, yet in time valuable information appeared in the report of Pero de Covilhã, one of the spies. He saw for himself not only the Indian coast of Malabar and the big Muslim trading-ports, but also the Arabs on the east coast of Africa and the black native population as far south as Sofala, on the latitude of modern Bulawayo. In addition, he learnt from the Arabs that it was possible to sail to the west from this east coast, but he was unaware that a short while before, within a thousand sea-miles of Sofala, his countryman Dias had had to turn his two small caravels back to Lisbon.

Bartolomeu Dias was an overseer at the royal Guinea warehouses in Lisbon. Little is known of his lfe, and in contemporary documents no mention is made of him or his connection with Africa. By 1481 he was already in charge of one of the ships in the first expedition to Guinea under the patronage of the new sovereign, João II, and on 10 October, 1486, he was given the caravel *S. Cristovão*, one of the little ships with which he was to sail for Africa the following year.

Apparently there was very little preparation for this voyage, which was to be of such significance in the history of the southernmost extremity of Africa. It is to be assumed that Dias, like Cão before him, had a mariner's compass and the same navigational instruments which had been used since the first of the Navigator's voyages, and with which, besides wind direction, degrees of latitude only could be ascertained. An astrolabe was used to determine latitude by observing the movement of the sun across the meridian at midday. At this time, around 1484, mathematicians, under orders from the Portuguese crown, were working systematically on improved declination tables of the sun's altitude for use south of the Equator, and more efficient astrolabes were being taken on the voyages to Africa.

It is from fragmentary data only, mainly from four Italian maps which appeared before 1502, and with difficulty, that the course of Dias's voyage can be ascertained. With his two caravels, each of approximately one hundred tons,

4

and a nameless little cargo-vessel, he left the Tagus in July or at the beginning of August, 1487, to return about December, 1488, after sixteen months and seventeen days. Except when he crossed the Gulf of Guinea, he hugged the coast of Africa.

From the first week of December, 1487, Dias sailed along the arid Namib coast of South-West Africa, and his progress can be determined chronologically because of his habit of naming places according to the festivals of saints in the Catholic calender.

After visiting the modern Walvis Bay, the caravels had by Christmas day entered the wide bay now known as Lüderitzbucht. They had left their supply-ship behind. The southward voyage continued as far as the Namaqualand coast, where European eyes saw for the first time in the misty interior the mountains that were later to be called the Pakhuisberg, Kapteinskloof and Cedarberg.

It must have been during the first week of the year 1488 that the Dias caravels, in the face of a strong south-easter, were deliberately taken off course – and not driven along by a storm, as traditionally was believed for a long time – for more than a thousand miles into the Atlantic Ocean by their pilot, Pero d'Alenquer. Then a southerly course was set along a latitude which took the ships past the unseen Cape, before they were swung northwards to reach land again.

The sight, during the first days of February, of the African coast west of Mossel Bay must have been a moment of triumph for Dias. At last, for the first time, south of the equator, the coast ran in a new direction, which indicated that the "southern shore" of this African continent had finally been reached after more than seventy years, and that the passage to the India of the priest king and the glamorous riches of the East was now in sight.

Mossel Bay was named *Aguada de São Bras* by these first circumnavigators of Africa, and to the Portuguese this fountain of Saint Blaise remained the only harbour of importance on the southern coast of Africa for more than a century. During Dias's first visit it was also the scene of the first contact between Europeans and the native Hottentots, a meeting unfortunately marred by violence.

The last dramatic stage along the south coast ended in personal defeat and disappointment for Dias. Royal orders compelled him to consult his fellow travellers about whether or not to continue the voyage. The weight of their opinion, which probably was expressed in a meeting which took place in the bay now known as Algoa Bay, forced Dias to turn his ships in March, 1488, after a river-mouth, generally accepted to be that of the Great Fish River, had been reached. This was a point nearly 1260 miles further than the last stone cross erected by Diego Cão.

Although for Dias this must have been an exasperating decision, time was to prove its wisdom. The defects of his small ships, the lack of provisions, the distance to the real India – the coast of Malabar – and above all the relentless enmity of Islam in the Indian Ocean, meant that Dias probably would never have returned from his travels, even if he had reached his destination.

On his return voyage he erected *padrões* at three places, starting at Kwaaihoek, west of the Bushman's River mouth, where the cross of Saint Gregory was raised on the 12 March, 1488. Fragments of this, the oldest evidence of European contact with South Africa, were discovered in 1938 and 1939 by the historian Eric Axelson, and can be seen in a reconstructed form in the library of the University of the Witwatersrand.

A second limestone cross was erected on 6 June, 1488, in the vicinity of Cape Point, which according to contemporary evidence was named *Cabo de Boa Esperanza* by Dias himself, and not, as some believe, by King João II. This was the Cape around which Dias had unwittingly sailed on his outward voyage. This most southern tip was the only part he actually saw of the Cape peninsula. The return voyage proceeded without interruption from Cape Point to Lüderitzbucht, where, before Dias sailed for Europe, the third *padrão* was erected in July, 1488, on the bay named, successively, *Angra das Voltas*, *Golfo de São Cristovão*, and *Angra Pequena* by Portuguese sailors.

The discoverer of Southern Africa was received unobtrusively by his sovereign, and lived without recognition or reward until he met his death in the South Atlantic Ocean in 1500, on another voyage to India in the service of his king. It is possible that the sensational fact of his circumnavigation of the Cape was assessed at its true value in Lisbon, but deliberately underplayed at the time. It brought with it no proof of the proximity of India, nor prospect of profitable trade. The seafarers told only of an unattractive, desolate southern land which, in the words of a contemporary, "yielded nothing to delight the heart of man", and where, moreover, the sea was full of dangers.

Da Gama sails round the Southern Land and reaches India

Nine years were to pass after Dias's homecoming before a Portuguese ship was once more to brave the stormy seas of the Cape. The main reason for this delay was that African trade had already brought Lisbon considerable prosperity, the symbol of which was the royal Guinea warehouse, the *Almazem de Mina*. There was no reason to seek further afield for wealth along an ocean-route which, apparently, merely extended beyond the safe tropical areas to arid regions of little promise.

The leading advocate of further attempts to reach India had always been King João II himself, but at this time he was mourning the death of his son and successor, and suffering increasingly from the kidney disease from which he was to die in 1495. In March, 1493, he was further troubled by the news the Genoese Cristoforo Colombo brought to Lisbon of an India he had discovered in the service of the rulers of Spain – in the west, however, not in the south where Cão and Dias had searched for it. The "Indians" that Columbus brought with him as proof of what he said were indeed neither negroes nor orientals, and on the whole there was sufficient reason for serious doubt as to whether a search to the south was still justifiable and, whether there could still be any value in the 1455 papal concession to Portugal of all regions eastward *ad Indos*

6

when the goal had apparently already been attained by Columbus's voyage to the west. The political struggle which João II had to conduct against Spain and the extremely biased Pope Alexander VI was settled in Portugal's favour in 1494, by the designation of Spanish and Portuguese overseas spheres of interest as specified in the Treaty of Tordesilhas. This treaty again assured Portugal of the route southwards, shortly before John the Perfect was succeeded by his brother-in-law, Manuel the Fortunate.

Manuel I, who ruled Portugal until 1521, and whose reign was to witness the flowering of a Portuguese trading empire extending from Brazil to the Malayan Archipelago, was truly the spiritual heir to the Great Navigator. Immediately after his accession to the throne he so effectively argued with those opposed to further voyages to the south that preparations were begun for the expedition that was to reach the destination Dias had aimed at.

The two ships of the new expedition – *São Rafael* and *São Gabriel* – were nearly three times the size of Dias's caravels, and were called *naus;* each had twenty cannon of various calibre and was thus well-armed. The light caravel *Berrio* was to accompany the two large ships as a look-out ship, and there was also a heavy cargo-vessel for provisions and supplies. The ships were provided with the latest means of measuring latitudes, improved astrolabes, including one that could be erected on land to obtain more accurate readings, and the services of Dias's experienced pilot, Pero d'Alenquer.

The man to whom the King in 1497 gave the command, as captain-major, of the ships that were to reach India via the Cape, was thirty-eight year old Vasco da Gama (1460 – 1524), a bachelor and the son of a magistrate in the coastal town of Sines. Da Gama was quite different from the gentle Dias. Apparently he did not have much knowledge of navigation; in this sphere he had to rely on his pilots. But he was a stern disciplinarian and loyal servant of his king. He was an irascible man who could be ruthless in the execution of what he considered to be his duty. The oath which Da Gama solemnly swore on the cross before his sovereign, in which he undertook "to go out to discover the oceans and countries of India and the East", sustained him throughout his voyage.

His departure from the Tagus on 8 July, 1497, was colourful. It was surpassed in splendour only by his return more than two years later, about August, 1499, as the hero who had charted for Portugal the sea-route to the coast of Malabar around the Cape, key to the riches of the East.

As was not the case with Dias's expedition, a *roteiro* or log-book of Da Gama's historical voyage has been preserved. From this it appears that his first contact with the coast of Southern Africa was determined by the new route he followed.

On his outward voyage Da Gama was the first to attempt to avoid the doldrums by sailing out at immense hazard across the Atlantic Ocean in a wide arc from the Cape Verde Islands towards the coast of the as yet undiscovered Brazil, and then back south past the Cape with the aid of the west wind. This mighty game of chance with the ocean lasted ninety-three days until land was

7

sighted again somewhere south of the Orange River. Either intentionally or because of the current Da Gama, on the 7th November, 1497, landed in the bay he christened St. Helena Bay. Here he saw Hottentots for the first time.

Da Gama, like Dias, then found himself faced with the necessity of sailing directly into the raging south-easter – the voice of the giant Adamastor in the famous epic *Os Lusiadas* by Luis de Camoës. He sailed round the Cape directly into the wind without swerving to the west. He landed at *Angra de São Bras*, where he saw the "brown people" again during a stay of thirteen days and bartered cattle before continuing his voyage past the *Rio de Infante*, the furthest point reached by Dias.

Traditionally, Da Gama gave the name *Terra do Natal* to the coast around the Kei River on Christmas Day, 1497, although this was not recorded in his log-book. This name, which initially referred to the coast of Pondoland, was later in the Portuguese period extended to cover a larger area, stretching from a starting-point (*Ponta Primeira*) at the Kei River, through a central point (*Ponta do Meio*) at the Umzimvubu River, to the furthest point (*Ponta Derradeira*) which was probably the Bluff at Durban.

There is no record of Da Gama seeing any Bantu on this coast; it was only during the first weeks of 1498 that he met black people, probably a Tsonga tribe, north of the mouth of the Limpopo, and half a century passed before a shipwreck on the Natal coast brought the Portuguese into contact with the Nguni Bantu.

On the way to his great triumph – the reaching via the Cape of the Malabar coast in May, 1498 – Da Gama penetrated the Mohammedan world of commerce, and in the old island city of Mozambique the first "ships of the Franks" caused amazement and afterwards bloody conflict with the "Moors". Da Gama established the pattern of future voyages to India, using Mozambique as a halfway station on the long run from the east coast of Africa across the Indian Ocean. In the years to come Portuguese ships, sailing according to the strict timetable of the monsoon season, were to use Mozambique as a landmark on the south-east coast of Africa.

Da Gama returned from India without costly cargoes or valuable trade treaties, but the sea-route round the Cape which he had charted with ruthless persevererance was a priceless gift for Manuel I. Portugal could now exploit the unparalleled riches of the Indian trade as a royal monopoly which, as a weapon against Islam, enjoyed, moreover, papal protection against Christian competitors. The Sultan of Egypt's time-honoured role as middleman in the spice trade began to diminish with the development of the Cape route. Proud Venice watched the disappearance of its mighty medieval trading power based on the distribution of Eastern wares, as the king of Portugal moved the centre of the spice trade to the city of Antwerp on the Scheldt, and the rich moneylenders of Germany flocked to ensure that Lisbon had the financial backing required to secure the treasures of India.

For two decades after Da Gama's first voyage Manuel developed his Indian empire "in the service of God our Lord and to our own advantage", as he once put it. Each year fleets sailed round the Cape to drive Islam from its bases in the Indian Ocean, and load rich cargoes on the coast of Malabar. In 1500 Pedro Álvares Cabral sailed with a fleet in which Bartolomeu Dias also sailed, the latter meeting his death on the outward journey. The third voyage (1501 – 1502) was that of João da Nova, who built a small chapel at Mossel Bay. This was the first building erected by Christians in Southern Africa. Later during this voyage João da Nova was the first to see the "river of the lake", the *Rio da Lagoa*, in the bay to which Lourenço Marques was to give his name in 1544. The city which developed on this bay was to replace the city of Mozambique during the latter half of the nineteenth century as the centre of the Portuguese province of Mozambique.

Da Gama, now an admiral and raised to the nobility, commanded the fleet of 1502. He sailed from the Gambian coast to Sofala in one immense haul lasting ninety-nine days, without touching the Southern African coast on his outward voyage.

The 1503 fleet consisted of three squadrons, each commissioned to pursue the bloody war against Islam which Da Gama had begun with fire and sword. One of these squadrons was commanded by Antonio de Saldanha, who in the spring of 1503 sailed, through a navigational error, into the bay that is now called Table Bay.

The significance of the Cape to the Portuguese

After this first recorded visit the *Aguada de Saldanha* kept for a century the name of the man who was also the first white man to climb Table Mountain. This bay became an alternative watering-place to Mozambique, but because of the established sailing routes was only used in exceptional circumstances. All the great empire builders of Portugal's *Estado da India* sailed round the Cape during Manuel's reign, and one, the viceroy Francisco d'Almeida, who had shortly before brilliantly established Portuguese authority in the Indian Ocean, perished miserably on his journey with some of his superior officers during a skirmish in March, 1510, with Hottentots in Table Bay.

The Cape sea from the Natal coast to Cape Point, with its unpredictable storms and dangerous currents, was as perilous, particularly for the heavily laden homeward bound ships, as the Cape natives were hostile. The Portuguese did not desire or acquire any geographical knowledge of Southern Africa on their voyages along the despised coast, with some few exceptions of course, such as the detailed account of the famous pilot, João de Lisboa, of the south coast and adjacent mountains. Names were given to some places but only a few survived, e.g. Agulhas, Infanta, Recife and St. Sebastian's Bay.

The wealth and prosperity of the era of Manuel I did not end with his death in 1521, but signs of corruption, incompetent management and decay were already discernible in the days of glory. During the thirty-six years' reign of the gentle João III, the fleets continued to sail round the Cape of Storms while the crown serenely amassed its profits.

9

As yet there was no rival for the monopoly which Portugal had captured by force in the Indian Ocean and had established as far as the most distant spice islands of Indonesia. Sporadically French pirates waylaid the richly laden ships on their last lap to Europe, and this encouraged the Flemings and the English to begin nibbling at the Portuguese monarch's proud monopoly. But it was a hardy system, and many generations loyally served the royal treasury. Until 1578 Portugal poured her wealth and noblest blood into North Africa in her struggle against the Moors of Morocco.

The same factors that originally prevented Southern Africa from being of prime interest to Portugal continued operating throughout the sixteenth century. First, the destination of the shipping routes was the coasts of Mozambique and Malabar; there was therefore no need for halfway stations in the southern bays of Africa except as emergency ports and watering-places, nor need for any contact with Table Bay and the west coast of Southern Africa, neither of which was usually visible on either the outward or homeward voyages.

Furthermore, in comparison with what the east coast of Africa and the East itself could offer, there were no possibilities of trading in Southern Africa. Ivory was found in quantities sufficient for commercial purposes as far north as the bay of Lourenço Marques, and fever-riddled Sofala's gold from the interior was to be found even further north. Again, the native populations of Southern Africa were primitive barbarians, who were always inclined, moreover, to be hostile towards the Portuguese. Contrasted to these conditions were the magnificent cultures of the Arab dominated east coast of Africa and the west coast of India with its century old advanced civilisation, whose rulers could conclude agreements and conduct business.

The main deterrents to the exploration of the coasts of Southern Africa, however, were the sea and the gales. The land discovered by Dias and Da Gama was a nightmare to the sailor. Its storms, from Natal to Agulhas, were a constant threat to every Portuguese who fought to pass the stormy Cape. This land was merely there to by-pass, not to visit and get to know.

Therefore the Portuguese seafarers, whose voyage by the Cape route was practically unbroken until the end of the sixteenth century, learnt almost nothing about the country which they knew as "Western Ethiopia" (as against *Ethiopia Oriental*), and which was South East Africa, i.e. Mozambique and its interior as far as the Zambesi. João dos Santos was the only one to describe it, in 1609, from personal experience.

Portuguese knowledge of this area was otherwise derived from the bitter experiences of castaways on parts of the coasts of Pondoland and Natal, where heavy galleons such as the *São João* in 1502 and *São Bento* in 1554, loaded with riches, had run aground on the "coast of torments". It was Manuel de Mesquita Perestrelo, survivor of the Saint Benedict disaster, who in 1564 wrote about his gruelling experience, thus producing the first printed matter to deal exclusively with Southern Africa. He was also commissioned by his young king, Sebastian, to record in more detail the early coastal investigations of Barbudo and Quaresma (1506), João de Lisboa (1513), and the learned Dom João de Castro

(1538). In 1575–1576 he compiled a full account and map of a tour of inspection from the Cape to Inhambane.

The southern tip of Africa still had not been properly named. It was part of the empire over which the Portuguese kings of Avis ruled until 1580, and afterwards Philip II and his Spanish descendants, all legitimate successors to the throne. But it was never more than an incidental, anonymous and unesteemed portion of the Portuguese trade empire. When Lisbon planned a display of imperialism in Africa in 1569 to parallel Spain's empire-building in South America, it was the Zambesian territory that was selected for the tragic debacle of Francisco Barreto's expedition to the land of Monomotapa. The unwieldy Portuguese royal monopoly on Indian wealth was beginning to disintegrate in a slow reaction to cumulative causes, but the empire was to withstand the attacks of its trade enemies until long after the Dutch colony at the Cape had become a reality.

New circumnavigators and competitors

Many factors caused the Portuguese monopoly of the Eastern trade to totter dangerously. There was corruption in the Indian service and a shortage of manpower. The unwieldy and overloaded ships were an easy prey to English and French pirates or heavy seas. Portions of the royal monopoly were leased to strangers: in particular the perspicacious Dutch who distributed the spices quickly realized the possibilities of the Indian trade and before long began to filch the trade round the Cape from its jealous guardians.

As important as the story of the gradual supercession of the Portuguese as the sole navigators round the Cape are the political events in Portugal after 1578. The Avis dynasty that began in 1385 with the father of the Navigator died out in 1580, and the king of Spain, a son of Manuel's daughter Isabella, immediately legitimately claimed the Portuguese throne. In this way two kingdoms were united, and Portugal acquired as its ruler the same Philip II of Spain who was the arch-enemy of the Netherlands in its struggle for independence, and the enemy of the England of the first Elizabeth.

Admittedly the great Portuguese trading empire showed no immediate signs of disintegration, but the people who now sailed the Cape sea-route lacked the inspiration of a monarch who had himself traditionally been the leader and patron of overseas enterprise. Until 1640 they were to be "Spaniards"; the Protestant enemies they inherited from Spain did not care a rap for the pontifical protection of Lisbon's spice monopoly, and eagerly converged on the interests of the new Portuguese subjects of Philip II.

The spice trade was attacked on two fronts. First, the returning Portuguese merchantmen, unwieldy and heavily laden, were pirated on their last weary lap from the Cape Verde Islands to Lisbon. Long before 1580 the French Huguenots and the English had already begun to join in this pillage. Secondly, there were attempts to attack the spice trade directly at its source. Here the swift-sailing English were the initiators. Francis Drake, on his voyage round the world, reached "the Islands of the Spiceries" via South America, plundering all the way, and on his way home from the Moluccas passed "the fairest Cape" in June 1580.

This magnificent seafaring feat was repeated by Thomas Cavendish, who reached Java in 1587, and arrived home to learn that the Invincible Armada of Philip II had just been dealt a humiliating defeat by Elizabeth's captains.

English attacks were aimed mainly at Spain's interests in the New World, but in 1591 some London merchants fitted out three ships to sail the "true way" to India, round the Cape. They were the first to manage this since the half-forgotten voyage in 1529 by two Huguenot brothers from Dieppe, Jean and Raoul Parmentier.

During the time the English first spent at the watering-place "Saldania" in August and the beginning of September, 1591, they met the Hottentots – "certaine blacke savages, very brutish" – and collected sea food and wild sorrel for sailors ravaged by scurvy. On the voyage along the east coast the commander, George Raymond, died, and James Lancaster took charge. He reached Ceylon and Sumatra, but in 1594 arrived back in England without ships or crew. Elizabeth's merchants sent a second unsuccessful expedition, led by Benjamin Wood, around the Cape in 1596. In the same year the Dutch launched their first assault against the Portuguese monopoly. In spite of the inauspicious inception of the trade with India the English founded an East India Company in 1600, and the following year Lancaster – later Sir James Lancaster – once more was in the bay at the foot of Table Mountain, this time as commander of the company's first fleet to the East.

In the end it was the Dutch, and not the English, who destroyed the Portuguese monopoly in the East during the half century before the establishment of a colony at the Cape. The appearance of Dutch ships in the seas around the Cape was a natural development of the rolegenerations of Dutch, encouraged by the two Iberian nations, had played as distributors in Europe of wares imported from India. This role continued even when Spain became an enemy of the Netherlands after 1568. The carrying trade was doubly advantageous for the alert Hollanders and Zeelanders in that it gave their small country economic power, and simultaneously provided an opportunity for learning the potential value of the spice monopoly, which the Portuguese had kept so secret.

The stimulus for the Dutch to discard the role of middleman and to set out themselves to tap the sources of Portuguese prosperity came from the policy of Philip II as sovereign of Portugal. In the decade that followed the unification of the kingdoms of Spain and Portugal the traditional trade with Lisbon and the Spanish ports was made more difficult for the Dutch, and by 1590 had become quite impossible.

This was the signal for the Dutch to become openly aggressive with the ships of the Portuguese, with whom they had been on good terms for almost a century. It became their explicit aim to trade directly with the spice islands – the Moluccas, and not India. In 1592 nine Amsterdam merchants sent the brothers Cornelis and Frederik de Houtman to Lisbon to gather "secret information" about the route around the Cape, which information had been carefully guarded since the days of Dias.

The two brothers from Gouda did return with some ocean maps, but the man who made possible the first Dutch voyage to the east in 1595 was Jan Huyghen van Linschoten of Enkhuizen.

His wanderlust carried him to Goa as a Portuguese employee, where entirely on his own initiative he collected, in the course of about five years, an imposing range of records of all aspects of Portuguese trade and trading regions, as well as the navigational instructions for the route around the Cape.

Van Linschoten's great book *Itinerario ofte Reijs-boeck . . . naar Oost ofte Portugaels Indien* was published in time for Cornelis de Houtman to take it with him when, on behalf of the Amsterdam "Compagnie van Verre (Landen)", he set out for the Cape on 2 April, 1595. His four ships reached the bay of São Bras on 4 August. This was the first Dutch contact with the coast of Southern Africa.

The Portuguese first port of call on the way to the East had been Mozambique. The Dutch, however, chose the Sunda Straits between Java and Sumatra as their gate-way to the spice archipelago. Therefore the two watering-places, São Bras and Saldanha, were very important to them as the only stops on the month-long voyages to East India, as against "Hither India", the Dutch name for the sub-continent of India to which the Portuguese had sailed. This explains why the English and, especially, the Dutch wreckers of the Portuguese monopoly made increasing use of the Cape harbours and preferred to anchor in Table Bay. This was the new name given to this bay by Joris van Spilbergen in 1601, when its first name was transferred to modern Saldanha Bay.

The Portuguese, heralds of European culture in Southern Africa, were forced off the scene by their rivals soon after 1600, but they retired with honour. This small nation of less than a million people, with courage, perseverance and daring, opened nearly half of the globe to the western world before it had to start withdrawing in the face of the greater wealth and larger numbers of its competitors.

The Dutch attempt to capture the Moluccan trade started with a series of fleets sent to East India by rival companies – the "fore-companies" – round the Cape and Cape Horn between the years 1595 and 1602. To avoid the adverse effects of competition, the companies were united on a federal basis in 1602 as the United Netherlands Chartered East India Company. This company was granted a charter by the States-General of the Netherlands, which remained the sovereign authority over these overseas enterprises.

The Dutch East India Company, with its six autonomous chambers under a main directorate, "the Seventeen" or Lords Majores, became the instrument of Dutch activity in the East. In the Malayan Archipelago itself a permanent administration, headed by a governor and a Council of India, was established after 1609, a permanent headquarters was established at Batavia, in Java, after 1619, and a large number of comptoirs with their own commanders were founded during the decades prior to the establishment of a comptoir at the Cape.

From the beginning Table Bay – for a long time still referred to as Saldania by English travellers – was a regular port of call for passing English and Dutch ships, and for the time being friendly relations were officially maintained between the two nationalities. Ships left mail for one another in Table Valley under stones inscribed with names and instructions, as can still be seen in a "post-office" collection which was unearthed in Adderley Street in the twentieth century and which is preserved in Cape Town. The peaceful bay was a rendezvous for ships that had been separated at sea, somewhere for the sick to convalesce, and occasionally a repair-shop for ships damaged at sea.

As early as 1613 the English had considered founding a colony in Table Valley; after 1616 Dutch visits became more frequent, and by 1619 the possibility of building a joint fort or two forts in Table Bay was being discussed at a high level by the Dutch and English companies. Before any decision had been reached the English flag was hoisted without warrant in 1620 on the ridge of Signal Hill or Vlaeberg, at the foot of Lion's Head, by Captains Andrew Shillinge and Humphrey Fitzherbert, who proclaimed that Table Bay was now under the sovereignty of James I of England.

England did not, however, respond to this attempted occupation. There was a similar lack of response from the Netherlands to the strongly-worded demand compiled in Table Bay by the most active supporter of the Dutch against the English in the East, Jan Pieterszoon Coen, that the Dutch should establish a colony at the southern extremity of Africa.

An accidental circumstance – the stranding in Table Bay of the *Nieuw Haerlem*, a ship on its homeward journey in 1647 – once more focussed attention on the Cape and its possibilities as a refreshment station for the ships of the Dutch company. The south-easter drove the fully-loaded *Haerlem* on to the beach, probably in the vicinity of Milnerton, on the afternoon of 25 March, 1647. A square fort, the "vasticheyt (fastness) Zandenborgh", was knocked together from salvaged wood and as much of the cargo as possible was saved. The captain sailed on another ship leaving sixty sailors behind under the command of the junior merchant, Leendert Janszen, to await the next homeward bound fleet.

Janszen kept a log-book of this unusual visit which continued until the arrival of a fleet under Wollebrandt Geleijnsen de Jongh on 15 March, 1648. On his return Leendert Janszen and one of his companions, Matthijs Proot, were requested to submit a report to the Directors concerning the suitability of Table Bay as a site for a company station.

The "Remonstrantie" by Janszen and Proot was dated 26 July, 1649, and contained strong recommendations for starting a refreshment station which would pay its way, and whose garrison could live and trade peaceably with the Hottentots, help prevent shipwrecks round the Cape, and protect fleets from surprise enemy attacks. In 1650, on the strength of this document, the directors decided in principle to erect "a rendezvous and fort" at the Cape, and to have instructions drawn up for its commander.

These instructions were drawn up in 1651, and a capable commander was sought. Matthijs Proot was approached, but he did not accept the post; then Jan Anthoniszoon van Riebeeck, a merchant formerly employed by the company, offered his services. He had been a passenger in the fleet that took the crew and cargo of the *Haerlem* on board in Table Bay during 1648. Van Riebeeck was thirty-two years old and eager to re-enter the Company's service.

He was asked to comment on the "Remonstrantie" by Janszen and Proot. The thorough way in which he, in his "Nadere Consideratie" of June 1651, critically yet sympathetically evaluated the possibilities for a station at the Cape must have contributed considerably to his being appointed to command the proposed refreshment post at the Cape.

In the Company's extensive organisation, which had been functioning for half a century, the establishment of another little fort with a garrison of about a hundred men at the southern end of a country about which, apart from Table Bay and Mossel Bay, little more was known than when Dias sailed back to Portugal in 1488, did not attract undue attention. It was merely a utility measure, part of routine expansion in the interests of the company's traffic at sea.

There was no talk of establishing a colony, and still less were there any idealistic considerations. That the humble task delegated to Van Riebeeck in 1651 would lead to the birth of a new nation and the development of a country with vast natural resources was something only the future would reveal.

2. The Arrival of Van Riebeeck at the Cape

The Cape and the precious return fleets

A new period in the history of Southern Africa began as the *Drommedaris* and the *Goede Hoope* anchored in Table Bay on Saturday the 6 April, 1652. For more than fifty years countless ships had been anchoring in this bay whose mountains had witnessed both joy and tragedy. Often the sailors of passing ships met here and recovered from the ravages of scurvy. Storms frequently wrecked ships and the sailors were unable to reach the safety of the shore.

The history of all the dramatic events that took place at the foot of Table Mountain has yet to be written.[1] In the Journal of the Castle at Batavia it is related how in 1636 the ex-Governor-General H. Brouwer suppressed a mutiny amongst the crew of his fleet and threw eight of the ringleaders overboard into Table Bay.[2] The ninth ringleader was keel-hauled three times and banished to Robben Island. It is not related how long he managed to stay alive.

Not only were the seas along the African coast freakish, but the behaviour of the native population, the roaming Hottentots, was unpredictable. Sometimes they were in Table Valley and eager to barter their cattle; at other times they would have nothing to do with visiting sailors. In 1638 they murdered merchant Cornelis Specx and fourteen of his crew when they ventured too far from their ships.[3]

Although the Cape had played a certain part in the life of those who sailed to and from the East before 1652, it was only when the *Drommedaris* and the *Goede Hoop* arrived on April the 6th, the *Reyger* on April the 7th and the *Walvis* and *Oliphant* on the 7th of May, that people came to the Cape with a definite aim in mind and clear duties to perform. Among the new arrivals there were also women and children. The man in command, Jan van Riebeeck, arrived at the Cape on the *Drommedaris* with his wife, Maria de la Queillerie, and a son almost eight months old. Van Riebeeck was born on 21 April, 1619. In 1639 he went to

---

1. An excellent anthology of many of these events has been gathered by Major R. Raven-Hart in *Before van Riebeeck, Callers at South Africa from 1488 to 1652*, Cape Town, 1967.
2. *Dagh-Register van 't Casteel Batavia*, 21 Junie 1636. (Also Major R. Raven-Hart: *Before Van Riebeeck*, p.144). On p. 129 in The Journal we read: ... "dat den 17en do < 17 March 1636 > ... by sententie door gemelten Generael Brouwer ... in de Tafelbay acht levendich overboort geseth ende een (naer dat driemaal gekielhallt was) op het Robben eylandt gebannen".
3. The story is told in *Rijksgeschiedkundige Publicatiën: Generale Missiven der V.O.C.* 1, 1610 – 1638, edited by Dr. W. Ph. Coolhaas, p. 731: "Die van de *Son* hebben 14 man daeronder den coopman Cornelis Speckx aen gemelte Cabo verlooren, sijnde van d'inwoonderen vermoort, alsoo niet nae behooren op hoede waren ende hun te verre t'landtwaert in vertrouwden op hoope van beesten te becomen, welcke in groot getal van die van Saldania achter den Taeffelbergh waren gedreven". This happened on 30 April 1638.

16

the East as a junior surgeon in the employ of the Dutch East India Company and visited many strange places during his eight years service. Journeys to Atjeh, Japan and China had a formative influence on him. He was accused of participating in private trade and this was responsible for his return to Europe. On his return home he visited the Cape with the fleet of Wollebrandt Geleynsen de Jong. From his writings it appears that he had also visited Barbados and Greenland.

When he arrived at the Cape in charge of the new settlement Van Riebeeck's instructions were clear. He had to build a fort to be known as Fort de Goede Hoop. This had to be large enough to house eighty men, who would garden and plant fruit trees, and ensure that there were arable and pasture lands. They were to erect a flag mast from which to signal ships, and build pilot boats so that fleets could be piloted safely into the bay. They were instructed to keep their costs low.

From the information available it appears that the most important aim of the undertaking was to ensure the safety of the fleets and to provide them with fresh produce. Strict instructions were given to live at peace with the native inhabitants and any foreign subjects who might settle at the Cape. The council of Seventeen felt that the Cape was large enough to permit more than one nation to live there, each within its own demarcated area.

The organization which controlled the Cape was known as the Dutch East India Company. The management of the Dutch East India Company, or as it was called in Dutch the V.O.C., was in the hands of the Council of Seventeen, which was composed of seventeen directors who met for six consecutive years in Amsterdam and then for two years in Middelburg. The seventeen directors were chosen from sixty directors, merchants who were divided into six management bodies. These bodies were known as Chambers and each Chamber equipped its own ships and recruited its own crews. The twenty merchants of the Chamber of Amsterdam sent eight members, the twelve merchants of the Chamber of Zeeland sent four members and the merchants of each of the Chambers of Rotterdam, Delft, Hoorn and Enkhuizen sent one member to the Council of Seventeen. Each of the Chambers, except that of Amsterdam, in turn nominated the seventeenth member of the Council. This precluded Amsterdam from ever having an absolute majority.

In March, 1602, the States-General, the highest authority in the Netherlands, granted extensive powers to the V.O.C. by means of a charter. This charter gave the Company a trade monopoly from east of the Cape of Good Hope to the Straits of Magellan; it could enter into contracts with princes and potentates and was allowed to appoint governors, soldiers and judicial officers to rule in the territories it had conquered; it could build forts and recruit soldiers.

The first place where the Council of Seventeen used their full powers was Djacarta, established in 1619 and renamed Batavia in 1621. Here a Governor-General, assisted by the Council of India, was appointed. These men also exercised authority over the Cape. Thus Jan van Riebeeck had to report everything that happened at the Cape to the Governor-General and Council of India.

This meant that the Journals in which the daily events were entered had to be sent both to Amsterdam and Batavia. The same rule applied to the Resolutions or minutes of the Council of Policy, the "Placaten" or Laws, the petitions, instructions and letters written at the Cape.

The first five years

While he was still on board the *Drommedaris* Van Riebeeck had begun acting as Commander of the settlement he was to found at the Cape. Here he wrote the prayer which was to become known as Van Riebeeck's prayer in the resolution book. We also find the resolutions of 30 December, 1651, and 20 January and 29 March, 1652, in his own handwriting. When, however, work at the Cape started in earnest on Monday morning the 8th April, he no longer had time to write down the resolutions himself. When the ships had left, there were with him at the Cape according to his own records only ninety poor ignorant people, who expected him to guide them in everything. Everyone, whether builder, gardener, farmer, carpenter, plasterer or blacksmith, expected guidance and advice from the Commander.[4] Small wonder that only fifteen days after his arrival he was longing for "several hard-working Chinese", as he could not hope to cultivate one hundreth part of the fertile land he saw around him with so few hands.

Although Van Riebeeck pointed out in his first letter to Batavia that there was enough work at the Cape for a thousand men and that in times of sickness he only had sixty and sometimes no more than fifty able-bodied men to do all the work, it is remarkable how much he did achieve and how many obstacles were overcome during the first year. After a long drought at the Cape that first year the ground in which the foundations for the fort had to be dug was rock hard, and the naming of the four points or ramparts could only take place on the 15th of May. The ramparts were named after the four largest ships in the fleet which had brought the settlers to the Cape, and the fort itself was to be known as the Fort de Goede Hoope.

When extremely heavy hail and rain ushered in the winter everyone was still living in leaky wooden huts and canvas tents. The first vegetables and other plants were washed away; many, including Van Riebeeck's wife, became ill and the wife of the senior surgeon died. Work on the fort almost came to a standstill and Van Riebeeck's Journal records, that "at present life here is becoming sad and miserable".[5] Nevertheless the fort was ready to receive the first family on the 4th June and on the 6th of June a son, Bernert Willemsz, was born to the sick-comforter. On the 3rd of August the northern rampart, Reijger, was completed and everyone moved into the fort where the roar of the lions sounded less frightening.

4. In C.493, vol. III: *Letters Despatched, 1652 – 1661*, 5 March 1659, p. 881, Van Riebeeck writes: that the men whom he had to help were so unskilled that he was forced to be in turn "ingenieuer, graver, hovenier, boer, timmerman, metselaer, smith etca".

5. Thom, H. B.: *Journal of Jan van Riebeeck*, vol. 1, p. 44.

After the first winter everything started to improve. A large variety of vegetables was well suited to cultivation at the Cape and the crew of the yacht *Goede Hoope* were treated to Cape-bred chickens and fresh vegetables. By September the fort was in reasonable state of defence. When the Hottentots came with cattle, sheep, ostriches, ivory and genet skins they were encouraged to visit the fort and came in increasing numbers. The first butter was churned on the 26th of December and Van Riebeeck opened a try-house at the mouth of the Salt River. The barrels of train-oil were later to be protected by Dijnhoop, a small fort.

When the first homeward-bound fleet from Batavia arrived at the Cape under Admiral Gerard Demmer in March, 1653, Van Riebeeck was able to supply it with cattle, sheep, cabbages, carrots and milk, and the Admiral was very satisfied with the state of the fortifications. Van Riebeeck pointed out that his own people were exhausted from the continual work and begged Demmer to allow two hundred of his sailors to help for a few weeks in completing the fort. Demmer was willing to help feed the people at the Cape with rice, meat and bread from his ships but did not want his sailors to work. They also were exhausted after the long journey and had to rest. Later when Van Riebeeck found fleet commanders who agreed to allow their sailors to work he was seriously reprimanded by Governor-General Johan Maetsuijcker who reminded him that the Cape was not founded to make convalescent persons ill, but to make the sick well.

When the first naval war against England was in progress the Council of Seventeen allowed Van Riebeeck to strengthen his garrison with twenty-five men from passing ships. Besides fifteen women and children there were now one hundred and thirty-six men at the Cape and Van Riebeeck was convinced that in time something valuable could be made of it. At the same time, in a letter to the Council of Seventeen, he expressed his regret that they had not yet thought fit to transfer him to India on promotion, and asked that his salary be increased from ƒ75 to ƒ150. On the 15th April, 1654, the Council of Seventeen replied to this letter informing him that they were giving him the title of Commander and raising his salary to ƒ90 per month, adding that they would not neglect to consider his transfer at a more opportune time. In the meantime they felt that he was doing good work at the Cape.

Van Riebeeck began his second year at the Cape with enthusiasm. More ground was prepared for cultivation and the gardens were enlarged. Vines, trees and plants were imported from Brazil, St. Helena, Batavia, Ambon, Japan, Spain, France, Mauritius and Madagascar. Van Riebeeck interpreted the permission to increase his garrison very freely and soon had one hundred and fifty and then one hundred and seventy men at the fort. Finally Maetsuijcker wrote on the 7th November, 1654, to inform him that he must reduce the garrison by fifty men. Before this instruction had to be carried out, however, the work had progressed well. The wooden houses on the square inside the fort were replaced by one square house built of stones quarried locally. The walls of this house were four feet thick and its wooden beams had been brought from the woods with great difficulty. The residential quarters were on the second floor and the ground floor was used for storage. The fort itself was completed by the end of 1653 and the walls withstood at least that year's winter rains.

In other respects it was not a prosperous year for the officials at the Cape. On Sunday, the 19th of October, 1653, the Hottentot, whom the Dutch called Herry, the chief of the small band of Strandlopers or Watermans, murdered the herdsman David Jansz and stole almost the whole of the settlers' herd of cattle, sheep and pigs. Van Riebeeck was deeply shocked that Herry, whom he had employed as an interpreter, fed from their table as a great friend and clothed in European attire, should do such a thing. Although Herry was pursued he was not captured. Food became scarce and when in the autumn of 1654 the home-ward-bound fleet did not touch at the Cape with the necessary provisions, Van Riebeeck began to worry because his people were starting to go hungry. A galliot was sent to Saldanha Bay to fetch penguin eggs and fish. Another galliot, the *Tulp*, was sent to St. Helena to contact the homeward-bound fleet there and obtain rice for the Cape. Yet another galliot, the *Roode Vos*, was sent to Mada-gascar and Mauritius. With the coming of the third winter some of Van Rie-beeck's men became rebellious because there was ever more work and less food. A certain Jan Danielz of Veurne, nick-named "the doctor", began carrying two knives and muttering dark threats to the effect that he would know on whom to use them "if it happens again like last year that we get so little to eat but have to work just as much". Van Riebeeck acted immediately: Jan Danielz was sen-tenced to one hundred strokes and then to be keel-hauled. After this he had to work in chains for six months without remuneration. He survived these punish-ments and was pardoned in August, 1654, when the joyous tidings that the Peace of Westminster had ended the first naval war against England reached the Cape. When it is realized that the earth walls of the fort could not stand up to the winter rains this joy is understandable. One of the ramparts, the Walvis, had already collapsed on the 1st August, 1654, and in June of the following year Van Riebeeck had to concede that the fort was deteriorating and that in due course it would be necessary to build a stone fort.

In peace-time, however, the rebuilding of the fort at the Cape was not the Council of Seventeen's chief concern. This was that passing ships should be well provisioned from the settlement and that the Cape should become self-supporting as soon as possible. As far as the first aim was concerned good progress was being made by the fourth and fifth years of Van Riebeeck's stay at the Cape. Not only were Dutch fleet commanders and their crews well catered for but the English and French were also heartily welcomed, entertained at the Commander's table, and sent on their way with many provisions. As appears from the Journal entry of 12 December, 1655, their sick were also cared for in the Company's hospital. Van Riebeeck records that those concerned expres-sed their gratitude and promised to make proper compensation for everything.

However, the hope that the Cape would become self-supporting was not realized. The attempt to export seal-skins failed and no precious metals were found. The wind damaged the wheat and Van Riebeeck could not succeed in getting rice to ripen at the Cape, so rice had to be imported. As the work increased so did the number of officials which meant that more food had to be imported and the company's expenditure rose accordingly. In his first letter to Batavia Van Riebeeck proposed, as a suggested solution, that some free burghers, from India or the Netherlands, should come to the Cape and help with the work.

A few years later the Council of Seventeen concluded that this was the only answer to the problems of the Cape. In a letter dated 6 October, 1654, they wrote that a certain sea-captain, David Claesz Swaegh, had told them that Hout Bay would be a suitable place to settle a few Dutch families. On the 28th April, 1655, Van Riebeeck replied that it was unnecessary and undesirable for free burghers to live so far from the fort. The banks of the Versse River, later known as the Amstel and yet later as the Liesbeeck, would be a more suitable place for a settlement, since the wind was not so strong there as in Table Valley. He suggested that the burghers should sell their products to the company at fixed prices and that they should be allowed to supplement their income by hunting and fishing, keeping pigs and poultry, and possibly brewing beer. To help them get on their feet it would also be necessary to sell them slaves. Three months later he wrote to the Council of Seventeen stating that several officials at the Cape had declared themselves willing to become free burghers but that farming families from the Netherlands would also be welcome.

The directors had already given Van Riebeeck permission, in a letter of 30 October, 1655, to set officials free. They expressed their satisfaction, in a letter of the 12th October, 1656, at there once more being sufficient produce and sheep to provision the ships at the Cape, but reminded Van Riebeeck that it was high time that the Cape was self-supporting. They felt that the best way of achieving this goal would be by giving work to the free burghers, who would, as unpaid labourers, be able to work for less than did the officials.

As far as the transfer of work was concerned a trial was begun when ten dairy cows were leased on 1 October, 1655, to the gardener, Hendrik Boom, whose wife had farmed in the fatherland. Van Riebeeck realized, however, that the settling of free burghers at the Cape was a radical change in the policy of the settlement, and he approached the matter with much circumspection. In May, 1656, the first grain was sown at a place called Rondebosje, or the Ronde Doorn Bosjen. This venture was successful and so was a second experiment. On 5 December, 1656, Van Riebeeck took all the Dutch women at the Cape by wagon to Rondebosch to show them how well the wheat, tobacco and beans were growing.

The free burghers

On the 3rd February, 1657, Van Riebeeck delivered wood to Rondebosch to build a fort with which to protect the wheatlands of the free burghers. This small fort was known as Coornhoop. Two days later he received a letter, dated 12 October, 1656, from the Council of Seventeen with instructions to release eight or ten men to manage the farming. In the same letter he was informed that his salary had been increased to ƒ130 but that the Directors were not prepared to transfer him to the East at this stage. The Seventeen added that, as the trade with Angola and Madagascar would probably become important in course of time and as Mauritius was on the point of being brought under the administration of the Cape, they had decided that Van Riebeeck's stay there for a longer period would be desirable and, indeed, necessary for the Company. At the same time they informed him that Rijkloff van Goens would visit the Cape on his return journey to India and would report on what had been achieved there. As Commissioner he would on arrival be chairman of the Council of Policy, the governing body at the Cape.

When the Council met on 21 February, 1657, before the arrival of Van Goens, the free burghers were divided into two groups. Steven Jansz van Wageningen and three others named their farms The Hollandsche Thuijn or The Dutch Garden. This group was also known as Stevens Colony and was nearer to the fort than the other group, Harmans Colony, where Harman Remajenna and four others had named their farms the Green Field.

On the 16th of April Van Goens, who was at the Cape from the 17th March until the 19th April, signed detailed instructions, which he then handed to the Commander. In accordance with the wishes of the Council of Seventeen he instructed Van Riebeeck to have not more than one hundred officials at the Cape and to reduce this number to seventy as soon as possible. He expected that with this small complement Van Riebeeck should first build two guardhouses, and then later a small fort at Bosheuvel, a breakwater for the ships in Table Bay, and a cattle pen at Rondebosch, and also that he should especially encourage agriculture and enlarge the Company's garden. Van Goens did, however, permit Van Riebeeck to use the crews of passing ships if he could obtain the approval of those in charge of the ships. Eventually new storerooms were to be built in the fort and a canal dug across the peninsula to keep the Hottentots out of the area inhabited by the Whites.

In the matter of the free burghers, the tenth letter of release was issued during Van Goens's stay at the Cape. He impressed upon Van Riebeeck the necessity of encouraging the free burghers wherever possible. They were to be allowed to barter with the Hottentots. Their ploughs were to be repaired without charge for three years by the Company's blacksmith. He withdrew the permission previously given to Steven's Colony to grow tobacco, on the grounds that it would be detrimental to the Company's sale of tobacco at the Cape. It is remarkable that Van Goens had already in 1657 warned the Company not to grant the same privileges to the officials as to the free burghers; if the officials enjoyed the same privileges as the free burghers the latter would not be able to make a living. Finally everybody was allowed to fish but nobody was allowed to hunt without the express permission of the Commander.

In accordance with the Company's practice elsewhere, Van Goens appointed Steven Jansz van Wageningen as the first burgher councillor. He was to be seated between the second deputy and the sergeant if any of the free burghers came to trial. This was in accordance with the Company's principle that the accused had to be represented on the bench by someone of his own class. The following year Hendrik Boom, who had also become a free burgher, was appointed by Van Riebeeck as the second burgher councillor. Every year one of the burgher councillors retired and a new one was appointed by the Commander and the Council from a list of four names.

Van Goens also drew up regulations concerning slaves. When slaves arrived at the Cape the free burghers were to have first choice. The officials, however, were to see to it that no one spoke to the slaves in Portuguese.

Van Goens and Van Riebeeck also had long discussions about the Company's Hottentot policy. They agreed that to exterminate or transport the Hottentots would be barbaric and unchristian. For this reason guardhouses and small forts were to be built as a defence against sudden attack but meanwhile everything possible should be done to obtain their goodwill. If they persisted in robbing and stealing, the offenders should be sent to Robben Island. If the guilty party could not be found, fellow tribesmen should be detained until the culprit was handed over. When murder was committed and the criminal was apprehended, the death sentence should, if possible, be carried out by his own people. These instructions of Van Goens were important because they were in fact later put into effect.

The generosity with which the free burghers were treated, on the recommendation of Van Goens, bore good fruit. The muster roll shows that in 1658 there were already fifteen farmers, two tailors, two hunters, one doctor, three try-workers and fishermen, one woodcutter, two carpenters and twenty-four labourers. There were ninety-one officials and twenty-two women and children. With the ten convicts and sixteen slaves there were now one hundred and eighty-nine people to be fed at the Cape. Commissioner Johan Cunaeus who visited the Cape in 1658 felt that this was more than enough and as long as the settlement was dependent on the Company for food the number should not be increased. The officials, who had been forbidden by Van Goens to have their own gardens, were permitted by Cunaeus to grow vegetables on condition that the ground be returned to the Company when the officials left the Cape.

The Commander also was given a land grant but apparently not on condition of returning it to the Company on his departure. This land was behind Lion's Head but he soon exchanged it for land behind the Windberg.[6] He called his land Bosheuvel. The Deeds and Transport Notices show that Van Riebeeck also owned land to the south of the small fort Coornhoop and between the Salt River and the land of Hendrik Boom. One of these farms was known as Uijtwijck.[7] On it Van Riebeeck built a house, outbuildings, a cattle post and cultivated some arable plots. Not only did he sell wheat from his farms but,

6. Böeseken, A. J.: *S.A. Argiefstukke, Belangrike Kaapse Dokumente*, vol. 1, pp. 13 – 14.
7. In Deeds Office: Transporten en Schepenenkennis, 1652 - 1662, Deed of Transfer of land called Uijtwijck, 15 Dec. 1661.

according to the inventory he made before leaving the Cape, he also had 1,244 fruit trees and several thousand vines growing on Bosheuvel. He was anxious to sell this farm to the Company before leaving the Cape but when this did not come to pass Jacob Cornelis van Rosendaal leased it and later, in November, 1665, bought it for 1600 guilders.

It is noteworthy that Van Riebeeck was able, in a time of scarcity, to cultivate almost as many morgen as the officials. Though he worked hard on his own farm he did not neglect his supervision of the free burghers; as a matter of fact they benefited from his knowledge of farming. He was able to justify their complaints, at the end of 1658, about the low prices the Company was paying for their produce but, on the other hand, he was not disturbed by their threats, as the settlement did not depend on their labour alone. But despite his own hard work Van Riebeeck was forced to admit, during the course of 1661, that the free burghers at the Cape could not produce enough for their needs. Rice had to be imported and the more burghers there were the more rice was needed. Consequently the Council of Seventeen, in a letter of the 23rd August, 1661, ordered that only officials who intended to farm should be released from the Company's service and that the number of free burghers had to be kept as low as possible.

Nevertheless in May, 1662, when Van Riebeeck and his family prepared to board the *Mars* for their journey to Batavia he could look back with satisfaction on his ten years' stay at the Cape. He advised his successor, Zacharias Wagenaer, to strive to live in peace with the Hottentots so that the Dutch could explore the interior without fear of attack. He should ensure that there were always sufficient provisions for the ships and should encourage the breeding of cattle, sheep and pigs. All the good advice which had been given to him, such as how to feed the population from the produce of the farms and how to serve the Company best in the cheapest way, Van Riebeeck now gladly passed on to his successor and he also left behind the knowledge he had gained over a period of ten years. No fewer than fourteen Hottentot tribes are described in his official report. Some he knew from personal experience and others by hearsay only. In another document the times of planting, pruning and harvesting are recorded in great detail and Van Riebeeck refers to his *Hoveniers Almanack*, in which he wrote further particulars about the land and farming.

In Van Riebeeck's report of his stay at the Cape there is hardly a discordant note. He was especially satisfied at the way in which the first difficulties with the Hottentots had been overcome. He was satisfied too that it was possible completely to protect the cattle of the Company and the free burghers from the raids of the Hottentots with the help of the small forts, Kijckuijt, Keert de Koe, Houdt de Bul and the Ruiterwacht, and a hedge of bitter almond trees. An increasing number of mounted guards also made it impossible for the Hottentots to flee into the interior with stolen cattle.

It is remarkable that Van Riebeeck does not say anything about the conversion of the Hottentots to Christianity. At the beginning of the Resolution book he wrote a prayer which amongst other things expresses the hope that a true Reformed Christian Belief may be propagated amongst these "wild and brutal people". He later added the words "if possible" as if he had begun to doubt whether it were possible. In fact only one Hottentot girl, Eva, who had been taken into his home and educated there, had been converted to Christianity before he left for Batavia.

The two sick-comforters during Van Riebeeck's stay at the Cape were Willem Barentz Wylant and Van Riebeeck's brother-in-law, Pieter van der Stael. They said the evening prayers and preached the sermon on Sundays. The former left on the 10th of March, 1656, and the latter arrived on the 5th of March, 1656. Holy Communion could only be held and children baptized when a minister arrived on one of the passing ships and stayed at the Cape for a few days or weeks. During the whole of Van Riebeeck's term of office at the Cape the sacraments had to be administered by such ministers as fleetingly visited the Cape. Thus the Cape was founded to provide for the physical welfare of the fleet and the fleet in its turn contributed to the spiritual welfare of the Cape.

3. The Settlement under the Van Der Stels

Free burghers or officials?

Jan van Riebeeck's successor, Zacharias Wagenaer, as he signed his name whilst in the service of the Company, was the son of a Dresden city magistrate. He was born in 1614, and started his career in 1633 with the famous Amsterdam cartographer, Joan Blaeu. When he succeeded Jan van Riebeeck in 1662 he had already served seven years in the West India Company and twenty years in the East India Company. He displayed great interest in flora and fauna, and although he tried in vain to cultivate rice, which had to be imported into the Cape from Japan, Java, Arrakan and Siam, he nevertheless succeeded admirably in providing the huge fleets with meat and vegetables. Even the fleet of Pieter de Bitter, with a crew of about 3,000 men, which was anchored in Table Bay for more than forty days, had no complaints about the provisions Wagenaer supplied.

Wagenaer himself, however, often complained bitterly about the Cape and its inhabitants. Three months after his arrival he informed the Seventeen that he could not agree with what Jan van Riebeeck had "written, testified and hoped" concerning the free burghers who, according to Wagenaer, were, with the exception of six or eight, lazy and dissolute. He earnestly requested, therefore, that a minister be sent to the Cape and, in a letter of 21 November, 1663, went so far as to ask the Directors to remove no less than sixty-seven free burghers from the Cape and replace them with more diligent families. Although the Directors did not immediately comply with his request, the incompetent burghers were gradually sifted out and by the close of the seventeenth century only ten or twelve of the original free burghers still had descendants at the Cape. Concerning the free burghers who were at the Cape in 1699, Daniël Heins, one of the Commissioners, noted that he had to say in all sincerity that he had never come across more obedient and dutiful subjects than these people, "of whom the most prominent", he said, "assured me that they would never consider returning to their fatherland".[1] Much water still had to flow under the bridge, however, before it was decided who would play the most important role at the Cape, the free burghers or the officials.

When the winter rains of 1663 caused Van Riebeeck's fort to collapse in five or six places, Wagenaer suggested to the Seventeen that at the place where annually thousands of "Christian people came to refresh and restore themselves a well proportioned stone fortress" should be erected. Several of Wagenaer's

---

1. Film W 315 in the Cape Archives, with the microfilm of Kol. Arch. 4018, oo. 117 – 1184. (Rijksarchief, The Hague).

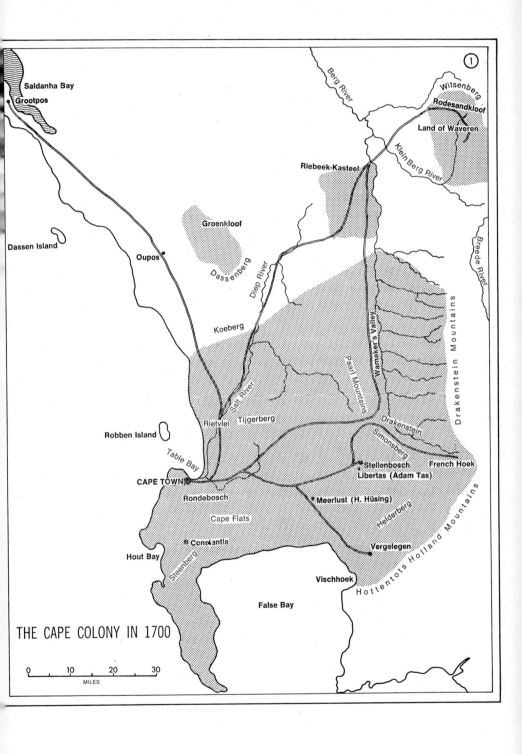

THE CAPE COLONY IN 1700

Saldanha Bay
Grootpos

Witsenberg
Rodesandkloof
Land of Waveren

Berg River

Klein Berg River

Riebeek-Kasteel

Breede River

Dassen Island

Groenkloof

Oupos

Dassenberg

Diep River

Koeberg

Wamaker's Valley

Paarl Mountains

Drakenstein Mountains

Salt River

Rietvlei   Tijgerberg

Robben Island

Drakenstein

Simonsberg

Table Bay

Stellenbosch
Libertas (Adam Tas)

French Hoek

CAPE TOWN

Rondebosch

Meerlust (H. Hüsing)

Helderberg

Cape Flats

Vergelegen

Constantia

Hout Bay

Steenberg

Vischhoek

Hottentots Holland Mountains

False Bay

0   10   20   30
MILES

suggestions bore fruit, for before his departure the first minister, Joan van Arckel, was sent to the Cape, and in August, 1665, the land for the new five-pointed Castle was allocated. The corner-stone was laid on 2 January, 1666.

Although the Directors had obviously decided that the Cape was important enough to be defended, their attitude to the settlement as a whole was negative. Journeys to the interior were encouraged only if they were profitable. During the sixties and seventies no thought was given to expansion or colonization. When one of the Company's officials, Georgius Fredericus Wreeden, of his own accord learnt the Hottentot language, and compiled a list of words, "for the time being using Greek characters", the Seventeen were not enthusiastic. They were prepared to print his list and "honour" him with a reward of 100 rix-dollars, but added that it would be much more useful if "the inhabitants were to learn our language rather than we theirs".

When Cornelis van Quaelbergen (27 September, 1666 – 18 June, 1668) succeeded Wagenaer the Republic of the United Netherlands was waging its second war against England. The Directors decided, even before the Peace of Breda was concluded in July, 1667, that the dangers of the conflict were over as far as the Cape was concerned, and the soldiers who were helping to build the Castle could therefore be employed elsewhere. The French had to be watched, however, and when the French admiral De Montdevergue was too cordially entertained by Van Quaelbergen, the latter was replaced by Jacob Borghorst (18 June, 1668 – 25 March, 1670). Like the free burghers, all these Commanders owned land and did some farming. Thus Borghorst bought cattle, sheep and wagons from the departing Commander and other officials. However, in April, 1668, the Directors decided that officials would no longer be allowed to farm. Borghorst sold his sheep and wethers for ƒ3,722 and his wagons and oxen for ƒ1,450. Owing to ill-health he had previously requested to be allowed to leave the Cape. He now repeated his request, and on 25 March, 1670, was succeeded by Pieter Hackius. Hackius, who was in constant bad health from the time of his arrival, died on 30 November, 1671.

Since the Directors were aware of a new struggle which was approaching against England and Louis XIV of France, Isbrand Goske, on the way to the East as Commissioner, signed instructions in February, 1671, that the building of the Castle be resumed. Three hundred men were taken from the ships to assist in this task, and on 2 October, 1672, Goske landed at the Cape as Governor in order to supervise the work in person. By this time the inhabitants knew that the unrest in Europe had materialized into war. In the event of the enemy attacking the Cape it was decided that all the wives and children of the free burghers were to be evacuated to the Company's first outpost, Hottentots-Holland. The officials would then march against the enemy under five standards, the free burghers being divided into two companies.

Although the garrison had been enlarged to four hundred and twenty men progress in building the Castle was slow; but when, on 13 July, 1674, the news reached the Cape that peace had been concluded with England on 6 March, 1674, four of the five ramparts were already completed. The fifth rampart and the seaward gateway were completed by Goske's successor, Governor Johan Bax, called Van Herentaals (13 March, 1676 – 29 June, 1678). Not until after the death of Johan Bax was it decided to call the ramparts Oranje, Nassouw, Catsenellenbogen, Buren and Leerdam in honour of Prince William the Third. The ceremony of naming the ramparts took place on 26 April, 1679, while Commissioner Dirk Blom was at the Cape.

Still no positive steps had been taken towards the colonization of the Cape but the number of free burghers gradually increased as their families grew. A letter to the Directors mentioned that in 1679 there were sixty-two families, with one hundred and seventeen children at the Cape. Amongst the eighty-seven single men only twenty-two were agriculturists. The others were artisans, fishermen and inn-keepers. By 1679 the number of people at the Cape other than officials had increased to four hundred and eighty; this included one hundred and ninety-one slaves and thirty servants. After the garrison had once more been reduced by sixty the free burghers exceeded the paid Company officials in number.

As the Castle was nearing completion and the threat of an invasion had passed, the Directors decided that it was not necessary to send an official of the rank of governor to the Cape. The highest authority at the Cape would once more be a commander, and the person chosen for this post was Simon van der Stel, who assumed duty on 12 October, 1679.

Simon van der Stel

The new Commander had been born on 14 October, 1639, while his parents, Adriaan van der Stel and Maria Lievens, were on their way to Mauritius, of which Adriaan had been given command. Maria Lievens was a daughter of Hendrik Lievens, a sea captain, and Monica da Costa. Simon van der Stel spent the first five and a half years of his life on Mauritius, where a sister, Maria, was born. During May, 1645, the family left for Batavia. There Simon and his sister were baptised on 3 January, 1646. Another sister, Adriana, was born in Batavia. A few months later, on 16 May, Adriaan van der Stel was killed in Ceylon during a campaign against Rajah Singh. Simon's mother later married a sea captain in Batavia, and died there in 1652. In 1659 Simon sailed to Holland with the fleet of Pieter Sterthemius to further his studies.

Details of these studies have not as yet been discovered. He married Johanna Jacoba Six on 23 October, 1663. They had five sons and one daughter. The three older children, Wilhelmus Adrianus, Adriaan and Catelina, were born in Haarlem in 1664, 1665 and 1667 respectively, while Frans, Hendrik and Cornelis were born in Amsterdam and baptised in the "Zuiderkerk". According to deeds discovered in the Amsterdam City Archives, it appears that Simon was a property owner and businessman, and was greatly interested in the making of wine and brandy.[2] Through his wife he was related to the well-known Six

2. Böeseken, A. J., *Simon van der Stel en sy Kinders* (Cape Town, 1966).

family, and the very wealthy Van Waverens. When the armies of Louis XIV invaded Holland he was given command of a company of infantry. Possibly the long absence from home estranged him from his wife; possibly after the Peace of Nijmegen, which was concluded during August, 1678, he longed for a more adventurous life than that of an Amsterdam merchant. He may also have started thinking about the future of his children. Whatever it was that made him decide to leave Holland, it is certain that his appointment during March, 1679, as Commander of the Cape must have been a great joy to him. In May, 1679, he embarked on the *Vrye Zee*, with his six children and his wife's youngest sister, Cornelia Six.

Simon van der Stel was welcomed on 12 October, 1679, by Hendrik Crudop, the acting Commander at the Cape. At the time of his arrival the officials and free burghers with their wives, children, slaves and servants numbered seven hundred and sixty-seven souls. Only twenty-two families were actively engaged in agriculture, and consequently the Cape was not self-supporting. Large quantities of rice had to be imported annually. Therefore van der Stel's principal problem was how to produce enough wheat to feed the population of the Cape. This received his immediate attention. After the most pressing shipping business had been settled he and a few members of the Council rode into the interior between 3 and 8 November. After a vist to Hottentots-Holland, where the south-easter blew fiercely, he decided to start a new settlement on the banks of the Eerste River. He was the first person to pass the night on a "little island" in the river, and had it noted in the Journal that he would call the settlement Stellenbosch because of its trees he liked so much.

This settlement, of very personal interest to van der Stel, was unlike the outposts founded by the Company. There the ground was tilled by officials, or they leased it temporarily to free burghers, as was the case at Hottentots-Holland. In Stellenbosch the first free burgher started working independently as early as 1679. In May, 1680, the Commander could inform the Directors that a number of "free persons" had established themselves at Stellenbosch. The number increased gradually. In 1681 a fifth of the wheat harvested at the Cape was produced by Stellenbosch, in 1682 a third; in 1684 forty families harvested three thousand and twenty-one bags of wheat. As yet there were only free burghers living in Stellenbosch. In 1682 Van der Stel appointed four of them to act as Heemraden and to settle any disputes amongst themselves. After the visit of Hendrik Adriaan van Reede, who was sent from Holland as High Commissioner, the first official was sent to Stellenbosch. He was given the title of "landdrost", and in 1687 a church, a council-house and a residence for the landdrost were built. The rapid growth and success of the settlement were principally due to the zeal and energy of Simon van der Stel.

In the Journal and Letters there are many indications of the energy and perseverance with which the Commander undertook his task. First he made the Castle habitable, and during June, 1680, he moved into it with his children and sister-in-law. He started a saw-mill at Hout Bay. He visited Robben Island to organise the fishing and attend to the treatment of convicts. He started a brickyard at De Kuijlen. The moat around the Castle was deepened by blasting, the rampart Leerdam was repaired, and visitors were entertained hospitably and lavishly at the Castle. He also punished dishonesty amongst officials and captains of visiting ships, thereby making many enemies.

He used his knowledge of wine-making to help the free burghers improve the quality of their wines. The reception of the Cape wines in Batavia and Amsterdam, was not, however, encouraging. Batavia admitted that they had a "reasonably good taste", but advised Van der Stel to use them at the Cape, so that he would have no need of Spanish or French wines from the East-bound ships. In Amsterdam, too, the prices fetched by the Cape wines were not satisfactory.

During the first years of Van der Stel's administration attention was chiefly centred on ensuring sufficient meat and other provisions for the crews of the passing fleets. The organisation of the garrison and the burgher militia also demanded attention. Here Van der Stel's experience as a captain of the mercenary guards in the war against Louis XIV proved invaluable. There was also a new factor to complicate life at the Cape. This was the arrival in March, 1681, of high-ranking Orientals. The Council of Batavia had banished these people to the Cape, and urged the Commander to take particular care that they did not escape or fall into the hands of the French, Danes or English. Van der Stel protested that he did not have enough people to guard such political prisoners, but the Batavian authorities ignored his complaints and advised the Commander of the Cape to spread the prisoners out around the country so that they would have little opportunity to conspire against the Company.

Almost every year the fleets to and from the East brought to the Cape a Commissioner who held a higher rank than that of the Commander, and who had to report on the Commander's activities and assist him wherever possible. It should be noted that these high officials almost invariably commended Van der Stel. As early as 1681, Rijckloff van Goens, the younger, reported that the local harvest could at last supply all the Cape's needs, and that rice had to be imported only for the slaves. However, both he and his father, Rijckloff van Goens, senior, who visited the Cape the following year, urged Van der Stel to plant more trees. They also advised him to do everything in his power to diminish the annual losses sustained by the Company at the Cape.

The search for minerals was one way in which the Commander attempted to carry out the instructions to minimize the Company's costs. He knew how to smelt ore, and personally examined the ore brought from the north by Oloff Bergh in 1682 and 1683. He hoped that there might be copper or silver in Namaqualand, but he also considered the possibility of deposits closer to the Cape. Thus during November, 1683, the Commander travelled through Simon's Valley along the mountains as far as Crusenvliet, climbing to the top of the mountain to investigate the rumoured presence of minerals there.

As far as his personal life was concerned, the first years of Simon van der Stel's sojourn at the Cape were not happy. His sister-in-law died in May, 1681. The directors criticised his personal expenditure and the way in which his sons were employed. Consequently he advised his eldest son to return to Holland. Later his daughter and his sons Adriaan, Hendrik and Cornelis also left the Cape, so that only Frans remained. In 1683 Van der Stel was already showing more interest in his country residence, Rustenburg, where he had planted new vineyards and many trees, than in the silent Castle. The year 1685 was a turning-point in his life, and simultaneously was a decisive year in the history of Southern Africa. When High Commissioner Hendrik Adriaan van Reede visited the Cape at the beginning of 1685, the Directors were as yet not sure what they were going to do about the Cape. They still had not decided whether it would be better to use the free burghers or the officials to supply their fleets and defend the Cape against attack, but a clearer policy was beginning to take shape. In 1682 Governor-General van Goens had instructed Simon van der Stel to oppose all miscegenation at the Cape. Van Reede whole-heartedly agreed with this policy. He went a step further, and stipulated that children of slaves should be taught by their own teachers. He also considerably improved the lot of the slaves at the Cape by providing better clothing and housing for them. There had been marriages between Dutchmen and emancipated female slaves at the Cape, but after 1685 these were prohibited, except when the female slaves had Dutch fathers. A school established solely for the children of burghers and officials, fitted well into this policy.

Van Reede and Van der Stel understood and respected each other. The High Commissioner supported the Commander in his punishment of dishonest officials, but at the same time advised him not to be too peremptory in his treatment of his fellow-councillors. He commended Van der Stel for his care of the Company's sheep and cattle, and for the way agriculture had improved during his administration. His report points out that during 1685 no less than 370 morgen had been cultivated and that a harvest of 2,400 bags was expected, which would be sufficient to feed the slaves and the garrison and, possibly, to send a surplus to East India. The High Commissioner was also pleased with the viticulture.

Two matters, however, did not please Van Reede. He would have liked the Commander to plant more trees, and to improve the standard of building. Hottentots-Holland especially, was severely criticised. The house and stables were so primitive and dilapidated that they were quite unfit for use. This particular farmhouse had been built before Simon van der Stel's arrival at the Cape, and he agreed that it should be rebuilt. Van Reede stipulated that the walls should be stone, and the house, pens, stables and other outbuildings should be protected by a surrounding wall, with everything neat and practical. This would teach the free burghers how to build farm-houses and how to protect their farms from wild animals. All stone walls were to be covered with clay mortar, and whitened with lime. In this manner Van Reede contributed to what was later to be called the Cape-Dutch style of architecture.

The High Commissioner's main problem was how to turn the Cape into a profitable possession for the Company. He approached this problem from various angles. He tried to economise. He also tried to increase the income from the sale of monopolies. Furthermore he suggested that there should be a vigorous prospecting for minerals. He gave Van der Stel permission to lead an expedition to the north. In the next chapter we shall see how eagerly the Commander made use of this concession.

Not long after the departure of Hendrik Adriaan van Reede the Directors decided to make the Cape a permanent settlement, and to encourage free burghers to settle there. In order to encourage French refugees to emigrate to the Cape attractive terms were drawn up, and approximately one hundred and fifty Huguenots availed themselves of the opportunity. Van der Stel was also allowed to encourage Hollanders and others off passing ships to settle at the Cape as farmers. In October, 1686, he distributed twenty-three smallholdings to such people and the new settlement was called Drakenstein in honour of the High Commissioner. Eighteen months later the first French arrived in the *Oosterland* and they, and others who reached the Cape during 1688 and 1689, were settled on smallholdings among the Dutch and German free burghers. A piece of ground between Drakenstein and Stellenbosch was given to their minister, dominee Pierre Simond, while Paul Roux was appointed their lay-reader and schoolmaster. An attempt was made to incorporate the French as quickly as possible with the Hollanders, and although the Directors allowed them to have their own church council they were not allowed to form a separate community of their own. The children quickly learnt to speak the language of their friends, and after twenty years there were only a few elderly people who could understand nothing but French. Although in the eighteenth century the French were requested to include translations with their letters to the Government, they were never prohibited from speaking the French language amongst themselves. The younger generation, however, used their mother tongue less and less, and so the language of this minority group gradually disappeared at the Cape.

During the last decade of the seventeenth century the increase in population was due not to immigration but to a rising birth-rate. Nearly every Sunday couples were married, and babies baptised. When Wilhem Adriaen van der Stel took over the administration of the Cape, in 1699, its population had risen to 402 men, 224 women and 521 children.

Wilhem Adriaen van der Stel

After an absence of more than fourteen years, Wilhem Adriaen van der Stel must have been pleased to arrive back at the Cape as Governor. With him came his wife, Maria de Haese, and his children. He was as industrious as his father, and immediately began planting the trees he had brought from Holland. He was thirty-four years old and quickly adopted policies that differed from those of his father. Like his father he journeyed inland to survey suitable smallholdings for free burghers who were willing to penetrate deeper into the interior. In November, 1699, he rode through Stellenbosch and Drakenstein until he crossed the Ubiqua Mountains, which overlooked a beautiful valley. This he called the "Land van Waveren". Despite his father's warning against moving free burghers further into the interior, he issued many grazing licences. The new settlement thus became a community of cattle farmers. They were under the administration of the landdrost of Stellenbosch. When they were attacked by the Ubiquas, or Bushmen, in 1701, everybody, Cape officials and free burghers as well as burghers from Stellenbosch and Drakenstein, forty men in all, came to their aid and helped to recapture their cattle and drive off the Ubiquas.

No other noteworthy events took place during the first years of Wilhem Adriaen's administration. On 12 February, 1700, his meat contract with the Company was extended for ten years while Commissioner Wouter Valckenier was at the Cape. The Commissioner also saw to it against Van der Stel's wishes that the free burghers were informed that cattle trading with the Hottentots was no longer prohibited. This gave the free burghers a right which they keenly exploited. Van der Stel wished to trade with the Hottentots himself and on behalf of the Company, and did not like this competition. In October, 1702, a number of free burghers arrived at the Castle with two thousand head of cattle, which, it was rumoured, had been stolen from the Hottentots. This gave the Governor reason once again to prohibit cattle trading. In a letter to the Seventeen Van der Stel admitted, however, that the "most important and pious" citizens did not take part in these authorised expeditions for trading cattle in the interior.[3] As Van der Stel was accused by the free burghers of maintaining fifteen cattle posts in the interior, and admitted to eight, his motives were not above suspicion. If the free burghers were prevented from trading the officials would have no competitors.

However, the fight between the free burghers and officials which broke out three years later was mainly over rights of land ownership. When Wilhem Adriaen van der Stel arrived in the Cape, most of the officials had land on which they farmed. His father, Simon van der Stel, had built a beautiful house at Constantia on land which he had obtaiend from Hendrik Adriaan van Reede. The Commissioners Daniël Heins and Wouter Valckanier gave Simon van der Stel more land in 1699 and 1700, and a fine farm to Frans van der Stel. The former secundus, Andries de Man, the fiscal, Johan Blesius, the surgeon, Willem ten Damme, the new secundus, Samuel Elsevier, the pastor, Petrus Kalden, the sick-comforter, Albert Coopman and the captain of the garrison, Oloff Bergh, all possessed plots and most of them had farms. The prohibition against officials owning land, which dated from 1668, was thus completely disregarded by the time Wilhem Adriaen van der Stel came to the Cape. Together with Frans van der Stel and Simon van der Stel the new Governor received a plot from Daniël Heins in the Table Valley. Then in the following year, after surveying the country personally, Wouter Valckenier granted the new Governor 400 morgen in the vicinity of Hottentots-Holland. This farm Van der Stel called "Vergelegen".

Although he could, with a change of horses, cover the distance between

---

3. C. 507: Uitg. Br., 20 March 1702, p. 418 (Cape State Archives).

Vergelegen and the Castle in six hours, it is clear from the daily journals and the resolution book that Van der Stel spent increasingly less time at the Castle. In 1700 the Council of Policy met eleven times, whereas in Van Riebeeck's days it had met at least fifty-two times a year. This was indeed seldom enough, but in 1701 the Council met only seven times, in 1702 six times and in the ensuing two years five times each year. Even so, Van der Stel did not altogether neglect the work that had to be done at the settlement. In 1703 a new stable was completed at the Castle, and in April, 1703, he could inform the Seventeen that "the new church on the Heerengracht, except for the tower" had been completed.

Nor was Van der Stel idle at Vergelegen, as can be seen from his own records and the official journals. He was not satisfied with the 400 morgen which had been allotted for his farm. He therefore gave his head gardener adjacent land of over 100 morgen, which he then "bought" from him. During the course of a few years a homestead with outbuildings, such as slave quarters, a barn for the wine press and stables, was erected. There were hundreds of slaves on this farm, as well as a number of European servants. Later, when he tried to jusitfy his actions at the Cape in his *Korte Deductie*, he admitted that some of them were on the Company's payroll. As Governor he had the right to make use of servants in Company pay.

In the *Korte Deductie* he also admitted to owning a hundred thousand vines and eight cattle posts across the mountains, and to buying 2,600 sheep. The free burghers maintained that he actually owned considerably more. The extent of Van der Stel's farming is, in fact, hardly relevant. It was the fact that he and his fellow officials, as well as Simon and Frans van der Stel who had been officials, were farming so successfully, that disturbed the free burghers. The officials on the other hand regarded the free burghers as irresponsible farmers who neglected their fields and did nothing to combat soil erosion or outbreaks of scab among their sheep.

Simon van der Stel was worried about the standard of agriculture at the Cape, the shortage of trek oxen, and the possibility that there would be insufficient meat for the hospital and passing ships. He advised his son to prevent the free burghers from moving inland and to allow officials who had been in the country some time to settle as free burghers and to farm, as he and his son Frans were doing.

Wilhem Adriaen, however, preferred solving the problems inherited from his father in his own way. He encouraged rather than discouraged free burghers to become cattle farmers and to venture further into the interior. However, he wished to prevent them from trading with the Hottentots, as he was trying to build up both his own and the Company's cattle stocks. Whereas Simon wanted to free officials so that they could go farming, Wilhem Adriaen could see no reason why an official had to resign from the Company if he wanted to farm. His own father had farmed for fifteen of the nineteen years during which he governed the Cape. Other Governors and Commanders had done the same.

Meanwhile the citizens were very much aware of what the officials were doing. They felt that the officials wanted to work the free burghers out of the produce market. The richer citizens were particularly aware of this threat. When the Governor, in an attempt to increase the income from the wine contract, awarded it to one instead of to four free burghers, the free burghers' resentment at the high-handed attitude of the officials came into the open. Henning Hüsing, who had already complained to the Seventeen about the Governor and the officials at the Cape, began, with Adam Tas, who did all the secretarial work, to collect further complaints. They pointed out that the new owner of the wine contract, Johannes Phijffer, was a friend of the Van der Stels with insufficient capital to pay for the granting of a contract which gave him the monopoly of the wine trade. He would thus do exactly as he was told by the officials, who had made it possible for him to obtain the contract.

While the free burghers waited for a reply to their first letters to the Seventeen and the Governor-General and Council of Batavia, Tas was industriously collecting as many complaints as possible against the Governor and his friends. He finally embodied them in a letter of complaint containing thirty-eight points, which was signed by sixty-three free burghers. The Governor was attacked and also Frans van der Stel and the parson, Pieter Kalden. Samuel Elsevier's large farm was also mentioned.

The officials, of course, were perfectly aware of what was brewing among the free burghers. In fact, some of the free burgher's feelings were only too apparent from their behaviour. Thus the former burgher councillor, Jan Rotterdam, remained seated on Sunday, 11 October, 1705, when the rest of the congregation rose, as was the custom, when the Governor and his family entered the church. Van der Stel regarded this as a serious matter, and convened a meeting of the Council of Policy for the next day. Deputies were sent to Jan Rotterdam, and were received in an insulting manner. Van der Stel and his Council decided to send the old man to Batavia to appear before the Council of Justice. By December it was known among the free burghers that the Governor had received a letter from Batavia. He knew that Henning Hüsing, Jacobus van der Heiden, Jan van Meerland and Adam Tas were his chief enemies.

A fierce struggle began. Henning Hüsing lost his profitable meat contract on 19 December, 1705. Although this was in accordance with an order issued by the Seventeen, Adam Tas was unaware of this, and declared in his diary on 25 December that " . . . the Governor has arranged matters to his satisfaction now, he's found the trick to sell his sheep and those of some of his friends besides". This, as the free burghers explained to the Seventeen in their letter of complaint against the Company officials, was the actual consequence of the Seventeen's order.

The return fleet from the East brought more news in 1706. Adriaan van der Stel, a member of the Council of India, informed his brother of the matters pending against him, and Wilhem Adriaen began taking countermeasures. He hurriedly sent out officials to ask whether the free burghers still had any wine to supply to the Company and, equally hurriedly, a "testimonial" was drawn up in which the Governor's "merciful and meek manner" was praised. People were invited to the Castle to sign the testimonial. Many did, "even Blacks", Adam

Tas noted. Afterwards, landdrost Starrenburg went to Stellenbosch and Draken-stein to collect more signatures. At the same time Van der Stel was also acting more drastically. On 28 February, before sunrise, Adam Tas was arrested and his desk was taken to the Cape. This enabled Van der Stel to establish the exact nature of the complaints against him. He decided that the time for leniency was over, and acted mercilessly. On 8 March, the Council of Policy decided to send Henning Hüsing, Jacobus van der Heiden, Pieter van der Bijl, Ferdinandus Appel and Jan van Meerland to Holland in the return fleet. They and other Cape citizens were granted a "hearing" in the hope that they would withdraw their complaints, or at least modify them. Van der Heiden, who was one of the most intractable witnesses, was thrown in the so-called Dark Hole of the Castle, a cell without any light whatsoever. The other four were sent to Europe on the return fleet. Meerland died during the voyage, but Hüsing, Appel and Van der Bijl submitted "a humble supplication, as well as the free burghers complaints" to the Seventeen.

While a commission of inquiry was investigating the matter, Wilhem Adriaen was issuing summonses to many Cape free burghers. Nine who refused to obey the summonses were banished in absentia to Mauritius for five years, and fined 200 rixdollars each. This was in August, 1706. By the end of the year not one of them had been taken into custody. Although Van der Stel finally succeeded in apprehending three of the nine, his power to revenge himself on them was ended on 17 April, 1707. The letter he received on that day was quite unambiguous. It was signed by the Seventeen on 30 October, 1706, and summoned the Governor, the secundus, the landdrost and the parson, Petrus Kalden, to Amsterdam. It banished the free burgher Frans van der Stel from all the Company's possessions. All the other officials were categorically forbidden to own land or to trade. The free burghers had been completely victorious.

On his return to Europe Van der Stel did his utmost to prove that he was innocent of all the accusations made by the free burghers. He defended himself at great length in what he called the *Korte Deductie*. It appeared anonymously, and was answered at even greater length by a number of Cape citizens, in what they called the *Contra Deductie* which appeared in 1711. These two publications started much controversy. Not to this day has either side categorically proved the innocence or the guilt of Van der Stel and his officials.

It was obviously important for Van der Stel to establish whether or not he was guilty of the accusations made against him. It was equally important for the future of South Africa that it should be decided at the beginning of the 18th century whether there was room at the Cape for farmer-officials as well as free burghers who were agricultural and cattle farmers. The free burghers had proved that the officials by abusing their powers had gained an unfair advantage. The Governor admitted that the advantage had been on the side of the officials, but maintained that the free burghers were exaggerating. In the years which followed the free burghers' vistory over the officials, the former proved that they were well able to satisfy the needs of the fleets, hospital and garrison.

The free burghers learnt a valuable lesson from their clash with the officials.

Whenever one of the officials subsequently obtained land by marriage or inheritance, he was immediately asked either to become a free burgher or to sell his land. As we shall see in the next chapter, the number of free burghers gradually increased in the course of the eighteenth century, and although the number of officials increased as well the rate of their increase was far slower. The Cape was to be colonized, not by a succession of officials, like the Company's possessions in the East, but by Europeans who had found a permanent home on the continent of Africa.

4. The Lure of Africa

Expeditions of discovery before 1700

Upon reading Jan van Riebeeck's Journal one is immediately struck by the restless fervour with which almost from his first day at the Cape the Commander began to explore his surroundings. People in Europe at that time had only a superficial knowledge of the coast of Southern Africa. They knew nothing about the interior and credited the wildest tales. Van Riebeeck, however, lost no time in beginning personally to acquaint himself with his new environment. Almost every day, on foot and later on horseback, he roamed the coast from Table Bay to Hout Bay. He sent fast galliots such as *De Roode Vos, The Swarte Vos* and *De Tulp* up to Saldanha Bay and, later on, up the East Coast. In 1655 Jan Jacobsz, commanding the galliot *'t Nachtglas*, was commissioned by the Seventeen to explore the island Tristan da Cunha.

Van Riebeeck expected a great deal from these ventures, particularly from the voyages along the East Coast. After consultation with the cartographer Martinus Martinio, he expected not only to reach the kingdom of Monomotapa and Butua, but also Ophir, where it was believed King Solomon had obtained his gold. One of Van Riebeeck's most dynamic officials, Fredrick Verburgh, was twice sent to Madagascar. He returned from the first voyage in December, 1654, with nothing to show for his pains; he and the crew of *De Tulp* perished on the second voyage. Rijckloff van Goens, who visited the Cape as Commissioner in 1657, criticized what he called the "airy notions" of the Commander. If, he said in his report, the men who left in *De Tulp* – there were twenty-five of them – had been employed in agriculture, the Company would by now have been in a position to export wheat to Madagascar.[1] He nevertheless did encourage Van Riebeeck to journey into the interior in an attempt to disclose "the secrets of Africa". He optimistically supposed that it might be possible to reach the river Spirito Sancto and the "City of Monomotapa" overland. Van Riebeeck did not share his optimism. In 1655 he had sent ensign Jan Wintervogel northwards. He reached Saldanha Bay overland. In September of the same year Willem Muller, a corporal, was sent into the interior with nine soldiers and the interpreter whom the Dutch called Herry. The expedition reached the Hottentots-Holland, mountains where Herry outwitted the others and was the only one to take advantage of this second land journey.

It is not surprising therefore that Van Riebeeck attempted no official expeditions inland in 1656. Next year Van Goens urged him to do so and promised

1. C.700: Memoriën en Instructiën, 1657 – 1685, p. 13. (Cape State Archives) (Translated from the original Dutch).

*f*150 to the first man to reach the Spirito Sancto. However, even without the incitement of a reward, there were many men eager to explore Africa's interior. As the first travellers had been well received by the Hottentots Van Riebeeck had no difficulty in later finding volunteers for further ventures. The first expedition after Van Goens had left the Cape set out in the spring of 1657. The fiscal Abraham Gabbema left with six officials, eight free burghers, one white servant and four Hottentots. Theirs was the first expedition to reach the Berg River. Their food and trading goods were carried by pack oxen. They were better equipped than previous expeditions, but they returned with only seven cows, three calves and forty-one sheep.

The free burghers blamed the officials for their failure to obtain more cattle and asked whether they might not, without the Company's servants, themselves organise an expedition into the interior. They wished to ascertain whether they could on their own obtain more livestock from the Hottentots.[2] Van Riebeeck approved the idea, provided the free burghers abided by Van Goen's condition that they should not pay more for the cattle than the Company was prepared to pay. Nine days after their departure on Sunday, 18 November, the eight free burghers who had gone trading on their own initiative returned to the fort with – as Van Riebeeck noted not without satisfaction – "a lean cow, three calves and forty-seven old and young, bad, mad sheep".[3] He therefore suggested that they stay at home and farm rather than roam the countryside. This injunction was to be repeated by many subsequent authorities at the Cape.

Expeditions under proper supervision of Company officials were however essential, in order to obtain sufficient cattle from the Hottentots. In 1658 Jan van Harwarden was sent four times with this aim in view. In February he and fifteen soldiers returned with only eleven cows and forty-five sheep. In October he fared even worse: he managed to get only three head of cattle, two calves and nineteen sheep. It appeared that his pack oxen could not carry enough copper, tobacco and pipes to barter successfully. In November Van Riebeeck introduced an innovation. Drawn by six oxen and loaded with trading goods, the first ox-wagon headed for the interior on 2 November. Using a wagon proved a sound idea, for Van Harwarden and his seventeen soldiers returned on 8 November with two hundred and three sheep and twenty-five head of cattle. These men went back to the Hottentots between 10 and 16 November, and returned with one hundred and five sheep and eleven head of cattle. Seven free burghers, who were explicitly said not to be farmers, traded with the Hottentots from 6 to 9 November, but returned with only thirty sheep. The various traders, sent primarily to barter goods for cattle, explored new parts of Africa purely incidentally. Thus on 21 March Jan van Harwarden told Jan van Riebeeck that he had "found the pass over the mountain range of Africa, against which the Berg River lies and through a kloof of which it flows from the far

2. Bosman and Thom: *Journal of Jan van Riebeeck*, vol. II, 1656 – 1658, 8 November 1657, p. 181. (Translated from the original Dutch).

3. *Ibid.*, 18 November 1657, p. 185. (Translated from the original Dutch).

interior".[4] Historians later agreed that Jan van Harwarden and his men were the first to see the valley which was later known as the "Land van Waveren". In this case the opening up of the interior was incidental to the economic necessity of obtaining sufficient cattle for the fleet.

In the following year seven free burghers, led by the free burgher-hunter Christiaen Jansz van Hoesem, were allowed to leave for the interior in search of the Namaquas. They were away from 3 February to 7 March and reported that they had been ninety miles[5] into the interior but had to turn back when they came to a great tidal river and therefore must have been close to the sea. Van Riebeeck questioned them and came to the conclusion that they could have been no more than thirty miles inland, which meant that they must have turned back near the mouth of the Berg River. From May, 1659, until May, 1660, further expeditions north were not considered feasible because the Company was waging war on the Caapmans. Not until November, 1660, did Van Riebeeck decide to send the cadet Jan Danckaert on an expedition to Monomotapa. He had the reputation of being a good engineer and "geometrician". Seven more cadets and five soldiers volunteered to accompany him. Among them were George Fredricus Wreede, who was later to compile the first list of Hottentot words, and Pieter Meerhoff of Copenhagen, who came to the Cape in 1659 and was later to become an important explorer.

The party left on 12 November, and did not return to the Fort until 20 January, 1661. They said that they had reached a big river on 8 December, 1660, and had seen between two hundred and three hundred elephant. From this time on their journal constantly refers to the Elephant River. In the high mountains to the north-east of the river the expedition began to falter when Christiaan de Soete would no longer lead the oxen, and Pieter Roman refused to carry the pick-axe.[6] Van Riebeeck was justified in remarking that Jan Danckaert did not have sufficient authority over his men and wrote the expedition off as a failure. Ten days later he was equipping a new expedition to continue where the others had left off.[7] The new venture was more successful. Twelve men under Pieter Cruijthoff reached the territory of the Namaquas, who were described as giants wrapped in cured animal skins and wearing iron and copper beadwork.

As the Namaquas appeared to be a particularly friendly people, Van Riebeeck decided to send another expedition as soon as possible to make peace between them and the Saldanhars, with whom, it was rumoured, the Namaquas were constantly clashing. At the same time the expedition was to use its merchandise

---

4. *Ibid.*, 21 March 1658, p. 244. (Translated from the original Dutch which in this case is clearer: "de passagie gevonden hebben over 't vaste geberghte van Affrica daer de Bergh-revier tegenaen leght ende met een clooff diep uyt het landt deur compt lopen").

5. Thirty Dutch or German miles were equal to somewhat more than one hundred and twenty-five English or South African miles.

6. Bosman and Thom: *Journal of Jan van Riebeeck*, vol. III, 1659 – 1662, 23 December 1660, p. 318.

7. *Ibid.*, 30 January 1661, p. 323.

to try to entice the Namaquas to the Fort. Pieter van Meerhoff, eight officials and two Hottentot interpreters left the Fort on 21 March, 1661, and returned on 20 April. They all received good rewards, particularly when it was established that they had been a six days' journey deeper into the interior than their predecessors. However, Van Riebeeck was not yet satisfied with what had been done to reveal the secrets of Africa. In November, therefore, he commanded sergeant Pieter Everaert, the head of the Cape militia, to visit the Namaquas with Pieter Meerhoff and Cornelis de Cretser, who was to keep a journal. They were accompanied by eight cadets and two soldiers, some of whom were making the journey for the second, and others for the third time. When this party returned to the Fort on 13 February, 1662, they told Van Riebeeck that on account of a severe drought they had been unable to make contact with the Namaquas. On the outward journey one of the party had been killed by an elephant, while on the return journey the sergeant and another member of the expedition had fallen ill. Despite their comparative failure, they were all rewarded in the customary manner, for, as Van Riebeeck noted in his journal, he wanted "to keep up the spirit of the volunteers".[8]

Wagenaer, Van Riebeeck's successor, reaped the reward of this policy, for when, in September, 1662, he considered that the time had come to send another expedition to the Namaquas there was no lack of "curious volunteers", who were willing to begin where the others had left off.[9] Wagenaer sent out Pieter Cruijthoff with twelve men and a wagon "progressively to explore the land of Africa even further".[10] Although it was Cruijthoff's second journey north and many of his companions knew the interior equally well they made no new discoveries. Illness and disputes with Hottentots hampered the expedition and it returned on 1 February, 1663, with no new facts. However, by September of that year there were more "able volunteers" than were needed for another expedition. Wagenaer decided to send Jonas de la Guerre with fifteen men, whom he described as "the fastest and liveliest fellows, accustomed to inconvenience and quite fearless".[11] They took a wagon and six oxen which could also serve as pack animals, and departed confidently on October 11, 1663. They returned without the wagon on 22 January and said that according to their estimates they had been within eight to ten days' journey of the great river Vigiti Magna. On this, as on previous occasions, they had been forced to return through lack of water.

Thwarted by the water difficulty, Wagenaer paid attention to other matters. Overland expeditions to the north were not attempted again until 1682. Cornelis van Quaelberg traded with the Hottentots in the immediate vicinity of the Fort and nowhere else. His wife even accompanied one of the parties. Later Hieroni-

8. *Ibid.*, 16 February 1662, p. 476: as Van Riebeeck put it: iiv . . . to keep the volunteers eager for such an enterprise . . . ".

9. Böeseken: *Resolusies van die Politieke Raad, 1651 – 1669*, 9 September 1662, p. 288.

10. *Ibid.*, 9 September 1662: "om dit rijck van Afrika progressivelijck nader en nader te laten ontdecken", pp. 288 – 289.

11. *Ibid.*, 27 September 1663: "16 van de gaeuwste en fluextte quanten (die ongemack gewent en voor geen kleijn gerucht verveert en zijn)", p. 308.

mus Cruse crossed the Hottentots-Holland Mountains, traded with the Hessequas and reached the Gouritz River. This intrepid traveller even got as far as Mossel Bay.

Two months after his arrival Jacob Borghorst, who succeeded Quaelberg on 18 June, 1668, sent a small, light sailing vessel, the *Voerman*, to search for possible harbours, rivers or anchorages along the East Coast. Corporal Hieronimus Cruse and fifteen men accompanied him with instructions to land at Mossel Bay and to return to the Castle overland while the *Voerman* and its crew were to explore the coast and harbours of Terra de Natal. The crew of the *Voerman* did not do well and got no further than the Bay of St. Francis. However, Cruse and his men visited the Attaquas and returned to the Castle with a reasonable amount of cattle. Borghorst was so pleased that he immediately sent Cruse back to trade with the tribes who had the most cattle. He had a fight with the Bushmen or Sonquas and earned the respect of the surrounding Hottentot tribes, for the Bushmen were dangerous enemies who left nobody in peace and fought hard to keep their hunting ground for themselves alone.

The Seventeen were not pleased that all attempts to explore the north had been abandoned. In 1669 Borghorst, to comply with their wishes, sent the *Grundel* out to explore the west coast, north of the Cape. The steersman of the *Grundel* was a well-known cartographer who charted the west coast up to Angra Pequena. Up to this time, the end of the sixties, all parties travelling in the interior had gone wherever they wished in perfect safety. In 1670, however, some white hunters were murdered. The Hottentots maintained that the Sonquas were responsible, but some Chainouquas came to the Castle claiming that Gonnema, chief of the Cochoquas, was the culprit. There was nothing much Pieter Hackius, who had succeeded Jacob Borghorst on 25 March, 1670, could do, as he had only a small garrison at his disposal and was moreover in bad health. Isbrand Goske, who arrived on 2 October, 1672, was in a more favourable position to react positively to aggression, since he had been given a larger garrison with which to protect the Cape against possible attacks from enemies of the Republic. When Gonnema attacked three big-game hunters in November, 1672, once again the Cape authorities were unable to retaliate, this time because an attack from overseas appeared to be imminent. In 1673, however, another hunting party was attacked by the Hottentots and Hieronimos Cruse, assisted by Elbert Diemer and eighteen free burghers, was sent out on horseback to punish the Hottentots. They were absent from 6 to 25 July, and returned to the Castle with eight hundred head of cattle and nine hundred sheep.

Other Hottentot chiefs, amongst whom Claas, alias Dorhá, chieftain of the Chainouquas, offered to help attack Gonnema and also asked for Dutch support should they attack him. A joint attack was launched in March, 1674. Wouter Mostert was placed in command of fifty free burghers. Ensign Cruse commanded fifty soldiers and was Commander-in-chief, having under him, also, the chiefs Claas, Coopman, Schacher and Cuiper with four hundred Hottentots. They aimed at surrounding Gonnema and intended to punish him. They did not succeed, however, and he escaped with his tribe, but had to leave eight hundred head of cattle and four thousand sheep in the hands of his attackers. Gonnema revenged himself by doing his utmost to prevent the Hottentots in the interior from trading with the Europeans, and in November, 1675, he launched an unexpected attack on Schacher and Cuiper. Once again Schacher was aided by Goske and once again Gonnema fled to the mountains, but was not followed because his pursuers had to return to work their farms.

Although Goske had a garrison of 462 men, he left Gonnema in peace. His successor Johan Bax resumed the attack on Gonnema. He had noticed that whereas previously two or three people could travel in perfect safety fifty an sixty miles, now it was not safe for as many as twelve men to move more than twenty miles from the Castle. He had been in command only two weeks when he heard that three free burghers had been murdered on the banks of the Breede River. At once he sent fifty infantry and twenty-seven horsemen under Hiero-nimus Cruse, as well as some Hottentots who were Gonnema's enemies, to deal with him. In October, 1676, Gonnema once more proved to the Council that he knew the interior better than the officials and consequently made good his escape. It was therefore decided to send Captain Dirk Jansz Smient and Lieutenant Cruse with a group of soldiers, free burghers and Hottentots after Gonnema, who, they were told, was lying up near the Berg River with his cattle. This party accomplished nothing either, though they took some cattle from the chieftain Kees, who was looking for grazing-land with some of Gonnema's cattle near Saldanha Bay.

As the officials could obtain sufficient cattle from the tribes along the east coast, they were in a position to ignore Gonnema. This he did not like and in June, 1677, he sent emissaries to the Castle, asking why nobody came to trade with him. As the free burghers wished to be able to hunt safely in the interior once again, a sergeant, two corporals and eighteen soldiers were sent to trade with Gonnema, after a ceremonious peace had been concluded on 25 June.[12] A lively trade soon sprang up once more and when Simon van der Stel took over in 1679 he was able to state that "we live in peace" with "our neighbours" the Hottentots. He sent out regular trading parties to obtain meat, the Hessequas supplying most of the cattle.

Encouraged by Governor-General Rijckloff van Goens, who visited the Cape in 1682, Van der Stel also sent expeditions to explore "more and more African countries at the southern point". He repeatedly requested permission personally to lead such an expedition into the interior. In 1685 the High Com-missioner, Hendrik Adriaan van Reede, finally acceded to his request after Van der Stel had assured him that the undertaking would not be dangerous.

Among the fifty-seven members of the party were Frans van der Stel, Hendrik Claudius, the apothecary and artist, and Isaacq Schrijver, the well-known traveller.[13] This was so far the biggest expedition to have explored the sub-

---

12. Böeseken: *Resolusies van die Politieke Raad, 1670 – 1680*, 25 June 1677, pp. 190 – 191.
13. Böeseken: *Simon van der Stel en sy kinders*, p. 74. A list of names of all the participants in this expedition can be found in the Archives at The Hague in Kol. Arch. 4001, pp. 1105 – 1107.

continent of Africa. The Commander travelled in a coach drawn by six horses. Trading goods and a dinghy had been loaded on eight wagons. There were also seven more wagons, fourteen riding horses and two hundred and eighty-nine draught and pack oxen. Seven free burghers accompanied the party up to the Elephant River. The party was away from 26 August, 1685, to 24 January, 1686, and returned with drawings of plants and animals, a good map and lively descriptions of their experiences. On 5 September a rhinoceros of "incredible size" charged the Commander, whose blunderbuss failed to go off. Fortunately the shouts of the other hunters deflected the animal's course, and the party travelled on in peace to look for Monomotapa and its treasures.

To get to know the country that they inhabited the party undertook more than Van Goens had required of them. They carefully mapped mountains, swamps and rivers. They sketched hares, birds, freshwater fish, scorpions, snakes, worms, insects, plants and roots, flowers and thorns. While others rested Van der Stel climbed mountains. On 1 October the party sighted the first strange camp fires, and the next day Van der Stel slaughtered some sheep for a few Sonquas to whom he gave bread, rice and brandy, "with which they made merry, dancing, singing and shouting in the strangest manner".[14] On his birthday, Sunday, 14 October, he was surrounded by Hottentots and he made a pact with them that the Dutch and the Hottentots should "always live with each other in good and prosperous peace".[15] The expedition's two small cannons fired joyous salutes and the Hottentots honoured the Commander by singing and dancing.

Van der Stel found the Hottentots to be fickle; copper, he determined, was too far from the sea to warrant profitable exploitation; and he did not find the river Vigiti Magna, or Eijn, as the Hottentots called it. Despite these negative results Van der Stel did much positive pioneer work on this expedition. One drawing shows how he drew wagons into a circle to act as a protective shield in case of attack, as the Voortrekkers were to do a century and a half later. He also learnt much about the interior with its flowers and blind flies, endless plains and shortage of water, eerie mountains and capricious inhabitants. He was beginning to feel what many of the officials and free burghers at the Cape already felt, that they could not live anywhere else other than at the southern point of Africa, which region was beginning to win their hearts and was to become their childrens' land of birth.

Since Van der Stel's party discovered no gold and silver in the interior of Africa there was no need to follow the advice of Van Goens, who had recommended them not to make public any such finds "because that often reverberates around the world among the enemies of our nation" which would "encourage them the more to disturb and plague us".[16] As yet there was nothing

14. Waterhouse: *Simon van der Stel's Journal and his expedition to Namaqualand, 1685–1686*, p. 35 (Translated from the original Dutch).
15. *Ibid.*, p. 45 (Translated from the original Dutch).
16. C.700: Memoriën en Instructiën, 1657 – 1685, p. 383 (Cape State Archives) (Translated from the original Dutch).

in Southern Africa to arouse the cupidity of other nations and officials and free burghers could peacefully explore the country, thereby increasing their knowledge of their environment.

Information about the east coast was provided chiefly by the crews of shipwrecked vessels. Survivors of the shipwrecked crews from the *Stavenisse*, *Good Hope* and *Bona Ventura* had much to tell about the natives between Terra de Natal and the Cape. Isaacq Schrijver also met Hottentot tribes on his journey to the Inquas in 1689 and brought back a detailed description of the Bantu. He realised that the Bushmen and the Hottentots belonged to different ethnic groups and that the Bushmen were the more dangerous.

The hunter

Though free burghers who entered the interior on their own initiative were prohibited from trading with the Hottentots, they were allowed to hunt, and the officials found it impossible to prevent a hunting party deep in the interior from changing into a bartering expedition. In 1693, therefore, Van der Stel drastically revised the "placaten" or laws about trading with the Hottentots. In future no-one was allowed to receive cattle from the Hottentots in exchange for money, tobacco, brandy, arrack, guns, powder or lead; in addition, nobody was allowed, alone or in company, with or without wagon or cattle, to cross the mountains of Hottentots-Holland, Rode Zand, Elephant's Path, or any mountain leading to the Sonquas, Hessequas, Ubiquas, Grigriquas or Namaquas.[17] Persons caught on the other side of the mountain would not only have to pay a fine, but would also have all their possessions and cattle confiscated.

The efforts to keep the free burghers on this side of the mountains failed, even in Van der Stel's time. The discouraged governor records in the instructions to his son that many farmers, in spite of strict and repeated injunctions, insisted on participating in the "prohibited cattle trade". When the Seventeen decided to stop trading with the Hottentots towards the end of the 17th century they instructed the Governor to rescind the prohibition on bartering. Unmarried adventurers in particular used this concession to open bartering with the Hottentots. At one stage rumours reached the Castle that a group of forty-five men had used force to take cattle from a group of Hottentots. Wilhem Adriaen van der Stel ordered a judicial inquiry. The permission to barter was withdrawn but nobody was punished. According to Wilhem Adriaen this was because so many burghers were concerned in the matter, but according to the free burghers it was because the officials were also guilty of such malpractices.

After Wilhem Adriaen left the Cape trading was once again thrown open, but in the twenties of the 18th century more complaints about the behaviour of free burghers in the interior were received. The Seventeen decided to punish all the free burghers "as disturbers of the common peace and violaters of

---

17. Jeffreys: *Kaapse Plakkaatboek*, part I, p. 283 (Translated from the original Dutch).

justice and freedom"[18] in accordance with the "placaten" of 19 October, 1697, and 27 October, 1702. In April, 1727, Pieter Gysbert van Noodt once more prohibited barter and the ban was never lifted again.

Hunters, however, were still permitted at certain special times of the year to hunt big and small game. In the 17th century there were many hippopotami in the Berg River. The free burghers were so eager to obtain hippopotamus blubber for themselves and their slaves that by the eighties of the 17th century they had to travel as far as the Elephant River to find any of these beasts. Elephant, too, became scarce, and in the 18th century elephant hunters were often away for over a year in their efforts to find sufficient ivory to make their trips worthwhile. Many of them travelled quite fearlessly into the far interior, and got to know the native tribes well. Some, however, like Hermanus Hubner and his five companions, who were murdered by a Xhosa tribe under Palo, paid dearly for their audacity. Big game hunters penetrated eastwards as far as and beyond the Fish River, and the elephant hunter, Jacobus Coetsé, was probably the first European to cross the Orange River in 1760, and later to reach what is now South-West Africa overland.

The cattle farmer

Even before Simon van der Stel became Commander there were farmers who farmed exclusively in sheep and cattle, and grazing licenses had been issued to people without any fixed property. Simon van der Stel did not wish cattle farming to develop as an independent form of farming and discouraged it by legislation. Among other things he decreed that every free burgher who possessed cattle also had to possess some immovable property such as a plot of land or small farm. He also would not allow anyone to trek with his cattle more than eight days' distance from his farm.

All Simon van der Stel's "placaten" forbidding farmers to trek to distant pastures with their cattle in times of drought were ineffective. Wilhem Adriaen realised this and, although he did not immediately rescind his father's regulations, he encouraged rather than opposed the cattle farmers. After his first journey into the interior he realised that many free burghers were living on farms that were too small for them. New plots were made available "in a beautiful valley, distant from the Castle about 18 to 20 hours on horseback".[19] This valley he called 't Land van Waveren. The new farms were still fixed property, but, though fertile, they were too far from the Cape market to be of practical agricultural use. As a result the free burghers in 't Land van Waveren had to rely almost exclusively on cattle as a means of subsistence. Before Wilhem Adriaen left the Cape he informed the Seventeen that the free burghers who had gone inland had herds of cattle and flocks of sheep that were in excellent condi-

18. Jeffreys et al.: *Kaapse Plakkaatboek*, part II, pp. 129 – 130.
19. C.509: Letters Desp., 1704 – 1707, p. 583. (Cape State Archives) (Translated from the original Dutch).

47

tion. Consequently, the meat at the Cape was better and cheaper than it had been before. Therefore he advised the Seventeen that the free burghers should not be ordered to return to their allocated farms, as the "Placaten" ordered them to do.[20] The result of this attitude of Wilhem Adriaen and his successors was soon apparent in the ever increasing livestock of the free burghers.[21] More and more grazing licences were issued, often for periods of three, four, six or nine months. Some of the farmers who obtained grazing licences also possessed farms, but the further they left the settled areas behind, the more often they possessed nothing but loan land. Often the grazing rights on a farm were extended for a number of years. On such farms the farmers built houses, known as the "opstal". Not being the owner of the land, when they left they sold the "opstal" to the person who obtained the grazing rights on the farm. This form of land tenure was known as the loan place system.

Up to 1714 the cattle farmer paid nothing for a grazing licence, but in July, 1714, Governor Maurits Pasques de Chavonnes and the Council of Policy decided that "all those who request permission for the loan of any land as grazing-land for their cattle, will have to pay in the coffers of the Honourable Company six rixdollars for half a year and for a whole year twelve rixdollars". In addition the farmers had to pay a tithe on any crop obtained from such farms.[22] In 1732 the recognition fees were doubled and a new system of land ownership was introduced enabling farmers to own "adjoining land" for fifteen consecutive years in full ownership. The new system, however, did not have sufficient advantages to take the place of the loan place system.

One of the most important features of the loan place system was that it encouraged rapid expansion into the interior. In the first half of the 18th century the cattle farmer who had become a trek farmer encountered virtually no resistance on his advance into the interior. Many Hottentot tribes had succumbed to a widespread smallpox epidemic, so that large tracts of uninhabited land offered excellent prospects for cattle-farming. In 1717 cattle farmers reached the banks of the Breede River, and by 1730 those who had gone east were at the Great Brak River, while others were moving down the Langeberg, north of Kogmanskloof. In the north the areas in the vicinity of the Elephant and Doorn River were inhabited. In 1734 the Company's farthest outpost was erected in the Riet Valley on the Buffelsjagts River. Its purpose was to protect the cattle farmer and Hottentots against the rapacious Bushmen. The cattle farmer, however, rarely waited for protection and confidently penetrated ever deeper into the vast continent of Africa.

One of the problems which developed with the rapid advance of the cattle farmer was the difficulty, if not downright impossibility, of keeping in touch with schools and the church. The church nearest to the ever expanding border was in Drakenstein. It had been built in 1720. There were no schools for children

20. *Ibid.*, p. 583.
21. P. J. van der Merwe: *Die Trekboer in die Geskiedenis van die Kaap-Kolonie*, pp. 57 – 59.
22. *Kaapse Plakkaatboek*, part II, p. 31. (Translated from the original Dutch).

who could not attend school in Cape Town or in one of the smaller towns. Parents had to teach the children themselves or use itinerant schoolmasters. The gravity of the situation is revealed by the report of Gustaaf Willem, Baron van Imhoff, who journeyed a short way inland in 1743. He disapproved of the rapid advance into the interior and tried to halt it by instituting a new land tenure system. Freehold farms of 60 morgen would be made available, but anyone who wanted more land – and what cattle farmer would be happy with 60 morgen? – would have to pay the usual recognition of 24 rixdollars per year. As the system never was popular it did nothing to stem the advance of the trek farmers. Even fixing boundaries and ordering cattle farmers to return within them had little effect.

Van Imhoff's instruction that more churches should be erected in the interior had greater practical value. Thus the Rev. Arnoldus Meiring held the first service in the new church in the Land van Waveren in 1743 and two years later the Rev. Rutger Andreas Weerman delivered his inaugural sermon in the church of Swartland. One of the new sick-comforters, Abraham Schietekat, who had to read sermons on Sundays was sent to Grootvadersbosch across the Breede River. His main duty was to take charge of education.

The Governor and Council of Policy realised that schools and churches were not all that the border farmer lacked. Thus it was decided to place the territory across the Breede River as far as Mossel Bay, where the furthest farms were to be found, under the jurisdiction of a local court. Johannes Theophilus Rhenius was accordingly appointed deputy magistrate. He was instructed to establish, with the assistance of four heemraden, a local court for the cattle farmers in the far-flung districts or "De Verre Afgeleegene Districten" as was the official name. This was in 1745. In the following year an official residence was built, known as the drostdy, called Swellendam, in honour of Governor Swellengrebel and his wife Wilhelmina, née Ten Damme.

New boundaries were fixed between the districts in 1745 and the Great Brak River became the eastern border of the Cape. The farmers, however, continued to move even further east with their cattle. In the north, too, where no boundaries had been determined the trek into the interior began to swing east because water was scarce. The Great Karoo began to exert its fascination and would for many years remain an area without boundaries. Even further north in the Roggeveld and the Nuweveld the farmer trekked east with his cattle, while the Swellendam people between the Langeveld Mountains and Swartbergen in the Little Karoo moved in the same direction. About 1763 cattle farmers from various places began to look for grazing in the area known as the Koup. By this time there were quite a few who were not sure whether their recognition fees should be paid to the magistrate at Stellenbosch or at Swellendam.

Authorities at the Cape who had cared little for the cattle farmers began to realise that the time had come to investigate matters in the border areas. The governor did not know the outlying districts at all, but in 1768 the secundus J. W. Cloppenburgh undertook a journey into the interior and found among the inhabitants of the border what he described as "an almost complete lack of religion and obedience and consequently of good behaviour". The remedial measures he recommended were impractical, but in 1771 the Cape Government made an effort to discourage further expansion into the interior. The Gamtoos was now proclaimed the eastern border of the Cape and the landdrost of Swellendam was ordered to command everyone who had settled east of the river to return within the boundary which had been proclaimed. Such an order, however, was not worth the paper it was written on, for by this time many of the more enterprising border farmers were already protecting their livestock and goods against the attacks of Bushmen and Hottentots in the Camdeboo, while others in the south were making their first contacts with the cattle-owning Bantu. Cape authorities did not object to farmers settling in the Camdeboo, but they did not relish the thought of the illegal cattle trade which would be the inevitable consequence of the border farmers settling too close to Kaffirland.[23]

Thus the attitude of the Cape authorities towards their subjects differed from place to place, from one group to another and from time to time. On the one hand there were the officials who did not remain long in the country and knew little or nothing of the interior, and on the other the farmers who increasingly identified themselves with the African continent and had never known another home.

23. P. J. van der Merwe: *Die Trekboer in die Geskiedenis van die Kaap-Kolonie.* pp. 146 – 151.

5. The Company and its Subjects

The Governors and the Council of Policy

The first free burghers at the Cape were scarcely settled on their small farms when Commissioner Van Goens pointed out that "it would not be possible for the freemen to exist if the officials were to enjoy the same privileges".[1] It was often necessary for this principle to be repeated by other officials. When the Governor and nearly all the members of the Council of Policy disregarded it at the beginning of the eighteenth century the burghers rebelled and were supported by the Council of Seventeen.

The lesson that the burghers learnt from their dispute with Wilhem Adriaen van der Stel and his officials was that constant watchfulness had to be observed. Thus the slipshod way in which the secretary Pieter de Meyer handled the administration of title-deeds and other matters decided a few burghers to complain to Commissioner Abraham Douglas, so that in 1716 the officials were once again accused of appropriating too much power and becoming big land-owners. The chief offenders were Pieter de Meyer, who owned a few hundred morgen of land and sold firewood to the Company, Johannes Swellengrebel, a junior merchant and dispenser, landdrost Nicolaas van den Heuvel, who had large vineyards and sold wine to the Company, and the quartermaster Jan Brommert, who delivered vegetables and fruit from his farm to the ships.

Commissioner Douglas also investigated other complaints against the Governor and Council of Policy. His findings were not in favour of Maurits Pasques de Chavonnes and his officials. The Commissioner accused the Governor of issuing and signing title-deeds without the knowledge of the other Council members, of giving land to his son-in-law, and of making the burghers pay considerable amounts of money for their papers of freedom. The Directors maintained that the Commissioner did not have sufficient proof to bear out all his charges, but they viewed Douglas's accusations against secretary Pieter de Meyer in a serious light. The latter was summoned home "without title and salary". Jan Brommert was ordered to sell his farm, but was later allowed to become a free burgher, as was Johannes Swellengrebel. Douglas's inquiry stopped all high officials from farming. Every one was given the choice of either becoming a farmer or remaining an official without land. In 1721, however, the members of the Council of Policy were given permission to own a vegetable garden of 1½-2 morgen during their stay at the Cape. Although a

---

1. C.700: Mem. and Instr., 1657 – 1685, 16 April, 1657, p. 9. In the original document Van Goens wrote that "niet mogelijck is dat de vrije luijden hier souden connen leven, so de dienaeren deselfde preëminentien hadden".

few officials later owned gardens slightly larger than the specified area there was never again any serious transgression of this regulation. Even the minister, the Rev. F. le Sueur, whose wife inherited land in 1746, was told that he would have to resign from the church if he wanted to keep the ground.

De Chavonnes, who remained in office until 1724, proved an excellent Governor once these matters had been rectified by the Commissioner. He dutifully carried out the Directors' orders to increase the Company's revenue at the Cape. In 1714 quitrent was levied on farmers who owned loan-farms; during the same year stamps for use on notarial deeds were introduced; and in 1715 the first excise-duty was imposed on local wine, so that the wine-farmer had to pay one rixdollar on every cask of wine he delivered to the Company. Later Van Imhoff raised this excise duty to three rixdollars.

Other important measures introduced by De Chavonnes included the school ordinance, in August, 1714, and the regulations for goldsmiths and silversmiths, in July, 1715. A friend of the Governor, the Rev. Lambertus Slicher, became rector of the first Latin school in Cape Town. The deputy governor, the minister and the captain were appointed as school superintendents to administer education under the Governor and his Council. When Commissioner Becker was at the Cape in 1717 it was decided that all schoolmasters had to be tested by the clergy. This meant that the authorities had some control over the itinerant teachers who did so much to keep the inhabitants of the interior in contact with civilization.[2] The Latin school very soon failed, however, as parents at the Cape frequently sent their young sons to Europe to complete their studies.

Governor de Chavonnes did not personally undertake any long journeys into the interior. When the Rev. P. van Aken accused some burghers of stealing cattle from the Hottentots the Governor asked landdrost M. Bergh to investigate the matter. The evidence that the landdrost collected against the burghers was so contradictory that the Governor and Council concluded that the Rev. van Aken's accusation could not be substantiated.

The following incident shows how much the attitude of the Governor and the Council of Policy could influence the development of the country. In 1717 the Seventeen sent a questionnaire to the Governor and his Council members. One of the questions they asked was whether in future more slaves or more white labourers should be sent to the Cape. Each member of the Council of Policy was asked to give his answer in writing. Only one member strongly advocated importing white workers and reducing slave labour, so the advice of the majority of the Council was followed and after 1717 the number of slaves at the Cape increased rapidly. The fear that encouraging white immigration would lead to greater poverty of the individual was prevalent at the Cape during the eighteenth century.

De Chavonnes received the Company's highest title, namely that of Coun-

2. Vide J. L. M. Franken: "Huisonderwys aan die Kaap, 1692 – 1712" and J. Hoge: "Privaatskoolmeesters aan die Kaap in die 18de eeu". Both published in *Annals of the University of Stellenbosch*, July, 1934.

cillor-Ordinary of India, and subsequently remained in office at the Cape for three more years until his sudden death on 8 September, 1724, when his second-in-command, Jan de la Fontaine, became acting Governor. De la Fontaine, who had been at the Cape since 1710, was given the rank of Junior Merchant in 1713, thereby becoming a member of the Council of Policy. He was liked by everyone, and most people at the Cape were disappointed when the Directors decided to appoint Pieter Gysbert Noodt to succeed De Chavonnes. Governor Noodt reached the Cape on 25 February, 1727. He was a military man and no stranger to the Cape. In 1718 he had stayed at the Castle as De Chavonnes's guest with a view to improving the fortifications. About six weeks after his return as governor, in accordance with orders from the Directors, he strictly prohibited all trade with the Hottentots. The fiscal, the landdrost and officials at the Company's outposts were instructed to confiscate wagons and goods of burghers suspected of bartering. Again by order of the Directors he investigated the possibility o* building a road across the Hottentots-Holland mountains to facilitate fetching wood from the forests on the other side of the range. In November, 1727, he inspected the forests in the vicinity of Rivier Sonder End, but concluded that the Hottentots-Holland mountains made it too difficult to transport wood from the interior to the Cape.

Another problem with which Noodt had to contend was that of desertion among the soldiers of the garrison. Discipline at the Castle was strict, and when, in April, 1729, thirteen men deserted, four of the eight caught were hanged for resisting arrest. On the day of execution Noodt died suddenly of a heart attack, and Jan de la Fontaine once again became acting Governor. Everybody was pleased when the Directors this time agreed to appoint him as Governor. He held office from 8 March, 1730, until 31 August, 1737.

Attempts to open up the African continent continued. In March, 1721, an attempt to take possession of Rio de Lagoa for the Company was launched. The undertaking failed miserably, however, and on 30 December, 1730, the garrison of one hundred and thirty-three soldiers that had occupied Fort Lydsaamheid returned to the Cape.[3] There was still much unexplored territory between Delagoa Bay and the Cape. Jan de la Fontaine, however, seldom visited the interior himself. The longest journey he made was to Mossel Bay, when he was accompanied by his secretary Ryk Tulbagh, quartermaster Jacobus Möller, the ensign Rudolph S. Alleman, and five burghers. They left on 7 July, 1734, but after a beacon had been erected at Mossel Bay heavy rains made it impossible for the party to travel further, so that they were back at the Castle on 2 September.

After twenty-eight years as a Company official, Jan de la Fontaine requested to be allowed to return to Holland with his children. He was succeeded by the deputy Governor, Adriaan van Kervel, who had acted as secretary of the Council of Policy from 1719 to 1725. He had then become fiscal, and later

3. For further details see C. G. Coetzee: "Die Kompanjie se besetting van Delagoabaai": *Archives Yearbook*, 1948, part II.

deputy Governor. His experience made him the obvious choice for governor. When he died after three weeks in office the choice of his successor was more difficult because the second-in-command, Hendrik Swellengrebel, who had been born at the Cape, had been promoted to the rank of Senior Merchant after the fiscal, Daniël van den Henghel, who therefore maintained that his seniority gave him the right to be appointed Governor. When the Council of Policy's vote on the matter resulted in a tie, Van den Henghel objected to Tulbagh's vote for Swellengrebel on the grounds that the two men were brothers-in-law. Tulbagh maintained that for nine years he had voted according to his conscience, and still did so. At Christoffel Brand's suggestion the lot was cast and Daniël van den Henghel was elected as acting Governor until the Seventeen could make their wishes known. When the Directors received the reports on this matter they decided that Swellengrebel should be appointed Governor, although he had not been a Senior Merchant for as long as his rival.

Hendrik Swellengrebel was a competent Governor from 14 April, 1739, until 27 February, 1751, when he returned to Europe. Before he assumed duty there had been trouble with some Hottentots who had complained to the Castle that they had been robbed of their cattle by farmers of the Olifants River area. The matter had been investigated, and the Hottentots proved right. They were placed under the protection of the Company, and were given back their cattle. The farmers were angry and ignored orders both to appear before the landdrost and to appear before the Council of Justice. A Frenchman, Etienne Barbier, became the leader of a group of the dissatisfied farmers. On 1 March, 1739, with a band of armed horsemen, he fastened to the church door a document which accused the government of tyranny and stated that Barbier and his followers would no longer pay taxes.

This uprising was not Van den Henghel's only problem in the period before Swellengrebel assumed office. In the north the Bushmen had become actively hostile. Many farmers had been forced to abandon their properties, and the acting Governor had decided to raise a large commando, promising an amnesty to all those who helped him in the campaign against the Bushmen. Barbier's followers had seized the opportunity. He himself had remained in hiding, but was finally caught, sentenced to death and executed in November. Once more all barter with Hottentots and Bantu was strictly prohibited.

Swellengrebel became Governor during these disturbances, but notwithstanding its stormy beginning his term of office passed peacefully. In September, 1740, even the Bushmen came to the Castle to promise that they would make no further raids. An attempt to convert the Hottentots to Christianity was begun in Baviaanskloof, where Georg Schmidt, one of the Moravian missionaries who had come to the Cape in July, 1737, was teaching the Gospel. This station was later called Genadendal. When he baptized five Hottentots in 1742, the Council of Policy considered the matter and decided to forbid Schmidt to baptize any more converts. Schmidt felt that his work would be without value unless he could administer the sacraments, and so in January, 1744, he requested to be allowed to return to his land of birth.

The intolerance of the Governor, the Council of Policy and the ministers towards Schmidt and his work extended to the Lutherans as well. In 1741 a survey was made to ascertain how many people, at the Cape and in the outlying districts, professed the Lutheran belief. The Lutherans earnestly requested to be allowed to establish their own church at the Cape. In 1742 their request was refused by the Governor and Council "with one voice". Dr. J. Hoge, who has recorded the history of the Lutherans at the Cape,[4] points out that the minister, Franciscus le Sueur, and the deputy Governor Tulbagh, had both married daughters of Johannes Swellengrebel, and were among the most fervent opponents of the Lutherans. It was not until nine years after the death of Ryk Tulbagh that the Lutherans succeeded in building their own church at the Cape, and were granted "the same freedom of public worship as was enjoyed by those of their persuasion in Batavia".

Ryk Tulbagh as Governor, 1751 – 1771

When Ryk Tulbagh became Governor he had already been in the Company's service for more than thirty years. He was baptised on 14 May, 1699, when his father, Dirk Tulbagh, and his mother, Catharina Cattepoel, were living in Utrecht. Soon afterwards the family moved to Bergen-op-Zoom, where Ryk went to school during his early years. Ryk's father died early, so his uncle helped him to attend school until he was sixteen. Afterwards he had to fend for himself, and he entered the Company's service.

He came to the Cape in 1718 on the ship *Terhorst*, and was made an assistant in the office of the Secretariat. In 1722 he was promoted to chief clerk of the Secretary of the Council of Policy. A year later he was promoted to warehouse superintendent, and in 1725, when Adriaan van Kervel became deputy Governor, Tulbagh was appointed Secretary of the Council of Policy. At the same time he was promoted to vendue-master. A devout churchgoer, he was a deacon in the Reformed Church until the end of 1725, and became an elder in 1726. At this time he held the rank of a Junior Merchant, and after 16 September, 1728, he signed the resolutions of the Council of Policy not only as its Secretary, but also as a Council member. He now became a member of the Council of Justice as well, and thus served society in various capacities. Through his marriage with Elizabeth Swellengrebel he became still more closely associated with the group of officials who administered the Cape, and in 1732 he received the title of Merchant.

When Hendrik Swellengrebel became Governor on 14 April, 1739, Tulbagh was appointed deputy Governor and became *ex officio* chairman of the Council of Justice. He was also promoted to the rank of Senior Merchant.

When Swellengrebel requested to be allowed to leave the Cape the Council of Policy wished Tulbagh to succeed him, as his faithful service over many

---

4. Vide J. Hoge: "Die Geskiedenis van die Lutherse Kerk aan die Kaap", p. 36 in *Archives Yearbook*, 1938, part II.

years had given him the experience to fill the highest office in the country "for the benefit of the community and the well-being of this colony". The Council of Seventeen acceded to the Council's wishes, and on 27 February, 1751, Tulbagh was sworn in as Governor. He was later given two more distinctions: in 1754 he was honoured with the title of Councillor-Extraordinary of India, and on 21 October, 1766, he was informed that henceforth he was to be addressed as Councillor-Ordinary of India.

Since his wife had died on 13 October, 1753, and the couple had had no children, Tulbagh was alone at the Castle. Frequently, however, important visitors relieved his solitude. The last visitor to stay at the Cape while the Governor's wife was still alive was Abbé Nicolas Louis de la Caille, the famous French astronomer, whose visit lasted from 19 April, 1751 to 8 March, 1753. Tulbagh also helped the astronomers Charles Mason and Jeremiah Dixon, who were at the Cape from 27 April to 3 October, 1761. Every year the fleets brought high officials to the Cape, among whom were commissioners Joan Gideon Loten and Librecht Hooreman.

Among the important visitors that Tulbagh entertained at the Castle on behalf of the Company were the English soldier and statesman, Lord Clive, the English explorer, Captain James Cook, and the French author, Bernardin de St. Pierre. Some of the visitors stayed in the Company's summer-house in The Gardens. Others preferred to lodge with one of the free burghers. Thus Lord Clive lived with the burgher Petrus Johannes de Wit, while the author of *Paul et Virginie* stayed at the Neethlings' house.

That Tulbagh impressed such travellers in their interviews with him is apparent in several of their journals. One of the travellers who visited the Cape shortly before Tulbagh's death writes of him as "the father of the country at Africa's extremity, who, after more than fifty years' sojourn there, really knew the true interests of the inhabitants and the nature of the country, and who was well-beloved by all for his gentle and paternal rule".[5]

The variety of Tulbagh's interests is apparent in all the glimpses we have into his life, from the orders he gave his gardeners to his collection of books. In 1752, 1753 and 1754 he sent the gardener Hendrik Christoffel Prisky to the interior "to find and collect plants, vegetation, herbs and insects".[6] Later Johan Andries Auge was sent out on a similar mission. Collections of plants and seeds were carefully sent overseas. One of the best collections of Cape plants was incorporated in the herbarium in Leyden. In 1762 the Professor of Botany at this University, David van Rooyen, informed Tulbagh that he had "never obtained such a beautiful, extensive and, to him, so informative as well as desirable a collection as this one from the Cape".[7]

Tulbagh's collections of plants made him well-known in Europe. The famous

5. Vide J. S. Stavorinus: *Reize van Zeeland over de Kaap de Goede Hoop* . . . part II, p. 321. Although Stavorinus gave this description of Tulbagh in the account of his travels between 1774 – 1778, he had also visited the Cape during the last year of Tulbagh's life.
6. C.703: Mem. and Instr., 18 Dec., 1752, 25 Sept. and 13 May, 1754. (Cape State Archives).
7. C.488: Letters Received, 14 March, 1672, p. 389. (Cape State Archives).

botanist Carolus Linnaeus named one genus of Liliaceae *Tulbaghia*. The Governor likewise dedicated himself to developing the beauty of the gardens in the peninsula, and travellers, such as the Swede Carl Peter Thunberg, write in high praise of the plants, trees and animals that had been collected and tended by Tulbagh in the Company's garden. Thunberg was very disturbed that, after Tulbagh's death, many beautiful trees, amongst them chestnuts, were chopped down to make place for oak trees, while many of the animals from the interior that Tulbagh had protected in the zoological garden were let loose and killed by wild animals.

Tulbagh loved books, and it is fitting that the first library at the Cape was founded during his term of office. This was in September, 1761, after the death of Joachim von Dessin, Secretary of the Orphan Chamber, who left his collection of books and manuscripts "for the general benefit". He also left a legacy of 1,000 rixdollars, the interest of which was to be used for buying new books. Van Dessin's books and manuscripts numbered 3,856 volumes. That Tulbagh himself was also a booklover is evident from his will, which left his French books to Josephus de Grand Preez, his Dutch books to Pieter Hacker, and his law books to the Secretary of the Council of Justice.

Extant official documents from Tulbagh's term of office show that he was a hard worker. The first important task he undertook was the codification of the Slave Laws. The increasingly bad behaviour of the ever-growing number of slaves necessitated a stricter enforcement of existing laws. As the laws of almost a hundred years of slavery at the Cape were very confused Tulbagh sorted them out into one Slave Code. This "placaat" was published in September, 1754. Death was the penalty if slaves assaulted their masters. If slaves were disrespectful to their masters they could be tortured or put in chains. These laws also applied to female slaves.

Apparently slaves were much addicted to gambling, which frequently involved them in fights. To prevent such fights and other disturbances slaves were prohibited from going round in groups of three or more. Guardians of the law were authorised to break up any gatherings of slaves, if necessary by using their canes to drive members of a group asunder. Slaves were not allowed to be out in the streets after ten o'clock at night without some kind of light. No slave could bear arms, and those that raced horses, wagons or carriages through the streets could be punished. To reduce noise Tulbagh prohibited slaves from cracking whips, singing in the streets at night, and whistling loudly to attract the attention of other slaves indoors.

Concerning the work of slaves, it was laid down that they had to dispose of refuse and other filth by dumping it in the sea. Under no circumstances were they allowed to sell liquor for their masters. Only comestibles could be sold from house to house or in the streets by slaves. This regulation was necessary to prevent the sale of stolen goods.

In the streets no insolence by slaves was tolerated and because of the danger of fire no one, whether official, free burgher or slave, was allowed to walk around with a lighted pipe in his mouth. No slave was allowed within the boundaries of the cemetery at the funeral of a white person, and when a slave was buried six, eight or ten pairs of slaves were allowed to bury their relation or friend. The number depended on the status of their master.

The life of slaves at the Cape was not without hope. Many of them plied their trades and saved enough to buy their freedom and that of their loved ones.

The group of freedmen who had been slaves at the Cape were treated as the equals of the white population in all respects. Only once did Tulbagh make a law restricting freedom in any way. This aimed at preventing the wives of freedmen from dressing too smartly, and was in accordance with the standard sumptuary laws of the time.

Tulbagh's so-called sumptuary laws had very little to do with him; they were merely enacted during his rule. This was by order of Governor-General Jacob Mossel, who sent to the Cape a copy of the 124 Regulations issued in Batavia to restrain the extravagances of the officials in the East. The Cape officials were to adapt the regulations to local conditions. Tulbagh, who was working day and night combating the second serious smallpox epidemic, delegated three of his councillors to carry out this adaption.

The commission concluded that many of the regulations abolishing the use of carriages and horses by junior officials were not applicable to the Cape. On account of the poor weather at the Cape they decided that all councillors should be allowed to own carriages and horses, but only the Governor was to be allowed to decorate his carriage with coats of arms, figures and gold paint. Moreover, only the Governor and members of the Council were to be allowed to dress their coachmen in livery. The number of horses to each coach or carriage was not to be limited as in Batavia, since the commission felt that the bad roads and long distances warranted four, six or more horses, which therefore could not be regarded as a luxury. They also maintained that no vehicles at the Cape were kept solely for pleasure.

In the matter of dress, the Commission applied only a few of the Batavian regulations to the Cape. Officials below the rank of Junior Merchant, who had never served on any governing bodies, and their wives were not allowed to use parasols. Men below the rank of Merchant were not allowed to go to the Castle with a parasol in fine weather. Thus the use of a parasol (or "kipersol") was obviously a status symbol! For the rest, the commission adopted no more of the Batavian regulations concerning male dress but added a few new regulations regarding the dress of their wives and daughters. Women married to men below the rank of Junior Merchant were not allowed to wear velvet or silk-embroidered capes, and nobody – definitely nobody – at the Cape was allowed to adopt the latest fashion of dresses trailing on the ground! Slaves had to be soberly dressed, but because of differing climatic conditions the regulations of Batavia were not to be applied to the Cape slaves. The display of pomp and splendour at funerals was also curbed.

While the officials were busy changing and adapting these laws, Tulbagh and the doctors were strenuously engaged in fighting the small-pox epidemic of 1755. All large gatherings, such as the annual artillery exercises, were cancelled;

the clothing of infected persons was burnt, the hiring out of black clothes for funerals and the partaking of refreshments after funerals were prohibited. Fresh air and clean bed-clothes were considered vital. An "advertissement" or announcement warned "that those found negligent in these respects would be fined 50 rixdollars".[8] When the epidemic ended in 1756 and no more people died of the dread disease a day of prayer was declared. The epidemic greatly reduced the population of the Cape as can be seen from the figures sent annually to the Directors. Notwithstanding natural growth and the high birth rate the population decreased from 6,110 to 5,123 free burghers and officials, and from 6,279 to 5,787 slaves in one year. It was not until 1760 that the population regained the ground lost in the disaster of 1755.[9]

Although Tulbagh attempted to apply stringent health measures to incoming ships small-pox struck at the Cape for the third time in 1767. Though there were fewer deaths more than five hundred people died, and it was not until March, 1770, that the Directors could be informed that the disease had run its course.

Tulbagh took strong measures to prevent panic in crises such as the outbreak of war or fire. He also introduced other positive measures to improve the way of life at the Cape. To prevent traffic accidents wagons drawn by eight horses had to be led by a slave. Roads were improved, and in 1771 Tulbagh commanded Lieutenant-engineer Carel David Wentzel to level the streets and recover the costs from the house-owners. With its burgher watch, and its effective measures against fire and other hazards, the town at the foot of Table Mountain was a pleasant place in which to live.

Although Tulbagh, after he became Governor, no longer went into the interior himself he let slip no opportunity of improving his knowledge of its inhabitants. On the last day of February, 1752, the biggest party since Simon van der Stel's journey to the north was sent inland by Tulbagh in a north-eastern direction. Thirty-seven officers and soldiers were under the command of Ensign August Frederik Beutler. Eleven wagons were taken care of by twenty-five Hottentots. The surveyor and cartographer, Carel David Wentzel, and a second mate, Peter Clement, went to map the expedition, while Carel Albrecht Haupt was in charge of the log-book. A surgeon, a botanist, a blacksmith and a wainwright also accompanied the expedition.

The journey went well. The Fish River was reached on 2 June, and three days later the party was on the banks of the "Chijs Chamma", which was described by Haupt as the border between the land of the Hottentots and "het Caffersland". When it entered Bantu territory some free burghers joined the expedition, but all the Hottentots remained behind for fear of the Bantu. The Kei River was described as the border between the Tembu and the Xhosa, who lived to the east of this river.

8. *Kaapse Plakkaatboek*, vol. III, p. 17.

9. J. J. F. Joubert: *Die Kaapkolonie onder Ryk Tulbagh, 1751 – 1771*, pp. 131 – 132. (Unpublished M. A. thesis, Univ. of Stellenbosch 1942).

The expedition reached the Qora River, but its members decided on 10 July, to go no further. Their instructions to return via the "Copper Mountains", which Simon van der Stel discovered in 1685, were regarded as "regt dollemans werk" or pure madness by the leaders of the expedition, since the country was in the grip of a fierce drought. Even by following well-known routes they did not arrive back at the Cape until November, after an absence of eight months.

Information on the interior was often supplied, in the eighteenth century as in the seventeenth, by elephant hunters. In 1760, Tulbagh gave Burgher Jacobus Coetsé permission to hunt elephant. Tulbagh was especially interested in what Coetsé found north of the "Grootrivier", later known as the Orange River, and decided "to follow up the aforementioned discoveries made by Coetsé in a more detailed way, as soon as such expeditions could be undertaken without considerable expense to the Hon. Company".[10]

The opportunity for one such expedition arose when Captain Hendrik Hop requested permission to explore the interior with a number of volunteers. Tulbagh acceded to his request and sent the gardener, Jan Andries Auge, the surgeon, Carel Christoffel Rykvoet as minerologist, and the surveyor, Carel Frederik Brink as cartographer and scribe, with the expedition. This group explored the interior to the north of the Orange River, but drought and fatigue at last forced them to return to the Castle. Like Simon van der Stel, they found evidence of no mineral other than copper.

The Governors and the border farmers

Although the journeys to the interior did not financially benefit the Company, the topographical and geographical facets gathered gave the officials a better idea of the vastness of the interior and of the location of its various inhabitants. Most officials at the Castle who had little or no knowledge of the interior were perturbed by the rapid advance of farmers beyond the borders of the Cape. In 1770 Ryk Tulbagh and his Council stipulated that the boundaries of the border district of Swellendam were to be the Gamtoos River in the east and the Swartbergen in the north. The new farms that were to be issued at Bruintjies Hoogte were to be included in the district of Stellenbosch.

The officials at the Cape were to a large extent ignorant of the needs of the border farmers. After the death of Ryk Tulbagh, and during the seventies of the eighteenth century, most members of the Council of Policy were complete strangers to the Cape. Pieter, Baron van Reede van Oudtshoorn, who was designated as Tulbagh's successor, knew the Cape well, but died at sea in January, 1773. Joachim, Baron van Plettenberg, who was sworn in as Governor on 18 May, 1774, had been at the Cape since 1767, and was therefore better informed that his second-in-command, Otto Luder Hemmy, who came to the Cape in 1774. The fiscal, Willem Cornelis Boers, also arrived at the Cape in

10. C.347 Letters Despatched, 6 March, 1762, p. 275. (Cape State Archives).

1774, while Damiaan Hugo Staring was appointed quartermaster in 1773, and became a member of the Council of Policy in 1778. The Captain of the garrison, Robert Jacob Gordon, who was later to become very familiar with the interior, came to the Cape in 1777. The only member of the Council of Policy during the seventies who knew the Cape well was the secretary of the Council, Olof Martini Bergh.

Although the officials no longer farmed as they did at the beginning of the eighteenth century, many of them succeeded in amassing considerable fortunes at the Cape. Thus Damiaan Hugo Staring, together with the quartermaster, Hendrik Möller, and a retired burgher-councillor, Jacob Alexander la Fèbre, established the firm of La Fèbre & Cie. This firm made much money from the timber trade.[11] Though many free burghers at the Cape also became rich, there were nevertheless deep-rooted antagonisms between the higher officials and the burghers. The burghers began to regard the officials as foreign intruders who came to the Cape merely to enrich themselves before leaving again. Although marriages between officials and daughters of free burghers did occur, the Governor had the right to prohibit such marriages.[12]

A still greater gulf existed between the free burghers of the town and the inhabitants of the rural areas. Governor van Plettenberg realised that in order to administer the country soundly it was necessary to know the interior and its inhabitants better. When difficulties concerning border arrangements came up for discussion in the Council of Policy, Van Plettenberg informed the Council that he had decided to undertake a journey himself "to the most outlying regions as far as they are occupied". Landdrosts were instructed to hold draught-oxen and horses in readiness at certain points of the proposed route and Van Plettenberg left the Castle with a small party of officials on 3 September, 1778.

The diary which records which farms sheltered the party unfortunately tells little about the inhabitants of the farms. It does, however, record other interesting facts. On the tenth day after their departure the expedition met the first Hottentots, two men with their women-folk and children. The journey through a "barren, and uninhabited veld" is described as long and tedious. It began "at the foot of one of the Karroo mountains where the Touws River flowed past" as far as the Gamka or Leeuwen River. Until 24th September the expedition continued through the "barren, dry and desolate veld", with its clay, stones and shrubs. The travellers saw thousands of springbok but few people. They did not arrive at the "Cambdebo's River" until 24 September, when the grassy plains where the farmers had found grazing for their animals were finally reached.

Only a few of the farms of this area are described in much detail. With Johannes de Beer the party rested for two days. This farmer irrigated his wheat-fields and vineyards through a conduit from the Swart River. The Governor noticed,

---

11. A. Staring: *Damiaan Hugo Staring, een zeeman uit die achttiende eeuw*, pp. 53 – 54.
12. *Kaapse Plakkaatboek*, vol. III, pp. 100 – 101.

too, that there were no Hottentot kraals left, but that everywhere Hottentot families lived with the farmers on their farms.

Near the Sneeuberge firewood and timber were so scarce that the farmers dwellings were extremely primitive, consisting of "a single low-walled room without partitions",[13] which also served the farmers as storehouses. The roofs were straw, and yet, despite their poverty, the farmers always had a Bible and often other religious books, and regularly held family prayers. The Governor had it recorded that these distant border families were "usually . . . moral, reasonably skilled and ardently wished for" a minister and a landdrost.[14] The farmers who lived near the Sneeuberge also complained very much about the "Bushmen-Hottentots", who stole their livestock and murdered their herdsmen.

On Christiaan Opperman's farm the expedition saw Bushmen drawings of human beings, wild asses, eland, baboons, ostriches and pigs. Hendrik Cloete's farm is described as one of the best situated farms in the whole of the Cambdebo, while Willem Prinsloo's farm, which was reached on 15 October, had the most agreeable situation – on the banks of the Bos River – in the entire region through which they had travelled. Beautiful ironwood, beech and yellowwood trees grew on this farm, the soil was suited to grain cultivation and afforded excellent grazing for livestock.

From this farm Van Plettenberg sent Captain Robert Jacob Gordon, who in 1777 had journeyed far into the interior with Lieutenant William Paterson, on ahead to the Bantu chieftain Koba. According to the travellers' journal Gordon spoke the Xhosa language. They returned to the Governor's camp a few hours later with Koba and twenty-eight Xhosas, including two of Koba's sons. The visitors entertained the governor with singing and dancing.

The border farmers had complained to Van Plettenberg that "the Kaffirs who had previously always kept themselves at a distance of about one day's journey east of the Great Fish River" had for the past few years been crossing the river with large herds of cattle in search of pastures. After Van Plettenberg had personally negotiated with the Xhosas, it was agreed that in future they would remain east of the river. It was only later realised that Koba did not have the authority to make such an important agreement. Only Rarabe, the paramount chief of the Bantu tribes, could agree to such a settlement. On the return journey, the bay which had been variously known as "Baaij Content, de Baij Angola, de Keurbooms Riviers- en de Pisangriviers Baeij", was named Plettenberg Bay.

When Van Plettenberg and his party reached the Castle on 26 November, 1778, the Governor knew nothing of the problems which awaited him. Secretly the burghers at the Cape were already quoting the writings of Locke and other European philosophers, where they found proof of their right to "oppose their

---

13. George McCall Theal: *Belangryke Historische Dokumenten*, p. 12.
14. *Ibid.*

rulers".[15] Thus while the interests of the farmers in the border districts were beginning to clash with those of the Bantu, the free burghers at the Cape had come into contact with political philosophies which convinced them of their "natural" right to govern themselves. The Cape was consequently about to enter upon a period of strife.

15. C. Beyers: *Die Kaapse Patriotte, 1779 – 1791*, pp. 206 – 207.

6. Domestic Strife and International Warfare, 1778 - 1795

Characteristics of the period

During the last eighteen years of the Company's regime, affairs at the Cape were very disturbed, both domestically and internationally, but this does not mean that previously there had been no strife. There had been conflicts between free burghers and officials, between border farmers and Hottentots as well as Bushmen, and between various people and parties responsible for the government and administration of the Cape. War had been waged between great powers such as Britain and France, and the Cape had armed itself to withstand attack. During the last period of Company rule, however, four new factors entered the old situation to produce exceptional disturbances.

The first new factor was the clash between the border farmers and the Xhosa who were moving steadily in a south-westerly direction on a wide front. This began a period of conflict between the White man and the Bantu in the history of South Africa, a conflict which has not even yet been satisfactorily resolved.

The second new factor was the irruption of revolutionary democratic theories among the colonists at the Cape. For the first time it was apparent that European ideas were being modified at the Cape to suit local conditions. The first signs of a new attitude appeared in the people of the Peninsula, then in the people of Graaff-Reinet and Swellendam. In the latter sectors relationships with Non-Whites were also an important consideration.

The third new factor was the acceleration of the Company's decline, which accompanied that of a sharply divided Netherlands Republic. This disintegration affected all spheres of life at the Cape; in particular it weakened the Company's control. The greater the distance from the centre of government in Cape Town the weaker the control of the Company, generally speaking. The state of affairs in the Netherlands therefore had a direct bearing on the affairs of the border farmers.

The fourth factor, allied to the third, was the two massive attacks on the Cape Peninsula by the British navy. These aimed at conquering the Cape by attacking its seat of government. The first onslaught was only withstood with the help of a force of French marines. When at the end of the period of Company control overseas support was not forthcoming, the Cape could not withstand a second attack and fell into new hands.

It is thus clear that the last years of the Dutch East India Company's regime at the Cape were quite complicated. From one point of view they were the end of nearly one-and-a-half centuries of Company occupation, from the establishment of a refreshment station at the Cape to the British conquest of the Cape during the French Revolutionary Wars. From another they saw the beginning of move-

ments highly significant for nineteenth century Southern Africa, such movements as the aspiration of the Whites for democratic self-government and their
clash with the Xhosas on the historic eastern frontier.

Few truly radical changes had been made at the Cape during the long period
of Company government. In fact, the Company's policies were characterized by
an extreme conservatism which was close to stagnation, and affected all aspects
of life at the Cape. The mercantile policy of the Company controlled everything:
the monopoly system had to be maintained and protected at all costs. Only such
industries as the Company could not run profitably or properly itself were
assigned to the free burghers, and, if it seemed advisable to do so, the Company
would at any stage resume control of such industries. The Company always saw
that it obtained the maximum possible profit from the private enterprise of the
free burghers. As far as the Company and most of its officials were concerned,
the free burghers were a necessary evil.

From 1778 to 1795 there was an ever-widening gap between the Company's
theory of control as set out above, and its practice. The Company was apparently
governing the Cape more or less according to its old system; actually a new
situation was developing behind the scenes. While in the Netherlands "the
decrepit mercantile creature" was being attacked first by middle class capitalists
and then by the lower classes, the so-called "Patriots" at the Cape began protesting vehemently against the Company's economic system, first to the Council
of XVII and later directly to the States-General.

To effect a permanent change in the economic system of the Cape the Cape
Patriots desired an appreciably greater measure of democratic self-government,
particularly in the central governmental bodies. A democratic system of government would be their safeguard against the whims of privileged Company
officials who were amassing personal fortunes under the protection of the
monopoly system. In their demands for democratic representation the Patriots
were particularly concerned with establishing the right of the well-to-do classes
of Cape free burghers, who according to their lights had no adequate say in
economic and political matters, despite their constant efforts to obtain recognition. The Patriots wished to end the economic domination of the small circle of
officials and some privileged free burghers. Some officials, amongst them those
whose "salary was written off" (they were no longer on the Company pay sheet),
were half-way between free burghers and officials; they wanted to enjoy the free
burghers' privileges without assuming the accompanying responsibilities. These
people competed unfairly with the free burghers. Furthermore, through
marriage, nepotism and mutual back scratching, these officials could draw a few
ordinary free burghers into the privileged circle under the cloak of the worn-out
monopoly system. This put most of the settled community of free burghers,
particularly those in and around the Peninsula, at a tremendous disadvantage,
for they could not share in any of these profitable privileges. The privileged
free burghers, whom the Patriots called the "Mamelukes", also enjoyed excessive
privileges in the social and cultural spheres. The "Mamelukes" could become
comparatively rich, although they could not always display their opulence at the

Cape because of the sumptuary laws. They were able to entertain visitors, who were often business associates or of scientific and cultural significance, in fitting style in attractive mansions on their estates in the Cape Peninsula. They were able to give their children a reasonable education by employing private tutors or sending them to Europe. The group was also well represented in ecclesiastical posts. They were in close touch with the main stream of Western civilisation in all its aspects. The Patriots, however, were in a less fortunate position: they had insufficient funds of their own and there were no government funds at the Cape to establish the necessary schools and churches.

As the old order drew to an end so did the continuously conservative policy of the Company behind which the Mamelukes had sheltered; the nineteenth century was to begin with new aspirations for democratic self-government. The Patriots were the vanguard of nineteenth-century democracy in the Cape and the Cape farmers on the Xhosa border were the predecessors of the Voortrekkers. In the second quarter of the nineteenth century the two groups were to combine to provide southern Africa with its twentieth century outlines. The independent spirit of the border farmers was the source of the desire for republican independence, to begin with in the nineteenth and later in the twentieth century. The development of various enterprises under the Company's monopoly system prepared the way for the visionary entrepreneurs who were to become the mining magnates and captains of industry of the nineteenth century.

While the protective shell of the Company's policies remained the Patriots in the western Cape struggled in vain to introduce reforms. The first major changes were only effected through foreign intervention. In the west the Company's authority, backed by professional soldiers and strong fortifications, was too strong for any local rebellious forces the Patriots could muster. In an area far removed from the Company's direct authority the first irruption of violence occurred where the white border farmers and the Xhosa clashed on a wide front. The border farmers were accustomed to taking care of local government and military matters themselves, and in practice all that was necessary to maintain order on the border was that officials should provide the necessary arms and ammunition. Any actual official intervention, which possibly might have prejudiced the interests of the border farmers, could easily have resulted in their repudiating the Company's weak authority altogether. The stronger British military authority would have been able to end the insurrection immediately, even if only by cutting the border farmers off from their indispensable supplies of arms and ammunition.

Some of the causes of the disturbances at the Cape were domestic; others had external sources, but interacted with the first. Thus, there was potential unrest at the Cape, but it was stimulated into open violence by outside influence. Ideas about democratic self-government coming from the Netherlands, North America, Britain and France added fuel to the fire of the Patriots' enthusiasm. Philanthropic ideas about the christianization, moral advancement and protection of the non-Whites came from Western Europe. The first-mentioned ideas stimulated the desire for greater local control, the latter discouraged it, but both caused unrest.

There were also purely foreign factors which contributed to the disturbances at the Cape. Towards the end of the eighteenth century the Dutch Republic began applying a policy which was to endanger itself and its colonies. This policy was partially the consequence of sharp differences of opinions within the Republic itself, which held all the potentials of civil war and resulted in the intervention of foreign powers. The marked weakening of the Netherlands and of the Company, which had become ever more closely identified with the state, appreciably increased the risks attendant upon a break with their traditional ally, the British. The acquisition of France as an ally instead of England did not ensure permanent and effective protection against the attacks of the British navy on Dutch colonies, particularly where the strategically placed Cape was concerned. By the end of the eighteenth century the British navy was supreme at sea. A naval war inevitably meant an attack on the Cape. As various Cape officials were well-disposed towards the British, internal tensions and conflicts at the Cape were to increase during the British attacks.

As a result of the intense naval warfare during the American War of Independence shipping traffic at the Cape increased appreciably. This provided the Cape with a badly needed though temporary market, and for the moment rebellion subsided, since the strongest reason for dissatisfaction had fallen away, at least for a while.

However, temporary affluence accustomed the inhabitants of the Peninsula to a higher standard of living. It brought new merchants and shipping interests to the Cape. Enterprising young North Americans arrived under their own flag for the first time. Apart from there being more French visitors there were also more Scandinavians. All these factors further weakened the Company's monopoly system. Private Cape merchants found it increasingly easy to develop into cosmopolitan merchants. Company officials acted as agents for overseas mercantile houses or became independent merchants. Thus the Company in its last few years was forced officially to open its ships to private trade so that the diminishing profits of the monopolies could be made good by freight and excise duties. Next the Commissioners Nederburgh and Frykenius allowed the colonists the private ships they had always desired, and also the privilege of armed trading voyages to the east, west and north along the African coast. However, these concessions came too late. The European naval war had brought too many strongly armed cruisers on to the high seas. The poorly armed small ships of the Cape merchants, who did not have unlimited capital resources, were simply no match for the cruisers. Cape ships were seized at various points along the routes, and were an irreparable loss to the local merchants.

From the point of view, in 1795, of the almost 20,000 white colonists at the Cape these small Cape ships represented all the many opportunities which the hundred-and-fifty-years-old Colony was losing. However, the last eighteen years of the Dutch East India Company focussed attention strongly on these relatively few White colonists. They were as yet divided, clumsy, weak in many respects and searching for a common purpose, but they were being well schooled for the role they were to play as South Africans in the nineteenth century. The White Afrikaner – the Bolander and particularly the frontier farmer – had become thoroughly conscious of his identity. The eighteen years of conflict with the Company were a formative period which prepared him for a far fiercer and more effective struggle against a much stronger European power.

The Cape Patriots

The Cape Patriots were the first to attempt to revolt against the Company in the period under discussion. After the death of Governor Tulbagh, who knew and understood the Cape Colony and its inhabitants, the Cape colonists had to deal with new officials, who were mostly young and inexperienced men (see Chapter 5). Some of them wished merely to get rich quickly and live in luxury, and made no attempt to further the interests of the Company. Thus it is understandable that their actions often were detrimental to the interests of the free burghers. Thus some officials, J. F. Kirsten, D. van Ryneveld and C. Brand, had a profitable private trade with visiting ships in their own as well as in Company supplies, even making use of the Company's wagons and oxen. Brand, who had a post in False Bay, formed the trading company Cruywagen & Co. in association with a few ex-members of the burgher council and some officials, while the La Fèbre Company was particularly active in Table Bay. That Company interests were not protected by the officials did not disturb the free burghers, however, since it gave them an excellent opportunity for complaining about the officials (some of whom treated the free burghers with contempt) to the higher authorities of the Company.

That highly placed officials at the Cape were once again, as they had done in the era of W. A. van der Stel, threatening the livelihood of the free burghers under Governor Joachim Baron van Plettenberg, despite express instructions to the contrary from the Council of XVII, was only one cause of the free burghers' dissatisfaction. The influence of European philosophers such as Locke, Grotius and Pufendorf encouraged the burghers to make their first demands for the political rights which would guarantee their economic interests. Anonymous pamphlets, such as *De Magt en de Vrijheden eener Burgerlijke Maatschappij verdedigt door de gevoelens der voornaamste regtgeleerden opgedragen aan het oordeel der Caapse Burgerij* (The Powers and Freedoms of a Civil Society defended by the Opinions of the most important Jurists brought to the attention of the Cape Citizenry) were distributed at the Cape. The above pamphlet was being circulated as early as May, 1778. It maintained that the welfare of the people was the highest law and, on the basis of an inalienable right by God and in nature, the people were legally entitled to substitute a new regime for an oppressive one. Pamphlets were distributed and secret meetings of malcontents were held.

When the extremely unpopular Independent Fiscal Mr Willem Cornelis

Boers, a nephew of the Company's advocate, had a free burgher living in Cape Town, C. H. Buytendag, arrested in January, 1779, and banished to Batavia without a trial, the simmering dissatisfaction came to boiling point. To the oppressed Cape burghers this was a matter of principle on which the whole community should voice its opinion. After the local authorities had been approached to no avail various "representatives" decided to send four authorized delegates to the Netherlands. These were an ex-member of the burgher council, Jacobus van Reenen, an ex-burgher lieutenant, Barend Jacob Artoys, and two burghers, Nicolaas Godfried Heyns and Tieleman Roos. In Holland, on 9 October, 1779, they compiled a bulky petition or "memorie" in the name of 404 Cape burghers and personally handed it to the Council of XVII a week later.

This important document was made up of three parts. The first described the difficult circumstances under which the Cape burghers lived. Because prices fixed by the Company were too low and there were no other markets for their produce the farmers could not make a proper living. Cattle farmers who were being victimized by the avarice of officials were travelling forty days' journey into the interior to escape Company control. The second part contained a list of complaints against the most important officials. Among other things, it was maintained that officials were exploiting the Company's outposts to their own advantage.

The third part, which consisted of thirty-seven articles recommending various reforms, is significant. For example, the powers of the Independent Fiscal were to be curtailed in many respects. A burgher should be arrested only by another burgher and then taken to the "Burgerwaghuis" (Old Town House). Burghers were never in future to be banished to Batavia, and Buytendag was to be allowed to return. Burghers were to be sent overseas, and then only to the Netherlands, only with the permission of the burgher councillors. When matters affecting burghers were discussed by the Council of Policy seven burgher councillors had to be present. These burgher councillors also had to report annually to the Council of XVII on the circumstances of their fellow burghers. Burghers and officials were to be equally represented on the Council of Justice, and the eldest burgher was to act as vice-president. To replace the old system of co-opting the petition demanded the right of free election for all bodies on which burghers were represented, members of the bodies having the right to elect their own successors, who would then have to be accepted by the Governor and the various bodies. The petition also requested the right of appeal to the Netherlands instead of to Batavia. This suffices to show how the most important items of a political nature involved demands for a greater measure of self-government for the burghers.

The articles dealing with economic matters among other things requested the right to have two ships come annually from the Netherlands, carrying the burghers imported goods, while on their return voyage they would carry Cape produce which would be sold on the open market. The Company could then impose its own import and export duties. The burghers also requested permission to send a few ships with Cape produce to India, from where they would return with eastern merchandise. They also wanted to take part in the profitable slave trade to Zanzibar and Madagascar. The petition goes on to suggest that it would be of mutual advantage if the free burghers were to trade directly with the Company without the intervention of so many officials. This would simultaneously lower the Company's administrative costs and assure the burghers of lower buying prices. To prevent the landdrosts of Stellenbosch and Swellendam from encroaching on the interests of the burghers they were to be forbidden to possess any wheat, cattle farms or vineyards. The burghers wanted to provision ships as soon as they arrived, and not after an interval of three days. Officials who left the Company's service were to be registered as free burghers within six weeks and then had to accept the usual responsibilities of a free burgher. The Company should abolish its outposts, and was not to raise any new taxes. More schools and churches were to be built in rural areas. In conclusion, the burghers asked for copies of the Council's instructions so that they could determine whether the instructions were being carried out as the Directors of the Company intended.

After they had received the petition in 1779 the Directors gave senior officials the opportunity of defending themselves in writing. The Governor denied that the Cape was falling into a decline, and argued that the petition had not been drawn up by the representatives of all the citizens. He alleged that only a small number of the almost 3,000 Cape burghers had actually signed the petition, and that virtually nobody from the rural areas was among them. Van Plettenberg resigned, as did some of the other officials, but because of the American War of Independence he remained at the Cape until February, 1785.

The Dutch Republic was participating in the American War of Independence from the end of 1780 up to May, 1784, and the state of war to a large extent determined the procedure followed with the petition of 1779. Communications by sea between the Cape and the Netherlands were slow and uncertain. When the brilliant French admiral, De Suffren, succeeded in reaching the Cape in 1781 with a strong fleet, just before the British commander, Johnstone, a prosperous war boom developed at the Cape. Although De Suffren kept his fleet at the Cape for only three months, he left the Pondicherri regiment behind on his departure. The Luxembourg regiment, which was in the pay of the Company, further strengthened Cape defences in May, 1782. The presence of these military forces temporarily created such a favourable market for the free burghers' produce that in turn they could afford French luxuries on a large scale. The dissatisfied Cape free burghers could now no longer claim there was an economic depression at the Cape.

Nevertheless the burghers drew up their *Nadere Memorie* (Detailed Petition) as a further complaint. It was dated 17 April, 1782, and signed by Jacobus van Reenen, B. J. Artoys and N. G. Heyns. Once again they demanded the right to appoint members of various civic bodies themselves, subject only to the approval of the Governor and burgher councillors, but not subject to the approval of officials. To prevent oppression of the burghers no-one was to hold office as member of the Council of Policy and of the Council of Justice at the same time. The burghers thus favoured a division of governmental powers.

It was only in December, 1783, that the Directors of the Company made their first decisions about the petition of 1779. The free burghers were not to be represented on the Council of Policy, but the Council of Justice would henceforth have six instead of three burghers. The chairman would always be an official and the right of appeal would still be to Batavia and not to the Netherlands. Once again, as was the case after the struggle with W. A. van der Stel, officials were strictly forbidden to possess or rent farms, to keep cattle, to grow wheat, or to produce wine. The structure of the monopoly system would remain unaltered, the lease system would remain and the burghers would not be allowed to trade with the Company's own ships. They were allowed to sell as much farm produce as possible to foreign ships, and once the Company had seen to its own needs the burghers' surplus produce would be bought by the Governor at prices to be determined by a commission of three burghers and three officials.

The Directors replied to the other requests towards the middle of 1785. They denied free election to civic bodies, but burghers would have free access to the Court of Justice and the secretariat. Henceforth they could not be forced to take service with the Company; and they were no longer to be banished to Batavia only: they could choose between Batavia and the Netherlands.

Faced with these unsatisfactory results the burghers continued their meetings. In November, 1784, "Committed Representatives" were sworn in. By the end of the next month these representatives had prepared a preliminary address, intended for the Chairman of the States-General of the Dutch Republic. The appointment of Mr. J. J. Serrurier as Boers's successor had given the Cape a much more hateful, vicious Independent Fiscal. Further actions by the authorities led to further petitions, all of which were submitted to the States-General in May, 1785.

When it became clear that the new Governor, Lieutenant-Colonel C. J. van de Graaff, a friend of the Stadholder's, was not prepared to make concessions to the burghers, they chose M. A. Bergh, Johannes Roos, J. H. Redelinghuys and J. A. Bresler to put their case to the States-General. However, there was disagreement among the four representatives which led to Bergh's resignation. The remaining three representatives submitted a petition in April, 1786, in which the States-General was requested to provide fixed laws and proper procedures for the law courts. Where the economy was concerned, the representatives demanded effective protection against the whims and despotism of officials. Though the plight of the Cape burghers elicited a sympathetic response in the Dutch Republic, nothing more was achieved; the States-General was not prepared to intervene in Company matters.

The Cape burghers called themselves "Patriots" in emulation of the party in the Netherlands which opposed the Orange party. Both were inspired by the democratic ideals emanating from the British and French philosophers of the Enlightenment, men such as Locke and Price, Montesquieu and Rousseau. The successful American Revolution encouraged all patriots to persevere with their own democratic revolutionary struggle. As with the Patriots in the Netherlands the Patriots at the Cape sought affiliations with the French, whereas supporters of the Orange party preferred Britain as an ally. Again as with the Patriots in the Netherlands the Patriots at the Cape failed in their attempts. In 1787 a Prussian army invaded the Netherlands, suppressed the local Patriots and restored Orange authority. The Cape Patriots failed to attain their basic aims principally because the Company authorities, who were hand-in-glove with the Netherlands Republican government, were simply not prepared to act against their own interests by granting the desired democratic and economic reforms.

Yet the Patriot movement is of considerable importance in the history of South Africa. The basic democratic idea that the people themselves were to appoint and dismiss their government appeared at the Cape for the first time; stemming from it came other ideas such as the following: representatives of the people were to guard the interests of the free burghers, the principle of free election was to be instituted, governmental powers were to be separated, and inviolable laws were to protect the people or permanent inhabitants of the Cape against official whims. The term "volkstem" (voice of the people) was used for the first time; it was again used later among the rebellious frontier farmers of Graaff-Reinet and Swellendam, and much later by the Voortrekkers in the nineteenth century. The term "Patriot" was not merely a grandiose, self-laudatory expression of patriotism, but reflected a true love of a country – the Cape – by a people, its permanent inhabitants. These terms are therefore significant symbols of the local patriotism which was being born at the Cape.

In many respects local patriotism at the Cape grew most rapidly in the interior, where the farmers had to face common problems and dangers arising from their contact with the non-White races. The policy of the Company towards the Hottentots, Bushmen and particularly the Xhosa perceptibly hastened the growth of patriotism in the frontier regions.

The Company, the farmers and the natives

In the last eighteen years of the Company's regime the tribal system of the Cape Hottentots had virtually disappeared (see Appendix 1). Many Hottentots were impoverished and possessed no cattle. Many who no longer adhered to a chief became itinerant hunters or, like the Bushmen, turned into marauders. Some went to farms as badly paid servants or, in the nineties, settled on mission stations. A new community with new problems was developing, and this meant that the Hottentots, the farmers and the Company had to make some adjustments in their attitudes. Lured by brandy and tobacco, the Hottentot was being absorbed into the white rural or border communities in a subordinate position. The white farmer's contact with the Hottentot was complicated, however, by the Hottentot being not only an unskilled labourer but simultaneously a potential convert to Christianity who as such could compete with the so-called "born Christian" in the social sphere.

72

The Company was therefore obliged drastically to revise its policy towards the Hottentots. Whereas originally it had been indifferent towards the independent Hottentot tribes who supplied it with cattle, it now began to protect the detribalised Hottentots from a white, Christian ruling class which were opposed to the hopes and aspirations of individual Hottentots. The Hottentots were made subjects of the Company, learned how to handle fire-arms, and were taken on commandos. The landdrosts were instructed to ensure that the Hottentots were not oppressed and in particular that they were never prevented from complaining to the authorities. Often attempts to protect Hottentots were opposed by the farmers. In the nineties, when Moravian missionaries in the Swellendam district once again began to convert Hottentots and spoke up on their behalf to the authorities, opposition among the farmers flared up strongly.

Slaves mixed freely with the Hottentots and so added considerably to the Coloured population. In order to turn the offspring of this mixed parentage into a sound labour force under proper control, the government approved a measure which compelled children of such unions to work for a specific employer up to the age of twenty-five. This indenture system was later extended to other Coloureds.

Those Hottentot tribes who were not content with this gradual absorption into the white community moved north. Among them those who were later known as the Griquas (formerly the Grigriqua or Chariguriqua) and the Korannas (formerly the Kora or Gorachouqua) were particularly important. Both tribes had been partially westernised while in the Cape Peninsula and had then moved away from Dutch influence and control. Strengthened by what they had picked up of Western culture, such as the use of the horse and the gun, they were able to hold their own so well against Bushmen and certain Bantu tribes that they were later to establish themselves firmly on and to the north of the Orange River. Trek farmers and Voortrekkers were later to co-operate with them at times but more frequently there were clashes between the two groups.

The Bushmen were always a problem on the border (see Appendix 1). Some trek farmers in the Camdeboo and along the Sneeuberge found that the Bushmen stubbornly defended their traditional hunting grounds using poison arrows as weapons, and some farmers had to retreat to the south. The Bushmen dealt with the northern farmers by making lightning attacks on their cattle and then retreating to the safety of rocky fastnesses and caves in the mountains where the mounted farmers could not follow them. They murdered Hottentot herdsmen, and at night attacked farms and sometimes burnt down the farm houses.

The Company authorities could offer little protection to the farmers on the remote northern border. They were given guns and ammunition and could organise themselves into commandos to pursue the Bushmen systematically. They were allowed to shoot the adults, make out indentures for surviving children and recapture cattle. Hundreds of Bushmen were killed; as they were assimilated only with difficulty very few were taken into the colonial community. They were attacked by the Hottentots and Bantu as well as by the Whites. Historically the Bushmen are significant because they obstructed the northward drive of the trek farmers during the last three decades of the eighteenth century. Field Corporal Albertus van Jaarsveld reported to the landdrost of Stellenbosch on 15 November, 1779: "There had never been such an irruption of the Bushmen as now, for here we see Bushmen daily, and though we make every exertion, we cannot overtake them, the country is so rugged and hilly . . . and . . . please to see sir, the number of cattle that have been carried off recently".[1] In an attempt to avoid the Bushmen the farmers even left the north-eastern border, moved to Bruintjieshoogte and trekked across the Fish River into the country of the "Caffers".

Whites had been in contact with the Xhosa from early in the eighteenth century, but it was only in the period under discussion that a stable border, approximately from Bruintjieshoogte to the sea, was established between the Xhosas and the trek farmers (see Appendix 1). This eastern border of the Cape Colony was the first of many established between the White man and the Bantu; consequently it is particularly significant. The basic reason for the long series of border clashes in the east was that both races were cattle farmers and wanted the same grazing grounds. As their customs concerning land ownership were totally different, as explained in Appendix 1, there were bound to be misunderstandings which could develop into armed clashes. The two groups also competed fiercely for game. While the trek farmers ate venison to save their cattle stock, the Xhosas hunted game mainly for the skins. The Xhosa were accustomed to visiting farmers for weeks on end, and expected to be well entertained from the farmers' scanty stores. The isolated farmers found this custom a great strain. The farmers also felt unsafe among the Xhosas who far outnumbered them, and increasingly the farmers came to regard the Xhosa as a threat to their safety. Of all the natives of Southern Africa, the Xhosas were the most interested in tilling the soil in a primitive fashion. They were at an appreciably higher cultural level than many of the other tribes, and were also economically and politically superior. They were well-organised under traditional chiefs, and well-armed with the throwing and stabbing assegai. It is thus understandable that they could for many years effectively oppose the relatively small number of isolated border farmers, although the latter possessed fire-arms and fought on horse-back or from wagon laagers.

The immediate causes of the first armed clashes between the farmers on the eastern frontier and the most westerly Xhosa tribes from 1779 onwards cannot be established with any certainty. It would seem, however, as if there was a lack of authoritative control on both sides of the thinly populated and remote border area. As a result unruly elements could act contrary to a border policy which was vague in any event. Adventurous White hunters and cattle barterers stole Xhosa cattle in Xhosa territory, while the armed activity of lesser Xhosa

1. To the Landdrost of Stellenbosch, from the English translation of D. Moodie: *The Record or a series of official papers relative to the condition and treatment of the Native Tribes of South Africa*, III, (a photostatic reprint, A. A. Balkema, Amsterdam and Cape Town, 1960), p. 87.

chiefs frustrated the paramount chief's attempts to arrive at a peaceful border settlement. Consequently a feeling of impending doom spread among the White border farmers and suggested one of two extreme reactions. Either the farmers could organize an attack by experienced commandos on the western Xhosa tribes, or they could abandon their farms and retreat westwards. The Xhosa point of view is not clear; amongst other things they objected to cattle thefts by the Gonaquas Hottentots whom, they subsequently alleged, had been sheltered by Whites (see Appendix 1).

Whatever the immediate causes of the first clash between the Xhosas and the border farmers, the elements of friction in their relationship were so intrinsic that a hundred years of sporadic warfare was to follow. As the White farmer moved first north and then, after sixty years, north-east, mainly because of unrest on the Xhosa border, his Bantu policy in Southern Africa was of necessity determined by his early years of contact with the Xhosa. Relations on the eastern Cape border are therefore of fundamental significance in the history of Southern Africa.

When Governor Van Plettenberg visited the Suurveld in 1778 he found various groups of Xhosas there with their cattle. In trying to effect territorial separation between the Xhosa and the trek farmer along the Great Fish River, he reached agreement with a few subordinate Xhosa chiefs that they would remain east of the river (see Chapter 5). However, he did not discuss this border question with Rarabe, the paramount chief of the territory. Trouble was therefore inevitable, and it came the next year when the Xhosa drove large herds of their cattle across the border in search of grazing. The first clashes took place near Bruintjieshoogte. Cattle thefts increased so much along the whole border that many farmers had by the end of 1779 abandoned their farms on the Fish and Bushmans rivers. Two farmers' commandos were organised in 1779 and 1780 to follow the Xhosas into their own country. Then the Governor and Council of Policy appointed Adriaan van Jaarsveld as commandant of the eastern border. In accordance with the Company's attempts to economize he was instructed to make lasting peace with the Xhosa and to ensure that the border farmers no longer bartered cattle in Xhosa territory. During May and June, 1781, Van Jaarsveld, with a mounted commando of ninety-two men and forty Hottentots, drove all the Xhosas back into their territory. Contrary to his instructions he took 5,300 head of cattle from the Xhosa and divided them among the members of the commando and other farmers who had suffered stock losses. That was the end of the first "war".

The farmers in the far eastern regions had for years been demanding their own minister and landdrost. It was only in 1786 that M. H. O. Woeke was sent to the new district of Graaff-Reinet and only in 1792 that the Rev. J. H. von Manger, the first minister, arrived there. The important Graaff-Reinet district had been made up of the eastern parts of the districts of Stellenbosch and Swellendam, and was separated from the latter by the Gamtoos River. The important eastern border now ran along the Tarka and Baviaans Rivers, and down the Fish River to its mouth.

The establishment of the Graaff-Reinet drostdy is significant because although the Company had now extended its protection to the troubled eastern border, as had been requested, the Company officials reduced the farmers' powers to defend themselves. It was Company policy at all costs to keep the peace on the remote border. On the one hand the Company wished to economise, and on the other, for philanthropic reasons, to protect the Xhosa against injustice from the farmers. Under certain circumstances the execution of this policy made life extremely difficult for the small number of border farmers. During the last years of the Company's regime a series of crises developed on the eastern border, until ultimately the border farmers completely repudiated Company authority.

Landdrost Woeke tried unavailingly to keep the trek farmers and Xhosas apart. Both groups wished to graze their cattle beyond the border and often the farmers traded illegally with the Xhosa for their cattle. In order to be able to act punitively Woeke asked for fifty or sixty soldiers, which the authorities were not prepared to provide. In 1789, the landdrost decided that there were too many Xhosas west of the Fish River and ordered the officers of the burgher force to move the Xhosas back across the river. Before this order could be carried out the authorities decided that negotiations should be entered into to settle the matter. This course was attempted, but meanwhile the large number of Xhosas west of the border increased the farmers' anxiety. The Xhosas would not relinquish their claims on the Suurveld as grazing ground. By the nineties, cattle thefts by bands of marauders were the principal cause of friction on the border. Large numbers of Xhosas were by this time living among the farmers, even as far west as the Sundays River. Representations to landdrost Woeke to order the expulsion of the Xhosas had no effect. In May, 1793, the unpopular H. C. D. Maynier became landdrost of Graaff-Reinet. He was of a philanthropic turn of mind and espoused the Company's passive, peaceful policy towards the Xhosas. By this time many families had left the border area. The remainder adopted defensive measures. A precipitate commando attack by the farmers aided by the Xhosa chief Ndhlambe provoked a devastating retaliation from the Xhosas in which they occupied the whole area between the Swartkops and the Fish River. Many cattle were taken, farm houses were burnt down, a number of farmers and servants killed, and of the one hundred and twenty farms all but four were devastated.

Maynier prohibited further commando attacks on the Xhosa and tried in vain to prevail upon the Xhosa to return over the border and restore the stolen cattle. Then he tried, with an inadequate force and again without success, to eject the Xhosa. More burghers from as far afield as Swellendam were called up and ordered, as far as possible without unnecessary bloodshed, to push the Xhosa back over the border and recover the stolen cattle. Maynier could count on the support of only a small number of the Graaff-Reinet people under him because their leaders did not trust his policy with the Xhosas. Thus his main strength in the subsequent attack on the Xhosas was a powerful Swellendam commando. They patrolled the Xhosa territory somewhat fruitlessly while hostile Xhosas launched attacks from the strategic position of the overgrown banks of the Sundays and Bushmans rivers.

The commando was unable to achieve what it set out to do and peace negotiations were opened with the Xhosa. Only 4,000 of the stolen cattle, to be distributed among the burghers as compensation, were found. Unrest in the border area continued: the Xhosa did not leave and cattle thefts increased. Maynier refused to protect the farmers. His recommendation that no violence should be used against the Xhosa was accepted by the Company. The policy of territorial segregation was to be imposed with all possible mildness. In future farmers' commandos were only to act in self-defence, and then only with Maynier's permission. The landdrost was to try to win the goodwill of the Xhosas through the usual yearly presents. As the authorities were determined not to approve further armed attacks on the Xhosa, and the Xhosas refused to move east over the Fish River, the policy of territorial and economic segregation could not be put into effect.

Many of the border farmers now found their position untenable: the Company would not protect them, and they were not allowed to protect themselves. The only course open to them appeared to be to repudiate their unsympathetic government.

The dying Company was no more successful in connection with the problems of the western Cape Colony than with those in the east. Its attempts at reform were inadequate and belated. It was concerned only with short term remedial measures, and was therefore ineffective.

Fruitless Company reforms and the reactions of the burghers

The last ten years of the Company's rule at the Cape are characterised by the acceleration of the Company's decline, and the remarkably inefficient efforts of the authorities to improve matters. By the end of the American War of Independence the Company was in debt to the tune of 49½ million guilders. At this stage the fortification expert, Lieutenant-Colonel C. J. van de Graaff, was sent to the Cape as Governor in 1785. He lived luxuriously on a salary of 18,000 guilders a year, and spent enormous amounts on batteries, forts and ramparts, apart from his expenditure on mercenaries. The new Governor clashed with his officials, neglected his administrative duties and did not satisfy the citizens. He spent so much paper money that there were more than a half-million rixdollars in circulation by August, 1791, and its value was steadily diminishing. When the Council of XVII realised what was happening at the Cape, and in particular that the Cape deficits had increased so much that the Company was seriously debilitated by the Cape (the Company's debt now being 80 million guilders), drastic economies were put into effect in 1790. All building at the Cape was stopped immediately, the privileges of officials were curtailed, slaves and outposts were sold and the Wurttemberg Regiment was posted to Batavia. Governor Van de Graaff was recalled and left the Cape in June, 1791. The Cape was still not adequately protected against foreign invasion and, according to the Company's books, deeply in debt.

The States-General now intervened in the Company's affairs. In November, 1791, a reform commission was sent from the Netherlands, and arrived in the Cape in June, 1792. The commissioners, Nederburgh and Frykenius, spent about fifteen months investigating matters in and around the Cape Peninsula, but found it extremely difficult to institute constructive long-term reform measures. Among other things they drastically cut expenditure by abolishing certain offices and giving the remaining officials more onerous duties, although they did increase the salaries of these officials. They attempted to increase income by imposing new taxes, such as the unpopular auction fees, charging pier and crane fees for ships, charging new customs duties on imports, which increased the cost of living at the Cape, imposing an unsuccessful tax on vehicles kept for "comfort and pleasure", and imposing a tax of 5% on all movable and immovable property of senior Cape officials returning to the Netherlands. Furthermore, transfer duties on fixed property were raised from $2\frac{1}{2}\%$ to 4%. Naturally officials as well as free burghers were bitterly dissatisfied with many of these reforms. Most of them did not, in any case, decrease the burden of the Company.

Since the commissioners had been told to discover ways of enabling the burghers to make a better living, and they knew that they actually made the lot of the burghers more difficult with their new tax policies, they sought elsewhere for other means of improving matters. The export of wool was encouraged by adapting the freight fees to the price which the wool fetched in the Netherlands. Furthermore, wealthy entrepreneurs were encouraged "to undertake whaling along the coasts and in the bays of the Cape of Good Hope, where the English and North Americans were practising it with much success".[2] An old request of the burghers was conceded: they were thenceforth to be allowed to take part in the lucrative slave trade along the eastern coast of Africa and with Madagascar. Nederburgh and Frykenius also finally, in November, 1792, allowed the burghers free trade in their own ships; this also the burghers had repeatedly requested. The importation of spices, sugar and coffee was, however, to remain a Company prerogative.

For the first time the free burghers were allowed to export their own products in their own ships to an overseas market, and to import other products, with certain exceptions, in exchange. However, a profitable local shipping trade could not be built up overnight. It required considerable capital, commercial and navigational experience and peaceful times. No such favourable factors obtained at this time. The burghers were also dependent on the Company to supply them with suitable vessels at reasonable prices. O. G. de Wet bought *De Zeenimph* for 15,000 guilders, but it sank in a storm, causing heavy losses among the shareholders. *De Dankbare Africaan*, which had been bought by J. J. de Vos for 14,400 guilders, made coastal voyages around the Cape and also

2. Echte stukken etc., Instructions for C.C.G.G., Art. 7, p. 144, quoted by Dr. A. J. Böeseken: *Die Nederlandse Kommissarisse en die 18de Eeuse Samelewing aan die Kaap* (in Archives Year Book for South African History, 7th year, 1944, p. 193).

undertook profitable trips to the East Indies; however, in this case, disagreements among the shareholders caused losses. This ship was later captured by the British. Another small ship, which was optimistically named *De Hoop op Welvaart* (Hope of Prosperity) by three Van Reenens, called at St. Helena Island among other ports. At the beginning of 1794 the Cape burghers were allowed to extend their trade to Australia, as long as the return journey to Batavia was made via Timor only. In 1795 they were granted the additional right to ship Chinese trade goods in Batavia. *De Herstelder* left for Europe in April, 1795, with the products of the Cape whale and seal industry, but was taken by a British privateer near Norway.

This official recognition of and aid to private enterprise came much too late, however. The war brought commerce and shipping to and from the Cape almost to a standstill. Well-armed British cruisers found the defenceless Cape ships an easy prey. Had these concessions been made in the early eighteenth century the burghers would have made good use of them. The excellent strategic position of the Cape in the southern hemisphere, lying as it does midway between the East and the European harbours, would have given the burghers a great trading advantage. Indeed Cape wholesalers and retailers had long been quietly trading on an international level and, with the help of Company officials, building up capital. There was an active correspondence with North America, London, Amsterdam and other cities in Europe and the East, goods were shipped back and forth in the Company's and foreign ships and clearances effected. But the restrictions to which the Company subjected this trade and the uncertainties of peace as well as of war prevented a substantial accumulation of capital.

The attempted reform of Nederburgh and Frykenius thus did little to pacify the free burghers. Their position became even more precarious. One of their problems was the shortage of hard cash which, because of the Company's policy, was rapidly leaving the Cape. In consultation with the Council of Policy, the commissioners decided to establish a loan bank in April, 1793, where the burghers would be able to obtain money at 5% interest. This did not mean an increase in cash, however, for only depreciated paper money was available. The commissioners were under no illusions about the ineffectiveness of their measures. Again and again they were confronted with possibility of the Company's total bankruptcy. Nederburgh was simply trying to "keep matters out of confusion pending the imminent fall of the Company".[3]

The commissioners reported that most of the Cape's inhabitants were impoverished and lacked any means of remedying the matter. By February, 1794, the Burgher Councillors complained once again about the desperate circumstances of the free burghers. Late in 1795 J. F. Kirsten recorded that the burghers of Stellenbosch were so dissatisfied that they were about to follow the example of Graaff-Reinet and Swellendam and rebel against the Company. He

---

3. S. G. Nederburgh's "Consideratien over de toestand waarin de Oostindische Compagnie zig in dit ogenblik bevind . . . ", 7 March, 1791, quoted by A. J. Böeseken in *Die Nederlandse Kommissarisse*, p. 188.

added, furthermore, that had the British occupation fleet not arrived at the Cape, the Cape district would have joined the other districts in revolt.[4] "I do not suppose", Kirsten continued, "the Annals of Turkey can produce an equal parallel of Tyranny and Extortion".[5]

Whereas the reactions of the burghers in the Peninsula and its vicinity were restrained by those armed forces the Company still possessed, the frontier farmers of Graaff-Reinet and Swellendam had far more freedom to vent their dissatisfaction. The commissioners realised only too well that the Company's administration of the remote districts was highly unsatisfactory and that there were bound to be violent reactions to its inefficiency. Yet they did nothing to investigate the frontier problems, let alone suggest solutions. They never went further afield than Stellenbosch.

Rebellion at Graaff-Reinet and Swellendam

The actual policy concerning the border districts was determined within the general framework of Company policy by Commissioner-General J. A. Sluysken, who was left in control at the Cape when Nederburgh and Frykenius sailed in September, 1793. The unpopular landdrost on the remote Xhosa border, Maynier, also gained local power and, as we have already seen, played a dominant role there. His policy was ultimately to cause rebellion. By the beginning of 1795 an important group of border farmers had begun to feel that their position was intolerable. Late in January farmers signed an agreement and on 6 February, 1795, certain "heemraden", ex-"heemraden" and burgher officers, supported by armed farmers, ordered the landdrost to leave the drostdy. Democratic and revolutionary terms and ideas were familiar to these people. They called themselves the general voice of the people ("algemene volkstem") and elected representatives to look after their interests. These representatives now met with the "heemraden" and burgher officers to appoint their own officials. Burgher lieutenant C. D. Gerotz was appointed provisional landdrost. Sluysken sent a commission under O. G. de Wet, President of the Council of Justice, to persuade the rebellious Graaff-Reineters to recognise Company authority again, but his efforts were unsuccessful. The rebellious farmers refused to obey the Company's laws or to pay its taxes.

On 17 and 18 June, 1795, the Swellendam district followed Graaff-Reinet's example, protesting especially against the Company's economic and Hottentot policies. About sixty armed burghers under a self-elected "national commandant", J. P. Delport, forced landdrost A. A. Faure and his assistants to relinquish their posts and appointed Hermanus Steyn as "National Landdrost". The rebellious burghers established a revolutionary "National Convention" as their main executive body. Theirs was not a declaration of complete independence;

---

4. Refer article 13 of Kirsten's memorandum in C. F. J. Muller: *Johannes Frederik Kirsten oor die toestand van die Kaapkolonie in 1795*, (Pretoria, 1960), p. 60.

5. *Ibid.*, p. 63 (article 19).

they merely repudiated the authority of the Company while electing to remain under the flag of the Dutch Republic.

A month later at an important meeting the members of the National Convention formulated their attitude to Company policy. They declared their firm intention of governing themselves, because "We have been long enough in the Yoke of Slavery and are now resolved to venture the last drop of blood for our dear Fatherland and resort under a Free Republic".[6] Thus ended the Company's control of the two border districts. Under Sluysken the armed forces of the moribund Company were already resisting a British fleet in False Bay and the authorities had been hoping for support from the Swellendam forces. There was, therefore, no question of their sending troops east to subjugate the rebellious "Colonies".

The first British conquest of the Cape

Prince William V fled from Holland to England in January, 1795, and revolutionary French forces assumed control of the Republic of the United Netherlands. The Batavian Republic was established. A strong British fleet was quickly fitted out to occupy the Cape before the French got there and sailed with a letter from the Prince of Orange which requested Sluysken to receive the British as friends. When Admiral Elphinstone arrived in False Bay in June, 1795, with troops under the command of General Craig, Sluysken opposed the British forces. Burghers from the outlying districts were mobilized. Lieutenant-Colonel C. M. W. de Lille was sent to Simonstown with a small force, but was soon recalled to Muizenberg. This meant that a strong British force could land unopposed at Simonstown. Early in August De Lille put up a half-hearted defence of Muizenburg with 200 infantrymen from the garrison, 200 mounted burghers, 150 pandours and 120 gunners, against a superior force of 1,600 British. Shortly afterwards De Lille retreated to Wynberg. There were British sympathisers among the senior Company officials and officers, and badly organized withdrawals of the regular troops caused the burghers to lose confidence in their commanders. They saw that Wynberg was not being properly fortified or defended. Sluysken could have counter-attacked with his approximately 2,500 men before Major-General A. Clarke arrived early in September in fourteen more ships carrying large reinforcements. When a further quick retreat from Wynberg followed, the burghers suspected a number of their commanding officers, among them De Lille, Van Baalen and Gordon, of treason. They refused to retreat further to the fortified line between Fork Knokke and Devil's Peak, and many went home.

Sluysken capitulated at Rustenburg on 16 September, 1795. By agreement Cape laws and customs were to remain unaltered; no new taxes were to be levied; internal free trade and more generous overseas trade were envisaged;

6. Quoted by Dr. C. Beyers in A. J. H. van der Walt *et al*, editors, *Geskiedenis van Suid-Afrika*, I, (Cape Town etc. 1952), p. 182.

and the Company's paper money was guaranteed. In this way the rule of the Netherlands East India Company, which had lasted for nearly one-and-a-half centuries at the southern tip of Africa, came to an end.

7. Transition, 1795 - 1806

In the history of South Africa the years between 1795 and 1806, which saw the turn of a century, were a period of political transition which determined whether Holland, France or England was to govern the Cape. The uncertainty concerning the future of the Cape, which was a consequence of the French Revolution and the Napoleonic Wars, was in fact only finally resolved by the treaty of London in 1814, but by the time England had occupied the Cape for the second time in 1806 it had become quite clear who was in future to control this territory.

In the period between 1795 and 1806 the Cape was governed first by the British and then by the Batavian Republic. The first British regime was conscious of its temporary nature, and did little to alter Cape institutions and customs. The Batavian regime was characterized by drastic reforms and an enlightened spirit of government, but was far too short to change the Cape permanently. The period of transition was not entirely without significance, however, since existing problems, such as those of the eastern border, were to assume new proportions, while principles, such as the independence of the Supreme Court, were established which to this day are still recognised in South Africa.

The first British administration, 1795 – 1803

In 1795 the British assumed control at the Cape, which then had a population of 16,000 – 20,000 Whites, 17,000 – 25,000 slaves and an estimated 14,000 Hottentots – a heterogeneous community of differing characteristics, colours, standards of living, morals and habits. There were differences even among the Whites who were spread over a large area. The merchants and officials of Cape Town, the settled agricultural community near Cape Town, and the pioneer cattle farmers of the frontier districts had little in common. These divergences and racial differences among the Whites, the presence of the Bantu on the eastern Cape borders and economic troubles were to create many problems.

At the beginning of the English occupation the Cape was under the military government of Generals Craig and Clarke and Admiral Elphinstone. The last two left in November, 1795, leaving Craig in sole charge. The strict, but humane and honest administration of Craig ended in May, 1795, when crown colony government was instituted at the Cape and Earl Macartney became governor. Macartney was an excellent administrator, but too conservative and inflexible to gain the colonists' loyalty. He tolerated no insubordination and would billet soldiers on whoever disobeyed him. Loyal citizens were well treated, however, and there was much social activity under the aegis of the

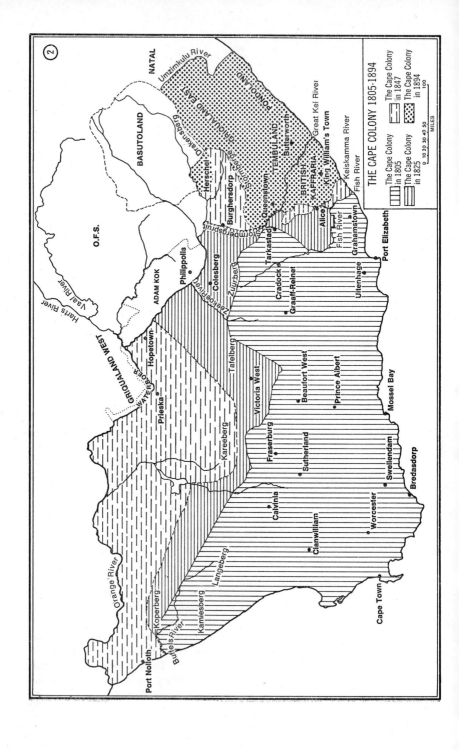

THE CAPE COLONY 1805-1894

charming Lady Anne Barnard, wife of the Colonial Secretary. In November, 1798, Macartney retired for reasons of health and Major-General Francis Dundas took over command at the Cape, except for a short interlude (December, 1799 – April, 1801) during which Sir George Yonge was governor. Dundas continued the blend of the strict and lenient policies of his predecessors, but Yonge abused his power, was incompetent and corrupt.

Under the crown colony government inaugurated by Macartney government was absolute and direct. The old Council of Policy disappeared and all civil and military powers were in the hands of the governor, an arrangement which the British retained at the Cape until 1828. Craig replaced the old College of Burgher Councillors, or Commission of the High Court, with a Burgher Senate. This body consisted of six members: the governor filled vacancies from names which the Burgher Senate submitted to him. Excepting in judicial matters the Burgher Senate had approximately the same duties as the old body, such as advising the governor on matters concerning the colonists and managing municipal affairs in Cape Town. It is doubtful whether the Senate was of any use to the colonists. For example, Macartney refused its request that more slaves should be imported to alleviate the acute labour shortage, and it also clashed with the governor on matters of lighting and improving the streets of Cape Town.

In matters of judicature the British government improved on the existing Council of Justice. Administration of justice remained in the hands of un-qualified judicial officials, but their numbers were reduced to a president and seven members at fixed salaries. The governor and deputy governor served as a court of appeal; in some cases appeal could be made to the Privy Council in London. Barbaric punitive measures such as the rack were abolished. The privilege of fixed salaries was extended to other officials. In this way the fees and additional earnings which had previously made up such a large and obscure part of every official's income were eliminated. Only the fiscal was still entitled to part of the fines imposed by the supreme court. In the outlying districts local government continued unchanged, except that the judicial powers of local courts were extended. The new regime wished to conciliate the colonists and for this reason, and because the British occupation was temporary, preferred not to change too many of the existing institutions.

In contrast to its actions in constitutional matters, the first British regime was lenient in the economic sphere. The economic policy of the new masters was healthier and more profitable to the colonists and merchants than that of the Dutch East India Company. The British authorities were soon made aware of the economic instability of the Cape. The first crop of wheat was satisfactory and Craig made the mistake of exporting the surplus grain. When the next crop was poor famine was imminent and Craig hurriedly had to import wheat and even issue paper money to the value of £50,000. Despite such errors the arrival of the British did herald an economic revival. The many troops in the Colony and the war in Europe brought prosperity to the Cape merchants and farmers. Furthermore Macartney alleviated the colonists' burdens by abolishing the most oppressive monopolies and by writing off land taxes that were in arrears. Although essential agricultural products still had to be sold to the government at fixed prices, as in the Company's days, colonists and merchants, on the whole, were better off than before.

The first British regime, in accordance with the conditions of capitulation, did not impose new taxes. Yonge trespassed in this respect by instituting hunting licences and increasing the excise on brandy, but these taxes were soon repealed. In spite of his shortcomings Yonge tried to promote agriculture by establishing a department of agriculture which also ran an experimental farm. Successive crop failures, however, caused the loss of an investment of thousands of pounds in the farm. It could not even properly satisfy the needs of its employees. The only positive result of the experiment was that the colonists became acquainted with English iron ploughs.

As far as external trade was concerned the Cape was in a unique position. In the beginning British navigation laws operated at the Cape as in all other British colonies, but in December, 1796, the British government passed a special law which allowed free entry into the Cape of all goods from British colonies, while goods from well-disposed foreign powers were allowed entry on payment of import duties. The Cape was therefore in a privileged position. Although imports exceeded exports by nearly £300,000 per year, this amount was made good in the hard cash which came into the country through the troops and passing ships. During the first British regime about 170 ships entered Table Bay and Simon's Bay annually. This was appreciably more than the eighty-six ships which had visited the Cape in 1794, although admittedly there were times under the Company when there had been a heavy pressure of shipping, for example, an average of 164 per year during the period 1785 – 1789. The Colony's income also rose quickly from 1796 onwards, but salaries took a heavy toll .The governor, for example, received £10,000 per year and the other more important officials collectively £14,700.

On the eastern Cape frontier the friction between the colonists, the Hottentots and the Bantu was to afford a true test of the British regime. Under the previous regime there had already been clashes between White and Bantu and in the districts of Graaff-Reinet and Swellendam the colonists were in revolt against the Company. The new regime had to restore order, but the people of Graaff-Reinet did not wish to take the interim oath of loyalty and thereby lose the independence they had won from the previous regime.

Under certain conditions Graaff-Reinet would subject itself to British authority. Among other things, the government had to recognise its officials and military officers and supply them with ammunition so that they could protect their lives and property. General Craig was sympathetic but had to put down the rebellion; not only to ensure order and equable colonial administration, but also particularly because it was imperative that the supply of meat from the interior should not fail. Nevertheless, Craig was willing to recognise the Graaff-Reinet landdrost, Carl Gerotz, until such time as Frans Bresler, nominated by the British, could take over. Bresler, however, was a Company official who had entered the service of the British, and this the people of Graaff-Reinet did not like. They considered him a traitor and would have preferred a British land-drost. When Bresler raised the British flag before the Graaff-Reinet drostdy on 22 February, 1796, the burghers hauled it down again and refused to take the oath of allegiance. They were determined to remain loyal to the Batavian Republic, and Bresler returned to the Cape a month later.

Craig could not overlook this hostile demonstration. He therefore stationed 300 troops under Major King at Stellenbosch from where they would be able to advance on Graaff-Reinet, recruited a Hottentot corps for inland service and prohibited the delivery of any supplies to Graaff-Reinet. Yet General Craig hesitated to set about subjugating the people of Graaff-Reinet immediately. His hesitation was partly due to a widespread hostility among the colonists, even among those who had taken the oath of allegiance. In the words of Lady Anne Barnard, many had taken the oath in the frame of mind of: "We must swear, for they are the strongest".[1]

At this point Craig also had to turn his attention to defending the Cape against outside attack. It was known that a Dutch naval squadron under Admiral Lucas was on its way to the Cape. It was possible that this squadron, with the help of a French squadron and the Cape colonists, would reconquer the Cape. Craig, however, acted with dispatch and forced Lucas to capitulate at Saldanha Bay since he did not receive the expected French help, was troubled by mutiny among his sailors who supported the House of Orange, and also heard that he could expect little help from the colonists. The capitulation of Lucas and a serious shortage of ammunition contributed to Graaff-Reinet's accepting British authority by the end of 1796. Craig reappointed Bresler as landdrost and pardoned the people of Graaff-Reinet, with the exception of the district surgeon, Jan Woyer.

Woyer fled to Batavia on a Danish ship and convinced the Governor-General, Van Overstraten, that Graaff-Reinet only lacked ammunition to overthrow the British government. Van Overstraten therefore sent the ship *Haasje* to Algoa Bay with ammunition and other supplies. The *Haasje*, however, had to put into Delagoa Bay for repairs and when its destination and purpose became known an English ship, the *Hope*, captured her in May, 1797.

On the eastern frontier of the Cape tension between White and Black mounted. Consequently, Macartney seconded John Barrow, his secretary, to Landdrost Bresler to investigate conditions on the border. Barrow's *Travels into the Interior of Southern Africa* show that he was not capable of making an objective judgement, because he was greatly prejudiced against the frontiersmen, whom he considered to be reckless, ignorant and brutal. Nevertheless, Barrow had to help Bresler to restore order, to foster the colonists' confidence in the government and to exact obedience to the new administration.

Bresler and Barrow, on Macartney's instructions, continued the Company's

1. Lady Anne Barnard (H. J. Anderson ed.): *South Africa a Century ago (1797 – 1801)* (Cape Town, 1924), p. 15: Anne Barnard to H. Dundas, d.d. Cape Town, 10 Aug., 1797.

policy of racial segregation. Burghers who had left their farms because of threatening Xhosas were encouraged to return to them. If they did so within four months, they would be exempt from recognition money for six years. The problem was, however, that tribes who had fled from the Xhosa chieftain Gaika were living in the Suurveld on the Colony's side of the border and refused to return to their side of the Fish River, although Gaika recognised the border and promised not to molest the Xhosas of the Suurveld if they should return to his territory. This promise did not, however, succeed in persuading the Bantu to move back to Gaika's side of the border. The situation on the eastern border thus remained tense, and to make matters worse various frontiersmen at Graaff-Reinet again became rebellious.

The arrest, early in 1799, of Adriaan van Jaarsveld, the previously mentioned leader and an esteemed burgher of Graaff-Reinet, on the charge of forging a receipt of the Orphan Chamber, ignited the situation on the eastern border. The accusation against Van Jaarsveld was justified, but the people of Graaff-Reinet, who had lost their confidence in the government and its officials, believed that the charge was merely a pretext to constrain their leader and make him atone for his earlier activity in Graaff-Reinet affairs. They knew that Macartney had already banned Commandant Petrus Delport, Swellendam's leader, without a hearing. Encouraged by reports that the Cape Town garrison was weakened because troops had left for India and because fire had destroyed many horses and military supplies, a group of Graaff-Reinet citizens broke into open rebellion, freed Van Jaarsveld and besieged the drostdy.

In Cape Town a few people sympathized with the rebels. One such sympathizer was the teacher Edeman, who requested French aid from Mauritius. The French sent an old frigate, the *Prudente* manned by volunteers, to Algoa Bay, but she was taken by a British man-o-war on 9 February, 1799, before she reached her destination. A second French attempt to render aid also failed when the *Preneuse* arrived in Algoa Bay in September, 1799, but was driven off by two British ships, the *Camel* and the *Rattlesnake*. By this time the Graaff-Reinet rebellion was already over. Not all the people of Graaff-Reinet supported the rebellion, and when General Vandeleur appeared in March, 1799, to quell the revolt the small group of dissidents capitulated without resistance. Van Jaarsveld and nineteen others were arrested and tried on a charge of high treason. Marthinus Prinsloo and Van Jaarsveld were condemned to death and the others sentenced to exile and penal servitude. The government did not, however, carry out the death sentences. Van Jaarsveld died in goal and when the Cape was returned to the Batavian Republic in 1803, all the other prisoners were freed.

The civil unrest of the Van Jaarsveld rebellion gave Bantu and Hottentots an opportunity to plunder farms and steal cattle. The fact that ammunition deliveries to Graaff-Reinet had been prohibited by the British government aggravated the situation. The behaviour of the Hottentots also gave cause for alarm. Previously they had welcomed the support of the Whites against the cattle-stealing Bushmen. As land became increasingly scarce, and doubtless also enticed by the

White man's goods, more and more Hottentots took service with the Whites. Some employers treated them badly and created tension between the races. The ineffectual maintenance of law on the eastern border increased the friction. At Vandeleur's arrival the Hottentots, believing that the authorities would welcome their co-operation against their White employers, joined his troops. Vandeleur disarmed them, however, and when the Hottentots noticed that many of the troops had returned to Cape Town they became suspicious of the government and joined the Xhosas. This Hottentot-Xhosa alliance was dangerous since the Hottentots knew the fighting tactics of the Whites and in many cases possessed firearms.

While Vandeleur was returning from Graaff-Reinet to Algoa Bay his party was unexpectedly attacked by a Xhosa tribe who probably thought that the troops had come to drive them out of the Suurveld. The indignant Vandeleur was determined to teach the Xhosas a lesson, but from Cape Town came an order issued by the acting governor, Dundas – probably influenced by such people as Barrow – that peace was to be effected with presents, promises and a conciliatory attitude. The Xhosas, however, did not understand a policy of appeasement and merely considered it a sign of weakness. Consequently the Xhosas and Hottentots wreaked havoc. By the end of July, 1799, they occupied the whole of the southern half of the Graaff-Reinet district.

At his wit's end Dundas himself, accompanied by soldiers and burghers, went out to the border, not to make war but to apply his policy of appeasement per-sonally. Honoratus Maynier, who had incurred the displeasure of the frontier farmers even in Company days, assisted Dundas in his negotiations with the Xhosas and Hottentots. They did in fact achieve a peace treaty in October, 1799, according to which the non-Whites were to cease their marauding activities. The Xhosas, however, could remain in the Suurveld unmolested. Further-more, Dundas appointed Maynier resident commissioner for Graaff-Reinet and Swellendam. He left Maynier the support of some dragoons and Hottentot soldiers, with instructions to oppose armed action against the Hottentots and cattle rustlers. In case of future trouble, Fort Frederick was built at Algoa Bay and a garrison of 350 men was stationed there.

Dundas's and Maynier's policy for maintaining law and order on the frontier was intrinsically sound, but its failure was a foregone conclusion because the means for effecting it, such as a police force, were lacking. The result was chaos, aggravated by the burghers still being suspicious of Maynier because of his behaviour during the Company's regime. In October, 1801, they besieged Maynier in the drostdy and, under Tjaart van der Walt and other responsible leaders, drew up petitions which set out their grievances against Maynier. In response the authorities despatched Major Sherlock to Graaff-Reinet with a body of troops to restore order, and recalled Maynier to Cape Town. A com-mission of enquiry acquitted Maynier of the charges brought against him, but he was not sent back to the frontier.

Maynier's return to Cape Town satisfied the burghers, but did not solve the problems on the eastern frontier. Something more decisive was required. In

1801 Dr J. T. van der Kemp, a missionary, established a reserve for vagrant Hottentots on the Swartkops River, and during the next year further efforts were made to settle the Hottentots. The frontier farmers, however, were already demoralised and not eager for commando service. They distrusted the government and did not want to leave their families on the farms while they went on commando. A further setback occurred in May, 1802, when the able Tjaart van der Walt was killed in action. Without his leadership the commandos which were called up could not restore peace. It began to look as if the eastern districts would fall into the hands of the Blacks.

By 1802 only a full-scale military action could save the situation on the eastern frontier. Dundas was not prepared to undertake this, as it was already known that the Cape was to be handed back to the Batavian Republic. He therefore went to the border in the middle of 1802, persuaded the warring parties temporarily to leave each other in peace, and called up a commando of burghers to keep an eye on matters while the troops withdrew to Cape Town. Thus the first British occupation ended without a solution to the thorny border problem having been discovered. Dundas felt that the greatest obstacle to a solution was that the Colony was too large. Even Yonge realised that the four districts into which the Colony was divided were too extensive for efficient administration and, on the advice of the fiscal, Willem van Ryneveld, he recommended subdivision of the districts and the institution of circuit courts as well as of a better educational system. The British government in London, however, rejected these proposals since they would entail unnecessary expenditure in a colony which was merely a temporary possession.

In spite of the temporary nature of the first British occupation there were some who thought of the Cape as permanently important to Britain because of its strategic position on the sea route to India and its role in the struggle between France and England. Thus Macartney pointed out that the Cape Colony was of small commercial value and that it would be an expensive undertaking to keep it, but "its chief importance to us arises from its geographical position, from its forming the master link of connection between the western and eastern world, from its being the great outwork of our Asiatic commerce and Indian empire, and above all from the conviction that, if in the hands of a powerful enemy, it might enable him to shake to the foundation, perhaps overturn and destroy the whole fabric of our oriental opulence and dominion".[2] Others, however, argued that it was unneccessary to possess the Cape as long as Britain was supreme on the sea. The British cabinet and parliament were divided as to the value of the Cape, but ultimately the Cape was given back to the Batavian Republic at the Peace of Amiens. In February, 1803, the Cape once again changed hands.

2. G. M. Theal: *Records of the Cape Colony*, II (London, 1898), p. 114: Macartney to Dundas, d.d. Cape Town, 10 July, 1797.

The Batavian period, 1803 – 1806

In contrast to the Dutch East India Company, which had regarded the Cape merely as a halfway station between Europe and the East, the Batavian Republic in 1803 gave the Cape the high status of a Dutch colony. The new colony was directly under the Batavian government in the Netherlands and in the care of the Asiatic Council, the body which was responsible for the administration and defence of the Dutch colonies. The Asiatic Council, in contrast to the authorities of the first British regime which principally and deliberately implemented a temporary and negative policy, wished to follow a thorough and constructive colonial policy at the Cape. With this in mind Advocate J. A. de Mist, a member of the Asiatic Council, composed a memorandum even before the Peace of Amiens, in which he set out principles for the government of the Cape after its retrocession to Holland. The memorandum was so well received that De Mist was appointed as commissioner to take over the Cape from the British and to organise its government and administration. J. W. Janssens, a pensioned military officer and at the time secretary-general of the war cabinet, would act as governor and accompany De Mist to the Cape.

De Mist's memorandum contains suggestions for political, administrative, economic and social reforms. "All the sins of the past, those of omission and those of commission", De Mist wrote, "can now be wiped out as with a damp sponge, with one stroke of the pen all the old contentions can be blotted out and forgotten; and on the clean white page may be written the new Charter for this settlement, framed with wisdom, mildness and discretion, but always tempered with a proper firmness. Thus this Colony may be given a new lease of life, and, by God's mercy, may become in time one of the most important possessions of the State".[3] His recommendations were based on what he had found in official documents and travel journals, and not on a personal visit to the Cape. After facing the situation at first hand, De Mist was to modify some of his opinions. Among other things, he found that Barrow's *Travels* did not present an objective impression of White and non-White, and that the Cape colonists lived in a conservative world which had not to any great extent been influenced, as had been the Batavian Republic, by the enlightened ideas of revolutionary France. This is not to say that De Mist wanted to bring about a complete change at the Cape. Even though his memorandum takes as its point of departure the people themselves he believed that only a strong central government could look after their welfare. In addition, he preferred to act, not according to the revolutionary principle of destroying everything in existence, but to base future development on existing good.

The central government which De Mist instituted at the Cape Colony was intended not only to be a strong executive, but also to prevent abuse of power. The powers of the government were curtailed to eliminate abuses, but not to

3. Gie, S.F.N.: *The Memorandum of Commissary J. A. de Mist* (V.R.S. 3, Cape Town, 1920), p. 172.

such an extent as to render the government ineffective. Everything depended on a balance of control between the governor on the one hand and the officials on the other. The governor was responsible for defence, safety, peace and order, and was to supervise the administration. He was assisted by four officials nominated by the Batavian government, of whom two had to be Cape colonists. These officials would also be departmental heads of (1) agriculture and stock-breeding, (2) finance, (3) trade and commerce, (4) shipping and fisheries, and under the chairmanship of the governor they formed the Political Council. Up to September, 1804, however, when De Mist relinquished his post as commissioner, the governor was subordinate to the commissioner.

Continuing his policy of attempting to eliminate the possibility of abuses, De Mist placed financial management in the hands of an Accounting Chamber, which in status was just below that of the Political Council. The Accounting Chamber, whose members were appointed from the colonists by the Asiatic Council, controlled all funds and was responsible for them to the Asiatic Council. The Political Council therefore could not abuse the country's treasury. By instituting the Accounting Chamber, De Mist also expressed the principle of no taxation without representation. Indeed, it was essential to grant the colonists representation in the Accounting Chamber and on the Political Council, since the elements of representation which had existed in the Burgher Senate during the first British regime and the College of Burgher Councillors under the Company had disappeared. The Burgher Senate was replaced by a Community Council of seven members who had to be inhabitants of Cape Town or its district. The Community Council was concerned mainly with municipal duties in Cape Town and its district. It therefore no longer was a link between the government and colonists as the College of Burgher Councillors and the Burgher Senate had been.

The next important change was in the judicature. De Mist separated judicial and executive authority and entrusted the former to a Council of Justice, consisting of six members with legal qualifications, a secretary and an attorney-general, who replaced the fiscal and public prosecutor, and who was no longer entitled to part of the imposed fines. Appeal could be made to the Supreme Court at The Hague. Thus the judicature was quite independent. Furthermore, De Mist instituted a government office to administer estates, a function previously fulfilled by the secretary of the Council of Justice. The Orphan Chamber continued unchanged.

These institutions could effectually control Cape Town and its environs. De Mist's vision, however, also penetrated further inland. He realised that to be strong a central government should be supported by efficient local government in the districts. Previous governments had particularly neglected the interior of the Cape, and therefore Janssens and De Mist travelled round the country to obtain first-hand information about the rural areas and their needs. They found the Colony to be too extensive for efficient administrative and judical control through the existing division into the four districts of Cape Town, Stellenbosch, Swellendam and Graaff-Reinet. Consequently two new districts,

Tulbagh and Uitenhage, were established. Landdrosts were appointed for all six districts. They were each to be assisted by six citizens, as "heemraden", and a secretary. They fulfilled administrative functions, solemnized marriages and acted as a court of justice with limited powers. Each district was subdivided into wards or field cornetcies with a radius of about thirty-six miles. Each ward had a field cornet who received no salary but was exempt from tax. His most important duties were to maintain law and order, publicize official orders and proclamations, hold post-mortems, arrest criminals and, on the order of the landdrost, call up the burghers of his ward for commando service. Efficient communication with the interior was also essential to the smooth running of the administration as a whole. Consequently, in Januray, 1805, a postal service was instituted to carry letters between Cape Town and all the drostdys.

The central and local governments instituted by De Mist were undoubtedy improvements on those of the first British regime and the Company's rule. There was more chance of their being successful than with any of the previous forms of government, particularly because the demands made by the Cape Patriots during the last years of the Company's reign had been acceded to in certain respects. Among other things the Patriots had asked for the executive and judical powers to be separated and for a voice in the central government, even if this last was not yet based on the principle of free elections.

The Batavian regime also instituted reforms in religious and educational matters. In his church ordinance of 1804 De Mist extended equal legal protection to all religious bodies which acknowledged a supreme being, in other words to the Reformed Church, Lutherans, Anglicans, Roman Catholics, Mohammedans and others. But he made the church subservient to the state and the government reserved the right to oppose any religious doctrine it considered dangerous. The government also provided ministers for the Nederduits-Gereformeerde Kerk and paid them, and the governor had to approve the members elected to the church council. The conservative colonists, however, did not approve of De Mist's liberal religious tolerance. They were also opposed to De Mist's arrangement that a landdrost and two heemraden could solemnize marriages in the country districts. To them, marriage was a sacrament which could only be solemnized in church, even if it entailed much trouble and long journeys to reach a church. The colonists were also dissatisfied because the authorities took the responsibility for educational matters away from the church.

During their journeys Janssens and De Mist had noticed the shortage of educational facilities and that those that did exist were not uniform. Consequently De Mist promulgated a school ordinance aimed at placing education on a firm foundation, obtaining the necessary funds to finance education and providing educational facilities for Cape Town and its well-populated environs, and for the outlying districts. Control of education was entrusted to a commission of seven members who represented the Political Council, the Orphan Chamber, and the Nederduits-Gereformeerde and Lutheran churches. In the outlying districts the landdrosts and ministers were honorary members of the commission and they could give advice on matters concerning their districts. The Political Council controlled educational funds. This school ordinance placed education under the state; the direct influence of the church was eliminated. Up to 1806, however, few of these plans were put into effect.

In the economic sphere the Batavian regime tried to balance expenditure and income. This could be done by improving the Cape Colony's crops and wines and its stock-breeding. However, the authorities were soon to learn that they could not rely on agricultural products for export. The Colony's climate and rainfall were too uncertain. The cultivation of wheat for export was encouraged, but three successive bad crops necessitated importing rice from India to augment the local shortage of wheat. Viticulture was more reliable, but the quality of the wine was poor. A German viticulturist was therefore imported from Europe to improve the quality of wine produced at the Cape, but the efforts to make wine a profitable export did not succeed. Generally speaking problems such as drought, lack of transport and labour shortages made agriculture difficult at the Cape, and no profitable agricultural export was developed.

A product which could certainly be developed into an important export was wool. With this in mind the government in 1804 appointed a commission to promote stock-breeding. The commission particularly encouraged the breeding of wool sheep, but found it difficult to persuade the colonists to change from the familiar fat-tailed sheep to a wool sheep. Even so, progress was made, but because of the short term of the Batavian regime wool farming showed no immediate results. It was only much later that the production of wool was to increase in importance.

Free trade had been De Mist's aim, but after his arrival at the Cape he found that free trade was not possible, particularly because of the war-torn condition of Europe. The Cape colonists were therefore, as before, dependent on the Cape market for the sale of their produce. De Mist also had to relinquish his plan for decreasing the amount of paper money and replacing it with coins. Indeed, the war and a chronic shortage of money – the average annual revenue for the years 1803 – 1806 was 396,638 rixdollars – forced him to issue 300,000 additional rixdollar notes which brought the total of notes in circulation to 2,086,000. This meant that the rixdollar depreciated by about twenty per cent.

The monetary shortage also contributed to the Batavian Republic's not being able to embark on a strong frontier policy. The authorities could little afford to defend the Cape against internal as well as external attacks. With Europe at war, the Batavian regime was forced to follow a conciliatory policy in the interior, as its predecessor had done. The inland journeys of De Mist and Janssens had given them a clear picture of the eastern border problem and the relationship between White and non-White. They realised that the alliance between the Hottentots and Xhosas was dangerous and somehow had to be broken up. They effected this rupture by attending to the grievances of the Hottentots, among which was their lack of land. In consequence several missionary societies were granted land on which the Hottentots could live; for example a farm of 7,000 morgan was given to the missionaries Read and Van der Kemp for a mission station at Bethelsdorp. Furthermore, Hottentot captains, such as Klaas Stuurman, were persuaded to live some distance from the Xhosas, down the Gamtoos River.

The Batavian regime welcomed the idea that Hottentots should enter the service of the colonists, but wanted to prevent employers from taking the law into their own hands. Hottentot employees had to be treated justly and labour contracts had to be drawn up if a Hottentot worked for a colonist for longer than three months. The authorities also expected the missionaries to encourage diligence among the Hottentots. The missionaries did not come up to expectations. Janssens wrote in January, 1805: "Generally the missionaries are wretches without enlightened precepts – they do great harm and I attempt in vain to find out what good they do".[4] Small wonder, therefore, that the government did not allow the Hottentots on the mission stations to have any contact with other natives inside and outside the colony. This was to prevent industrious workers being influenced by the laxity of the mission stations.

On the eastern border the Batavian regime followed a policy of absolute separation between White and non-White. Captain Lodewyk Alberti, who was stationed with his troops at Fort Frederick, had to implement this policy. His force, however, was too small for any decisive action. There was the problem, as under the first British occupation, of there being many Xhosas in the Suurveld who refused to return to their side of the Fish River border for fear of Gaika. Janssens did in fact negotiate with these Xhosas, as well as with Gaika, who was prepared to accept his refugee subjects. In spite of this, the Xhosas remained in the Suurveld, and though Alberti wished to drive them out, he could not do so. Alberti, however, enjoyed the confidence of the frontier colonists and the Bantu and was thus able to maintain law and order on the border.

The enlightened Batavian government was opposed to slavery and wished to end it. Because of the serious labour shortage the slaves could not, however, be freed at once. The government thus planned a slow process of freeing them, in which children were freed at birth. Before this plan could be implemented the Cape Colony once again passed into British hands.

The British occupation of the Cape in 1806 was again a direct result of the war in Europe. The Batavian Republic, which was in fact a satellite of France, had scarcely taken over the Cape when in May, 1803, war once more broke out between England and France. There was a possibility that the British would re-occupy the strategically important southern point of Africa, and Janssens had to prepare for this eventuality. But he also had to send some of his best troops to Batavia and the mercenaries, estimated at 1,500, who remained at the Cape could not effectively defend it against attack. Janssens therefore organised a citizens' militia from among the colonists and included the Hottentot regiment of 600 pandours, serving under White colonists as officers, in his plans.

---

4. Translated from the original Dutch quoted in J. P. v. d. Merwe: *Die Kaap onder die Bataafse Republiek*, 1803 – 1806 (Amsterdam, 1926), p. 263, from a letter by Janssens to the Asiatic Council, d.d. 5 Jan., 1805.

The long-awaited attack on the Cape only materialised once the danger that Napoleon would invade England had abated. Very early in the new year of 1806 the signallers on Lion's Head reported the arrival of a British fleet of sixty-one ships under Sir Home Popham, with General Baird and 6,700 troops on board, which threatened the continuance of the Cape Colony as a Dutch dependency. On 7 January Baird's main force landed at Bloubergstrand, where Janssens resisted him with a force of 2,000 men. The result of the clash, which took place on 8 January, near Rietvlei on Bloubergstrand, was a foregone conclusion. The defenders were no match for the superior numbers of the attackers. Two days later part of the defending force capitulated and on 18 January, 1806, Janssens and the rest of his force laid down their weapons.

According to the conditions of capitulation the burghers could return straight to their homes. The soldiers were taken prisoners-of-war, but would be sent to the Netherlands at British expense. The new authorities undertook to respect private property but confiscated all the property of the Batavian government. Paper money would provisionally remain in circulation, the official religion would be respected, and all existing rights and privileges of the inhabitants were guaranteed. In March, 1806, Janssens and the garrison left for Holland, and with their departure Southern Africa saw the last of Dutch authority.

De Mist and Janssens had been deeply concerned about the welfare of the Cape Colony. Some of their arrangements, such as the solemnization of marriages, admittedly had been unpopular with the colonists. A certain amount of inevitable dissatisfaction could be ascribed to the Batavian regime, enlightened as it was, being insufficiantly familiar with the mores and customs of the Cape communities to avoid all mistakes. It did not apprehend that a new nation with its own views was developing at the Cape. However, the Batavian authorities did act in the interests of their subjects and for the first time at the Cape a government made some attempt to keep the development of the outlying districts in mind. The term of office of the Batavian regime was however too short for any results of its numerous reforms and regulations to become apparent. The return of the English meant that the enlightened theories of Batavia would be replaced by more conservative British ideas.

8. A New Regime, 1806-1834

Great Britain and the Cape Colony

The second British occupation of the Cape in 1806 had far-reaching effects on the history of South Africa. Up to 1795 the Cape had been a Dutch colony. From 1806 onwards the nature of the Cape colony became even more complex than before due to a number of new factors: British rule, followed by the coming of British people who brought British views, ideas and culture. These factors were to be of paramount importance in the subsequent history of the country.

From 1806 to 1834 the Cape was a crown colony completely under the control of the British Government. The British colonial policy of the time had been greatly influenced by the momentous events in Europe and America during the late eighteenth and early nineteenth centuries. The excesses of the French mob strengthened the reactionary tendencies of the British ruling classes, and made it difficult for them to understand or sympathize with the aspirations of the common people, at home or in the colonies. These tendencies partially explain the harsh treatment of the Slagtersnek rebels, for example. Furthermore, the loss of the American colonies caused Britain to minimize the value of colonies. The only reason the British occupied the Cape in 1806 was to safeguard Britain's lucrative trade with India. The Cape interior was considered to be a barren territory not warranting any expenditure. The large war debt which Britain had incurred during the Napoleonic wars necessitated an imperial policy of economy. This economizing resulted, among other things, in reductions of the garrisons at the Cape which in turn obliged the Cape frontiersmen to defend themselves. Most of the factors determining British colonial policy tended to push the Cape into the background. The philanthropic factor, however, focussed attention on the Cape. However, the philanthropy of that time was discriminatory. At times it sought to further the interests of the coloured races at the expense of the Whites. This aspect of the British colonial policy was the Afrikaners' greatest source of grievance.

In 1806 the Cape Colony after one hundred and fifty years of restricted development, was an extensive area inhabited by a sparse white population of nearly 26,000, a large slave population of about 30,000 and a Hottentot population of approximately 20,000. The frontier districts, isolated by the lack of roads, were primitive and constantly harassed by plundering Bushmen and Bantu. In comparison with other colonies founded elsewhere in the seventeenth century, the Cape was economically and constitutionally retarded. It had no such staple product, as the sugar of the West Indies, which would have enabled it to participate in world trade and ensured that it had champions in the British Parliament. The White population at the Cape had unique problems. In most of the territory the rainfall was low and erratic and the land infertile. The abundance of wild life which made it a hunter's paradise also made it difficult to establish permanent settlements. The large native population was a very real danger. Economic racial integration had existed at the Cape from the earliest times. It helped create an economy based on non-White labour and militated against large scale White immigration. The threat of the marauding Bushmen in the northern frontier districts was later to be completely overshadowed by the vigorous Bantu attacks on the eastern frontier. Indeed it soon became apparent that the Bantu were to be the greatest challenge to the materially weak White civilization which had firmly taken root in a strange environment.

The administration of the Cape

British authorities regarded the Cape as the Gibraltar of the Indian Ocean. As late as 1815 Somerset described it as "an outwork to India"[1] and in 1839 Christopher Bird complained about "the utter insignificance of this Colony, and the consequent contempt in which it, and all that belongs to it, are held".[2] In addition the Imperial authorities, much influenced by the philanthropic concepts of the time, paid heed to writers such as Barrow, who stated: "Such men (the Boers) will never become civilised until they are ruled with a rod of iron".[3] Consequently the traditional policy of conciliating conquered colonies was applied less sympathetically at the Cape which had to safeguard the route to India. The administration aimed more at securing a centralized efficiency.

Consequently the terms of the 1806 capitulation were less liberal than was usual with the British. The customary guarantee to preserve the rights, privileges and religion of the Dutch colonists was given but there was no guarantee that "laws and usages" would continue, nor that new taxes would not be levied.

In 1814 British rule of the Cape was confirmed in the Convention of London. The only clause affecting the Cape Dutch was one which stated that Britain would not discriminate against former Dutch subjects.

The administration of the Cape was thus more autocratic than that of any other British territory, excepting the penal colony of New South Wales. The Cape governor had powers which were not granted to his colleagues anywhere else. For example, his power to introduce constitutional changes was unique. All legislative and executive authority was vested in him, for the Council of Policy was abolished. The judicature was subordinate to him in that he could appoint and dismiss all members of the Council of Justice except the president, and all authority in both criminal and civil appeal courts was vested in him. In both these courts, instituted by Caledon, he was assisted by assessors, but they only acted in an advisory capacity. His actions were all subject to the approval

---

1. Theal: *Records of the Cape Colony*, X, p. 130, Somerset—Bathurst, 19 June, 1815.
2. D'Urban Papers: Bird—D'Urban, 4 March, 1839, Cape State Archives.
3. *An Account of Travels into the Interior of Southern Africa*, pp. 136, 137.

of the Colonial Office, but his decisions were seldom queried. He was also the highest military authority.

Gubernatorial autocracy was tempered only by the benevolence which generally characterized it. The College of Burgher Councillors continued as the Burgher Senate, but it no longer was the mouthpiece of public opinion.

There was considerable English opposition to the Roman-Dutch legal system. British principles of justice exercised some influence on the two appeal courts, but the rest of the administration of justice, as far as the officials and legal practice were concerned, remained Dutch in principle. The governors favoured the anglicization of the judiciary, but they were not prepared to introduce radical changes until the future of the Colony had been finally decided.

Even prior to 1814, before British rule became permanent at the Cape, the authorities were eager to establish sound administration which would ensure law and order for Whites and non-Whites. The administration of an extensive colony with poor communications was rendered more difficult by its being divided up into only six districts. The efficiency of local government was increased when Governor Caledon created three additional districts, Clanwilliam, George and Caledon. Caledon was not, however, aiming only at ensuring obedience to the law; he also wished to use the old Dutch institution, the College of Landdrosts and Heemraden, to familiarize Afrikaners with British concepts, particularly with philanthropic ideas. Consequently the policy of gradually appointing British officers as landdrosts was introduced.

Another improvement which the Earl of Caledon instituted at the Cape was the establishment in 1811 of the Circuit Court. Two or more members of the Council of Justice annually visited the outlying districts to hear those cases which fell outside the jurisdiction of the Colleges of Landdrosts and Heemraden. The Circuit Court became a permanent and useful institution. It facilitated and improved the administration of justice in the interior. This was very necessary after the weak rule of the Company. The Circuit Court reported on the work of the landdrosts as well as on educational, religious and social conditions in the country. It was moreover an integral part of the policy of centralization since it brought the population more directly under the control of the governor. It is apparent from their reports to the Colonial Office that governors also used the Circuit Court to protect the coloured races and slaves and to propagate British ideas.

As had been the case during the first British occupation of the Cape, loyal Dutch officials were retained in their positions. This was part of the traditional British policy of conciliating conquered people. Furthermore there was the practical consideration that loyal, submissive Dutch officials could help disseminate British ideas since such officials usually enjoyed the confidence of the Cape Dutch population. All governors at the Cape also wished, however, to implement the traditional policy of anglicization and to bring the conquered colony into line with the mother country. Three months after taking the oath of office Cradock formulated his policy: "I therefore anxiously hope that, in whatever Directions we may receive from Home ... there will appear the

Desire to assimilate the Institutions of this Country to those of England".[4] Writing to his superior the Colonial Secretary, Cradock expressed himself even more strongly. He considered the overwhelming numerical superiority of the Dutch population in relation to the British to be a danger, advocated large-scale British immigration and maintained that British interests would best be served "by the cautious and progressive introduction of the same laws, the same principles, and the same institutions of the parent state".[5] He also was convinced that anglicization would promote the welfare of the conquered people.

Cradock, a zealous reformer, paid attention to the old system of loan-farms, under which, on payment of a nominal fee, farms of about 3,000 morgen could be obtained. This system had certain advantages as long as land was plentiful and extensive farming was the order of the day. Since the seventies of the previous century, however, expansion northwards had been temporarily halted by the activities of the Bushmen, and the Bantu prevented Trekboer expansion beyond the Fish River. Land became scarcer and more intensive farming on smaller farms was necessary. To encourage more intensive farming and also to obtain a denser population on the frontiers, Cradock issued a proclamation in 1813 stating that holders of loan-farms could convert them into quitrent farms by paying considerably higher rentals. All future grants of land would be based on this new system and all quitrent farms had to be properly surveyed. The reaction was unfavourable for farmers were quite satisfied with the old loan-farm system. They could see no reason why they should accede to the higher costs associated with the new system. The measure was, however, of importance for the future; it placed agriculture on a sounder economic basis and eventually it did encourage more intensive farming methods.

In 1814 Holland finally surrendered the Cape to Britain and the new administration was immediately faced with the threat of the economic collapse of the Colony. In most parts of the country economic development was as erratic as the rainfall. During the war years the economy had been artificially stimulated by the large garrisons which provided a ready, though temporary, market for Cape produce. From 1816 Britain was obliged to follow a policy of strict economy and the Cape garrison was reduced from 4,000 to 2,400. The Cape sank deeper into debt; the value of the rix-dollar declined; prices rose steeply and the already negligible trade diminished still further. The death of Napoleon on St. Helena in 1821 and the subsequent departure of his entourage meant that another market was closed to the Cape.

As a conquered colony the Cape had not yet become fully integrated into the imperial economic system; although the restrictions of the Mercantile System were enforced the Cape did not yet share its advantages. Above all the Cape produced no staple commodity for which there was a great demand abroad. The wool industry was still in its infancy: in 1826 the value of wool exports was only

4. C.O. 1616: No. 29, Cradock – Alexander, 6 Dec., 1811, Cape State Archives.
5. Theal: *Records of the Cape Colony*, VIII, p. 221, Cradock—Liverpool, 31 Dec., 1811.

£545. The small White population, the vast distances and the lack of communications prevented any significant trading activities in the interior, where a primitive barter economy was still in operation to a large extent.

The issue of paper-money, which had been initiated by Van Plettenberg at the time of the American War of Independence, had been continued during the first British occupation of the Cape and the Batavian period. Baird and Caledon increased the amount of paper-money in circulation by more than one million rix-dollars. The inevitable result was that the value of the rix-dollar fell from 44s 2d in 1806 to 1s 6d in 1825. In the latter year the authorities introduced the British monetary system into the Cape as part of their policy of achieving imperial uniformity in this connection, and the value of the rix-dollar was fixed at 1s 6d. This deflationary measure ultimately benefited the Colony, but the immediate effects were disastrous for the wealthy classes at the Cape.

In 1814 Cradock was succeeded by Lord Charles Somerset. This member of the influential, aristocratic Beaufort family was the prototype of a Tory reactionary, and his advent inaugurated a new era. His influential family connections, his autocratic tendencies – particularly his aversion to any opposition – together with the fact that the Cape was now a permanent British possession, encouraged Somerset to act more forcefully than his predecessors.

After his return from England at the end of 1821 Somerset's rule became so autocratic that it necessitated the service of the notorious "*Oliver the Spy*". This state of eaffairs was probably the result of two factors, conditions in Britain where action had reached its peak, and the opposition Somerset received from the Brritish Settlers at the Cape. These settlers, who were familiar with parliamentary institutions, would not stomach Somerset's despotism. The arrival at the Cape in 1819 of the missionary, Dr. John Philip, who evinced great interest in poitics, i ntroduced new factors into the situation. Philip's representations cominlg on top of the complaints of the Settlers and the intervention of Wilberforce and the philanthropists led to the appointment in 1823 of the Commissioners of Inquiry, Colebrooke and Bigge.

In 1824 the appearance of the first journals other than government publications quickened the struggle for a more liberal administration. The Rev. Abraham Faure and one of the leaders of the Settlers, Thomas Pringle, obtained permission from Bathurst despite Somerset's opposition to publish a quarterly in Dutch and English. A printer, George Greig, also proposed to publish a weekly journal. They agreed that all matters of political and personal controversy should be excluded from their publications. The bilingual quarterly, *The South African Journal* and *Het Nederduitsch Zuid-Afrikaansch Tijdschrift*, as well as the weekly, *The South African Commercial Advertiser*, edited by Pringle, Fairbairn and Greig, made their first appearances early in 1824. The English journals soon antagonized Somerset. Somerset ordered the fiscal to impose a censorship which Greig refused to accept. The *Advertiser* ceased publication and Greig was banished. Soon Pringle's *Journal* was also in disfavour. Both Greig and Pringle joined the agitation in London against the autocratic Governor. The Colonial Secretary, Bathurst, authorized the *Advertiser* to begin publishing again, but in

1826 it was once more banned. After Fairbairn had gone to London to continue the struggle a new and less reactionary government finally issued an ordinance in 1828 which laid the foundations of the freedom of the press. Publishers in future were to be free of the control of the Governor-in-Council and were only to be subject to the laws of libel. This was an important step towards democracy.

As a result of the complaints which had reached the Colonial Office Bathurst established a Council of Advice at the Cape in 1825. This did not limit the governor's authority to any significant extent for the Council was composed solely of officials dependent on the governor's favour, who could only discuss matters proposed by the governor; in addition the Council could only act in an advisory capacity. Nevertheless the mere fact of the Council being established was an acknowledgement that the complex affairs of the multi-racial Colony could no longer be left to the discretion of one person. In 1827 two colonists were appointed to the Council, but they were retired officials and were not true representatives of the colonists.

In Canada the policy of anglicization had been applied immediately after the conquest of the French colony in 1763. At the Cape it was only implemented on a large scale after the arrival of the 1820 Settlers. British settlers at the Cape had many grievances – some valid – in respect of the Council of Justice and they did not hesitate to voice them. The governor's dominant position in the judicature was justifiably regarded as conflicting with the constitutional principle of the separation of the powers of government. Understandably the office of fiscal was also criticized, for as Crown prosecutor he had the right to claim one-third of all fines imposed and in addition his position on the bench was next to that of the chief justice. English disapproval of Dutch as a language medium was less justifiable, but nevertheless understandable in view of the ideas of the time.

Cradock had sent reports of a number of criminal cases to Bathurst to expose the alleged shortcomings of the law at the Cape. While it is true that the Cape law did not judge white and coloured by the same yardstick, it must be remembered that nobles and labourers did not always receive equal treatment in the Europe of that time either. Cradock also lost sight of the fact that Cape criminal law was mild in comparison with the harsh British penal code.

In 1816 Goulburn, Parliamentary Under-Secretary for Colonies, made one of the rare declarations of colonial policy in the House of Commons, in which he stressed the fact that English laws and principles were introduced into the colonies in such a manner that conquered peoples could not take exception. The government considered that the right time for introducing English laws and principles in the Cape was after the arrival of the Settlers who also demanded their introduction.

The Commission of Inquiry's most important report was published in 1826. On the basis of this report the first Charter of Justice was proclaimed in 1827 and the second in 1834. These were the first effectual limitations of the governor's authority for, although executive and legislative powers were still vested in him, he lost his judicial powers and an independent judiciary was now ensured. A High Court of Justice took the place of the Council of Justice. Roman-Dutch law was retained but it was proposed in the future gradually to introduce British legal principles. Trained lawyers were to be appointed by the Crown; that they were trained in British law but had to interpret Roman-Dutch law was not considered to be anomalous. The High Court was to consist of a Chief Justice and three puisne judges, all being appointed from Britain. Criminal cases were to be heard before a judge and jury. The legal procedure and language medium were to be English. An Attorney-General was to replace the fiscal.

The advantages of these far-reaching changes outweighed the disadvantages and the Cape Dutch did not regard them as a source of grievance. Indeed the jury system met with such favour that a similar system was later established in the Boer Republics. However, the Commissioners of Inquiry, strongly influenced by philanthropic ideas, also abolished old institutions which had expressed the colonists' attitude to the relations between the Whites and non-Whites. The Colleges of Landdrosts and Heemraden were abolished: resident magistrates and commissioners were to take over the College's judicial and administrative functions respectively. The powers of the field-cornets were curtailed, the Burgher Senate was abolished and in 1834 the Orphan Chamber was also abolished. With these developments the last vestiges of collegial self-government disappeared. The conservative Cape Dutch, concerned about their former rights as burghers, mourned their passing. Some of the institutions, particularly those of the Landdrosts and Heemraden, were revived during and after the Great Trek.

As far as legislative and executive powers were concerned, centralization reached its peak with these changes. The factors responsible for these developments were the reactionary tendencies in Britain, philanthropic concern for the welfare of the coloured races in the event of the colonists receiving autonomy, distrust of the Cape Dutch White majority, and the problems which had arisen in Canada after the introduction of representative institutions. In 1830, however, the Whigs were returned to power in Britain and in 1832 the First Reform Act was passed, which was a definite step towards democracy. At the Cape, with the Dutch newspaper, *De Zuid-Afrikaan*, taking the lead, the agitation for the introduction of representative government gathered force and the old battle cry of "no taxation without representation" began to be heard. These tendencies found a response in British governing circles, particularly among friends of the Settlers.

Eventually, in 1834, the agitation produced some results, partially because it was felt that after the emancipation of the slaves the Whites could be trusted with more self-government. An Executive Council, comprising the four leading officials, and a Legislative Council, consisting of the same officials and from five to seven respected colonists appointed by the Governor, were established. Although this step was a great improvement on the Council of Advice, it did not approximate to representative government for there were still no elections. Nevertheless there was freedom of debate in the Legislative Council, and except for a long reserved list legislative initiative was vested in that body. In addition no ordinance was valid without having received the approval of the Legislative

Council. The foundations of a sound democratic administration were being laid: the judiciary was already independent and the latest development defined the legislative and the executive authority more clearly.

The Cape Dutch

By the time of the second British Occupation of the Cape in 1806 this group had already acquired the characteristics of an embryo nation. A century and a half of weak Company rule had left the Cape Dutch, and more particularly the Trekboer element of the interior, largely to their own devices. They had to open up the interior, protect themselves against the indigenous races, make their own roads and be responsible for the education of their children. Consequently they developed into a self-sufficient and individualistic people. Their chief requirement of any government was that it should leave them in peace. In their isolation they developed their own language.

The British policy towards the Afrikaner was based upon the broad British colonial policy for dealing with conquered White population groups. The first principle of this policy, manifest in Canada and the West Indies, was one of conciliation towards the French, Spanish and Dutch inhabitants of those territories. This magnanimity, which granted representative institutions to the French-speaking Canadians within thirty years of Canada becoming a British possession, was initially not part of British policy in the Cape Colony. This was owing to many reasons: Britain showed little interest in the interior, there was no rival power in close geographical proximity to the Cape, as was the case with Canada; the Cape guarded the valuable trade-route to India; the unfavourable image of the Dutch colonist projected by a succession of English philanthropists; and philanthropic concern about the treatment of the coloured peoples in the Cape Colony.

The second, more enduring principle, of the British policy towards foreign White elements in British colonial acquisitions was anglicization, and this was applied inexorably in South Africa. Colonial authorities at this time were blind to the fact that small national groups were very aware of their identity. The colonial powers of Europe were convinced of the superiority of their own cultures and institutions, and believed that they were benefiting those they conquered by re-moulding them in the image of the mother country. It was also felt that imperial interests would be endangered by foreign White elements within the empires.

Anglicization only began to be fully implemented at the Cape after 1820, because of the temporary nature of the British occupation before 1814, and the absence of any significant British population group before 1820. Most Dutch officials at the Cape had little knowledge of English. Nevertheless, in 1813, Cradock stressed the importance of knowing this language and announced that in future official appointments would be dependent on a knowledge of English; it was only later, however, that this policy was applied consistently. Many Dutch-speaking officials of overseas and local origins were employed in the civil

104

service, partly as a conciliatory measure and partly for practical considerations. The only condition was that their loyalty to Britain had to be above suspicion. Anglophils such as W. S. van Ryneveld and J. A. Truter (later Sir John Truter) rendered valuable and faithful service to the British administration. Many of the Dutch officials working in the civil service rapidly became anglicized. From the outset, however, the higher posts with the best salaries were reserved for British subjects who were appointed from the mother country. Nepotism played a role in these appointments.

From 1814, and especially after the arrival of the British Settlers, English-speaking officials were appointed in increasing numbers. That they were favoured in many ways caused resentment among Hollanders and Cape Dutch in Cape Town. The absence of a free press forced these latter to vent their feelings in satiric diatribes, which were posted up at night on the high stoep of a house, which belonged to a man called Dreyer, at the corner of Longmarket Street and the Heerengracht. One of these read as follows:

> O Heere der heere!
> Wie zal hier in Afrika weer regeere;
> Alle die uit Engeland zijn gebannen;
> Worden hier groote mannen;
> En ons arme Hollandsche gezellen
> Kan men de ribben op het lyf al tellen.
> O heere, wilt ons toch verlossen
> Van al die Engelsche ossen,
> En leidt ons toch naar wenschen,
> Ons arme Hollandsche Christenmenschen.[6]
> Amen.

The imperial policy towards foreign churches in conquered colonies is of interest. Despite the fact that there was not yet complete religious toleration in England – for instance only members of the state Church of England were appointed to official positions – a more liberal policy was followed in the colonies.

One of the terms of the 1806 surrender had been that "Public Worship as at present in use shall also be maintained without alteration".[7] This meant that De Mist's Religious Code would remain in force. De Mist, imbued with revolu-

---

6. "O Lord of lords!
   Who will again rule here in Africa;
   All those who are exiled from England;
   Become great men here;
   And we poor Dutch fellows,
   Can count the ribs on our bodies.
   O Lord, will you not deliver us,
   From all the English oxen,
   And lead us to our wishes,
   We poor Dutch Christian people,
             Amen.
   Noted by Meurant: *Sixty Years Ago*, p. 29.
7. *Kaapsche Courant*, 11 Jan., 1806, Articles of Capitulation, 10 Jan., 1806.

tionary ideas, had regarded the church primarily as an instrument for maintaining order in the state. This coincided with the Tory attitude in general and Tory obsession with centralization in the state in particular. Under the previous regime the Dutch Reformed Church had not been privileged in any way, although churches of this denomination were more numerous than any other in Cape Town, while in the *platteland* areas there was no other church.

The governors were instructed to ensure that the rights of the Dutch Reformed Church were respected. This church was, nevertheless, still subservient to the state and even as early as Baird's term of office it was made clear that the state would not hesitate to exert its authority. When the landdrost of Tulbagh informed the local minister, the Rev. Ballot, that he had to stable Baird's eight horses on a certain Sunday, Ballot, on the grounds of his Sabbath duties, demurred. He was then peremptorarily summoned to Cape Town and, even after drafting a letter which acknowledged guilt, was not allowed to return to his home and parish before he had sworn absolute obedience to the government. Another incident of the same kind occurred later, on which occasion the Rev. Von Manger of Cape Town was threatened with the withdrawal of his salary and being transferred to Uitenhage: once he had suitably reaffirmed his allegiance to the government no action was taken. The absolute subservience of a church which had considerable influence with its members was vital to the authorities, who recognised that such a church could be of great use to the secular powers.

The office of the Political Commissioner who represented the state on the Cape Town church council was an anachronism dating back to the time when the Dutch Reformed Church was the state church. The British regime, however, not only retained the institution but gave it additional powers, despite the objections of the church. Baird declared bluntly that the governor, as the representative of the crown, had to be recognized as head of the church in all respects. Somerset further strengthened the hold of the state over the church by appointing the landdrosts as Political Commissioners in their respective districts. As the church was the most important bastion of Afrikaner consciousness it is not surprising that the authorities determined to make it a tool of the conqueror. So, for example, Cradock ordered prayers for the British royal family and for British victory in the war to be read at every service.

As early as 1808 the Colonial Secretary had suggested that English-speaking Calvinist ministers should be used to fill vacancies as they occurred in the Dutch Reformed Church. He considered this would help to disseminate British ideas in general and philanthropic concepts in particular, but to begin with, in accordance with the policy of conciliation, every effort was made to find Dutch and Cape Dutch ministers for the churches.

After 1820, however, the chronic shortage of ministers provided the opportunity for filling vacancies in the Dutch Reformed Church with English-speaking ministers in accordance with the policy of anglicization and Scottish Presbyterian ministers were sent to the Cape. Somerset's view was that as both the Scottish Church and the Dutch Reformed Church were Calvinist there could be no objections on doctrinal grounds to such a move. The Rev. George Thom who was on leave in England was called in to advise on this matter. He was in favour of the move, pointing out that beyond Cape Town there were not more than four hundred persons who could speak English. He felt this position should be rectified and his remarks reflect the main aim of the government in its policy towards the Dutch Reformed Church.

Education was obviously the most effective means of implementing anglicization and before 1820 all governors attempted, without much success, to ensure that English was used more generally in schools. After 1820 the Cape Dutch thirst for knowledge and the shortage of teachers (Thom, incidentally, had instructions to recruit teachers as well as ministers) provided the authorities with their opportunity. Goulburn, the Parliamentary Under-Secretary for Colonies, stated that Bathurst agreed with Somerset "as to the expediency and propriety of gradually superseding the Dutch Schoolmasters by Englishmen of a superior class, as affording both the best means of making the English language more general in the Colony and improving the manners and morals of the people".[8] The importation of English and Scottish ministers and schoolmasters aimed not merely at teaching the Afrikaners the English language, but also at changing them into Englishmen. To attract pupils to the numerous schools established by English schoolmasters it was decided to charge no fees.

Bathurst announced his intention of making English the only official language in the Cape Colony, and Ellis, the Colonial Under-Secretary at the Cape, compiled a memorandum advocating a more rapid implementation of anglicization. He stated that as the Cape was now an integral part of the British Empire it was essential that all ties with Holland should be severed.

After Bathurst had instructed Somerset to proclaim that English was now the sole official language, the policy of anglicization, which had been considered for so long, finally received full official sanction in July, 1822, when Somerset's Language Proclamation was published. English would be the sole language used in government offices from 1 January, 1825, and in the law courts from 1 January, 1827; correspondence with the Colonial Secretary in Cape Town had to be conducted in English as from 1 January, 1823. The preamble justified these steps on the grounds that English was already well known by the Dutch colonists from their contact with English-speaking fellow-citizens, and that the Scottish ministers and English schoolmasters would improve their knowledge of English still further.

The anglicization policy provoked no positive reaction among the Cape Dutch. The official class, dependent on the government, ensured that they and their children learnt English. The more prominent Cape Dutch families in Cape Town and its surroundings speedily acquired a sound knowledge of English and attached considerable value to this achievement. Although Cape Dutchmen such as these, for example the Van der Byls and the Cloetes, sometimes became completely anglicized, they were the exceptions. Most of the Cape Dutch

8. C.O. 1305: No. 348, Goulburn—Somerset, 10 Feb., 1822, Cape State Archives.

remained true to their church and to Dutch, the language of their church. This was the crux of the matter: the Dutch colonists were not particularly concerned about the Dutch language as such, but they were strongly attached to their church and its language was Dutch.

Although there were indications that colonists living in the interior were beginning to appreciate the advantage of knowing English, the anglicization of the public service hardly affected them because they seldom had contact with the authorities. Although the well-informed Cape Dutch went to some trouble to learn English, there were limits to the lengths to which they were prepared to go. For example, the free English schools, where Dutch was not taught, failed to achieve their object because they often lacked pupils. The anglophil Sir John Truter, in a report on the first synod, warned Somerset in 1824 "that an apprehension is fast spreading among the public, that their children will not be allowed to receive any further instruction in Dutch, and that the language is to be totally prescribed".[9] In 1836 the Rev. Robertson, who had been one of the imported teachers, informed D'Urban that the schools would only succeed in disseminating English if "the very natural prejudice of the majority of the population in favour of the Dutch language"[10] were taken into account. He recommended that Dutch should also be taught and that religious instruction should be given through the medium of Dutch.

The main purpose behind the policy which aimed at completely anglicizing the Cape Dutch population was not realized. Many Dutch colonists became bilingual in the course of time, but retained their allegiance to their own language. They came to accept British democracy, British political liberalism, the British Crown and the Imperial connection, but they did not lose their identity.

The British Settlers

The authorities considered that large-scale British immigration into the Cape Colony would solve many of their problems. Britain, severely affected by the Napoleonic wars and carrying the burden of a large war debt, wished at all costs to avoid continual clashes on the colony's eastern frontier. In 1809 Major Collins, who had been sent by Caledon to investigate frontier conditions, recommended that the English population on the frontiers should be increased. After the Frontier War of 1812 Cradock instructed the frontier farmers not to return to the conquered Zuurveld. Instead English garrison towns would be established there and they would spread "the blessings of British liberty and benevolence".[11]

From the imperial standpoint the presence of large, foreign White populations in the colonies was not sound policy and Cradock considered the Dutch-speaking

9. Dreyer: *Boustowwe*, III, p. 267, Truter—Somerset, 30 Jan., 1825.
10. C.O. 795: Annexure No. 8, 8 Feb., 1836, Cape State Archives.
11. Theal: *Records*, IX, p. 7, Cradock—Vicars, 14 Nov., 1812.

inhabitants of the Cape to be a danger in this respect. The anglicization of the Cape Dutch and the large-scale immigration of British citizens, who in time would assimilate the Cape Dutch, were the obvious solutions.

The first step in this direction was taken in 1817 when two hundred unmarried Scottish artisans were brought to the Cape Colony by Benjamin Moodie of Swellendam. Because there was a shortage of skilled labour at the Cape this private undertaking was a great success, and it led to a press campaign in Britain in which the roseate prospects of emigration to the Cape were stressed. Thousands of British subjects were emigrating to the United States of America, Canada, Australia and New Zealand for social, economic and political reasons. In 1819 the Imperial parliament granted £50,000 to divert some of this stream of settlers to the Cape. At a time when state-aided emigration was rare and when Britain was in financial straits, this was evidence of the importance which the Government attached to it.

Somerset, who was on leave in England, had described conditions at the Cape in a favourable light. Prospective settlers were told that they would each receive a farm of fifty morgen which was large by British standards. They would not have to pay any rent for the first ten years and the government also would provide a free passage to South Africa. Agricultural implements, seed and rations would be sold to settlers at cost price. To many the Cape sounded like the Promised Land, but more than 3,000 settlers were soon to be faced with the harsh realities of living not only in a strange country, but also in the undeveloped Zuurveld.

About 90,000 applications were received. Heads of parties, with whom the government made all arrangements, had to be responsible for at least ten emigrants. Every adult male had to deposit £10, repayable in three instalments. Neither the leaders nor their followers were selected carefully. The most serious consequence of this was the fact that among those selected there were too many poverty-stricken city-dwellers and not enough farmers. Such people could not make successful pioneers, who had to be able to lay out farms, tame nature, and deal with wild animals and plundering natives.

The Settler's arrival at the Cape was very badly organized. In the first place the government had told the settlers little about local conditions. In addition, Sir Rufane Donkin, the Acting Governor, expected only 2,000 and the arrangements for the reception and initial settlement of the travel-worn immigrants were inadequate.

Each family was taken to its destination by wagon and then left to fend for itself. Shelters had to be contrived hastily on the rolling grass-plains. The cultivation of the land also presented difficulties; it soon became apparent that the Londoners in particular were not suited to agriculture. Some of the immigrants soon lost heart and left their farms for the towns to become goldsmiths, porcelain-workers, shoemakers, etc.

Those who persisted in their efforts to farm soon became acquainted with the exactions of the South African climate. Their first crops were destroyed by a type of rust; they had used up their initial deposits and they were faced with famine. They had to mortgage their farms to obtain more rations. Nevertheless some persevered, adopting the slogan of "up, man, and try, never say die". Drought, floods and locusts intensified their difficulties. To begin with the Xhosas were quiescent, but from 1821 onwards their attacks increased the Settlers' hardships.

The second grain crop was promising but again it was destroyed by rust. Somerset's return from England brought no relief, for he regarded them as radicals and banned public meetings. The failure of their third crop was ultimate proof that the Zuurveld was not suited to agricultural pursuits. The lack of a suitable market for the Settlers' produce also militated against intensive farming and the farms were too small for extensive farming. The exodus to Grahamstown gathered momentum. Of the 1,004 men who had settled in the Zuurveld in 1820 only 438 remained by 1823 and the ideal of a concentrated population on the frontier had not been realized.

From 1824 onwards conditions improved. The government was forced to reconcile itself to the idea, which Cradock had condemned, of extensive farming on the frontier. The Settlers' farms were considerably enlarged, the debts which they had incurred to buy rations were cancelled and direct taxation was discontinued until 1826. A section of the Settler community managed to make a living by trading. Ivory trade with the natives, which had been forbidden since the days of the Company, was once more permitted. Licensed traders, using Fort Willshire as their centre, bartered with the Xhosas on three days a week, and beads, buttons and colourful trinkets were exchanged for ivory and skins. Soon this trade was worth £40,000 a year.

Those Settlers who continued farming did eventually find a staple product suited to the area. The production of fine wool had not succeeded elsewhere in the Colony. The Settlers' efforts in this field were so successful that fine wool production became the most important industry of the area and contributed significantly to the economic development of the frontier districts.

The Settlers and their children soon began to play a leading role in Cape affairs. They were opposed to the system of administration which permitted Somerset's despotic rule. Their agitations contributed to his recall and resignation, the anglicization of the administration, the freedom of the press, and the establishment of the Executive and Legislative Councils.

The influence of the Settlers was to be very significant for South Africa. For many years their relations with the Dutch Colonists were amicable. When the Settlers arrived at the Cape the Cape Dutch were to all intents and purposes exclusively farmers. The British Settlers and their descendants helped develop the South African economy in general, and trade and industry in particular. The two white population groups complemented each other.

The Hottentots

In 1806 the position of the Hottentots was unsatisfactory. Legally they were still independent tribes controlled by their captains. They were not regarded as

British subjects because, theoretically at any rate, they still occupied land which they owned. Actually, however, they had already been reduced to the status of a landless proletariat, although there were still some Hottentot kraals. Some tribes migrated northwards. Those who remained in the Cape had to sell their labour to Whites or seek refuge at mission stations such as Bethelsdorp. Regular work habits were not part of their nomadic tradition and they were not protected by the law in their service contracts with the Whites. During the first British Occupation the authorities were forced to pay attention to them because of the Hottentots' attempts to ally themselves with the Bantu.

After 1806 the British authorities also were concerned at the anomalous position of the Hottentots. Caledon's Hottentot proclamation of 1809 was the first comprehensive law aimed at defining the status and legal position of the Hottentots. This proclamation accepted that their detribalization was an accomplished fact; thenceforth they would be regarded as British subjects and the laws of the land would also apply to them. An effort was made to encourage steady habits of work among them and to curb their nomadic tendencies and vagrancy by stipulating that they could not leave their fixed place of abode without a pass from the field-cornet or landdrost. Their interests were also protected by a clause which stated that all contracts of service for a month or longer had to be registered before the fiscal, landdrost or field-cornet, and that no contract would be valid for longer than a year.

Caledon helped to civilize the Hottentots by inducing them to accept a more stable way of life; at the same time the proclamation aimed at ending the labour shortage, which had become especially acute after the slave trade had been stopped in 1807. Caledon's proclamation was the first labour legislation at the Cape. Cradock's proclamation of 1812 stated that Hottentot children, who had been supported by their parents' employer up to their eighth year, were to be apprenticed to that farmer for the next ten years, if the landdrost was satisfied that the employer was humane. The employer had to provide the children with food and clothes. The aim was to inculcate the habit of work among the Hottentots from an early age and to compel the employer to take suitable care of them. The employers were also expected, among other things, to provide instruction in the Christian religion. In 1819 Somerset augmented the Hottentot legislation by stipulating that Hottentot orphans with no means of support could also be apprenticed up to their eighteenth year.

The Imperial government, even in the undemocratic period before the 1832 Reform Act, was sensitive to the reactions of pressure groups. The philanthropists were one of the most powerful of these groups. Their leaders, influential men such as Wilberforce and Buxton and, in the Colonial Office, James Stephen, the Permanent Under-Secretary, and Glenelg, the Secretary of State, could not easily be ignored. Philanthropic ideas which stressed the universal equality of men and the inviolability of their individual worth generated a steady opposition to and condemnation of practices which forced non-Whites into subordinate positions under Whites in the colonies. The missionary philanthropists, who considered it their exalted duty to champion the cause of the "weaker" non-Whites in the British colonies, were bound to be involved in a violent clash of interests with the White colonists.

The authority of the Colonial Office and the influence of the missionaries ensured that philanthropic ideas would profoundly affect the Cape Colony. The awakening sense of responsibility towards indigenous races led to the formation of numerous missionary societies. Missionaries to the colonies played an important part in shaping public opinion in the mother country, for their messages and reports were read regularly in British churches.

There were sharp reactions in philanthropic circles to Caledon's Hottentot proclamation, which was seen as a reaction to the abolition of the slave trade in 1807. Dr Van der Kemp and the Rev. Read of Bethelsdorp considered the proclamation to be an attempt to perpetuate slavery in the form of forced labour.

Read began the agitation against the proclamation by writing to the headquarters of the London Missionary Society in England and accusing the colonists of treating the Hottentots cruelly, and the Governor and Landdrost Cuyler (of Uitenhage) of laxity in acting against the offenders. He maintained that in the Uitenhage district alone there had been more than one hundred unpunished murders of Hottentots. This letter was printed, circulated in Britain, and brought to the notice of the Imperial Government by Wilberforce. The Colonial Secretary ordered Cradock to conduct a thorough investigation into the allegations, and to punish any offenders severely.

Cradock was assiduous in carrying out these instructions. Read (Van der Kemp had died in the meantime) was given every possible assistance in collecting evidence. The Circuit Court of 1812, later known as the "Black Circuit" because of its specific purpose, spent more than four months investigating the allegations. More than fifty Whites were brought to court and more than one thousand witnesses were called. Notwithstanding Read's letter, only seventeen cases of murder, fifteen of assault and a larger number concerning charges such as the withholding of wages were heard.

Not a single murder charge was upheld by the court. Some fines were imposed for harsh punishment of servants and for lesser offences. The trials proved that there was little justification for the government's suspicions concerning the Dutch colonists' treatment of non-Whites. The judge reprimanded Read for his wild allegations and also sharply criticized the organization of the mission station at Bethelsdorp.

The Black Circuit caused a furore among the Cape Dutch. They considered it an affront that they should have been accused, even falsely, by non-Whites. They had been put to great inconvenience to answer the charges. Although most of them were acquitted they felt that their good name had been besmirched. The frontiersmen did not realize that the government's thorough investigation, which had largely absolved them from blame, had actually rendered a service to them and their descendants. They regarded the British government with distrust and the conviction that the authorities favoured the coloured races gathered ground among them; missionaries and mission stations were also regarded with suspicion.

The seething discontent among the farmers led to the unsavoury Slagtersnek episode. Their conviction that the authorities had a bias towards the Hottentots began at the time of the Hottentot rising of 1799 and was strengthened by the activities of the "Black Circuit". In a sense the Slagtersnek rebellion was the reaction of a few frontier farmers to British philanthropy. Chief Magistrate W. S. Van Ryneveld was aware of the explosive situation on the frontier when he advised the Cape government not to send "pandours" (Hottentot soldiers) into the interior again. Such an action, he warned, could lead to a renewal of disturbances: the government ignored the warning.

Several of the ringleaders of the rebellion were typical of the less desirable frontier element. Stockenström had said of Johannes Bezuidenhout and Cornelius Faber that they were not prepared to obey any authority; Stephanus Botma had been deported from the colony. They had spent most of their lives among the Bantu and had degenerated sufficiently to attempt to obtain help from Gaika. Living as they did in the Baviaan's River district (later Glen Lynden), one of the most isolated parts of the country, they were far removed from church and schools and in daily contact with the natives in their natural state. They had to some extent succumbed to the influence of a primitive environment.

A certain Frederik Bezuidenhout ignored repeated summonses to appear in court in connection with the alleged ill-treatment of his Hottentot servant. When Hottentot soldiers were sent to arrest him, he resisted and was shot dead. At his funeral his brother, Johannes Bezuidenhout, swore to avenge him and incited his friends to rebel. Only about sixty followed him and the rebellion was speedily crushed. Johannes, with his family, his brother-in-law Faber and the two Botma families, tried to flee into Bantu territory. Johannes's wife helped him until he was killed and she and her twelve-year-old son wounded. With that the rebellion came to an end.

Although most frontiersmen did not agree with the actions of the Bezuidenhouts, they sympathized with their motives. According to Stockenström, people were saying "that the Black nation was protected and not the Christians".[12]

From the government's point of view, too, the rebellion should not be considered in isolation. Somerset feared a repetition of the earlier rebellions. He was determined that vigorous justice should teach the frontiersmen to obey the law. Somerset, the Tory par excellence, wished to see the people of the Cape Colony subjected to the same stern discipline as the masses in Britain were.

Justice was wielded with a vengeance. Six of the ringleaders of the Slagtersnek rebellion were sentenced to death (one sentence was commuted to banishment for life); five were hanged (four having to ascend the scaffold a second time after the rope broke); all the other rebels were forced to witness the executions, and some were subsequently deported. The resentment against the government, especially among frontiersmen, had started during the first British occupation of the Cape; various measures including the "Black Circuit" intensified the

12. G.R. 16/5: No. 179, Stockenstrom—Cuyler, 5 Jan., 1816, Cape State Archives.

discontent which reached its first peak at the time of Slagtersnek. To some frontiersmen Slagtersnek became a symbol of oppression.

In the eighteen twenties philanthropists and missionaries, under the leadership of Dr John Philip, once again took up the cudgels on behalf of the Hottentots and agitated against the Hottentot legislation. The gist of the arguments against the legislation was that the Hottentots were placed in an inferior position, that coloureds were forced to enter the service of white farmers, that they were not able to move about freely and consequently could not better their salaries. The first complaint was justified, but that for the first time Hottentots had been given legal protection was disregarded. After 1809 they were no longer subjected to the whims of their employers. The second complaint also had substance, but it must be borne in mind that the habit of work is one of the foundations of civilization and that unless the Hottentots could acquire this habit they would not be able to improve their way of life. There are serious objections to all pass laws, but they were considered necessary in most colonies to induce a stable way of life among primitive races and to combat vagrancy and thieving. The pass laws did immobilize the Hottentots and this meant that it was not easy for them to move around in search of better wages. Nevertheless their wages after 1809 were not lower than they had been before. There are well-founded objections to the policy of apprenticing Hottentot children, and there were abuses. The system did, however, teach the children the value of regular work. Also, as the Commissioners of Inquiry found, it was usual for the Hottentot servants to attend the family prayers held in the employer's house; this was an important civilizing influence. Apprenticed children also attached their parents more closely to a specific employer.

Dr Philip, a fearless and zealous propagandist, became the spiritual leader of the philanthropists in the Cape. He was in close touch with Wilberforce and Buxton and also with the Commissioners of Inquiry. He was determined to use the philanthropic movement to achieve complete equality between Whites and non-Whites and believed that this was the best means of civilizing the coloured races. In 1826 he went to England and worked in close conjunction with Buxton.

His propaganda work, *Researches in South Africa*, was published in 1828. Among other things he stresses the alleged cruelty of the Boers towards the coloured races. Despite its inaccuracies the book greatly influenced the British governing classes. Philip rejoiced when the Fiftieth Ordinance was issued by the philanthropic Acting Governor, Bourke, in 1828. To a large extent it cancelled all existing Hottentot legislation. According to the ordinance there was to be no discrimination on the grounds of colour as far as free inhabitants of the Colony were concerned: there were to be no restrictions on the individual's freedom of movement and no person was to be forced into service, or to be limited to a fixed place of abode, or way of life, or work. At Philip's insistence the Imperial Government also stipulated that Ordinance 50 could not be amended or repealed without its permission.

The Fiftieth Ordiance increased vagrancy and theft, and intensified the labour problem. At the same time it did enable Hottentots to obtain better conditions of service. When the slaves received complete freedom in 1838 they too immediately obtained the freedom and equality which the Hottentots had obtained ten years earlier. To combat vagrancy and its attendant evils a draft ordinance was considered by the Legislative Council in 1834. Dr Philip and his son-in-law, Fairbairn, the editor of the *Commercial Advertiser*, were strongly opposed to it. All except one of the civil commissioners supported the ordinance, and it was passed by the Legislative Council, but the Colonial Secretary vetoed it.

The philanthropic policy towards the Hottentots further impoverished farmers, who had already been adversely affected by the costs connected with the new form of land-ownership and the fixing of the value of the rix-dollar at 1s.6d. Farmers were harrassed not only by Bantu cattle-raiders beyond the frontier but also by Hottentot thieves within the Colony. It has been calculated that between 8,000 to 10,000 of the 32,000 free persons of colour were unemployed vagrants.

It is worth noting that the Dutch colonists who remained in the Cape Colony and who did not take part in the Great Trek came to accept the concepts of British political liberalism, although never any form of social equality. The Fiftieth Ordinance was a turning-point in the history of non-White legislation in the Cape Colony; thereafter Cape legislation became "colour-blind". After 1828 there was no more discrimination on the grounds of race or colour, except in the case of Indians who were not considered an indigenous and assimilable element. The Cape Afrikaners, in time, came to accept this standpoint and in this respect the British anglicization policy had indeed been remarkably successful.

The slaves

Slavery at the Cape was almost as old as the Colony itself, and was part of its economic and social pattern. It was the least favourable aspect of an economy based on non-White labour, but it was not, however, the inhumane institution which it was elsewhere. This was owing to several factors: much of the country's assets was invested in slaves; slaves were an important source of labour in a land suffering from a chronic shortage in this respect; in general the White inhabitants of the Cape did not treat their servants with undue harshness. Even Barrow stated that slaves were usually well treated and Somerset maintained that slaves were probably the happiest section of Cape society.

The philanthropists classified the Cape with the West Indian colonies, where slavery existed in all its inhumanity. The philanthropic anti-slavery campaign was actually aimed at the slavery of the West Indian plantations, while at the Cape philanthropists tended to concentrate on the welfare of the indigenous coloured races. Although the West Indian plantation slaves were often treated like animals, slavery was defended in Britain by the powerful sugar interests. Most of the slaves in the British Empire were to be found in the West Indies, and slavery was defended in those colonies by local administrative bodies and a strong pressure group in British governing circles. The Cape consequently was affected by a series of slave regulations which did not take into account its vast distances, its sparse population and the humane way in which slaves were treated as domestic servants, farm labourers and skilled workers in this colony.

In 1787 the philanthropists founded the Anti-Slave Trade Committee and in 1807 their power became evident when the slave trade was abolished in the British Empire. To prevent slaves being smuggled into the Colony Somerset in 1816 proclaimed that all slaves at the Cape had to be registered. In 1820 Bathurst ordered the British Settlers not to be allowed to use slave labour. In 1823 the Anti-Slavery Society was founded under the leadership of Buxton, and the first of a series of slave regulations, which continued until 1832, was issued. These Imperial regulations aimed at alleviating the lot of slaves in various ways. Their hours of work were limited to such an extent that they were less than those of many labourers in Europe and Britain. The food, clothing and treatment of slaves were carefully prescribed. Slave Protectors were appointed to enforce these regulations precisely. The right of the owners to inflict punishment was limited: records of all punishments had to be entered in a punishment book and, after the book had been attested to, it was inspected by the protectors twice a year.

Slave owners were offended by these regulations. Most of them had always treated their slaves well. Their suggestion that slavery should gradually be abolished by freeing slave children at birth was ignored. The regulations undermined the authority of the owners and increased the lack of discipline among the slaves. A feeling of helpless indignation spread among the slave owners.

The demonstration of the philanthropists' power reached its zenith in 1833 when the British Parliament passed the emancipation act which abolished slavery at the Cape from December, 1834. British taxpayers would carry the burden of the £20,000,000 which was to be paid as compensation to slave owners. Ex-slaves at the Cape would be apprenticed to their masters for four years. Nobody at the Cape objected to slavery being abolished but the methods employed greatly increased the grievances of the Dutch colonists who were the chief owners of slaves.

The new governor, Sir Benjamin D'Urban, had to carry out the provisions of the emancipation act. Commissioners were appointed to assess the number of slaves and their value. According to their report there were 35,745 slaves valued at £3,041,290. The first disillusionment for the people at the Cape was the announcement that they had been allocated only £1,247,401 as compensation, but there were further shocks to follow; compensation would only be paid in London and it would be paid in British government stock. Furthermore, all the administrative costs of the emancipation would be deducted from the compensation money and each claim had to be accompanied by stamps to the value of £1.10s. Having no business connections in London and being inexperienced in such matters, many Cape Dutchmen sold their claims to agents for a trifle. Because they distrusted the British Government's attitude toward them, many of them were convinced that it was intended that they would ultimately receive no compensation. In the end slave owners received approximately £41 for every £100 they had invested in slaves.

The abolition of slavery was in every way estimable. In the long run it benefited the Cape economy but its immediate effects were disastrous. Poverty-stricken Dutch colonists were further impoverished. The situation was made more critical by there being no law at the Cape to combat vagrancy. In 1838, after the apprenticeship period had elapsed, many slaves would join the thousands of vagrant Hottentots.

The Bantu

During the triangular conflict between Bantu, Boer and Briton the British Government made serious, although at times shortsighted, attempts to solve the eastern frontier problem. They wished to establish law and order throughout the colony but various factors hampered them. The Colonial Office, which exercised supreme power, could hardly be expected to understand the conditions on a distant frontier; because of her financial obligations incurred by wars and high costs of empire, Britain was unable to spend much money on an insignificant colony; the British government also had to contend with the representations of the philanthropists. In addition, with the exception of Somerset, few governors remained at the Cape for any length of time. A governor had hardly shed his preconceived ideas about the territory and adopted a more balanced viewpoint, than he would be succeeded by a new governor. Consequently British frontier policy was characterized by vacillation, and this was interpreted, by the Bantu in particular, as weakness.

On the eastern frontier a critical situation had been created by the Xhosas' renewed encroachment on the Zuurveld and by their continual thieving and violence. In 1809 Caledon sent Major Collins to investigate conditions on the frontier. He recommended that the Xhosas should be driven over the frontier, the Fish River, and that English inhabitants should be settled thickly on the frontier. Because of the Napoleonic wars which were still raging and its bias towards the non-Whites, the Colonial Office wished to avoid any action which could lead to war. Caledon was instructed to win the confidence of the Xhosas. This was a policy which had often proved fruitless. Caledon, therefore, in spite of the letters received from the landdrosts in the frontier districts, instructed that no commandos were to be raised and that frontiersmen were only allowed to shoot at Xhosas in self-defence. It is interesting to note that, already at this early stage, Cuyler, the Landdrost of Uitenhage, warned the authorities of the danger of the frontiersmen becoming disloyal to the British government. In this case the government's conciliatory policy towards the non-Whites was stronger than that towards the conquered White race. Caledon admitted to his successor, Cradock, that his policy of conciliation towards the Bantu had failed; he suggested that action should be taken.

This advice was heeded. Cradock, who was a soldier, called up the commandos within a month of assuming office, and ordered the Bantu to be driven over the frontier. Under the energetic leadership of Lieutenant-Colonel Graham and with the aid of about a thousand troops this order was carried out with determination. The so-called Fourth Frontier War was already over by February, 1812. Cradock's frontier settlement was largely based on two main concepts. He wished to effect complete separation between the Bantu and the frontier farmers and he wished to implement Collins's recommendation concerning a dense English population on the frontier. A Hottentot regiment using what was later known as Grahamstown as its headquarters was to patrol the Fish River area. The plan to settle British inhabitants on small farms on the frontier only materialized in 1820. Cradock also allowed the spoor law to be enforced. The spoor of stolen cattle could be followed, but only cattle which belonged to Whites could be reclaimed.

Cradock's abilities were to be severely tested by South Africa's fundamental problem, the native question, and his task was not made any lighter by the attitude of the Colonial Office. The Colonial Secretary, Liverpool, outlined the role which the Colonial Office intended to play. He reminded Cradock of Macartney's conviction that the Natives were forced to adopt violent measures by the actions of the "Dutch settlers". He also expressed the hope that "the disgraceful proceedings against the misguided natives" had already been suspended.[13] Bathurst, Liverpool's successor, ordered that troops were only to be used to defend the harbours of the peninsula, and that parts of the Zuurveld were to be given to the Xhosas if clashes could not be avoided in any other way. After Cradock had visited the frontier he referred to "the good and unoffending conduct" of the frontiersmen in contrast to "the faithless and unrelenting disturbances of the peace" on the part of the Bantu.[14] A disconsolate Cradock tendered his resignation.

Somerset on his 1817 visit to the frontier found that the farmers had been forced to abandon the eastern part of the Zuurveld to the Xhosas because of periodic raids and murders. These occurred despite the continual patrols which made heavy demands on the farmers. Somerset carried the spoor law a stage further. He explained to Gaika and other tribal chiefs that the Bantu principle of joint responsibility would be applied. The headman of the kraal to which the spoor of the stolen cattle were traced would be obliged to surrender as many cattle as had been stolen. Somerset also intended to station a larger garrison on the frontier, but when he returned to Cape Town he received Bathurst's instructions to economize which meant, among other things, that the number of British troops at the Cape would be reduced from 4,000 to 2,400.

Somerset recognized Gaika as the supreme chief of the Xhosas and helped him in his hour of need, after he had been defeated by his rival Ndlambi. Ndlambi took his revenge by invading the Colony and wreaking havoc. In Grahamstown a handful of defenders stubbornly withstood the attack of 10,000 warriors, and so the Fifth Frontier War started (1819). Again the burgher commandos had to support the troops. This, according to Somerset's glowing report, they did with dedication and self-sacrifice. The crux of Somerset's

13. Theal: *Records*, VIII, p. 216, Liverpool—Cradock, 20 Dec., 1811.
14. *Cape Town Gazette*, 8 Jan., 1814, Government Proclamation, 7 Jan., 1814.

118

frontier settlement was the creation of a neutral belt between the Fish and Keiskamma Rivers. This territory was to remain unoccupied and would be patrolled to prevent clashes between frontiersmen and Bantu. A dense White population, eventually partly attained with the coming of the British Settlers, would, it was felt, further safeguard the frontier.

The philanthropists opposed this annexation of Bantu territory. Under the leadership of Dr Philip and inspired by the arrival of an increasing number of missionaries humanitarianism now also focussed its attention on the non-Whites beyond the frontiers. That these tribesmen were being oppressed by the Whites was an easily acceptable belief because the Whites were the "Cape Boors", whom travellers and missionaries had portrayed in such unflattering terms. Somerset was influential enough to ignore the philanthropists in general, and that included Philip. The arrival of the philanthropic Acting Governor, Bourke, in 1826, completely changed matters, however. As far as non-White affairs were concerned Philip's word was now often law, particularly after the publication in 1828 of his *Researches in South Africa*.

Bourke issued instructions that military action against Xhosa thieves had to cease. The spoor law, as applied by Cradock and Somerset, was repealed. The impractical condition was laid down that stolen cattle could only be followed and recovered as long as they were in sight. Even Bathurst was surprised at this reversal of frontier policy. Bourke also abandoned the policy of absolute segregation which had been enforced by his predecessors. Ordinance 49 of 1828 stated that Bantu who had been issued with passes were allowed to enter the Colony to look for work.

Cole (1828 – 1833) added to the impression of vacillation by once more putting Cradock's measures into operation. The spoor of stolen cattle could be followed, but no Bantu cattle could be taken to compensate the farmer for cattle which could not be traced. Inconsistency also characterized the policy as far as the neutral belt was concerned. Makomo and his Xhosa followers were allowed to settle there, only to be driven out again in 1829, and in the same year the Kat River Hottentot settlement was established there. Cole also decided to settle Whites in the area to strengthen the defence of the frontier. In 1831 the Colonial Secretary, Goderich, approved the settlement of Whites in the former neutral belt, provided that Dutch Boers were excluded.

In 1830 Philip launched his campaign against the commando system. He maintained that in most cases the commandos were only interested in loot, and that they had reduced many innocent Bantu to poverty-stricken vagrants. He maintained that it needed only the word of any mendacious Boer that his cattle had been stolen for a commando to be sent into Bantu territory. If the Bantu offered opposition they were shot down like dogs. Buxton set the efficient philanthropic machinery in motion in England, and in 1833 the Secretary of State banned the brutal commandos, as he called them. With insufficient troops on the frontier, the frontiersmen were now defenceless against Bantu attacks.

When D'Urban assumed control at the Cape in 1834 conditions were critical on the eastern frontier. Philip was in close touch with the new governor. The philanthropists were now insisting on a completely new approach towards extra-terrtiorial tribes. Treaties were to convert them from enemies into allies. The first such treaty was signed with the Griqua Captain Andries Waterboer in December, 1834.

By Christmas of that year the disastrous Sixth Frontier War was already raging. Thousands of warriors operating in small units devastated a wide front in the frontier areas. The immediate causes of the war were the activities of military patrols endeavouring to recover stolen cattle. The fundamental causes were the vacillations over the spoor law, the occupation of the neutral territory, and the Bantu interpretation of these vacillations as evidence of the White man's weakness.

The war caused great losses and suffering. Twenty-two colonists and about eighty Hottentots were murdered, 456 houses were burnt down, and it was alleged that 5,700 horses, 115,000 head of cattle and 162,000 sheep were stolen. The losses were estimated at £300,000. Under the leadership of D'Urban and Lieutenant-Colonel Smith (later Sir Harry Smith) burgher commandos and troops launched counter-attacks and ended the war.

D'Urban's frontier settlement was approved by the colonists. The territory between the Keiskamma and Kei Rivers was annexed as the Province of Queen Adelaide. D'Urban's initial intention was not to allow any Xhosas to remain in the territory. It was impossible, however, to expel all the Xhosas from the area and certain well-disposed tribes were allowed to remain. They would be British subjects and would be under the authority of a British Resident and government agents. Tribal chiefs would retain certain powers and harmless native customs and laws were retained. White and non-White inhabitants of the area increased, which meant that they had only limited land for farming. Both groups were forced to practice more intensive agricultural methods. Mutual dependence made it imperative that co-operation should replace rivalry.

D'Urban's dispatches to the Colonial Office did not give a full and an immediate detailed account of conditions on the frontier. In the meanwhile Philip and the philanthropists had not been idle. Philip sent many letters and a bulky memorandum dealing with the causes of the war to Buxton and to the Colonial Secretary, Glenelg. Philip insisted that a House of Commons committee should revise the whole frontier system. His demands were acceded to, and the Aborigines Committee under the chairmanship of Buxton was convened and immediately started gathering evidence. Stockenstrom, the former landdrost of Graaff-Reinet and commissioner-general of the frontier districts, condemned the old system and this made a great impression. The philanthropists agreed with him and proclaimed emphatically that the treatment of the Bantu was a blot on Britain's good name. It was demanded that a new policy, based on friendship instead of coercion, should be enforced because it would be more humane, cheaper and profitable. Philip, accompanied by two converts, a Bantu and a Hottentot, left for England.

It did not need much to convince Glenelg and Stephen, the Permanent Under-Secretary for Colonial Affairs, because they both belonged to the inner circles of the philanthropic group, the "Saints", as their enemies mockingly named them. Apart from that D'Urban had neglected to keep them fully informed. Glenelg announced his decision to D'Urban in his dispatch of 26 December, 1835, in which he maintained that the recent Bantu aggression was fully justified in the light of the actions of colonists and colonial governments over many years. The annexed territory, the Province of Queen Adelaide, had to be returned to the Bantu, and Stockenstrom, in the capacity of lieutenant-governor of the Eastern Province, with the assistance of missionaries, would conclude treaties with the headmen. This decision was the logical outcome of philanthropic policy, which in respect of British administration was launched by Macartney and Barrow and continued by Liverpool, Bathurst and Goderich.

The financial factor, that is the British policy of economy, was responsible for the government being unwilling to defend the frontiersmen. At the same time the philanthropic factor made it impossible for the colonists to defend themselves. In 1795 the two frontier districts had thrown off the yoke of the Company because of a similar dilemma. Now, in 1835, the reversal of D'Urban's frontier settlement decided many colonists to cast aside British authority in a peaceful rebellion, the Great Trek.

9. The Period of the Great Trek, 1834-1854

In South Africa the two decades from 1834 to 1854 were dominated to such an extent by that phenomenon known to contemporaries as the exodus of emigrant farmers, that these twenty years can justifiably be called the period of the Great Trek. The historical significance of the central event of this period is that it concluded and gave meaning to years of transition stretching from the seventies of the eighteenth century to the fifties of the nineteenth century. It transformed the nature of the white settlement in the southernmost part of the African continent: a relatively undeveloped refreshment station became the adolescent South Africa, whose horizons were widened by having attained extensive access to two oceans and a vast potential hinterland north of the Limpopo. Moreover it laid the foundations for the subsequent establishment of the Union and later Republic of South Africa. When, in 1854, the Great Trek was brought to a logical close by the Bloemfontein Convention, South Africa, in its mature twentieth century guise, was already clearly recognizable.

It should not, however, simply be assumed that all South African historical events between 1834 and 1854 were directly influenced by the Great Trek. Many important trends in southern Africa having little or only indirect connection with the Trek, are also discernible in this period. For example, the Trek had little bearing on the other great population movements of this period, the extensive non-White migrations in various parts of southern Africa and the increasing flow into southern Africa of White immigrants from Europe. The problems inherent in the relations between White and Xhosa farmers on the Cape eastern frontier, which had been one of the causal antecedents of the Trek, continued long after the Great Trek had taken place. The decision to grant more autonomy to the Cape Colony was not necessarily a direct consequence of the Trek and the economic prosperity experienced at this time in various parts of South Africa was only partially caused by it. It was partly as a cause and partly as a result of the Great Trek that missionaries greatly increased their efforts throughout southern Africa.

In this chapter the Great Trek as a unique phenomenon in South Africa's past receives most attention, but the above factors, which are also integral aspects of the period under discussion, have not been entirely neglected.

What was the Great Trek?

The Great Trek has been interpreted in many different ways. Prof. W. M. Macmillan categorically labelled it "the great disaster of South African history".[1]

---

1. *The Cape Colour Question* (London, 1927), p. 247.

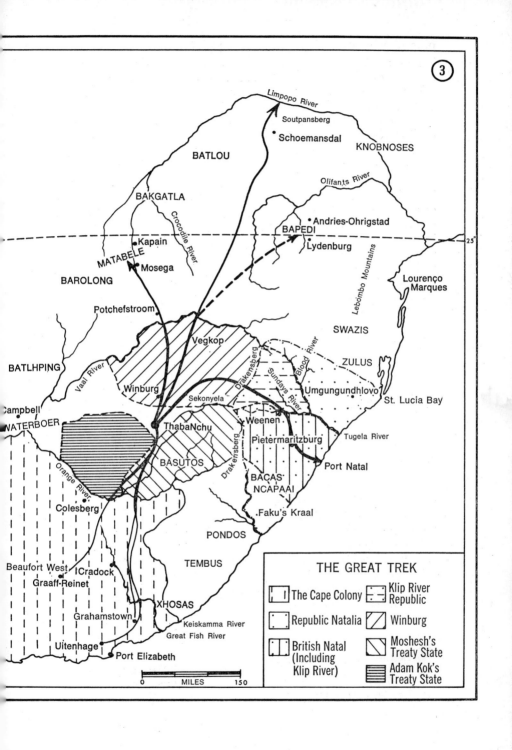

③

THE GREAT TREK

The Cape Colony	Klip River Republic	
Republic Natalia	Winburg	
British Natal (Including Klip River)	Mosesh's Treaty State	
	Adam Kok's Treaty State	

Limpopo River

Soutpansberg

Schoemansdal

KNOBNOSES

BATLOU

Olifants River

BAKGATLA

Crocodile River

Kapain

Andries-Ohrigstad

BAPEDI

Lydenburg

MATABELE

Mosega

Lourenço Marques

BAROLONG

Lebombo Mountains

Potchefstroom

SWAZIS

Vegkop

BATLHPING

Drakensberg

Blood River

ZULUS

Vaal River

Winburg

Sundays River

Umgungundhlovo

St. Lucia Bay

Campbell

Sekonyela

WATERBOER

Orange River

ThabaNchu

Weenen

Pietermaritzburg

Tugela River

BASUTOS

Drakensberg

Port Natal

Colesberg

BACAS

NCAPAAI

Faku's Kraal

PONDOS

Beaufort West

ICradock

TEMBUS

Graaff-Reinet

Grahamstown

XHOSAS

Keiskamma River

Great Fish River

Uitenhage

Port Elizabeth

0   MILES   150

25°

Prof. E. A. Walker saw it as "the central event in the history of European man in southern Africa" and as "that long series of flights from the oncoming nineteenth century in British uniform . . . ".[2] A little later Prof. L. Fouché described it as "fundamentally a desperate protest against equality between black and white".[3] "Tactically", Prof. C. W. de Kiewiet stated five years later, "the Great Trek represented a decision to give up the frontal attack and undertake an outflanking movement . . . The Great Trek indissolubly linked the future of all South Africa with the Boer race".[4] Dr. D. F. Malan's speech at the inauguration of the Voortrekker Monument in 1949 perhaps best expresses the Afrikaner viewpoint: "As a heritage the Voortrekkers left us a greater South Africa . . . Their infinitely greater achievement was that they left to posterity not only a country, but a country which at the same time was the bearer and future nursery of a national soul. If the foundations for an independent South African nationhood were gradually laid in the old Colony since the days of Adam Tas, and if for this reason it to some extent already then existed, then the Voortrekkers with their struggles and suffering and their great achievement built on them and practised that independent nationhood to such an extent that they can almost be regarded as its creators".[5]

Outwardly the Great Trek was an organised exodus of many thousands of Afrikaans-speaking frontier farmers from the British Cape Colony to neighbouring territories to the north and north-east; one of the reasons why this movement was unique was that these trekkers had no intention of ever returning to the Cape. The Great Trek fits into the pattern of similar nineteenth century migratory movements elsewhere in the world. On the North American continent white settlers moved westwards in steadily increasing numbers; they also emigrated in many directions to Australasia and the thousands of islands in the Pacific. Considered against this broad historical background, the Great Trek was merely a considerably accelerated process of white colonization, which, nevertheless, within a few years, more than doubled the territorial expanse of Western civilization in southern Africa. Its occurrence in the thirties of the nineteenth century was one of the last of a long series of non-white and white migrations in southern Africa.

Attracted by prospects of good grazing and hunting grounds and spurred on by tribal conflicts, various non-white peoples had already migrated to southern Africa (see Appendix 1). From the late seventeenth century European colonists from Table Bay had been gradually moving to the north, to the north-east and to the east of the Cape; by the late eighteenth century these colonists, who had become half-nomadic trekboers, had come into increasing conflict with Bushmen hunters and Xhosa farmers along a wide front in the north and north-east of the Cape (see Chapter 6).

2. *The Great Trek* (London, 1934), pp. 8 and 374.
3. "Causes and consequences of the Great Trek", in *The Star*, 12 Dec., 1936.
4. *A History of South Africa* (Oxford, 1941), pp. 53 and 56.
5. *The Star*, 16 Dec., 1949.

Although the British authorities were opposed to expanding the Cape Colony further to the north after 1824, they were nevertheless compelled to move the Cape frontier to the Kareeberg, the Orange River and Stormbergspruit, since they wished to keep most of the trekboers within the Colony. By the mid-twenties of the nineteenth century some trekboers had decided to settle permanently in Transorangia, principally to relieve themselves of the necessity of regular moves out of the drought-stricken northern districts of the Cape Colony. Many settled in groups along the banks of the Modder River. In the meanwhile other trekboers continued to make seasonal treks in search of grazing, or for hunting purposes, often as far as 200 miles north of the Orange River. On the eve of the Great Trek some of these trekboers had journeyed beyond the Modder River and had even reached the Vaal River; it is possible that some of their hunters had even visited the western and southern Transvaal.

A long time before this, Hottentot and Bastard groups had also migrated northwards across the Orange River. There these semi-westernized Korannas and Griquas had established their own small states. The steadily increasing stream of British settlers who had begun to come to South Africa in the early nineteenth century (see Chapter 8) soon evinced an interest in Natal and Zululand. About this time a series of massive and complex Bantu migrations originated in those territories as a consequence of the activities of Shaka, the black Napoleon of southern Africa. These Bantu migrations to the north, west and south of Natal and Zululand started other new migratory movements which all helped to disrupt and depopulate vast, fertile stretches of southern Africa (see Appendix 1). These areas, Natal, Transorangia and parts of the Transvaal, were those which were to attract the Voortrekkers.

The Voortrekkers emigrated from the land of their birth, which was the Cape Colony. In contrast, however, with virtually all other white emigrants from South Africa, before and after them, they were not lost to the mother colony, but actually enlarged and strengthened it by establishing outposts of Western civilization further north in Africa. They were unique in that they did not emigrate to remote regions like America, Australia or central Africa. They were Afrikaner-Boer pioneers who established an independent democratic state bordering on the mother colony; in doing this they more than doubled the area of white settlement in Africa. Most Voortrekkers, although determined to leave British territory permanently, did not wish to sever all connections with the established white community in the south. During the late thirties, the vital Trek years, and also more than a decade later, there was constant communication between the Trekker territories and the old Colony: the inhabitants of both areas visited one another; reciprocal trading relations involved transporting goods and products over land and by sea; the Voortrekkers maintained their cultural ties with the Colony; "aftertrekkers" strengthened the forces of the earlier Voortrekkers.

The Great Trek was no spontaneous folk-migration. It was the best solution which a group of Afrikaner frontier leaders could devise to enable a portion of Cape frontier society to withdraw from a situation which, from their point of view, had become intolerable. First, however, the revolutionary trek doctrine had to be propagated: there was no immediate general acceptance of the trek idea and it was only after a period of gradual and hesitant evolution that the movement assumed the form familiar to us. Most of the Voortrekkers came from the frontier districts: this would seem to indicate that the grievances of the farmers there were more pronounced than those of other groups, but it also reveals the importance of the gradual evolution of the trekboer in the eighteenth and early nineteenth century in preparation for the Great Trek. That evolution gave the Afrikaner farmer physical and psychological mobility: it became a normal procedure for him to load his possessions on to his ox-wagon and to drive his cattle further into the interior in a never-ending quest for better loan-farms. A distinction should be drawn, however, between the Great Trek and the trekboer movement, although at the time the two phenomena were not regarded as separate migrations. The Great Trek cannot simply be regarded as an acceleration of the trekboer movement. The trekboer, whose decision to trek into the interior was prompted entirely by material considerations, remained a *loyalist* who continued to regard the British constitutional and religious institutions in the southern Cape as his. The Voortrekker, on the contrary, was a *rebel* who looked towards the far north and north-east and whose ambition was to become a permanent inhabitant of an independent republic, so that he could solve his problems without interference from the British. There was a radical difference, then, in the spirit of the two movements. The trekboer movement was still under way when the Great Trek started, yet there was no direct connection between the great exodus of emigrant farmers and the earlier movement; the two movements continued to develop along parallel lines. What did happen, however, was that certain trekboers, such as Paul Kruger and his family, became Voortrekkers.

The Great Trek is still generally regarded as the crucial event in South African history. Its significance is that by occurring in that specific form and at that particular time, it influenced the course of future events in South Africa in a special way. That it can be interpreted in many different ways has already been indicated by the quotations cited earlier in this chapter; the possibility of widely varying interpretation perhaps arises from the main population constituents in South Africa having been affected by it in very different ways. Even today it is by no means clear what the long-term results of the Great Trek will be; the unpredictable developments of the later twentieth century may necessitate a radically new interpretation.

The Afrikaner regards the period of the Great Trek as his heroic epoch, the source of his national inspiration: during this period his first republican traditions, his identity, and the basis of his non-White policy were established. English-speaking historians – some of whose views have been quoted already – generally view the Great Trek as a catastrophe which divided South Africa and that it was the consequence of short-sighted policies and actions. Such historians stress the negative aspect of the Boers' flight from their difficulties in the Cape and consequently consider the Trek to have created serious and enduring South

African problems. Such Bantu historians as have expressed opinions on the matter have categorized the period of the Great Trek as a time of White conquest. During that period the differences among the non-Whites were aggravated by the activities of the Whites. The white conquerors had the organization and military power to gain them the control in an extensive area over the land, labour and cattle of the non-Whites. Although the Great Trek was to all intents and purposes a physical emigration, it should also be regarded as a recalcitrant reaction on the part of the frontier farmers to British authority; in fact it was basically a rebellion against the British.

Causes

Before any assessment can be made of the measure of success achieved by this rebellion, it is obviously necessary to define the Voortrekkers' aims and to determine to what extent those aims were realized. This, in the first instance, entails an analysis of the causes of the Great Trek. It is, however, not only necessary to investigate those conditions at the Cape from which the Voortrekkers wished to escape, but it is also particularly important to consider the positive policy which they intended to apply in the interior.

On the eve of the Great Trek there was widespread dissatisfaction among various constituents of the Cape population. The Coloureds were uncertain of their precise place in white society. The Afrikaners of the western districts had been affected most severely by the emancipation of slaves and their control over their coloured labourers had also been weakened. The British Settlers on the extremely exposed southern flank of the Cape-Xhosa frontier had suffered from war losses and frontier disturbances, nor was it easy for them to maintain a reasonable standard of living, since they had insufficient control over their labour and were not permitted to own slaves.

But it was the Afrikaner farmers on the eastern frontier who were affected most adversely by British policy; they were also in a position to react more effectively than any other section of the population. From the late eighteenth century onwards generations of eastern frontier farmers had suffered severe losses in the series of Xhosa wars, and this had given rise to one of their traditional grievances.

Walter Currie, an English inhabitant of Bathurst, visited the disturbed Olifantshoek in the Uitenhage district in April, 1836, and reported that the Boers there were loath to accept his assurance that conditions would improve. A Boer stated "that in his father's lifetime and his own they had been 5 times clean swept out by Kaffirs . . . that for protection, the future would be like the past, indeed he thought they were worse off than fifty years ago; in those old times when they were robbed they redressed themselves, but now their hands were tied while the Kaffirs were loose".[6] The unrest on the eastern frontier con-

---

6. G. M. Theal (ed.): *Emigration Documents*, p. 114. To Sir B. D'Urban, 26 April, 1836 (South African Public Library, Cape Town).

tinued and the ruinous losses suffered through wars and thefts were repeatedly stressed as both an underlying, long-term cause and as an immediate cause of the Trek. Early in 1838 a prominent farmer from the vulnerable Uitenhage district, who had by then already trekked beyond the northern boundary of the Colony, commented on his experiences: "What have the frontier farmers not endured from the Kaffirs from time to time and particularly during the last unexpected invasion? Since 1811, I have served the British Government as a burgher many years without receiving the slightest reward". After he had succeeded in re-establishing himself by dint of hard work "the Kaffirs came and robbed me of everything, as was the case in 1819 and again in 1834 ... What have I left after many years of striving and hard work? Literally *nothing!*"[7]

To overcome these difficult conditions on the Xhosa frontier, the Boers requested whole-hearted government support, but as regular British troops were seldom available in sufficient numbers, the frontiersmen were forced to rely on the protective or punitive power of burgher commandos. However, even the commando system could only function effectively if the government supported it with weapons and ammunition. In the decade before the Great Trek the frontier farmers received no such support from the British authorities, partly because of prevailing British policy of economy and partly because of philanthropic considerations (it was feared that the Bantu would be unjustly treated). The commando system was thus actually rejected in principle (see Chapter 8). Consequently the Afrikaner frontier farmer developed a profound distrust of the British government. In 1839, J. N. Boshof (later president of the Orange Free State) pointed out that Glenelg's well-known dispatch, in which he blamed the Whites for the outbreak of the Sixth Frontier War, had profoundly shocked the Afrikaner farmers. Boshof went on to ask "what was now wanting to confirm the suspicions which they had long entertained, that the total ruin or annihilation of the White population would be looked upon with indifference?" He reported that many Natal Voortrekkers had expressed bitter complaints about this matter and that they had asked, "What confidence could we longer have in such a Government?"[8] The ruinous losses on the frontier reached a peak during the Sixth Xhosa War; furthermore the Boers had to supply their own horses and equipment and leave their possessions unprotected while they went on commando. Another severe shock was that their hopes of receiving compensation for their losses were disappointed; furthermore the government which had refused to compensate them still demanded the usual taxes. These experiences confirmed the opinion of Afrikaner farmers that the existing conditions on the frontier made it impossible for them to live there.

A further difficulty for the farmer was that he could not obtain sufficient trustworthy servants and farm labourers. Because of philanthropic pressure government regulations were promulgated which gave the frontier farmer less

7. Anonymous letter, *De Zuid-Afrikaan*, 16 Feb., 1838 (Translation).
8. J. Bird (ed.): *Annals of Natal*, I, pp. 508 – 9 (letter of 17 Feb., 1839 to *The Graham's Town Journal*).

control than ever before over his coloured labourers. Many labourers who left the farms became lawless vagrants, sometimes operating in gangs (see Chapter 8). The difficulties of making a living in most frontier districts were aggravated by the slaves being emancipated under conditions unfavourable to their former owners. Admittedly there were not nearly as many slave-owners in the eastern districts as there were in the western districts; nevertheless prominent leaders, such as Gert Maritz, suffered heavy losses from the freeing of the slaves.

J. H. Hatting, Sr., a well-known Voortrekker, later maintained that: "In this way the Boers were completely deprived of labour and they and their children had to do all the work and look after the cattle so that farming in the Cape Colony was no longer to be endured".[9]

In April, 1836, Piet Retief, writing on behalf of the inhabitants of Winterberg and Koonap, summed up the implications of this shortage of labour: "The increasing insubordination and desertion of these manumitted slaves, now apprenticed labourers, and others of the Colored Classes, on entering into service, are other grievances of great magnitude ... To this may be added the great distance of the seat of magistracy from their habitations, a circumstance which has a powerful effect in producing this insubordination, it being impossible that the masters for every offence of an Apprentice, or other Servant, can undertake a journey of 2 or 3 days to the nearest magistrate ... The only alternative is they are deprived in most cases of the services of their Servants, and which in the present distressing times cannot fail to have a most prejudicial effect upon their agricultural pursuits in general".[10]

In addition to the constant heavy losses from the continual disturbances on the eastern frontier and the difficult situation as far as labour was concerned, the frontier farmer complained about the lack of sufficient cheap land. At this time the normal shortage of land on the eastern frontier was aggravated, probably more so than at any other time in the Cape, by the financial and philanthropic aspects of British policy in the decade and a half before the Great Trek. Furthermore many farmers were uncertain whether it would be worth their while to improve their farms; many of them had not yet, after many years, received their title deeds from the incompetent, poorly-paid officials. Materially the frontier farmer was simultaneously afflicted by shortages of capital, labour and land, and this was largely because of British policy; furthermore a feeling of apprehension, which had become almost chronic, had been engendered in him by the unstable conditions on the frontier.

However, the grievances of the Afrikaner frontier farmer were not confined to material matters alone. There were two other main causes of his dissatisfaction: the British policy of equality between White and non-White and the former's lack of self-government. The frontier farmer was profoundly disturbed by many aspects of the philanthropists' policy of racial equality. Generally

9. G. S. Preller (ed.): *Voortrekkermense*, I, p. 115 (Translation).
10. Grahamstown Archives 213: Miscellaneous Letters, 1836, Retief to Campbell, 11 April, 1836 (Cape State Archives) (Translation).

speaking the Afrikaner's attitude towards the non-Whites was based on three main concepts: he distinquished on religious grounds between the White Christian and the non-White Heathen; he was very much aware of the physical differences between the European and the indigenous races of Africa; he differentiated between Whites and non-Whites according to their respective positions in the existing social structure (the Afrikaner had little in common with his non-White servant, his farm labourer or his former slave). It is not surprising therefore that the Afrikaner was profoundly affected by the British policy which did not countenance differentiation between the races; nor is it surprising that he reacted so strongly to that policy.

This point is well illustrated by the words of Field-Cornet C. V. Buchner, a loyal burgher official from the Lower Bushman's River area, on the southern flank of the eastern frontier, who did his utmost to counter the trek idea. In reporting that his district was rapidly becoming depopulated, he stated: "I am now beginning to think that there won't be 30 men left in the ward by next year, but thieves and vagabonds in large numbers won't be lacking ... the Africanders cannot stomach the unbridled behaviour of the Blacks and that and nothing else is the main reason for the exodus".[11]

The words of a well-informed Voortrekker woman, Anna Steenkamp, a niece of Piet Retief and someone who moved in influential Trekker circles, are also relevant in this context: "The shameful and unjust proceedings with reference to the freedom of our slaves; and yet it is not so much their freedom which drove us to such lengths as their being placed on an equal footing with Christians, contrary to the laws of God, and the natural distinction of race and colour, so that it was intolerable for any decent Christian to bow down beneath such a yoke; wherefore we rather withdrew in order thus to preserve our doctrines in purity".[12] That this state of mind was prevalent in the Cape Colony is confirmed by other incidents. A Scottish minister in the Dutch Reformed Church, the Rev. A. Smith, encountered much dissatisfaction at the official British policy of equality among the members of his congregation in the eastern frontier settlement of Uitenhage: objections were raised against the publishing of banns and the marriages of Hottentots in the Church. An itinerant missionary, J. Kretzen, came across a housewife in Swellendam who argued "but the Bible does state that this people (the Hottentots) must serve us".[13] Other complaints concerned the baptism of Coloured children in the Dutch Church and the fact that there was no differentiation between races at Nagmaal. (The latter practice had already, before the thirties, provoked sharp reactions from Afrikaners elsewhere in the Cape Colony.)

Despite the feeling of identity which had been evolving among Afrikaner

11. L. G. 102: C. C. Uitenhage, 1836 – 1837, annexure in No. 169, Buchner to Civil Commissioner Uitenhage, 4 Aug., 1837 (Cape State Archives) (Translation).

12. „'n Paar Saamwerkers": Die Dagboek van Anna Steenkamp (Pietermaritzburg, 1939), p. 10 (Translation).

13. Swellendam 3/8: Kretzen to Church Council, 4 July, 1845, p. 1 (N.G. Church Archives, Cape Town) (Translation).

farmers since the eighteenth century, British policy in the early thirties of the nineteenth century had not permitted them to play any real part in the administration of their country. They never had had much say in the central administration of the Cape Colony, but they were sorely aggrieved when their important share in the local government of the remote frontier districts, which had been an accepted custom since the early years of Company rule, was restricted. The experienced frontier official, Andries Stockenstrom, who had been Landdrost for sixteen years and Commissioner-General for six years in the eastern districts, before his appointment as Lieutenant-Governor, in discussing the causes of the Great Trek, cited the following: "the Boers . . . disapproved of the administrative change by which the Board of Heemraden was abolished and the Colony deprived of the only shadow of representation in it . . . "[14] (see Chapter 8). The judicial powers of the Field Cornets, who were appointed from the ranks of the burghers, were also restricted because of philanthropic considerations; and officials from overseas were appointed to protect the non-Whites against the frontier farmers. That decisions were made which closely affected the Afrikaner frontier farmers, particularly in matters concerning the non-Whites, without their being consulted was deeply resented by the farmers. When the President and members of the Natal Volksraad explained to the Governor, Sir George Napier, why the emancipation of the slaves was a cause of the Great Trek, they stated: "And that in a manner so that we were not consulted as to the best or most suitable way in which it could be carried out . . . All these evils we ascribe to a single factor, namely that we were not granted a representative form of Government".[15]

Naturally the Afrikaner frontiersmen who trekked did not all do so for the same reasons. Some of them, such as the De Klerks and De Beers, still bitterly remembered Slagtersnek (see Chapter 8). Others resented the policy of anglicization as it was being applied in the courts, schools and churches; the introduction of English as the only medium in government institutions was regarded not only as an inconvenience but also as a cause of added expense. Because the anglicization policy was not as yet being rigidly applied, this matter did not, however, provoke widespread discontent among the Afrikaners. The frontier districts, particularly, were still so predominantly Dutch that the practical application of the official anglicization policy would have caused the complete disruption of local government. Thus before and during the Great Trek, Dutch was still being used extensively in official documents and correspondence, and unilingual Dutch field cornets were still being appointed.

An attempt has been made to analyse the various causes of the Great Trek separately, but it must always be remembered that there was interaction between the different material and non-material factors which began to convince the Afrikaner frontier farmer from the late twenties, that his situation had become

14. C. W. Hutton (ed.): *The Autobiography of the late Sir Andries Stockenstrom* (Cape Town, 1887), II, p. 62.

15. J. H. Breytenbach (ed.): *Notule van die Natalse Volksraad (volledig met alle bylae daarby), 1838 – 1845*, Suid-Afrikaanse Argiefstukke, Natal No. 1 (Parow, 1958), p. 392 (Translation).

intolerable. His government neither protected him nor permitted him to protect himself properly. Gradually he began to feel the necessity for drastic action. The particular solution eventually decided upon by the Afrikaner leaders was a mass emigration to the territory to the north and north-east of the Cape Colony. If the intricacies of their problem are recalled, it will be realised that this was indeed an ingenious way out of the farmers' dilemma. Their peaceful rebellion embarrassed the British government to such an extent that for years it hesitated between action and passivity, and gave the people of the Great Emigration the priceless chance of successfully overcoming the awkward problems of its beginnings.

One of the early difficulties of the Voortrekkers was that relatively few Whites actively associated themselves with the movement in favour of emigration. Although there was widespread discontent everywhere in the Cape Colony, the supporters of the movement were mostly found among the inhabitants of the eastern frontier districts. That the discontented British Settlers in the east and the discontented Afrikaners in the west did not react in a similar way to their problems was probably mainly because the English had not gone through the trekboers' conditioning experience in mobility, and the Afrikaners in the western districts and on the norther frontier had not been harassed by a series of Xhosa wars. Consequently most of the Voortrekkers came from eastern frontier districts such as Uitenhage, Albany, Somerset East, Cradock and Graaff-Reinet. Virtually no English Settlers joined the Voortrekker exodus and from the northern frontier it was only the farmers of the Beaufort West district who joined the Great Trek in any appreciable numbers. Of the western districts only Swellendam provided an appreciable number of Voortrekkers. Up to 1840, the estimated number of emigrants from the sparsely populated eastern districts was not more than 20% of the white inhabitants of that area, and probably only about 9% of the total white population of the whole Colony; altogether only about 6,000 people trekked into the interior.

Shaping

It is not known when the trek idea began nor who was responsible for its inception. Most probably the belief that such a movement would solve their problems gradually began to take shape in the minds of various Afrikaner frontiersmen in the early thirties of the nineteenth century. The trek concept contains negative as well as positive elements. On the negative side is the implication of flight from the disturbed eastern frontier districts where conditions were becoming intolerable. To the mobile Afrikaner frontiersmen a solution in the nature of a trek would have been attractive and acceptable. Adventurers, traders, hunters, missionaries and trekboers had often talked of the northern and north-eastern areas of southern Africa. Articles in newspapers, magazines, and travel books also aroused interest in those areas. That there were relatively thinly populated, attractive and healthy regions and potential farm-lands to the north must have been brought to the notice of the frontier leaders. The Boer leaders knew that tribal wars among the indigenous inhabitants in the interior had virtually depopulated extensive stretches of territory north of the Orange River and in Natal; they also believed that some of the remaining Natives would welcome the Afrikaners as protectors or allies. As opposed to the situation on the colonial eastern frontier, the farmers would have sufficient suitable non-White labour and, in particular, they would acquire fertile land cheaply. The Afrikaners could apply their own native policy. The experiences of the Griquas has shown that good fire-arms and fast horses made it possible to live safely in the territory to the north of the Cape Colony. Small wonder then that the early exponents of the trek concept believed that to trek would be the ideal solution to the problems of the Afrikaner farmers on the eastern frontier. As soon as they crossed the Cape frontier they would be free of British control and consequently could follow their own ideas in spiritual and material matters in their own state; in-deed, as their leaders gradually realized, they would be able to put into effect the ideal of complete democratic self-government as advocated by the old Cape Patriots and as practised in North America at that time. To the Afrikaner fron-tiersman, who had been waging a struggle on two fronts for three generations, on one hand against an unsympathetic foreign government and, on the other, against a preponderance of non-Whites in the remote interior, welcome new prospects were suddenly revealed. The idea of an Afrikaner state, founded by Afrikaners as a consequence of the plight of the frontier farmer stimulated a nascent Afrikaner national feeling. It acted as a clarion-call to the hesitant con-servative frontiersman, and aroused the imagination of the idealist. It trans-formed the Trek from a reckless rebellion into a divinely inspired mission in Africa. In July, 1837, Piet Retief and Gert Maritz wrote to Governor D'Urban: "we . . . wish to be recognized as a free and independent people".[16] A year later Andries Pretorius wrote to the sympathetic Rev. Van der Lingen concerning the Trek to the North . . . "so we will become a people working for the glory of His Name".[17]

The realization that a trek offered a peaceful solution to their problems and that it would finally terminate the frontier tension made the trek idea acceptable to many Afrikaners – at any rate, more acceptable than the only other apparent alternatives such as emigration overseas or to the western districts, or an armed uprising in the Colony. However, the first Trekker leaders had considerable handicaps to overcome. Few of them had had administrative experience. The vast distances between the far-flung farms and the variety of the Afrikaners' farming activities – for example cattle farming on the Uitenhage coastal plain and sheep-farming on the plateau further inland – were other factors which would easily lead to differences of opinion particularly concerning the trek route. It was also not easy for the leaders to discuss the establishment of their new state while they were still in the Colony, for if news of these discus-sions were to reach the ears of the British authorities the farmers would have

16. Facsimile in G. S. Preller (ed.): *Voortrekkermense*, II, p. 282 (Translation).
17. H. S. Pretorius and others (eds.): *Voortrekker-Argiefstukke, 1829 – 1849* (Pretoria, 1937), p. 27 (Translation).

been regarded as rebels and could have been treated in the same way as the Slagtersnek rebels. Furthermore, the transportation of arms and ammunition across the Cape frontier had to take place secretly so as not to transgress the laws of the land openly, and possibly have the whole movement hindered by court cases.

By the eve of the Great Trek the frontiersmen were well acquainted with the two main routes they could follow into the interior. They could either move over the open northern plains beyond the Orange River which had been cleared by Mzilikazi's impis or in a north-easterly direction towards Natal. The latter was the shortest route but it was through Kaffirland which was occupied by tens of thousands of Bantu. It would be a hazardous undertaking through difficult country. The alternative longer route would lead first through the familiar Transorangia territory, then eastwards towards the unknown Drakensberg passes and over the highest mountain range in South Africa. The ultimate advantage of a north-easterly trek was that the Afrikaners would have their own harbour, Port Natal, on the Indian Ocean, which would be an extremely valuable trading link with the outside world. But there were also elements of uncertainty connected with Natal, the main one being that the British traders and hunters who had been living there for about a decade might request the British government to annex the territory. If the British authorities agreed, the Voortrekkers would once more find themselves living under British rule.

Because the original organizers of the Great Trek kept their plans secret we do not know how they set to work. We can, however, assume that it was probably those who led the vanguard of the first trek, who planned the trek. Louis Trigardt and Hans van Rensburg, the fearless but impetuous pioneers who opened up the way to the Transvaal Lowveld and Portuguese East Africa, emigrated in 1835; Andries Hendrik Potgieter, the constructive founder of a settlement in the far North, left the Cape at the end of 1835, or the beginning of 1836; Gert Maritz who was inclined to be irascible, was a gifted administrator, who had been a legal agent, wagon-maker and farmer in Graaff-Reinet, trekked in September, 1836. In Maritz's case it is known that he had been active in the early arrangements for starting the Trek.

During 1834 the organizers of the emigration decided that they must obtain more information concerning the best areas for Voortrekker settlement. The individualistic Piet Uys from Uitenhage took the initiative and in September, 1834, led a large and important commission of prominent frontier farmers from Albany and Uitenhage on a trek to Port Natal along the coastal route. Some of the members of this trek were Jacobus Uys, Johannes Stephanus Maritz (Gert Maritz's brother), Johannes de Lange, the renowned scout, and Gert Rudolph. After an intensive survey of conditions in and around Port Natal, Uys and his company returned to the Eastern frontier, which was again at war, early in 1835. Uys reported that Natal would be acceptable as a Trekker settlement. According to Willem Jurgen Pretorius from the Graaff-Reinet district, who also trekked later, further reconnaissance expeditions went to the Soutpansberg, on which expedition he was sent, and to the present-day South-West Africa. Later in 1836

134

the first great wave of Voortrekkers began to roll northwards, after the pro clamation of Colonial Secretary Glenelg's unfavourable (for the Afrikaner frontiersmen) eastern frontier settlement. This proclamation was issued at the same time as the frontiersmen realized that there would be no redress of their other frontier grievances and that the newly appointed, philanthropically-minded Lieutenant-Governor, Andries Stockenstrom, would not provide them with any adequate protection against frontier unrest.

For a variety of reasons the initial reaction of the British authorities to the extremely complex new problem presented by the Voortrekkers was indecisive. British policy-makers, such as Glenelg, Governor D'Urban and Lieutenant-Governor Stockenstrom, did not view the problem in the same light and conse-quently they not only expressed widely divergent views concerning frontier conditions and grievances, but also suggested widely different solutions to the problem. The Governor was virtually alone in considering the Great Trek to be detrimental to the Colony and in doing his utmost, as far as the authorities and frontier conditions would permit him, to remedy the grievances of the frontier farmers as speedily as possible. The Lieutenant-Governor regarded the Great Trek as an accelerated and enlarged version of the trekboer movement and believed that it was impossible for the British government to arrest this move-ment permanently. According to him the Great Trek was as inevitable as the earlier, smaller movements and he did not hesitate to say publicly that there were no British laws which could prevent the Voortrekkers from leaving the Colony. Lord Glenelg was inclined to endorse the views of his experienced, philanthropic Lieutenant-Governor. The rebellious Voortrekkers, therefore, were regarded as loyal trekboers and the *Cape of Good Hope Punishment Act* of 1836, which had been drawn up to control the trekboer movement, was now employed against the Voortrekkers. This was a futile decision. No Voortrekker was ever charged in a Cape Court with crimes committed beyond the borders of British territory. Although the British Government ostensibly exercised supreme power in and around Southern Africa, its initial steps to combat the Great Trek were half-hearted and ineffectual.

Because of this state of affairs the earliest Voortrekkers steadily gained con-fidence in crossing the Cape frontier with fire-arms and ammunition in defiance of the colonial laws. The temperamentally erratic Stockenstrom not only openly declared that the British authorities could not prevent the Trekkers from emigra-ting but also clashed with the Governor and many frontier officials over this matter. Late in 1836, he also completely antagonized the frontier commandant, Piet Retief. When Retief, respected and enterprising, decided to join the Voor-trekkers already in Transorangia, the trek idea received a considerable boost. A large company followed him across the frontier and many other frontiersmen became convinced that, after all, trekking was the only answer to their problems and began preparing to leave the Colony.

Retief further influenced the farmers in favour of trekking in the succinct exposition of his own motives in his famous Manifesto. In the same document he set forth a policy for establishing an independent Voortrekker state in the north. He urged other frontiersmen to exchange the unrest of the British-Xhosa frontier for a peaceful existence in an Afrikaner state. In that state "proper relations between master and servant" would be maintained and life and property would be protected. The laws of the new state would be made generally known. "We quit this colony", Retief stated, "under the full assurance that the English government has nothing more to require of us, and will allow us to govern ourselves without its interference in future". Cape newspapers reprinted the Manifesto after it had first appeared on 2 February, 1837, in *The Graham's Town Journal*, together with a list of 366 new Voortrekkers. This was a milestone in the development of the Great Trek.

When it became known that Retief was trekking northwards, many of the several thousand Voortrekkers between Thaba Nchu and the Vet River eagerly awaited his arrival. By the winter of 1837 much had already happened to the Voortrekkers and soon weighty decisions would have to be made. Hendrik Potgieter had tried to maintain contact with his predecessor in the Soutpansberg, Louis Trigardt, and had led a reconnaissance expedition to the far north, even trekking beyond the Limpopo; this northern territory was always to exert a unique attraction on Potgieter.

Meanwhile Mzilikazi had observed the approach of many Voortrekkers with great suspicion; they came from the same direction as that from which he had previously been threatened by the Griquas and Korannas, who had also been mounted and armed with guns. Near the Vaal River the Matabele overwhelmed and killed some small groups of hunters and an advance guard of Trekkers. Potgieter formed a fortified laager and on or about 16 October, 1836, at Vegkop the Trekkers repulsed several thousand of Mzilikazi's warriors, who suffered heavy losses. Many of the small company of defenders received assegai wounds, however, and the Matabele captured all their cattle. In January, 1837, Potgieter and Gert Maritz took Mzilikazi's headquarters at Mosega and brought back many of the captured cattle. Their commando, consisting of 107 Trekkers and a number of Bastards, drove the Matabele far to the north; three American missionaries, including the Rev. Daniel Lindley, returned with the Voortrekkers to their settlement. A provisional, primitive Voortrekker administration had already been established at Thaba Nchu.

By the time of Retief's arrival, Potgieter and Maritz were no longer working well together. At a people's meeting (volksvergadering) in April, 1837, the Transorangia Trekkers elected Retief as their leader under the familiar title of "Governor"; he was also to be their commander-in-chief. Maritz retained his judicial powers and was also the president of the "Council of Policy"; that is, he was chairman of the highest administrative body, which was later to become known in the Republic of Natal as the Volksraad. There was as yet no separation of the three powers of government, yet the beginnings of differentiation are already evident.

Since no minister of their Dutch Reformed Church had seen his way clear to accompanying the Trekkers, final arrangements in the field of church administration could not yet be made. The Cape synod had deplored and condemned the

136

Trek, and had indirectly censured the participants. This was not only because the ministers were all British officials, but also because the church feared that the Trekkers' Christian civilization would degenerate in the remote interior. Under these difficult circumstances Retief and other Voortrekkers were forced to use the services of an ex-schoolmaster and former missionary of the London Missionary Society, the Hollander, the Rev. Erasmus Smit. The somewhat pathetic Smit, who had trekked with his brother-in-law, Gert Maritz, was sixty years old, sickly, over-sensitive and addicted to strong drink.[18] Consequently many Voortrekkers, especially those who knew him best, were unable to accept him as their minister. This was a source of considerable friction among the Trekkers. Various attempts were made to obtain the services of other more acceptable ministers, even English-speaking missionaries, such as the Wesleyan, the Rev. James Archbell and the American Presbyterian, the Rev. Daniel Lindley.

The Trekkers also had to decide on the ultimate destination of the Great Trek; this was another source of differences of opinion. Potgieter considered that the risk of a British annexation of Natal eliminated that territory as a possible area for Voortrekker settlement. Because he had decided on the far north as his ultimate destination, he sought constantly, with restless energy, to establish a link with the outside world through the Portuguese east coast harbours. He wished to sever virtually all connections with the British Cape Colony. However, kindred spirits to Potgieter, the followers of Hans van Rensburg and Louis Trigardt, were to show what happened to small groups encountering hostile Natives in the territory to the north, and to reveal the lethal effect on man and beast of the tropical diseases of the east coast plains. By the middle of 1836 Van Rensburg and his entire party had been murdered by Natives near the Limpopo, while two years later Trigardt and most of his followers were to die of malaria at Delagoa Bay. Meanwhile the intrepid Potgieter continued insisting that the Voortrekkers' salvation lay in the far north where they would be free of all British control, for north of latitude 25° south they would even be outside the jurisdiction of the *Cape of Good Hope Punishment Act*. However, Mzilikazi's Matabeles had to be expelled from the western Transvaal before a Voortrekker state could safely be established in the north. Piet Retief, Gert Maritz and Piet Uys, who had finally left Uitenhage in April, 1837, and their numerically strong parties considered the depopulated, extremely attractive Natal coastal plain and its hinterland between the Tugela and Umzimvubu rivers to be the most suitable area for a Voortrekker settlement. Port Natal, the only good harbour on a long dangerous stretch of coastline, was the key to the whole area. Retief and Uys had already met many of the British hunters and merchants from Natal in Albany and Uitenhage, and Uys had renewed acquaintance with them on his trip to Natal. Retief and Uys counted on receiving

18. The tragic life-story of Erasmus Smit, in which the elements of spiritual idealism, Afrikaner nationalism, human weaknesses and grinding poverty were commingled, must still be written.

the whole-hearted support of these settlers. The Voortrekkers also knew that the British government had refused to accede to the settlers' request to annex Natal.

Because of all these circumstances and also because the Voortrekkers had come from various districts and were inherently individualists, the appointment of Retief as "Governor" in no way eliminated all dissension. Furthermore, in May, 1837, Retief had confirmed Erasmus Smit's position as minister of the Trekkers in the face of considerable and unabated opposition. The question of the destination of the trek was provisionally resolved by a compromise: the Afrikaners would trek in both directions, so that the Matabele danger could be eliminated while Port Natal was being acquired. From the Suikerbosrand, near the present Heidelberg, towards the end of October, 1837, a powerful commando of 330 men advanced against Mzilikazi's headquarters. The fierce fighting which started on 4 November, and which lasted about nine days destroyed the Matabele empire in the Transvaal; Mzilikazi was forced to found a new state beyond the Limpopo. By the time that Potgieter, Uys, Gert Rudolph and their men (among whom was Andries Pretorius who was visiting the Voortrekkers) had returned to their laagers, Retief had already left on an extremely important mission to Port Natal and Dingaan's capital. From 6 October, 1837, when he and fifteen men left his laager near the Drakensberg passes, the "Governor" had run into many complex problems. To begin with, the full support which he had hoped to receive for his undertaking from all the leaders of the Voortrekkers, was not forthcoming. Secondly, he found the task of getting his ox-wagons down to Port Natal through an unknown Drakensberg pass and along a rough pioneer's road the most taxing ordeal of his entire trekking experience. When they arrived at the port on 19 or 20 October they were welcomed as future neighbours by most of the British settlers who lived there with their Bantu followers. Alexander Biggar, who was particularly well-disposed towards Retief, emphasized that the establishment of a Voortrekker state would safeguard the settlers against Dingaan and consequently promote trade. Biggar informed Retief that on 21 June, 1837, the missionary, Captain A. F. Gardiner, had received the territory between the Umgeni River, the Drakensberg and the land of Faku, from Dingaan on behalf of the British king, but that most British settlers rejected Gardiner's philanthropic policy and his authority over them in terms of the Punishment Act. Retief's next problem was to find a policy acceptable to the few settlers who had already been granted rights in the region of Port Natal. How could he reassure them that they would not be engulfed by the Voortrekker state; and how would the policy he chose be received among the other Trekker leaders?

Retief had to tread warily in his negotiations with Dingaan. Apparently Retief paid a successful visit to the Zulu king at the beginning of November, 1837. Dingaan declared that he was prepared to grant Retief an extensive area between the Tugela and the Umzimvubu, on condition that Retief restored to Dingaan the cattle stolen from him by Sikonyela; this would prove that the cattle had not been stolen by the Trekkers. When Retief returned to the Boer laagers in Northern Natal shortly after this meeting, he was confident that his mission had succeeded and that it augured well for the future.

His optimism was not shared by other Trekker leaders. Their opposition in this connection and also concerning the Trekker administrative institutions, increased the pressure on Retief to conclude his negotiations with Dingaan as soon as possible and virtually at any cost; then his policy would be justified. Retief surprised Sikonyela and returned victoriously to his laager early in January, 1838. After an unsuccessful attempt to induce more men to accompany him, he travelled to Ungungundlovu on 25 January with a select band of 70 Whites and 30 Coloured outriders. Despite warnings, Retief decided to brave the wiles of the treacherous Dingaan (who had obtained his throne by cunningly murdering his brother, Shaka) in an attempt to obtain a magnificent, strategically situated homeland for the Voortrekkers, and to consolidate his own position as their leader; it was an injudicious decision. Retief's 100 horsemen arrived at Ungungundlovu on 3 February, 1838; on 4 February Retief drafted a treaty which was signed by Dingaan on 6 February. At the farewell function which followed the signing of the treaty Retief's entire unarmed company was overwhelmed by Dingaan's soldiers in a surprise attack and killed at Dingaan's command.

Just as Retief's decision to trek and his Manifesto had been a significant point in the early development of the Great Trek, so his dramatic death marked a second such point in the Natal phase of its development. Dingaan's chief motive in killing Retief was fear of the magic of the mounted Voortrekkers' markmanship—distance apparently did not concern them. They were the men who had so easily defeated and scattered the force of his old enemy Mzilikazi, whose empire Dingaan had repeatedly, but unsuccessfully, tried to conquer. Dingaan also interpreted some of Retief's actions as a direct threat to his own position. First there was the well-intentioned but injudicious letter which Retief had sent to Dingaan from Port Natal on 8 November, 1837, in which the Trekker leader had told Dingaan of what had happened to Mzilikazi and informed him that God did not allow wicked kings to live long. Then Dingaan had become suspicious because Retief had not handed over the fire-arms captured from Sikonyela together with the cattle. Dingaan's agents, who had accompanied Retief to supervise the return of the cattle, also may have reported that even before the treaty had been signed Retief's followers were streaming down the Drakensberg passes in large numbers. Dingaan's traditional policy – like that of Shaka – was not to tolerate strong neighbours. In view of his knowledge of the whereabouts of the Trekker laagers, and since he had got their leader in his power, he had decided to use his tactical advantage in carefully planned and sudden attacks on a wide front. After the attack on Retief, Dingaan immediately sent his impis during the night to overwhelm the Trekker laagers along the Upper Tugela. So 1838 became the Great Trek's year of crisis; the entire Trek project was in dire danger of disintegration.

After Dingaan's first surprise attacks early in the morning of 17 February, 1838, with thousands of warriors on the scattered and thus extremely vulnerable laagers along the Bloukrans and Bushman's River, the Zulu spearhead broke against the well-fortified laager of Gert Maritz on the afternoon of the same day. Altogether nearly 300 white Trekkers and more than 200 of their Coloured servants were killed. Tens of thousands of sheep, cattle and horses were driven away and Maritz's subsequent counter-attack did not recover many of them. The news that the future of the Great Trek was in jeopardy in northern Natal rapidly spread to Transorangia and even to the Cape Colony. Maritz started preparing a strong commando to send against Dingaan. The British settlers from Port Natal and their non-White followers also planned an attack on the Zulus.

Both expeditions failed lamentably. Apart from the sound tactics and courage of the Zulus, the defeat at Italeni must be ascribed mainly to serious dissensions among the Natal Trekkers, who sent a powerful commando of nearly 350 men under the joint leadership of Hendrik Potgieter and Piet Uys to Zululand in April, 1838. Faulty liaison between the leaders led to the deaths of Piet Uys, his twelve-year-old son, Dirkie, and nine others, in a Zulu ambush beyond the Buffalo River. This severe defeat caused Potgieter and his valuable group of fighting men to move westwards to seek fulfilment of his old ideals on the Highveld. There, on 13 June, 1838, in exchange for cattle, Potgieter obtained the territory between the Vet and Vaal rivers from the Bataung captain, Makwana.[19] The Voortrekker town of Winburg was subsequently founded in the southern portion of this territory.

Six days after Italeni, thirteen British settlers and about a thousand of their Bantu followers were killed by the Zulus on the Lower Tugela. One of the results of the deaths of the main leaders of the Port Natal settlement was that Gert Maritz and Karel Landman, who had arrived with his party from Uitenhage after the Zulu attacks, were shortly afterwards able to occupy the harbour in the name of the Natal Volksraad without any opposition from hostile settlers. The settler Alexander Biggar was appointed landdrost and the young Scottish Trekker, William Cowie, field-cornet. Karel Landman was now the Chief Commandant of the Natal Voortrekkers.

The Great Trek reached its nadir in the difficult winter of 1838. Unable to attack again, the Natal Voortrekkers maintained their positions in fortified laagers. Between 13 and 15 August Dingaan, despite the cold, launched a surprise attack with about ten thousand Zulus on the laager on the Bushman's River. After a desperate assault on what became known as Veglaager, the impis retreated, but the Voortrekkers again lost many cattle. Some Trekker parties, such as that under Karel Landman, established and fortified themselves on the coast round Port Natal and so protected the harbour. The settlement of the Greyling party

19. Authoritative writers have erred in this connection. See E. A. Walker: *The Great Trek* (London, 1934), pp. 118 and 226; H. B. Thom: *Die Lewe van Gert Maritz* (Cape Town etc. 1965), p. 145; A. J. H. Van der Walt and others, D. W. Krüger (ed.): *Geskiedenis van Suid-Afrika* (Cape Town etc., 1965), p. 204. From Potgieter's letter to Sir H. Smith, dated Potchefstroom 15 May, 1848, it is clear that Potgieter acquired the territory only after his return from Natal (See H. S. Pretorius and others (eds.): *Voortrekker-Argiefstukke, 1829 – 1849*, R 141/48, p. 317, also R 17/38, p. 26).

near the coast was to be of importance with regard to the subsequent establishment of the Voortrekker town of Pietermaritzburg, named after Pieter Retief and Gert Maritz.

Maritz's health had deteriorated to such an extent that on 23 September, 1838, he died at the age of 42. Only Karel Landman remained of the prominent Natal leaders. Sickness and a shortage of food were other problems with which the Natal Trekkers had to contend. Their difficulties were somewhat alleviated, however, when the aid requested from the Colony arrived in the form of provisions, equipment and men.

Some time before the arrival in the Tugela Valley, on 22 November, of Andries Pretorius, the promising new leader from Graaff-Reinet, steps had been taken to organize a great commando against Dingaan. Pretorius was no stranger to the Trekkers: he had acted as their scout in Transorangia, the Transvaal and Natal. He had accompanied the second expedition against Mzilikazi for some distance; he had previously visited Port Natal and had acquired a farm there; he had met Retief after his return from Sikonyela and had learnt of his plans for the future. Pretorius had also tried to obtain the services of a minister for the Trekkers, and while still in the Cape Colony he dreamt of an Afrikaner "volk" (people) fulfilling their destiny in the north. When the Great Trek is considered as a whole, Pretorius emerges as one of the leaders who contributed most to the success of the Afrikaner Emigration. From the time that this brilliant organizer and talented soldier, after careful consideration, first identified himself with the Trek until his death, almost at the end of Great Trek period, he was constantly making constructive contributions towards its furtherance.

Two days after he was appointed Commandant-General on 25 November, 1838, Pretorius led his mounted force with their ox-wagons into Zululand. On 15 December he showed a fine appreciation of tactics in placing his wagon laager between a deep stretch of a tributary of the Buffalo River (later to be known as Blood River) and a large ditch. Pretorius's force consisted of about 470 men, reinforced by British settlers and their Bantu followers. The Zulu force of about 12,500 armed with shields and assegais could not withstand the devastating fire of the Voortrekker guns and two small cannon. Some days before the battle, which was fought on Sunday, 16 December, 1838, the Voortrekkers had taken a solemn vow or covenant that if God granted them victory in the coming fight they and their descendants would always commemorate the day of victory and would build a church to His honour. This vow inspired them in one of the largest and most decisive battles ever fought between Blacks and Whites in South Africa. More than 3,000 Zulu dead testified to the overwhelming defeat inflicted on Dingaan's elite regiments. But the Battle of Blood River was more than a great military victory: it was the foundation of the short-lived Republic of Natal, and the commemoration of the Voortrekker victory at Blood River on the Day of the Covenant created a new and enduring Afrikaner tradition which was to continue long beyond the early nineteenth century.

The way to Ungungundlovu was open; near Dingaan's former capital Pretorius found the bodies of Retief and his men and the treaty on which the

Voortrekkers were to base their claim to Natal. Although the Zulus nearly succeeded in neatly ambushing the Boers at the Battle of the White Umfolozi, on 27 December where Alexander Biggar, among others, was killed, Zulu morale had already begun to crumble. Dingaan was unable to return to his capital, and after his brother, Mpande, had joined forces with a trekker commando, the Zulus under Dingaan were finally defeated at Maqongo in February, 1840; Dingaan fled north where he was killed.

The Republic of Natal

In a certain sense the Trekker victory over Dingaan ended the shaping of the Great Trek. The Trekkers had finally found, after a search which had begun in 1834, a northern territory suitable for their cattle-farming and agricultural pursuits. Now the period of settlement could begin. The focus of the Trek had moved to beautiful Natal (the first choice of most of the Trekkers) and its valuable, strategically situated harbour where the fundamental structure of a state had already been established in the Republic of Natal. This republic is important for at least two reasons: it was the earliest republic in the history of South Africa and it only existed for four years. The history of this republic principally consists of the attempts of inexperienced cattle-farmers and agriculturists, with their knowledge of the limited Cape institutions, to establish a new and extremely democratic political structure and to govern themselves according to their own lights.

The Natal Voortrekkers were exposed to constant direct and indirect pressure from the British government which once more wished to subject them to British rule. The possibility of Voortrekker independence being strengthened by association with the French, American and Dutch governments through the visits of foreign ships to Port Natal, particularly disturbed the British authorities. Obviously, too, the native policy of the Trekkers was subjected to close scrutiny. Philanthropic missionary pressure ensured that the Voortrekker use of native labour, and their negotiations with the Zulus concerning such matters as compensation for Zulu losses and the acquisition of land, would receive close attention; their attitude towards the Baca and Pondo tribes to the south of Natal would also be watched carefully. The British government also had to consider the possibility of the Boers causing Bantu tribes to be driven southwards and thus aggravating the chronic tension on the Cape eastern frontier; this might greatly increase the already heavy British military expenditure.

Although for some time British policy towards the Voortrekkers in Natal was indecisive, financial considerations finally compelled the authorities to take positive steps. Sir George Napier, Sir Benjamin D'Urban's successor, wished to apply Lord Glenelg's philanthropic policy. After he had failed in an attempt to ban the export of arms and ammunition to Port Natal, he decided to occupy its harbour with a military force. The new governor hoped to end the Trek with this direct intervention, or at the very least to bring it under British control by gaining possession of its port of supply. In December Major Charters's force landed at Port Natal. The Natal Volksraad vainly protested against Charters's seizure of military supplies at the port. The next British commander, Capt. Jervis, was unable to arrange a lasting peace between the Volksraad and Dingaan. By the time Jervis and his troops left Port Natal in December, 1839, the Volksraad's alliance with Mpande had strengthened the Voortrekkers' position.

The Republic now became more stable; its Volksraad had more authority and had regained control of the Trekkers' military supplies. The Republic's boundaries were established between Zululand, the Drakensberg and the Umzimvubu. A more peaceful existence for the republicans seemed assured. Gradually they were able to leave their widely dispersed fortified laagers and devote themselves to caring for their vast farms. Thus the surviving Voortrekkers were finally able to reap some reward for their suffering. Attracted by the good prospects in Natal, many *after*trekkers from the Colony came to strengthen the original republican body. Not only farmers, but also townsmen, arrived in Natal by sea from the Cape. There were lawyers, medical doctors, salesmen and merchants, land-speculators and scientists among those who came. Trade between the Cape and Natal began to flourish. In 1838 goods to the value of £200 were exported from Natal to the Cape; in 1839 this figure had risen to £4,800. Natal imports from the Cape showed an even more rapid increase from £5,900 in 1838 to £14,700 in 1839 and to £17,000 in 1840. When the Trekkers' cash supplies were exhausted, and they had few products to export, however, trade began to decline.

In this way a new community was developing in Natal. Gradually the primitive, mobile groups of frontiersmen became integrated into a complex, and more stable social structure. This process required more administrative officials than could be supplied from the ranks of the Boers. Consequently the Republic had to use men who were not fully identified with the Trek spirit; this resulted in internal clashes which weakened the Republic. The central government of the Republic consisted of an elected Volksraad of 24 members, with a president or chairman, and a commandant-general as the military commander-in-chief. There was no sound executive power and this was to hamper the smooth functioning of the machinery of state. The Cape titles of "Governor" and "Council of Policy" disappeared. For local government the old and tested institutions of Landdrosts and Heemraden which had existed in the Cape frontier districts, were introduced. Contact with the Trekkers on the western Highveld was re-established. After Pretorius and Potgieter had agreed, in 1840, that the entire Trekker territory would be controlled by the Natal Volksraad, it was decided by the Volksraad in 1841 that an Adjunct Council of 12 members would be established at Potchefstroom. Potgieter was appointed Chief Commandant west of the Drakensberg. It was now possible for the Voortrekkers to concentrate more on civil matters: their mobile phase had apparently ended. Permanent arrangements were also made in church affairs. The Rev. Daniel Lindley, who had been a missionary among the Matabele and Zulu, was established at Pietermaritzburg as minister for all the Voortrekkers east and west of the Drakensberg. This practical American Presbyterian minister was as attracted to the

Voortrekkers as they were to him. Lindley, because of his American experience, could see the relations between Whites and non-Whites in better perspective than many of his contemporaries.

After the British had withdrawn from Port Natal, Napier paid much attention to establishing a new policy towards Natal. Although much pressure was being exerted on the British government to annex the territory, Napier did not lose sight of realities and consequently was not prepared to countenance an occupation of Natal lightly, which would be contrary to Britain's financial interests. Any strong positive action such as annexing Natal as a British Colony, establishing an administration there, and maintaining a permanent garrison in the area, would have entailed more expense than Britain was prepared to incur at this time. Nor could such a course of action be justified on the grounds that the income from the new colony would cover its expenses. Only when a new situation arose in Natal would there be sufficiently strong arguments to advance in favour of annexation.

Sir James Stephen, Britain's philanthropically minded Permanent Under-Secretary for Colonies, expressed the British reasons against annexation in the following terms: "it is very ill policy to enlarge this ill-peopled and unprofitable colony (the Cape Colony), and that to make a new settlement at Port Natal . . . would be merely to throw away so much money, and to multiply our relations and responsibilities towards barbarous tribes, from which nothing could ever come, but the consumption of treasure – the waste of human life, and a warfare alike inglorious, unprofitable and afflicting".[20] When the Secretary of State, Lord Stanley, laid the matter before the British Cabinet, it was decided that the commitments of the imperial treasury were already sufficiently heavy, and that to increase Britain's expenditure by annexing Natal would merely be to add to her already heavy financial burden.

Napier, as the spokesman of British policy in South Africa, was never prepared, however, to go to the other extreme of recognizing the independence of the Trekker state. He considered the Trekkers to be British subjects under the jurisdiction of the *Cape of Good Hope Punishment Act*. Since he recognized neither the Republic nor its officials, the repeated requests of the Natal Volksraad for official British recognition and eventually for closer co-operation between Britain and the Republic, were consistently rejected by the Governor.

With Zulu control of the area south of Zululand ended, thousands of uprooted Natives streamed into the Republic. To ensure that unrest, similar to that which had caused them to emigrate from the Cape eastern frontier, did not develop in their new state, the Volksraad began to consider measures for applying the Trekker policy of racial differentiation and territorial segregation. In December, 1840, Pretorius led a punitive expedition against the Baca tribe in the south. This act disturbed the Pondos and their Wesleyan missionaries who had a chain of mission stations stretching from that area nearly to the Cape

---

20. Memorandum, 31 January, 1842, quoted by H. L. Hall: *The Colonial Office* (London, 1937), pp. 171 – 2; C.O. 48/214 in the Public Record Office, London.

eastern frontier. Consequently, the Wesleyan superintendent, the Rev. William Shaw, made strong representations to Napier requesting that Faku should be protected.

The Cape apprenticeship system under which native children were placed in the service of white employers for a certain time had been brought to Natal by the Trekkers. Although there were regulations to prevent abuse in this system philanthropists and missionaries accused the Trekkers of perpetuating slavery. In September, 1841, the Rev. J. Archbell came to the defence of the Voortrekkers by denying this allegation in *The Graham's Town Journal*. The Volksraad's dilemma about labour was that, whereas in the Colony the Boers had lacked sufficient non-White labour, in Natal they were inundated by thousands of potential, but uncontrollable labourers. An attempt was made to solve the problem by instructing landdrosts to ensure that no farmer had more than five Bantu families living on his farm. It was, however, difficult for the authorities to get the poorly paid or unpaid officials to apply this measure effectively in the extensive territory, or to prevent non-White labourers from contravening it.

Because of the increasing numbers of Natives in the Republic, the Volksraad in August, 1841, decided to apply their policy of segregation by moving thousands of Bantu to the southern boundary of Natal. Napier viewed this step as a new and serious threat to the Cape eastern frontier; the pressure set up by this movement might force the Xhosas over the Cape frontier where renewed military operations would necessitate heavy British expenditure. First the Governor decided to send British troops to the Umgazi River near Natal's southern boundary. Later Captain T. C. Smith was ordered to march to Port Natal with 250 men and a few cannon; at the beginning of May, 1842, he raised the Union Jack at the Voortrekker port.

Napier also wished to prevent foreign ships from calling at Port Natal. In August, 1841, the American brig *Levant*, under the command of Captain Holmes, had traded a little with Natal, but even this had caused consternation in British commercial circles. Shortly before Captain Smith's arrival the visit of the Dutch trading vessel, *Brazilie*, under the command of Captain Reus, to Port Natal between 26 March and 24 April, had caused something of a sensation in certain British circles because of their suspicion that the Dutch government or even the government of her rival, France, was attempting, as they were doing elsewhere, to undermine British supremacy in south-east Africa.

The arrival of the British troops accentuated the increasing hostility between the Republicans and the few British settlers. It will be remembered that Piet Retief had to handle the British settlers at Port Natal with considerable finesse during his first visit there in 1837. Although their joint expedition against Dingaan's impis had forced the two groups to unite temporarily, no lasting bond had been forged between them. The Zulu attack on Retief and his 100 men had made many Trekkers suspect that the British missionaries, Gardiner and Owen, or some of the hostile settlers at Port Natal, might have incited Dingaan; otherwise, they concluded, such a radical action was inexplicable. This unfounded suspicion took firm root among the Afrikaners. It was therefore not surprising that many Voortrekkers believed, and not altogether without reason, that certain British inhabitants of Natal undermined their Republic by sending unfavourable reports to the Cape and by conspiring to aid the British government whenever they could. The arrival of Captain Smith widened the breach between Afrikaner and Briton.

Open conflict then ensued between Smith's forces and the Boer forces led by Pretorius. The Trekkers repulsed Smith's badly planned night attack at Congella and inflicted comparatively heavy casualties on the British force. Pretorius then besieged their camp. While Smith withstood the siege, Dick King, a British settler from Port Natal, rode six hundred miles to Grahamstown to obtain help for the British. Late in June the British relief force, under Lieutenant-Colonel A. J. Cloete, landed at Port Natal. The raising of the siege ended the Boers' military resistance in Natal. On 15 July, 1842, the Volksraad, sitting at Pietermaritzburg, signed the terms of capitulation. Although the Republicans ater renewed heated negotiations, Napier and the British Cabinet were adamant that British authority could not be withdrawn from Natal. This attitude was partly the result of the imperial authorities now having more money at their disposal to cover the heavy cost of establishing Natal as a British colony, and partly because they believed that in time the development of Natal's natural resources would cover many of her expenses. They also hoped that the threat of a military force in the Xhosa's rear would help to reduce British military expenditure on the Cape frontier. Other factors already mentioned, such as the effective protection of the Natal Natives, the elimination of foreign intervention in Natal, and the pacification of the Cape frontiers were also stressed as reasons for the annexation. The decisive argument was that, despite the heavy expenses involved, it was politic for the British to establish their rule in Natal, for, as various pressure groups maintained, if Natal were left to the Voortrekkers the British government would be saddled with an even greater financial burden in the future.

The imperial government made its decision in December, 1842, and announced it to South Africa in 1843. Gradually British control and administration was more firmly established in Natal, until the Volksraad and the shadow republic disappeared in October, 1845 (see further Chapter 11).

The second Trek

The second Trek, from Natal, occurred for basically the same reasons as the first Trek from the Cape Colony. As had been the case on the Cape eastern frontier, many Afrikaners were disturbed by the implementation of a British policy, which adversely affected them materially and otherwise; they felt they had been rendered defenceless against the non-Whites and that their position as the bearers of European civilization was being seriously threatened. There were nevertheless, some differences between the conditions existing in Natal and the conditions which had existed in the Cape Colony. Whereas the emancipation of slaves was not a factor in the Natal situation, Afrikaner national consciousnes

146

had developed since the thirties. As a result of the Trekkers' experiences and achievements as a group in the face of tremendous pressures, new Afrikaner national traditions had arisen; the martyrdom of Piet Retief, the courage of Marthinus Oosthuizen, the heroic death of Dirkie Uys, had all enriched the heritage of Afrikanderdom. In addition there was the new vow which the "volk" commemorated annually. One of the basic conditions of the new British regime was that there was to be no differentiation between Whites and non-Whites in Natal; once again, to the Afrikaners, this policy meant a threat to life and property. Although the Volksraad continued to legislate for some time, it had little influence in Natal. The British land policy, in particular the meticulous surveying of farms and allocations of land, created the same kind of complex problems as it had in the Cape. Despite all these factors, many Afrikaners did not wish to leave Natal and continued for some years to hope that conditions in the territory would improve. Towards the end of 1845, however, when British colonial administration was formally inaugurated in Natal with the appointment of the philanthropically inclined Martin West as Lieutenant-Governor, the second Trek began to take shape.

The Trekkers' discovery of a way to the sea via Natal had only been achieved through much effort, suffering and sacrifice. Most of their leaders had died in Natal, many hundreds of Trekkers had been killed in war, by sickness, and by exposure; tens of thousands of the cattle, which they needed to start a new life had been lost. That their Republic of Natal, the territory on which most of the Trekkers had set their hearts, had been annexed by Britain so soon after its establishment, made a serious psychological and material impact on the Afrikaner. They had created national traditions, but in Natal were once more living under the Union Jack.

The second Trek, like the first, was not a spontaneous movement; the idea of it had first to be propagated. There were "first" Trekkers, such as Willem Hendrik Jacobsz, "after" Trekkers such as Andries Pretorius, those who remained in Natal, like Karel Landman, and some, like Carel Buchner, who returned to the Cape Colony. The Trek from Natal strengthened the weak Trekker communities of the west and north-west interior, but the second Trek, by re-introducing mobility, also disturbed the new-found stability of these settlements, and disrupted their peaceful and relatively primitive cattle-farming and agricultural pursuits. Lands which had only recently been tilled were repeatedly abandoned so that new farms could be occupied. Moreover, new problems concerning new tribal boundaries, the divergent aims of the Trekboer loyalists and the Voortrekkers and the renewed British interest in their territory and activities, were to be encountered on the western Highveld. The Voortrekkers were now concentrated in the north of Transorangia and the Transvaal; their only way to the sea was the hazardous route through the hot, malaria and tsetse-fly infected eastern Lowveld to the Portuguese harbours on the Indian Ocean.

Up to 1842 the Great Trek was a peaceful reaction to British authority: from 1842 its nature changed to one of violent rebellion. The Republic of Natal was only surrendered after a fierce military clash between the Voortrekkers and British regular troops led by an officer who had fought at Waterloo. There had also been friction and clashes with the British settlers in Natal, and the Afrikaners suspected that the Natal British had incited Dingaan against Retief. Trekker reinforcements from the west made a vain attempt to save their Republic. The rebellious feelings of the Trekkers grew and resulted in further military clashes. This phase was ended in 1848 by the final defeat of the republicans at the desperate Battle of Boomplaats. There could be no more fighting, but the Afrikaners would trek again to the west, to the north, and to the north-east if their negotiations with Britain failed.

The period of violent republican resistance was also the period in which the two Boer republics originated. The territory of these republics was gradually established as the Trekkers settled on the western Highveld, and in the eastern and northern Transvaal. In the western Transvaal, Potchefstroom, a pleasant spot, well supplied with water, had become the focus of the Voortrekkers' settling since 1838. In 1842 the Rev. Daniel Lindley confirmed 100 Trekkers and baptized nearly 200 children there. Smaller concentrations of Voortrekkers settled round Suikerbosrand, the Magaliesberg, the Apies River, and Fonteinedal. As will become apparent later in this chapter, new Transvaal towns were usually founded by Hendrik Potgieter, the pioneer of the north, some of them being established because of the pressure of new Trekker waves from the British territories.

The violent phase of the second Trek was characterized by constant and increasingly determined British efforts to control it. In the process Britain became steadily more involved in the Trekker territories. This enhanced her prestige and satisfied the philanthropic missionaries, but her new military and administrative responsibilities increased her financial burdens. As British expenditure continued to increase, and when it began to seem as if the new territories were not going to be profitable, Britain began to doubt the wisdom of her policy. Her attempted pacification of the interior had involved her in a series of clashes between Voortrekkers, Trekboers, Griquas, Barolongs and Basutos.

At this time the endemic unrest on the Cape-Xhosa boundary once again flared up into the Seventh Frontier War or the War of the Axe (1846 – 1847). This marked the end of Stockenstrom's Treaty State System. Sir Peregrine Maitland's attempts to conclude treaties with Kreli, paramount chief of the Xhosa, and Faku, the Pondo chief, had not produced any frontier stability. Both of Maitland's successors, Sir Henry Pottinger and Sir Harry Smith, still had to wrestle with this extremely complex and expensive problem.

A change in British policy towards the Voortrekkers began when the authorities were forced to move troops which could be ill spared from the Cape eastern frontier to Transorangia because of Britain's new responsibilities in that area. A further important factor which modified British policy was the profound dissatisfaction felt in many quarters at the slow progress in converting the South African indigenous races to Christianity. Although there were more missionaries in a wider area than ever before, they were not conspicuously effective.

148

There were few lasting civilizing influences discernible, other than that the Native was deeply concerned with exchanging his assegai for a firearm.

To enable Britain to defend extensive frontiers effectively, her government began to consider an alternative policy; this entailed accepting the Voortrekker as an ally against the Native. The influence of the missionary-philanthropists had declined, so that the Voortrekkers were no longer viewed primarily as the violators of the rights of the non-White. The new British attitude was only one step removed from the British Convention policy of the early fifties which granted constitutional recognition to the independent Boer republics. Britain was still able to maintain her supremacy over a much enlarged South Africa because the republics were cut off from any direct access to the sea. Events in Transorangia and the Transvaal during the forties and fifties must be analysed within this particular framework; only then does it become clear why Britain, with her overwhelmingly powerful military and naval resources in and around southern Africa, did not subject the Voortrekkers in the interior to her rule.

As has been indicated, on the eve of the Great Trek there were already many trekboers living in the south of Transorangia. Among them clashes had developed in the south-western portion of the territory between the trekboers on the one hand and the Griquas and Bastards on the other, mainly over land-ownership. Supported by missionaries of the London Missionary Society the Griqua chief, Adam Kok, tried to defend his interests around Philippolis. To the east, the Basuto chief, Moshesh, tried to extend his authority from Thaba Bosigo to include the fertile territory west of the Caledon River. Moshesh came into conflict not only with Whites but also with other Bantu chiefs, such as the Barolong chief, Moroko, who was supported by Wesleyan missionaries, and Sikonyela to the north. Occasionally Moshesh acted on the advice of the Paris Evangelical missionaries who had converted his people to Christianity, but more often this ruler, one of the shrewdest diplomats in South African history, himself formulated the policy which enabled him to lead his people successfully through a maze of difficulties.

The particularly heterogenous character of the population of southern Transorangia caused endemic disturbances which made the British government attempt to pacify the area. Circumstances favoured British intervention. The trekboers wished for British protection because they had lost contact with the republican Voortrekkers, who principally occupied the Winburg territory between the Vet and Vaal rivers and the Drakensberg. Under the leadership of Potgieter the republicans of Winburg had formed a bond with the Trekkers of Potchefstroom. After the Natal Voortrekkers, who were aided by Jan Mocke and others from Transorangia, had failed to preserve their Republic, their federal tie with the Trans-Drakensberg Boers was severed. In 1843 the republicans on the western Highveld established their own administration and a year later declared their independence. Potgieter and his burgher council claimed that their authority extended to the Orange River, and the republicans accepted the Thirty-three Articles of 1844 as the basis of their constitution.

All the elements necessary for a violent conflict were present in southern

Transorangia. This caused the British once more to extend their authority, which meant that a second Trek began in this territory too. In October, 1842, Judge William Menzies was informed at Colesberg that Jan Mocke and his Voortrekkers were on their way to Allemansdrift on the Orange River, to proclaim a republic north of the river. Since the British government had not authorized him to annex any more territory, Napier was compelled to repudiate the Judge's annexation of the vast area up to the 25th degree of latitude. To pacify the territory the Governor ordered a strong force to Colesberg a few months later. Although a firmer policy was being followed in Natal, where the first annexation of an important Trekker territory had taken place, Napier decided merely to conclude treaties with Adam Kok and Moshesh in November-December, 1843. The Governor was attempting to establish subsidized buffer states which would help protect the Cape northern frontier without the expenditure of vast sums of money. As Adam Kok's ally the British authorities were, however, soon compelled to help the Griquas against the Whites. This policy of protecting non-Whites against Afrikaners had already led to reactions among Afrikaners on the Cape eastern frontier and in Natal. In southern Transorangia it was to have the same effect: it even converted some trekboer loyalists into rebels. White opposition to Adam Kok increased until British regular troops defeated an armed Trekker force at Swartkoppies in May, 1845. In June of that year Governor Maitland crossed the Orange to conclude a new agreement with the Transorangia chiefs at Touwfontein: their territories were to be sub-divided and Whites could hire farms in one portion only. In January, 1846, a British resident was to be stationed at Bloemfontein to control the Whites, but the authorities did not give him sufficient support to enable him to pacify his remote and extensive territory. More clashes between White and non-White were almost inevitable and involved Britain yet further in the affairs of Transorangia. At the same time these developments accelerated the second Trek to Winburg and to the Transvaal.

In the meanwhile Potgieter was still searching for a way through Portuguese territory so that a new harbour could be established on the Indian Ocean. In 1845, with this possible harbour in mind, he founded a town in the north-eastern Transvaal, which he hoped to use as a centre from which to re-establish contact with the Dutch who for trading and other purposes had sent the *Brazilie* to visit Port Natal. The new settlement was also completely outside the jurisdiction of the *Punishment Act*. It was called Andries-Ohrigstad and attracted hundreds of Boers from various parts of the interior who had participated in the second Trek. Although Potgieter's position was strengthened by the concentration of so many Whites at a strategically important point, the situation also created many problems, for he was opposed by the leaders, such as J. J. Burger, of the so-called Volksraad Party. Poor roads, malaria, the tsetse fly and internal dissensions prevented Potgieter from establishing his port, despite the earnest efforts which led him and about 100 of his men to reconnoitre the far north and north-east and attack Mzilikazi in the vicinity of the Matopos. Early in 1848 he and his followers established themselves at the new settlement of Schoemansdal in the Soutpansberg, an unhealthy region which was also menaced by thousands of Bantu.

But this settlement still did not mean that the second Trek was over, for in the same year, 1848, Pretorius again contributed something of value to it. He had eventually been forced to abandon all hope of leading the life he wished in Natal when his attempt to negotiate with the High Commissioner, Pottinger, at Grahamstown had failed. Pretorius first trekked to the Magaliesberg. He then advanced, at the head of the largest commando he had as yet led, against Sir Harry Smith in southern Transorangia. This move had been necessitated by Smith's annexation in February, 1848, of the whole of the territory between the Orange River, the Vaal River and the Drakensberg as the Orange River Sovereignty. The experienced British general moved his superior force quickly and in August decisively defeated Pretorius at Boomplaats. Smith's further attempts to consolidate British authority and frontiers in southern Africa and to gain control of the best Trekker routes to the East Coast seemed to indicate that he had obtained a firm control over the Great Trek. Admittedly there was a further great Afrikaner exodus northwards which greatly increased the number of the Transvaal Voortrekkers, but it was this very event which disrupted the activities of the Transvaal Trekkers, particularly those under Potgieter and Pretorius. These two men, the last of the great Voortrekker leaders, became isolated with their die-hard supporters, and ultimately even estranged from each other. Smith, south of the Vaal, was confident that he had solved the most important British problems through the creation of the Orange River Sovereignty.

The Conventions grant constitutional recognition

The annexation of the vast area between the Orange and the Vaal was a severe blow to the Voortrekkers, as had been the annexation of Natal five years earlier. Due to their constant trekking many Afrikaner farmers had become impoverished; many had died young from living in unhealthy regions. Many had been forced to abandon the territories which had been their first or their second choice; clashes of personality resulted, and administrative disruption.

After attempts had been made at Hekpoort in the Magaliesberg and on the Olifants River to unite the Transvaal Voortrekkers, it was decided at Derdepoort in May, 1849, that they would all be controlled by one Volksraad. The implementation of the decision to establish "a United Bond of the whole community of Voortrekkers this side of the Vaal"[21] was frustrated, however, by the absence of Hendrik Potgieter. Although Andries Pretorius had outstanding military talents, and was respected by the Trekkers, the Volksraad was opposed to continuing the office of commandant-general or chief commandant. Later, in January, 1851, when the Volksraad did recognize military leaders, no fewer

21. Quoted by F. A. van Jaarsveld: *Die Eenheidstrewe van die Republikeinse Afrikaners*, I, Pioniershartstogte (1836 – 1864), (Johannesburg, 1951), p. 100.

than four commandants-general were appointed. In the western Transvaal Andries Pretorius was in command of the Mooi River, Magaliesberg and part of the Marico district, while J. A. Enslin commanded another part of the Marico area. Hendrik Potgieter was appointed commander of Soutpansberg in the far north, and W. F. Joubert of Lydenburg, which had replaced the unhealthy Ohrigstad as the chief settlement of the north-eastern Transvaal. This gave the remote Transvaal settlements an extremely ineffective and unstable type of administration (see Chapter 13), which prevented their taking any firm, united action against the British government or the Native tribes.

In the meanwhile the British government had become entangled in serious difficulties in the extensive interior of its southern African possessions. Britain's financial obligations had not diminished, as had been predicted; on the contrary they had increased considerably. The outbreak of the Eighth Frontier War in British Kaffraria meant that Sir Harry Smith had also to use his inadequate military forces against rebellious colonial Hottentots. Many eastern frontier farmers were no longer at all enthusiastic about undertaking commando duties, and this helped to make it impossible for Smith to continue defending the Orange River Sovereignty. Without considerable British military and financial support, Major H. Warden, the British Resident, was unable to maintain peace, particularly as far as Moshesh was concerned. In June, 1851, Warden's attempt to enforce his frontier settlement with his weak local forces resulted in his being defeated by the Basutos at Viervoet. Because the British government considered that precedence must be given to continuing the Eighth Frontier War and because the British Commissioners, Hogge and Owen, feared that Pretorius might intervene in the affairs of Transorangia, the British authorities were prepared to negotiate with Pretorius at Sand River in the north of the Sovereignty.

The British government was now convinced that Smith's defensive policy would merely increase Britain's financial commitments. They felt they should make allies of Voortrekkers, who would help protect Britain's extensive frontiers in southern Africa. These then were the British reasons for the Convention which was concluded at Sand River on 17 January, 1852. Its recognition of the independence of the community north of the Vaal was, in fact, the first official British recognition of a Trekker republic (see further Chapter 13). Britain guaranteed that no trade restrictions would be imposed on her new ally, not even on ammunition, and that she would repudiate treaties which she had made with natives north of the Vaal River. After the passage of eighteen years one of the chief aims of the Great Trek into the far north had finally been realized, but the Transvaal Trekkers were still disunited even as far as the Convention, which was a consequence of Pretorius's initiative, was concerned, because of their ineffective administration and private quarrels. Potgieter and his followers only accepted the Convention some time after it had been concluded.

British military and financial commitments in southern Africa had increased so much during these years that Sir Harry Smith was in disfavour and in January, 1852, was recalled to Britain. The new High Commissioner, Cathcart, was ordered to give precedence to ending the Cape Eastern Frontier War; by the end of 1852 he had done much towards achieving this purpose. However, when he attempted to attack Moshesh with his force of 2,500 regular troops, he was defeated at Berea Mountain on 20 December, 1852. This setback virtually sealed the fate of Smith's sovereignty, particularly since Britain's commitments in Europe were increasing. Cathcart then proposed that a British commissioner should be sent to the Sovereignty to investigate the possibility of establishing a Trekker buffer state in that territory; the alternative was for 2,000 additional troops to be sent to Transorangia. In March, 1853, the Imperial government informed Cathcart that it accepted his first proposal.

In the meantime, Hendrik Potgieter, after being reconciled to Andries Pretorius, had died on the Day of the Covenant, 1852; about seven months later Pretorius, the last of the great Voortrekker leaders, died at the age of fifty-five. New leaders, among whom were sons of these men, were to come to the fore to try to solve the problems of the republicans.

In the midst of considerable tension among the heterogenous groups in the Sovereignty, the special commissioner, Sir George Clerk, started drafting a measure to grant independence to the territory. Many English-speaking property owners, traders and professional men strongly opposed this step. As early as June, 1850, they had established a weekly newspaper called *The Friend of the Sovereignty*. Church and missionary circles and Trekboer loyalists also opposed this move. Clerk nevertheless forced the issue and on 23 February, 1854, the Bloemfontein Convention was signed. For the first time the British flag was withdrawn from a territory in southern Africa which Britain had annexed and British subjects, under protest, were deprived of British citizenship. In this way the second Trekker republic was established. The Bloemfontein Convention was modelled along the same lines as the Sand River Convention, but it was more revolutionary and defined boundaries and other matters more precisely. Britain repudiated her various treaties with non-White chiefs in Transorangia (see Chapter 12). In this manner all republicans in the interior north of the Orange and west of the Drakensberg were accepted and supported by Britain as her allies against the indigenous races. The Bloemfontein Convention brought the Great Trek, after twenty years, to its logical conclusion.

The significance of the Great Trek

The Voortrekkers, who had already been honoured with this title, had apparently realized the basic aims of the Great Trek by 1854. After a twenty year struggle for official constitutional recognition their former government had now eventually allowed them to give up their British citizenship. They could now rule themselves according to their own lights: to the Voortrekkers this primarily meant that they could determine their own relations with the non-Whites. There was no restriction on their labour legislation, except that they might not practise slavery; consequently they could ensure that they had an adequate supply of cheap non-White labourers. The availability of much cheap land had already been ensured and there were many more millions of morgen lying fallow to the north. The most democratic states yet known in southern Africa were founded by the Voortrekkers and they were to serve as stimulus to constitutional demands of southern colonists which were still under British control. The Great Trek which had originated peacefully and which had developed into an armed rebellion, had succeeded in its third phase. The Voortrekkers were accepted and supported as allies against the indigenous forces of black Africa.

The eighteenth century democratic concepts of the Cape Afrikaner and the new national and religious traditions acquired by him in Natal were to provide the basis for his new life in his own republics during the late nineteenth century. Although many of the Cape and Natal Afrikaners remained loyal to the British Crown, and were to be anglicized in language, culture and customs, they were usually still very much aware of the British attitude to their republican fellow Afrikaners in the interior. There was a profound, mutual interaction in constitutional, social, cultural and economic spheres between Afrikaner British subjects in the coastal colonies and the Afrikaner republicans on the Highveld and this was to remain a constant feature of South African life. Many British subjects, such as J. H. Brand, T. F. Burgers and J. C. Smuts, were to play significant parts in the development of the republics throughout the late nineteenth century. There was an almost chronic shortage of political leaders among the approximately 20,000 White Transvaalers and 15,000 White Free Staters who were nearly all farmers. These men had to carry their early experiments a stage further and learn to govern themselves. They were also culturally backward and socially isolated. For some time, too, the financial position was to remain desperate, largely because the chief means of subsistence, cattle-farming and agriculture, were so primitive. It was to be some time before they would benefit from the Industrial Revolution, the effects of which had already begun to be felt in the Cape Colony.

On closer examination, however, it will become apparent that the Voortrekkers did not entirely succeed in achieving all their aims. They did not have a sufficiently numerous population to back them, because not nearly enough persons had been persuaded to trek from the sparsely populated Cape eastern frontier districts; consequently, only a few strong settlements could be founded further north. All the Trekker territories remained thinly populated: no Trekkers settled in the Trans-Limpopo area or in present-day South-West Africa. From the point of view of the white man there were almost unlimited prospects of expansion in South Africa during the second quarter of the nineteenth century. Because of their lack of numbers, the Afrikaners were unable to take advantage of these opportunities at a time when they were otherwise able to act at will.

The British government lost a great opportunity of retaining a firm control over southern Africa. The constitutional differences and the widely divergent non-White policies of the various South African states were later to cause the British authorities much embarrassment. The Great Trek it is true, encouraged economic progress; it resulted in the promotion of sheep-farming, in the opening up of great new markets which laid the foundations for future economic

154

advancement, and in the gradual development of maritime activity along the south-eastern coasts of Africa. At the same time the periodic economic rivalries between the two coastal colonies and the two interior republics, adversely affected the whole of southern Africa. Furthermore, although the British had relaxed their control over the Voortrekkers, the Afrikaners had still not obtained their own port, the key to true independence. It was therefore still possible for Britain to exert pressure on the interior of southern Africa whenever she wished to do so. Towards the end of the century, the Voortrekkers and their republican heirs once more lost their independence and were subjected once again to British rule.

The various indigenous tribes of the interior had been only temporarily subjugated by the guns, horses, ox-wagons, better organisation and Calvinistic determination of the Voortrekkers. Apart from the Matabele, the Bantu had nowhere been defeated decisively. The Zulus, for example, with better leaders and guns were once again to resist white control long before the end of the century. The Bantu were now confronting the Whites across many more and much longer frontiers. The fifty year old Xhosa-Boer frontier situation was multiplied many times over throughout south-east Africa. Furthermore, there were tens of thousands of non-Whites permanently settled among Whites in Trekker territories.

Most long-term results of the Great Trek must be sought not in the nineteenth but in the twentieth century. The full significance of this Afrikaner movement can still not be properly estimated. While the Bantu migrations of the early nineteenth century undoubtedly dwarfed the Great Trek as far as sheer numbers were concerned, the fundamental significance of the Trek – according to our present interpretation – was far greater. The white Great Trek settled the regions depopulated by the black Great Trek and in so doing crowned the white movement with a reasonable measure of success. By the time of the conventions the way had been prepared for the inception of the Republic of South Africa which, more than a century later, was to come into being as the eventual realization of an early nineteenth century republican ideal.

In the sixties of the twentieth century it is abundantly clear that the Afrikaans-speaking South African, with his republican constitution, his political leadership, his unique non-White policy and his national and religious traditions, is greatly indebted to the period of the Great Trek, his first heroic epoch. And it is at least as highly important that it was also during this period that the Afrikaner became seriously estranged from his main white ally in a black continent, the English-speaking South African. For more than a century this estrangement was to remain a constant fundamental factor of South African history. Britain's annexation of the Trekker republics half a century after the Conventions had been signed was accompanied by an unprecedented white death-toll which was to bring the deep-seated and fierce Afrikaans-English enmity to the surface again.

In conclusion the Great Trek must also be seen as the earliest seizure of power in South African history by a white group acting on their own initiative. Beginning in the middle thirties, developing in the late thirties and early forties and concluding in the mid-fifties of the nineteenth century, the Great Trek enabled the Voortrekkers to a large extent to free themselves from European control. Seen in this light, the Great Trek is unique in at least one aspect: it has been the only successful rebellion in the history of South Africa.

10. The Cape Colony, 1853-1902

Towards the middle of the nineteenth century the Cape Colony was still, despite the emigration of thousands of Voortrekkers, by far the leading state in the south of Africa, but in constitutional, administrative, political, economic, cultural and educational fields the Cape was still an undeveloped crown colony. This chapter outlines the Cape's main line of development in the second half of the nineteenth century, and also attempts to illuminate various relations between the Cape Colony and the northern states.

Constitutional and political development

The Legislative Council which Sir Benjamin D'Urban instituted at the Cape in 1834 functioned up to 1853 in spite of public opposition. Although the citizens began to agitate for a more representative form of government shortly after the establishment of this Council, the British government, for various reasons, was not prepared to accede to their requests. But from 1846 onwards various factors produced a more sympathetic British attitude towards self-government and Sir Harry Smith was asked for a report on self-government at the Cape Colony. He entrusted the task to William Porter, Attorney-General at the time, who drew up various proposals with the co-operation of the Colony's judges. By March, 1848, these had been sent to England. After studying the proposals, the Queen, in 1850, issued letters patent to the Cape Legislative Council authorizing it to go into the matter more thoroughly.

Because of the British decision to use the Cape as a penal settlement, feelings rose to such a pitch in 1849 that most of the nominated citizen members of the Legislative Council resigned. The leading spirit of the Anti-Convict Movement in Cape Town was John Fairbairn, but English and Afrikaans-speaking people together protested against the proposed disembarkation of the *Neptune's* 282 undesirable immigrants. Various people resigned from public bodies and boycott movements were begun. There was even intimidation and assault, and the new members ("popular members") of the Legislative Council resigned in turn. Early in 1850 circumstances forced the *Neptune* to sail for Tasmania. This constitutional crisis showed without a doubt that the Colony was capable of expressing a strong public opinion and that the two white population groups could act in concert.

A draft constitution could now be drawn up by the Legislative Council, but members of the *ad hoc* committee quarrelled so much that finally Porter prepared this draft as well. The Eighth Frontier War (1850 – 1853) further delayed the matter, and the revised "Cape of Good Hope Constitution Ordinance" was only sent to London in December, 1852. It went in spite of agitation by the

Eastern Province members, under the leadership of Godlonton, who wanted a separate government. Because of various governmental upheavals in England the ordinance was only ratified about March, 1853, after the statutory deletion of the franchise qualifications to which there were objections. The British Government in accordance with Ordinance No. 50, would have no racial discrimination. At that time the total population of the Cape was estimated at 350,000 and although the non-Whites were by far in the majority, few of them would have qualified for the franchise.

The new constitution took effect on 1 July, 1853, and apart from a few important revisions, remained the constitution of the Cape Colony up to 1910. According to this constitution, the Legislative Council consisted of the Chief Justice as President and fifteen elected members, eight of whom had to be from the Western Province. The members, elected for ten years, had to be enfranchized citizens at least thirty years of age and in possession of unencumbered property worth £2,000 or immovable and/or movable property to the value of £4,000. The Council held its sessions in the Supreme Court building until the present Parliament building was opened in 1885.

The Legislative Assembly consisted of forty-six elected members, who were elected for five years. Any franchized voter in the twenty-two constituencies could stand for election. The Assembly had to meet at least once a year at a place determined by the Governor. (Once, in 1864, it even met at Grahamstown when Wodehouse was trying to curry favour with the Eastern Province group.) According to Art. 89 English would be the official language of Parliament and Dutch-speaking people were thus excluded from the debates. Any male British subject over twenty-one, provided he had not been found guilty of specified crimes, could vote if he lived in a building worth £25 or earned over £50 per annum.

The legislative competence of the houses was identical, but financial measures could only be introduced by the Governor in the lower house. The Governor also had other extensive powers: in fact, legislation was largely subject to his pleasure. The constitution did not provide for responsible ministers. The chief officials who were nominated by the Colonial Secretary attended the sessions as heads of departments. They had no vote and were responsible only to the Governor. It would therefore be merely a matter of time before there would be clashes between the executive and legislative authorities in this "representative government". That the first years saw no serious conflict must be ascribed mainly to the improvement in economic conditions and the tact of Sir George Grey.

There were no parties during the first parliamentary election, but the Eastern Province group advocated separation, changing the capital to Grahamstown and revising the franchise qualifications. To the first parliamentary sessions – held in a Freemasons Hall in Parliament Street up to 1885 – must be credited among other things the excellent Divisional Council law which remained in force with few revisions up to 1889, the jury system for civil matters, and the "voluntary principle"[1] which was brought up in Parliament for the first time by the liberal group under the leadership of Saul Solomon.

The most contentious matter of the fifties was the old one of the partition of the Colony into the eastern and western provinces. The appointment in 1836 of a Lieutenant-Governor for the Eastern Province did not help matters, since this official had limited authority only. The Eastern group, under the leadership of an influential publisher, Robert Godlonton, feared domination by the "Afrikaner" majority of the Western Province, and did not support self-government for the Cape. On the other hand, the Eastern Province was so sparsely populated, so poor and so preoccupied with military matters that Saul Solomon's motion for keeping the Cape Colony an undivided colony was readily accepted by all.

The period during which Sir Philip Wodehouse was governor at the Cape (1862 – 1870) was characterized by his tactlessness, autocratic and high-handed actions, hostility to any movement for separation of the Eastern from the Western Province and incredible constitutional clashes. To all these sources of friction must be added a trade depression, viticultural diseases, droughts, a world-wide economic recession and increased taxes for the estimated 181,000 Whites in the Colony.

Wodehouse, who had been requested by the British government to effect federation of all South African states under a strong federal government, had at the beginning of his term of office an unfortunate first parliamentary session. With a view to decreasing British defence expenditure – which had passed the £3 million mark in 1850 – and to cutting the Free State off from the sea, Wodehouse advocated the incorporation of the economically dependent British Kaffraria into the Cape Colony. Because of its increasing deficits, the Cape parliament voted against the proposal, and this resulted in an exasperating constitutional deadlock. Molteno, Saul Solomon and others demanded that responsible government should be introduced at the Cape before contentious incorporations were debated. But three years later the imperturbable Wodehouse got his way when, in 1865, the British Government authorised him by means of the "Kaffrarian Annexation Act" to incorporate British Kaffraria in the Cape with or without the permission of the protesting Cape parliament. Although Wodehouse's move was followed by a motion of no confidence, British Kaffraria became an integral part of the Cape Colony in April, 1866. The Legislative Council was enlarged to twenty-one members, and the Lower House to sixty-six.

Wodehouse's policy and actions not only antagonised all factions in the Cape Assembly – the Separatists, the Westerners, the Kaffrarians and the self-government group – but also extra-territorial governments. For example, the Free State was alienated by the annexation of Basutoland (1868) just when the Boers wanted to punish Moshesh for alleged aggression. Wodehouse firmly believed

---

1. "Voluntaryism" implied the abolition of state aid to churches. The liberal group brought the matter up in Parliament almost annually until it was accepted in 1875. See *Cambridge History of the British Empire*, Vol. VIII, 1963, pp. 372, (*n*.4), 388.

that only the Imperial government could keep the peace in South Africa and that there should be no hesitation in repudiating the conventions with the two Republics if this would promote British policy.

Actually, it was financial measures and Wodehouse's zealous attempts to substitute an autocratic form of government for the constitution which produced the worst clashes. As a result of the agricultural and economic depressions of the sixties, the Cape treasury in 1866 already showed a deficit of £100,000 and parliament had to insist on austerity measures. The Assembly would have no part in proposed increased taxes on wine and wool.

The next year promised to be better, but despite good crops and the discovery of diamonds, and the fact that Britain had abandoned her intention of saddling the colonists with defence matters, new clashes could not be avoided. Consequently the determined Governor proposed an amendment of the constitution which would give him a subservient one-chamber parliament (without "responsible government"), a proposal which was rejected in the Assembly by a large majority.

The new parliament of 1869 was even more strongly opposed to Wodehouse's policies and further constitutional clashes, and even a motion of no confidence, followed. Parliament was therefore dissolved. The new election was fought on constitutional questions, which is why the 1870 parliament summarily rejected the Governor's constitutional amendments and tax proposals, notwithstanding the national debts already having reached £1,420,000. Once again a constitutional stalemate was reached between executive and legislative powers and it became clear that the 1853 constitution would never be able to function under Wodehouse. Only "responsible government" with parliamentary authority could end the constitutional crises, but the colonists themselves were sharply divided on the matter. Granville, the British Colonial Secretary, had meanwhile, however, shown quite clearly that the colonists would have to decide finally whether they wanted self-government or an imposed autocratic government.

As a result of the chronic constitutional deadlock, Wodehouse was replaced in 1870 by Sir Henry Barkly, who was a passionate advocate of self-government. He believed with the Imperial government, that "responsible government" would spare the British taxpayer and would simultaneously be a basis for the consolidation of all the South African states. It goes without saying that Molteno's 1871 motion for self-government – similar to his motion of 1860 – had the Governor's approval and blessing. Although the motion was rejected in the Upper House by three votes, the industrious Molteno attained his objective the following year – despite strong opposition from Godlonton's separatists – when the Upper House, after various political manoeuvres, approved his motion by one vote. At that time the Cape, thanks to diamonds, wool and ostrich feathers, was experiencing a period of economic prosperity. Furthermore, the opening of the Suez Canal made the Cape less important to Britain, and the Colonial Office was no longer quite so opposed to recommending self-government for the Cape.

With the passing of *"The Constitution Ordinance Amendment Act, 1872"* the Cape's constitutional struggle ended. Because of constitutional amendments concerning salaried appointments under the Crown, the executive thereafter were all members of one of the two houses and responsible to the Assembly. As soon as the executive forfeited the confidence of parliament, they had to resign.

On 1 December, 1872, the first "responsible" cabinet was formed, with J. C. Molteno, "the lion of Beaufort" as Prime Minister, Dr. H. White as Treasurer, J. H. de Villiers as Attorney-General, C. A. Smith as Commissioner of Crown Lands and Public Works and C. Brownlee, later the author of the Transkei native policy, as Secretary of Native Affairs. In this way the British cabinet system was introduced into the Cape, and the Cape Colony achieved complete colonial self-government, that is, parliamentary government with ministerial responsibility.

The Governor's position was radically altered. As representative of the British government, he now had to execute his duties on the advice and with the approval of the local ministry. As High Commissioner he still, of course, possessed extensive powers in extra-territorial areas.

In future the Colony would naturally also be responsible for its own defence and for the maintenance of domestic peace. Furthermore, the new constitution eliminated the Separatist movement, particularly after the constitutional amendments of 1874 when the redelimitation of constituencies ended the unnatural political grouping. On the recommendation of Justice J. H. de Villiers, the Legislative Council after 1874 consisted of twenty-one elected members, who were elected for seven years, three for each of the seven circles into which the Colony had been divided.

Although the Cape Colony, for various reasons, had to wait nearly twenty years for responsible government, the new constitution encouraged a greater political maturity and created a favourable climate for the federation of Southern Africa which had become such a great necessity. This matter of federation was unfortunately bungled a few years later by the arrogance and tactlessness of Lord Carnarvon. The Cape government's independent and wise view on the matter of limiting the Imperial factor in Southern Africa afforded an opportunity for approaching the problems of this territory on a national basis. For the Transkei territories, which by 1894 had all been incorporated in the Cape Colony, the constitution was important because it made it possible for the Colony to evolve a native policy of differentiation without Imperial interference. The new constitution also corrected the Colony's financial policy, since a "responsible" cabinet could henceforth devote its attention on a "national" basis to the complex matters of diamonds, communications, customs, etc. Finally, the constitution, true to the spirit of self-government, caused political parties to appear which were to leave their mark on the development of the Cape Colony.

The Afrikaans-speaking people, who by 1872 made up nearly three-quarters of the White population, supplied only about one-third of the parliamentary representatives. Britain's policy of anglicization since 1806 had achieved its objective in the fields of language, education and religion. Government, administration of justice and commerce had become completely English but the rural

161

Afrikaner, in spite of losing his interest in the public affairs of the country, continued to retain his identity. The part played by the Imperial government in South Africa, particularly in such matters as the incorporation of the diamond fields and its policy towards the two Republics, was however, to nurture an Afrikaner national consciousness and reawaken the political interest of the Cape Afrikaners.

The "Genootskap van Regte Afrikaners" (Association of True Afrikaners) was established in Paarl in 1875. Under the influence of this society, whose aims were "om te staan ver ons taal, ons nasie en ons land"[2], "Di Afrikaanse Patriot" – the first Afrikaans newspaper – was founded in 1876. It was this newspaper which, under the leadership of the Rev. S. J. du Toit of Paarl, advocated the foundation of the Afrikaner Bond in 1879 after the British annexation of the Transvaal. This body was to play an important role in the Cape political groupings up to the end of the century.

The foundation of the Bond was preceded by the establishment of various agricultural societies. These societies wanted not only to nurture a feeling of economic solidarity among the Cape Afrikaners, but also to concern themselves with cultural matters, education, the federation of South African states and the efforts to get Dutch accepted as the second official language in parliament and in the schools. The economic aspects of the agricultural societies were later united by J. H. Hofmeyr (Onze Jan) – chiefly as a result of the unpopular Customs Act (1878) – into the strong "Zuidafrikaansche Boeren Beschermings Vereeniging" which did in fact also later have political aims.

In the field of journalism there were also movements to promote the Afrikaner cause: "De Zuid-Afrikaan", Hofmeyr's paper, and "Het Zuid-Afrikaansch Tijdschrift" which were established to promote Dutch, did much to inform the Afrikaner and develop his point of view.

Hofmeyr, who to begin with did not support the Afrikaner Bond, did feel, however, that the Afrikaners' political aspirations should somehow be coordinated so that they could work towards "the salvation of a united South Africa".[3] After the first Anglo-Boer War the Bond grew rapidly, particularly after the merging of the Bond and the "Beschermingsvereenigings" between 1882 and 1883, and Afrikaners from the Cape to the Limpopo drew together to pursue the ideal of a united South Africa, political and social. There is no doubt that the powerful Bond, with its slogan: "Afrika voor de Afrikaners" and Hofmeyr's strong leadership, nurtured Afrikaner nationalism and solidarity. The effects began to be felt in 1882, when Hofmeyr, with the help of the Scanlen ministry, succeeded in getting Dutch recognized as the second official language in Parliament. Indeed, after 1884, the Bond, because of its strong representation in the Assembly, became very powerful. From this time on matters such as protective tariffs for the farming community, the excise on brandy, the Bantu

2. G. Dekker: *Afrikaanse Literatuurgeskiedenis* (Cape Town, 1961), p. 14.
3. Quoted by A. J. H. Van der Walt and others: *Geskiedenis van Suid-Afrika*, II (Cape Town, 1955), p. 639 (Translated).

franchise and the "independence" of the Cape Colony could be arranged to the satisfaction of the Afrikaners.

In the early eighties Cecil John Rhodes, the imperial and economic col entered the Cape political arena (see Chapter 14). His organizational abilit financial successes on the diamond fields, caused him to found the De Company, which merged with other companies, in 1888, to form the *De Beers Consolidated Mines, Ltd.*, a gigantic organization, which would later, together with "The Consolidated Gold Fields of South Africa", make Rhodes the richest and most influential man in South Africa.

In 1881 Rhodes became the Barkly West representative in the Cape Parliament. In order to realise his ideals, which involved extending the British Empire over the whole of Africa and federating the Southern African states, he needed the support of the Afrikaner Bond. He gradually became intimate with Hofmeyr, particularly after the latter had spoken out against republicanism and positively affirmed his loyalty to the British Crown. At that time Hofmeyr wanted at all costs to eliminate the Imperial factor in South Africa, i.e. the power of the British Government to interfere in South African affairs to the embarrassment of a self-governing colony. Rhodes maintained diplomatically, yet categorically, that this attitude reflected his own purposes. In this way he eventually misled many Afrikaners.

Because of the Transvaal's interest in the internal affairs of Bechuanaland in the years 1882 and 1883, two small republics – Stellaland and Goschen – were established on the so-called western border of the Transvaal Republic. Rhodes, who wanted to keep this "Suez Canal" to the territories north of the Limpopo open for Imperial use, insisted in the Cape parliament that the Cape should interfere in this matter. This "missionary road" he described as vital to the Cape's commercial interests, particularly because of the interest of the Transvaal (and Germany) in the same territory. The Cape and the Afrikaner Bond were not particularly interested in this matter and vacillated so much that Rhodes insisted on Imperial intervention. This meant that the Transvaal was excluded from the western territory. Thus, Rhodes's diplomacy and political manoeuvering and General Warren's show of power with 4,000 troops outwitted Kruger, and a British protectorate was proclaimed over Bechuanaland.[4] Rhodes's way to the north was safe and the Free State was almost surrounded by British territory, a situation through which Rhodes later hoped to force Imperial federation on the Free State and the other South African states.

It is significant that Rhodes, despite his activities in Bechuanaland which had involved Afrikaners, did not alienate his influential Afrikaner Bond friends. He pointed out that he had safeguarded the Cape Colony's trade interests and he also impressed them with his dream of a united South Africa. He asserted that the Cape Colony, because of its position, would play a leading role in any such future federation. Rhodes subsequently supported the Bond increasingly in important matters such as the use of Dutch in the courts and the civil service,

4. The southern part of Bechuanaland was only incorporated in the Cape Colony in 1895.

religious instruction in the schools, the repeal of the excise duties and the establishment of protective import tariffs; in fact, Rhodes identified himself to such an extent with the aspirations of the Afrikaner Bond that he was soon nicknamed "the young burgher".

The Rhodes-Hofmeyr alliance reached its climax after the general election of 1888. In 1890 when Rhodes became premier with the support of the Afrikaner Bond, after the fall of the Sprigg cabinet, he declared that he would devote himself to "South African politics" only. With the help of Hofmeyr and the Bond, Rhodes – the personification of financial power – had now been made a statesman and had achieved financial and political power of a kind previously unknown in South African politics. An informal and approachable Imperialist, Rhodes associated with Afrikaners on easy terms and continued to promote Afrikaner interests. He was no negrophil and helped pass the Franchise Act of 1892, which raised the qualifications for voting rights, and safeguarded the white voter in the Cape Colony. He also greatly helped with the Scab Act (1894). Although this law aimed at protecting the chief source of prosperity of most Afrikaners, it was for many years unpopular in rural areas. In agriculture Rhodes assiduously fostered the interests of the farming community; he obtained the services of experts and introduced improvements at the Cape, as evidenced by the importation of Arab horses and Angora goats.

Understandably Rhodes's confidence increased as his financial and political influence grew. After his Bechuanaland success, he contemplated acquiring Matabeleland, the "balance of Africa", as the next step towards the achievement of an "Africa British from Cape to Cairo". Through his mediation the Moffat Treaty of 1888, which excluded all the foreign powers from control in Matabeleland, was signed with Lobengula. However, the Transvaal had the previous year already signed a similar treaty with the chief. Rhodes's acquisition of the profitable Rudd concession for mineral development was soon followed, in 1889, by the floating of the British South Africa Company. This made inevitable the British occupation of Matabeleland and Mashonaland in the next year (see Chapters 13 and 14).

The British moves in the lands north of the Limpopo thwarted Kruger's plans for northward expansion and isolated the Transvaal yet further. At the same time, Rhodes's action considerably widened the rift between the Transvaal and the Cape Colony, although the Cape Afrikaners were not enthusiasitc about Rhodes's plans for expansion and felt the Transvaal had been treated unjustly. Tactfully Rhodes explained, among other things, that as a "Cape colonist", he merely wished to eliminate the Imperial factor. To prove his good faith, he offered Afrikaners an interest in the new territory; some even took shares in the British South African Company which was founded to administer and develop the territory. The alliance between Rhodes and Hofmeyr therefore continued despite the doubts of some Afrikaners.

With the Swaziland Convention (1890), which destroyed Kruger's plans for a road to the sea and about which Hofmeyr adopted an anti-Transvaal attitude, the rift between the Cape and the Transvaal widened, and the Afrikaners' disapproval and criticism of the Rhodes-Hofmeyr alliance grew apace. Even the harmony within the Rhodes cabinet which had prevailed since 1893, began to wane. Hofmeyr, the hope of Afrikanerdom, was bitterly and increasingly attacked. He was accused of treason since he seemed to connive at Rhodes's imperialist aspirations. At the same time, Rhodes had been growing more and more arrogant and impatient of any opposition, particularly after his efforts to buy Delagoa Bay had finally failed in 1894.

Before long the soaring ambitions of Rhodes brought him a staggering setback. Possibly he took the support of Hofmeyr and the Bond too much for granted. The Bond had once again supported him in the question of the Transvaal drifts (1895), and this possibly encouraged him to carry the "divide and rule" tactics, by which he attempted to implement his Imperial aspirations and plans for federation too far by a coup de main (see Chapter 14).

The sensational Jameson Raid in December, 1895, was an attempt of the Rhodesian police under the leadership of Leander Starr Jameson to occupy Johannesburg in concert with an Uitlander insurrection organized by the Reform Committee. The raiders hoped to capture the Pretoria arsenal and establish a provisional government so that the British High Commissioner could force Kruger to make large concessions to the Uitlanders. Today there is no longer any doubt about Rhodes's moral and financial complicity in the raid, or about the foreknowledge of the British government and the High Commissioner in Cape Town concerning this matter.[5] Hofmeyr and the disillusioned Bond, who viewed the treacherous raid as an attack on all Afrikanerdom rapidly became alienated from the English-speaking population of the Cape. The latter also closed their ranks by establishing the South African League which aimed at perpetuating British authority in South Africa. The Jameson Raid drew the Afrikaners closer together and helped formulate their ideals as never before. The Afrikaners' prestige in Europe also increased, as evidenced by the enthusiastic congratulatory telegram sent to Kruger by the German emperor after the victory over Jameson's intruders.

After excitement about the Raid had subsided somewhat Rhodes, who had resigned as premier, regained some of the ground he had lost and mercilessly condemned his former Bond allies ("my tools"). He still believed in the ultimate unification of South African states, but now he was convinced that it could be effected only through direct intervention by the Imperial Factor. Kruger's policies, according to Rhodes were too conservative and isolationist. In 1897, Chamberlain, an accomplice in the Raid, who had in the meantime taken over the Colonial Office in England, sent Sir Alfred Milner as High Commissioner to South Africa with instructions to attend to matters in the Transvaal, that is to say, to work out a reform programme according to a British formula (see Chapter 14).

In the Cape Colony the Sprigg government was weakened because it had

5. See J. G. Lockhart and C. M. Woodhouse: *Rhodes* (London, 1963), pp. 292 – 302, 314, 316 and 319.

lost the support of the Bond without gaining that of the pro-British Progressives. In the second half of 1898 the Sprigg ministry fell, over the intended redelimitation of rural constituencies. In the strenuous election fight which followed, the Bond and the moderate English-speaking people obtained a small working majority, enabling W. P. Schreiner of the Bond to form a government. This political defeat infuriated the South African League, the Cape Imperialists and the Progressives. It was clear that Milner was determined, particularly after his belligerent speech at Graaff-Reinet, to maintain British prestige and authority in South Africa, by force if necessary. The threat of war increased as war mongers and anti-Afrikaans newspapers became vociferous. The Afrikaner Bond at the time was too pacific. Schreiner, who went out of his way to avert disaster, persuaded President Steyn, at a hint from Hofmeyr, to organise a conference of the most important parties in Bloemfontein in May, 1899. Unfortunately the conference, because of Milner's stubbornness about the franchise question, had no positive result. Subsequent attempts by Schreiner, Hofmeyr and the Free State also came to nothing because Milner believed that the Cape government was not his reliable ally, but was trying to save the Transvaal from a thorny position.

Schreiner now attempted to hold the Colony on a middle course, whereupon Milner summarily ordered him to stop supplying arms to the Transvaal. Even after the outbreak of war in October, 1899, Schreiner tried to limit the Cape to a defensive role, hoping to avoid a general rebellion among the Cape Afrikaners. At the same time he avoided constitutional clashes with Milner.

Shortly after the outbreak of war, various districts in the Northern Cape were occupied by Free State Republicans, and many Colonials joined the Republicans. When the Boer raiders had to withdraw in 1900 to defend the Republics, the first rebellion in the Northern Cape came to an end. Hundreds of rebels were imprisoned to await trial, while in some cases property was confiscated and destroyed.

The Schreiner government was in an unenviable position: on the one hand it enjoyed the trust and support of Afrikaans-speaking people, on the other it had to co-operate in Milner's war effort. The cabinet, like the people, was divided about the part the Cape should play in this effort, but the long-awaited division came only in June, 1900, on the question of amnesty for the Cape rebels. Schreiner, who did not fully support the war and who was deeply concerned about the role the Imperial government was beginning to play in Cape politics, resigned in June, 1900, rather than possibly see the constitution which had been obtained at such cost, abrogated by Britain. However, the new Sprigg ministry acted with extreme moderation both in and outside parliament as a result of the actions of the Schreiner group. The members of this group were known as the "Adullamites".

Outside Parliament matters had also reached a boiling point. Afrikaners became feverishly active. They organised war relief funds, national congresses, vigilance committees, deputations and petitions and they even tried to effect conciliation and peace.

It has been said that the Worcester Congress of the Afrikaner Bond (December, 1900), which was attended by thousands of Afrikaners, instigated the second Republican raid of December, 1900, under the leadership of Hertzog, Kritzinger and De Wet. This raid, launched to relieve the pressure on the Republics and to stifle the cry of "the war is over" in England, was the great hope of the Republics. At one stage it was even believed that the independence of the Republic would be determined in the Cape!

In spite of the strict enforcement of martial law in the Cape many Colonials joined the Republican raiders. The Sprigg ministry retaliated by forming a defence force of town guards and "District Mounted Troops" of limited fighting ability. By the second half of 1901 almost the whole of the North-West had risen in rebellion and considerably complicated matters for General French who was responsible for British military operations against raiders and rebels; particularly disturbing for him was General Smuts's projected mass attack on the Western Province (see Chapter 15).

As a result of the generally chaotic conditions, the Cape Parliament, after its sitting in 1900, did not meet again until August, 1902. This was after repeated attempts had been made, mainly by Milner, to suspend the Constitution. The Suspensionists, whose plans were finally scotched by the Imperial Conference in London (1902), believed that the suspension of the Constitution would enable the Imperial government to break the powers of the Bond, dispose of the rebels to its satisfaction, effect conciliation and enforce federation.

The results of the war were not as devastating for the Cape as for the two Republics. The armies did not follow a "scorched earth" policy in the Cape, but even so there was considerable material loss in some districts. Post-war depression hit the Cape particularly hard and there was very slow moral and material rehabilitation. The war emphasized the alienation of Afrikaans and English-speaking people and helped produce the distasteful racial political groupings of the twentieth century.

Native policy

Chapter 9 explains how industrious philanthropists and liberals in Britain disrupted Sir Benjamin D'Urban's plans for the Eastern Frontier which had been acceptable to the Cape colonists, and so had caused such dissatisfaction among the border farmers that the "flower of the eastern border" had trekked north. The philanthropic policy, known as the Glenelg Treaty System, which was followed from 1836 to 1846 and which was intended to pacify native tribes with concessions and treaties and to bring them into a British sphere of influence, offered no permanent solution to border problems. The increasing raids from Kaffirland continued and made conditions untenable for the frontier farmers. Both Sir George Napier and his successor, Sir Peregrine Maitland, were forced drastically to revise the treaties with the native chiefs so that punitive expeditions could act with more authority, but conditions continued unsafe on the Eastern Frontier in the forties. A series of border incidents paved the way for the long and expensive War of the Axe (1846 – 1848), a war which was the direct result of the dubious Glenelg System.

Sir Harry Smith (1847 – 1852), the new governor and High Commissioner of the Cape, (the latter being a new office which empowered him to act in extra-territorial matters as well) was chosen by Lord Grey, British Minister of the Colonies, to promote his policy of assimilation and civilization at the Cape Colony. This policy, which from 1846 was a reaction to philanthropism, aimed to bring independent native tribes under British protection and white guardianship in order to civilize and detribalize them.

Smith's border measures after the Seventh Frontier War clearly indicated that the old policy of territorial separation had ended. The "conquered territory", called Victoria East, was annexed to the Cape Colony, and the northern part, under the White magistracy of Calderwood, was given to the loyal Fingos. British Kaffraria, the former "province of Queen Adelaide", would be administered as a separate British Crown Colony. The treaty system was ended dramatically by the new "Inkosi Inkulu". The native tribal chiefs were to be assisted by magistrates, garrisons and native police. The goodwill and co-operation of White missionaries were obtained and they returned to the badly damaged mission stations to continue their work.

Smith's arbitrary measures on the border, particularly his discouragement of tribal traditions such as the lobola system, his undermining of the chiefs' and witch-doctors' authority, his new system of land tenure and his institution of a tax system, were used by agitators such as Unlanjeni to foment further trouble in the Ciskei. When the fractious Sandile, chief of the Gaikas, was replaced by a White magistrate (Brownlee), armed violence erupted. Thousands of Gaikas, Tembus and Kat River Hottentots banded together and streamed across the border, leaving havoc in their wake. Among other things, three of Smith's military settlements for ex-servicemen on the Tyumie River were barbarously destroyed on Christmas Day, 1850.

This Eighth Frontier War (1850 – 1853) began disastrously for Smith, who at the time was occupied with important Free State matters. At one stage the burgher commando system collapsed and reinforcements from Britain were late. Despite reverses and losses such as that of the *Birkenhead* with 437 soldiers in February, 1852, on Danger Point, Smith had, by March, 1852, gained control of the situation by adopting a policy of destruction. His successor, the veteran Cathcart, nevertheless found it necessary to reorganize the whole defence force, establish a police unit and mobilize the burgher commandos in order to drive the natives out of the Amatola strongholds. By the beginning of 1853, Kreli's country, the Transkei, was totally devastated. Ten thousand head of cattle had been taken and the £2 million war was over.

Cathcart's border measures were chiefly military, defensive and negative. The confiscated territory of the Tembus and the rebellious Kat River Hottentots was given to Whites and loyal Fingos. The policy was thus one of changing borders, displacing tribes and locating Whites and loyal Natives in previously hostile areas. Cathcart wished, in fact, to create a military buffer state of White settlers, Hottentots and loyal natives between the Cape Colony and British Kaffraria in Victoria East and extend it towards Queenstown and the Amatola Mountains. British Kaffraria would still be administered as a native reserve by Xhosa and Tembu tribal chiefs under the strict supervision of White magistrates. Kingwilliamstown always housed a strong military contingent of soldiers and police to support the Chief Commissioner. Like Smith, Cathcart believed that it was safer to keep native tribes in reserves and then, through indirect government, christianize, civilize and administer them, than to dam them up beyond the new Eastern border, the Kei River. The war, however, had been so expensive that Britain for the moment wanted no further territorial gains; hence the Conventions of 1852 and 1854 which recognized the two Boer buffer states on the Cape's northern borders (see Chapter 9).

By the middle of the nineteenth century, therefore, no solution had yet been found for the Eastern Frontier problem. Colonial Ministers followed each other too rapidly for any kind of continuous policy to be established. Also the various border measures were too related to the military situation to be permanent. The incorporation of native territories between the Fish and Kei Rivers and the settlement of Whites among the natives automatically created new problems.

The next new Cape Governor, Sir George Grey, introduced yet another method of dealing with the Eastern Frontier and the colour problem. Grey, who assumed office in December, 1854, and who had been much praised for his "constructive" approach to the Maori problem in New Zealand, was to apply in South Africa a revised form of this policy. This was expected to provide a positive solution to the South African native problem. Grey aimed at detribalizing, educating and befriending the native. Attempts were made to substitute the quitrent system of land tenure for the native system of communal tribal ownership, while the salaried chieftains were still to be "assisted" by White magistrates. Natives who could not subsist off their land had to help develop their country by building roads, schools and hospitals. In this manner, for example, the industrial and trade schools at Lovedale, and Healdtown were established, as well as hospitals such as the Grey Hospital at Kingwilliamstown; it was hoped they would help to wipe out ignorance, superstititon and witchcraft. The education and instruction of young natives were to follow the so-called "Practical Suggestions" of 8 February, 1847.[6] Improved wages were to hasten the economic integration of the Natives.

British Kaffraria was reserved for the Gaikas as a separate British territory under the personal supervision of the High Commissioner. In order to hasten the commercial, civilizing and assimilation policy a dense mixed population ("partly Europeans, part Natives") was desired on the border, for only through the integration of Black and White, in Grey's opinion, would the natives develop industrious, friendly and civilized communities which could be incorporated into the White cultural, agricultural and economic order.

6. Refer A. E. Du Toit: *The Earliest S.A. Documents on the Education and Civilization of the Bantu* (Communications of the University of S.A., C.47, Pretoria 1963).

The British government, wishing to prevent expensive Eastern border clashes and reduce its financial responsibilities, approved of Grey's civilizing policy and even voted an annual £40,000 to carry it out. This amount was later drastically reduced because of the Crimean War and the Indian Mutiny (1858).

Once again, however, the Eastern Frontier was restless. The presence of Whites, interference with tribal customs, the agitation for lost rights and the demand for more land in over-populated areas unsettled the more primitive Natives. Grey tried to view the problem in broader perspective since the border in the Eastern Cape was the most sensitive sector of the Cape borders. Being a strong advocate of a common native policy for the whole of Southern Africa Grey continually tested the reactions of the northern states to the idea of a federation of South African states.

The unrest on the Cape border would most likely have come to a disastrous head in the course of 1857 if it had not been for an incredible Xhosa national reaction to European civilization, an incident known as the Xhosa Suicide. One of their leaders, Kreli, egged on by Moshesh who wanted attention diverted from his Free State activities, had it bruited about that a girl, Nonquase, and her uncle, Umhlakaza, who was a witchdoctor, had received messages from their ancestral spirits to the effect that if the dissatisfied Xhosas were to destroy all their cattle and provisions, dead heroes, cattle and supplies of grain would appear out of the earth on a specified day, 18 February, 1857, and the White intruders would be blown into the sea. The ringleaders apparently intended so to inflame the imagination of their followers with this fabrication that they would hysterically attack in mass across the colonial border. When the cattle and supplies were destroyed, and the appointed day brought no ancestral abundance great famine and suffering were inevitable. Tens of thousands died, but about 30,000 streamed across the border in search of food and work.

The depopulation of British Kaffraria and the resultant disintegration of the Xhosa gave Grey an unexpected opportunity. The expected war on the Eastern border was averted and Grey's financially impracticable policy saved from total failure: between 1857 and 1859 a few thousand Whites could emigrate to the depopulated areas and thus protect the border, and speed up the economic integration of the Native. In 1857, for example, the Cape parliament voted £40,000 with which nearly 2,300 ex-servicemen from the "British German Legion" were settled at Berlin, Frankfurt, Hamburg and other localities. The scheme failed as an agricultural experiment, mainly because this type of ex-soldier immigrant either left the land or again enlisted for service in India. In addition to a few hundred farmers from the Western and Eastern Provinces, a further 2,300 German immigrants settled in British Kaffraria between 1858 and 1859. They immigrated in consequence of a contract which Grey concluded with the Hamburg firm, Godeffroy & Son, by which it agreed, for £50,000 to induce about 4,000 German farmers to emigrate to South Africa.

Although the British government subsequently stopped Grey's unauthorized immigration schemes, Whites were settled over a wide area as far as East London. The dissatisfied Fingos and Tembus were even moved out of British

Kaffraria across the Kei River to make room for the Whites so that in fact native territory was being expropriated. This resulted in an overflow of Natives into the Ciskei. For example, in 1858, the stubborn Kreli and his followers who obviously could not be assimilated, were driven over the Bashee River as far as Bomvanaland. The Transkei territory between the Kei and Bashee Rivers was kept clear by the police as a British domain and kind of no-man's-land, but after 1864 this supervision ceased for financial reasons. British Kaffraria, which included East London, was governed like a British crown colony after 1860, with a Lieutenant-Governor as its head and magistrates with wide authority over every tribe. In fact, there was "indirect government" for the purely Native area.

The desperate condition of the Free State Griquas at that time gave Grey the chance of solving the Griqua problem and extending British influence yet further. The Griquas under Adam Kok sold their Philippolis territory to the Free State after the Bloemfontein Convention (1854) and thus in effect became stateless. In 1861 Grey allowed them to emigrate to the "no-man's-land" which later became known as Griqualand East, where as "British subjects" they would form a buffer against the troublesome Moshesh and some coastal tribes, and simultaneously further the British policy of assimilation and integration. In their new homeland, where they would have their own constitution, the impoverished Griquas were able to rehabilitate themselves completely before Griqualand East was annexed in 1874.

By the sixties Britain was determined to reduce its Colonial expenses. Not only did she drastically reduce the annual allowance for Grey's Eastern Border policy, but she also put out unmistakable feelers concerning the federation of the self-governing and independent British territories. Such a federation would save administrative costs and reduce British responsibilities. The Colonial Office, however, was not particularly eager to entrust the fate of millions of non-Whites to the Cape Colony, particularly as it was not yet self-governing. For at least a decade Britain vacillated between her desire to economize and her sense of responsibility towards the non-Whites. The necessity for closer co-operation between the South African states which, according to British thinking, would lead to the repudiation of the conventions, was to grow ever more evident, since contradictory policies could not continue indefinitely.

Sir Philip Wodehouse, Grey's successor, inherited a stormy Eastern Frontier. The economic depression and the changed attitude of the British government, compelled Wodehouse to a certain extent to abandon Grey's policy of expansion. Even before the British government ordered the evacuation of the Transkei, Whites were not allowed to buy land there; later, in 1865, Tembus and Fingos were settled there to pacify them by giving them more living space. The undefined borders between the tribes in this area later produced open warfare between the Tembus and the Galekas, so that in 1873, the former gave their territory to the British government. A further departure from Grey's policy was the passing of the Imperial Act in 1865 which, for economic reasons, authorized the incorporation of British Kaffraria into an unwilling Cape Colony.

After 1870 the Imperial agitation for bringing all the native areas in South Africa under a centralized authority attained a new peak. It was for this reason that Sir Henry Barkly so vehemently advocated the annexation of the independent republics. The annexation of the diamond fields in 1871, the later acquisition of native areas and Carnarvon's federation scheme, made it evident that a centralized native policy and economic integration were two of the main motives of the British government.

Sir Bartle Frere, British High Commissioner in southern Africa between 1877 and 1880, endorsed the civilizing and economic integration policies of his precedessors. It was during his period of service that the Cape was expanded further, which led to many native and other areas[7], because of domestic and political matters, being drawn into the Cape Administration by 1894.

This incorporation of native territories into the Cape began as early as 1865 with the integration of British Kaffraria. In 1879, after the Galeka War, Griqualand East, Fingoland and the District of Idutywa were incorporated into the Colony, to be followed by Port St. Johns (1884), British Bechuanaland (1885), Tembuland, Bomvanaland and Galekaland (1885), the Mount Ayliff District (1886) and Pondoland (1894). Within the space of a quarter of a century, therefore, the contact between Whites (missionaires, traders, officials, soldiers and farmers) and non-Whites had grown to such an extent that the assimilation of the Natives according to Grey's policies was an accomplished fact. Segregation had lost its territorial character, and although the traditional social colour bar remained, cultural assimilation and economic integration hastened by the discovery of diamonds and gold progressed rapidly. This accelerated assimilation was, however, to result in a clash of racial ideologies between Afrikaner nationalism and the Cape liberal tradition.

Basutoland warrants particular mention. After the Imperial incorporation of this territory in 1868 it was entrusted to the Cape Colony in 1871 by High Commissioner Barkly, but the internal administration of this "autonomous" mountain territory never really got into its stride. Many Basutos who went to the diamond fields acquired guns and Premier Sprigg, aware that there was considerable anti-White propaganda in the territory was forced to apply the Peace Preservation Act (1878) to compel the Natives to hand in their firearms. This led to a long and drawn-out war, in which the Sprigg ministry appeared in a sorry light. It also caused an unprecedented constitutional crisis which brought the Scanlen ministry into power and confused the Basuto matter even further. As a result Basutoland, at the request of the Cape government, was handed back to Britain in 1884. Thus Britain acquired an "island" in the heart of South Africa which was to create thorny problems for future South African governments.

The denationalization of the Natives, effected by the disruption of territorial,

7. In 1880 Griqualand West was incorporated into the Colony and in 1884 the strategic Walvis Bay followed, after its annexation by Britain in 1878 as a result of internal strife in the vicinity.

political, economic and social barriers, created complex problems. Justice in native areas had to be administered according to the Colony's laws and according to traditional tribal law, and this produced many complications until a native criminal code and civil legal system for the Transkeian Territories could be organized in the last quarter of the century.

The essence of "the Native problem" was the administration of native landed property rights. In this sphere there had been much confusion since the sixties. The Natives found it difficult to accept individual landownership for this undermined the authority of the tribal chief. In accordance with various laws which were promulagated from time to time (e.g. in 1870, 1873, 1876, 1878 and 1879) the Bantu could live on private land as squatters, or on crown land, or in misson reserves where plots were available, or in locations where property ownership was allowed. Various commissions, of which the "Cape Native Laws and Customs Commission" of 1883 was the most important, investigated the highly complex matter of Native residential and property rights. The commissions' recommendations appeared in the Native Location Act of 1884 and the amended Act No. 33 of 1892, which aimed at attaining greater clarity and uniformity and an improved administration.

The well-known Glen Grey Act of 1894 promulgated the subdivision of Native land into property plots held in quitrent tenure in the Glen Grey district and thus implemented the principle of individual property rights. The idea was to reconcile the Native tribal system and the civilized demands of a White community in such a way as to facilitate the detribalization of the Native and at the same time find an economic use for state land. But many of these measures only increased the difficulty of administration, particularly as they clashed with the traditional tribal system of communal ownership.

In order to direct the many policies and to rationalize the administration, the Glen Grey Act of 1894, "a native Bill for Africa", was passed. In the same year the Transkeian Territories Council System – an administrative system for which officials such as Brownlee, Blyth and others should be given credit – was created for the Glen Grey area. According to this system, local government was to be effected in two ways, by subordinate location councils and by district councils. The former were nominated councils of three members who were to supervize matters such as water, grazing and veld fires while the district councils of twelve members under the chairmanship of a magistrate, could impose local taxes for divisional council work, involving such matters as dipping tanks, irrigation works and health services. Gradually the act, in revised form, was applied to all Transkei districts, and by the beginning of the present century the whole of the territory as an administrative unit was being controlled to the natives' advantage. The United General Council of the Transkei Territories or the "Bunga", which was established in 1895, was a council intended to introduce limited self-government and offered the native the opportunity to control his own areas and in his own interest keep in touch with the various government measures. Thus a progressive form of administration took shape in the Transkei that had further possibilities in it for Bantu advancement and betterment.

With the development and incorporation into the Cape of Bantu areas, it was inevitable that the question of native franchise would be raised sooner or later. In 1872, the franchise, subject to certain landed property qualifications was given to all males, irrespective of race or colour; but after 1879 when contact between White and Black had increased, the question of the Native franchise necessitated administrative and political readjustments. The growing "Kaffir Vote" became a cause for anxiety after 1887, when the constituencies of Griqualand East and Tembuland were formed and the Native voters already formed more than 40% of the voting body. The Franchise Act of 1887 and the Franchise and Ballot Act of 1892 still did not recognise a colour bar. But property provisions (£75) and literacy (i.e. a test of civilization) would – according to the Rhodes principle of equal rights for all civilized people – obtain throughout the Colony as a requirement for election registration. Communal land ownership and the individual property ownership of the Glen Grey Act would not, however, qualify a Native for the vote. In this way the swamping of the voter's roll by "blanket kaffirs" was avoided and the franchise question was solved, at least for the nineteenth century.

In this way the relationship between Black and White developed through various stages in the second half of the nineteenth century. The earlier military measures on the frontier had become complex political, administrative, economic and social problems. These problems and their solutions are an important part of Cape history. The absence of a common native policy in Southern Africa during the nineteenth century was not destined to make them any simpler for the generations of the twentieth century.

Economic development

The Cape, with the exception of parts such as the Western Province and the Malmesbury area, is not really an agricultural area. Yet up to 1870 more than 90% of the population were employed in agricultural and stock-breeding. Wine, which was about half of the Colony's exports in the first half of the nineteenth century, was in 1850 surpassed as a major export by wool and hides as a result of the reduction of preferential tariffs. By 1865 Cape wine had virtually disappeared from the British market. But wine production, despite tremendous price fluctuations and vineyard pests, increased until in 1890 it amounted to over six million gallons. This was not, however, nearly enough to satisfy the demands of the growing South African population. Maize and wheat production also rose gradually, but was not sufficient for domestic requirements.

Until the end of the nineteenth century stock-breeding was, because of climatic, geographic and marketing conditions, the most intensive industry in the Cape. The wool industry was so well entrenched by 1850 that the years between 1850 and 1870 are rightly called the wool period of the Cape. In 1864, wool production had risen to 36 million lbs. and made up three quarters of the Colony's exports. Despite this, South African wool was by European standards, inferior until shortly before the end of the nineteenth century, chiefly because of such factors as inferior stock, droughts and inexpert sorting.

Industry developed slowly in the Cape and the Colony was not in the least self-sufficient. The most important developments were in secondary industries such as the baking, wine, clothing, and wagon-building trades. This state of affairs was chiefly the result of the scarcity of journeymen, bad communications, lack of good markets and the industrialization of Europe. By 1852, with the exploitation of Namaqualand copper, the dignified early era of capitalism in the Cape had been replaced by a restless spirit of speculation. Many companies were established. The copper boom and the recession of the fifties lead to the floating of the stable "Cape Copper Company" in 1863, which was to operate for a long and fruitful period.

In 1855 the Cape parliament, like that of England, passed the Customs Tariff Act which abolished all preferential and differential rights. The resultant free trade brought an increased customs income – by 1860 this was already the Cape's main source of revenue – as the importation of textiles, metals and general goods increased steadily. These imports were generally taxed at $7\frac{1}{2}\%$ *ad valorem*. Up to 1870 the rest of the national income was derived mainly from taxes on business transactions, rents, the sale of crown land and fines. The civil population was not taxed directly, although the Natives paid poll tax. Fiscal money had for years been spent almost exclusively on administration, and social services and public works therefore received little attention. The only exception was the railway building programme which was mainly responsible for the government debt. This stood at £23½ million by 1890.

In 1841 the paper rixdollar which had been the Cape currency for fifty-nine years was replaced by sterling, which by 1881 was so firmly established that the Colony was placed on the sterling gold standard. This stability was to have an important influence on Cape banking. Long before the end of the nineteenth century the state monopoly of banking had been ended by the establishment of private district banks such as the Cape of Good Hope Bank. By 1862 there were no less than twenty-nine of these banks which, in some cases, controlled a reserve capital of over £1 million and paid dividends as high as 20%. After 1860 a feature of the monetary and credit system was characterized by the disappearance of most of the district banks and the establishment of strongly capitalized Imperial banks such as the London and S.A. Bank (1860) and the Standard Bank (1862). The disappearance of the smaller banks was a consequence of careless credit extension, competition, economic depressions, amalgamations with the Imperial banks, over-speculation on the Witwatersrand, and even droughts. By 1891, for example, only the Stellenbosch District Bank had survived the crises which had stengthened the Imperial banks. These banks played an important part in financing the various transactions which followed the discovery of diamonds.

Poor communications hampered developments at the Cape for much of the nineteenth century. In the interior main roads and passes such as the Bains Kloof and Michell's Passes, were only properly cared for after the institution of the

175

divisional councils in 1855. Weekly postal and passenger services were operating by the forties, but the ox-wagon was for a long time to remain the most important trading vehicle in the interior. The penny postal service of 1853 and the government telegraph service were extended over the whole of the Cape by 1864. The monthly mails between England and the Cape, which were inaugurated in 1851 and took 42 days, grew quickly from 1857 when the postal contract was given to the "Union Line", which entered into fierce competition with other steamship lines. By 1868 there was a fortnightly, and eight years later, a weekly, postal service between England and the Cape. This post was carried jointly by the Union and Castle companies.

Despite the opening of the Suez Canal in 1869, shipping traffic and foreign trade around the Cape increased rapidly in the last quarter of the nineteenth century, mainly because of the economic and financial development of Southern Africa and the increased speed of sea travel. By the nineties the voyage from England to the Cape took only fourteen days. England was the most important trader with the Cape throughout the second half of the nineteenth century, but from the eighties on Continental Europe and America also began increasingly to trade with the Cape. Thanks to improvements to Table Bay harbour between 1860 and 1869, the building of more lighthouses after the sixties and the initiative of private enterprise, coastal shipping had increased rapidly. By 1896 there were at least a dozen coasters serving South African ports only.

After 1870 the agriculture and stock-breeding and, in fact, the entire economy of the Cape entered a new phase as a result of the new markets opened up in the interior by the mines. The economic development of the Cape after 1870 was further affected by its increasing integration with developments in the Republics and Natal. This integration, which caused South Africa to develop into an agricultural and mining country, was the most important economic trend of the last quarter of the nineteenth century.

The discovery of diamonds between 1867 and 1870 radically changed the Cape's economy. Not only did it increase buying power, but it also stimulated markets in the interior and created new fields of employment. Tens of thousands of enterprising immigrants and their capital were attracted to the diamond mines, and imports and transport changed rapidly. The Bantu, who made use of the new opportunities for employment, saw their old communal way of life disintegrate to be replaced by an entirely different social and economic pattern of life. The discovery of diamonds also aroused a spirit of speculation and caused the diamond crisis of 1881 and the depression of 1882 – 1886.

The seventies in the Cape Colony are marked chiefly by an extraordinary prosperity. The economic boom particularly stimulated the export of agricultural products such as wool, hides and feathers. By 1878 the period of reckless over-speculation, easy credit and optimistic industrial investment reached its zenith. Exports and the banks' total discounts had practically doubled in a few years. The glittering financial edifice which had been constructed on diamonds and trade with the interior began to collapse in 1881: bank credits were summarily restricted, while the stock exchange caused anxiety and reduced buying

176

power and imports by millions. The discounts of Cape banks, for example, fell by 71.5% in 1887. Consequently, the number of insolvencies rose to astronomic figures, while government revenue decreased alarmingly. This, the worst economic depression of the nineteenth century at the Cape, showed to what extent the Cape had already been integrated into the capitalist system.

The recession ended when the Witwatersrand began working its gold mines. The opening of these mines had far-reaching economic and political consequences in the Cape and Southern Africa. The hitherto unsurpassed gold boom period (1886 – 1889) was followed, just as the diamond boom had been, by a serious recession. The market value of some shares fell by 60%. The Cape banks were hit particularly hard by the decrease in deposits and discounted bills, and several district banks, among them the Cape of Good Hope Bank, had failed by 1892. By the nineties the Cape economy was once more progressing steadily as evidenced by the appreciable increase in Cape railway revenue, exports totalling over £6 million,[8] increasing imports and higher state revenue.

In the last quarter of the nineteenth century the Cape Colony's industrialization received an impetus. During the nineties there were altogether 2,000 small industries (e.g. mills, waggon-building shops, breweries and furniture factories) which satisfied local demand and which employed 18,000 labourers who earned about £2½ million. The increase of import duties between 1864 and 1884 from 7½% to 15% stimulated the retarded but insufficiently protected manufacturing industries. Industrialization progressed too slowly, however, particularly because of the flow of labour and capital to the mines and the excellent export markets for wool and diamonds.

Railway development in the Cape was very closely associated with economic and political development. The first railway lines in the Cape Colony were completed in 1863 by the Cape Town Railway and Dock Co. These lines ran from Cape Town to Wellington and Wynberg. Because of the depression this private company could not undertake large projects, but the exploitation of diamonds necessitated a railway line to Kimberley, 650 miles at an estimated cost of five million pounds. The Cape government therefore stepped in, took over private railway and telegraph lines and, between 1873 and 1885, built three main lines at a cost of £14,250,000 from Cape Town, Port Elizabeth and East London[9] via De Aar to Kimberley. This made government control of the railways and the development of the Cape's economic structure accomplished facts. After the discovery of gold the railway race to the Witwatersrand began. The Cape railway reached Johannesburg in 1892, but three years later there were also rail links with three other ports – Port Elizabeth, Durban and Lourenço Marques. It is therefore understandable that fierce competition concerning harbour, transport and customs tariffs would develop between the different lines. As early as 1884 various attempts were made by the Cape and the Transvaal to regularize matters. The Free State and the Cape Colony, having together

8. Wool export from the Cape Colony amounted to over 73 million pounds (weight) in 1896.
9. The East London line via Rosmead and Stormberg only reached Kimberley in 1892.

built the railway line to Vereeniging via Bloemfontein, arranged matters to their own satisfaction with their customs treaty of 1889, in terms of which internal free trade was accepted and three quarters of the import duties on imported Free State goods were given to the Free State by Colonial ports. The general *ad valorem* rate was fixed at 12%. After the completion of the Lourenço Marques line in 1894, however, the Cape line which up to then had been virtually monopolizing transport to the Rand, was threatened by serious deficits. The Transvaal began increasing the tariffs levied on the Cape lines which crossed its territory and imposed heavy taxes on Cape products. When the Cape Town conference of 1895 failed, the Cape railway administration arranged a road transport service between the Vaal River and the Witwatersrand which precipitated the "drifts crisis" and British interference. However, an ultimatum obliged Kruger to open the drifts once again. There was no time for further arrangement before the outbreak of war (see Chapter 15).

In summing up, we may say that the development of the mining industry after the discovery of gold and diamonds dominated the Cape economy from 1870 and had various consequences: increased production; population growth; impoverishment; migrations; increased revenues from imports and exports; greater national incomes; depressions; railway development; a customs union; improved markets; the growth of finance and banking and the development of a typically capitalist point of view. After 1870 the old economic order was completely ousted by capitalism, industrialism and mining.

Educational, religious and other developments

The necessity for a central control of education in the Cape Colony in the thirties caused Sir George Napier in 1837 to instruct Sir John Herschel, the well-known astronomer and educationist, to investigate educational matters in the Colony. One result of this investigation was the publication of the important Government Memorandum of 1839 in which a department of education under the supervision of a general superintendent was envisaged. The Cape's first Superintendent-General of Education was Dr. James Rose-Innes, a Scottish educationist connected with the South African College, who managed, despite insufficient funds and innumerable problems, to lay the foundations of the Cape Department of Education.

The establishment of a central education department and the appointment of a Superintendent-General of Education were visionary undertakings which led to important educational developments: they gave direction and prestige to the backward and undeveloped educational system in the Cape. They were also to have a far-reaching influence on the establishment and administration of various other education departments in Southern Africa.

As a result of the abovementioned developments government aided schools were established; the so-called first and second class non-sectarian schools for the primary and secondary education of Whites in all the major centres. This new principle was four years later extended to rural areas where third class

178

government-aided schools were established. Private schools, using English as a medium, could also obtain state aid.

Education in these Government schools had to be secular from the outset and teaching was through the medium of English, although Dutch could be taught in the elemenatry classes. The Superintendent-General of Education would inspect all schools. The new dispensation not only placed all schools, including the later state-aided missionary (B schools) and native schools (C schools), under effective control, but local interest and responsibility in education was also stimulated. Teachers at these schools were usually imported Scottish teachers and/or students of established schools.

Developments in higher education lagged far behind those in elementary education. It was through the efforts of Sir George Grey and Langham Dale, successor to Rose-Innes, that interest in this educational field was aroused in the fifties. To begin with there had been only the South African College and Diocesan College in Cape Town. Now such institutions as St. Andrews College, the Grey Institute and the Graaff-Reinet College were established. Although they only did advanced school work for many years, they did pave the way for university education. The Board of Public Examiners, which conducted B.A. and M.A. examinations from 1858 onwards, also played its part in co-ordinating and controlling higher education in the Colony.

Ten years after the appearance of "De Kerkbode" (1849) a decision by the Synod resulted in the establishment of the Theological Seminary at Stellenbosch to train clergy for the Dutch Reformed Church and counteract the many liberal and British-oriented ministers. Ministers of the Dutch Reformed Church in most cases promoted education unselfishly mainly by their sympathetic supervision, helping to establish schools and training colleges, and their efforts to get education in the mother tongue accepted.

As a result of alleged abuses concerning the subsidizing of schools and the general control of educational matters, the Watermeyer Commission was appointed in 1861. In 1863 it published an authoritative report and most of its recommendations were embodied in the Education Act of 1865 (No. 13). Together with the "Schedule of Regulations", these two documents rightly became the cornerstones of the Cape Colony's educational system up to 1905. According to this Education Act, the old "Established Schools" had gradually to make way for a system of government aid. The system for trainees and inspections was placed on a sound footing, and the mission schools reaped great financial advantages. The disregard of Dutch and the enforced use of English as the teaching medium in all state-aided schools – third class schools also had to use English after they had been functioning for a year—made the schools into a political instrument. Afrikaners were taught to believe that English was their salvation and thus came to despise their mother tongue and lose their national pride. The Education Act of 1865, although it contained no new principles for the 140 supported schools and 5,000 pupils of the time, systematized and furthered the existing arrangements.

However, the Act, apart from the language clause already mentioned, had other shortcomings. Initiative in establishing schools was left to local enterprise so that conservative and backward districts often did not benefit from the Act. Salary guarantees too were a heavy burden on those of the community willing to give them. Finally, the Act came dangerously close to the dubious system of recompense by results. Its system was extended ten years later by "Good Service" allowances and awards of "payments by results" which had been operating at private farm schools from 1884.[10]

Up to 1841 non-White education was the responsibility of the many overseas missionary societies and, although the government gave financial aid, the societies kept their hold on non-White education throughout the nineteenth century. Many missionary schools, however, were attended by White children; in 1882 there were still 6,000 White children in mission schools. It also became customary after 1861 for non-White children no longer to attend government schools, mainly because the Whites objected.

The increased allowances voted in the Act of 1865 implied increased government control over the 211 mission schools and institutions attended by more than 24,000 children, but the societies resisted this secularization. The Act of 1865 was the most important educational legislation for non-Whites up to 1910.

The systematic neglect of Dutch after 1865 once again caused several larger private schools, which tried to do without government aid, to be established. This movement originated with the Synod of the Dutch Reformed Church and individual ministers, but ironically it was not long before English became the main feature of these schools while their education was patterned on the English system. The Stellenbosch Gymnasium[11] had to change its name shortly after its establishment in 1866 in order to qualify for government aid. Well-known girls' schools such as the Good Hope Seminary (Cape Town), the Huguenot Seminary (Wellington) and Bloemhof (Stellenbosch) which were established in the early seventies by the efforts of the Dutch Reformed Church had English principals and were obviously English-oriented.

The conservative rural Afrikaners did not long tolerate the neglect of Dutch. Under the leadership of A. Pannevis, C. P. Hoogenhout, the Rev. S. J. du Toit and others, a language society – Die Genootskap vir Regte Afrikaners – and the "Patriot" movement were born in 1876. The latter became a national movement for language and political rights. Articles in "De Zuid-Afrikaan", "Het Volksblad" and "Het Zuid-Afrikaansche Tydskrift" nurtured national consciousness among thousands of Afrikaners and played an important part in elevating Afrikaans to a written language and obtaining official recognition for Dutch. In 1882 Dutch was recognised, with English, as an official language of Parliament[12] and two years later it was recognised in the lower courts.

10. An Education Pension Scheme was instituted in 1887, a measure which promised higher status and security for the teaching profession.

11. This school was known as the Victoria College from 1887 onwards, and was the institution from which the University of Stellenbosch was to develop.

12. In the same year Dutch was recognised as an educational medium in Government schools.

180

The language struggle reached its height in 1890 when the "Zuid-Afrikaanse Taalbond" was founded and the national congress in Cape Town demanded equal rights for Dutch and English at school and in elementary examinations.

In the prosperous seventies there was renewed interest in higher education, which, among other things, resulted in the abolition of the Board of Examiners in 1873 and the foundation of the University of the Cape of Good Hope. This was an examining and controlling body which awarded degrees but left teaching to the existing colleges. In the following year the Higher Education Act, which regulated Higher Education well into the twentieth century, brought welcome financial relief which the Act of 1865 had not provided. The ideal of a teaching university, as recommended by the De Villiers Educational Commission of 1879 and the Ross Report of 1882, was only realized in 1900 when the old South African College began giving lectures.

Residential and industrial schools through which the efforts of the Dutch Reformed Church had been functioning since 1873 were only a minor educational force because, as with the schools for poor white people ("poor schools"), they were soon stigmatized. The private farm schools of the eighties were the result of the contentious Ross Report of 1882: five children more than six miles from the nearest third class school were sufficient to begin a state-aided farm school. In 1887 there were 179 of these schools teaching 1,300 children. Secondary education, which up to 1865 had been relatively neglected, progressed rapidly from 1870 because additional allowances were made available. The teaching which the existing colleges had been providing since the fifties was taken over by the first and second class schools after 1890.

During the last quarter of the nineteenth century the administration of local school committees attracted much attention. Matters such as financing, compulsory education, the guarantee system and the insecure position of the teachers were discussed, among others, by the Education Commission of 1879 and in the Ross Report of 1882. When Dr. Muir, the new Superintendent-General of Education assumed office in 1892, the educational machinery for more than 105,000 children, White and non-White, was in fact so antiquated that immediate efforts were made to plan some departmental reorganization.

The result of this planning was a streamlining and extension of the Education Department: statistics and reports were properly kept, an improved "Education Manual" was provided and a regular "Education Gazette" was published from 1901 onwards. Another important step was the reorganization of the inspection system. Matters such as "educational surveys", school libraries, nationalization of school buildings, improvement of curricula for primary and secondary classes, the establishment of technical high schools, the extension of the high school system, the establishment of departmental handbooks and examinations, and improved training for teachers were all given attention.

Possibly Muir's greatest triumph was the institution of district school boards and compulsory education. The School Board Act, which was passed in 1905, provided for roughly 100 school board districts, each with a school board of eighteen members, which board was given wide powers in local educational matters.

Thus the appointment of a Superintendent-General of Education in 1839, the passing of the Education Act of 1865 and the School Board Act of 1905 were the three most important milestones in the development of the Cape's educational administration.

After the termination of government control over the Dutch Reformed Church in 1843, the church had to resist fierce attacks from liberal sources; simultaneously, circumstances in the north resulted in the foundation of the Nederduits Hervormde Kerk (1853) and the Nederduits Gereformeerde Kerk (1859). The Cape Synod had also decided in 1857 that because of "the weakness of a few"[13] separate services would be held for White and non-White, a decision which was to have far-reaching consequences, particularly after the Dutch Reformed Mission Church was founded in 1881. In addition to the above-mentioned churches in the Cape there was also the influential Anglican Church which was divided into three Sees in 1853 and became "The Church of the Province of South Africa" in the seventies. It made valuable cultural contributions chiefly through its church schools.

The South African Public Library which was founded by Lord Charles Somerset, opened in 1822, and through later donations, among others from Sir George Grey, became one of the best libraries in Africa. The most influential newspapers in the second half of the nineteenth century were undoubtedly "De Zuid-Afrikaan" (1830), "The Graham's Town Journal" (1831), "The Cape Argus" (1857) and "The Cape Times" (1876). There was hardly any impressive literature, but authors and poets such as Cooper, Schreiner, Huet and S. J. du Toit may be deemed the heralds of the South African literature of the twentieth century.

In the field of art and music there was very little activity, but by contrast science developed on a broad front: for example, Sir David Gill of the Royal Observatory chartered the southern stars from 1879, and Marloth's "The Flora of South Africa" has achieved world renown. The world-famous Botanical Gardens at Kirstenbosch were founded by H. H. W. Pearson, while the South African Museum, which was re-established in 1855 by Layard, already had a unique collection of fossils and stone implements by the end of the last century. Research scientists such as Bowker and Bleek were responsible for authoritative works in fields such as entomology, archaeology and philology.

Conclusion

Thus the Cape Colony remained the leading state in Southern Africa throughout the second half of the nineteenth century. The Imperial government considered the Colony to be of such strategic importance that it was used as an observation

13. Printed *"Acta van die Sinode"*, 1857, p. 60.

post from which the British High Commissioner could keep an eye on Imperial interests.

In a period of fifty years the White population exceeded the 400,000 mark, and the undeveloped Cape Colony also went through stormy political times to achieve political and constitutional maturity. The awakening of the Afrikaner's national consciousness and the political grouping and circumstances prevailing at the end of the century were largely responsible for developments in twentieth century South Africa. With the growth of the diamond and gold mining industries, the economy of the Cape Colony underwent a transformation. A more complex system evolved and the Colony became partially industrialized with the financial and commercial characteristics of a modern capitalist state.

The Colony gained in prestige through the steady development of its educational system over half a century. Not only was provision made for education at elementary, secondary and higher levels, but far-sighted education policy and enlightened legislation were sound examples for other Southern African states.

In less than forty years the complex military and frontier problems had developed into a characteristically South African native policy based on differentiation. In the twentieth century, *mutatis mutandis*, this would form the basis for an envisaged permanent solution.

11. Natal, 1845-1902

On 31 May, 1844, Natal, which had been annexed by Britain on 12 May, 1843, became a district of the Cape Colony. The government for this district which was instituted in April, 1845, only came into operation in December of that year. The governing body, consisting of a lieutenant-governor assisted by a council of five members, acted in an executive capacity only. Legislative authority remained with the Cape government, and the lieutenant-governor of Natal corresponded with the Imperial government through the Cape governor as intermediary. Martin West, previously resident magistrate for Albany, was the first lieutenant-governor. One of his council members was Theophilus Shepstone as diplomatic agent for the Natives. He was to become a key figure in the native administration of Natal.

Apart from the few English traders and the British garrison, in 1845, the White population of Natal consisted principally of about four hundred Voortrekker families who had remained in Natal despite the annexation of the Republic of Natalia. Among them was Andries Pretorius, living on his farm "Welverdient" near Pietermaritzburg. West would have to reconcile these Voortrekkers to British authority, which would not be an easy task since they were already dissatisfied because they had no voice in the government of the district. West's native policy and the fact that not all their land claims were admitted were to alienate them yet further.

By 1845 there were about 100,000 Bantu in Natal, most of whom had streamed into the country from Zululand after the British occupation of Natal in 1842. They were a burden and a threat to the Whites. They squatted everywhere, even on Boer farms, went about armed, thieved, and were reluctant to enter service contracts. This was another of the problems West would have to solve. West knew that the Zulu chief Mpande would punish the fugitives if they were sent back to Zululand and so could not consider such a step. He feared that the cattle which the fugitives had brought with them – according to Zulu tradition the property of the chief – would be forcibly reclaimed by Mpande. Fortunately for West, Mpande was not pugnacious. However, it was imperative that something be done about the Bantu in Natal; accordingly West appointed a location commission on 31 March, 1846.

This commission recommended that a number of locations or reserves should be established for the Bantu, amongst which were the Zwartkop, Umvoti, Inanda and Umlazi locations, and made various suggestions for their control. Inevitably there were objections to the locations, particularly because they were in White territory and even included inhabited farms. For example, the Zwartkop Location was close to Pietermaritzburg near Pretorius's farm. "As a result of these decisions, namely that such an inundation of murderous and rapacious people will be living in our midst", Pretorius wrote to West in 1846, "every one of us will have to leave our beloved homes with tears in our eyes rather than risk our lives and property."[1]

Even the British government was dissatisfied with the commission's recommendations, since the commission wanted the British Treasury to advance money for the appointment of a White superintendent and a White officer with a police force for each of the locations. Earl Grey, the Secretary of State for the Colonies, decided in December, 1847, that the Bantu chiefs would have to control their subjects themselves until such time as Natal could afford to bring the Bantu under British law and administration. At this stage there was already widespread dissatisfaction among the Natal Voortrekkers because of the native policy and because their land claims had not been met.

The annexation proclamation of May, 1843, stipulated that land would be given only to those who could prove that they had lived on their farms during the twelve months before the arrival of Henry Cloete, the special commissioner to investigate land claims. Some Whites, however, had voluntarily left their farms and others had been ordered by the authorities to leave them because of the danger of living among thousands of Bantu. Consequently Cloete divided the claimants for land into three classes: in the first class were those who satisfied the condition of occupation and so could claim farms of 6,000 acres; in the second class were those who, for an acceptable reason, could not satisfy the occupation condition and so could claim farms of 2,000 acres; and in the third class were the doubtful cases which had to be investigated individually.

West believed that the Whites would remain in Natal if their land claims were settled, and he even went so far as to obtain the Cape governor's permission to grant 6,000 acre farms to claimants in the second class, while those in the third class could be promised farms. There were, however, so many delays in granting and surveying the farms that few of the Voortrekkers – by now thoroughly suspicious – were certain of what land they owned by the end of 1847. Only eighteen title deeds had been issued, although 650 claims had been made in 1846 and 1847.

By the end of 1847 the uncertainty concerning land and their dangerous position among the Bantu induced most of the Voortrekkers to think of trekking out of Natal. But they made a final effort to rectify their grievances by delegating Andries Pretorius to see Sir Henry Pottinger, the British High Commissioner and Governor of the Cape. Pottinger, who was at Grahamstown because of the Eighth Frontier War and was on the point of leaving South Africa, refused Pretorius a hearing. Dismayed and offended, Pretorius returned to Natal where in his absence the Voortrekkers had already determined to trek.

---

1. Translated from the original Dutch quoted in M. C. van Zyl: *Luitenant-goewerneur Martin West en die Natalse Voortrekkers, 1845 – 1849* (Archives Year Book for S.A. History, 1955, II), p. 135.

That the Voortrekkers decided to leave Natal without waiting for Pretorius's report must be ascribed to the complications which developed during 1847 in the Klip River area, between the Tugela and Buffalo Rivers. Fearing an attack from the Zulus on the other side of the Buffalo River, the Klip River farmers had negotiated with Mpande after twice fruitlessly asking the government at Pietermaritzburg for protection. When Mpande assured them that they were occupying land belonging to the Zulus, the farmers bought the Klip River area from him in about May, 1847. They elected their own government in which Andries Spies was commandant and held the highest office. However, according to a treaty which Mpande and Henry Cloete had concluded in 1843, the Klip River area belonged not to the Zulus but to Natal. Mpande was apparently under a misapprehension and in August, 1847, at the insistence of West he accepted in writing the Buffalo River as the border between Zululand and Natal. Armed with this agreement, West felt he was in a position to label the Klip River farmers as rebels and hence considered it necessary to demand from them an oath of loyalty to the Queen.

The Klip River farmers refused to take the oath and therefore were obliged to leave Natal. They spread rumours that a Zulu impi was about to enter Natal, and caused the Voortrekkers south of the Tugela, who were already alarmed because the Klip River area, their buffer against the Zulus, would be depopulated, also to decide to trek. The bad news Pretorius brought back with him about his attempt to see Pottinger merely confirmed their decision to trek, and there was now no stopping them. Even the visit of Sir Harry Smith, Pottinger's successor, to the already trekking Natal Voortrekkers early in 1848 and his efforts to settle their grievances could not persuade the majority to stay. Possibly they were correct in feeling that British government in Natal would not satisfy them, because by the middle of 1849 only sixty-three people had acquired title-deeds, and although two new locations, the Umzinyati and Impafana, were announced in 1848, there were delays in moving the Bantu and they remained scattered among the Whites.

West's government, which ended with his death on 1 August, 1849, was not successful. His personality was weak, his health poor, he was of a philanthropic mind and besides, he was fighting insurmountable problems. The worst of these problems was a financial one. The British government wanted to keep Natal with its harbour out of the hands of the Voortrekkers, but was reluctant to contribute financially towards the development of Natal. Natal could not help herself because no profitable minerals had as yet been discovered, trade was limited, mainly because of the lack of roads, and there was little agriculture because of the Bantu threat. The most essential funds had to be borrowed from the Cape Colony and by May, 1849, Natal already owed over £7,000. The financial problems chiefly delayed the implementation of the native policy and the surveying of farms, and thus created grievances which robbed Natal of much of its White population.

Furthermore, West and his council had no legislative powers. Even in urgent cases they had to wait for approval from Cape Town and, at times, London. This problem was partly solved in 1848, when a council of three officials, which could assume legislative powers in matters of urgency, was instituted.

After the death of West immediate efforts had to be made firstly, to increase the White population of Natal and secondly, to move the Bantu to their locations. The latter aim was achieved without much difficulty, but about one third of the Natal Bantu continued living on crown land and private farms. In June, 1849, all Bantu were placed under traditional Bantu jurisdiction. In the absence of magistrates for the locations, chiefs had to administer the law themselves, but appeal could be made to the lieutenant-governor, who was the chief of all Bantu, and the executive council. In 1850 magistrates were appointed for four of the locations after an annual hut tax of seven shillings had been instituted at the end of the previous year. Funds for the appointment of sufficient magistrates and a police force, and for the erection of schools to civilize the Bantu, were simply not available. There were only a few missionaries to try to exert a civilizing influence.

The locations were not very popular in Natal. The farmers looked upon the locations in their midst not only as a threat to their peace, but also as an evil which drained off Bantu labour from the farms. This attitude on the part of the farmers led Theophilus Shepstone, the head of native affairs, even to consider segregating the Bantu in a single large area, where it would be easier than in scattered locations to civilize them through the medium of magistrates, police and trade schools. Shepstone wanted to establish about 50,000 Bantu south of the Umtamvuna River with himself as supreme chief, but Sir George Grey, the Cape Governor, rejected this plan as he feared its repercussions on the eastern border of the Cape. The Natal colonists themselves planned to break up the existing big locations into a larger number of smaller ones, but even had the British government approved of this idea, there were not enough troops in Natal to put it into effect.

Even the British government realised that native affairs in Natal had to be attended to and ordered Benjamin Pine, West's successor, to investigate them. The commission Pine appointed in September, 1852, heard much evidence and criticized the location policy, but its results were negligble. The most important were that the location magistrates were henceforth known as assistant magistrates, to avoid any appearance that the Bantu were dependent on White government, and that Shepstone's status as Diplomatic Agent for the Natives was changed to Secretary for Native Affairs.

Fortunately for Natal the Bantu were not disposed to rebel and Shepstone had influence with the chiefs. Chiefs who did in fact revolt, as Sidoyi and Matyana did in 1857, lost their chieftainship. This helped to ensure that for many years the Bantu would not dare openly to resist the government. Nevertheless, the thousands of Bantu were a constant threat to the handful of White Natalians. Consequently, in 1848 and after, when many Voortrekkers had left Natal and only about 2,000 Whites remained, assiduous efforts were made to encourage White immigration into Natal. Immigrants were essential for agriculture, particularly for growing cotton, which, it was hoped, would make Natal prosperous.

In 1848 Jonas Bergtheil, a Durban merchant and controlling director of the *Natal Cotton Company*, sent for thirty five German families to cultivate cotton. These Germans, who settled in the vicinity of Durban, soon found that it was more profitable to grow vegetables. In the ensuing years Joseph C. Byrne, an Irish speculator, launched a scheme which brought about 2,500 British immigrants to Natal. The Australian goldfields later enticed many of them away again, but by then they had established the basis for an English-oriented Natal and played a part in founding towns such as Pinetown, Verulam, Richmond and Ladysmith. There were other schemes to draw immigrants, while some came on their own initiative. Before the end of 1851 the White population of Natal had increased by between four and five thousand. Then the stream of immigrants ceased. By 1856 Natal had about 8,000 White inhabitants.

Economically the young pioneer district was still in trouble, but matters were improving. The new settlers experimented successfully with various products such as cotton and coffee. In 1852 Edmund Morewood produced the first sugar cane on his farm Compensation on the north coast and so launched a profitable industry. There was trading with the Orange Free State and the South African Republic and many immigrants specialised in cartage work. In April, 1854, the Natal Bank was established with a capital of £20,000 which reflected the general confidence in Natal's future.

In the cultural field too there was visible progress. Charitable, political, agricultural and commercial societies were founded, and the Natal Association not only offered free library services, but also arranged public lectures. Journalism was so active that at one stage Natal was publishing six newspapers. Two of these, the *Natal Witness*, established in 1846 in Pietermaritzburg, and the *Natal Mercury*, established in 1852 in Durban, still exist. By 1855 there were two state schools, about eight state-supported schools and various private and church schools.

In the fifties, local as well as central governmental powers were extended. As early as 1846 Pietermaritzburg had a council of commissioners and ten years later this town, as well as Durban, was granted full municipal management. Pine and Grey also prepared Natal's secession from the Cape Colony. In 1856 provision was made for this and for a legislative council of four officials and twelve elected members. The right to elect members in this form of government had been tested in a few other British colonies, but was an innovation in South Africa. Apart from the Bantu, Natal was overwhelmingly British and there was no danger that any other nationality would attain a majority. The electoral qualifications, at Grey's recommendation, were high so as to exclude Bantu from the franchise. Accordingly all men with immovable property of £50, or who rented property for £10 a year, could vote.

The new constitution came into operation on 24 March, 1857, when John Scott opened the first session of the Legislative Council at Pietermaritzburg. The council could pass laws and control Natal's finances, subject to approval by the lieutenant-governor or the Queen. In the same year Natal got a supreme court of three judges, from where appeals could be made to the Privy Council in London. Natal thus obtained a limited form of representative government and outgrew its origin as an appanage of the Cape Colony.

The young colony

In the first years under the new constitution it was obvious that, above all, the young colony needed many white immigrants and capital from Europe. At that time many people were emigrating from Britain, but most of them preferred countries where they did not have to contend with thousands of Bantu. In spite of this Natal nearly doubled her White population in the decade after 1856.

The new settlers came mainly from Britain and the Cape Colony, but there were also some ninety Hollanders under the leadership of T. W. Colenbrander, who settled in Natal in 1858. The immigrants came on their own initiative or through immigration schemes. In 1857, for example, the Natal Legislative Council voted funds to finance immigrants from the United Kingdom. Relations or friends had to vouch for these immigrants, however, and guarantee ten pounds towards the immigration costs of each immigrant. This scheme operated up to 1868 and brought about 2,000 British subjects to Natal. There were other schemes which were not so successful.

The most promising, but most unsuccessful, of these schemes was the *Natal Land and Colonization Company* which was founded in England in 1860 with the purpose of buying land in Natal and then settling White people on it. The Company did buy the land, 250,000 acres at fifteen shillings per acre, but did not attain its second objective. Instead of being used as farms for Whites, the land was rented to Bantu at an annual rent of five to twenty eight shillings per hut. This scheme attracted so many Bantu that it was most profitable, but it was dangerous to try to remove the Bantu from the farms. Many other property owners, particularly speculators, followed the example of this company. Consequently increasingly less land was available for White immigrants and Natal virtually became a vast Bantu location with patches of White settlement scattered through it.

In 1869 and 1870 old and new settlers were lured to the diamond fields. Among them, for example, was the young Cecil Rhodes, who for a while had been growing cotton with his brother Herbert in Natal. The number of Whites in Natal did not, however, decrease. According to Theal the number of inhabitants in 1872 was about 17,500 Whites, 300,000 Bantu and 5,800 Indians. Six years later the number of Whites had increased to 22,000 and the Indians to 12,800. These figures show the increase in Whites, but point particularly to the arrival of the Indian element in the population.

When the first Indian, Babu Naidoo, arrived in Durban in 1855, nobody had any idea that any of his compatriots would follow him to Natal. Although the cultivation of sugar cane and cotton inevitably suggested Indian labour, public opinion in Natal, as well as in the legislative council, was initially opposed to importing Indians. The sugar industry, however, had to have a steady supply of labour and was in danger of failing because the Bantu only desired to work occasionally and were not dependable. In 1859 the Natal government was forced to agree that indentured Indian labourers, who had been employed successfully in places such as Mauritius, should be brought to Natal. Although the first arrivals in 1860 were of a poor quality and although funds for public works had to be curtailed to cover the importation of the Indians, it was clear that the project, from the point of view of labour problems, was a success.

The Indians, including women, were initially imported at government's cost and indentured to employers for three years. They had to be paid ten shillings a month, with an increase to eleven shillings in the second and twelve shillings in the third years, and be provided with free lodging and rations on a fixed scale. Employers had to repay three-fifths of the passage and other importation costs to the government. After three years the Indians either had to be indentured for another two years or could buy their freedom for £2.10.0 for each of those two years. After five years they were free to live and work as they chose, and after ten years' residence in Natal entitled to a free passage back to India or to crown land to the value of the passage. From 1864 onwards the Natal government paid one-third of each Indian labourer's passage, extended the period of indenture to five years and fixed the wages for the fourth and fifth years at fourteen and fifteen shillings per month respectively.

The importation of Indians cost the Natal government over £24,000 during the period 1860 – 1870, and the employers nearly £53,000. As far as the sugar industry was concerned, this was a good investment, since Indian labour undoubtedly helped increase production from 1,173 tons in 1859 to 7,622 tons in 1870; it rose as high as 10,172 tons in 1874. A new element in the population also meant, however, that Natal Whites would have to contend not only with a Bantu problem, but also with an Indian problem. This matter will be considered in more detail later.

The following were the principal factors in the Bantu problem. In addition to the locations which by 1864 had been increased to forty-two, covering 2,050,880 acres, and the mission stations of which there were twenty-one by 1864, covering nearly 175,000 acres, the Bantu also lived on crown and private land, which could otherwise have been farmed by enterprising immigrants. The tens of thousands of Bantu constituted a potential danger to the White minority should there be any disturbances. Apart from their annual hut tax, the Bantu contributed virtually nothing to the development of Natal. On the whole, the Bantu were content at a bare subsistence level, pursued their primitive way of life and showed little interest in paid employment. In fact, the Bantu women did all the hard work, while the men would from time to time relinquish their carefree life to work briefly on a farm or elsewhere. Nobody but the lieutenant-governor could force them to work. In his capacity as supreme chief of the Bantu he could call them up for public work at fixed wages. This practice, however, was open to abuse, since the chiefs who had to draft the labour only made those available against whom they had a grudge.

As more and more magistrates were appointed in the locations they gradually encroached upon the chiefs' barbaric powers. By 1872 there were almost forty mission stations, but there was little evidence of their exerting a civilizing influence. There was therefore a real danger of a Bantu uprising, though the Bantu were generally peaceable, partly because of Shepstone's policy of maintaining tribal ties. One tribe would never make common cause with another which thus reduced the possibility of a concerted insurrection. That Bantu were permitted to settle on private farms and crown land also created good will, as it must have made the Bantu feel the Whites were not trying to displace them.

Another factor which kept the Bantu peaceful was the steps the government took to deprive them of access to firearms and liquor. From 1859 onwards, for example, Bantu had to register all firearms and sale of hard liquor to them was prohibited in 1863. Possibly Shepstone's hold on the chiefs was the most important factor in the successful control of the Bantu. As long as the chiefs were loyal to Shepstone and the government there was little chance of dissatisfaction among their followers. Should a chieftain cease to be loyal, a rising like that of Langalibalele in 1873 could well occur.

Langalibalele, according to the Bantu the most powerful rainmaker in Natal, was chief of the Hlubi tribe and lived in the north-western part of Natal, bordering on Basutoland. In 1873 Lieutenant-Governor Pine ordered him to send eight of his men to Pietermaritzburg to register rifles which they had obtained on the diamond fields. Langalibalele, however, sent only five of the men and subsequently insulted government messengers.

Langalibalele's impudence caused restlessness among the Bantu and compelled the Natal government to send an armed force to arrest him. He escaped to Basutoland and fired on the patrol which pursued him. The Basuto chief Molapo, afraid of the consequences to himself, surrendered Langalibalele. Members of the Hlubi tribe who continued resistance were subdued. Fearing that the incident might unleash general uprisings, the Natal government used drastic measures. The property and land of the Hlubi tribe were confiscated and a special court tried Langalibalele and banished him to Robben Island. A protest was headed by Bishop J. W. Colenso, whereupon London decided that Langalibalele was to be held as a state prisoner on the farm Uitvlugt near Mowbray. Langalibalele returned to Natal in 1886 and died three years later.

The rising of Langalibalele was not without repercussions for Natal. In London, Lord Carnarvon, Secretary of State for the Colonies, believed that Shepstone's system of ruling the Bantu through their chiefs without westernising them, and with the chiefs wielding almost unlimited power, was no longer satisfactory. The uprising also convinced Carnarvon that his idea of a uniform native policy within a federation of South Africa was the right one. Consequently Carnarvon recalled Pine and sent Sir Garnet Wolseley to Natal as special commissioner, with far-reaching powers to reform the Natal constitution and the native administration.

When Wolseley took his oath of office at Pietermaritzburg on 1 April, 1875,

Natal had constitutionally progressed beyond the legislative council instituted in 1856. In 1865 the franchise was revised in order to make it difficult for the Bantu to obtain the right to vote. If a Bantu satisfied the property qualification, had lived in the Colony for twelve years, had for seven years been discharged from living under Bantu law, and in addition possessed a certificate of good behaviour signed by three voters and a magistrate, he could apply to the lieu-tenant-governor for the right to vote. The lieutenant-governor could, however, still refuse the vote. How difficult the Bantu found it to obtain the vote, or how little interest he had in obtaining it, is indicated by there being up to 1876 no applications for a discharge from Bantu law. Of course, a Bantu applying for such a discharge had much to lose and had to serve a long probation before being discharged from his traditional law. Among other things, he was allowed only one wife, whilst Bantu law allowed him as many as he liked. However, it was possible for the Bantu to obtain the vote, but by 1893 only three enjoyed this privilege. Coloureds, on the other hand, could vote if they satisfied the normal terms of enfranchisement.

Membership of the legislative council had also been modified. In 1869 the Protector of Immigrants, later replaced by the Colonial Engineer, was added as an official member, and two legislative members were given seats on the execu-tive council as well. Four years later the number of elected members was in-creased by three. At Wolseley's arrival the legislative council thus consisted of five official and fifteen elected members. In the previous year the legislative council had requested responsible government; Wolseley, however, "drowned their liberties in sherry and champagne".[2]

It was London's intention that Wolseley was to change the Natal native administration without opposition from the elected members of the legislative council. This meant that the numbers of official and elected members would have to be about equal. Wolseley succeeded, with the council's approval, in changing the constitution so that the council's membership for the next five years would consist of fifteen elected and thirteen non-elected members. The non-elected members were five officials and eight nominated non-officials who had been resident in Natal for at least two years and owned immovable property of £1,000. By entertaining lavishly at parties where wine and champagne flowed freely, Wolseley made himself popular and won the confidence of the Natalians. In this way he succeeded in robbing them of their constitutional freedom. The composition of the council was now such that the non-elected members, who were compelled to support government policy, were assured of a majority if only two elected members supported them. This could easily happen as there had long been differences of opinion between members of the coastal and of the inland areas.

Even with his now almost unlimited powers, Wolseley did not effect drastic changes in Natal's native policy. Lack of troops prevented him from seriously curtailing the powers of the chiefs. Besides, he found that Natal's native admini-

2. F. Maurice and G. Arthur: *The Life of Lord Wolseley* (London, 1924), pp. 126 – 127.

stration was not as bad as had been believed. He instituted a Bantu High Court of one judge which could hear appeals from the Magistrate's courts in the locations, and from which appeals could even be made to the Supreme Court. He also appointed a commission to codify Bantu law, abrogated the hated marriage tax of five pounds which had been levied in 1873 and increased the hut tax to fourteen shillings to make good this loss.

These measures, as well as the severe punishment meted out to the Hlubi tribe, helped keep Natal tranquil. Wolseley's main purpose was to prevent a racial war and stabilize Natal for the intended South African federation. Matters did not proceed as expected, however, because in Zululand, Natal's northern neighbour state, a crisis arose which in 1879 was to unleash war between Britain and Zululand.

Ever since the outbreak of the Anglo-Zulu War its causes have been much debated. Some maintain that the war was forced on the Zulus, others that chief Cetshwayo, who was very like his bellicose uncle, Shaka, was a threat to all the Whites of South Africa. Possibly the war was a direct consequence of Lord Carnarvon's plans for a South African federation. The Zulus, who refused to recognize the borders of the Transvaal or Natal, and Cetshwayo, who was belligerent and according to Shepstone and others, able to influence other Bantu tribes and instigate a general uprising of the Bantu, would have to be taught a lesson before federation could become possible. The Zulus, however, were not easy to defeat and from 10 January, 1879, when British troops entered Zululand, up to Cetshwayo's apprehension on 28 August, 1879, Britain paid highly in lives and money. At Isandhlwana Zulu warriors destroyed nearly an entire batallion of regulars and volunteers. It was only at the battle of Ulundi on 4 July, 1879, that the tide turned against the Zulus.

This expensive war changed British colonial policy and contributed to the Liberal Party's victory over the Conservatives in 1880. British imperialism was tempered. In Natal many colonists wanted Zululand to be annexed and thrown open to White occupation. This would compensate for the volunteers and the £250,000 which Natal had had to contribute to the war. But Zululand was not annexed. Sir Garnet Wolseley, High Commissioner for South-East Africa, made an arrangement with the assistance of Sir Henry Bulwer, the Natal Lieutenant-Governor, which was aimed at destroying the unity of the Zulus. He banned Cetshwayo, who united them, to Cape Town, and divided Zululand into thirteen districts for each of which he appointed a chief who governed under the supervision of a British resident. In the opinion of Wolseley, the Zulus would no longer be dangerous.

In agriculture Natal was successful in some ways and unsuccessful in others. Coffee, tea, cotton, maize and other products were successfully cultivated, but not always permanently so. Thus cultivation of coffee prospered up to 1870, when nearly a thousand tons were produced, but then plant diseases and labour problems began to undermine this industry. Cultivation of cotton, which was maintained for thirty years, was abandoned by 1875, mainly because of the fluctuation in the overseas demand. In contrast sugar remained in demand and by 1872 sugar cane already covered 6,280 acres and eighty three mills were operating to produce 8,638 tons of sugar.

The Natal government also tried to promote inland trade. Not only were they concerned with the trade itself, but also with handling as many goods as possible in Durban harbour, since customs was Natal's main source of revenue. An important attempt to increase the traffic through Durban was made in 1867, when import duties were lowered below those of Cape Town. The sand bar at the entrance to the Durban harbour was a great problem, however. Initial efforts, undertaken at great cost, to prevent the sand accumulating were not successful. In 1878 the government accepted the plan of Sir John Coode to narrow the harbour entrance and deepen the channel. After about one million pounds had been spent on the harbour Coode's plan finally succeeded. To transport goods over the sand between the Point and Durban, a local company built a railway of nearly two miles – the first in South Africa – which was opened in 1860. Seven years later the first lighthouse shone out over the Indian Ocean from the Bluff. Roads and bridges were also built to improve traffic routes to the inland republics, but it was soon evident that rapid means of transport had to be provided.

The first fast vehicle in Natal was a coach which from 1860 plied between Pietermaritzburg and Durban. To begin with the distance of fifty-eight miles was covered in about eleven hours, including a rest pause for passengers at Halfway House. Later, when the coach travelled daily the time was cut down to about six hours. The need for railways, however, became increasingly urgent as time went by since Natal had to hold its own in the advance of commerce and the general progress in South Africa. In 1875 the government approved a railway line between Durban and Pietermaritzburg, which would include sidelines to Isipingo and Verulam. On New Years Day, 1876, Sir Henry Bulwer turned the first sod of the Durban-Pietermaritzburg line. This line, constructed over difficult mountain terrain, was completed on 1 December, 1880, and the first train steamed into Pietermaritzburg to the strains of "See the Conquering Hero comes" from a military band.

The economic setback which South Africa experienced in the sixties also affected Natal. After 1857 there was reckless speculation. Money was plentiful, various banks opened branches and private agencies even invested money from England. Sugar farmers, traders and others borrowed on a large scale without considering the inevitable repayments. By 1865 the crisis had come and many Natalians went bankrupt. The Basuto War in that year, which damaged Natal's trade with the Orange Free State, once again emphasised the importance of inland trade.

After this conditions improved somewhat although credit was not easy to obtain without security. The discovery of diamonds increased trading opportunities and these Natal traders grasped eagerly. Not only imported goods, but also local products such as sugar and coffee, found their way to the diamond fields at good prices. It appeared that Natal was about to progress in all directions.

After the Anglo-Zulu War the history of Natal is marked by general progress. The most important advances were in the economic field, where railways had become a safe investment, and in the constitutional field, where the colonists at last obtained responsible government. The population also grew. The increased number of Indians augmented the colony's labour potential, but, on the other hand, created new problems. Besides, unrest in Zululand not only created a dangerous situation on Natal's northern border and hindered trade with the Zulus, but roused fears that it would spread to the Bantu in Natal.

The changes Wolseley had in 1875 made in the membership of the legislative council lapsed in 1880, when the number of councillors was once again made up, as it was in 1869, of twelve elected members and five officials. As early as February, 1880, the legislative council was in favour of responsible government, which the British government would only grant if Natal undertook to handle its own defence. The voters in Natal argued that they were the only community in South Africa which had not yet achieved parliamentary government. But they were not prepared to take over defence matters and thus in the election of 1882 they voiced disapproval of responsible government. The Natalians were loath to accept responsibility for their own defence principally because of complications in Zululand.

Wolseley's policy of 1879, far from making peace, only created disorder in Zululand. Broadly speaking, it divided the Zulus into two camps: those supporting Wolseley's thirteen chiefs and those opposing them. The latter, which included relatives of the banished Cetshwayo, such as his brothers Ndabuko and Shingane, and his chief induna, Myamana, and who were known as the Usutu, endeavoured to have Cetshwayo repatriated. In contrast the appointed chiefs, particularly Usibepu and Uhamu, who did not want to lose their positions, preferred Cetshwayo's absence. Clashes naturally followed and Zululand was far from quiet.

Consequently Natal, with unrest on its border, did not want to surrender the protection afforded by the Imperial troops. The legislative council preferred to try to enlarge its membership and extend the franchise. This was done in 1883. The qualifications were changed so that male inhabitants who did not possess or rent immovable property, but who had been resident in the colony for three years and earned £8 a month, could vote. The membership of the council was increased to thirty. Twenty-three of these were elected, five were heads of departments and two were nominated by the governor from leading colonists who owned land to the value of £1,000 and had been Natal voters for at least two years. In 1889 a further elected member was added.

After ignoring the question of responsible government for eight years, Sir John Robinson once more attacked the matter in 1890, this time with the support of an earlier opponent, Harry Escombe. Two elections were fought over the issue, and on 10 May, 1893, the legislative council passed a law to institute responsible government. Two months later the British government approved law. It provided for a parliament of two houses, a legislative council of ven members nominated for ten years and an elected assembly of thirty-seven members, chosen for four years. Executive power rested with the governor and a cabinet of not more than six members. Ministers had to be members of one of the houses, but the legislative council could furnish no more than two ministers. Anyone who satisfied the franchise requirements could be elected to the legislative assembly, but members of the legislative council had to be at least thirty years of age, have been living in Natal for ten years and own immovable property to the value of £500.

To a certain degree the institution of parliamentary government paralleled Natal's material progress from 1880 and was connected with the peace which had been assured on its northern border. The production of sugar increased and there were other products that were profitably cultivated. Coal mining became important too, particularly in the light of the near completion of the Durban harbour works, and the extension of the Natal railways. Durban could become a coal depot for steamships. With this goal in view, and in order to retain its hold on inland trade, the Natal government wanted to build a railway which would link Natal with the Free State and Transvaal, as well as run through the Natal coal fields. Consequently in 1883 a start was made with the railway extension from Pietermaritzburg via Newcastle to Charlestown on the Transvaal border, and this line was opened on 7 April, 1891. In 1892 a branch line, which swung away to the Free State north of Ladysmith and went to Harrismith, was completed. Connecting Durban with up-country areas not only accelerated trade but also resuscitated small towns such as Ladysmith, Dundee and Newcastle. Energy and time which had previously been spent on carrying goods could now be devoted to farming, which meant that this improved as well.

In 1886 the discovery of gold on the Witwatersrand emphasised the necessity of a rail link between Durban and Johannesburg. The line up to Charlestown was of some use, since from there goods were taken to Johannesburg by freight wagons, while passengers went by coach, but the ideal solution would be to extend the Natal railway to Johannesburg. This was necessary if Natal did not want to lose ground to the projected rail links from Delagoa Bay and Cape Town to the Rand. Efforts to reach agreement between Natal and the Cape Colony concerning uniformity of customs tariffs and rail extension to Johannesburg failed since Natal refused to increase its tariffs. By the time Natal came to its senses, the Cape line had already reached Johannesburg while Natal's line still only went as far as Charlestown. Furthermore, the Transvaal government was reluctant to extend the Natal railway. Natal's trade began to suffer, and even the development of its coal fields could not make good the loss. The realisation that Transvaal would be disposed to be more friendly towards a self-governing colony was the final factor which encouraged Natal towards responsible government. One of the first tasks which Natal's responsible government undertook was to extend its railways. In October, 1895, Johannesburg and Durban were linked by rail and the Natalians could relax.

This rail link and the improved Durban harbour immediately benefited Natal.

For example, in 1896 railway revenue was more than double that of 1895 (£1,136,000 in 1896 and £526,500 in 1895), owing mainly to the increased goods traffic between Durban and Johannesburg. Natal, with its harbour and railway, became the most important distributor of imported goods. With its improved harbour facilities, extra traffic could be handled with ease. In 1899 734 ships totalling 1,397,306 tons docked at Durban, compared to 98 ships totalling 25,961 tons in 1869. In 1869 imports amounted to £380,000 while exports totalled £363,000 as against £5,359,000 and £3,027,500 respectively in 1899. Customs dues remained Natal's main source of revenue and in 1902/1903, when the total income of the colony was just less than £4,350,000, revenue from customs had already passed the £1,000,000 mark.

In Zululand hostilities continued during the eighties. The British government did not want to spend money on restoring the peace and in 1882 decided to re-instate Cetshwayo as chief of the Zulus. Sir Henry Bulwer, Governor of Natal, would not tolerate this and tried to prevent Cetshwayo's opponents from being placed under his jurisdiction. With the help of Melmoth Osborn, British resident in Zululand, he arranged matters so that Cetshwayo was re-instated as chief of the central part of Zululand only. The northern part was placed under Usibepu, while the southern part, the Zulu Reserve, was under the authority of a British resident commissioner. These arrangements, however, failed just as Wolseley's had failed. Enmity between the Usutu and anti-Usutu was so deep that clashes could not be prevented. The situation developed into a battle between Usibepu and Cetshwayo. On 21 July, 1883, Cetshwayo was defeated at Ulundi and fled to the Reserve. Chaos followed, and even Cetshwayo's death on 8 February, 1884, did not settle matters.

The Usutu finally asked Coenraad Meyer and other Boers to attempt to restore peace. A few Boers, aware that the British government did not want to intervene, therefore went to Zululand in April, 1883, established that Dinuzulu should be Cetshwayo's successor, and helped to vanquish Usibepu. They were given land in exchange for their services, and in August, 1884, proclaimed this territory the New Republic. The Boers' intervention and particularly the idea that they might gain control of St. Lucia Bay in Zululand and thus acquire their own harbour finally forced the British government to act. On behalf of the British government, Sir Arthur Havelock, the Natal Governor, therefore negotiated with the New Republic Boers, fixed a border between the Boers and the Zulus and annexed the rest of Zululand on 19 May, 1887. This still did not solve all the problems. The Usutu refused to agree to the annexation and, under the leadership of Dinuzulu and his two uncles, Ndabuko and Shingane, revolted in 1888. This uprising was suppressed and the three leaders tried and sent to St. Helena. After this conditions in Zululand improved and there was more confidence in Natal to apply for responsible government. But Natal still did not want to lose the security afforded by the British garrison and made an agreement with the British government that the troops would remain in Natal for five years after the institution of responsible government.

Natal's economic revival brought an influx of immigrants. In October, 1880, for example, there were already 734 new settlers as against the 287 of the previous year. More Indians also arrived, not only indentured ones, but also many who came at their own expense and established themselves, mainly as traders. These, as well as those who had served their periods of indenture and had not returned to India, were known as free Indians. They constituted a particular problem for Natal.

As they were small landowners, traders and labourers, the free Indians prevented Natal from absorbing more White immigrants. The Indians also began to compete with the Whites. This elicited protests from the Natalians. In 1885 a commission appointed by the government to investigate Indian immigration found that the Whites in general were opposed to the "presence of the free Indian as a rival or competitor, either in agricultural or commercial pursuits".[3] The interests of the sugar growers weighed so heavily, however, that it was only in 1894 that the Natal Parliament decided to repeal the government's annual contribution towards Indian immigration. Pressure was also brought to bear on Indians whose period of indenture had lapsed, to return to India. A law of 1895 stipulated, among other things, that each indentured Indian who had not returned to India after five years or had not indentured himself again, had to take out an annual license of £1.10.0.

In spite of these measures Indians continued to immigrate into Natal in large numbers and by 1897 White antagonism to them was so strong that an attempt was made to prevent some few hundred free Indians from landing at Durban. Consequently the Natal government passed bills which not only limited the immigration of free Indians – a test of competency in a European language was demanded – but also restricted Indian traders. In 1896 Indians were also excluded from the franchise when a bill was passed which made it impossible for non-Whites and their descendants who did not come from a country with parliamentary institutions to register as voters.

Despite opposition and restrictions, the sugar magnates continued to import indentured Indians up to 1911. Free Indians continued to enter up to 1913, when the Union government prohibited further immigration. The numbers of Indians thus increased steadily by immigration. This increase, as well as a high birth rate, meant that by 1902 the 49,000 free Indians and 26,000 indentured ones outnumbered the 73,000 Natal Whites.

Natal made excellent progress in the field of education. By 1883 96 per cent of Natal's White children were at school; in the Cape Colony the figure was only 65 per cent. Of the more than 260 schools in existence in 1897 only fifteen were fully state schools. The rest were state-supported private schools. There were also a number of private schools which refused state aid. These schools slavishly imitated the British public school system and were patronised by parents who considered that the state schools were not maintaining the true British tradition. Others preferred church schools because they regarded state schools as "godless". Provision was also made for non-White education. By

---

3. Quoted in *The Cambridge History of the British Empire*, VIII (Cambridge, 1936), p. 550.

1894 7,139 Whites, 5,064 Bantu and 2,600 Indians were at school. The accelerated educational pace was particularly noticeable after 1877. In this year an education bill provided for the Colony's educational needs and an education board was instituted. After the institution of responsible government in 1893 educational matters were placed under the aegis of a minister.

Greater Natal

In 1845 the borders of Natal were defined as the Tugela River with its tributary, the Buffalo River, in the north, the Drakensberg in the west, the Umzimkulu River in the south and the Indian Ocean in the east. To begin with there was room enough for White and non-White, but it was possible that at some time there would not be enough space for the population. The Natal government therefore had to pay some attention to ensuring ways of expanding, particularly in the west towards Basutoland, in the south towards Pondoland and in the north towards Zululand.

In 1866 Natal incorporated part of Pondoland as the Alfred district. Before the British annexation of Basutoland in 1868 the Natalians had also desired this territory, but failed to acquire it. As early as 1861 Lieutenant-Governor Scott recommended that Zululand be incorporated into Natal as he feared that the South African Republic would obtain a hold over it. The British government, however, was opposed to territorial expansion and Natal was powerless to undertake it on her own. Even so Natal always looked covetously at Zululand and after the end of the Anglo-Zulu War of 1879 her desire for it grew. Natal would have been satisfied with a British annexation of Zululand, which could then have been incorporated at a later date into Natal.

Curiously enough the Natal legislative council did not take much interest in Zulu affairs during the eighties. In general the Natalians felt that the British government was implementing the wrong policy in Zululand and should be left alone to extricate itself from the troubles it had brought down on its head.

On 15 July, 1885, the legislative council for the first time expressed the wish in a number of resolutions that Britain should immediately annex Zululand, solve the Zulu problems and then incorporate the Bantu territory north of Natal up to the Portuguese border into the Colony. These resolutions were made because the council feared that the Boers would acquire Zululand. When Governor Havelock, on top of everything, began to negotiate with the New Republic without consulting the Natal legislative council, the council insisted that Natal be allowed to annex Zululand. This demand was disregarded however. In 1887 the British government annexed Zululand, excluding the New Republic, as a British colony quite separate from Natal.

In Natal the hope then arose that the New Republic would unite with Natal, but this hope died when in 1888 the New Republic united with the South African Republic to become the Vryheid district. There was still the chance that Natal might acquire the colony of Zululand. But the British government would not agree to this incorporation, principally because Natal was not self-governing. The Natalians had to prove able to govern themselves before they could be given further responsibilities.

They obtained parliamentary government in 1893, but even before their capacity could be tested the question of incorporation with Zululand once more came to the fore. This was because philanthropists were bringing pressure to bear on the British government to repatriate Dinuzulu, Ndabuko and Shingane, who had been exiled to St. Helena after the Usutu rebellion in 1888. Towards the end of 1894 the British government made secret arrangements for the repatriation of the exiles. Neither the British Resident Commissioner in Zululand, Sir Marshall Clarke, nor the Natal Governor, Sir Walter Hely-Hutchinson, expected the repatriations to have any repercussions in Zululand. In fact, Hely-Hutchinson, considered that Dinuzulu's return would end unrest in Zululand, and create conditions healthy enough to attract the Natal Bantu into Zululand.

Natalians in general feared that Dinuzulu's return would only create unrest in an otherwise peaceful Zululand. Consequently Hely-Hutchinson, who was in the unfortunate position of being governor of Natal as well as of Zululand, and who did not particularly want to antagonise his Natal ministers, deemed it essential that the Natal cabinet should endorse the repatriation measures. There had already been indications that these measures would be opposed by the Natal cabinet, since Prime Minister Sir John Robinson had, in May, 1894, indicated that the incorporation of Zululand into Natal would have to precede repatriation of the exiles. He expected Dinuzulu's return to start trouble in Zululand and obviously believed that Natal was more capable than the British government of coping with any problems. Cetshwayo's repatriation in 1883 by the British government and the consequent strife was still fresh in everyone's memory. Robinson reflected the attitude of his cabinet and they were so adamant that the British government was temporarily obliged to shelve the repatriation of the exiles.

A factor which reinforced the Natal cabinet's conviction that incorporation with Zululand should precede Dinuzulu's return was the annexation of Pondoland by the Cape Prime Minister, Cecil Rhodes, and his remarks about Natal, which aroused fears that he would annex Zululand to the Cape Colony. The Natalians had hoped for at least a part of Pondoland if any annexation in this area was to take place. Rhodes, however, in 1894 annexed the whole of Pondoland to the Cape Colony, and declared that Natal with its narrow-minded parliament and scanty White population could have no part in Pondoland and should indeed surrender the Alfred district south of the Umzimkulu to the Cape Colony. These actions and remarks aroused the Natalians and when in 1894, with the publication of the Pondoland correspondence, it became known that the Cape Colony had secretly obtained approval from the British government as early as 1892 for its annexation of Pondoland there was, according to Hely-Hutchinson, "a widespread impression that a similar surprise may be in store for Natal as regards Zululand".[4] As a result the Natal cabinet insisted on Britain promising that Zululand would be incorporated into Natal.

4. Quoted in M. C. van Zyl: *Die Uitbreiding van Britse Gesag oor die Natalse Noordgrensgebiede 1879 – 1897* (Archives Year Book for S.A. History, 1966, I), p. 265.

This promise the British government made in July, 1894, but the Natal cabinet – unjustly – were still suspicious of Rhodes and pressed for a speedy incorporation, maintaining that only then would it be right for Dinuzulu to return. In this manner Natal obtained a hold on the British government since Dinuzulu's repatriation could not be shelved indefinitely – he had been told in 1894 that he would be repatriated. The obvious expedient was to agree to incorporation, but the British government did not think the time ripe for such a step. Possibly it argued that responsible government had not yet been properly tested in Natal. The real reason, however, appears to have been that the British government first wanted to use Zululand to extend its sphere of influence in the Bantu areas between Zululand and Portuguese East Africa, viz. the Cispongola territory in the south, the Transpongola territory in the northwest and Tongoland in the north-east. These areas were desired because of their situation on the eastern seaboard.

As early as 1888 and 1890 the British government had incorporated the Cispongola territory piecemeal into Zululand to prevent Sordwana Bay from falling into foreign hands. Further annexation was to follow, as the South African Republic wished to reach Kosi Bay on the Tongo coast, via Swaziland and Transpongola. With his eye to Kosi Bay, Native Commissioner J. J. Ferreira acquired the districts of the Transpongola chiefs Zambaan and Mbegisa for the South African Republic in 1887. In Tongaland, however, Ferreira came off second-best because Governor Havelock had already signed a treaty with the Tongas that they would grant land or concessions to Britain only. Nor could the South African Republic further extend its control over the Transpongola territory because, according to the London Convention of 1884, any such move would have to be approved by the British government. The South African Republic also began to take an interest in the affairs of Swaziland.

After years of negotiation the South African Republic gained control of Swaziland in February, 1895, but a few months later the British government annexed the Transpongola territory for Zululand and proclaimed Tongoland a protectorate. The main motives were to cut the Republic off from the sea, to prevent a foreign port on the eastern seaboard from competing with Durban harbour, and to maintain Natal's trade route through Zululand and Zambaansland to Swaziland – Natal trade with Swaziland amounted to over £70,000 per year. Although the Natalians were directly concerned in these annexations, they would not openly admit to complicity. They were afraid that their rail communications with the South African Republic, among which the extension of the Charlestown link to Johannesburg was vital to Natal, would be adversely affected. Therefore the British government had to effect the annexations pretending that Natal had nothing to do with them. With Zululand as a British colony, quite independent of Natal, the Transpongola territory could easily be incorporated into Zululand. Had Natal already controlled Zululand, the Natal government would not have been in a position to oppose the claim of the South African Republic to the Transpongola territory. Consequently Zululand could not be incorporated into Natal before the Transpongola territory had been annexed to Zululand.

In 1896 the Natal government once more brought up the question of incorporation with Zululand, but the British government, because of the repercussions of the Jameson Raid, did not consider the time ripe. But Joseph Chamberlain, the British Secretary of State for the Colonies, still wanted to send Dinuzulu back to Zululand. Once again the Natal ministers insisted that Dinuzulu should only return after Zululand's incorporation. Chamberlain, however, first wished to complete the annexation of Tongoland. In the beginning the Tongas were opposed to the annexation of their country, but as a result of clashes between them and the Portuguese, annexation was concluded on 22 November, 1897, and incorporation into Zululand on 27 December, 1897, without any further opposition. Meanwhile, the British and Natal governments had agreed about the incorporation of Zululand in Natal, which occurred on 30 December, 1897. Seven days later the Zulu exiles, Dinuzulu, Ndabuko and Shingane, landed at Durban and left for Zululand immediately.

There were various conditions under which Natal took over Zululand. Among others, the existing system of landownership had to be maintained for five years so that sufficient land for Zulu settlement could be claimed during that period. Thereafter the Natal government was free to do as it pleased with the land which had not been reserved for locations. This arrangement was not quite to the taste of the Natalians, as they argued, in the words of Hely-Hutchinson, that "both in the interests of the advancement of the natives, and the interests of public order, it is not advisable that the natives should be collected into one vast reserve".[5] In contrast to the trend in South Africa at the present day, they argued that Whites had to live among the Bantu to civilize and control them. The idea of filling the unpopulated areas of Zululand with surplus Natal Bantu, most of whom were Zulus, in order to make more land available for White settlement in Natal never seems to have struck them.

The incorporation of Zululand meant that the area of the Natal Colony was nearly doubled. The Natal government now had in its care, in addition to the 535,000 Natal Bantu, a further 188,000 Zulus. After the Anglo-Boer War Natal was once again enlarged by the addition of the Transvaal districts of Vryheid, Utrecht and part of Wakkerstroom. In 1904 nearly half of Zululand, which since 1897 had reached north to the Portuguese border, was opened to White settlement. Except for the locations reserved for Bantu inhabitants, there was no territorial segregation between White and Bantu in greater Natal.

5. *Ibid.*, pp. 271 – 272.

12. The Orange Free State

The founding of a republic

Seldom in history has a state been so ill equipped for self-government as was the Orange Free State when, on 23 February, 1854, the Bloemfontein Convention was signed by representatives of the White population of the area between the Orange and Vaal Rivers and the British Special Commissioner, Sir George Clerk. Since 1848, when the Orange River Sovereignty was proclaimed by Sir H. G. Smith, various vain attempts had been made to establish law and order among its variety of inhabitants, Whites, Griquas, Korannas, Barolong and Basuto. Most disagreements were based on rights of land ownership. The British authorities, mainly because of the financial implications, were unable to reconcile the differing land claims and so, for the first time in history, the British Empire surrendered one of its possessions in Southern Africa.

The clause of the Convention which stipulated that the people of the Orange River Sovereignty would in future "be in all respects a totally free and independent nation" (translated from the original Dutch) and exempt from their fealty to the British Crown, must have sounded sweet to those who had been trying for a decade or longer to gain their independence. However, there were no overt signs of joy when the old Batavian tricolour, for lack of the Orange Free State's own colours, replaced the Union Jack on the fort. In the outlying districts the day passed almost unnoticed and in Bloemfontein the preponderantly English population, because it resented the British evacuation, boycotted the independence ceremonies.

Those, however, who accepted the responsibility for establishing and running a new government, did so with some misgiving. Their position was aptly described a few years later in *De Tijd*: "A powerful country took illegal possession of us and contemptuously tossed us aside when their arbitrary action failed to pay. They left simple people standing in an extensive, open country, surrounded by enemies on all sides, without judges, without soldiers, without money, divided by ignorance, exploited by fortune hunters and derided by a colony whose buffer they were".[1]

The historic nature of 23 February, 1854, did not escape the signatories to the Convention. As the Acting President, J. P. Hoffman, declared in a circular: "This day was one of the strangest, even unique, in world history, and for us the day our independence was born. What we become on this day, we were given unasked . . . ".[2] From the beginning the "Provisioneel Gouvernement"

---

1. *De Tijd*, 27 Feb., 1866, translated from the original Dutch.
2. *The Friend of the Sovereignty*, 25 Feb. 1854, translated from the original Dutch.

aimed at "maintaining internal unity and order and external peace" – an ideal for which the Orange Free State always worked.

The work of government was begun courageously, but it seemed that in the first five years every effort to progress and to found a new stable state was foiled. Tension and war between the Orange Free State and the Basuto on her eastern border, bad droughts, locusts, plagues, lack of money and experience, internal strife, disloyalties and constant changes of heads of state, often made the young republic powerless to combat internal disturbances or foreign attacks, and often even endangered the very existence of the state.

The provisional government retained the existing administration and also elected twenty-nine representatives to decide how the country should be governed. At the meeting of the Volksraad on 28 March the drafting of a constitution was regarded as its first and most important task. Using the French constitution of 1848 as a model, as well as some clauses of the American constitution, this group of unsophisticated Boers, for many years deprived of regular schooling and inexperienced in constitutional matters, succeeded with the help of some "Uitlanders" in fully expressing all the democratic and republican beliefs of the Afrikaner people. Although the constitution was wholly revised on two occasions it always remained essentially unchanged and the basis on which the "model" republic of the Orange Free State was built.[3]

Originally the constitution laid down that every person who had resided in the state for six months would be given citizenship and be entitled to vote at the age of eighteen.

The ultimate legislative authority was vested in the Volksraad whose members represented the field cornetcies and main towns of the various districts. Members were elected for four years and half would retire every two years. The Raad could pass no laws preventing the inhabitants from peacefully assembling in order to petition the government to introduce, revise or revoke a law. Religious and educational matters were in the hands of the Raad, while the Dutch Reformed Church was the state church.

All executive and administrative authority was vested in the State President and he was elected by the nation for five years. He was responsible for his actions only to the Volksraad. He was assisted in his duties as head of state by the Executive Committee which consisted of the Government Secretary, the landdrost of Bloemfontein and three non-official members. In addition to declaring or repealing martial law, this body could exercise the right of clemency in all criminal sentences.

The field cornets and commandants for the wards and districts were elected by the burghers, who became liable for military service at the age of sixteen. In times of war these officers elected a commandant-general from their ranks. To avoid the disagreements which had previously arisen in Natal and the Transvaal over this office, he was required to relinquish his post once a war had ended.

3. Vide Scholtz, G. D.: *Die Konstitusie en die Staatsinstellings van die Oranie-Vrystaat*, pp. 1 – 17, and Van Schoor, M.C.E. en Van Rooyen, J. J.: *Republieke en Republikeine*, p. 103 et seq.

The constitution also stipulated that justice would be administered according to Roman-Dutch law and that private property, personal freedom and the freedom of the press would be guaranteed.

With this constitution and an administration based mainly on the Cape-English example, the Free State elected its first president, Josias Philip Hoffman. Although his political views were supported more by the loyalists than by the dyed-in-the-wool republicans, it was his particularly friendly relationship with Moshesh which brought him the presidency. It was hoped that he would be able to stop Basuto plundering parties by adopting a conciliatory attitude towards the Basuto chief.

Eloquent, reasonably facile with his pen, sufficiently self-confident despite his being a cripple, and assisted by the competent and also crippled Dutch schoolmaster, J. J. Groenendal as Government Secretary, Hoffman showed in the single year he held office that he possessed many statesmanlike qualities. The Free State completed its first year of independence without having had to mobilize its forces. It had also resisted M. W. Pretorius's first attempt to establish closer connections between the republics on either side of the Vaal River.

It was apparent, however, from the so-called "gunpowder episode" that President Hoffman lacked the requisite tact and insight to lead a people who had divergent views about their political future. From a superficial point of view it would seem that Hoffman was forced to resign as a result of a gift of gunpowder to Moshesh and Adam Kok, which was not fully explained in the Volksraad. Actually the Raad was not only disturbed by this philanthropic gesture, but also in the opinion of the republicans who sought affiliations in the north, Hoffman was too compliant with the wishes of the so-called English party. This was comprised of the English-speaking part of the population, particularly from Bloemfontein and Smithfield, who for their part wished to establish connections with the Cape Colony.

Years of endeavour: the establishment of a civil service

The people of the Free State were better pleased with their second choice of president. Johannes Nicolaas Boshof was a man of wide experience in government administration, acquired first in the Cape civil service and later in that of Natal. With enthusiasm and self-sacrifice he began the difficult task of bringing order to the confused fiscal matters and civil service of the Republic. With the support of the Volksraad he introduced a series of well-planned ordinances and administrative measures which stabilized the entire administration. It was mainly owing to his work and insight in founding the Free State civillservice that the composer of the Free State national anthem was moved to incude the words "op orde, recht en wet gevest" (based on order, justice and law).

Boshof's strong administration had two results. It gave later presidents confidence to continue his work, and his success in producing order in government matters was what first stimulated a national consciousness and a sense of pride in the Free State. This created a new political climate which President Brand in particular could utilize to maintain and increase the Free State's independence.

In spite of his good work Boshof was to have five difficult and often unpleasant years as president. His efforts to maintain the independence of the Free State involved him in clashes both with those who desired union with the Transvaal and those who desired union with the Cape Colony. The latter, the "re-annexationists", grasped every opportunity for discrediting the republic in the eyes of the Colony. For example a fierce agitation erupted over the death sentence of one C. L. Cox who was found guilty of murdering his wife. The English people of the Free State, using the invalid argument that as a British subject he was not subject to Free State jurisdiction, also claimed that he was sentenced because of racial animosity. They even appealed to Sir George Grey, but he flatly refused to become involved in the matter since he had full confidence in Boshof's government and the Republic's legalsystem. The argument concerning anti-British prejudice was also spurious, as the Free State government had proved its confidence in the British by appointing many to several important government posts.

On the Free State's second birthday its new flag and coat of arms were to be appropriately celebrated. These symbols of nationhood had been presented to the republic in a gesture of goodwill by William III of the Netherlands, at the request of the Hoffman government. Not knowing of this request, the Boshof government had commissioned a design for the great seal which was incorporated into the coat of arms. In the midst of the birthday celebrations M. W. Pretorius arrived in Bloemfontein with a delegation to annex the Free State on the grounds of promises made to his father by the British government. His claim was denied, and when he doubted the authority of the Free State government, he was summarily ordered to leave the republic. During the next year tension in the Free State and between the two republics was to increase at an alarming rate. The "re-annexationists" found much to hope for in Grey's federation plans for southern Africa and therefore strongly resisted union with the Transvaal, while those who desired this union used various illegal strategies in the northern areas in an attempt to force the Boshof government into such a union. However, there was also a strong group supporting Boshof's point of view that the two republics should continue separately and "compete with one another in the struggle for a true Christian civilization, and good government".

In 1857 fears of mutual interference brought Free State and Transvaal commandos face to face at Renoster River, and fratricidal bloodshed was only averted at the last moment. A peace treaty was concluded between the two states, each acknowledging the other's independence. Pretorius relinquished his claims and the Free State undertook not to interfere with the Transvaal's internal affairs. The treaty established a basis for close co-operation between the republics, but such co-operation only became a reality in the eighties.

The Free Stater's lack of discipline under martial law caused Boshof to decide on stricter military service for the burghers. This evoked such a sharp reaction among his people that, together with other matters concerning which there was friction between him and the Volksraad, it led to his resignation. The people of Bloemfontein particularly were so dismayed at this that Boshof withdrew his resignation. The Basutos on the eastern border were openly hostile, and he realized that the republic could not afford to look for a new president at this stage.

In their search for more land, the Basutos in the east had been increasingly trespassing over the border, and had plundered White cattle and property. All the letters, negotiations and personal mediation of Sir George Grey could not convince Moshesh that he had to control his subjects, and particularly his subordinate chiefs. After all promises to return the stolen cattle had come to nothing, the Free State declared war on Basutoland on 19 March, 1858. To begin with the Free State fared well, but when it became clear that the siege of Thaba Bosiu was going to be a lengthy one, Boshof began looking for allies. The Transvaal would only help if such help would increase the likelihood of the Free State uniting with the Transvaal. Grey sympathized with the Free State, to the extent that he even made a donation towards the erection of a training-college, but he could only act within the framework of British colonial interests. He prohibited the Cape colonists from helping the Free Staters as he hoped that the war would force the Free State to accept his plans for federation.

When to Boshof's dismay the burghers began deserting the commandos in large numbers he had no choice but to agree to an armistice with Mosesh on 1 June and to accept Sir George Grey as mediator. In spite of the compensation the Basutos were made to pay, the war had almost broken the Free State financially. In order to improve matters in case the Basuto's should renew their attacks, the Free Staters by a majority vote decided to join the Transvaal. However, when Grey, in an effort to preserve the possibility of federation, on his own responsibility declared that this would mean a contravention of the conventions, the decision was not put into effect. In their desperation the Free Staters swung to the other extreme, and the Volksraad decided to join a British federation. When the British government, basing its policy on "no further expansion" and the maintenance of the conventions, would not fall in with Grey's plans, the Free State found itself still in a precarious position.

Further trouble awaited the Free State. In May, 1858, the Koranna captain, Skeelkoos, attacked Boer families in the western Free State. Men and unarmed women and children were murdered and thousands of sheep and cattle stolen. A commando had to be mobilized to clean out the marauders permanently from their strongholds on the Vaal River.

In spite of the political uncertainty and threats of war the republic did make some progress on the socio-economic level. In 1856 the census had shown a total White population of 12,859 in five districts. Three years later there were indications that the population had nearly doubled, mainly through immigration. The growth of the republic was also reflected in the gradual increase in the government's revenue and expenditure. Despite all setbacks, and owing to Boshof's strict austerity measures, the republic remained solvent.

It was mainly the Free Staters' lack of patriotism, loyalty and determination which made Boshof decide that he would serve them no longer. Notwithstanding his optimistic administrative policy, he was too sensitive a man to endure petty pin-pricks and political rebuffs, and once again he resigned the presidency to return to life on his Natal farm.

An attempt to unite the two republics

Partly because there was a strong group in the Free State in favour of unification with the Transvaal, and partly because the rest of the population, their hopes dashed by Britain's rejection of the federation plan, saw no other solution to their problems Marthinus Wessel Pretorius, President of the South African Republic, was elected President of the Orange Free State as well. As a practical pioneer leader in his own environment this farmer no doubt had his virtues, but it had already become apparent in the Transvaal that as statesman he lacked the ability and vision to realise the dreams of his father, who had hoped for one republic north of the Orange River. For a time the younger Pretorius was able to maintain the union between the two republics. The Free State had by a large majority decided to merge with the Transvaal, but the South African Republic had not been eager to unite with the Free State for fear that the Sand River Convention which guaranteed its independence would be nullified. After six months Pretorius was forced to relinquish his Transvaal presidency. He continued to make efforts to unite the Free State and the South African Republic, but the Transvaalers' unwillingness to join such a union thwarted his attempts. Only towards the end of President Brand's term of office did a close association of the republics become an active political issue.

His tact in dealing with Natives made the Free State hope that Pretorius would be able to control the Basutos. Although the so-called Warden Line restricted his tribe's property, Moshesh did nothing to stop continuous and wide-spread cattle-rustling from the farms of Free State burghers. By repeatedly visiting Moshesh, especially after a particularly unpleasant murder of a White farmer, Pretorius did succeed in maintaining a precarious peace on the eastern border of the Free State. Moshesh obviously realised that war with the Free State would also entail war with the Transvaal. In order to reduce cattle-rustling, Pretorius wished to institute a regular border patrol, but the poor finances of the Free State prevented this measure from being put into effect. Contrary to the Bloemfontein Convention the British High Commissioner interfered in the Bantu question, to the dismay of the Free State. However, Pretorius requested Sir Philip Wodehouse to redefine the border, although this had already been done in the years of the Sovereignty. The border would only finally be established in President Brand's term of office.

A particularly noteworthy action of Pretorius was that which ended the years of arguments about the property rights of Whites in the inalienable Griqua lands. When the British government offered Adam Kok's Griquas a new home in the no-mans-land which was later to be known as Griqualand East, the Free

Staters eagerly seized the opportunity, and bought the remaining Griqua territory around the Philippolis and the Campbell territory of Cornelis Kok for £4,000. Although the Free State since becoming a republic had been on very good terms with the Griquas, as with the Barolong who lived near Thaba Nchu, the emigration of the Griquas removed all possibility of friction and freed more land for the continuous stream of immigrants from the Cape Colony.

In spite of the problems which the young republic had to face during its early years there was a definite, if slow, improvement in its economy. The simple, self-sufficient, and mainly agricultural economy was able to withstand even the worst droughts of living memory in 1860 and 1862, as well as violent hailstorms and floods in certain areas. The towns grew steadily with the influx of foreign population, mainly of British and Dutch, and villages such as Boshof, Kroonstad, Bethulie, Jacobsdal and Philippolis also developed in the nine years following the inception of the republic. By 1860 imports from the Colony and Natal amounted to £250,000 but of the import duties levied on goods destined for the Free State in British ports, the republic received nothing. As the Free State's growth depended largely on its increasing its revenue, the Volksraad delegated Pretorius, and the Government Secretary, J. Allison, to negotiate for a part of this revenue in Cape Town. The mission failed. The British government was not for many years to relinquish this economic hold on the republics.

Pretorius's periodic absences from the Free State to settle problems in the Transvaal meant that the Free State administration lacked continuity and also caused a crisis in government finances. The 1863 financial year ended with a deficit of £12,500. After first refusing to accept Pretorius's resignation, the Volksraad then decided to accept it. If Pretorius was anywhere effective, it was in the less spectacular fields of state jurisprudence and administration. At least the judiciary, education, prisons, and defence had been placed on a sounder footing. The failure of Pretorius's efforts politically to unite the Free State and the Transvaal was made apparent shortly after his resignation, when 1,550 Free State burghers petitioned that the Free State was not able to contend with the Basuto threat. The Volksraad, however, under the acting president, J. J. Venter – who had helped to found the *Gereformeerde Kerk* in the Free State – supported the point of view expressed in a counter petition, signed by 1,014 burghers, that the Free State should not under any circumstances surrender its independence.

J. H. Brand, the architect of a model republic

The party who wished to keep the Free State independent and whose slogan was 'Vrij zijn wij en vrij willen wij blijven" ("Free we are and free we wish to remain") was supported by the weekly paper, *De Tijd*, and a number of influential Dutch. It reflected the feelings of most of the Free State burghers for the next twenty-five years. These people knew very well that the continued existence of their republic depended entirely on their choice of the next head of state. The election of the able Cape advocate and member of parliament for Clanwilliam, Dr Johannes Henricus Brand, as the fourth State President of the

Free State, ensured not only the future of the republic, but was also to bring it unforeseen glory. For twenty-five years this superb statesman, polished diplomat and brilliant administrator was to officiate as State President in such a way that his people honoured him with the title "Vader des Volks" (Father of the People). His friendly personality, his integrity, his legal background, his visionary and thorough powers of organization and his remarkably clear insight into the politics of his state and southern Africa as a whole, meant that he would not only solve many of the republic's problems systematically and permanently, but also that he would so develop the whole system of government that the Free State would come to be regarded as a model republic.

Although Brand wished to promote cordial co-operation among the states and colonies of southern Africa, he always insisted that the Free State must in every way advance its independence. Only so could she enter the broader field of the general political, economic and social problems of southern Africa on an equal footing with the other states. For this reason he gave priority to solving the difficult Basuto problem, since it was retarding the republic's progress towards political and economic self-sufficiency.

Initially he adopted the honourable method of negotiating with Moshesh to induce the Basuto to withdraw from where they had settled as much as twenty miles inside the republic's boundaries. When, however, the Basutos argued that they did not know precisely where the boundaries were, Brand immediately followed the same tactics as his predecessor, and induced the British High Commissioner to establish the eastern border of the Free State beyond all doubt. In October, 1864, the old Warden Line was confirmed with minor alterations.

When various of Moshesh's subordinate chiefs, encouraged by certain missionaries of the Paris Missionary Society, refused to recognise the established border and some burghers died in the ensuing clashes, Brand persuaded the Volksraad to declare war on the infiltrators. Border violations had to be stopped once and for all. This would not be an easy task because the Basutos had smuggled in many guns and they were well ensconced in their mountain fortifications. The Free State commandos, under commandants Fick, Wepener and De Villiers, were now well disciplined, and were also inspired by President Brand's personal encouragement. The murder of some Transvaal transport-riders by the Basuto brought the South African Republic into the war and a commando under Paul Kruger gave valuable aid. Soon the commandos had reached Moshesh's redoubt, but after a half-hearted attempt, in which Louw Wepener died heroically, to take Thaba Bosiu, the burghers exhibited the same poor morale as had afflicted them in earlier campaigns. Only President Brand's arrival prevented a complete collapse of their lines. The policy of everywhere confiscating the Basuto's cattle and of destroying their crops did, however, now begin to take effect. Moshesh now requested Wodehouse to place the Basutos under British control. Wodehouse strongly recommended that this should be done, but the Imperial government was still opposed to any form of territorial expansion in South Africa.

Wodehouse did, however, succeed in making things difficult for the Free State. When Brand, planning a final death-blow to the Basutos, promised Cape colonist volunteers farms in whatever territory was conquered, Wodehouse announced that he would stop the supply of all weapons and ammunition to the Free State if she made use of foreign aid. He acted in this way for fear the Free Staters would totally conquer the Basuto, and despite his threat being contrary to the Bloemfontein Convention. Because the war had an extremely detrimental effect on trade in the Cape Colony, he offered his services for negotiating a peace. His offer was turned down. It was only when Molapo, one of Moshesh's strongest allies, surrendered, that the Basuto chief sued for peace with the Free State. In the Treaty of Thaba Bosiu (April, 1866) Moshesh not only agreed to pay compensation, but allowed the Free State to annex the conquered territory. While Wodehouse gravely doubted whether the Basuto would be able to maintain themselves on what remained of their territory, Brand wished to divide the conquered territory into farms as quickly as possible so that it could be populated as a strong buffer against further Basuto trespasses. Because of the earlier political interference of some French missionaries, the Volksraad decided, at the request of the burghers, that all French mission stations inside the republic's boundaries would have to be vacated. Obviously the innocent as well as the guilty were involved in this evacuation, and this move of the Free State was to provoke sharp reactions, even overseas. According to traditional policy Molapo was allowed to keep his tribal territory for his subjects, but to maintain peace a White commandant was appointed to his kraal in a supervisory capacity. No Whites could enter Basuto territory without permission, and only the Dutch Reformed Church was allowed to proselytize in the area.

President Brand was lenient, and allowed the Basuto to harvest their crops before they had to leave the conquered territory. This enabled Moshesh once more to infiltrate his warriors into the area, and a commando had to be mobilized to remove them all. Two of Moshesh's subordinate chiefs, Mopeli and Letsie, requested to be allowed to become Free State subjects. The former was finally settled in Witzieshoek under the same conditions as Molapo, but when the latter treasonably instigated murders in the conquered territory two strong commandos under Commandants Joubert and Pansegrouw once more took the field in July, 1867. A different spirit now motivated the men, that of teaching Moshesh and his chiefs a final lesson. Even in a short time President Brand had succeeded in awakening a spirit of self-reliance among the Free State people, and had created in them a determination to defend their freedom. A few sharp fights and the systematic destruction of the Basuto's crops caused Moshesh considerable dismay and he once again appealed for British annexation. Wodehouse who, by obstructing the Free State in various ways, had prevented it from dealing the Basutos a decisive blow, finally persuaded the British government to annex Basutoland on the grounds that the Free State's actions endangered all relations with the Natives in southern Africa and that in attacking Basutoland it was probably looking for a passage to the sea. In March, 1868, at a point when the confident and victorious Free State commandos were poised to deliver

Moshesh's deathblow, Wodehouse intervened to annex Basutoland for Britain (see Chapter 14).

The incensed Free State sent a deputation to Britain to protest against the annexation and the repeated breaches of the Bloemfontein Convention, but met with no satisfaction. Nevertheless, in the Free State there was great joy at the end of the long struggle which had cost the state and burghers so many lives, so much property, money, time and energy, and had so retarded the republic's economic development. Brand declared during the London conference in 1876: "The Free State has no native problem: we have already settled it. The Whites are against the natives as two against one". The White Free Staters did keep the Basuto subordinate chiefs under White control in their tribal areas, but the republic never considered the Natives in the Free State to be a "problem". All arrangements and relations with the indigenous non-Whites were determined by the principles of differentiation and guardianship. Within limits, their social welfare, christianization and education were cared for. At Thaba Nchu the traditionally friendly relations between Maroko and his Barolongs and the Voortrekkers were continued throughout the years of the republic. The Barolong always gratefully acknowledged the Free State's protection against the hostile Basutos. On Maroko's death in 1880, there was a struggle for succession of such proportions that in 1884 Brand insisted to the Volksraad that the area be placed under Free State guardianship. The Barolong were disarmed, but kept their full territorial rights.

Meanwhile the treasury had reached a crisis. To make money available for essential and new services, Brand had advised the Volksraad to have paper money, the so-called "blue-backs", printed. The paper money, to a face value of £30,000, was backed by the value of government farms and property. War costs soon absorbed this money, and it was decided in 1866 to issue another £100,000 in "blue-backs". The Basuto War, however, devalued the paper money to half its face value, and Cape Colony traders refused to accept it as legal tender. After the war against the Basuto, the republic's economy was still shaky, but the discovery of diamonds and the receipt of a part of the customs tax levied on Free State goods in British colonial ports, meant that the paper money could be withdrawn. By 1875 only about a quarter of the notes were still in circulation, and at full face value. Brand and his Volksraad had weathered the crisis.

The problem on the eastern border had hardly been solved when the Free State found itself with a problem of equal dimensions on its western border. When in 1867 diamonds were discovered in the district of Hopetown, and shortly afterwards on the banks of the Vaal River and near Dutoitspan and Vooruitzicht, thousands of fortune-hunters from all parts of the world converged on the area between the Orange and Vaal Rivers, where the diamond city of Kimberley would eventually arise. On the strength of British actions during the years of its Sovereignty, various clauses of the Bloemfontein Convention, and President Pretorius's purchase, in 1861, of territories from the Griquas, including the Campbell grounds west of the Vaal River, the Free State claimed with full justice that the territory between the Vaal and Orange Rivers belonged to her

In order to confirm this claim beyond all doubt, it was proclaimed anew in 1870, and Free State officials were appointed to maintain law and order among the diggers. These arrangements were approved by the diggers themselves.

However, a Colesberg solicitor and adventurer, David Arnot, claimed all the land, which included the diggings, in the name of the Griqua captain, Nikolaas Waterboer. This claim was based on an old treaty which Governor D'Urban had concluded with Nikolaas's father, Andries Waterboer, and the fact that Adam and Cornelis Kok were his subjects and could carry out no territorial transactions without his permission. Waterboer's claims, however weak and uncertain, if upheld would limit the westward expansion of the Boer republics and ensure British domination in southern Africa. They were therefore strongly supported by Richard Southey, the Cape Colonial Secretary, who urged Waterboer to place the whole of his territory under British control. When the South African Republic incompetently submitted its claim to the triangular area between the Vaal and Harts Rivers to the arbitration of Lieutenant-Governor Keate of Natal, Keate did not limit himself to his brief, but determined that all the ground west of the Ramah-Davidsgraf Line, which was Free State ground, also belonged to Waterboer. Shortly after his arrival the prejudiced Sir Henry Barkly, Britain's new High Commissioner, proclaimed as British the whole of the territory which Waterboer claimed in order to keep the thousands of diggers in check and to protect the so-called territorial rights of the Griquas. In fact, the land in question had been bought by unprincipled speculators and when later, in 1878, the Griquas were joined by other tribes in a rebellion against the loss of their ground, they were cruelly suppressed.

President Brand was quite willing to submit the property rights of the Campbell territory to foreign arbitration, but consistently fought Britain's right to occupy the Free State territory between the Orange and Vaal Rivers. This had meant not only the loss of the world's richest diamond mines, but also of 143 inhabited farms. As the Free State could not take up arms against this new British demonstration of power, Brand, despite serious illness, defended the Free State's rights untiringly, tactfully and with perseverance for more than four years, verbally and in writing. Brand seldom received any reciprocal courtesy or helpfulness in his correspondence and negotiations with Barkly. In order to publicize her case, Advocate H. A. L. Hamelberg was sent to Europe as diplomatic representative of the Free State. This did succeed in somewhat embarassing Britain, while the trade and diplomatic agreements which she had made with the U.S.A. and some European powers, as well as the appointment of consular officials, also reduced any prospect of Britain annexing the Free State once again. In the Free State even those who had previously been in favour of re-annexation by the Cape Colony, now supported Brand to a man and defended the Free State's rights and integrity. *The Friend of the Free State*, which was reluctant to drop all Carnarvon's federation plans, found in 1875 that it had a competitor. A new weekly paper, *De Express*, appeared, which was greatly to stimulate the emergent Afrikaner nationalism in the two republics.

The British occupation of Griqualand West had meanwhile been permitted by the Free State, but she suggested foreign arbitration to settle the matter. The British, however, feared to lose the economic advantage of the diamond area as well as their dominating position in southern Africa, and all Brand's suggestions concerning arbitration were either ignored or deferred. The decision came from an unexpected quarter. In 1876 the Cape territorial court decided that the respective claims of the South African Republic and the Free State to the areas in dispute were justified in all respects, and that the annexation had taken place without the permission of the Griqua people. Brand immediately went to London to claim the diamond areas between the Vaal and Orange Rivers, but it was clear that Britain was prepared to undo the wrong only by paying compensation and keeping the land. The Free State could not enforce the return of the land, and Brand had to be satisfied with an amount of £90,000, said to be the amount of damages the state had sustained. Britain's attitude embittered many Free Staters and even Transvaalers, and ensured that the Free State would have no part in the confederation scheme which Lord Carnarvon was at that stage trying to force on southern Africa. The shape of the new British imperialism in southern Africa brought the two Boer republics closer to each other and re-awakened their desire for closer unification.

Obviously the Free State benefited from the phenomenal prosperity of the diamond fields, mainly through the increased trade in food and transport. Apart from temporary recessions, serious droughts, and periodic plagues of locusts, economic crises in the republic were things of the past. Most of the £90,000 which had been received in damages from Britain was used to establish a state bank which flourished through all the years of the republic. Brand's wise financial policies also ensured that government revenue always exceeded expenditure, so that the state, like its people, could begin to establish capital funds. This enabled the republic to pass out of its pioneering stage and develop into a modern state.

From the day he took office to the day of his death, Brand passionately promoted education. He made the Volksraad realize that the state should, as far as possible, train its own youth to fill the increasing number of vacancies in its professional fields. It was particularly the interest of the Dutch Reformed Church (N. G. Kerk) that caused educational matters to improve in the seventies. The talented Dr J. Brill from the Netherlands was appointed as principal of Grey College which with the Eunice Insitute for young women offered the only advanced education in the Free State, and the government obtained the able Scotsman, Dr John Brebner, to head educational matters from 1874 until the late nineties. Although there were continual complaints that education in the Free State was far too English-orientated, and in many ways little was done to promote an Afrikaans culture in the republic, the system itself was surpassed by few others in the world at that time.

Since he was a legal man it was natural for Brand to show particular interest in the administration of justice. In 1872 he succeeded in establishing a separate appeal court. This court after three years was made into a full supreme court with F. W. Reitz as the first Chief Justice. Brand also insisted on an efficient civil service and appointed his officials with great care. For many years he had to draw his people from the Cape Colony. To assist his own genius for administration he had the services of the able F. K. Höhne and, from 1879 onwards, P. J. Blignaut as government secretaries. The far-sighted Brand was also continually introducing legislation in the Volksraad to modernize and develop the state's public services. His progressiveness always won the whole-hearted co-operation of his chief officials and the Volksraad; at the most it was tempered only by some healthy conservatism on the part of the Volksraad.

However strongly Brand defended the independence of the Free State, he had equally strong convictions about not allowing it to become isolated. In addition to establishing diplomatic relations with the outside world and healthy trade relations with adjacent territories, he particularly exerted himself to acquire modern communications such as the telegraph and railways for the Free State. By 1879 the capital of the Free State had been connected telegraphically to the British colonies in southern Africa, but as far as the building of railway lines was concerned, Brand was to struggle with the Volksraad for more than ten years before he could persuade them to relinquish their prejudices against this new mode of transportation. Not only were they deterred by the cost, but they also feared that railways would provide a means for the British colonies to obtain a stranglehold on the republic. In 1888, however, the chairman's casting vote decided the Volksraad to extend the railway line from the Cape Colony to Bloemfontein.

By the beginning of the eighties Brand had become an eminent statesman, and it was hardly surprising that he was asked to act as intermediary in 1881 when the Transvaalers inflicted severe reverses on British troops. Although Brand would have preferred the Free State to maintain a strict neutrality in this affair, he could not prevent hundreds of Free Staters from going to the aid of the Transvaalers. Despite the high regard the people had for their State President, these years saw the beginning of a marked political estrangement between them and him. Because of his Cape-English background, Brand had no particular love for the Transvaal, and despite Britain's new imperialist policies always worked to strengthen the ties between the Free State and the Cape Colony. Brand, like various other Cape statesmen, believed that close economic co-operation would eventually see the birth of a united southern Africa, if needs be under the British flag, but with complete self-government. Although he was no advocate of Rhodes's imperialism, he did nothing to promote the growing Afrikaner nationalism among his own people. Through his sharp criticisms of the Afrikaner Bond, which aimed at unifying all Afrikaner endeavour as a sectional movement and through accepting a British title to promote friendly relations between the two white sections of the population, he began finally to drift away from the majority of the Free Staters. Most Free Staters believed that the two Boer republics had to move closer to each other to enable their national aspirations to withstand the rising tide of British imperialism. When gold was discovered on the Witwatersrand, and Kruger offered to share with the Free State the advantages which an independent way to the sea would have for the two republics, Brand preferred to maintain the Free State's economic independence without estranging the British colonies. The most he was prepared to do, was to conclude a new treaty of trade and friendship with the South African Republic. The changed economic situation in South Africa had, in any case, given Brand the whip hand in concluding in 1888 an extremely advantageous customs agreement with the British colonies, while simultaneously arranging for the construction of railway lines which would favour the Free State. When he died in 1888, President Brand had contributed much to the now flourishing Free State. It was unfortunate that he had become estranged from his people during his last two terms of office. Yet nevertheless, he had, without consciously shaping the Afrikaner's political views, strengthened Afrikaner republicanism. The years from 1864 to 1888 made the Free State a republican prototype which not only elicited admiration from overseas, but proved to the supporters of republicanism how well democracy could be served by a republican form of government.

Reawakening of the desire for Afrikaner unity

Chief Justice F. W. Reitz who succeeded Brand, curiously enough had nearly the same background as his predecessor. Reitz also went to school in Cape Town and studied law in Europe. He served on the Free State bench from 1874, but even as a judge it was clear that he differed diametrically from Brand in his political views. As an outspoken Afrikaner and strong supporter of the original ideals of the Afrikaner Bond, he stubbornly resisted the notion, which existed even in the Boer republics, that the English language and culture were superior to those of the Afrikaners, and he openly advocated strengthening the ties of blood and tradition with the Transvaal by political means.

One of Reitz's first tasks was to ratify Brand's provisional customs agreement with the Cape Colony, according to which the Free State was to receive three-quarters of the customs duty on imported goods passing through the Cape Town harbour. In the first year the Free State received the enormous sum of £130,000 from this source. This enabled the Free State to erect numerous new schools and made possible the compulsory schooling necessary to combat the illiteracy of the poor, which tended further to impoverish them. During Reitz's term of office, the number of pupils in the schools rose from 2,000 to 5,800.

Next, Reitz turned his attention to the Transvaalers, who now dominated the economic scene to such an extent that he had to plead powerfully for the South African Republic not to institute an increased rate on the import and transport of Free State goods. This was agreed in 1890 in a revised treaty of trade and friendship. In return the Free State signed a political treaty with the South African Republic which guaranteed lasting peace between the two states, and stated that each would come to the help of the other should the independence of either be threatened. During these negotiations the matter of a closer association between the two republics was raised, but however strongly President Reitz and the editor of *De Express*, Carel Borckenhagen, may have felt about it, nothing further came of this idea during Reitz's period of office.

Reitz also obtained the assurance of the South African Republic that the Johannesburg market would not be connected to the Cape railway through Bechuanaland. To make full use of the advantages of this market, the laying of the main line from Norvalspont to Viljoenskroon was speeded up. On 17 December, 1890, the first train steamed into Bloemfontein admidst great celebrations, and the Vaal River was reached eighteen months later. As the Free State could not alone bear the expense of the line, the Cape Colony was initially responsible for its operation. Nevertheless, the completion of the new line meant a new impulse for the Free State, and the prejudice against railways vanished so quickly that districts began to compete to get branch lines.

Reitz's presidency, which was characterized by the same non-party politics as that of his predecessor, was tranquil, particularly because the policies of the head of state were in full accord with the sentiments of most of his people. Furthermore, his period of office coincided with a period of peace and prosperity throughout Africa. How well the Free State prospered is apparent from the fact that the White population of 78,000, chiefly farmers, since agriculture and cattle raising had remained the basis of the Free State economy, harvested in one year, over 200,000 bags of corn and 180,000 bags of mealies, as well as sheared 60,000 bales of wool. The Free State was not only self-sufficient in food, but had surplus food to export to the markets of Johannesburg, Cape Town and Kimberley. The erection of a new Raadsaal in 1890 – 1893, a symbol of "the steadfastness, the dignity, the virtues and the aspirations of the nation", as President Reitz expressed it, reflected the progressiveness of the republic's government and administration. President Brand's excellent civil service improved steadily under Reitz's tutelage.

Although the capital of the republic was populated and developed chiefly by English-speaking people, to such an extent that Anthony Trollope described it as the most English town in South Africa, there was a markedly harmonious co-operation between Boer and Briton. In the religious field as well there was, in contrast to the situation in the Transvaal, a tolerance upon which foreigners freely commented. Although the Dutch Reformed Church was the state church it never enjoyed this position to the detriment of other religious bodies. The Dutch Reformed Church, however, in addition to its proselytizing work and its great interest in education and combating poverty, contributed greatly towards the establishment and growth of the numerous Free State towns which had begun shooting up even in Brand's time.

Possibly it is characteristic of Reitz's term that the republic's first codified law appeared in 1891. Nearly every page breathes the spirit of the original constitution as exemplified in the legislation and government regulations passed over more than a generation. One of the most important laws, which attained its final form in Reitz's time and determined the subsequent population pattern, was Ordinance 29 of 1890, according to which Asiatics in future were no longer allowed to settle in the Free State. In conformity with the Volksraad's sympathetic and tolerant attitude, the law would not apply to Asiatics who were already established in the Free State.

M. T. Steyn and the triumph of republicanism

When in 1895 President Reitz resigned for reasons of health, another legal man, this time a son of the Free State, succeeded him. President M. T. Steyn, who originally had adhered to Brand's political views, probably began to absorb Reitz's opinions when he sat on the Free State criminal bench. When Steyn assumed control of the Free State, the Jameson Raid, which exposed Rhodes's brand of imperialism, had just occurred. It was Steyn more than any other statesman in southern Africa who realized that only the unification of the whole of Afrikanerdom under one republican flag would stem the tide of aggressive imperialism. In this opinion he was supported by most of the Free State burghers, as evidenced by their rejection of closer co-operation with the British colonies. This attitude was also supported by Steyn's uncle, J. G. Fraser, the unofficial leader in the presidential elections of the strong English communities in Bloemfontein and other towns. In practice Steyn's policy meant that he would maintain and strengthen republican principles in southern Africa through the closest possible co-operation with the South African Republic. Separately at first, and then jointly, the two republics had to be strengthened internally in every possible way. Systematically Steyn devoted himself to developing the Free State republic, spiritually, culturally, economically, politically and agriculturally, in such a way that it would be able to join a greater Afrikaner community as a model state, and, if needs be, as its leader. Under Steyn's brilliant leadership and inspired statesmanship, backed by the talented Abraham Fischer in the Executive Council and a remarkable number of able members of the Volksraad, amongst them H. Klein, the Free State was to reach its peak of development.

Because he considered that the progress of the country depended on the crop grower and the cattle farmer, Steyn concentrated on promoting scientific farming methods. Cericulture was greatly improved, irrigation was attended to and an agricultural council, a state experimental farm and an agricultural college were established. The prosperity of the farming class was not only essential in itself, but also afforded a refuge for the growing number of poor Whites. However, a series of droughts, of which that of 1897 was the worst, and the great rinderpest epidemic in the same year, caused an influx to the towns of impoverished farmers. When the epidemic subsided by the end of the year, it had killed nearly 45,000 head of cattle.

In the educational field existing schools were attended to and given increased aid, while the children of indigent parents were particularly cared for so that they could learn a trade and enter life independently. For this purpose in Bloemfontein an industrial school was established whose pupils were absorbed mainly by the railway workshops and other industries in the town. Although Steyn

218

insisted as adamantly as his predecessors that all Free State children were to learn English, he and the Volksraad took steps to prevent Dutch from being ousted from the schools. They realised that the disappearance of Dutch would have a denationalising effect which had already become evident. Since overseas universities, or the English-orientated Cape University were absorbing the Free State and Transvaal matriculants, Steyn strongly advocated the establishment of a university for the two republics. This would obviate their having to rely on foreigners to fill their higher executive posts. Only the outbreak of war prevented this ideal from being realized.

The danger inherent in the foreign control of the main railway line running through the Free State to Johannesburg had been strongly emphasised by the Jameson Raid. President Steyn therefore recommended to the Volksraad that the government should take over the line, which it did in 1897 at a cost of £169,000. Railway profits, however, soon made good this outlay and even financed the construction of branch lines.

The Free State's progress in virtually every sphere now enabled Steyn to devote himself to the matter of closer unity with the South African Republic. In 1897 President Kruger visited Bloemfontein, and a new agreement between the two republics was reached. The treaty of trade and friendship which had previously been drawn up at Potchefstroom was redrafted in greater detail and gave the Free State far more trade advantages. The political treaty, moreover, was extended to the extent that the two republics always were to keep each other informed of matters which could threaten their peace or independence. Citizenship was to be granted to anyone who might emigrate from one republic to the other. A Council of Deputies was established, a federal body, which had to meet regularly to discuss matters of common interest to the two republics, such as defence, a possible federal government, uniform legislation, mutual trade, a joint appeal court and a single monetary system. Only the outbreak of the war prevented ultimate unification between the two republics. In tightening the ties between two sister republics, Steyn had no desire to generate racial hatred or acquire undue advantages; he simply wished to foster and guarantee Afrikaner nationhood.

Steyn's close rapprochement with the South African Republic did not mean that he wanted to detach his state from the British colonies. He realised that the Free State could not deny its ties of blood and spirit with the Cape Colony, and that the goodwill of the Cape Afrikaners had to be retained to realise the ultimate ideal of a united South Africa under a republican flag. His effort to establish an inclusive customs agreement among all the southern African states and colonies, as J. H. Hofmeyr, leader of the Afrikaner Bond had done, was a failure, but a new customs agreement with the Cape Colony in which Natal later joined, was even more advantageous to the Free State, and resulted in increased trade between the Free State and the British colonies.

Meanwhile the threat of war in southern Africa was growing daily. Steyn realized that if the Free State was to fulfil its obligations towards the South African Republic it would have to improve its own defences. The commando law was changed so that, should the two republics have to defend their independence by force of arms, a joint council of war could be established. Inspection of arms (the "wapenschou") and rifle practice was made compulsory for all burghers between the ages of eighteen and forty. The Free State Artillery Corps, which had been established by President Brand, and was under the command of Captain Albrecht, was also brought up to its full strength of about thirty guns. Many Mausers, which replaced the Martini-Henry or "poena" (a light rifle), were imported, together with the necessary ammunition. By 1899 the Free State could muster more than 23,000 fully armed men.

President Steyn's gigantic efforts, up to the last moment, to avert the war between Great Britain and the South African Republic are related elsewhere. Once war was declared Steyn decided the Free Stater's were obliged to support the Transvaalers' struggle for their independence. To those who advocated Free State neutrality he declared, "I prefer to lose the independence of the Orange Free State honourably, rather than keep it in dishonour and disloyalty".[4] That he was supported in this opinion by the majority of his people, is evidenced by the fact that thousands of loyal burghers under the leadership of Steyn and General C. R. de Wet, and backed by the moral support of their wives and children, fought to preserve their republican ideals against all odds up to the bitter end.

4. Oberholster, J. J. and Van Schoor, M.C.E.: *President Steyn aan die Woord*, pp. 81 – 82 (translated into English).

13. The South African Republic

Recognition of Transvaal independence

The Sand River Convention was signed on 17 January, 1852, by the representatives of Britain and the Transvaal. This Convention did not create a new state or government, it merely recognised the sovereign independence of an existing state north of the Vaal River which was from September, 1853, known as De Zuid-Afrikaansche Republiek (The South African Republic) in accordance with a decision of its Volksraad. In signing the Convention, Britain also undertook to maintain a policy of non-intervention in the affairs of the new republic and to attempt no further expansion into territory north of the Vaal.

Problems of government and the drafting of a constitution

Britain's recognition of the new state did not eliminate the problems which were besetting the South African Republic. These problems were mainly of a constitutional and governmental nature, but there were also economic matters which required attention. It was the task of the men who had been elected to lead the republic to solve these problems as soon as possible so that the state could be established on a firm footing.

One of the gravest deficiencies was that the state had no proper constitution or governmental machinery. It was being governed in a tradition which stemmed from the Great Trek, and more especially by the so-called *Thirty-three Articles* of 9 April, 1844, which were often referred to as the first Transvaal constitution or Potgieter constitution. This constitution was reaffirmed by the Transvaal Volksraad in 1849, but it was not really a constitution at all. In fact, it contained little more than a number of rules concerning the exercise of public justice, and some civil regulations and one stipulation concerning the annual election of Volksraad members. Government was by a single body, the *Volksraad*, which not only was the legislature but also held the highest judicial power. Furthermore, because of its limited constitutional knowledge, false ideas about the inter-relationships of the various functions of government, and resultant fear that the head of state might develop into an autocrat, the Volksraad also tried to retain the executive power. This was a most unhealthy situation and the history of the Volksraad and its actions before and after Sand River proves without a doubt that it was certainly incapable of efficiently performing all the functions of government. Nor did the Volksraad have any fixed seat and this also contributed to the inefficiency of the government. It met every three months at different venues in turn, usually at Lydenburg, Rustenburg and Potchefstroom, which meant that it had no permanent government office or address.

The Volksraad performed its executive duties in only the most perfunctory manner, and the chief commandant or commandant-general, to begin with Hendrik Potgieter and later Andries Pretorius, had perforce to begin acting in an executive capacity. This displeased the Volksraad, but whoever held the post of commandant-general came to be regarded, by the outside world as well, as the chief of state. Thus it was Andries Pretorius who negotiated with the British authorities towards the end of 1851 concerning their recognition of the Transvaal's independence and who signed the Sand River Convention as the Transvaal's representative. He had the Volksraad's permission but it was only given at the last moment when this body was faced with a *fait accompli*. After the death of Andries Pretorius on 23 July, 1853, his office passed to his son, Marthinus Wessel Pretorius, the most important commandant-general in the Republic, who from the beginning exerted himself to find solutions for the problems of the young state.

High on M. W. Pretorius's reform programme was the drafting of a proper constitution for the South African Republic, but yet another pressing problem had to be solved first. His country's population was not only geographically isolated and in various groups, but there were also political differences among them which dated mainly from the years before 1852. There was a group in the north, living in the Soutpansberg with the settlement of Schoemansdal as their centre. They were under the personal leadership of Commandant-General Andries Hendrik Potgieter, which leadership passed to his son, Piet Potgieter (died in 1854) on his father's death on 16 December, 1852. In the north-east another group lived in the vicinity of Lydenburg. This group, whose commandant-general was W. F. Joubert, was not merely satisfied with the existing system of government by the Volksraad, but supported it emphatically and was utterly opposed to the creation of a separate executive authority. Another group from the district, later known as Utrecht, on the Buffalo River initially lived outside Transvaal territory, but later joined the Lydenburg community. The biggest group, however, was in the west, in an area stretching from Potchefstroom to Marico and Rustenburg. This group recognised the authority of Commandant-General A. Pretorius, and they transferred their allegiance to his son, M. W. Pretorius, when the father died. Before a constitution and a strong central government could be achieved, it was essential to dispose of all differences and to promote unity of purpose among all these various groups. M. W. Pretorius was to attend to these tasks, but another matter arose to hamper his attempts at unifying the country. Trouble developed in the field of religion.

Difficulties in this connection were initially purely theological but soon began to be felt in governmental spheres. They originated in the following manner. No legitimate minister had accompanied the Voortrekkers from the Cape because of a government ban and the unsympathetic attitude of the Cape Church towards the Trek. This meant that by 1852 there was still no permanent minister in the South African Republic. In this year Rev. J. H. Neethling of the Cape Church visited the Transvaal, and the Transvaalers discussed with him the possibility of obtaining their own minister. Rev. Neethling laid down one condition, namely that the Transvaal congregations be incorporated into the Cape Synod, which was accepted by the Transvaal Church Assembly as well as by the Volksraad. The request, which was made in accordance with this condition, was approved by the Cape Synod in October.

In 1853, however, after the arrival of the first permanent minister for the South African Republic, Rev. Dirk van der Hoff, matters took quite a different turn. First the General Church Assembly, of which Van der Hoff was the chairman, decided in August, 1853, in Rustenburg that the Nederduits Hervormde Kerk would be the only church recognized in the South African Republic, which meant that no incorporation into the Cape Synod could take place. The reason for this decision was that many Transvaalers, among whom was Pretorius himself, feared that any such incorporation might lead to an extension of English influence in the Transvaal church affairs with possibly detrimental effects on the Republic's freedom and independence. This decision caused a schism in the church, which was aggravated when Van der Hoff quarrelled with the Church Council of Lydenburg over the attempts of a Hollander, J. A. Smellekamp, to get another minister for the South African Republic from the Netherlands. When the Volksraad intervened by putting Smellekamp on trial, sentencing him to a heavy fine and finally banishing him from the country because he did not pay it, the Lydenburg Church Council severed their connection with Van der Hoff as their minister on 31 August, 1853, and decided to apply for incorporation into the Cape Synod. This schism in the church greatly hampered Pretorius's efforts to create political unity in the Transvaal.

However, reasonable progress was being made in drafting a constitution. In January, 1857, the Volksraad accepted the draft of Jacobus Stuart, a Hollander, as the constitution of the South African Republic, subject to a few alterations. This constitution provided for legislative authority to be vested in a Volksraad whose members were to be elected by the people; an executive authority vested in a president (later state president) as chairman of an executive council which would comprise the commandant-general and other members; a judicial authority; and an army, which would be the responsibility of the commandant-general. Both he and the state president would be elected directly by enfranchised citizens, the state president for a five year period of office, the commandant-general, initially, for an unspecified term, which in 1889, however, was established as ten years and in 1896 as five. In January, 1857, however, the Volksraad, in contravention of the specific provisions in the recently accepted constitution elected M. W. Pretorius as the first president, and Stephanus Schoeman from Soutspansberg as the first commandant-general, of the South African Republic. When the oath of office was ceremoniously administered to Pretorius on 6 January, the new flag of the Republic the "Vierkleur", was raised at Potchefstroom for the first time.

The fact that a constitution had been achieved was in itself a memorable event, but it did not automatically make for unity, because Lydenburg refused to accept it. Its members in the Volksraad proclaimed Lydenburg a separate republic, which Utrecht joined the following year. Thus there was now, in addition to the religious schism, a political division among the people of the Transvaal which was to last until April, 1860, when Lydenburg rejoined the South African Republic. The Soutpansberg faction also objected to the constitution. The newly elected Commandant-General S. Schoeman, refused to accept office. These difficulties were, however, in due course ironed out through negotiations and minor amendments to the constitution, and on 16 February, 1858, the constitution could finally be ratified by a Volksraad in which Soutpansberg was also represented. Thereupon Schoeman also accepted office as Commandant-General, and the South African Republic had finally achieved constitutional stability.

The term of office of M. W. Pretorius

Meanwhile, Pretorius was trying to realize yet another of his political ideals, which was to unite the South African Republic and the Republic of the Orange Free State (O.F.S.). These efforts nearly started a war between the two republics in 1857; in 1858 they caused the Governor of the Cape, Sir George Grey, to intervene, contrary to the Conventions; finally they resulted in the election of M. W. Pretorius as President of the Free State as well, where he was inaugurated in February, 1860. (The actions of Pretorius concerning the unification of the two republics and his presidency of the Orange Free State are discussed in Chapters 14 and 12 respectively.) Pretorius's acceptance of the presidency of the Orange Free State had unpleasant and even grave repercussions for the South African Republic. In the first place, when the six months leave, which the South African Republic had granted Pretorius to carry out his plans in the Orange Free State had expired, the Free State Volksraad requested an extension of the leave; whereupon the Volksraad of the South African Republic demanded that Pretorius resign one of the presidencies because the constitution forbade the president to hold more than one office at the same time. Pretorius resigned his Transvaal presidency, and a member of the Executive Council, J. H. Grobler, was nominated as acting president. This situation caused great confusion and, finally, civil war, since Pretorius's supporters and those who advocated the unification of the two republics disagreed with the decisions of the Volksraad These people decided at a large meeting at Potchefstroom that the existing Volksraad no longer enjoyed the confidence of all the people and that new elections should therefore be held, that Pretorius should be allowed to retain both his presidential posts and that he be given a year's leave to implement his unification plans, and that Commandant-General Schoeman should act as president in the interim. During the following years there were people who attempted to act on these decisions, while the Volksraad took counter-measures Feelings ran high among the population, and soon there were two armed camps the Volksleër (People's Army) representing the dissatisfied faction, and the Staatsleër (State Army) under he leadership of Commandant Paul Kruger. On 5 January, 1864, open warfare broke out, but the next day M. W. Pretorius

224

offered from the Free State to act as intermediary. The parties agreed to a new election, in which M. W. Pretorius was once again elected president of the South African Republic. He resigned as president of the Orange Free State, and this ended all the quarrels, which had, in fact, been caused by Pretorius in the first place.

During the next few years of his presidency, Pretorius had to attend to various threats from Bantu tribes. First there was the hostility of the Zulu chief, Cetshwayo, who in 1865 mobilised his impis when he refused to recognise the validity of Mpande's gift of a strip of land made previously to the Republic and which the latter needed to gain access to the sea. Fortunately a clash was avoided, but the situation was tense enough to force the Boers to concentrate in laagers on the border for some time. In the north, however, the situation was much worse. In 1864/5 the Shangaan chief, Mzila, across the Portuguese border, became hostile, while the tribes in the Soutpansberg, within Transvaal territory, in 1867 broke into open revolt, armed with guns and ammunition supplied by gun-runners. The commando which was immediately despatched under Commandant-General Paul Kruger failed to subdue the revolt. This had far-reaching consequences, for most of Schoemansdal, one of the oldest settlements in the Transvaal, fell into the hands of the Bantu, who thus lost much of their awe of the Europeans.

From the day he became Commandant-General in 1854, M. W. Pretorius had always exerted himself to improve the Republic's poor economic position. There was a scarcity of ready cash amongst the population, and the state treasury was virtually empty. The basic necessities of life, virtually all of which were imported through the ports of the Cape and Natal, were extremely expensive because of the customs duties imposed by these two colonies. This handicapped the treasury because it could hardly tax these goods once more. Thus in 1854 Pretorius began to consider the possibility of opening negotiations, particularly with the Natal government, to obtain for the Transvaal some of the customs dues imposed on goods destined for the Republic. His attempts were unsuccessful, however.

Once this line of approach had proved unprofitable, he began to consider the idea of acquiring a port for the Transvaal, as had the Voortrekker leaders before him. In 1858/9 he began negotiating with the Zulu chief Mpande for a strip of land through Zululand which would give the South African Republic access to the sea. This would enable the Republic to penetrate up to St. Lucia Bay, but neither this nor any subsequent effort was successful. The British government finally thwarted all such hopes in September, 1861. During 1865 – 1866 Pretorius once again attempted to obtain concessions concerning import duties on goods destined for the Transvaal, but all his attempts to negotiate directly with the British Colonial Office and the Natal government were unsuccessful. He therefore began to concentrate on the Portuguese coast. He aimed to make use of a settlement established in 1864 in the Eastern Transvaal by a Scots adventurer, Alexander McCorkindale, by agreement with the Republic. Pretorius wanted McCorkindale's help to obtain a free passage to the mouth of the Maputa River, where he intended establishing a port. Great things seemed to be afoot when in September, 1867, McCorkindale produced a complete plan for the harbour, and for the re-organisation and modernisation of the South African Republic's administration, finances, education, judicial system, etc. Although the Republic entered into a contract with McCorkindale for building and equipping the proposed harbour, this ambitious scheme also came to nothing. Pretorius was under the impression that the southern part of Delagoa Bay, including the mouth of the Maputa, did not belong to the Portuguese. Thus with the permission of the Volksraad in 1868 he proclaimed that the borders of the Transvaal now extended westward up to Lake Ngami and eastward along the Maputa up to the sea. Pretorius wished to expand the Transvaal westward to encompass the northern area where Karl Mauch, a short while previously, had discovered gold. Portugal and, particularly England, who wanted at all costs to prevent the Republic from obtaining an independent seaport, protested so sharply at the territorial proclamation, uttering threats and taking certain steps that the proclamation was never implemented and finally was entirely forgotten.

As there were no longer any prospects of obtaining a port, Pretorius made use of what Portuguese goodwill there was left to conclude a pact of "peace, friendship, trade and borders" with Portugal in 1869. This treaty was very important to the South African Republic. It offered the Republic immediate and most generous trade terms in exchange for its recognising Delagoa Bay as Portuguese property, which also meant that Portugal had officially recognised the Republic, which example was in due course followed by other powers.

One other significant event occurred during Pretorius's term of office, but its outcome was disastrous for him personally. This was the discovery of diamonds between the Vaal and Harts Rivers in 1870. Although there had never been a formal demarcation of the western border of the Transvaal, the Republic had always considered the territory in which diamonds were discovered to be its own. In fact, before diamonds were discovered, the Transvaalers never for a moment entertained the thought that the territory might not belong to them. When Potgieter had conquered the territory north of the Vaal by defeating Silkaats in 1837, the Transvaal had claimed all the chief's land, which in effect had no borders and nobody had ever contested this claim. As time passed Transvaal farmers occupied farms westward along the Vaal River and up to the Harts, and Transvaal magistrates for many years exercised their power in that territory. Finally, the Transvaal government had already begun to establish townships in that area, of which Bloemhof was one. This was the position when diamonds were discovered, whereupon the Griqua chieftain Nicolaas Waterboer also laid claim to the land as did the Barolong and Batlapin chiefs who were instigated by White agents. A further development was that the British magistrate of Kimberley was instructed by acting High Commissioner Hay to exercise his authority in the new diamond area.

President Pretorius unexpectedly found himself in an awkward situation and, since he was convinced of his Republic's just claim, he willingly assented, as did all the other claimants, to submitting the whole matter to the arbitration of Lieutenant-Governor Keate of Natal. However, he committed a grave error by signing a document without previously informing the Volksraad and obtaining their permission. In this document he undertook to abide by the decision of the arbitration court. In 1871 the court decided against the South African Republic after an incompetent presentation of the Transvaal case by Pretorius and the State Attorney, Fred Kleijn, and awarded the diamondiferous area to the other claimants. The Transvaal Volksraad was extremely dissatisfied and refused to accept the judgment. The most important reasons for their refusal were, first, that Pretorius had acted unconstitutionally in signing the document of submission without first referring to the Volksraad, and secondly, that two of the arbitrators were interested parties who could not be trusted to make an impartial judgment. Barkly attempted to protest at the South African Republic's refusal to withdraw from the contested area, but when he got no results, the area was quietly left to the Republic. For Pretorius, however, the outcome of the matter was disastrous. His unconstitutional action engendered such dissatisfaction that in 1871 he was compelled to resign as State President of the South African Republic. Although Pretorius did not thereupon disappear from the Transvaal political scene, his resignation ended a definite era in the Republic's history.

The term of office of T. F. Burgers

After their experiences with the diamond fields, the people of the South African Republic were determined not to elect another unlettered man to the presidency, and President J. H. Brand of the Orange Free State was asked to stand as a candidate in the forthcoming election. Brand, however, recommended the Rev. T. F. Burgers of Hanover, who accepted nomination. To make such a candidate acceptable, however, the constitution had to be amended (1) by deleting the provisions which stipulated that a candidate for presidency had to be a citizen of the Transvaal and (2) by amending the provision which stipulated that a candidate for the presidency had to be a member of the Hervormde Kerk in such a way that to be a member of a Protestant church was sufficient.

Burgers was elected with a large majority over the other candidate, Wm. Robinson, and sworn in as State President in Pretoria on 1 July, 1872. The new President did not face a pleasant prospect. The Transvaal was going through a particularly difficult period. There was confusion and dissatisfaction concerning the loss of much territory through the Keate award; the financial and economic conditions of the state were deplorable because, apart from there being no money, trade was totally underdeveloped because there were no trading facilities and particularly because the Transvaal did not have its own port or indeed any access to the sea; education was extremely poor; and finally, the Bantu tribes within and immediately beyond the Transvaal borders were restless and truculent. All these and other matters were clamouring for attention. Burgers was competent, energetic, idealistic, and eager to attack all problems, but his efforts to realize his ideals were to meet with serious and often insuperable obstacles. One of these was to be the attitude of the British, who wished to prevent the Transvaal from developing into an independent republic. This situation will be discussed in some detail later.

One of the first matters to which President Burgers attended was the question of the disputed diamond area. After thorough investigation he wrote to Sir Henry Barkly in December, 1873, and again in August, 1874, challenging the validity of the Keate Award with well-founded arguments. As a result the British did not insist on implementing the provisions of the Keate Award and the Republic continued to exercise its authority in the disputed territory. As far as the Republic's monetary matters were concerned, at the time Burgers became president there was in circulation paper money which had been issued at various times. But because there was no security to back them, the notes were hardly worth the paper they were printed on and merchants outside the Republic refused to accept them as legal tender while those within the Transvaal doubled the price of their wares. Burgers realised that in order to strengthen the country against Britain, financial matters would have to be put in order. He, therefore, with the approval of the Volksraad, borrowed £60,000 from the *Cape Commercial Bank*, substituted this for the worthless notes and arranged to repay the loan at £3,000 per year. The Republic could now once again obtain the credit outside its borders, which was essential to general economic development.

In 1873, when alluvial gold was discovered in the vicinity of Lydenburg, an improvement in the economic situation could be hoped for, but these goldfields were in their turn to create another problem for Burgers. The miners who converged on them were chiefly foreigners who were not well disposed towards Burgers and the Republic, and generally were strongly in favour of bringing the Transvaal into the British sphere of influence. In 1873 these diggers brought out their own newspaper, *The Goldfields Mercury*, in which they criticized the Transvaal in no uncertain terms. This was the second British orientated newspaper in the Transvaal. The other one, the bilingual *The Transvaal Advocate and Commercial Advertiser* which was published in Potchefstroom, was already in existence when Burgers became president. The only other paper in the Transvaal was the *Staatscourant*, and Burgers realised that a good Dutch paper, which would present the interests and viewpoints of the Republic, had become essential. Due to his efforts such a newspaper, *De Volkstem*, appeared in August, 1873. This newspaper was to play an important part in the future history of the South African Republic. It still is one of the most important sources for the history of the Republic.

In order to improve education in the Republic, the Volksraad in 1874 passed Burgers's well-known Education Act, the first of its kind in the history of the Transvaal. It provided for the establishment of farm and town primary schools and a secondary school or gymnasium at Pretoria, which would mainly train officials and teachers, who were urgently needed. Furthermore the act provided for parents to have a voice in educational matters through elected school commissions. In these respects it was a progressive piece of legislation, of significance for the Republic, but because of lack of staff it could not be implemented immediately. Only in February, 1876, were the first steps taken to put it into effect when W. J. van Gorkom from Holland was appointed as the first superintendent of education. The gymnasium was opened only on 5 May, 1876, in Pretoria, with four pupils and two lecturers, Dr E. J. P. Jorissen and Dr J. A. Roorda Smit, who was also the principal. Meanwhile, however, the Education Act was being used to discredit President Burgers with the electorate by those sections who favoured British domination of the Transvaal either through federation or annexation. This faction was supported by a conservative section of the Transvaal people and particularly by members of the Nederduits Gereformeerde Kerk. The burghers disapproved of the Education Act on the one hand because free-thinking teachers, particularly Van Gorkom, were being appointed to the schools, and on the other because of Article 26 of the Education Act which stipulated that the Bible would be read in every school and that Bible history would be taught, but that no religious instruction, which seems to have meant dogmatic teaching, would be given during school hours. In 1876 there were, amongst other things, allegations despite the above-mentioned article that the act banned the reading of the Bible and the teaching of Bible history during school hours, and that it threatened freedom of religion. Although many of the allegations were false they succeeded in making many Transvaalers, for whom the act was in fact too liberal, dissatisfied with Burgers. Resistance to Burgers's education policy was also obvious in that after the gymnasium had been established, those of British persuasion immediately established an opposition institution and primary school.

One of the Republic's major problems was that it had no direct access to the sea, which it had to have if the Republic were ever to become wholly independent. President Pretorius had already considered the possibility of making Delagoa Bay more easily accessible to the inhabitants of the Transvaal and in 1870 the Volksraad authorized the government to build a road suitable for "trek-en ander machines" from the centre of the Republic to the Portuguese border. Almost immediately after he had assumed office, President Burgers, however, suggested that building a railway would be a better idea. The Volksraad went into the matter and, after they had studied a memorandum compiled by G. P. Moodie, authorised the government on 31 July, 1872, to go ahead with the railway. Moodie obtained a concession for its construction, on condition that he was able to form a company for the purpose within a year. Meanwhile, Burgers was telling the Volksraad that the Republic, in order to guard its independence, might have to try to buy Delagoa Bay from the Portuguese. The Volksraad was enthusiastic about the idea, but it came to nothing because the fate of Delagoa Bay was at that time in the hands of President MacMahon of France, who was acting as arbiter following Britain's claim to the southern part of Delagoa Bay after Pretorius's 1868 border proclamation.

Moodie's concession for building a railway lapsed after a year, and the Volksraad approved their president's proposal that the state itself should undertake the project. As the Republic lacked sufficient funds, the Volksraad approved a foreign loan of £300,000 and the President was sent to Europe to negotiate for a loan. Burgers welcomed their decision, as he considered such a visit an opportunity to make the Republic more widely known in Europe. He was to leave on 16 February, 1875, and on the previous day P. J. Joubert was sworn in as acting president in Burgers's absence.

Burgers left the Cape at the beginning of April in high spirits. He went first to England, where he tried to improve relations with the British government but failed to raise a loan. The reason for his failure was that Britain was trying to thwart the Transvaal's plans, since they would interfere with Lord Carnarvon's plan for a South African federation (see Chapter 14 for details). Burgers did succeed in introducing his state to Europe, and aroused interest in the Transvaal, particularly in Holland, Belgium and Portugal. The plans for the railway did not, however, progress as smoothly as he had hoped, mainly owing to the subtle and effective propaganda from London which frustrated his efforts. In December, 1875, Burgers wrote to the Transvaal government, saying that endless obstacles were being placed in his way by "shameful intrigues from England" and that spies dogged his every movement. The railway loan which he hoped to float in Holland was consequently undersubscribed, when he had already concluded the necessary agreements with Portugal concerning the building of the railway and had made provisional arrangements with Belgian factories to supply railway material. Of the £300,000 required for the railway the loan finally only provided about £90,000, and Burgers had ordered about £63,000 worth of material in Belgium. Some of the materials were transported to Delagoa Bay, where they rusted away, while the rest lay in Flushing harbour, quite useless, and was finally sold at a great loss. The main reasons for the material not being used and the railway not being built, were the war against Sekukuni to which Burgers had to devote all his attention when he returned to the Transvaal and the annexation of the Republic in 1877. Also some of the people of the Transvaal disapproved of the whole railway matter, but this disapproval would not alone have been sufficient to halt the building of the railway. In any case, Burgers on his return to the Transvaal soon dispersed the dissatisfaction of these people.

When Burgers arrived in the Transvaal in April, 1876, he found public opinion to be running quite strongly against him as a consequence of effective English propaganda. To aggravate matters, the Bapedi chief, Sekukuni, who lived in the mountainous area near Lydenburg, had somehow obtained guns and ammunition and he became so aggressive, that, towards the middle of May, the Republic had no choice but to declare war on him. Apart from the fact that the country in general was not ready for a war, the moment was most unpropitious for Burgers in particular who feared that a war at this stage would interfere with his railway plans and the raising of the loan in Holland, and there was the possibility that it might also crystallize British intentions concerning the Transvaal. As he could not prevent the war, he determined to end it as soon as possible.

Burgers's first problem was to find an officer to command the campaign. The post of commandant-general had been abolished in 1873 and neither Paul Kruger nor Piet Joubert was willing to take command. The only way out was for Burgers to assume supreme command himself, at least nominally whilst the inexperienced M. W. Pretorius assisted by Niklaas Smit would be in actual charge of operations. Another problem was that the burghers, who had been growing increasingly cantankerous, did not respond well to the president's mobilization of the commando. After the first setback they simply went home, in spite of Burgers's pleading with them to stay. The British High Commissioner in South Africa, Sir Henry Barkly, made use of this opportunity to telegraph his superiors in Britain that Burgers had been defeated by Sekukuni, and that a meeting held at Lydenburg had decided to asked Britain to take over the Transvaal. The war could not be merely abandoned, however, and with the Volksraad's approval, Burgers left a number of paid volunteers in the vicinity of Lydenburg in an attempt to subdue the Bapedi. This move was successful and by the end of 1876 Sekukuni sued for peace. The English newspapers in South Africa and Britain made full use of this war to discredit Burgers and the Transvaal still further, and certain Transvaal ministers even joined the propaganda campaign. The Transvaal was accused of being too weak to govern itself, and unjust and cruel to the Bantu; there were open and passionate appeals for Britain to take over the country. These circumstances, however falsely represented were to give Carnarvon a useful pretext for putting his annexation plans into execution as quickly as possible.

Meanwhile Burgers was facing increased dissatisfaction among the Transvaalers themselves, particularly because of certain taxes which had been imposed. One of these, very much resented, was a tax which had been imposed to repay the interest on the railway loan, and in September, 1876, the government could not avoid imposing a war tax. This proved too much for the people to accept and by the beginning of 1877 it was clear that most people in the Transvaal wanted another president. It happened to be time for another election, and, amongst others, Paul Kruger was asked by many burghers to stand for election. At first Kruger refused because he was very conscious of his shortcomings, but in the end he decided to accept nomination because of the difficult times and general dissatisfaction. As it happened the election was not held because of the annexation of the Transvaal but there was every indication that Burgers would not have been re-elected.

In order to carry out his federation plans, Lord Carnarvon, the Secretary of State for the Colonies, had to annex the Transvaal, and he asked Theophilus Shepstone, the Secretary for Native Affairs in Natal, to proceed with the annexation as soon as he could. Shepstone acted immediately. On 22 January, 1877, he arrived in Pretoria with a small guard of twenty-five policemen and eight officials to discuss with President Burgers, as he had previously informed Burgers, certain Transvaal problems which were also of prime importance as regards the security of the British colonies. The English-speaking community received him with much enthusiasm and President Burgers entertained him, as emissary of the Queen of England, at a luncheon.

To begin with Shepstone did not divulge the true reason for his visit and

231

tried to win the goodwill of the government and the people by his cordiality. When he began discussions with the Executive Council, however, it quickly became apparent that the ostensible reasons for his visit had been mere pretexts, and he was forced to reveal the true purpose of his journey. He explained the British government's dissatisfaction with the state of affairs in the Transvaal, which was based mainly on the Republic's weak financial position, its inefficient administration and its lack of control over the Bantu within its borders. He also made it quite plain that if these matters were not remedied to his satisfaction, he would not hesitate to annex the country.

Burgers hurriedly caused the Volksraad to pass certain measures in order to meet Shepstone's objections in the constitutional sphere, and another of Shepstone's main objections fell away when Sekukuni sued for peace. Nevertheless, and despite Burger's formal protest against annexation on 11 April, the British High Commissioner proceeded on 12 April to execute his commission by annexing the Transvaal as British territory, after he had tried to impress the Transvaalers with the imminence of the Zulu danger. Burgers left Pretoria and the Transvaal in May 1877, and settled first in Cape Town and later in the Hanover district, where he died in December 1881. On 26 November, 1895, he was ceremoniously re-interred at Pretoria, on an occasion at which President Kruger was present.

Annexation, war and restoration of independence

The annexation of the Transvaal was quite unexpected and what is also surprising is that the Transvaalers did not simply haul down the British flag and hustle Shepstone and his small guard out of their territory. Precisely this was, in fact, what F. Wolmarans, who was in Pretoria with about four hundred armed burghers, wanted to do but the Executive Council prevailed upon them not to act.

The Executive Council argued that the Transvaal's general economic and political position was such that it would be better temporarily to acquiesce, rather than start a war. The Executive Council also believed that if the true facts about the Transvaal and the wishes of its inhabitants were made known to the British government, Britain would herself withdraw from the Transvaal. On 11 April, the day before the annexation, the government had decided to send a deputation to Britain to present the case of the Transvaal. The deputation consisted of S. J. P. Kruger and Dr E. J. P. Jorrissen (the latter at Kruger's request because of his legal knowledge and facility in several languages) who were to bring all matters to the attention of the British government. If this policy was not effective they were to seek the friendly aid and meditation of other powers.

That it was Kruger who was sent, and not President Burgers, is significant. It indicates that the Transvaalers had lost all confidence in Burgers, and that Kruger was regarded as the Transvaal's new leader. This former commandant-general, who had been nominated to the new office of vice-president in 1877 when the constitutional reforms were affected, had been an influential figure in politics while Burgers was president. For the next four years he was to lead the Transvaal's resistance to annexation.

Despite many misgivings among which his own total inexperience in diplomatic matters was not the least, Kruger accepted the responsibility of leading the mission and the deputation left for London and had its first discussions with Lord Carnarvon in July, 1877. In a series of four meetings Kruger did everything in his power to convince Carnarvon that most of the Transvaal's population was against the annexation. Carnarvon, primed by Shepstone with information on South Africa which maintained the opposite, would not accept Kruger's arguments and asserted that the annexation would stand. Neither did he accept Kruger's suggestion that the temper of the Transvaalers should be tested with a referendum because, as Carnarvon put it, such a referendum would in fact be nothing more than a vote about the annexation itself. The deputation returned to South Africa towards the end of 1877, after visiting the Netherlands to put the Transvaal's case there. Notwithstanding the terms of their commission, they visited no other European states.

On his return to the Transvaal Kruger immediately realized that the political situation in the territory had changed considerably during his absence. The dismay and apathy which had characterized the time immediately after the annexation had been replaced by a sober appreciation of what the annexation meant, and a perception, born of awakening nationalism, that united action was essential. Some hotheads wished to declare war immediately when Kruger reported back on his mission to about 1,400 burghers in Pretoria on 7 January, 1878, while others criticized the actions of Kruger and, more particularly Jorissen, in England. Kruger, however, pacified his critics, calmed the hotheads and once again expressed his conviction that Carnarvon was deluded and that if he could be convinced that virtually nobody in the Transvaal desired British annexation, the British government would withdraw from the Transvaal. It was decided at the meeting that a referendum would be held to obtain definitive figures which could be submitted to Carnarvon. They wrote to inform Carnarvon of their decision on the same day. On 4 April the various committees which had been circulating the petition drafted a document at Doornfontein which they intended submitting to Carnarvon. Of the signatures on the lists 6,591 were against and 587 for annexation, which the compilers felt was conclusive proof of their claims. The joint commission therefore immediately nominated another deputation consisting of Piet Joubert and Paul Kruger. They were to submit these details to Carnarvon, in the hope that they would be able to convince him that his information was false.

The second deputation in its turn did what it could to convince the new Colonial Secretary, Sir Michael Hicks-Beach, who had succeeded Carnarvon in the interim, that the Transvaal had a plausible case. Having been "informed" by Carnarvon and prepared by Shepstone, the Colonial Secretary refused to believe anything the Boer deputation told him or showed him and reiterated that the Transvaal would remain a British possession. He was not prepared to discuss the matter any further. Joubert and Kruger left London in October, 1878. In between negotiations they had also made short trips to Holland, France and Germany, where the Transvaal case attracted some considerable attention in the press.

Meanwhile in the Transvaal antagonism to Shepstone and his administration increased daily and the Boers became more and more determined on resistance. At a meeting at Wonderfontein on 10 January, 1879, when the deputation reported back to 2,000 or 3,000 burghers, there were many who wished to declare war. Once again Kruger pacified his people and assured them that the time was not yet ripe for defiance. All peaceful ways of achieving their independence must first be exhausted. No doubt Kruger felt that war should not be declared unless it was certain that the burghers would fight such a battle to the bitter end. Those who were present at the Wonderfontein meeting did, however, vow in a solemn oath to be loyal to their people and their country and, with their trust in God, to work until death for the restoration of their Republic's freedom. Piet Joubert was sent to the British High Commissioner, Sir Bartle Frere, who was in Natal at the time to acquaint him with the meeting's decision. Frere once again promised the Transvaal self-rule, but without independence, and that he would personally go to the Transvaal to hear from the inhabitants their precise grievances. There was now some new hope. Possibly Frere's personal knowledge of the Boers would help the British authorities to see matters in a different light.

On 10 April Frere arrived at Kleinfontein, on the road between Heidelberg and Pretoria, where between 4,000 and 5,000 burghers had gathered especially to meet him. He discussed matters with the Boer committee under the chairmanship of M. W. Pretorius. The negotiations began in a tense atmosphere. Frere did his best to convince the Boer leaders of the advantages of British administration and once again promised them self-rule, their own language, their own flag, the Vierkleur, and a survey for the construction of a railway line to Delagoa Bay; the Boer leaders would not be satisfied by anything less than the restoration of their freedom and independence. Frere, however, categorically told them that there was no possibility of such a restoration. He also refused the Boer leaders' request that they be allowed to plead their cause with the British government, but he did agree to send the Queen a new Boer petition, accompanied by a letter from him in which he would attest that the Boer leaders were honourable. Frere kept this promise and also added that the arguments of the Boers deserved serious attention from the British government. No reply to the petition was ever received, for which most or all of the blame must be attributed to other letters Frere wrote, in which he urged the British government to persevere with the annexation.

Even though the meeting at Kleinfontein therefore had no results in this respect, it did have some in others. A large number of burghers had spent a long time in one another's company; they had waited for Frere for over three weeks. They had learnt much and had become more united. Furthermore, the Republic of the Orange Free State which had previously, owing to President Brand's influence, merely expressed its sympathy with the Transvaal after the annexation in 1877, now, at the request of the Kleinfontein meeting, explicity condemned the annexation. The Orange Free State Volksraad adopted a resolution expressing the hope that the Transvaal would succeed in its attempts to regain its independence. Finally, the Transvaalers were heartened by the sympathy and active interest of the Cape Afrikaners. Even in Natal there was some condemnation of the annexation and of federation, mainly owing to the efforts of Alfred Aylward, editor of the *Natal Witness*.

In the meantime, there had been two important changes in the administration of the Transvaal. In March, 1879, Shepstone was replaced as administrator by Sir Owen Lanyon, who had no understanding of the Boers and their problems, and who made no effort to learn anything about them. These attitudes, combined with his utter lack of tact and his tendency to act autocratically, in direct contradiction of all promises of self-government, made him hardly a fit person to reconcile the Boers to the British annexation. The other important change was the dismissal in September, 1879 of Frere as High Commissioner for Natal and Transvaal, and the nomination of Sir Garnet Wolseley as Governor of the Transvaal and High Commissioner for the Transvaal and Natal. Just as Lanyon differed from Shepstone, so did Wolseley differ from Frere. He was no diplomat but a soldier who believed in firm action. Proof of this is his remark to Piet Joubert that the Vaal River would reverse its course before Britain would abandon the annexation, and his proclamation that the British government had determined that the Transvaal would permanently be an integral part of British South Africa. Wolseley asked Kruger to serve in the new government, in the hopes of neutralizing the resistance movement, but Kruger indignantly refused the offer.

By the end of 1879 patience was running out. After Wolseley's policy statement another meeting was held at Wonderfontein despite the governor's warning, or rather threat, in forbidding the meeting. Over 6,000 burghers attended the meeting declaring unanimously that the time had come to reclaim their country and re-establish their Volksraad and president. Kruger asked them to consider the matter once again and weigh the consequences, for he would prefer, if possible, to avoid force. The burghers, however, were now determined to act and possibly inspired by the Vierkleur which had been hoisted on the occasion, the following decision was formulated on 15 December:

"The time for petitioning the English government is past; this course offers us no salvation. The officials of Her Majesty the Queen of England have shut the door to Her Majesty and Parliament by their untruthful and false representations . . . We can therefore no longer speak to England because there is nobody who replies to us. This is the reason why we, the people of the Zuid-Afrikaansche Republiek, take the step of firmly stating:

1. that the People of the Zuid-Afrikaansche Republiek have never been Her Majesty's subjects, nor do they want to be; therefore everybody who calls us agitators is a slanderer;

2. that the People desire that the Government of the Zuid-Afrikaansche Republiek, whose activities have been suspended, resume them as soon as possible;

3. that the People desire that the Volksraad be reassembled as soon as possible".[1]

This decision was to be implemented by the existing committee, and another meeting, at which the Republic was to be re-instated, was arranged for 6 April, 1880, at Paardekraal.

Wolseley, who had just returned victorious from a bloody war against Seku-kuni, was highly indignant that his prohibition had been ignored. He arrested M. W. Pretorius and W. E. Bok, respectively chairman and secretary of the "Volkskomitee" (Peoples Committee), on a charge of high treason, but soon released them on bail for tactical reasons. Wolseley at this stage offered Pretorius a seat on the Executive Council which he, as Paul Kruger had done before him, summarily refused. Tension was increasing and the Transvaal leaders, who realised that implementing their manifesto would inevitably mean war, were now in an extremly difficult and responsible position.

Two matters, however, both vital to the Transvaal, delayed the immediate implementation of the manifesto. One was Governor Sir Bartle Frere's decision to introduce legislation at the next session of the Cape Parliament to provide for a conference on federation, at which the Transvaal would also be represented. If this happened it would end the Transvaal resistance movement, and to avert this possibility the "Volkskomitee" sent Kruger and Joubert in March to the Cape Colony to work against the proposed legislation. That the bill ultimately was not passed was therefore largely owing to the efforts of Joubert and Kruger. The other matter was the pending election in England. During his election campaign the Liberal Opposition leader, W. E. Gladstone, sharply attacked Disraeli's Transvaal policy, which he condemned outright. Before the above-mentioned deputation left for the Cape Colony on 10 April, 1880, the Transvaalers heard that Gladstone had won the election and had become Prime Minister. Once again their hopes rose, and Kruger and Joubert immediately wrote to Gladstone about restoring the Transvaal's independence. In June, while they were still in the Cape, Gladstone's disappointing reply arrived: he could not advise the Queen to restore the Transvaal's independence, but was prepared to grant the Whites complete local self-rule which would be realised most quickly and easily if the Transvaal were to become a member of a South African federation. Thus the hopes centered on Gladstone were dashed, and there was no further possibility of negotiating with Britain.

Back in the Transvaal, it was generally realized that the time for action had come, but it was also realized that the Boers were not well equipped for war. The absence of any further open defiance of the British administration, the reasonable manner in which the Boers paid their taxes, albeit under protest, and the lack of apparent dissatisfaction made Wolseley and Lanyon think that the Transvaalers had at last resigned themselves to British authority. In fact they

---

1. Translation of a proclamation published by the Government of the South African Republic, Annexure No. 4 *De Staatscourant gedurende den Vrijheidsoorlog van 1881*, Pretoria reprint, 1885, p. xi.

were using this as a time for preparation during which arms and ammunition were being bought in small quantities. The national meeting fixed for Paardekraal on 6 April, was put forward to 8 January, 1881, at which time Kruger and Joubert would report back to the Transvaalers.

During the final months of 1880 matters developed rapidly which necessitated the national meeting being put forward again, this time to 8 December, 1880. The developments were, among other things, the written declaration of Commandant P. A. Cronje and one hundred and twenty-seven of his burghers to the Potchefstroom magistrate that they were willing to pay the taxes they owed, but only to the *legal* government, and, particularly, the episode in November, of Piet Bezuidenhout's wagon. Piet Bezuidenhout refused to pay certain costs in connection with his summons, which exceeded the tax he owed. Thereupon Magistrate M. W. Goetz of Potchefstroom attached his wagon, but on the morning when the sheriff was due to sell it at a public auction in Potchefstroom, Commandant Cronje and a number of Boers seized the wagon and returned it to its owner. This was plainly an open act of defiance, and Lanyon felt that he could not simply let the matter pass. This was the incident that was to ignite the inflammable situation in the Transvaal. Kruger made it quite clear to the local Colonial Secretary, George Hudson, that now he could no longer control his people. The wagon affair was not merely a matter between the British government, Cronje and Bezuidenhout, but had come to symbolize the conflict between the British government and the Transvaal burghers. Hudson was only too well aware of this.

Notwithstanding the short notice at which the date for the national meeting had been put forward, and Lanyon's banning of it, there were between four and five thousand burghers at Paardekraal by 8 December, and the number increased to eight or ten thousand within a few days. On 10 December the People's Committee decided that the time had come to give effect to the above quoted resolution of 15 December of the previous year, viz. that the government should resume its activities and that the Volksraad should be convened. The decision was confirmed on the following day by the thousands of burghers present; the government was entrusted to Paul Kruger who had been elected Vice-President by the Volksraad in March, 1877, and Piet Joubert was elected Commandant-General. On 13 December the old Volksraad, which had not met since Aipril, 1877, assembled and entrusted the government of the country to the triumvrate of Vice-President Kruger, Commandant-General Joubert and W. M. Pretorius.

The Volksraad brought the Executive Council up to strength, attended to urgent financial matters and made Heidelberg the provisional seat of government. The Triumvirate immeditaely prepared a proclamation, issued in the name of the people on 13 December under God's guidance, which announced the restoration of the Republic's government and explained why this step had been taken. It also declared the Republic's willingness under certain conditions to co-operate with Britain, and to consider favourably the question of federation. Finally it proclaimed martial law. The reconstituted government then left for

Heidelberg and Commandant Piet Cronje went to Potchefstroom with about four hundred burghers to have the proclamation printed.

On 16 December, 1880, the Vierkleur was raised at Heidelberg and the Triumvirate demanded of Lanyon that he peacefully hand over the government of the country to them. Lanyon refused to do so and immediately took measures to suppress the revolutionary Boers by force of arms. He was well equipped for such a course, for during the annexation British garrisons had been stationed in all the major Transvaal towns. On the same day the first shots were exchanged between the British garrison at Potchefstroom and the Boers, and the War of Independence had begun. Two days later the British Special Commissioner in Potchefstroom capitulated, but Colonel Winsloe and his garrison, immediately outside Potchefstroom, withstood the Boer siege until 21 March, 1881, before they surrendered. On 20 December, 1881, the first major battle of the war occurred on the Honde River near Bronkhorstspruit. A detachment of the 94th Regiment, two hundred and fifty seven men under the command of Colonel Philip Anstruther, which had been summoned hurriedly from Lydenburg to Pretoria, was virtually destroyed in a twenty minute clash with Commandant Frans Joubert and about two hundred men. Colonel Anstruther was mortally wounded in battle.

The Triumvirate headed by Kruger soon had matters under control. Landdrosts were everywhere appointed to take charge of the country's administration and various administrative measures were put into operation; the British garrisons in the various towns were besieged to prevent their concentrating in Pretoria and Commandant-General Piet Joubert with the main Boer force went to Laing's Nek on the Natal border to ensure that General Sir George Colley, Governor of Natal, should not bring reinforcements into the Transvaal to relieve the garrisons. Thus the whole country was within a week administratively and militarily in the hands of the Boers and British administration had virtually ceased.

While on 28 January, 1881, Joubert successfully repulsed an attack by Colley, and Niklaas Smit again defeated Colley on 8 February, at Schuinshoogte near Ingogo, Paul Kruger, assisted by Jorissen and Bok as chief advisers took over the government of the country. He had not only to attend to the war and all its consequences, but also to many administrative, financial, political and other matters; he also had to control the Transvaal Bantu, who were still restless. In that difficult time the sympathy of the Afrikaners in the Orange Free State and the Cape Colony for the cause of their Transvaal kin greatly heartened Kruger. While the Orange Free State moved steadily towards active support of the Transvaal and the events in South Africa were being sympathetically reported in the European press, and even in some British newspapers, President Brand of the Orange Free State was strenuously endeavouring to end the war in the Transvaal. President Kruger was also willing to stop the war, but only if the annexation was rescinded and British garrisons were withdrawn from the Transvaal. Negotiations had been under way for some time when Colley made a desperate effort to invade the Transvaal. The results of this attempt were disastrous for the

British. On 27 February, 1881, the Boers fought the famous battle of Amajuba in which the British were defeated and Colley was killed. This battle ended the war.

Peace negotiations were conducted on Britain's behalf by a Royal Commission consisting of Sir Hercules Robinson (Governor of the Cape), Justice H. de Villiers (Chief Justice of the Cape) and Sir Evelyn Wood (Colleys' successor). Transvaal was represented by the Triumvirate while President Brand attended the negotiations in an advisory capacity as a friend of both sides. After about six months agreement was reached and the Pretoria Convention signed on 3 August, 1881. This gave Transvaal self-government, but not complete independence, for the Transvaal had to accept the suzerainty of the British Crown and a number of other conditions. It was stipulated that:

(1) Britain would control the foreign relations of the Transvaal and its agreements with foreign states;

(2) the British government would have the right to appoint a Resident in Pretoria who would, amongst other things, supervise the Bantu tribes in the Transvaal; Transvaal legislation concerning the Bantu would be subject to his approval;

(3) Britain would have the right to move British troops through Transvaal territory in time of war;

(4) Swaziland was declared independent of the Transvaal and the western border of the Transvaal was demarcated in such a way as to cause a loss of territory to the Transvaal;

(5) the Transvaal government would be responsible for the payment of all debts incurred before the annexation and for expenditure legally incurred in governing the country since annexation;

(6) the Convention had to be confirmed within three months by a legally elected Volksraad.

The Republic was not to retain its old name, but was to be known as the *Transvaal State*.

Both the Triumvirate and the new Volksraad were unenthusiastic in accepting these conditions, which were far more stringent than they had expected, but under prevailing conditions they had no choice. Most of the provisions continued to be constant irritations, and after Paul Kruger had been elected President of the restored Republic and sworn in during May, 1883, there was a general feeling that it was time to renew negotiations with the British government, particularly because of the Bantu attacks on the south-western border which had not been very well demarcated. The Volksraad re-opened negotiations by sending a deputation consisting of President Kruger, General Niklaas Smit and Rev. S. J. du Toit to London. The negotiations were successful and the British government was persuaded to accept a new Convention whose conditions were far more favourable.

This *London Convention*, which was signed on 27 February, 1884 (exactly three years after Majuba), restored the name *Zuid-Afrikaansche Republiek* and did not mention British suzerainty. It acknowledged the Republic's independence, and

239

the right of the Republic to have its own Bantu policy within its borders. As far as foreign relations were concerned, the only stipulation which remained was that all treaties with a foreign power or with Bantu tribes east and west of the Republic, were subject to Britain's approval. The Crown's right to move troops through the Transvaal fell away; the British resident would be recalled and replaced by a consul; the western border of the Republic was extended again and the national debt was decreased by the substantial amount of £131,000.

Realising that much had been gained, the Volksraad, although for obvious reasons it was not quite satisfied, ratified the new Convention on 8 August, 1884. The Republic was free and independent again, except for the stipulation about treaties with foreign powers, and President Paul Kruger and the Volksraad could turn their attention to furthering the progress of their state.

The term of office of Paul Kruger: the Triumvirate

In its ensuing history the South African Republic was, owing to various factors and circumstances, economically, politically and in other ways involved with states, governments and people outside its borders. In this connection its endeavours to obtain a port and the relationship between Kruger and Rhodes are particularly important. As these "foreign relations" are discussed in detail in Chapter 14, this section will refer to them only in so far as they may be necessary to the history of domestic affairs which is dealt with in the rest of this chapter.

After the restoration of Republican government in August, 1881, Vice-President Kruger moved to Pretoria to give state matters his undivided attention. First and foremost on his programme was the advancement of the Republic. There was little money, and the state's future financial obligations loomed large; the civil service had to be reorganised and education, which had always been one of Kruger's main interests, would also have to be completely reorganised on a christian national basis. Kruger had definite suggestions to offer about these matters, and these suggestions were approved during the first meeting of the new Volksraad in September 1881. Thus certain fiscal and financial measures, based on a policy of economy, were adopted and a system of concessions or monopolies was accepted to promote industry. The Rev. S. J. du Toit, who had won fame for the part he had played in the Genootskap van Regte Afrikaners, was, on Kruger's recommendation, appointed Superintendent of Education, which post he held until 1889. An education act (Act 1/1882) was passed. This act emphasised the responsibility of parents in the education of their children; stipulated that education had to be christian; made provision for primary, secondary and higher education, for financial support of education and for the "Nederduitse" (Dutch) language as medium of instruction. All these measures clearly revealed the objectives of Kruger's policy, a national economic system and a national educational policy as basic requirements for the well-being of state and people.

Mindful of the favourable conclusion of the conflict with England, which had been a hazardous undertaking for the Republic, and of the partial restoration of their state's independence, the government summoned the people to Paarde-kraal between 13 and 16 December, 1881, to thank God for their deliverance and to celebrate 16 December. This was the day on which the Battle of Blood River had been fought in 1838, and on which the War of Independence had begun in the previous year (1880). Between 12,000 and 15,000 people responded to the summons and Vice-President Kruger spoke on the first day of the assembly. During the ceremonies more stones were piled on the cairn which the burghers had raised when, on 14 December of the previous year, they had restored the government. The cairn was to commemorate their decision and their vows. These ceremonies expressed the people's gratitude to God and at the same time were powerful demonstrations of a new national consciousness which augured well for the future.

During 1882 it was decided to dispense with the Triumvirate and preparations were accordingly made to inaugurate a president and an executive council. Before this could be done, however, the government was faced with a serious challenge when Sekukuni, the restored tribal chief of the Bapedi, was murdered by his brother Mampoer. The murderer fled to a neighbouring chief, Mapoch (also known as Nyabel), who refused to hand him over to the Transvaal government. Action had to be taken immediately. Commandant-General Joubert attacked Mapoch in the difficult mountainous terrain of the Eastern Transvaal with about 3,000 burghers. He used extremely effective siege tactics which finally forced the two chiefs to surrender. Both were tried in court and condemned to death, but Kruger (who had meanwhile become President) exercised clemency in the case of Mapoch. The successful conclusion of the war against Mapoch contributed greatly to the prestige of the Republic, particularly in the eyes of its Bantu subjects, and consequently to the subsequent maintenance of law and order. It also meant much to Commandant-General Joubert who became a hero among the burghers. He was accepted as commandant-general until his death in 1899, even when it later became clear that he was not always equal to his task.

Meanwhile the government had immediately to face another problem on the western border. Clashes between various Tswana tribes about chieftainship and borders broke out while the Royal Commission was still determining the locality of the western border. As the Transvaal had no control over these tribes it could not act. However, as the clashes increased, there now arose the problem of the White volunteers, including some from the Transvaal, who joined the fight on both sides in the hope that the feuding chiefs would reward them with farms. This caused many complications and in October, 1881, the government forbade its people to interfere in these quarrels because such intervention could cause new trouble with the British. The continuous clashes and consequent disorder among the chiefs were the Transvaal's main reasons for its insistence, in 1883, that the Pretoria Convention be revised.

First presidential election

The first presidential election after the War of Independence was held at the beginning of February, 1883. The candidates were Vice-President Kruger and Commandant-General Joubert. Kruger was elected with 3,431 votes as against 1,171 for Joubert and the first state president of the restored Republic was sworn in on 9 May, 1883.

Kruger's domestic policy is of particular importance. He formulated it in his answer to the people's request that he should stand for election to the presidency. Briefly, Kruger's internal policy was based on the following: the development of the country's resources, particularly of agriculture, to the point where profits could be made by exporting goods; the promotion of free trade, which was to be encroached upon as little as possible by concessions; the promotion of industries, factories, and the mining of the country's mineral deposits by improving the Republic's transport system with roads and the *essential* railway between Pretoria and Delagoa Bay; the encouragement of immigration from Europe, particularly from Holland, within certain limits, however, to prevent the national identity from being submerged; the maintenance of a christian, just and civilizing policy towards the Bantu to control barbarity and turn the Bantu into happy and contented subjects of the Republic; the separation of church and state; and the promotion and development of christian education in the light of the text: "My people are destroyed for lack of knowledge" (Hosea 4:6). As far as foreign relations were concerned, Kruger endeavoured to maintain cordial relations with the suzerain power of Britain and favoured some kind of closer association among the South African states and colonies with a view to building a South African nation; the Republic, however, was to retain its independent status.

After the London Convention had been signed, Lord Derby told Kruger and his co-deputies that although the treaty had not yet been confirmed, they were free under its terms to negotiate with foreign states, i.e. without the intervention of the British government. They therefore left England for the Continent with the dual purpose of promoting the planned Pretoria-Delagoa Bay railway and investigating the possibility of establishing a bank in the Republic. It soon became clear that the establishment of a bank would have to wait until the railway plans had been realized, so they concentrated on the latter. Finally an agreement with the Portuguese government was signed on 17 May, 1884. In Portugal the deputation was received at court on three occasions and the King honoured Kruger by bestowing upon him the Order of the Great Cross of the Immaculate Conception. Particularly in Holland, and in Belgium, where royal receptions were held, the Transvaal deputation was received with much enthusiasm. In fact, it succeeded in establishing close cultural bonds with these countries. During this tour Kruger got to know the twenty-four year-old Dr W. J. Leyds, who agreed to become the Republic's State Attorney in the place of Jorissen, who had been dismissed by the Volksraad. The visits to France and Germany, where the deputation met Bismarck and Kaiser Wilhelm I, were also very important. Among other things, these visits resulted in reciprocal appointments of consular representatives, but most important of all was the recognition accorded to the South African Republic by the outside world. The deputation returned to its country grateful for and pleased about their achievements in England and Europe.

Railway policy and development

Back in their own country, whose independence was now virtually fully restored, President Kruger and his comrades could turn their attention to the domestic affairs of the Republic. At this stage the one matter of tremendous importance was the railway link planned between the Republic and Delagoa Bay. The matter became vital once gold was discovered in 1886. The discovery of gold changed conditions in all spheres of life in the Republic, and it and the struggle to obtain a railway link dominated the internal politics of the Republic until it went out of existence. At the heart of Kruger's policies, both domestic and foreign, was the question of independence, which, of course, brought the Republic into close contact with British policy and that of other states and colonies in South Africa. This contact and the economic and political relationships which resulted, are discussed in Chapter 14. Although they will therefore not be discussed very fully here, they will be referred to with the domestic matters of the rail link and the discovery of gold which are discussed below.

One of the most important purposes of the Boer deputation to Europe in 1884 was the promotion of a rail link between Pretoria and Delagoa Bay. Such a railway would, on the one hand, greatly further the financial and economic progress of the Republic and on the other it would make the Republic independent of the British colonies, Natal and the Cape, through whose harbours it had to import and export all goods. Such a railway had been the ideal of President Burgers, and Kruger regarded it as an economic and political necessity. Now that he had an agreement with the Portuguese he devoted himself for the next ten years to realizing the rail link despite all opposition and problems.

The first obstacle was the opposition of a number of Transvaalers who were against the rail plan because of the debt with which President Burgers had burdened the Republic. They also feared that the railway would deprive the transport-riders of their living. Once the mining of diamonds had begun in earnest transport-riding by ox-wagon to and from the diamond fields had become most remunerative in the absence of any other means of transport. President Kruger was aware of this attitude among the burghers when he asked the Volksraad to approve his concession to the Dutch engineers Johannes Groll and David Maarschalk, in terms of which they were to build the railway from the Portuguese border to Pretoria. But the tactful manner in which he presented his case overcame all the Volksraad's objections and they unhesitatingly approved the Dutch concession.

The holders of the concession had to float a company with the required capital as soon as possible. This, however, was not so easy, as the Transvaal's weak economic position did not attract investors. There was therefore a delay in forming the company, which made things very difficult for President Kruger, particularly after the discovery of the main gold reef towards the middle of 1886. A rail link with a harbour had become a matter of great urgency. The Cape Colony wanted to extend its line from Kimberley to Johannesburg, while Natal would have liked to see a link between Durban and the Transvaal. The Orange Free State was also willing to allow the Cape Colony to build a line, from Noupoort via Norvalspont, across Free State territory to the Transvaal. This would not only provide revenue for the Orange Free State but also give it the use of a railway line. (See Chapter 14 for negotiations about the construction of railways between the Transvaal, Orange Free State, Cape Colony and Natal.) Because of the delay in floating a company, his people began to urge Kruger to abandon the Dutch concession. Kruger was not opposed to a rail link with any of the other South African territories, but he insisted that the link with Delagoa Bay had to be built first, because such a railway, running on Transvaal territory most of the way, would benefit the Transvaal treasury in freight charges and import duty more than any other. Above all, this railway and the use of a Portuguese port beyond the control of the British would be a guarantee of the Republic's freedom and independence. The President would therefore not accede to the requests and suggestions of the Cape Colony.

In March, 1887, the government was obliged to warn the railway concession holders that they must implement the concession within six months or forfeit it. In the meantime the discovery of gold had made the Transvaal a better risk for investors and the holders of the concession were able to obtain Dutch and German capital. They formed the required company on 21 June, 1887 – the *Nederlandsch Zuid-Afrikaansche Spoorwegmaatschappij* (N.Z.A.S.M.). Work on the Republic's lifeline could thus be begun, but another obstacle caused yet further delay.

The N.Z.A.S.M. was to build the railway line from the Portuguese border, where it would link up with the line from Lourenço Marques to Pretoria. For building the part which would run across Portuguese territory, the Portuguese government had granted a concession to Colonel Edward McMurdo's English company. Since the materials and other equipment which the N.Z.A.S.M. required for their line would have to be transported on the Portuguese line, and since a tariff agreement for the whole line would have to be negotiated, a prior agreement with McMurdo's company about tariffs was essential. McMurdo, however, refused to consider any such agreement because he wanted to be able to dictate terms concerning the Transvaal section of the line. The attempt of the N.Z.A.S.M. to buy McMurdo's shares in the English company failed because of McMurdo's unreasonable demands. The lack of the required agreement compelled the Republic in July, 1888, to stop the N.Z.A.S.M. from proceeding with site preparations until such time as a reasonable agreement had been reached with the British company. After more than a year such an agreement was concluded by the Dutch company on 4 September, 1889. However, it was not made with McMurdo's company, but with the Portuguese railway administration which had in 1889 gained control of the line when their government confiscated it because the British company had not completed it in the allotted time. The confiscation was vitally important for the Republic since it eliminated British influence from Delagoa Bay and the vital railway. Meanwhile the N.Z.A.S.M. had completed the necessary surveys and the construction of the Delagoa Bay line across Transvaal territory began on 1 November, 1889.

Once these obstacles had been overcome the construction of the eastern line went well and the line was completed by the end of 1894. Thus was realised one of Paul Kruger's greatest ideals.

This must have been the end of a time of tension in the Republic, particularly since, as one delay followed another, external and internal pressure had been brought to bear on Kruger to permit rail links with the Orange Free State, the Cape Colony and Natal. Kruger refused to alter his plans, however, and although the Transvaal government did, under force of circumstances, assent to the extending of the Cape-Free State lines from the Vaal River and the Natal line from Charlestown to Johannesburg in 1892 and 1894 respectively, permission was only given once it was certain that the eastern line would be completed within the forseeable future. When this line was officially opened in July, 1895, the Cape Governor, Sir Hercules Robinson, declared quite correctly that this railway owed its existence to the will power and determination of one man – Paul Kruger. In his official speech, Kruger called the line "our national railway" which guaranteed not only the economic and political independence of the Republic, but which also drew the Republic and other countries closer together. The acquisition of the railway was an event of tremendous importance in the history of the South African Republic. Its inauguration, however, also meant the beginning of competition with other railways which developed into an intense struggle over tariffs, and at one stage almost resulted in war. (See Chapter 14 for details.)

Two other important rail developments, though in no way comparable to the eastern railway, should be mentioned. The first is the construction of the so-called *Rand Tram*, a light railway line from the Boksburg coalfields to the Johannesburg gold mines, which was opened in March, 1890. Its purpose was to supply cheap coal to the gold mines. In August, 1889, the Volksraad authorized the extension of this line as far as Krugersdorp. The other development was the construction of the essential line between Pretoria and Johannesburg. The President submitted a resolution concerning this project to the Volksraad in August, 1889, but it was so strongly opposed that all his persuasive powers failed to gain him a majority vote. Ultimately the two towns were linked in 1893 when the Pretoria-Vaal River railway was completed.

As the public began to perceive the advantages of the railway, prejudice and opposition decreased and in its last years the Republic devoted much of its attention to the construction of new lines. Thus in 1895 it was decided to build a railway from Pretoria to Pietersburg, particularly because such a line would be useful in controlling the northern Bantu tribes. This line was completed in 1899. Another essential branch line was built in 1896 to link Barberton with the eastern

245

line. Another line, for which a concession was granted as early as 1896, was envisaged to connect Ermelo with the eastern line near Machadorp. Because of the outbreak of war with Britain this link was never completed. Tenders for the construction of railways from Pretoria to Rustenburg and from Belfast to Lydenburg closed on 12 October, 1899, but by then war had broken out and nobody was concerned with building more railroads.

An event which caused far-reaching changes and complications in the history of the South African Republic was the discovery in 1886 of the main gold reef on the Witwatersrand, which climaxed a whole series of gold discoveries of varying significance. This discovery came at a time when the Republic's economic position was very shaky.

The discovery of gold and its consequences

The history of the discovery of gold is in itself a fascinating story which cannot, however, be told in detail here. The first gold discovery of any importance was that in 1873 of the rich alluvial deposits at Pilgrims Rest near Lydenburg. President Burgers proclaimed the territory a gold mining area and hundreds of fortune-hunters from the rest of southern Africa and overseas streamed into the diggings. These people, who caused Burgers much trouble and opposed him vehemently, gave the Republic a foretaste of the problems which such a foreign population element could create. In 1882 more gold was discovered in the De Kaap Valley. Here the rich Sheba Mine, which is still being worked, was discovered in 1885, which discovery caused Barberton to be founded nearby. Into this area, too, people began to stream from all over the world, particularly from Australia and within a short time there were about 10,000 persons at the gold-fields. Although much gold continued to be mined these fields decreased in importance once gold had been found on the Witwatersrand.

As early as 1876 the Witwatersrand was being prospected for gold, but without any remarkable results. After the annexation and the War of Independence the search was resumed, and considerable gold was found at the following places particularly:

1. at Kromdraai in 1882 by J. G. Bantjes and S. J. Minnaar, where the find was so promising that the government in 1885 declared the area a public gold mine, the first in the Witwatersrand area;

2. at Tweefontein, also in 1882, where in 1885 a battery with ten stamps was erected, the first machine in the Witwatersrand area to pulverise auriferous rock; and

3. on the farm Wilgespruit, in September, 1884, where the two brothers H. W. and F. P. T. Struben discovered a particularly rich reef which they called the "Confidence Reef", and which they began to mine, with the government displaying more interest in it than usual.

These finds were all surpassed by the discovery in May/June 1886 of the main reef at Roodepoort by J. G. Bantjes, and from then onwards events moved rapidly. Because of this major discovery, and because favourable reports had been received from other locations, the government in September, 1886, pro-claimed nine farms to be public gold diggings, Driefontein, Elandsfontein, Doornfontein, Turffontein, Randjeslaagte, Langlaagte, Paardekraal, Vogelstruis-fontein and Roodepoort. During September and October the Mining Commis-sioner, Carl von Brandis and the Assistant Mining Commissioner, Jan Eloff issued digging licenses and pegged out claims, so that everything was ready for work to begin on the goldfields.

Almost immediately many people began arriving at the new goldfields and soon diggers' camps had arisen. Before the end of 1886 the government had surveyed a township which they called Johannesburg. All these events shattered the previously peaceful life of the Republic and its population, who were pre-sented with new opportunities, but were also faced by new demands to be satisfied without delay or firmly resisted.

Financially and economically the discovery and mining of gold was obviously very advantageous to the Republic. The state had been in serious financial straits since its inception, and after the War of Independence it was additionally burdened by a large state debt. The taxes levied on the gold mining industry provided the government with a new source of revenue. Whereas ready cash had been scarce, gold mining and its ancillary activities put much money into circulation, enabling the people to pay their taxes. The increased export trade benefited the Republic and ultimately the Republic's financial position was so improved that it could readily obtain credit overseas. The earlier scarcity of money had been the reason for no independent bank having yet been established in the Republic, which had to rely on branches of Cape, Free State and Natal banks. The increased circulation of money now caused an increase in the number of bank branches, such as those of the Cape Commercial Bank, the Natal Bank, the Standard Bank, and the Bank of Africa, and new banks were established in the Transvaal, the Netherlands Bank in 1888 and the National Bank of the South African Republic (later the National Bank of South Africa) in 1891. Money poured into the Republic to satisfy the demands of the mining industry, companies were floated and, in general, capitalism ousted the original agri-cultural economy of the Transvaal.

Gold mining, with the influx of so many people into the gold areas, caused a whole series of towns, stretching from Randfontein to Springs, to be founded on the Witwatersrand before 1900. This growth of towns stimulated the demand for various other industries, while a large market for agricultural products sprang up within a few months. The development of this market caused a radical change in the life of the farmers, who had thus far produced mostly for their own use and for limited trade purposes. Now, however, they could cater for the urban market which offered good prices. This meant that they had to change and develop their methods of farming. The new type of farming, the gold mines, the other new industries and commercial enterprises all created a large demand for Bantu labour and gave the Bantu in their turn, opportunities to find a different type of life in a new world. A further important result of the development of the gold industry in general was the rapid growth of communications, railways in particular, not only in the Transvaal, but throughout the whole of South Africa (see Chapter 14). In the economic field, the discovery of gold thus effected a revolution in a very short space of time. This was another factor with which the government had to contend in running the country.

The "Uitlander problem"

As far as the people themselves were concerned, the discovery of gold also had far-reaching consequences. The original small population of the Transvaal had consisted mainly of Afrikaners, who were farmers and had a conservative, profoundly Christian, national tradition. What few foreigners there were in the Transvaal mainly concentrated on the Lydenburg goldfields, and they had had no influence at all. Now, however, a new cosmopolitan foreign population developed in the heart of the Republic, side by side with the Boer community for whose history, traditions, culture and ideals it had no sympathy. The new-comers were interested solely in gold, commerce, industry, money. They were soldiers of fortune, and from the outset there was a wide gap between the "old" and "new" inhabitants of the Transvaal. Most of the people who came to the goldfields failed to make their fortune, and often ended in miserable poverty. White unskilled labour had to find work in mines, factories and industries and was forced to compete with cheaper Bantu labour. Those people who were poorly paid or unemployed naturally congregated in cheap residential areas which soon became wretched slums. Various behavioral patterns new to the Transvaal, evolved in this society. The gambling and drunkenness, miscegenation, work and entertainment on Sunday were regarded by the Transvaal farmers as evils and public evidence of sin. The new life on the goldfields was in many ways a total violation of the traditional Boer way of life. The vast chasm between the old and the new in the Transvaal was evident as early as at the Paardekraal festival of December, 1866. This primarily religious occasion was attended by a large number of diggers, who invested it with a character totally different from its traditional one. Among other things, they erected unlicensed canteens and installed gaming tables neither of which ceased their activities even during the religious ceremonies. Such matters, and the diggers' foreign way of life, elicited stern strictures from Paul Kruger.

The communal way of life was also changed by the new turn of events in the Transvaal. Tens of thousands of Bantu came to work on the goldfields, never to return permanently to their homes again. They drifted away from their traditional tribal ties, becoming urbanised individuals trying to imitate the European way of life in all respects. (See also Chapter 14.)

The new developments on the Witwatersrand, the changes in commerce and industry, the sudden appearance of a number of new towns, the almost immediate influx of large numbers of people, all had a tremendous political influence on the Transvaal. In the first place the administration machinery had to alter and develop very quickly to cope efficiently with the new circumstances. This adjustment, as well as other essential formal ones, could fortunately be made.

The new population group, however, soon brought in its wake a much larger problem. President Kruger and the older citizens initially viewed the "Uitlanders", as the foreigners were called, as a threat to the morals and customs of the nation rather than as political opponents. Probably the memory had faded of the Uitlanders' part in undermining the Republic a decade earlier. But in February, 1887, when the President visited the goldfields on his annual journey through that part of the country, he began to get worried about these new people of his, although he had been cordially received. As was usual on these journeys, President Kruger gave the people an opportunity to tell him of their hopes and grievances. He heard mostly of their grievances. The miners complained because they could not obtain property rights to their stands, and because of the high licensing fees and import tariffs. They requested municipal self-government and claimed that they were being oppressed although they contributed most of the state's income.

President Kruger promised to consider their grievances. He did not intend to differentiate between the old and new populations and he expected the latter to concur with the old inhabitants and maintain the independence of the country. He promised everybody equal treatment. The Uitlanders' grievances and requests roused many fears in Kruger. There was the possibility that the foreigners would one day numerically exceed the old inhabitants, the attendant problem of governing with the support of only the minority of the population, and the danger this constituted to the freedom of the Republic should the Uitlanders insist on political rights. In 1886 the mining population of Barberton had already agitated for representation in the government of the country. In September, 1887, Kruger gave proof of his secret fears when he repeated his promise not to differentiate between the old and new population. The occasion was a second visit to the goldfields, but this time he made the reservation that equal treatment did not include enfranchisement and representation of the Uitlanders in the Volksraad. Yet Kruger and the government both knew that the demands which had begun to be made could not long be gainsaid. Yet such demands could not be satisfied in the simple and obvious manner, for this would not only subordinate the interests of the old population to those of the foreigners, but would also gravely endanger the independence of the Republic. Moreover, this matter was becoming urgent because the Uitlanders would have satisfied the legal requirements for naturalization after five years residence in the Republic. In order not to endanger their independence, and yet simultaneoulsy to satisfy the Uitlanders whom the Republic needed, the Transvaalers would have to find some suitable solution quickly.

In June, 1888, Kruger had already suggested to the Volksraad the possibility of instituting a second Volksraad as a solution to this thorny problem. After long deliberation the resolution was accepted in June 1890. The resolution was formulated in Act 4/1890, which made the existing Volksraad the First Volksraad and instituted a Second Volksraad. The Fist Volksraad was the highest authority, responsible for all matters of policy and for the independence of the state. The resolutions of the Second Volksraad were subject to the approval of the First, and it was responsible for controlling local matters which did not affect state policy: mining, roads, postal, telegraphic and telephonic services, patents and copyright, samples and trade marks, infectious diseases, company matters, insolvency, civil and criminal procedure, and any matter which the First Volksraad might refer to the Second. In elections for the State President and the First Volksraad, only those had the vote who had obtained citizenship before the new bill became law, or thereafter by birth and when they reached the age of sixteen. Thus Uitlanders could not vote for the First Volksraad; they could only vote for the First Volksraad if they had for ten years been *eligible* for election to the Second Volksraad. To be eligible to be so elected a person had to be at least thirty years old, enfranchised for at least two years immediately preceding the time of his election, a member of a Protestant church, resident of the Republic and owner of fixed property in the Republic. All citizens over the age of sixteen, that is, including all the foreigners who had been naturalized for two years, could vote for members of the Second Volksraad.

Apart from the facts that these measures did not always make for a cordial relationship between the two Volksraads and that the Second Volksraad soon insisted on an extension of its powers, they did not give the Uitlanders sufficient representation and could not prevent friction between the Uitlander population and the government. This friction resulted from the Uitlanders' many grievances, and in 1892 it ultimately gave rise to an organized Uitlander movement, the *Transvaal National Union*. Advocate Charles Leonard played a leading part in its establishment. Ostensibly the aims of the organization were the maintenance of the Republic's independence, the obtaining of equal political rights for the Uitlanders and the obtaining of satisfaction for Uitlander grievances. Actually its aim was the ultimate destruction of the Republic.

It should be made clear that originally not all the foreigners in the Transvaal were dissatisfied. Many of those of British origin were far more interested in becoming rich than in acquiring political power. In fact, one of the mining magnates, Lionel Phillips, said that the people cared nothing for the vote and that it would be difficult to arouse them against the Kruger government. There were, however, a number of Rand magnates who wanted to incite the heterogeneous masses on the goldfields, mine and factory managers as well as workers, and make of them malcontents who would help the magnates to gain their own economic and political ends. Leonard, in particular, well known for his earlier agitation against the Transvaal in the Cape, did much to foment discontent on the goldfields.

From its inception the *Transvaal National Union*, openly British orientated, agitated against the misgovernment of the Republic in general and of Paul Kruger in particular demanding an equal enfranchisement as the sole solution to its problems. It attempted to achieve its aims by means of public meetings, petitions to the government and the press. During the presidential election of 1893 it co-operated as closely as possible with the opposition to Paul Kruger led by Commandant-General Joubert and his "progressive" supporters, for this seemed the best way of removing Kruger, its biggest obstacle, in a constitutional manner. After the election, which Kruger won by 7,854 votes to Joubert's 7,009 and Chief Justice J. G. Kotze's 81 – Kruger's smallest majority ever, which undoubtedly reflected the influence of Uitlander propaganda – the *National Union* continued steadily to support the opposition to the President, in the Volksraad as well as in the Volksraad elections of 1895.

The year 1895 marked a deterioration in the relations which were already strained between the *National Union* and the Transvaal government. Early that year the *National Union* presented the government with a petition bearing 13,000 signatures, which insisted on fairer conditions for the vote. Shortly afterwards, in May, the government committed the tactical error of conscripting some Uitlander inhabitants of the Transvaal, all British subjects, for war service against the Bantu chief Malaboch in the Northern Transvaal. Some of them refused to comply reasoning that since they had no political rights in the state they could not be expected to perform compulsory military service. They were arrested and the Supreme Court held that, according to the laws of the country, they were liable for military duty. Protest meetings were held under the aegis of the *National Union*, the first while the conscription was still being carried out, and representations were made to the government. When these proved futile, the *Union* appealed to the British government, which immediately dispatched its High Commissioner in Cape Town, Sir Henry Loch, to Pretoria to negotiate with the South African Republican government. These complications completely altered the nature of the Uitlander problem: up to that time the relationship between the Transvaal and the Uitlanders had been purely domestic; now the appeal to London and London's decision to intervene in the internal affairs of the Republic dragged the matter into the field of foreign policy, and, in a certain sense, into international relations.

On 25 June President Kruger met Loch, the representative of the British government at Pretoria station, but a group of Uitlanders who were also there to meet Loch humiliated Kruger with a pro-British demonstration. They sang "Rule Britannia", unharnessed the horses from Kruger's coach and drew it, with Loch and Kruger seated inside, to Loch's hotel while someone waved a Union Jack from the coachman's seat. Loch entered the hotel with the Uitlanders, leaving Kruger on his own, and expressing no disapproval of the incident, whereupon some of Kruger's people pulled the President away in the coach. The incident caused a storm of indignation. Loch's negotiations, however, stopped the conscription of British subjects by the Transvaal government. Because of the explosive situation and at Kruger's request Loch did not accept the invitation of the *National Union* to visit Johannesburg, although its leaders were in touch with him and appealed through him for the protection of the British government.

Loch believed everything the Uitlanders told him and even considered with them the possibility of an armed uprising and its being aided and abetted by Britain. He wrote to President Kruger that the franchise question was a justified Uitlander grievance which should be settled by the Transvaal government; to

Lord Ripon, the British Colonial Secretary, he wrote that the political situation was so serious that an eruption was imminent. Loch's view was adopted by the British government as their official evaluation of the whole situation.

After these events, the situation in the Republic became increasingly tense. Further petitions were submitted to the government in 1895, bearing more than 35,000 signatures, many rather dubious, again requesting an extension of the franchise. Although the Transvaal Volksraad dismissed the requests after lengthy discussions, they served the other purposes for which they were intended, namely to impress the British government and people with the great political injustice to which the Uitlanders were being subjected by the Transvaal government. Meanwhile political agitation, particularly under Leonard and Phillips, grew in extent and intensity in Johannesburg and increasingly stronger representations were made for British intervention. The agitations resulted in the publication on 26 December, 1895, of the *National Union's* wordy manifesto written by Charles Leonard and addressed to the people of the South African Republic.

In the manifesto the *Union* reaffirmed its aims of maintaining the independence of the Republic, obtaining equal rights for all and removing all grievances, of which there was a long list. Some were justified, others were exaggerated or quite without foundation. The greatest source of dissatisfaction was, the manifesto cl aimed, that although the Uitlanders made up the majority of the Transvaal population (which was certainly not the case) they were excluded from having their say "in all matters affecting our lives, our liberties and our property", i.e. from the government. There were further complaints about, amongst other things, the dynamite monopoly which inflated the price of dynamite, the system of concessions in general, the price of coal, rail tariffs, import duties and other taxes which were regarded as excessive, the corruption which was supposed to exist in the Volksraad and among officials, the allegedly dictatorial powers of the President, the inadequate educational facilities for Uitlander children, the lack of recognition for English, Dutch being the medium in schools, the discrimination against Uitlanders on religious grounds, the state's administration of Bantu affairs which was said to be a "gross scandal and a source of immense loss and danger to the community", the lack of adequate self-government for Johannesburg, etc. The Uitlanders claimed they aimed to reform the existing republic into a "true Republic" by having a new constitution drafted by qualified representatives of the whole white population, by instituting a "fair" electoral law and representation in the Volksraad, by establishing equal rights for the Dutch and English languages, by making the legislative body responsible to the heads of the large departments, by removing all discrimination in the religious field, by making the supreme court independent, by instituting a liberal and comprehensive educational system as well as an efficient civil service, and by establishing free trade in all South African products. It is quite clear that this manifesto was intended to create the impression in Britain that the Uitlanders led a desperate life of unjust oppression in the Republic.

The Jameson Raid

Meanwhile C. J. Rhodes, the Prime Minister of the Cape Colony, had as early as 1894 begun to nurture the idea of making use of the Uitlanders in Johannesburg to bring down the government of the Republic. In spite of his policy of encircling the Transvaal with British possessions, in an attempt to cut the Transvaal off from the sea, including Delagoa Bay, Rhodes could not persuade the South African Republic to accept his ideal of a united South Africa under the British flag, even though he negotiated with Paul Kruger and proposed a South African customs union. (All these matters are discussed in Chapters 10 and 14.) Before 1894 Rhodes had paid little attention to the Uitlander movement. His idea of using the Uitlanders was encouraged by the increasing German interest in the South African Republic and Britain's favourable attitude towards his plans. In order to carry out his plans Rhodes organized an uprising in Johannesburg with the knowledge and approval of the British Prime Minister, Lord Rosebery, the Minister for Colonies, Joseph Chamberlain and the British High Commissioner in South Africa, Sir Hercules Robinson. The uprising was to be supported by a military raid into the Transvaal under the leadership of Dr L. S. Jameson. Once the uprising had succeeded, Robinson was to go to Pretoria, act as mediator between the Transvaal government and the *Transvaal National Union*, and institute a "Constituent Assembly". The Transvaal could then be changed into a self-governing British colony. Such a colony would be willing to join a federation of South African states.

Rhodes's plan was based on the belief that the Uitlanders constituted the greater part of the Transvaal population; according to him, there were 100,000 British subjects as against 14,000 Boers. The actual figures however, were roughly 150,000 Republican citizens and nearly 76,000 Uitlanders, of whom about 41,000 were English. Other factors which Rhodes and his co-conspirators did not take into account were the internal dissension among the Uitlanders, their lack of arms, and above all the absence of any enthusiasm for such an artificial uprising.

A few days before the uprising was due to take place in Johannesburg it became clear that it would be an utter failure. Jameson, meanwhile, with five hundred hand-picked policemen of the *Chartered Company*, was waiting at Pitsani on the western border of the Transvaal, prepared to advance on Johannesburg. The *National Union's* manifesto appeared in the press at the same time. Jameson disregarded messages that the uprising was delayed, and on the evening of 29 December, 1895, he crossed the border on his way to Johannesburg, resolved to play his part in the downfall of the Transvaal government. His men neglected to cut all the telephone wires, and the Transvaal government was informed of the whole situation by the following morning. They called up the western commandos under General P. A. Cronje. Even burghers who had not been summoned joined the commando from far and near. On 2 January, 1896, at Doornkop near Roodepoort, Jameson was confronted and forced to surrender to the Boers. Chamberlain and Robinson repudiated Jameson's raid so that his status became that of a freebooter. President Kruger magnanimously handed Jameson and his officers over to the British government for punishment. Jameson was sentenced to fifteen months imprisonment, of which he served a few months before being released on grounds of ill-health. Rhodes gave evidence to a British Parliamentary *Committee of Inquiry* into the Jameson Raid. However, the Committee glossed over the facts, and the complicity of Rosebery, Chamberlain and Robinson, which has been proved beyond doubt by contemporary researchers, did not come to light. Small wonder that the Opposition dubbed it the "Committee of No Enquiry".

Jameson's raid put the Johannesburg leaders of the uprising in a very difficult position, for they were now obliged to take some sort of action. Leonard, Beit and a few other leaders had left Johannesburg before the raid to seek safety elsewhere, as they were afraid of the consequences if anything should go wrong. The remaining leaders restyled the *Transvaal National Union* the *Reform Committee*, took over the government of Johannesburg and sent a deputation to Pretoria. Talks between Sir Hercules Robinson, who had meanwhile arrived in Pretoria, and President Kruger began on 6 January, 1896. President Kruger now had the whip hand. With about 12,000 burghers and the State Artillery standing by to ensure prompt obedience, he demanded the immediate surrender of all arms and granted an amnesty to all the insurrectionists except the leaders. Furthermore, he promised the Uitlanders, who had been misled by their leaders, that their grievances would be investigated and that a city council would be instituted in Johannesburg. It would be elected by the inhabitants, and take full charge of local affairs.

Arms were handed over on 10 January and peace and order were restored. The sixty-four members of the *Reform Committee* were arrested and their leaders, Lionel Phillips, John Hays Hammond, Frank Rhodes and George Farrar were sentenced to death by the Supreme Court on a charge of high treason, to which they pleaded guilty. President Kruger commuted the sentence to a fine of £25,000 each. The fines were paid by Cecil Rhodes.

The Republic versus Chamberlain and Milner

The Jameson Raid had significant consequences. They cannot here be discussed in detail but what they amounted to was that Afrikaner nationalism was stimulated throughout South Africa and became a powerful unifying force. This became apparent four years later, when the Transvaal was forced to declare war on Britain. On the other hand, the anxiety which the failure of the Jameson Raid and its immediate repercusisons aroused in the English orientated members of the community produced a surge of nationalism among them also, and South Africa was virtually divided into two camps. The period between 1896 and 1899 was thus a time of stress between Afrikaner nationalism and British imperialism, which finally came to a head in 1899 in the war between Transvaal and Britain. This war is discussed elsewhere (see Chapter 15) so it is not treated in any detail here.

The Uitlanders in Johannesburg were very subdued for a while after the failure of the Jameson Raid, but the British did not abandon the intention of drawing Transvaal into a South African federation under the British flag. In fact, their determination increased as the Republic grew ever more independent of the British colonies because of its gold and its own railway link with the sea. It was less and less interested in joining any kind of South African association. Furthermore the increasingly friendly relations between the South African Republic and Germany were a source of great anxiety to Britain. The German Kaiser's telegram to Paul Kruger, in which he congratulated Kruger on repulsing the Jameson Raid and restoring peace *without summoning the aid of friendly powers*, confirmed Britain's suspicions and further strained Anglo-German relations.

From the British point of view, there was one remaining way in which a South African federation could be effected. This was for Britain to intervene in the domestic affairs of the Republic and try to force the government to give the Uitlanders the vote. This was the policy which the British government adopted, being still under the impression that the Uitlanders formed the majority of the population. The policy was implemented by the Colonial Secretary, Chamberlain and Sir Alfred Milner, Britain's new High Commissioner in South Africa since 1897, who were determined to deprive the South African Republic of its independence, by force if necessary. (For details of the actions of Chamberlain and Milner see Chapter 14.)

Internal affairs

Thus far in this discussion the main emphasis had fallen on the railway and the Uitlander questions as the dominating and controlling factors in the history of the South African Republic after the War of Independence of 1880/1. Before this chapter ends, however, attention should be drawn to a few other matters, which so far have merely been referred to in passing. One of these is the opposition to Paul Kruger which developed in his own ranks from the time he became president in 1883. This opposition, led by Commandant-General P. J. Joubert, was particularly opposed to President Kruger's policy of concessions, the rail concession to the N.Z.A.S.M. being one of the chief bones of contention, and Kruger's appointment of Hollanders as officials in the administration of the country. Gradually the opposition developed into a "progressive" group (not party) which, amongst other things, advocated liberal concessions, including the franchise, to the Uitlanders. The progressive group was strongly supported by newspapers such as *The Star* and *Ons Land*. Proof of its growing influence was to be found in the results of the presidential election, quoted above, of 1893, as opposed to the election of 1888. The Jameson Raid and the resultant British attitude caused a decline in the influence of the "progressives", as reflected in 1898 in the tremendous majority of Kruger's re-election for the fourth time, although it took place in what was regarded as a period of crisis. Kruger got 12,864 votes, S. W. Burger 3,814 and Joubert 2,009.

A matter which was of prime interest to Kruger, and which had become vitally important to the developing Republic, was education. This had been left in a somewhat precarious state when Rev. S. J. du Toit resigned as Superintendent of Education in 1889. In May, 1889, the President offered improved prospects for education and emphasised that there would be religious instruction and education in the Dutch language. Secondary education particularly, left much to be desired, for of all the excellent projects envisaged by the Education Act of 1882, only the training college for teachers had been realised, mainly because of a shortage of funds. From 1889 onwards serious efforts were made to establish a university in Pretoria, which went as far as negotiations with Dr A. Kuyper in Holland. Various circumstances, particularly Kuyper's unwillingness to help find the required lecturers in Holland, ended the whole undertaking in 1891.

Had there been success in establishing this university in Pretoria where young Transvaalers could have been educated, it would probably have helped Kruger gradually to have begun appointing chief executives from his own ranks, thus neutralizing the criticism that he liked appointing Hollanders. Another matter, however, removed this point of criticism. This was the Jameson Raid and its consequences, for the change of attitude towards the Republic it produced among Cape Afrikaners made the President confident that they also would work for the maintenance of Transvaal independence. He therefore unhesitatingly began to appoint Afrikaners from the south to high civil service posts which had previously been held by Hollanders. Thus the former president of the Orange Free State, F. W. Reitz, was nominated as State Secretary in 1898 in the place of Dr Leyds, who was appointed as the Republic's Envoy Extraordinary and Minister Plenipotentiary to various European states. Another important appointment of this period was that of the young Cape jurist, Advocate J. C. Smuts, as State Attorney.

While Chamberlain's attacks on its independence absorbed all the Republic's attention and diplomatic ingenuity, Paul Kruger's government had to cope with an unexpected legal crisis in 1897, which complicated matters yet further. This crisis sprung from the right, which Chief Justice J. G. Kotze demanded in 1890, for the bench to test the validity of the Volksraad's legislation against the Constitution. Kruger considered the Volksraad to be the highest authority in the state, and viewed the Chief Justice's demand, advanced as it was at that particularly trying time, as some sort of political threat to the independence of the state. Therefore the Volksraad in February, 1896, passed legislation which authorised the President to ask the judges whether they regarded it as compatible with their duties and their oaths to give judgment according to existing and future legislation by the Volksraad, and not to arrogate to themselves the power to test any such laws and resolutions against the Constitution. Should a judge not consider this attitude to be compatible with his duties and oath the President was empowered to dismiss him from his office. This law was considered by the judges to reduce the independence of the Bench, and the whole episode was used by the Republic's enemies as "proof" of the legal instability which was said to exist in the Republic, although the differences between the

256

judges and the government were ultimately resolved. When President Kruger used his power in February, 1898, to dismiss Chief Justice Kotze because he repeated his claim to test the validity of the laws, his move coincided with the Uitlanders' explosion of wrath at the Volksraad's action against the report of the Industrial Commission of 1897. The dismissal of the Chief Justice was cited as being no less than the destruction of the independence of the Bench. Thus the legal crisis, which was no more than a purely internal matter, ideally suited the purposes of Chamberlain and Milner. They lost no time in exploiting it.

The episode regarding the Industrial Commission was one of the last events to disturb the Uitlanders. This commission, under the chairmanship of S. W. Burger (a "progressive" who was to become one of Kruger's opponents in the presidential election of 1898), investigated the complaints and problems of the mining industry and submitted its report in August, 1897. Influenced by the mining companies, it recommended a number of important concessions to the mining industry. Milner and the mining magnates were extremely pleased with the recommendations, but their hopes were dashed when, towards the end of 1897 the Volksraad, basing its decisions on the report of a commission of its own, did not accept all the recommendations of the Industrial Committee. Once more the Uitlanders were up in arms against the Transvaal government. Milner made full use of this opportunity as well.

War

In 1894 the war against Malaboch showed that the burghers of the Republic who were also its fighting force, were badly armed. Between 1887 and 1891 the Republic had bought about 13,000 second-hand Martini Henry rifles, of which about 9,000 had been distributed among the burghers, but this was hardly sufficient. The Jameson Raid again showed that many burghers were still totally unarmed while the rest possessed only old or obsolete rifles. Nor could the Republic rectify the matter.

The Jameson Raid had alerted the Republic to foreign threats, and its immediate consequence was the Transvaal's move to obtain arms. Over 73,000 modern German Mausers and their ammunition were bought in the three years after the raid, and heavy artillery, of which the Republic had very little, was ordered in France and Germany. The State Artillery was enlarged and forts were built in Johannesburg and Pretoria. This caused much criticism from the British, but the Transvaal was now to a certain extent in a state of preparedness.

Meanwhile negotiations about the franchise questions were taking place between Milner and the Republican government. As they progressed it became increasingly clear that Milner was aiming completely to destroy the Republic and that he was uncompromisingly bent on war. At the beginning of 1899 he made use, as Rhodes did before the Jameson Raid, of the Uitlanders to achieve his aim. He sent a petition with 21,684 signatures, listing the grievances of the Uitlanders, to the Queen. This petition was accepted by the British government. Thus the government of the Republic found itself directly confronted by the British government. The negotiations which followed were intended simply to gain time for Britain to move her troops as close as possible to the Transvaal borders, and it became ever clearer to the Transvaal that it would have to go to war to protect its independence. To prevent the British troops from encircling the Republic, the Republic was compelled to deliver an ultimatum to Great Britain, after prolonged consultation with the Orange Free State according to their agreement of 1897. Britain rejected this ultimatum and therefore war with Britain, which had not been sought by the South African Republic, broke out on 11 October, 1899.

14. States and Colonies in South Africa, 1854-1902

In the four preceding chapters the histories of the two British coastal colonies and the two inland Boer republics were discussed individually. This treatment should not be taken to imply that these states were quite isolated from one another and that they developed entirely independently of one another; obviously there were forces constantly at work which tended both to unite these states and also to produce clashes between them. Among these forces were the unification and federation movements, mineral discoveries and economic competition, and the rise of Afrikaner nationalism in counteraction to British imperialism. These factors and trends, which also exhibit a close relationship with the British colonial policy in respect of South Africa and which cannot be divorced from it, will be discussed in as far as they are relevant to two or more of the South African states and colonies.

Attempts at closer union, 1854 – 1872

After 1854 there were continuous attempts to close the gaps that had arisen from the territorial division of South Africa which followed upon the Great Trek. These attempts aimed either at uniting the two independent inland Boer republics, the Transvaal and the Orange Free State, or at drawing one or both of these republics into a federation with the British coastal colonies of Natal and the Cape. The Orange Free State was initially to play a crucial role in these activities.

The geographical position of the Free State Republic, contiguous to the Cape Colony, Natal and the South African Republic, would necessarily involve it in their problems. Furthermore, the inhabitants of the Free State were divided in opinion. Those in the north, the old Windburg republicans, wanted to unite with the Transvaal (the supporters of unification). The colonial elements in the south wished to join the Cape Colony (the supporters of federation). A third group wished the Free State to remain independent.

Those in the Free State who desired unification were strongly supported by the Transvaaler, M. W. Pretorius, who hoped to realise his father's ideal of founding one large Voortrekker state. In September, 1854, when Pretorius paid a private visit to Bloemfontein the supporters of unification attempted to use him to strengthen their position but the Free State Volksraad resisted their efforts. As a result J. J. Venter, a member of the Volksraad, introduced the policy that the Free State should continue as a separate republic but should enter into some kind of treaty with its sister state. The position of the Venter group was strengthened when J. N. Boshof succeeded J. P. Hoffman as president of the Free State. Boshof took a firm stand in relation to the other groups but this resulted in the supporters of unification asking for the support of Pretorius. Consequently clashes developed between Boshof and Pretorius.

Pretorius would probably have responded immediately to the call of the supporters of unification were it not that circumstances in the Transvaal at that time did not favour unification. There was political strife between the groups at Potchefstroom, Lydenburg and Soutpansberg. During 1855 and 1856 Pretorius succeeded in introducing a new constitution for the South African Republic, which provided for the inclusion in the Republic of territories other than the Transvaal. Lydenburg and Soutpansberg would not accept the new constitution. However, at the beginning of 1857 Pretorius was elected president of the Republic, albeit in an unconstitutional manner, and felt himself strong enough to attempt to secure the Free State and so to realise his ideal of a united republic north of the Orange River.

In February, 1857, Pretorius and the Transvaal State Secretary, M. A. Goetz, visited Bloemfontein to object to Free State legislation in terms of which the Cape and Transvaal owners of Free State farms had either to occupy the farms within six months or else to sell them. This, however, was merely the ostensible reason for Pretorius's visit. On 24 February he attempted to claim the Free State for the Transvaal. He argued that Queen Victoria had promised the Free State to Andries Pretorius, who had helped to gain the Free State her independence, but that the transfer had not been effected. M. W. Pretorius was therefore now claiming the Free State as the heir of Andries Pretorius.

The Free State government rejected Pretorius's claim and asked him to leave their state. He complied with this request but did not relinquish his claim, promising the supporters of unification that he would return with a commando to carry out his purpose. Boshof protested to the Potchefstroom government but it supported Pretorius's action and promised to help those who desired unification. Boshof reacted violently against the supporters of unification in his state which, in April, 1857, caused the Potchefstroom Council of War to demand that Free State persecution of the supporters of unification should cease. The Free State had to accede to this demand within twenty-four hours or the Transvaal would forcibly protect the supporters of unification.

In the meantime Boshof had been unsuccessfully trying to form an alliance with the Cape Colony; he had, however, succeeded in gaining the support of Lydenburg and Soutpansberg, who wanted to be rid of Pretorius's "illegal government". Boshof's reply to the Transvaal ultimatum was to proclaim martial law, take even stronger measures against the supporters of unification and enter into an agreement with Lydenburg and Soutpansberg to act together against Potchefstroom.

In May, 1857, Pretorius mobilized his burghers on the bank of the Vaal River and promised help to the supporters of unification in the Free State. The presidents of both the republics were therefore preparing for war. On 25 May the Free State and Transvaal commandos met at the Renoster River but an armed clash was averted through the mediation of Paul Kruger and others. The Vaal River Treaty, which recognized the independence of both republics, was signed. Lydenburg and Soutpansberg indeed were dissatisfied because the Free State had made peace without their knowledge but their resistance crumbled, and gave Pretorius an opportunity in 1860 to unite the Transvaalers under his leadership. (See also Chapters 13 and 14.)

With the First Basuto War in 1858 the unification movement which had been dormant in the Free State since the signing of the Vaal River Treaty again became active. The Free Staters were unable to defend themselves against the Basuto and when Sir George Grey, Governor of the Cape Colony, refused to help them, Boshof was compelled to seek help from the Transvaal. Pretorius hoped to use the emergency in the Free State to bring about a unification of the two republics. On the instructions of the Transvaal Volksraad he left for the Free State at the head of a commando. On 23 May, 1858, Pretorius met Boshof at Winburg and informed him that the Transvaal would help the Free State on condition that the two states united. Before agreeing Boshof wished to consult his Volksraad.

The supporters of unification had meanwhile not been inactive and in twenty-three petitions 1,445 people signed in favour of and 98 opposed unification. It seemed that unification was inevitable. However, in June, 1858, the Free State Volksraad in Bloemfontein received a letter from Sir George Grey which stated that Britain would not consider the conventions to be binding were unification carried through. This damped the enthusiasm for unification of both the Free State and the Transvaal. The independence guaranteed by the conventions was more important to them than unification.

Grey had his own plans for a federation which would fail if the two republics united. Boshof kept Grey well informed of the republics' aspirations towards unity. Grey did not wish to lose the chance of having the Free State in his contemplated federation because it linked the Cape Colony and Natal. He was afraid that the Transvaal would prevail upon the Free State to unite, and so urged the British government to adopt the attitude it did concerning the conventions. The British government knew nothing of Grey's federation plan but its stipulations did prevent the unification of the two republics and so promoted Grey's plans.

In the Free State conditions were favourable for federation. The knowledge that the British government would not agree to the unification of the republics made federation more acceptable to many Free Staters, while the movement received further powerful support from Advocate Hamelberg and *The Friend*. They pointed out that there was little advantage in uniting with the weak and poor Transvaal when federation with the Cape Colony, with its money and harbours, was possible. They also argued that because of the Basuto threat the Free State in its poverty and weakness could not remain independent. Even Boshof and his government favoured federation and Grey used every opportunity to propagate his plan. For example, he explained the advantages of federation to 300 Free Staters when in September, 1858, he mediated between Moshesh and the Free State. The idea of federation began to gain ground everywhere and on 7 December, 1858, the Free State Volksraad decided by a majority

261

of one to enter into negotiations with the Cape concerning federation. The Cape parliament was, however, scheduled to discuss this decision only in March, 1859, and in the meantime Grey would sound the British government on the matter.

Grey's opportunity came when Bulwer Lytton, the British Secretary of State for the Colonies, sought Grey's opinion concerning a possible federation of the Cape Colony and Natal, and a permanent South African policy based on the conventions. Lytton was looking for a policy which would ease the mother country's financial burden in the colonies. In his detailed reply of November, 1858, Grey condemned the convention policy and emphasized that the Cape Colony and Natal could not federate without the intermediate Free State. He thus advocated a federation of all the South African states under the British flag, with a governor appointed by the British government at its head. Grey further contemplated a federal parliament elected by the inhabitants of the various states with a responsible cabinet to assist the governor. The federal government would be responsible for matters of general interest while the existing state legislative bodies would be responsible for local government.

The most important reason for Grey's federation plan was the native problem which he felt could not be solved by a divided South Africa. He also argued that it was possible that the republics in the north would become so strong that they would overshadow the south and could even become dangerous from the economic and military points of view. In some respects Grey was crossing imaginary bridges before he came to them, but there was much to be said for his plan. There was a need for federation in South Africa and one of the republics even asked for it. It is probable that federation could have succeeded and possibly would have prevented much strife and bitterness.

Be that as it may, the British government, which remembered the expenses of the Orange River Sovereignty, did not accept the federation proposal. On 6 October, 1858, Lytton wrote: "In a federation with these Dutch Republics we have much to risk and nothing to gain – we reverse in it the old story of the giant and dwarf, in which the dwarf got the wounds and the giant the profit. It seems to me that, here, the dwarf would be thrusting her Dutch Nose into all sorts of Black Squabbles, from which the British Giant would always have to pull him (sic) out with the certainty of more kicks than halfpence".[1] The fear of expense wrecked Grey's federation plan.

The failure of Grey's federation scheme caused the unification movement to revive. In July, 1859, the Free State appointed a commission to discuss the matter of unification with the Transvaalers but the government in Pretoria would not commit itself as long as there was any danger of violating the Sand River Convention. The Republic desired unification but feared to lose its independence.

The unification movement was again stimulated when M. W. Pretorius, the Transvaal president, was elected president of the Free State as well. He took the

1. Quoted in C. W. de Kiewiet: *British Colonial Policy and the South African Republics 1848 – 1872* (London, 1929), p. 127.

oath of office in 1860. It would seem that Pretorius united the two republics, but actually this was not so. He therefore appointed a commission to amend the Free State constitution so that it would correspond with that of the Transvaal. He also consulted the Free Staters on the matter of unification and received 1,076 signatures for and 104 signatures against unification. However, there was still opposition to unification in the Transvaal.

The Transvaalers were afraid that the conventions would be rescinded should they unite with the Free State. For this reason the Volksraad granted Pretorius six months leave of absence to act as president of the Free State. At the end of this period the Transvaal Volksraad discharged Pretorius honourably from his presidency of the Republic. Pretorius considered the Transvaal Volksraad to be the main hindrance to unification and so turned to his supporters in the Western Transvaal. This move antagonised the Eastern Transvaal opponents of unification and caused civil war. Because of the chaos in the Transvaal Pretorius could not further his plans for unification. In April, 1863, he resigned from the presidency of the Free State and returned to the Transvaal. Enthusiasm for unification then flagged in the Free State because as *The Friend* stated "it was like trying to lean on a broken reed".[2]

The supporters of federation thus again came to the fore in the Free State and produced 1,550 signatures for and 1,014 against federation. They even, though unsuccessfully, sought the support of Governor Wodehouse. The Free State Volksraad, however, felt compelled "to do everything in its power to maintain the independence, freedom, honour and dignity of our republic".[3] In this frame of mind the Free Staters elected J. H. Brand as president. He was to protect the independence of the Free State by successfully opposing all movements aimed at closer union. (See Chapters 12 and 13.)

During the years from 1865 to 1870 the gulf between the two republics was widened by various incidents. In 1865, at Brand's request, the Transvaal sent volunteers to help in the Second Basuto War. The Transvaalers, however, went home before the Basuto were finally defeated and so aroused the distrust of the Free Staters. The Transvaal was also fighting Bantu tribes in the Waterberg, Soutpansberg and Lydenburg regions. Trouble with the Bantu in both the Free State and the Transvaal thus tended to cause both states to concentrate on domestic matters. The two republics were also disputing about their common border along the upper reaches of the Vaal River. This difference was only settled in 1870 when Lieutenant-Governor Robert Keate of Natal, acting as arbitrator, established the border at the Klip River. All these incidents built up a state of tension and increased the alienation between the two republics.

During 1870 and 1871 the desire for unification had revived but this time it was the Transvaalers who took the initiative. This reversal in the Transvaalers'

2. Quoted in F. A. van Jaarsveld: *Die Eenheidstrewe van die Republikeinse Afrikaners*, I, (Johannesburg, 1951), p. 294.
3. Quoted in E. M. Attree: *The Closer Union Movements between the Orange Free State, South African Republic and Cape Colony (1838 – 1863)* (Archives Year Book for S.A. History, 1949, I), p. 365.

attitude was mainly owing to the political disunity, poverty and weakness of the Transvaal under M. W. Pretorius, who in 1863 had again become president, as contrasted to the Free State which Brand had unified and developed financially and otherwise into a strong state, a model republic. Brand had also managed better than Pretorius in diplomatic exchanges with the British government concerning Basutoland and the diamond fields. The Transvaalers envied the Free Staters their prosperity and their president.

Since 1869 the Transvaal Volksraad had been receiving petitions from its people requesting unification with the Free State. The Keate Award concerning the diamond fields and Pretorius's subsequent resignation as president increased the desire for unification. Brand was consequently approached to become president of the South African Republic as well. The potential mineral wealth of the Transvaal, the possibility of a railway line to Delagoa Bay, and the Transvaal's free trade treaty with the Portuguese were used as bait. The Free Staters, however, considered the Transvaal to be impoverished and divided and did not want to unite with such a state. Brand associated himself with these sentiments and recommended that the Transvaal ask the Rev. T. F. Burgers to be president. The Transvaalers accepted this advice and thus acquired what they believed to be a "clever" president. Their need for unification was thus diminished.

Nevertheless the two republics did not drift apart. The need for co-operation between them was emphasized by British intervention in the interior, particularly in the matter of the diamond fields. In 1872, at the instigation of the Free State Volksraad, Brand negotiated with the Transvaal about a secret defence treaty and a friendship, trade and extradition treaty between the two republics. Because of Brand's caution and Burgers's ill-health the first-mentioned treaty came to nothing. The friendship treaty was concluded, however, and by drawing the republics closer together it partly satisfied their desire for unification. By this time the British had already staked a claim in the interior of South Africa.

New British interest in the interior

The convention policy by which Britain withdrew herself from the interior of South Africa was not popular everywhere and was sharply criticized by various British officials. William Porter, the Cape Attorney-General, was opposed to the Voortrekkers (whom he regarded as Cape and thus British subjects) being given their independence. Sir George Grey, who in 1854 was actually appointed governor of the Cape to implement the convention policy, also condemned it. According to him the British government, in its haste to be rid of financial responsibilities, had overlooked the fact that events in one area would have repercussions elsewhere. He maintained that in its own interests the major power in South Africa could not ignore events on the borders of its own possessions. For this reason he urged the British to intervene north of the Orange River and proposed the federation scheme which has already been mentioned. Sir Philip Wodehouse, Grey's successor, also considered the conventions to be a serious mistake and felt that the strongest power in South Africa should control the Boer republics.

Sir Charles Adderley expressed his opposition to the convention policy in the British parliament. He argued that in the history of the Roman Empire withdrawal from its possessions had been the first symptoms of its decline. Adderley was strongly supported by the philanthropists although their motives were quite different from his. Although the philanthropists were no longer as influential as they had been in the first half of the nineteenth century humanitarian ideas still influenced men greatly, and they availed themselves of suitable opportunities. They were violently opposed to the convention policy because it discriminated against the non-Whites. For example, the Whites were given arms and ammunition which were withheld from the non-Whites. The articles in the convention dealing with slavery provided the philanthropists with an opening for attack. They tried to prove that the South African Republic was engaged in the slave-trade and on these grounds insisted on British intervention in the Transvaal.

Some British officials wished to act on behalf of the non-Whites in the Transvaal because British policy concerning the republics was to some extent influenced by the belief that the Boers suppressed the non-Whites. But as long as colonial possessions were a financial drain and the British treasury depleted, the British government would not embark on a policy which would increase its responsibilities and expenditure. Nevertheless, resistance to the convention policy increased steadily so that by the end of the sixties it had been abandoned entirely. This change in British policy can be discerned in two events which occurred in 1868.

The first of these events was the annexation of Basutoland. The difficulties with the Basuto affected not only the Free State but the whole of South Africa. Basutoland had common borders with the Free State, the Cape Colony and Natal, and even the Transvaal became involved in the clashes with the Basuto. When at his wits' end Moshesh turned to Wodehouse, a man with philanthropic leanings, he was received sympathetically. Wodehouse recommended to London that Basutoland should be annexed and on 9 December, 1867, Buckingham Chandos, the Secretary of State for the Colonies, gave the necessary permission, on condition that Basutoland became part of Natal. Wodehouse would not agree to this since he feared that, like the Free Staters, the Natalians would take away the Basuto's land. He therefore proclaimed Basutoland a British territory on 12 March, 1868.

Wodehouse's motive for annexing Basutoland was, in the first place, that the Free Staters had taken too much of the Basuto's land. In their search for more living space the Basuto would thus become a threat to Natal and the Cape Colony. Annexation by the major power in South Africa would thus ensure security for Natal and for the Cape Colony and also join the two colonies together; at that time the colonies were not adjoining. The annexation would also re-establish trade, which had been disrupted by the Basuto wars, between the Cape Colony, Natal and the Free State. In addition the Cape Colony desired peace on its border because it was moving toward responsible government.

Lastly there was a strategic reason for annexation, namely, to prevent the Free State from expanding toward Port St. Johns to secure a harbour for itself. It is not certain that the Free State had any such intention, but Wodehouse suspected that it was so and wished to prevent any such move. (See Chapter 13.)

The second event of 1868 which helped to end the convention policy was linked with a proclamation issued in that year by M. W. Pretorius upon the discovery of gold at Tati. This proclamation extended the northern border of the Transvaal to Lake Ngami. This step did not conflict with the Sand River Convention but it aroused opposition in Natal, the Cape Colony and Britain. It was argued that a slave-owning country – although it had not been proved that the Transvaal did practise slavery – should not be allowed to obtain control over yet more non-Whites, or be allowed to develop into a bastion against future British development in the interior. Britain consequently instructed Pretorius to abandon his plans for expansion. In 1868, therefore, Britain discarded the conventions and was prepared to penetrate into the interior to fulfil the role of a major power in South Africa. The discovery of diamonds in 1870, in what was later known as Griqualand West, was the next development in South Africa that attracted Britain's attention. (See Chapter 14.)

Both the Free State and the South African Republic, as well as the Griqua chief Waterboer and a few Bantu headmen, claimed parts of the diamond fields. Both republics claimed the territory between the Vaal and the Harts Rivers but the Free State, because of the Sand River Convention, could not press its claim and so withdrew in favour of the South African Republic. But President Pretorius then agreed to arbitration and presented his case so poorly that the arbitrator, Robert Keate, Lieutenant-Governor of Natal, decided in favour of the non-Whites. President Brand, however, fought stubbornly for the Free State's claim to the remainder of the diamond fields. Waterboer then turned to the British government for help so that Britain annexed Griqualand West, including the diamond fields, on 27 October, 1871. Both republics thus lost the diamonds which they had hoped would relieve their financial straits. (See Chapters 12 and 13.)

The annexation of Griqualand West proved once again that Britain was not prepared to sacrifice her supremacy in South Africa. The diamond fields had to be possessed by Britain or the republics would become too strong and begin to dominate South Africa. The republics had to be kept weak so that they would be compelled to seek Britain's assistance. Federation was once more in the air and the British officials suspected that if the Boer republics were to grow strong they would never become members of a British federation. Britain, moreover, considered it to be a question of prestige to bring the approximately 50,000 British subjects on the diamond fields under British authority.

Griqualand West was also economically and strategically important to the Cape Colony. The diamond business and the other trade that accompanied it would break the depression being experienced at that time in the Cape Colony. One of the factors which had caused this depression was the opening in 1869 of the Suez canal which meant a loss of shipping and trade for the coastal colonies

British traders also believed that there were other great mineral deposits in the interior of Southern Africa. Griqualand West lay on the road to the north and this road had to be kept open for future British development of the interior. Border security was another reason for the annexation of Griqualand West. It was generally believed that the republics could not maintain order at the diggings and that any unrest there would affect the northern border of the Cape Colony.

The discovery of diamonds in Griqualand West had political as well as socio-economic repercussions throughout South Africa. The annexation of this territory aroused strong anti-British feeling among those Afrikaners who were opposed to co-operation with the British colonies. The open sale of arms and ammunition to non-Whites in Griqualand West was to have repercussions everywhere in South Africa, in such matters as the Langalibalele Rebellion in Natal, the Sekukuni War in the Transvaal, the Anglo-Zulu War of 1879 and the Basuto Rebellion of 1880 – 1881.

The adventurous, cosmopolitan population of the diamond fields disturbed the quiet life of the White rural communities. Crimes formerly unknown were committed. Capital and labour problems developed. Large capitalist undertakings such as "De Beers Consolidated Mines" were formed under the chairmanship of Rhodes. The mines needed labour and consequently non-White society was also disrupted as thousands of Bantu flocked to work on the diggings. This was the beginning of the detribalization of the Bantu which would later be accelerated by gold mining, the railways and other industries.

At first the Bantu returned home after working for a few months, but eventually they settled permanently in the cities. Here the Bantu, who had previously devoted himself to agriculture and animal husbandry and worked mainly as a farm labourer, entered industry and competed with the Whites for a place in the economy of South Africa. Economic integration was the result. In this way the diamond industry introduced problems for both the Whites and the non-Whites which would only be seriously attended to in the twentieth century. In fact, no attempt was made during the nineteenth century to formulate a general non-White policy for South Africa. Every state and colony had its own point of view and its own solution. Grey and Carnarvon did in fact advance this diversity of policy as a reason for federation. The conflict between the Boers and the British was, however, so dominant that little attention was paid to studying and controlling the relations between Whites and non-Whites.

The diamond industry further created new and previously unknown markets and after the depression of the sixties it materially benefited all the South African states and colonies. The greatest problem was to get products and trade goods to Griqualand West. Consequently the discovery of diamonds resulted in the erection of telegraph lines and the laying of railway tracks to Kimberley, the improvement and building of roads and bridges, and the growth of harbours. The diamond industry thus caused a break with the past in the shape of an industrial revolution. This revolution and especially the arrival of

267

artisans in Kimberley would later contribute to the relatively rapid development of the Witwatersrand gold mines.

The discovery of diamonds and the accompanying dispute over borders focussed British attention on the idea of a South African federation. While the annexations of Basutoland and Griqualand West indicated a new British interest in the interior of South Africa, it must be clearly understood that these areas were only annexed after strong and repeated appeals from officials in South Africa and that the British government would only agree to these expansions on condition that the existing colonies would bear the expenditure involved. The intention was that Basutoland should be attached to Natal and Griqualand West to the Cape Colony. However, owing to the actions of local officials both were originally annexed as separate colonies and it was only later that the Cape Colony took over their administration. The British government still wanted to economize and consequently Lord Carnarvon, the British Secretary of State for the Colonies, launched a federation scheme for South Africa.

Carnarvon's federation scheme

It was not only factors in South Africa which inspired Carnarvon's federation scheme. Countries such as the United States of America, France and Germany had begun competing with Britain in the industrial and commercial fields and Britain's initial advantage had begun to shrink. A spirit of imperialism had also developed in these countries; they had begun to desire colonial possessions. Colonies were necessary to provide raw materials for the factories and markets for the finished products of the factories. The competition for colonies changed British colonial policy. Whereas previously colonies had been considered to be millstones around the mother country's neck the dominant idea now was that colonies were necessary to keep the factories going. Britain had to obtain more colonies and existing colonies had to be bound more closely to the Empire to strengthen Britain's position among the other emergent colonial powers.

At the same time there was a tendency to attempt to lessen the financial burden of the mother country by making colonies responsible for their own expenditures. Consequently colonies had to be granted responsible government. They also had to co-operate more closely with one another to form a collective resistance to external and internal threats. The wars with the Bantu in South Africa were a particularly intolerable burden for Britain, but should the colonies and states in South Africa federate they could protect themselves, British troops could be withdrawn and this would bring about a large saving for Britain. Furthermore, at this time there was a strong tendency towards federation and unification; the federation of Canada had been effected in 1867 and Germany and Italy had been unified during 1870 and 1871.

In Carnarvon's view a federation in South Africa was extremely desirable Governors such as Grey, Wodehouse and Barkly condemned the convention policy and urged the maintenance of British supremacy in South Africa, which a federation would ensure. Carnarvon argued that in a federation disputes such as the border ones with the Basuto and those over the diamond fields would disappear. Also federation meant that a common non-White policy could be formulated and this would eliminate many problems. A federation would also secure the Southern African coast-line which was of great strategic importance to Britain. Britain was afraid that Germany might perhaps gain control of Delagoa Bay, establish links with the republics and so threaten British supremacy. Both Brand and Burgers had begun seeking access to the sea, which would not only ensure the economic independence of their states from the British coastal colonies but would possibly also lead to an alliance with a foreign power and the establishment of a balance of power in South Africa. It was thus in Britain's interest to draw the republics into a federation under the British flag.

Carnarvon realized that a South African federation could not be formed without the co-operation of the republics. He had to gain their goodwill. After the annexation of Griqualand West the republics were involved in a disagreement with Governor Barkly and were very indignant because he openly voiced his disapproval of them. Consequently Carnarvon repudiated Barkly and urged him to adopt a friendly attitude. Carnarvon further attempted to win President Brand's favour by offering the Free State £90,000 in compensation for the loss of the diamond fields. However, Carnarvon's attempts to eliminate anti-British feeling in the republics were to end in failure.

Carnarvon also began to work on the British colonies in South Africa with a view to federation. In 1875 he sent Sir Garnet Wolseley to be Lieutenant-Governor of Natal to amend the constitution of that colony in a way that would promote federation and ensure peace and quiet among the Natal Bantu – this was just after the Langalibalele Rebellion. Wolseley was successful and Natal became a willing tool of Carnarvon. In the Cape Colony, which Carnarvon wished to use as the key to federation, the situation was different, however. This colony had obtained responsbile government in 1872 and Molteno, its premier, opposed Carnarvon's plans because he considered them as a form of outside interference in the affairs of the Cape. In 1874 Carnarvon therefore sent the historian J. A. Froude to investigate the situation in South Africa and prepare the way for federation.

Carnarvon next wrote to Barkly on 4 May, 1875, instructing him to invite the South African states and colonies to discuss the native danger. The actual purpose of this meeting was to discuss federation. Carnarvon, however, made the mistake of suggesting who the delegates should be and also allowed the Eastern Province to be represented. The Cape government therefore refused to attend the meeting. The republics, which were still annoyed about the diamond fields decision, also refused to participate. (See Chapters 12 and 13.) Only Natal and Griqualand West were prepared to co-operate.

This rebuff did not deter Carnarvon. Next he convened a conference on federation for 3 August, 1876, in London; this also was a failure. Brand was present to negotiate the diamond fields question but he left when federation came up for discussion. Molteno was also in London but refused to participate in the conference and the South African Republic was not represented. Only

Theophilus Shepstone and Froude, representing Natal and Griqualand West respectively, were at the conference.

But still Carnarvon would not abandon his plans for federation. He now decided to forsake the friendly approach and to start acting forcefully. The South African Republic was the first state on whom he focussed his attention, understandably so since there was a good chance that the Republic would soon become extremely powerful. There were reports of rich mineral deposits, on the Lydenburg gold-fields for example, and with a railway to Delagoa Bay, for which President Burgers was assiduously striving, the Republic could become so strong that it would begin to play a leading role in South Africa. This Carnarvon wanted to prevent at all costs. Besides, once British authority was established in the Transvaal the recalcitrant Free State would be surrounded by British territory and so would be forced into a federation.

Carnarvon, however, disguised his real motives for the annexation of the Transvaal; he and his supporters emphasized the Transvaal's weaknesses rather than her strength. At this time the Transvaal was indeed very poor and the native danger was threatening. Burgers had done his best to develop the Transvaal in all spheres but he was too impractical and enlightened for the conservative nation whose president he was. Consequently most of his plans failed. When he personally led a commando to chastise the rebellious Bapedi chief, Sekukuni, and failed to do so, it was evident that the writing was on the wall. At this time the Zulus were also truculent about a border dispute between them and the Transvaal. The English gold miners at Lydenburg were pleading vehemently for annexation.

Carnarvon put forward all these events as excuses for annexing the Transvaal: It was bankrupt and too weak to govern itself; the Transvaalers were unable to handle the native danger and so jeopardized the whole of South Africa; the Boers suppressed and enslaved the non-Whites. Under these pretexts Carnarvon sent Theophilus Shepstone to the Republic with secret instructions to annex it if most of its inhabitants favoured such a move.

By the time Shepstone arrived in South Africa the Sekukuni War was over and the Zulus had calmed down. Nevertheless he went to Pretoria with twenty-five mounted police as a special commissioner of the British queen to discuss various matters. Shepstone stayed in Pretoria for several months studying the situation and artificially creating the climate which would facilitate annexation. At the eleventh hour Burgers tried to save the Republic by introducing various reforms but to no avail. On 12 April, 1877, Shepstone raised the British flag in Pretoria. Federation could now be taken further by Sir Bartle Frere whom Carnarvon had sent to Cape Town as High Commissioner, and possibly also to become the first governor-general of a united South Africa. (See Chapter 13.)

The results of annexing the Transvaal were, however, quite different from what Carnarvon and his successor, Sir Michael Hicks-Beach, had expected. Shepstone, who had been made the administrator of the Transvaal, developed into "a good Transvaaler" when he discovered that the Republic had had legitimate claims concerning the diamond fields and the Transvaal-Zululand border dispute, and had acted correctly against Sekukuni. He himself soon became involved in a war with Sekukuni. Neither he nor his successor, Sir Owen Lanyon, succeeded in establishing a sound administration in the Transvaal, so that the British rule did not satisfy the Transvaalers who had accepted the annexation under protest. It merely increased their dislike of the British and strengthened their opposition to federation. In May, 1877, the Free State Volksraad also protested strongly against federation, while 5,400 inhabitants of the Cape Colony lodged a petition with Frere against the annexation of the Transvaal. In August, 1878, when federation was discussed in the Cape parliament it was clear that conditions in South Africa did not favour such a move.

The last attempt to promote federation was the Anglo-Zulu War of 1879. Frere was convinced that Britain should obtain control of all the Bantu territories in Southern Africa before federation could be considered. In his opinion the Bantu were hostile toward the Whites because the Bantu believed that they could defeat the British. At the same time some Whites believed that all the Bantu leaders expected the Zulus to lead a revolt of the non-Whites against the Whites. To what extent this belief was correct and whether there were any signs of a Bantu nationalism is difficult to determine. It is doubtful whether there was any Bantu nationalism during the nineteenth century; no other tribe supported the Zulus during the Anglo-Zulu War. It was more likely that each Bantu group would have followed the example of another. If the Zulus had successfully challenged the British no doubt another group would also have dared to do so.

The Anglo-Zulu War was also aimed at winning the goodwill of the Transvaalers by removing the Zulu danger: " . . . the sooner the root of the evil, which I consider to be the Zulu power and military organization, is dealt with the easier our task will be", wrote Shepstone to Carnarvon more than a year before the outbreak of the war.[4] Once again results were different from what were expected. The expenses of the war were so great that the British government was chary of further territorial expansion and refused to annex Zululand. In 1880 and 1881 there was also a rebellion in Basutoland and unrest on the Cape's eastern border. Heavy financial burdens and the fear of incurring yet more made the British government extremely cautious. Moreover, in May, 1880, the Cape parliament voted against federation; this meant the end of Carnarvon's schemes. The repercussions of his plans had not yet, however, been fully felt.

The Transvaalers were disturbed at the loss of their independence and, after all amicable attempts to regain it had failed, they took up arms in 1880. Consequently, by signing the Pretoria Convention in 1881, Britain withdrew from the Transvaal. Carnarvon's plans for federation and the resultant Transvaal War of Independence of 1880 – 1881 also had another effect, namely they awakened Afrikaner nationalism. (See Chapter 13.)

Before 1881 there were few signs of an Afrikaner nationalism in South Africa. A feeling of identity did develop among the people who participated in the

4. Quoted in C. W. de Kiewiet: *The Imperial Factor in South Africa* (Cambridge, 1937), p. 215.

Great Trek but this was to be found particularly among the groups under certain leaders; the development of this group consciousness tended to prevent the growth of a general Afrikaner consciousness. Especially in the years after 1854 when Britain no longer concerned herself with the republics there were many examples of splinter parties, squabbling, confusion and even fraternal discord. This was especially so in the Transvaal of the sixties.

In the Free State politics ran on more stable lines but even here there was not much national consciousness. In the Cape Colony the Afrikaners were under British authority and subject to systematic anglicization. They had little contact with the Afrikaners in the north and it seemed that eventually they would be completely anglicized. The Afrikaners were thus dispersed and divided. They had no conception of nationality or of their own fatherland. There was nothing which would compel them to develop any such concepts.

Stimulation toward the development of an Afrikaner nationalism began in 1868; the longer it acted upon the Afrikaners the more intense was their reaction. This stimulus was the revival of British interest in the interior of South Africa, a return of the imperial factor which threatened the independence of the republics and roused them to action. The new Afrikaner attitude first became evident in the Orange Free State where a feeling of cohesion had already developed as a result of the struggle against the Basuto. The British annexation of Basutoland in 1868 and that of Griqualand West in 1871 aroused the indignation of the Free Staters. They realized that they stood to lose their independence and this gave them a common cause. The seeds of a national consciousness had been sown. (See Chapter 12.)

In the Cape Colony the Afrikaners also reacted against the British government's treatment of the Free Staters, especially concerning the diamond fields. Sympathy with the people in the north who spoke the same language as they did caused the Cape Afrikaners to become aware of their nationhood. They began to realize that they were being denied their rights of language and that they also had grievances. (See Chapter 10.)

The Transvaalers were aware of developments in the Free State. They had also lost diamondiferous territory but were to a large extent isolated from serious British threats and under Burgers they concerned themselves primarily with domestic wrangles. In 1877, however, they abruptly awoke to reality when the British flag was raised in their capital. Then only did the Transvaalers realize what they had lost. They forgot their previous discord and united to oppose the foreign intruder. At consecutive protest and national gatherings they formulated their common desires. They could trek no further, the land where they had settled had become their fatherland and they were determined to act together to regain its independence; they had to lose their freedom to discover its value. (See Chapter 13.)

The War of Independence brought Afrikaner national consciousness, whose signs were everywhere perceptible, to full maturity, as it united the Afrikaners against a common enemy. The Transvaalers depended on the help of the Free Staters and the Afrikaners of the Cape Colony for moral and material support,

Afrikaners, inside and outside the Transvaal, discovered their common identity. They began to dream of an independent South Africa in reaction to the scheme Carnarvon was trying to force on them.

The Transvaal War of Independence resulted not only in a national awakening among the Afrikaners but also in a political and cultural awakening, which assumed such forms as the Afrikaner Bond in the political sphere and the First Afrikaans Language Movement in the cultural. Afrikaner nationalism began to grow throughout South Africa, healed the divisions among the Afrikaners caused by the Great Trek, and became a factor which had to be taken into account after 1881. "Notwithstanding all earlier differences we feel that we are one nation with the same love of freedom, and the same hate of the oppressor" one Free State newspaper said of the Afrikaners.[5]

However, Afrikaner nationalism was not yet strong enough to break the political barriers between states and colonies and to unite Southern Africa. The Transvaal regained its independence with certain limitations and the Free State was free, but the Cape Colony and Natal were still under British rule. Moreover British imperialism was to become even stronger during the last years of the nineteenth century.

The policy of encirclement

With the re-establishment of independence in the Transvaal in 1881 and the London Convention of 1884 it appeared that Britain, as in 1854, was about to withdraw from the interior of South Africa. This, however, was not so; Britain could not allow the two Boer Republics to develop into powerful states and threaten British supremacy in South Africa. Britain now adopted a new approach and attempted to surround the republics with British territory to prevent any chance of their gaining independent access to the sea and the outside world. The republics had to be so restricted, economically and otherwise, that they would be compelled to seek closer union with the British colonies. The imperial factor as well as the Cape Colony and Natal were to play a part in this encirclement.

The policy of encirclement should not, however, be viewed merely as a narrow British South Africa policy. It should also be viewed against the background of the rising new imperialism and the consequent partition of Africa. There were two particular factors which aided imperialism. The first was nationalism, or people's awareness that they belonged to particular nations. This awareness was a consequence of Napoleon's conquests and became even stronger after his fall. Nationalism, amongst other things, was the reason for the unification of Germany and of Italy. Gradually another element began to develop in nationalism; people's love of their own nation developed into undue glorification of that nation. Each people considered their nation to be the leading nation and despised other nations.

5. Quoted in F. A. van Jaarsveld: *Die Ontwaking van die Afrikaanse Nasionale Bewussyn* (Johannesburg, 1957), p. 150, from *De Express*, 13 Jan., 1881 (translated into English).

This aggressive nationalism which developed into imperialism was common, expecially among the British who in those days were still one of the leading nations of the world; in the eighties it began to dominate their political thought. Imperialism was also fostered by books such as Professor Seeley's *The Expansion of England* (1883), Froude's *Oceana* (1885) and Dilke's *Problems of Greater Britain* (1890). Particularly widely read was Seeley's book whose premise was that the future belonged to the big countries and that England, which did not cover a large area, would only continue to exist if supported by a large empire. This work greatly influenced imperialists such as Joseph Chamberlain and probably also Cecil Rhodes. Soon powers other than Britain also became imperialist in their outlook.

The second factor which promoted imperialism was of an economic nature. As powers such as America, Germany and France became industrialized they tried to displace Britain as the leading trading power. Strong competition developed among the industrialists, who desired raw materials and markets. Colonies which could provide these advantages were therefore greatly desired. Apart from Africa there was little land not already occupied in the world. It is for this reason that after 1880 attention was focussed on Africa. The "scramble for Africa" had begun.

Imperialism and the partition of Africa profoundly affected South Africa. The occupations and annexations of the German, French, Italian and Portuguese powers spurred Britain on to secure more territory bordering on what she already possessed in her coastal colonies of South Africa. In addition to wishing to expand territorially it was also Britain's policy to strengthen her ties with those colonies she already possessed. In 1884 the Imperial Federation League was founded with the aim of federating all self-governing British territories. It was at the insistence of this organization that in 1887 the first conference of representatives of the most important British territories was held in London. At the instigation of Jan Hofmeyr of the Cape Colony, amongst others, this conference initiated a movement to turn the British Empire into an economic unit by introducing preferential tariffs instead of free-trade. This movement was not immediately successful but the urge towards closer economic co-operation which had also taken root in South Africa, was to affect the republics in their relations with each other and in their relations with the British South African colonies and Britain. This matter will be dealt with later.

Something else which stemmed from the partition of Africa and which affected Britain's policy in Southern Africa was the German occupation, in the early eighties, of the west coast of Africa north of the Orange River, the area later to be known as German South West Africa. The Cape Colony had also been interested in this territory, and in March, 1878, approximately 450 square miles at Walvis Bay had been annexed as British territory; before any more could be annexed the Germans staked their claim in the same area. The presence of the Germans on the west coast and their interest in other parts of Southern Africa was one of the main reasons for Britain's beginning to encircle the Boer republics.

The attempt to encircle the republics must also be seen as the consequence of a clash between a South African imperialism and a South African nationalism, as exemplified in Rhodes and Kruger respectively. As a young man Cecil John Rhodes came to South Africa to regain his health. The diamonds attracted him to Kimberley where he ultimately was instrumental in amalgamating the unorganized diamond diggings into a powerful company with much capital, the "De Beers Consolidated Mines". Later he acquired some mines on the Witwatersrand gold-fields which developed into the "Consolidated Gold Fields of South Africa". These successes ensured for Rhodes an income of more than one million pounds per year. He used this income and his contacts with world financiers to realize his life's ideal, which was to establish the British Empire firmly in Southern Africa. He even dreamt of a railway stretching from the Cape to Cairo across British territory. He also envisaged a federation of Southern Africa under the British flag. The two independent Boer republics, however, stood between him and the realization of this dream.

Rhodes's federation idea was supported in the Cape Colony by J. H. Hofmeyr, the leader of the Afrikaner Bond. The two men formed an alliance and with the support of the Afrikaner Bond Rhodes, who had entered Cape politics in 1881, became prime minister of the Cape Colony in 1890. Rhodes thus had political as well as financial power. (See Chapter 10.)

Rhodes's capitalist-imperialist ideal was opposed by the nationalist ideal of President Paul Kruger. Kruger united all Afrikaner nationalist forces. Although he lacked formal education he cared deeply for the interests of his fatherland, the Transvaal. He seldom discussed the subject of a unified South Africa, but when he did his attitude was always consistent with his statement in the 1883 election manifesto: "I will give my whole-hearted support to every attempt at closer co-operation between the states and colonies of South Africa which would result in the growth of a South African nation on condition that it does not entail the sacrifice of the rights and freedom of the Republic".[6] When he felt that the independence of the Transvaal was in jeopardy he refused to view matters from a wider South African perspective.

Kruger knew very little about international affairs and had to depend for a knowledge of such matters on the young Dutch jurist, Dr W. J. Leyds. Kruger's foreign policy, which was aimed primarily at countering the British threat to the Transvaal's independence, was designed to get rid of the London Convention; to prevent British intervention in the Transvaal's internal affairs; to extend the authority of the Transvaal at the expense of Britain's; to seek support from other European powers to counter British influence and to make the Transvaal economically independent of the British colonies, especially by acquiring a harbour for it. Kruger was to run into much opposition. His desire to expand the Transvaal and find it a way to the sea was to alert Rhodes and the

6. Quoted in G. D. Scholtz: *Die Oorsake van die Tweede Vryheidsoorlog, 1899 – 1902*, I, (Johannesburg, 1947), p. 110 (translated into English).

other imperialists and hasten their attempts to encircle the Transvaal. (See Chapter 13.)

The British government was also to play a part in encircling the republics although it was still very much concerned about expense and did not lightly undertake territorial expansion. After 1881 British policy tended to distinguish between imperial and colonial interests. When imperial interests were threatened the British government would act but the colonies were expected to look after their own interests or at least help the British government to do so. This policy resulted, among other things, in the Germans obtaining a foothold in South-West Africa. In this case the British government would not act for the Cape Colony and the Cape Colony hesitated to act on its own. The Germans exploited this situation but their arrival threatened imperial interests to such an extent that the British government was put on its guard and compelled to take action elsewhere.

The first opportunity for the British to act occurred on the western border of the Transvaal, where there were clashes between Bantu tribes and White volunteers were helping some of the chiefs. With the territory given them by Moshette and Massouw in payment for their services the volunteers founded the republics Goshen and Stellaland in 1882 and 1883 respectively. The Transvaal, which was dissatisfied with its western border as fixed by the Pretoria Convention, hoped ultimately to incorporate the two small republics and so open up possibilities for further territorial expansion to the west. This was precisely what the British imperialists, particularly Rhodes, then member of the Cape parliament for Barkly West, Sir Hercules Robinson, the High Commissioner, and John MacKenzie, a missionary in Bechuanaland, wanted to prevent.

When, in August, 1883, the Bechuanaland question was discussed in the Cape parliament, Rhodes said: "You are dealing with a question upon the proper treatment of which depends the whole future of this Colony. I look upon this Bechuanaland territory as the Suez Canal of the trade of this country, the key of its road to the interior. The question before us is this, whether the Colony is to be confined within its present borders or whether it is to become the dominant State in South Africa".[7] A year later the problem had still not been solved to Rhodes's satisfaction. He asked: "The Colony had built its railway for the sake of the trade, and were they going to allow themselves to be shut out from the future trade of the interior?" The Cape cabinet touched on another aspect with the decision " . . . that in view of the German annexations on the west coast and other threatened encroachments calculated to cripple the Cape Colony in its trade and otherwise, decisive measures should be taken for the maintenance of British authority in South Africa".[8]

Expansion by the Transvaal had to be opposed, the gateway to the north had to be kept open for the Cape Colony and perhaps the most important considera-

7. *Ibid.*, pp. 117 – 118.
8. Quotations in W. J. de Kock: *Ekstra-territoriale Vraagstukke van die Kaapse Regering (1872 – 1885)* (Archives Year Book for South African History, 1948, I), pp. 155 and 239.

ion, a wedge had to be driven between the Transvaal and the German colony of South-West otherwise Germany and the Transvaal might join forces. The result was that the British government sent Sir Charles Warren with an expeditionary force of 4,000 men to annex Stellaland and Goshen. In 1885 Warren placed the whole territory south of the Molopo River under direct British rule while the rest of Bechuanaland remained under the protectorate which had been proclaimed the previous year. This thwarted the Transvaal on its western side and kept the gateway to the north open for the Cape Colony.

Chances for the Transvaal to expand in a south-easterly direction towards the Indian Ocean through Zululand were also destroyed. The Boer intervention in Zululand and the founding of the New Republic has already been dealt with elsewhere (see Chapter 11). Official circles in Natal began to feel that the Boers were aiming to gain possession of the whole of Zululand and thereby not only cut Natal off from its hinterland but also reach the sea at St. Lucia Bay. The British government hesitated, however, to interfere with the Boers in Zululand. This hesitancy in British policy elicited the following comment from historian J. A. Froude in 1884: "The policy of Mr. Gladstone's Government involves the virtual abandonment of South Africa . . . (where) things are drifting towards the establishment of Dutch (Boer) supremacy . . . under the protection of Germany".[9]

Indeed the Germans as well as the Transvaalers were gazing longingly at St. Lucia Bay. Realizing this the British raised their flag at St. Lucia Bay in December, 1884, bought off the Germans and simply ignored the claims of the South African Republic and the New Republic. The British government was not, however, prepared to take any further action. It was only in 1887, when it became clear that the New Republic wanted to expand in the direction of St. Lucia Bay and that the Transvaal would eventually incorporate the New Republic and with it St. Lucia Bay, that the British government annexed Zululand. Cut off from the sea the New Republic continued until 1888 when it was incorporated into the South African Republic.

The British government procrastinated about annexing Zululand as they had not done about Bechuanaland. This was because the Cape Colony was willing to accept responsibility for Bechuanaland while Natal, though anxious to do so, was not politically or economically able to do the same for Zululand. Therefore the British government acted in Zululand only when imperial interests were threatened; St. Lucia Bay had to be kept out of the hands of the Germans and the Boers. Territorial expansion and financial obligations were only undertaken by Britain when they were absolutely essential. For this reason Sir Charles Dilke wrote in 1890: "I believe that the greatest of our dangers in South Africa is to be found in the desire of British governments to shirk responsibility, and their consequent inability to proclaim a definite policy, and in the difficulty of inducing Parliament to sanction a continuous expenditure without direct return".[10]

9. Quoted in M. C. van Zyl: *Die Uitbreiding van Britse Gesag oor die Natalse Noordgrensgebiede, 1879 – 1897* (Archives Year Book for S.A. History, 1966, I), p. 282.
10. C. W. Dilke: *Problems of Greater Britain* (London, 1890), p. 344.

In the area north of the Transvaal (Matebeleland and Mashonaland) it was no necessary for the British government to incur any expenses. Backed by hi British South Africa Company Rhodes could raise the British flag in the north without any cost to the British tax-payer. Kruger was also interested in this area and on 6 June, 1887, P. J. Grobler concluded an alliance with Lobengula, the Matebele chief, on behalf of the Transvaal. Rhodes, however, had already determined that the Cape Colony should control and develop the potentially rich Matebeleland through the gateway to the north (Bechuanaland) and neither the Transvaal nor Portugal could prevent him from carrying out his plans (See Chapter 10.)

The Portuguese claim to this area was based on the fact that both France and Germany recognized that the interior of Africa between Angola and Mozam bique fell within the Portuguese sphere of influence. Rhodes would not accept this because it would mean Portuguese influence would then stretch right across the African continent from east to west and prevent the realization of his dream of a road from the Cape to Cairo. He therefore sent the Rev. J. S. Moffat to Matebeleland and entered into a treaty with Lobengula on 11 February, 1888 The Rudd concession, in terms of which Lobengula relinquished the minera rights in his territory, followed on 30 October of the same year. In this way Rhodes gained control of Lobengula's territory; the Transvaal and Portuga protested in vain. In 1889 Rhodes founded the British South Africa Company Within a few years Lobengula had completely lost his territory and possible Transvaal expansion was obstructed in the north.

Believing that the Transvaal would be granted access to the sea at Kosi Bay on the east coast President Kruger, in May, 1889, relinquished all claims to wards the north. This was one of the greatest blunders of Kruger's political career; the London Convention did not restrict Transvaal expansion to the north but expansion to the east and west had to be approved by the British government. Kruger was blind to other possibilities because his attention was focussed on the uninhabitable and unhealthy coast of Tongaland and the inaccessible Kosi Bay. By relinquishing his claims in the north Kruger played into the hands of Rhodes and his supporters.

The Transvaal could only reach Kosi Bay via Swaziland, the Transpongola territory (the territories of Zambaan and Mbegisa), and Tongaland. It ha already been related elsewhere (see Chapters 11 and 13) that the Transvaal had obtained jurisdiction over Swaziland but that in 1895 Transpongola and Tonga land had become British territories and were later incorporated into Natal Britain did this to restrict the Transvaal yet further and to prevent it from obtaining the independent access to the sea which would bring it into close contact with the outside world in general and Germany in particular. Natal also was opposed to an independent state obtaining a harbour between Durban and Delagoa Bay. Natal's revenue was derived mainly from trade with the interior railways, and customs, and it therefore did not want any foreign rival north of Durban. (See Chapter 11.)

The restriction of the Transvaal's expansion to the east completed Britain's ncirclement of the Republic. Mozambique was now the only territory adjoining he two Boer republics not controlled by Britain. Rhodes knew that Delagoa Bay was the Transvaal's only chance of breaking through the British encircle-ment of her territory. For this reason he tried repeatedly to gain control of Delagoa Bay, but never succeeded. Meanwhile Kruger made use of the one remaining chance to break Britain's economic blockade of his state. The railway rom Pretoria to Delagoa Bay was completed in 1894. This access of the Trans-vaal to a non-British harbour greatly irritated the British Empire builders and also aggravated the prevailing economic unrest in South Africa.

Economic conflicts

The economic policies of the states and colonies in South Africa conflicted in many ways, partly because of their varying political policies. The Transvaal, for example, desired economic and political independence while the Cape Colony advocated unification with the other South African states. Politics and economics were not, however, always inter-related. The Free State, for example, was economically close to the Cape Colony while politically it was close to the Transvaal. Even the two British coastal colonies differed in their economic policies.

Economic clashes between the South African states were only to assume serious dimensions after the discovery of the Witwatersrand gold-fields. Before 1886 the republics, which did not have their own harbours, depended on the coastal colonies for exporting and importing their goods. The Republics repeatedly asked for a share of the import duties imposed on their goods in the harbours but their requests were always refused. The first tariff barrier was created in South Africa when, in 1881, compelled by economic depression, the Transvaal imposed an import duty on goods entering the Republic. These goods included certain South African products such as tobacco, mealies and liquor. Three years later the Cape replied by placing an import duty on Transvaal tobacco.

The Transvaalers, who were still struggling economically and had financial difficulties with the building of the Pretoria-Delagoa Bay railway, nevertheless realized that the Lydenburg and Barberton gold-fields demanded faster means of communication with the outside world, and proposed a customs union and free trade with the Cape in 1885 and again early in 1886. At the same time linking the Cape railway with Pretoria via Bloemfontein was suggested. The Cape Colony did not, however, respond to this suggestion and allowed a golden opportunity to slip through its fingers. This proposal, which was actually not in accordance with Kruger's ideals of independence, was not to be repeated again because the Witwatersrand gold-fields placed the Transvaal in a strong bargaining position and changed the entire economic situation.

The concentration of thousands of people in Johannesburg and the demand for mining equipment which followed upon the discovery of gold in the Re-public created an ideal market in the heart of the Transvaal. The Cape Colony

and Natal eyed this market covetously. They hoped for free import of their products and rail connections with the gold-fields. This time it was the coasta
colonies which were the suppliants and Kruger who had the whip-hand. He wa$
not averse to considering free import of certain products but would not hea
of a rail connection or a customs union; he would build his own railway t(
Delagoa Bay.

In 1887 the Cape Colony had sent a deputation to Pretoria to negotiate fo
free imports and a rail connection with the gold-fields but it was unsuccessful
to the distress of the Cape Colony which knew it was in its interests that th
Transvaal should look to the south for co-operation rather than to the east. Th
Cape Colony also had to guard against the Free State being persuaded t(
accept the Transvaal's policy. The presidents of the republics conferred a
Bloemfontein in October, 1887. Kruger was looking for co-operation in railwa
matters and proposed that the Free State should not allow the Cape railwa
right of way across its territory before the Delagoa Bay line was completed
The Transvaal in turn would not permit a rail connection with Johannesbur;
via Kimberley.

The Free State, because of its geographical situation, was indeed in a difficul
position. Brand was anxious to co-operate with the Transvaal politically bu
economically he was attracted to the Cape Colony because the Free Stat
depended on the Cape harbours with which rail connections were indispensable
There was also the danger that Johannesburg and Cape Town would be con
nected by rail via Kimberley which would be extremely disadvantageous to th
Free State. Brand considered it advisable, however, to reject the Transvaal'
proposals. Consequently the Cape Colony was offered a chance of co-operatin;
with the Orange Free State and Natal. A conference between these three state
was held in Cape Town in January, 1888.

The three states agreed about free trade in South African products, the imposi
tion of import duties on overseas goods and the building of a railway across Fre
State territory from Natal and the Cape. Natal and the Cape Colony could not
however, agree about common import tariffs. Natal wanted to keep the tariff
low in order to handle more goods in the Durban harbour while the Cape Colon
wanted to protect its own products by high import duties. Natal thus decided t
sacrifice the Free State trade in favour of extending its railway to the Transvaa
border. The Free State Volksraad only approved the extension of the Cape lin
to Bloemfontein and that only after the chairman had used his casting vote. Th
Cape conference was thus not very fruitful.

After the death of President Brand his successor, F. W. Reitz, and Kruge
convened a conference at Potchefstroom in March, 1889, where, besides ;
political pact, other treaties were also concluded between the republics. A trad
and friendship treaty provided for free trade. In terms of another treaty th
Transvaal agreed not to allow a rail connection from the south or the wes
without the consent of the Free State. In this way it was ensured that the Cap
railway to Johannesburg would cross Free State territory. The Free State in tur
undertook not to allow any railway line north of Bloemfontein without th

Transvaal's consent; this safeguarded the Transvaal's railway line to Delagoa Bay. (See Chapters 12 and 13.)

Reitz wished to co-operate with the Transvaal in all matters but he realized that the Free State was economically dependent on the Cape Colony, and so agreed to a customs union between the Free State and Cape Colony during a conference held in March, 1889, at Bloemfontein. Natal was also present at this conference but did not join the customs union because of the difference of opinion concerning import tariffs. The Free State also consented to the Cape Colony extending its railway line to Bloemfontein. There were thus three railway lines aiming at the gold-fields, from Delagoa Bay, Natal and the Cape Colony.

The Pretoria-Delagoa Bay line which was built by the *Nederlandsch Zuid-Afrikaansche Spoorwegmaatschappij* (N.Z.A.S.M.) would have been completed first had it not been for financial difficulties. Through Rhodes's intercession, however, the N.Z.A.S.M. obtained money from the Cape government in 1891 and later also from the banker Rothschild. This generosity of Rhodes and the Cape government was not unconditional, however. Kruger had to agree that the Cape line, which had reached Bloemfontein in 1890, could be extended to Johannesburg without delay and that it would remain in the hands of the Cape Colony until the end of 1894. The first Cape train steamed into Johannesburg in September, 1892. The Delagoa Bay line was only completed in November, 1894. Although the Natal line reached Charlestown in December, 1891, Kruger would not immediately allow it to be extended to Johannesburg. The Charlestown-Johannesburg section of this line was only opened at the end of 1895. The economic struggle did not end with the completion of the railways. Besides the differences concerning import duties there were also conflicts about railway tariffs.

The Transvaal retained its import duties except on certain products from the Free State. In 1890 the tariff was fixed at five per cent while certain products, such as cheese, coffee, sugar and alcoholic beverages, were subject to additional import duties. In 1892 the general import duty was raised to seven-and-a-half per cent but the additional import duty was reduced. These import duties annoyed the Cape Colony because it was anxious to get its products to the Johannesburg market. It therefore supported Rhodes in his advocacy of free trade and a customs union. Rhodes, however, could not succeed in breaking down the tariff barrier because Kruger realized that Rhodes wanted to draw the Transvaal into a united South Africa under the British flag.

Kruger wished to use the import duties to encourage industries within the Transvaal; he also wished to take his revenge for the British encirclement of his country which had robbed the Transvaal of its own harbour. At the signing of the first Swaziland Convention in 1890 Kruger was still prepared to join a South African customs union if his demand for a harbour for the Transvaal was met. He repeatedly refused to join a customs union when, after 1895, he had been deprived of the last chance to reach the sea at Kosi Bay. Besides political friction with the Cape Colony, the customs barrier of the South African Republic never produced a serious crisis. The rail tariff struggle, however, was to have different consequences.

When the Delagoa Bay line was completed in 1894 the Cape line had already enjoyed a two-year monopoly in transporting goods to Johannesburg. This had been a profitable source of income for the Cape Colony. In 1894, for example, this line had earned £2,713,000 of the entire Cape income of £5,390,000. Traffic to the gold-fields was responsible for most of these railway earnings. Having incurred a large debt in building this railway the Cape Colony obviously wished to retain its profitable traffic with Johannesburg, but the Delagoa Bay and the Natal line claimed part of the traffic. The Transvaal obviously would favour its own line. Natal accepted this policy but the Cape Colony would not do so, and at a conference in 1894 demanded half of the traffic to Johannesburg for the Cape line and one third for the Natal line. This meant that only a sixth would remain for the Delagoa Bay line, which was not acceptable to the N.Z.A.S.M. The N.Z.A.S.M. was prepared to give one third of the traffic to the Cape line. The Cape Colony consequently threatened to lower rail tariffs. This started the tariff war.

As a result of the Cape's threat Middelberg, the director of the N.Z.A.S.M. persuaded the Transvaal government to increase tariffs on the Vaal River-Johannesburg section of the line if necessary. This would mean that any savings from the reduced tariff in the Cape Colony would be offset by the increased tariff on the Transvaal section of the line. The Cape government was dissatisfied with this state of affairs and Rhodes even paid a personal visit to Pretoria but achieved nothing. Representatives of the Cape government conferred twice with Middelberg in Pretoria during November of 1894. The negotiations were unsuccessful, however, because the Cape Colony continued to claim half of the goods traffic.

Early in 1895 the Cape government lowered its rail tariff and the Transvaal replied by increasing the tariff on its part of the line. The Cape government countered this increase by off-loading its goods at Viljoen's Drift on the Vaal River and transporting them to Johannesburg by ox wagon. The fight had begun and not even the railway conference of April, 1895, which was attended by representatives of all the states and colonies, could end it. The Cape Colony reduced its claim to two-fifths of the goods traffic but the Transvaal would not accept this either. The only way in which the Transvaal could block the Cape was to close the Vaal River drifts to traffic. To take such a step, however, it would need the co-operation of the Free State.

With Reitz as its president the Free State was politically much closer to the Transvaal than during the presidency of Brand. Economically speaking the Witwatersrand gold-fields and the railways leading to them had opened up hitherto unknown markets for Free State products. Economic co-operation with the Transvaal was thus important to the Free State. In January, 1895, a representative from Pretoria had already discussed railway policy with Reitz and these discussions were followed by further negotiations in Pretoria in May of the same year. Closer political ties were discussed at this meeting which

resulted in 1897 in a political alliance between the two republics. In the economic field, the Transvaal was willing to create better facilities for importing
Free State products and was also prepared not to impose higher railway tariffs
on Free State products than on its own products, on condition that the Free
State agreed to the Transvaal's closing of the drifts across the Vaal River to
overseas goods.

On the recommendation of Middelberg the Transvaal government in August,
1895, proclaimed Viljoen's Drift and Sand Drift closed to the importation of
overseas goods as from 1 October. There was very strong reaction to this step.
Even the Free State government did not feel very happy about it. From Cape
Town Rhodes called on the British government for support. Joseph Chamberlain, the Secretary of State for the Colonies, responded to Rhodes's plea because
he considered the Transvaal to have contravened the London Convention. He
reprimanded the Transvaal government and was prepared to send an expeditionary force to remedy matters if the Cape government would bear half its
costs, provide some of the troops, and make its railways available for military
purposes. War, however, did not become necessary. The Transvaal had already
proposed a railway conference for November, 1895, and in view of this the drifts
were opened between 5 and 15 November. Because of Chamberlain's protest the
drifts were not closed again.

At the railway conference the Cape Colony still demanded two-fifths of the
goods traffic and Middelberg still was only prepared to agree to one-third.
Once again the negotiations ended in failure. In future no limitations would be
imposed on freight traffic and eventually the Cape traffic decreased in practice to
a third or less of the traffic to the gold-fields. Very little was achieved concerning
further customs unions or a uniform economic system. In 1898, when the Cape
import duties were lowered, Natal did join the customs union of which the
Cape and the Free State were members but the Transvaal still held back.
Kruger's aloofness, economic and otherwise, could not, however, save the
South African Republic. Since 1895 the British imperialists had been determined
to subjugate the two Boer republics.

Afrikaner nationalism versus British imperialism

By 1895 it was clear that Kruger would not associate himself with Rhodes's
ideal of a South Africa united under the British flag. The British policy of
encirclement had not succeeded in breaking the South African Republic economically. On the contrary the Republic became stronger and with the Witwatersrand gold-fields and the railway to Delagoa Bay it was possible that it
would become the leading state in South Africa. Kruger did not want to tie
himself to the British colonies in any way and continued to seek support from
Germany. Rhodes, who was in poor health at the time, began to despair of ever
realizing his ideal. He therefore tried to rush matters and towards the end of
1895 instigated the Jameson Raid.

In a letter which Rhodes wrote shortly after the Jameson Raid he stated that

Kruger was not the reason for the haste in this matter because Kruger was merely temporary; Rhodes's real fear was of the development of "a huge English-speaking republic in Transvaal which will absorb the North and leave the Cape out at the shank end of the Continent". His efforts for "union under the British flag under responsible government" and, as he formulated it, "to keep the north with the Cape whatever happens" were thus threatened by the same Uitlanders (foreigners) he was to use in his plot to overthrow the Transvaal.[11] If it is remembered that many of the Uitlanders were more interested in getting rich and having their grievances remedied than in hoisting the British flag, and that their contribution to the plot was half-hearted, it seems that Rhodes did have good reason for his fears. Later even Milner was afraid that the Uitlanders would be lost to the British flag!

Rhodes planned his campaign against the South African Republic carefully. Excepting through the route to Delagoa Bay the Republic in 1895 was already surrounded by British territory and there was a strong and dissatisfied British element, the Uitlanders, within the Republic. Rhodes could therefore now transfer his struggle with the Transvaal, which until 1895 had been restricted to its borders, into the very heart of the Republic. He merely had to incite the Uitlanders to revolt and then support them with an attack launched from an adjoining British territory. The British High Commissioner was then to hasten to Pretoria, arbitrate between the revolutionaries and the Transvaal government, and ensure that all White males obtained the vote for the election of a new government. Assuming incorrectly that the Uitlanders formed a majority within the Transvaal, Rhodes believed that the Republic would then be transformed into a self-governing British colony, which would considerably expedite his plans for a united South Africa.

Conditions in Britain also favoured Rhodes's plot. In 1895 there had been an important change in the government when a strong wave of imperialism had swept Lord Salisbury's Conservative Party to power. Joseph Chamberlain, an out-spoken imperialist, was the Secretary of State for the Colonies in the new government. Rhodes had nothing to fear from him; he was in fact well aware of the plot.

It is not necessary here to enter into details of Dr. L. S. Jameson's raid with an armed contingent from Bechuanaland and of the uprising in Johannesburg. (See Chapters 10 and 13.) Rhodes's plot failed abysmally and apart from international repercussions it had far-reaching effects in South Africa. Like Carnarvon's federation scheme and the annexation of the Transvaal the Jameson Raid worked against the development of any unity in South Africa. It made the republics yet more antagonistic to the idea of a South Africa united under the British flag. The gulf between Boer and Briton widened. Afrikaners throughout South Africa were drawn closer together by a powerful resurgence of Afrikaans nationalism. The Cape Afrikaners who had been somewhat estranged from the

11. Quotations in J. G. Lockhart and C. M. Wodehouse: *Rhodes* (London, 1963), pp. 341 – 342.

Transvaal by Kruger's economic policy once again felt a kinship with their fellow Afrikaners in the north. The Afrikaner Bond broke with Rhodes, which caused him to resign as Cape premier, and openly sympathized with the Transvaalers. The Free Staters regarded the Jameson Raid as an attack on their independence as well and drew even closer to the Transvaal. In March, 1897, the two republics entered into a political alliance in terms of which they would support each other with all available forces and means at their disposal should anything threaten their independence. In order to be prepared for any such eventuality the republics started arming. (See Chapters 12 and 13.)

The Jameson Raid and the Afrikaners' reaction also affected the English-speaking part of the South African population. The desire of the British policy-makers and imperialists to subjugate the republics was strengthened. The imperialistically inclined British in South Africa united under the South African League which was formed shortly after the Jameson Raid. The aims of this organization were the maintenance of British supremacy in South Africa and the achievement of equal political rights for all Whites in a united South Africa under the British flag. In the Cape Colony members of the League joined the Progressive Party under Sir Gordon Sprigg. (See Chapter 10.)

The Jameson Raid split South Africa into two sharply defined camps, that of those who wanted to ensure independent development and that of those who wanted to live under the British flag. The former had only themselves to depend upon, and theirs was a lonely fight. The Afrikaners still hoped, however, that some European powers would support them. Shortly after the Jameson Raid there were indications that Germany sympathized with the Transvaal, but nothing came of these hopeful expectations. The Afrikaners had to fight alone. By contrast the British camp was strong because the pace was to a large extent set by Britain.

The failure of the Jameson Raid was a set-back for Chamberlain who had to conceal his part in the affair. As long as the memory of the raid was still fresh he had to act carefully. He did not, however, forsake his desire to subjugate the Transvaal. He therefore set out to create the impression in the outside world that the Transvaal was a subordinate state. One of the weapons which Chamberlain used to justify his standpoint was Article IV of the London Convention, in terms of which the Transvaal had to submit all treaties entered into with foreign powers, apart from the Free State, to the British government for approval. Before 1895 the Transvaal government submitted treaties for ratification after the parties concerned had approved them. Chamberlain now demanded that the treaties be submitted before they were approved by the parties concerned. This would mean that the British government would have a voice in the conclusion of treaties even before the Transvaal Volksraad had made a decision, which would mean a diminution of the authority of the Transvaal government.

A virulent polemic about when treaties should be submitted for ratification then ensued. In 1897 when the Republic proposed that foreign arbitration should determine the interpretation of the London Convention Chamberlain

285

alleged that this could not be allowed because the Convention had not been concluded between two equal states. He claimed that the Transvaal was a subordinate state because the preamble to the Pretoria Convention, which placed the Transvaal under the suzerainty of Britain, had not lapsed. This argument was not legitimate but Chamberlain continued to assert that the Transvaal was a subordinate state and by so doing confused relations between the Republic and Britain.

Chamberlain also intervened in the internal affairs of the South African Republic and maintained that he could do so in terms of the London Convention. He protested against three acts adopted by the South African Republic in 1896, namely the Aliens Expulsion Act ("Wet op Uitsetting van Vreemdelinge"), the Aliens Immigration Act ("Wet op Toelating van Vreemdelinge"), and the Press Act ("Perswet"). These acts were another result of the Jameson Raid, which had made the Transvaal distrust foreigners and what it regarded as an inflammatory press. The government desired to have some means of firstly, deporting foreigners who disturbed public law and order, secondly, refusing admission to the Transvaal to foreigners who did not have passports and who could not support themselves, and thirdly, forbidding the distribution of printed matter which threatened the maintenance of law and order. Chamberlain claimed that these acts conflicted with Articles IV and XIV of the Convention. Through reinforcement of the troops in South Africa and a naval demonstration in Delagoa Bay he compelled the Transvaal government to revoke the Aliens Immigration Act. Chamberlain was prepared to enforce his will even if it meant going to war with the Transvaal.

In South Africa Chamberlain was ably supported by Alfred Milner who arrived at the Cape as High Commissioner in 1897. Milner considered himself to be a British nationalist but added: "If I am also an Imperialist, it is because the destiny of the English race, owing to its insular position and long supremacy at sea, has been to strike fresh roots in distant parts of the world".[12] He willingly expended all his energy in the interests of the British Empire. He regarded the Transvaal with its rich gold-fields as a threat to British supremacy in South Africa. With its gold the Transvaal could dominate South Africa and carry through a non-British union. Milner considered the Transvaal to be the centre of Afrikaner nationalism in South Africa. He believed that unless the Pan-Afrikaner idea was suppressed South Africa would eventually be lost to the British Empire. It is thus understandable that Milner used every possible means to eliminate the Transvaal threat to British supremacy in South Africa. He had hoped that internal problems would force Kruger to adopt reforms but this was not the case. When he was re-elected to the presidency of the Transvaal with an overwhelming majority at the beginning of 1898 Kruger's position was more secure than ever. In addition the Free State became more closely linked to the Transvaal by the political alliance of 1897, and in the Cape in 1898 W. P. Schreiner, with the support of the Afrikaner Bond, had taken over the control

12. Quoted in J. S. Marais: *The Fall of Kruger's Republic* (Oxford, 1961), p. 172.

of the government from the Progressive Party. According to Milner there was thus, "no way out of the political troubles of South Africa except reform in the Transvaal or war", and the chances of reform seemed slight![13]

Like Chamberlain Milner also constantly tested the actions of the Transvaal government against the London Convention. He objected, for example, to Cape Coloureds being included in the Transvaal Pass Law of 1896 and because the Transvaal would not grant property rights to Asiatics. Milner even intervened when the Transvaal government charged Bunu, the supreme chief of the Swazi, with the murder of his induna, Mbaba. These matters were, however, not sufficiently serious to produce a crisis, as Milner had hoped. He could, however, tackle the Uitlander question more forcefully in an attempt to achieve his goal.

An Uitlander agitation had been artificially created before the Jameson Raid; before the outbreak of the Anglo-Boer War this happened again. In 1899 the Uitlanders petitioned the British queen with 21,684 signatures concerning grievances about the franchise, the judicature, the administration, the local government, the police, public meetings and cultural and economic matters in the Transvaal. On the whole their grievances were exaggerated but Milner pounced on them as a reason for British intervention in the internal affairs of the Transvaal; his attitude was "reform or war".

Milner had already definitely decided to subjugate the Transvaal. He visited London towards the end of 1898 and talked Chamberlain over to his point of view. When he returned to the Cape early in 1899 he was determined that if Kruger did not attempt to alleviate the grievances of the Uitlanders he would press for war. With the Uitlander petition behind him he could now act. If the Uitlanders' complaints, especially those concerning the franchise, were settled a rapid and radical change in the character of the South African Republic could be effected. Like Kruger, Milner made the mistake of thinking that the Uitlanders formed the majority of the Republic's White population.

At Milner's insistence the British government reluctantly agreed to accede to the Uitlanders' request for British intervention. At the eleventh hour, however, Chamberlain agreed to a meeting between Milner and Kruger, which was arranged through the initiative of President Steyn and Premier Schreiner. At the conference held on 31 May, 1899, Milner demanded that the Transvaal grant rights of citizenship to foreigners after five years residence and that such rights be granted immediately to those who had already resided in the Transvaal for more than five years. Kruger's counter-proposal was the granting of citizenship rights after seven years residence and after two years to those who had already resided in the Transvaal for seven years. No agreement could be reached and the negotiations ended in failure. The Transvaal was later prepared to accept five years as qualification for citizenship on certain conditions unacceptable to Milner, amongst others that the British government should not intervene again in the internal affairs of the Transvaal. War was imminent.

13. Quoted in R. H. Wilde: *Joseph Chamberlain and the South African Republic 1895 – 1899* (Archives Year Book for S.A. History, 1956, I), p. 74.

The Orange Free State was in alliance with the South African Republic but this did not prevent Steyn from doing everything in his power to prevent war. Like Kruger he eventually came to feel that it was not merely the matter of franchise which was involved in the dispute but the independence of the Transvaal. The Free State therefore fully supported the Transvaal. The Cape Afrikaners, however, were in a difficult position. Although their nationalism prompted them to support the Transvaal, their loyalty as British subjects prevented them from openly doing so. The British in South Africa, however, generally supported Milner while public opinion in Britain largely favoured war. When Britain made further demands in September, 1899, Kruger answered with an ultimatum. War followed.

Initially the Anglo-Boer War of 1899 – 1902 united the Afrikaners in South Africa. Transvaalers and Free Staters fought side by side and many Afrikaners went from the Cape Colony and Natal to join the republican forces. As the war wore on some Afrikaners were induced to aid the British, and this resulted in much bitterness amongst the Afrikaners. The Bitter-enders and the Handsuppers were not to settle their differences for a long time to come. This war, which involved the whole of South Africa, was greatly to influence the future course of South African history.

15. The Anglo-Boer War, 1899-1902

Boer and Briton take up arms

When the forty-eight hour time-limit imposed by the Transvaal ultimatum to Britain expired at five p.m. on Wednesday, 11 October, 1899, the much-publicized diplomatic crisis of the preceding months became a state of war. The last desperate attempts to effect a reconciliation had failed and for almost thirty-two months armed force was to prevail over reason in South Africa.

President S. J. P. Kruger proclaimed martial law in the Transvaal, and President M. T. Steyn had no hesitation in mobilizing his burghers to support the Transvaal, in accordance with the treaty between the two republics. The republican generals had already received their orders. The Uitlanders whose presence in the Transvaal had been the cause of much of the dissension leading up to the war, left Johannesburg. Bantu miners were escorted out of the Transvaal and the gold mines were closed down for an unspecified period.

Most of the commandos had already been called up and were concentrated on the republican border. On the outbreak of war they began to move towards the four areas which were to become the battle fronts during the Boer offensive in the first weeks of the war: Northern Natal; the southern front which extended from the Basuto border along the Orange River as far, approximately, as Orange River station; the Orange Free State's western front, extending from the Vaal River to Derdepoort and which had Mafeking as its control point. A fifth front, the Transvaal's northern front, extending from Tuli to the Mozambique border, only became a combat area later in the war.

Except for a few regular units, such as the Transvaal police, or "Zarps", and the various well-trained and disciplined units of the Transvaal and Orange Free State state artillery, the Boer force was a people's army, an army without a uniform. The able-bodied men of a district were called up to form a commando under an elected commandant assisted by field-cornets, one from each ward of the district. The Transvaal had an elected commandant-general even in peace-time; in the Orange Free State a chief commandant was elected in times of war only. Traditionally the decisions of the republican officers commanding in the field were subject to a council of war (krygsraad). This system caused many serious delays and its disadvantages, like those of the practice of electing commandants and officers, soon became obvious. The final decisions on matters of strategy rested with the republican governments, who in the early stages of the war directed operations by telegraph from Pretoria and Bloemfontein.

Through force of circumstances the Boer commandos later in the war consisted not only of able-bodied men, but also of young boys, sometimes only eight or nine years old, and men of seventy and upward. In round figures

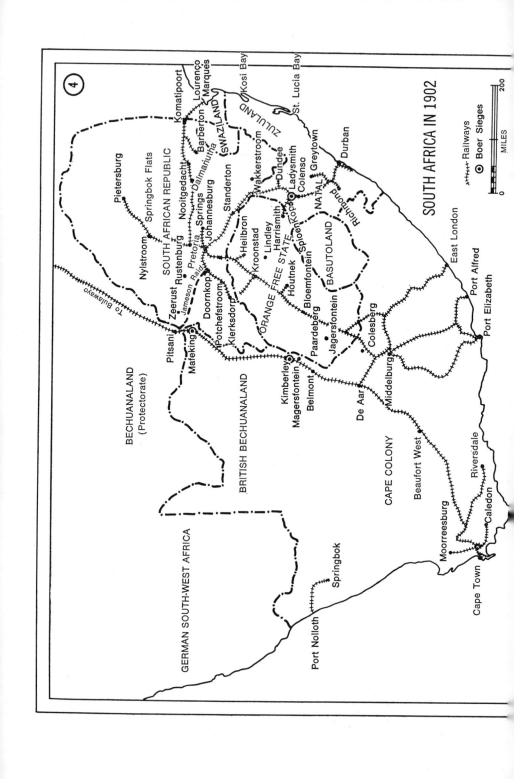

SOUTH AFRICA IN 1902

++++ Railways
⊚ Boer Sieges

0   MILES   200

GERMAN SOUTH-WEST AFRICA

BECHUANALAND
(Protectorate)

BRITISH BECHUANALAND

To Bulawayo

Pitsani
Mafeking
Zeerust
Jameson Raid
Rustenburg
Nooitgedacht
SOUTH AFRICAN REPUBLIC
Pietersburg
Nylstroom
Springbok Flats
Komatipoort
Lourenço Marques
Kosi Bay
St. Lucia Bay
SWAZILAND
Barberton
Dalmanutha
Pretoria
Springs
Johannesburg
Standerton
Wakkerstroom
ZULULAND
Dundee
Ladysmith
Colenso
Greytown
Durban
Doornkop
Potchefstroom
Klerksdorp
Heilbron
Kroonstad
Lindley
Harrismith
Houtnek
Spioenkop
NATAL
Richmond
ORANGE FREE STATE
Bloemfontein
BASUTOLAND
Kimberley
Magersfontein
Paardeberg
Jagersfontein
Belmont
Colesberg
De Aar
Middelburg
CAPE COLONY
Beaufort West
Port Nolloth
Springbok
Moorreesburg
Riverdale
Caledon
Cape Town
East London
Port Alfred
Port Elizabeth

the numbers of fighting men available in the Transvaal were about 30,000 and in the Orange Free State about 20,000; there were in addition 2,000 Afrikaner volunteers from the two British colonies. Altogether the potential fighting strength of the republics can be estimated at 52,000 men between the ages of eighteen and sixty, of whom 35,000 at the most could be mobilized in October, 1899.

Since the time of the Jameson Raid the republics had made no secret of their determination to arm themselves. To provide themselves with small arms they began importing two types of German Mausers to replace the older Martini-Henry and Westley-Richards rifles of the same calibre, but by the outbreak of war there were by no means sufficient Mausers to arm each burgher. During the course of the war Mauser ammunition ran out and eventually the Boers relied almost entirely on the Lee-Metfords they captured from the British. The republics had placed orders for artillery with Schneider-Creusot in France and Krupp in Germany. When the war broke out some of the orders had still to be delivered, and Dr. Leyds, the ambassador-extraordinary of the South African Republic in Europe, tried desperately, in most cases to no avail, to get the arms to South Africa. The Transvaal Artillery, under the command of Lieutenant-Colonel S. P. E. Trichardt, and the Orange Free State Artillery, under the command of Major R. Albrecht, had at the most seventy field-pieces, a mere handful compared to the many batteries of artillery, which included naval guns mounted on gun carriages, with which the British army was equipped. The Boer artillery, apart from a few obsolete guns, consisted of Krupp and Creusot field guns of 7.5 cm. and of four Creusot fortress guns of 15.5 cm., which became known as "Long Toms" and which were destroyed later in the war by the Boers themselves. The Boers also had Krupp howitzers and about twenty-two Vickers-Maxim automatic quick-firing cannon of 37 cm., the famous pom-poms which fired one pound shells. In addition the Boers had about thirty Maxim machine-guns of two calibres.

The Boer forces were at a serious disadvantage at the outset of the war because not a single commando was properly equipped or supplied; their commanders had to waste precious time and energy to attend to commissariat arrangements. Furthermore the Boer armies consisted of untrained civilians who had had virtually no fighting experience other than that obtained in small campaigns against Bantu tribes. Military discipline which would have curbed their natural individualism and the companionable informality of the traditional Boer commando was not a feature of the republican forces; the members of the commandos were accustomed to go home whenever they wished to attend to their families and farms and this practice continued in the first months of the war. Nevertheless the Boers were initially at a distinct advantage when opposed by the regular British army, despite the fact that these soldiers had gained experience in Britain's numerous colonial wars in Africa and India, and had received intensive military training. The Boers were familiar with the climate and terrain of their country and were excellent horsemen; in course of time it became apparent that infantry alone were ineffectual when employed against them. They were also excellent marksmen and this factor was proved to be of the utmost importance in a war in which machine-guns were to play a relatively minor role and static trench warfare was as yet unknown.

Although the Transvaal's ultimatum of 9 October, 1899 demanded that all British troops which since June had been massed on the borders of the Republic should be dispersed, the actual number of British troops in South Africa at the outbreak of war was not great. When Lieutenant-General Sir George White, V.C., arrived from India at the head of 12,000 troops and set up his headquarters in Ladysmith, there were altogether 27,000 British soldiers opposing the republican forces. Of these more than half were in Northern Natal, in the triangle demarcated by Charlestown, Mont-aux-Sources and Rorke's Drift which included the Dundee coal-fields. The rest of the British forces were widely scattered around the key Cape railway junctions, Stormberg, Noupoort, De Aar and the Orange River station (near Hopetown) while other forces were concentrated on Mafeking and Kimberley awaiting a Boer attack.

During the first most important weeks of the war there was little numerical difference between the Boer and British armies and consequently up to November the military balance was fairly evenly poised, but for the remainder of the war the British forces were considerably larger than those of the Boers. The British forces in South Africa at the outbreak of war were expected to remain on the defensive to withstand the initial Boer attacks until such time as the British high command was able to increase the number of its troops in South Africa to 50,000 by sending out an army corps under General Sir Redvers Buller, V.C. These reinforcements, it was planned, together with the local troops in the British colonies, were to launch a major offensive which, it was hoped, would soon bring the war to an end.

Already by the end of 1899 the events of the war had made it evident that many more troops were going to be needed in South Africa; within a few months (according to British returns) the number of British troops in South Africa had risen to more than 176,000 and from then on there were on the average never less than 151,000 in the country at one time, including 28,000 from the British dominions of Canada, Australia and New Zealand, and 109,000 irregular troops from Britain. By the time peace came 448,725 British troops had been used against the Boer Republics, a preponderance of at least four or five to one.

From 1896 the British War Office had been considering the strategy to be employed in a potential future war against the Republics and had taken into account the probability of republican invasions of the British colonies, which would give the Boers the initial advantage in the war. The basic principle of the British strategy was an advance along the Cape railway line, and not through Natal as in the 1880–1881 war, and as was expected by the Boer command in this one. The attitude which would be adopted by the Free State was the one uncertain factor in the British plans. If the Free State declared war on Britain immediately (as actually happened) the British could advance via

Bethulie and Norvals Pont; should the Free State stay out of the war, the British forces would have to invade the Transvaal by advancing along the Kimberley railway line and through Griqualand West.

In the first stage of the war, when the British would necessarily be on the defensive Kimberley would have to be held for reasons of prestige owing to the fact that it was the main town in Griqualand West, an area which was inhabited by a population who had strong republican sentiments. Colonel R. G. Kekewich therefore received orders to establish a garrison of 5,200 troops in Kimberley. Another 9,000 were placed in strategic positions to protect Buller's eventual line of march and to guard the border facing western Transvaal up to Mafeking, where Colonel R. S. S. Baden-Powell was to harass the Boers on the Bechuanaland border with two regiments and several thousand non-White auxiliary troops. The British desperately tried to convey the impression that they would attack in Natal, a subterfuge which effectively deceived the Boers until shortly before the main British attack was actually launched in February, 1900.

In the Cape Colony the cabinet of W. P. Schreiner, which was supported by the Afrikaner Bond, pursued an extremely tentative policy in order to fulfil its obligations toward the Imperial authorities without losing the support of the Colonial Afrikaners. It failed in both respects. The Boers did not realise the significance of their southern front and how easily they could have caused an uprising among the Colonial Afrikaners had they at the outset of the war immediately attacked the Cape Colony in force: such a course of action might have had a serious and disruptive effect on British strategic plans. When the Boers did eventually attack the Cape, it was done hesitantly and without determination despite the vehement adjuration of people such as the Transvaal State Attorney, J. C. Smuts, and Dr. W. J. Leyds, neither of whom could exercise any direct influence on the course of events. There was a widespread fear among British authorities that the northern and north-eastern Cape districts would revolt, but strangely enough no one seems to have considered the possibility of a strong Boer attack across the Orange River.

Boer strategy was based primarily on defending the two republics, but it was held that this could best be done from British territory, primarily in Natal where the British were expected to launch their main offensive. The war would also be waged defensively in the west, across the borders from the Molopo to the Orange River; in the south the drifts of the Orange River would also be guarded but initially the Boers had no definite plan to cross this river.

The first months: the war in British territory

While the British Parliament was budgeting for the first instalment of the amount of almost £200,000,000 which the war in South Africa would eventually cost and the Liberal opposition under Sir Henry Campbell-Bannerman was fiercely condemning the unjust war which had been forced on the Boers by

Chamberlain, Milner and the Salisbury government, the Transvaal commandant-general, Piet Joubert, invaded Northern Natal and the forces of General Piet Cronjé crossed the western Transvaal border at various points.

This was not a spectacular offensive; there were few indications that the Boer leaders realised the vital importance of gaining decisive victories in the first four or five weeks of the war before the flood of inexhaustible British reinforcements and supplies would begin to flow to South Africa. On 12 October in rainy weather, Joubert, with a force of 16,560 men, supported by Free Staters who came across the passes of the Drakensberg, launched a three-pronged attack on British territory in Northern Natal. He occupied Newcastle a few days later without having encountered White's main force of approximately 16,000 in and around Ladysmith or the Natal army, approximately 4,000 strong, under Major-General Sir W. Penn Symons in Dundee. Before the first shots were fired in Natal, General J. H. de la Rey captured the first British armoured train at Kraaipan, on the Kimberley line to the south of Vryburg on 13 October and Cronjé advanced on Mafeking from Ottoshoop with his force of 5,000 men.

Shortly thereafter Baden-Powell was surrounded by an overwhelming force of Boers who wasted valuable time and men in a useless siege which the astute and ingenious British commander withstood in masterly fashion for seven months. A little while later the Boers were to exhibit the same short-sightedness at Kimberley, and on the entire western front approximately 20,000 men were to be diverted to local operations in which some immediate success was achieved but which were of no ultimate advantage to the Boers.

On 20 October Joubert's left flank, consisting of commandos from Utrecht and Vryheid under General Lucas Meyer, were involved in an indecisive battle at Talana against the Dundee garrison. Owing to the lack of support received from General D. J. E. Erasmus, who was on the Impati Mountain, the Boers were forced to retreat across the Buffalo River. General Penn Symons was, however, fatally wounded in this battle. His successor, General J. H. Yule, evacuated Dundee and, partly because of Boer inefficiency, succeeded in reaching Ladysmith on 25 October by marching over Van Tonder's Pass, abandoning supplies, ammunition and wounded troops.

The Boer success at Dundee occurred at the same time as the first Boer defeat at Elandslaagte Station on 21 October. After Assistant-General J. H. M. Kock (a member of the Transvaal Executive Council) had defied instructions by advancing recklessly close to Ladysmith, his commando, together with the Hollander Corps and Adolf Schiel's German Corps were worsted in a fierce encounter. Kock was fatally wounded and died subsequently at Ladysmith; the German volunteer, Count Zeppelin, and Dr Herman Coster, a former State-Attorney, were also killed at Elandslaagte. The Boers suffered heavy casualties: 336 men of the force of nearly 800 were killed, wounded or captured. As the first British prisoners-of-war captured at Dundee, left for Pretoria, the first Boer prisoners-of-war were sent to the Island of St. Helena; subsequently the British authorities were to establish other prisoner-of-war camps on the islands of Bermuda in the West Indies, in Ceylon, and on the mainland of India.

The day after the battle of Elandslaagte the British troops evacuated the area and withdrew to Ladysmith while the Boers seized the railway. To cover the withdrawal of the Dundee force, White advanced against more than 5,000 Free Staters under General Andries P. Cronjé, at Rietfontein, who were in a position to prevent Yule from reaching Ladysmith. After he had achieved his purpose at the Battle of Rietfontein, White fell back on Ladysmith which was being threatened from all sides by the Boer forces, with Joubert's Transvaalers on the hills north and east of the town, and the Free Staters to the west. White's attempt on Monday, 30 October, to use the 12,500 men at his disposal to drive back the Boer commandos closing in on Ladysmith, ended disastrously for him. (The Battle of Lombardskop or Modderspruit.) The British defeat was doubly significant because north of Ladysmith a British attack against the right flank of the Boers also failed. In this engagement at Nicholson's Nek in which the entire force of Lieutenant-Colonel F. R. G. Carleton capitulated, acting Commandant C. R. de Wet of the Heilbron commando, came to the fore for the first time.

These battles fought on 30 October, which became known as 'Mournful Monday', cost the British forces 1,764 casualties, of which 1,284 became prisoners-of-war. Immediately thereafter Ladysmith was entirely surrounded. At the same time the Boer force, after some delay began to invest Kimberley, where Cecil John Rhodes, who had entered the town shortly before, was already showing signs of impatience. The commandos at the Orange River were ordered to invade the Cape Colony, and Sir Redvers Buller disembarked at Cape Town.

Five-sixths of all British troops in Natal were trapped at Ladysmith, and Sir George White was so important a military figure that his capture by the Boers might have had detrimental repercussions on the nationalist elements in India. The Boers were at the Tugela and the road was open, possibly as far as Durban, if they decided to advance so far into Natal.

The Natal situation was so serious that Buller was prompted to take the important decision to split his force, and to go to Natal personally to attempt to retrieve the position. Buller's force had originally been earmarked solely for the advance along the Cape railway; now Lieutenant-General Lord Methuen was instructed to advance along the railway from the Orange River to Kimberley with 2,000 men.

On the central front from Aliwal North to Norval's Pont where the Boer commandos had entered the Cape Colony in the first two weeks of November, several districts had been placed under martial law. Major-General W. F. Gatacre (advancing from Queenstown) and General French (who had managed to escape from Ladysmith and was to play an important part during the coming months as a cavalry commander) advancing from Noupoort, were to ward off the Boer threat to the Cape Colony.

On all fronts the Boers were fighting on British territory; they were to continue doing this for almost four more months. Yet the chances of the Republic winning the war were not as favourable as they seemed; the chance of gaining a decisive military and political advantage by means of a rapid advance was already irrevocably lost. Joubert in Natal was too cautious and lacking in initiative. Around Ladysmith were 6,000 Boers doing virtually nothing except guarding White, and Joubert would not consider a lightning advance on Pietermaritzburg and the Natal coast, which a younger general such as Louis Botha would have been eager to attempt. The Boer attack on Weenen, Estcourt and Mooi River petered out after the Battle of Willow Grange on 23 November. When Buller arrived in Pietermaritzburg, the Boers were withdrawing to await the enemy north of the Tugela, and Louis Botha had temporarily taken over the command from Joubert, who had left for Pretoria because of poor health.

The sieges of Mafeking and Kimberley tied down thousands of burghers on Cronjé's western front, while the Boer forces on the southern (Orange River) front advanced into the Cape, not as the vanguard of an extensive invasion, as the British War Office imagined, but as a defensive measure against British troop movements, about which President Steyn was uneasy. The invasion of the Cape by Boer commandos, who annexed territory along their route, caused many Afrikaners, including a few members of the Cape Parliament, to join the Republican forces.

Martial Law was proclaimed in Colesberg and the neighbouring districts. In this area as well as in Griqualand West and the Prieska district, there were widespread rebellions, which had to be systematically quelled by the British command during the following months.

The position of the Schreiner ministry, already distrusted and execrated because of its sympathy for the Boer cause, became increasingly difficult in view of the demands of the Imperial government at a time when many people regarded the Boer invasion as part of a 'Pan-Afrikaner Conspiracy'.

After the Boer commandos had occupied Colesberg and Aliwal North and had passed through Burgersdorp on the way to Stormberg, French arrived at Noupoort to assume command on the Colesberg front. He was to be engaged in this area until February 1900, with Gatacre on his right flank, while Methuen began to advance towards Kimberley on 21 November and Buller in Natal prepared to attack the Boer lines on either side of Colenso from his base at Frere. Methuen followed the railway line northwards and engaged the Boers who attempted to block his passage on three separate occasions.

At Belmont, on 23 November, he forced the Free Staters under Commandant Jacobus Prinsloo to retreat. The second battle took place on 25 November at Graspan, eight miles north of Belmont, where General J. H. de la Rey combined with Prinsloo in an action in which the casualties suffered by the Naval Brigade were as high as fifty per cent. De la Rey then withdrew to Modder River where Cronjé, who until then had been occupied at Mafeking, joined up with him. The third battle in the west was conducted from shallow trenches on the open plains at the confluence of the Modder and the Riet

Rivers where 3,000 Boers were attacked on 28 November. It was a defensive action in which the British suffered a series of setbacks. Cronjé then withdrew unnecessarily from this position northwards to Magersfontein, while Methuen remained at Modder River for twelve days. His progress had been satisfactory, but at this stage De la Rey, who was an excellent tactician, took up a position in the foot-hills at Magersfontein, with trenches in front of the foot-hills to enable his forces to fire over the plain.

In the second week of December 1899, the so-called "Black Week", the British army suffered three defeats in quick succession on the central, western and Tugela fronts. At Stormberg, after a gruelling night march, Gatacre was trapped near the railway junction by the Free Staters and rebels under General J. H. Olivier and on 10 December his force suffered severe casualties. Two days later Methuen launched his 12,000 men in a disastrous frontal attack on the Boer concentration at Magersfontein. On 12 December Cronjé and De la Rey, with their 8,000 burghers, repulsed the British attack in a bloody battle. Among the almost 1,000 casualties the Highland Brigade's losses were the heaviest, and included their commander Major-General A. J. Wauchope, who died early on the morning of 12 December. Methuen's depleted force fell back to the Modder River and in Kimberley, meanwhile, the tension between the military authorities and Cecil Rhodes increased. It was Rhodes's presence, after all, which was the main motive of the special British effort for the relief of Kimberley.

The heaviest blow suffered by the British was Buller's defeat at the Tugela on Friday, 15 December. Disturbed by the Boer victories at Stormberg and Magersfontein, Buller decided to launch a frontal attack, which he originally had resolved not to attempt, against the heart of Louis Botha's positions north of the river, positions which centred on Colenso and stretched west towards Spioen Kop, and east towards Hlangwane Hill or Bosrand. This reverse was on a far larger scale than that inflicted at Magersfontein; Botha's men succeeded in driving back the massive British infantry force of 23,000 men, support-ed by 42 guns, after six hours, mainly as a result of the devastating fire directed from the Boer trenches. Buller withdrew with 1,100 casualties and the loss of 10 guns and even contemplated leaving White to his fate in Lady-smith.

The jubilation in Europe and even among certain Boer sympathisers in Britain at the Boer victories was immediately dampened by the British com-mand's new line of action. Two British divisions were already at sea on the way to South Africa, and a third was nearly ready to sail. Buller, who retained his Natal command, was replaced as commander-in-chief in South Africa by the 67 year old veteran, Field-Marshal Lord Frederick Sleigh Roberts, V.C., the hero of Kabul and Kandahar. The new chief-of-staff was an equally distinguished soldier, Lord Kitchener of Khartoum, former Sirdar of the Egyptian army and the victor of Omdurman, a military organiser of note who would admirably complement the strategist Roberts, whose prestige in itself was an encourage-ment to the British in their hour of adversity. Upon his arrival in Cape Town on 10 January, 1900, Roberts immediately began planning his main campaign, which would be launched from the Modder River.

In the meantime, throughout January, rebellions which had been becoming more frequent in the Northern Cape and Griqualand West, were further stimulated by an expedition led by General P. J. Liebenberg of Potchefstroom. British troops suppressed uprisings at Upington, Douglas, Prieska, Hopetown, Philipstown and Kuruman, while on the otherwise quiet Tugela front, 4,000 Boers on 6 January, 1900 launched an heroic onslaught on Ladysmith from the south at Platrand (called Wagon Hill by the British). The British defenders showed equal bravery, and the attack was repulsed with heavy losses on both sides.

On the Colesberg front the British were in a more favourable position. In December French had advanced to confront the hesitant General Hendrik Schoeman, who, after Magersfontein, had to be helped by De la Rey. Once the dissension among the Boer commanders had abated, French faced stronger opposition until Roberts recalled him to Cape Town to be initiated into the next phase of the campaign. Major-General R. A. P. Clements assumed the southern command at a time when the Boer forces were withdrawing to counter the threat to Kimberley from the south.

After Buller had received reinforcements which raised the strength of his force to 30,000 men supported by 60 guns, he made a second attack on the Tugela. He also had under his command Lieutenant-General Sir Charles Warren (who, since 1877, had on various occasions served in South Africa) and the newly-arrived Fifth Division. When Buller began moving his forces on about 14 January, the Boer lines were stretched out far to the west; instead of attempting to outflank the Boers from the east at Hlangwane Hill, which eventually proved to be the only way to reach Ladysmith, Buller elected to order Warren to outflank them from the west, west of Spioen Kop and over Trichardts Drift. The capture of Spioen Kop and its subsequent evacuation on 24 January, 1900 was a tragedy of misunderstanding on the part of the British, and both Buller and Warren were responsible for this error of judgement. The desperate battle of Spioen Kop ended in victory for Louis Botha. Of the 1,653 British casualties, there were more than 300 dead, as against 50 dead and 120 wounded on the Boer side. The mutual recriminations and accusations and counter-accusations involving Buller and Warren lasted until 1902. In England this setback caused indignation especially as the relief of Ladysmith – the principal aim of all Natal operations – had not been effected.

While Buller, who despite his failures on the Tugela had never lost the confidence of his officers nor the affection of his men, was preparing for a third attempt to cross the river, Roberts explained his new plan of campaign to his staff. He had already planned its broad outlines in 1898. In the event of war against the Transvaal there was to be an advance to Mafeking by way of Kimberley; then, as Jameson had attempted in 1895, the attacking force would have to move in an easterly direction against the Rand and Pretoria. Roberts, however, had modified his plan since 1898: the eastward wheel would be carried out between the Orange and Modder rivers, directly towards Spring-fontein or Edenburg to force the Free Staters operating in Natal and on the southern front to return to defend Bloemfontein. After the battle of Spioen Kop Roberts once again amended his plan: he would try to relieve Kimberley *en passant* and would swing his force round to attack Cronjé from a more northerly direction than was originally intended. In the meantime Roberts attempted to convey the impression that he intended to launch his main offensive on the southern border of the Free State, from Norval's Pont and Bethulie. Roberts, with the unspectacular tactics which inspired little confidence in Milner, and which conflicted with all the principles laid down in voluminous British textbooks of military strategy, did in fact succeed in misleading the Boer commanders who had expected an attack from the south: when the energetic 'Bobs' arrived at Methuen's encampment at Modder River on 8 February "to cross the Tugela at Magersfontein" as he put it, he learnt of Buller's third failure to breach the Tugela lines.

An attack had been launched through Potgieter's Drift and 3,000 men under General N. G. Lyttelton, had directly attacked the Boer positions across the river at Vaalkrans. A handful of Boers under Commandant Ben Viljoen had defended the kop as long as possible despite a severe bombardment by 36 guns. After they had abandoned their positions, Buller had realised that Vaalkrans was after all not the key position, whereupon he had evacuated it and returned across the Tugela.

Meanwhile conditions in Ladysmith had become critical.

Roberts' advance: the turn of the tide

On 11 February, 1900 Roberts began to advance with clearly defined objectives: he was to use his force of 30,000 men, comprising four infantry divisions and French's cavalry division which was to play such an important part for the remainder of the war, to relieve Kimberley, destroy Cronjé's main force and to capture Bloemfontein.

French opened the operations brilliantly by adroitly by-passing Conjé's Magersfontein positions to relieve Kimberley on 15 February, and then re-joining the main advance against Cronjé, while the Boers, who had maintained the futile siege of Kimberley, fell back to Boshof. French had effectively proved the value of mounted troops, which were to play an ever-increasing role in the war. Altogether 350,000 horses were to be used by the British command during the course of the war; in fact both sides were to use horses extensively as the war developed.

Cronjé, who was still under the impression that Roberts would not leave the railway line, held his position at Magersfontein too long before suddenly deciding to move up along the Modder River with a cumbrous train of ox-wagons, and a considerable number of women and children who had gradually joined the commandos and whom he could not abandon. While Commandant-General Christiaan de Wet captured his first convoy of 176 wagons and 500 slaughter oxen from Roberts at Waterval Drift on the Riet River, the British army was busy pinning down Cronjé on the northern bank of the Modder River and encircling his encampment opposite Vendutie Drift, to the east of Paardeberg. In the ten day encounter known as the Battle of Paardeberg, the British were repeatedly repulsed by the Boers or attacked fiercely by De Wet from outside the encirclement in an effort to save Cronjé. Roberts suffered 1,442 casualties in these battles, before Cronjé, despite many pleas made to him to hold out while De Wet desperately tried to fight a way through to him, surrendered on Majuba Day, 27 February, 1900 with 4,000 burghers, mostly Transvaalers.

Cronjé's capitulation was a severe blow to the Boers and was to prove to be the turning point in the war; on the same day, 27 February, 1900, the Boers were also badly defeated on the Natal front. After Buller had made a fourth attempt on 21 and 22 February to gain a foothold on the other side of the Tugela, he, on 23 February, again launched a fierce attack against Botha's 5,000 Boers at Pieters Hill, and with an overwhelming force of 40,000, supported by 72 guns, captured the key position of the Tugela line on 27 February despite the Boers' heroic opposition.

The road to Ladysmith and its famished inhabitants was open. While White's force was being relieved, the Boers, their morale shattered, retreated in confusion until they reached the scene of the October battles, despite the entreaties of President Kruger himself, who had arrived at Glencoe. There, in the Biggarsberg, Botha finally succeeded in re-forming such lines as he could from those of his forces who had not returned home. Buller made no attempt to pursue the Boer force; he remained in Ladysmith from March to May, 1900.

All attention was now focussed on the Free State; the débacle of 27 February had also caused the Cape front to collapse, and by the beginning of March the commandos were retreating to Bloemfontein, with British forces under Clements, Gatacre and General E. Y. Brabant pursuing them across the Orange River.

During the week when Roberts rested his troops at Osfontein, the Boer commanders took stock of a situation extremely unfavourable to their forces. President Steyn made Christiaan de Wet chief commandant of the Free State; with the 5,000 men he was able to muster he was to attempt to block Roberts's advance on Bloemfontein. President Kruger journeyed from the chaos in Natal to Bloemfontein, and with President Steyn drafted a dramatic appeal, copies of which were sent to all European goverments, to the British Premier, Lord Salisbury, to stop the bloodshed and restore peace on a basis acceptable to both parties involved in the war.

Before any answer could come from London, Roberts's army began to advance on Bloemfontein. On 7 March at Poplar Grove, where De Wet had stationed his troops on either side of the Modder River, Roberts attempted to surround the Boers with an overwhelming force. De Wet, however, escaped without a single casualty and fell back on Abrahamskraal, with an extremely demoralised force. While De Wet was trying to organise the defence of Bloemfontein, De la Rey and others at Abrahamskraal and Driefontein provided the last opposition to the British columns advancing from the west on Bloemfontein.

The British occupied Bloemfontein without any opposition on 13 March. The Free State government was evacuated to Kroonstad and De Wet allowed his burghers to disband on the understanding that they would later voluntarily return to their commandos. Many of the disheartened laid down their arms while others elected to move to Kroonstad to continue the war. In the eastern Free State, the commandos were as yet largely unscathed, especially those of Olivier who had fallen back from the Cape.

On 12 March Kruger and Steyn's plea for peace was curtly rejected by Lord Salisbury. Great Britain was determined to subjugate the republics and did not fear the interference of the European powers. British supremacy at sea was unquestioned and she was at peace with all her Continental neighbours despite tension with France about the Nile Delta and periodic diplomatic friction with Germany.

Although public opinion in all European countries was fiercely anti-British, and although the press was frantically attacking British policy, the attitudes of the Continental governments towards England were determined by their alignment as members of the two opposing power blocs, the Triple Alliance (Germany, Austria-Hungary and Italy) and the Dual Alliance (Russia and France) and by their individual interests, which in no instance justified intervention in South Africa. Nevertheless there was continual diplomatic activity on the Continent regarding possible foreign intervention in the war in South Africa, with Russia taking a tentative lead in March, 1900. Dr Leyds, in Brussels, did his utmost to encourage intervention, by making numerous diplomatic journeys and negotiating through various channels. He also collaborated with the Boer deputation (A. D. W. Wolmarans, from the Transvaal, and Abraham Fischer and C. H. Wessels, from the Free State), who had been sent to Europe by the republics in March, 1900 in an attempt to negotiate peace. The Deputation visited various European capitals including St. Petersburg, and also Washington, and, although they continued to labour towards this end until the end of the war, they achieved no success.

In addition to the diplomatic efforts of Leyds and the Deputation, the embassy of the South African Republic in Brussels and Dr H. P. N. Muller, the Free State Consul General in the Hague, distributed literature, press statements and reports in support of the Boer cause, co-ordinated charitable collections, equipped ambulances and encouraged innumerable auxiliary organisations throughout the world to support the Boers.

With the fall of Bloemfontein, the conflict in the Free State almost instinctively became a mobile war as was also later to be the case in the Transvaal. At Kroonstad, on 17 March, at which Kruger and Steyn were present, a council of war decided to continue the war. General Joubert, too, was present at this meeting but died on 28 March in Pretoria and was succeeded as Commandant-General of the Transvaal forces by the 38 year old Louis Botha. The council of war subscribed to the policy of smaller commandos unencumbered by wagon trains, the use of more mobile units, and raids on the British lines of communications. De Wet had already demonstrated how effective such tactics could be, and within two weeks he was to do so again.

De Wet struck at Sannaspos on 31 March, at Mostertshoek on 4 April, and at Wepener, on 9 April. In those dark days for the Boer cause he kindled the flame of Boer resistance, persuaded many burghers to return to their commandos and began to perform the remarkable feats which earned him the reputation of being the most brilliant guerilla leader on the Boer side. De Wet, who seemed able to appear and disappear in an almost supernatural fashion, and who managed to elude the British columns for the next two years, was regarded by the British as the greatest personality produced by the war. On occasions he was referred to as the one man, who, with the exception of Napoleon, had imposed, up to 1902, the greatest burden on the British treasury.

An epidemic of typhoid among his troops and the enormous task of organising transport and supplies for the campaign against the Transvaal kept Roberts for six weeks at Bloemfontein. He now controlled the railway line to the Cape, and did not consider the possibility of further Free State resistance to be of such a nature that he would have to subjugate the territory completely before moving against the Transvaal. It was more important to attack the Transvaal before it had a chance to strengthen its defences.

Roberts next planned a broad sweep northwards on a line from Kimberley to Ladysmith. The divisions of Methuen and Hunter, consisting of 20,000 men would operate on the western flank along the Kimberley railway line. The main force of 43,000 men, under Roberts's personal command would advance in the centre straddling the central railway line, with French's cavalry supporting him. General Sir Ian Hamilton would advance on Roberts's right flank to keep the Boers in the North Eastern Free State at a distance. Simultaneously with this northward sweep Buller would march across the Drakensberg to the Transvaal Highveld with a force of 45,000 men. In addition Roberts left a considerable force under Generals Chermside, Rundle, Brabant, Pole-Carew and Kelly-Kenny in the Free State.

Louis Botha, who had assumed command of the Boers had scarcely 12,000 men and 28 guns, of which 8,000 men opposed the centre of Roberts's phalanx of khaki which began the long march to Pretoria on 3 May, 1900. So he adopted the form of battle which was to become characteristic of the Boers, that of constantly fighting, disengaging and falling back to fight again. By 3 May Roberts had reached Brandfort and on 12 May he was in Kroonstad. The Free State government had already fled to the North Eastern Free State and for months had been moving from one town to another. Ultimately President Steyn and his government joined De Wet and from then on stayed with him through all dangers and vicissitudes until the end of the war.

Roberts advanced to the Vaal River as quickly as French's 6,000 spent horses were able to move. Meanwhile he had sent Hunter's division on his left flank across the Vaal River, straight to Mafeking which was relieved on 17 May after being besieged for 213 days. This released Baden-Powell for operations in the Western Transvaal until later in the war he was given the task of establishing the South African Constabulary to keep the Boer commandos out of 'protected' areas.

While the British columns were everywhere crossing the Vaal River and the Free Staters by agreement were leaving the defence of the Transvaal to Botha and his Transvaalers, Roberts formally annexed the 'Orange River Colony' as British territory on the Queen's birthday, 24 May, 1900. Without much opposition the invading army advanced to Johannesburg as De Wet and his band launched spectacular attacks on the invaders' lines of communication at Biddulphsberg and Lindley.

The fall of Pretoria and after

Two days before Roberts rode into Johannesburg on 31 May, 1900, President Kruger and the Transvaal government left Pretoria and set up their seat of government at Machadodorp. In its last session on 7 May the Transvaal Volksraad had handed over the government of the republic to the Executive Council. Pretoria would not be defended; the guns had long since been removed from the forts around the town to be used elsewhere; war supplies were sent along the Delagoa Bay railway and the state attorney, J. C. Smuts, was instructed to remove the republic's gold supplies from Pretoria.

Botha fought a rearguard action against Roberts at Six Mile Spruit and then withdrew to the east. To the Boers this was a darker moment even than the occupation of Bloemfontein; even the steadfast Kruger wavered momentarily and his faith in the cause had to be bolstered by Steyn. Botha and the military leaders were discouraged and irresolute; if Roberts had sent French's cavalry eastwards instead of westwards from Pretoria, it is generally agreed, he would probably have been able to end the war immediately.

But within a week the Boers recovered their confidence. Botha and his officers learnt of De Wet's achievement on 7 June at Roodewal where he cut Roberts's precious rail link across the Vaal; and it was a week before communications were restored. De Wet also destroyed and captured large quantities of supplies, equipment and ammunition. On the same day Kruger issued a proclamation from Machadodorp in which he called on the burghers of the Transvaal to continue the struggle. Botha deployed his forces across the Delagoa Bay line where on 12 June, just east of Pretoria, he fought the Battle of Donkerhoek (Diamond Hill), before retiring eastward along the railway.

Buller in Natal had left Roberts in the lurch. He lay idle in Ladysmith with 45,000 men until 10 May when Roberts prodded him into attacking the restored Boer lines in the Biggarsberg. After encountering moderate opposition Buller moved towards Newcastle and the historic territory near Laingsnek. After Roberts had arrived in Pretoria, Buller advanced westwards over Botha's Pass, engaged the Boers at Allemansnek on 11 June and occupied Volksrust.

When he appeared on the Highveld, General Christiaan Botha (who was opposing Buller) and his force fell back on the Delagoa Bay railway and Buller moved westwards to Standerton eventually to join up with Roberts who was meanwhile waiting impatiently to begin using the Natal railway line. Roberts would rather have had Buller in the Eastern Transvaal in the rear of the retreating main Boer force.

Various circumstances detracted from Roberts's achievements. In Britain, the vehement Liberal campaign against the war received enthusiastic support from various womens' organisations. By mid-1900 rowdy protest meetings had become the order of the day, with David Lloyd George and Miss Emily Hobhouse, the energetic secretary of the womens' branch of the South Africa Conciliation Committee, well to the fore.

The situation in the Free State suddenly also assumed critical proportions. Roberts was forced to adopt the attitude that any resistance on the part of the Free Staters would be interpreted as an act of rebellion against the new government. Then came the first ominous decision to burn farmhouses near which destruction of the railway occurred, an admission of Britain's inability to end the war by military means alone. Although innumerable British brigades and columns interminably, and somewhat pointlessly, ranged far and wide till they were weary and footsore in pursuit of the Boer commandos they achieved little; nor did the four special mobile columns which were supposed to track down De Wet and the Free State government fare any better.

In the Cape Colony the "first rebellion" which had subsided in the north-east after the departure of Olivier and the Boer commandos, continued to smoulder in the far-flung triangle of territory defined by Hopetown, Kenhardt and Kuruman. Kitchener was sent to suppress it and Warren, the scapegoat of Spioen Kop, had to spend May and June, 1900 completing the task. In Cape Town, W. P. Schreiner's cabinet, which had been supported by the Afrikaner Bond, resigned on 13 June, 1900.

The setbacks suffered by the Boers, led to an intensification of Imperial pressure on the Cape government, which had resisted the proposed punishment of rebels by permanent disfranchisement. Sir Gordon Sprigg formed a government which was more responsive to Imperialist demands and had the so-called Treason Bill, which provided for the punishment of rebels, passed by the Cape Parliament. The Cape Parliament was not to meet between October, 1900 and 1902 and as the mobile war being waged in the north reached the Cape, martial law was also proclaimed in the Colony.

Before Roberts could advance eastwards in pursuit of Botha's main force and gain possession of the Delagoa Bay railway as far as the Portuguese border, Boer resistance in the Western Transvaal once more flared up. After the battle of Donkerhoek, General de la Rey, who had taken part in Botha's retreat from Brandfort, returned to the Western Transvaal. Under his command the forces of General E. R. Snyman (who had been at Mafeking) and General F. A. Grobler from Waterberg, moved into action against Baden-Powell, Smith-Dorrien, Carrington and later against Methuen. The area south of the Magaliesberg known as the "Moot" became the headquarters of De la Rey's force of approximately 5,000 men; and presently General J. C. G. Kemp, who had been with Botha, joined him.

Since the powerfully held areas around Johannesburg and Pretoria almost divided the Transvaal in two, the government at Machadodorp delegated the administration of the Western Transvaal to De la Rey and on 17 July the state attorney, J. C. Smuts, was sent to assist De la Rey in punishing traitors and in instituting local governing bodies. So the talented Smuts, who was later himself to be promoted to the rank of general, was initiated into the art of war by De la Rey. The pattern of war in the western districts followed the pattern established in the Free State by De Wet and his followers and swift blows were struck at Silkaatsnek, Dwarsvlei, and Onderstepoort (11 July), Selons River (21 July) and Carrington was driven back to Mafeking in August.

Toward the middle of June the pressure of the English columns began to force the Free State commandos, including De Wet who was accompanied by Steyn and government officials into the Brandwater Basin, south of Bethlehem, on the Basutoland border. For a while Fouriesberg became the temporary seat of government, but De Wet who was aware of the dangerous possibility that the 7,000 Free Staters in the area could be trapped in the Basin, decided that they could not stay there. On 15 June, guided by his expert scouts, Gideon Scheepers and Danie Theron, he escaped in characteristic fashion by leading his force comprising 2,600 men (including the Free State government) and 460 wagons through Slabbertsnek, one pass from the Brandwater Basin which was not blocked by the British columns. He then eluded the British columns between Bethlehem and Senekal, crossed the railway, and trekked over the Vaal River into the Transvaal. While Broadwood and the other generals began the "first De Wet hunt" (15 July to 17 August), Hunter trapped the inactive Free Staters, who, in De Wet's absence, had elected Marthinus Prinsloo as their commander-in-chief, instead of a more able general, the Rev. Paul Roux, whom De Wet had recommended for this office before his departure.

Although he could have broken through to safety, Prinsloo, on 30 July, 1900, with more than 3,000 men, surrendered to Hunter at Slaapkrans, in a capitulation which De Wet in his war memoirs was to refer to subsequently as "a dreadful act of murder committed against the government, the country and the people".

Some of Prinsloo's men, such as those under the command of Commandant Sarel Haasbroek, were able to fight their way out independently but the rest of the large force were sent as prisoners-of-war to the Diyatalawa camp in Ceylon. The number of exiled Boer prisoners-of-war was steadily increasing and fourteen overseas camps had been established to house them. Altogether 26,600 prisoners-of-war, including children of eight and nine years of age and old people, led a strange existence in these camps far from their homeland, until the middle of 1902, and in some cases even until 1904. They whiled away the long months of exile in different ways. Some showed an unusual aptitude for handcraft and made a wide variety of articles, others furthered their education;

most of them led a busy social life and participated in camp sports, while a few enterprising ones even circulated little camp newspapers.

From 11 July Robert's spearhead made contact at Witpoort with Botha's forces which had been retreating along the eastern railway to Middelburg; but an engagement was delayed by the news of De Wet's breakthrough to the west, which demanded Roberts's attention. In addition Roberts was held up by the leisurely progress of Buller, who was still at Heidelberg, and who reached Belfast only in August. On 25 August, Botha, at Belfast was awaiting the attack about to be launched by Roberts and his subordinates, French, Ian Hamilton and Pole-Carew, while Buller had also arrived after marching via Amersfoort, Ermelo and Carolina.

As at Donkerhoek, Botha drew up his men on either side of the railway line. He and his force of 5,000 men opposed Roberts in the last pitched battle of the war at Berg-en-Dal (Dalmanutha) on 26 and 27 August, 1900, a battle in which especially the "Zarps" distinguished themselves by their heroic resistance in the centre against an overwhelming force. Buller occupied Macha-dorp and Helvetia while the Boers dispersed towards Barberton and Lydenburg, from where they were eventually to inaugurate the war of movement in the Eastern Transvaal.

The Transvaal government moved to Waterval-Onder (where Kruger had been living for some time), and afterwards to Nelspruit where it was decided that Kruger, whose age prevented him accompanying the commandos, would leave for Europe to promote the cause of the republics there, while General Schalk W. Burger would act as Vice-President. President Steyn was present when the Transvaal president crossed into Portuguese territory. Steyn had been escorted by De Wet as far as the Magaliesberg, then had travelled through the Lowveld, north of the British forces. He was shortly to undertake the same hazardous journey back to De Wet and from this stage, Steyn, more than ever, became the main source of inspiration to the Boers in the field, in such measure that he may be said to have come to personify the spirit of Boer resistance.

Meanwhile, as early as 1 September, 1900, Roberts issued a proclamation annexing the Transvaal, while French, Pole-Carew and Buller tried in vain to subjugate the dispersed Boer forces in the Eastern Transvaal.

The War of Movement in full swing

Superficially it appeared as if the war was over and that from a British point of view all that remained to be done was to clear the country of some isolated Boer armed bands. Even Roberts was of this opinion, but events were to reveal that this was a serious error of judgment. By the spring of 1900 the war was being waged on a smaller scale; it had become a war of attrition waged against the British, planned by the Boer governments in the field and fought under the command of the chief republican officers De Wet and Botha. The transition from regular warfare to mobile war, first in the Eastern Transvaal and later in the Northern Transvaal where General Christiaan Beyers was operating, took only a few months, and in the meantime many dispirited Boers ("handsuppers") surrendered to the British. However, this tended to weed out the weak from the fighting ranks so that those who remained were the dedicated spirits. The remaining two-thirds of the war was fought with smaller commandos operating in territory which was familiar to them. Officers were no longer elected and generally commando discipline became more stringent. In future, all supplies, rifles and ammunition were to be captured from the British. The Boer command also decided largely to dispense with the use of artillery to ensure greater mobility.

Early in August De Wet had proved that he could completely evade 30,000 pursuers. After his return to the Free State he embarked on a renewed recruiting campaign among the laggards and waverers among the burghers. Many of these dug up their rifles and, breaking their oath of neutrality, rejoined the commandos.

Between 1 and 5 September, De Wet, to set a stimulating example, invested Ladybrand, and until October harassed one British garrison after another in the south. Untiringly he moved back and forth across the Vaal River at Schoeman's Drift, successfully attacked a British force on 24 October at Frederikstad in the Transvaal and provoked the 'second De Wet hunt", which was to have a surprising sequel: De Wet's decision to invade the Cape Colony. After he had lost his entire wagon train at Bothaville on 6 November he trekked through the Free State with 1,500 men, fought at Sprinkaansnek, occupied Dewetsdorp and advanced to the Orange River. The river was too full to ford with the entire force, but De Wet sent General J. B. M. Hertzog and General P. H. Kritzinger over the river with their two commandos. Hertzog reached the Atlantic coast at Lambert's Bay and Kritzinger reached the Willowmore district, while De Wet faced about, and, to the chagrin of his pursuers, escaped, and by Christmas 1900 had reached Senekal in safety after a truly epic trek.

In truth De Wet's expedition was part of a plan which had been evolved at a Boer conclave in the Magaliesberg in October, 1900 where future strategy had been discussed. This plan made provision for an invasion of the Cape Colony, and the destruction of the Rand gold mines – although this latter intention was never carried out. It had also earlier been agreed that Botha would invade Natal, while General Ben Viljoen would launch attacks along the Delagoa railway. These decisions were implemented, although Botha's advance on Vryheid was limited to unsuccessful attacks on various garrisons. British forces had not yet reached the Northern Transvaal, where Beyers was still able to move about unhindered. Pietersburg remained in Boer hands until April, 1901, when it was occupied by the British for the first time.

The British general election, the so-called "Khaki Election", which followed on the dissolution of the House of Commons on 25 September, 1900 was a bitter contest between the Conservatives and the "Little Englanders". On occasion the Liberals were accused of treason and the statement "a vote for the Liberals is a vote for the Boers", was adopted by the Tories as their election slogan. The Salisbury government was returned to power and their majority which was in the proportion of eight to seven, was interpreted as a mandate to finish the war in South Africa, despite the vehement attacks directed on government policy by the Irish members of the opposition and by Lloyd George, Morley, Harcourt and other Liberal spokesmen.

Despite the careful preparations made by Dr. Leyds before the republics' last trump card was played, Kruger's arrival at Marseilles on 22 November, 1900 and his subsequent tour of various European countries, produced no tangible results, although there was evidence of great sympathy for the Boer cause. Furthermore his attempt to visit Berlin without an invitation was regarded by the German Kaiser, William II as presumptuous. At Cologne the white-haired Boer leader was curtly advised to turn back.

For the rest of the war, Kruger resided quietly in the Netherlands. None of the pro-Boer pamphlets, or the pro-Boer organizations and demonstrations all over Europe, or the virulent and even obscene anti-British cartoons which appeared in many countries during the Anglo-Boer war, in any way influenced any government to come to the aid of the Boers.

It was well known that at the end of November, 1900 Lord Roberts was to be succeeded as commander-in-chief of the British forces in South Africa by his "military foreman", Kitchener. In the meantime Lord Milner's office of High Commissioner in South Africa was separated, in October, 1900, from his governership of the Cape Colony. He was to go to Johannesburg early in 1901 as the administrator of the two annexed Boer republics which were to be administered as British colonies.

When Kitchener assumed command of the British forces in South Africa he adopted new methods in an attempt to end the war. The tactical phase was over; systematic counter-measures were now to be applied against the mobile commandos. In 1901 Kitchener put the new methods into effect by simultanously introducing lines of blockhouses, establishing concentration camps for non-combatants (principally women and children), by organizing military "drives" by forces which were mostly mounted and deployed in columns instead of the traditional divisions and brigades.

Although De la Rey and Beyers had meanwhile soundly defeated Clements at Nooitgedacht near Rustenburg on 13 December and Kitchener himself had to go by train as far as Noupoort to help in the second De Wet hunt, he was still prepared to try a "peace" offensive against the Boers. In a proclamation of 20 December, 1900, he offered safe conduct to those individuals who wished to surrender, and established a Burgher Peace Committee which was to send out burghers who had already surrendered as emissaries to the various commandos. The experiment failed completely because the Boers regarded these collaborators as outright traitors and had at least one of them shot summarily by a firing squad.

In the last months of 1900 concentration camps began to be established, initially to give protection to the homeless women and children who were trekking around on the Highveld, and men who had surrendered. After the battle of Dalmanutha, however, concentration camps became part of the

British war policy which envisaged the systematic removal of women and children from their farms to prevent them aiding the burghers in the field by providing them with food or information. The official justification for this policy was that women and children were being evacuated from their homes to protect them from molestation by natives and to provide them with the necessities of life. A proclamation issued on 21 December, 1900 which coincided with Kitchener's peace manoeuvre, announced that men, women and children were to be removed from areas where commandos were operating.

The large-scale removal of women and children from the farms was merely one aspect of the pitiless British scorched-earth policy which was put into effect during 1901. The evacuation of the farms was accompanied by the burning of farm houses and the destruction of all means of existence.

Not only were poultry, sheep and cattle slaughtered or removed but anything that might provide food for the commandos, such as fruit trees, grain and other crops was destroyed.

The main issue however, still remained effective subjugation of the Boers in the field. At the beginning of 1901 Kitchener, in an attempt to achieve this object, built a vast network of blockhouses which eventually stretched from near Lambert's Bay in the Western Cape to Pietersburg in the Northern Transvaal. The first blockhouses were built to protect the railways against such redoubtable train-wreckers as Henri Slegtkamp, Jack Hindon and Karel Trichardt, who were particularly active along the Delagoa railway line. The lines of blockhouses also served the purpose of dividing the country into areas in which the commandos might more easily be brought to heel. For this reason, especially in the eastern Free State, the blockhouses were later erected at right angles to the railway. The blockhouses were made in different ways and of different materials, sometimes they were 200 yards apart with barbed-wire barriers between them. In the last phase of the war, swift mounted columns forming an unbroken line in sectors between the blockhouses, attempted to drive the Boers back against the railway, where the main line of blockhouses was situated.

The first major 'drive', before the erection of blockhouses, was carried out by French. With 40,000 men he swept the country between the Delagoa and the Natal railways eastwards across the Highveld up to the Swaziland border and back again from January to April, 1901. This force caused much damage and many women and children were taken to the camps, but the intention that French should inflict a shattering defeat on Botha's force was not realized. The Boer in the field had learnt to evade traps, and showed ingenuity in solving the difficult problem of surviving in a country which the enemy had stripped bare of the necessities of life. He made clothes from skins or canvas, or stripped enemy prisoners of their khaki uniforms and boots.

At the time when French was moving eastwards, the Boers were making their presence felt all over the Western Transvaal. Beyers ventured to approach to within a few miles of Johannesburg, crossed the railway at Kaalfontein and then moved east of Pretoria, crossing the line once more. Smuts was given command as general, left De la Rey and chose the Gatsrand as his field of operations. Here he achieved his first success at Modderfontein. De la Rey kept the English columns, particularly Methuen's force, busy in the Lichtenburg area, and Kemp was active in the vicinity of Krugersdorp.

The idea of invading the Cape Colony in force had been advocated constantly by Smuts. This scheme to carry the war into British territory once more, and to foment rebellion in the Cape Colony was put to the test by De Wet. On 6 January, 1901 he broke out of hiding at Doornberg, between Senekal and Winburg, and headed past Tabaksberg, Israelspoort, De Wetsdorp and Philippolis to Sand Drift on the Orange River, with the columns of Knox and Bruce Hamilton in hot pursuit. Thus the third or "great De Wet hunt" was inaugurated. General Lyttelton was even brought from the Delagoa Bay railway line to assume command of the operation which had to be carried out partially by train in an attempt to cut De Wet off. Before long the British military map once more looked like a confused spider web as the columns vainly scurried hither and thither.

De Wet moved westwards to contact Hertzog who was returning from his expedition to Lambert's Bay. De Wet was diverted east of Prieska by the swollen Brak River. He failed to meet Hertzog but somehow once more achieved the seemingly impossible; he threaded his way through the vast British forces in his path, crossed the Orange River at Botha's Drift, and returned to Senekal with President Steyn on 11 March, after a remarkable journey of 800 miles.

His raid did not provoke widespread rebellion in the Cape Colony; in fact this never occurred at any stage in the war, but the commandos of Manie Maritz started operating in the North Western Cape and those of Kritzinger, Scheepers, Wynand Malan, Lötter, Lategan, Edwin Conroy, Hugo, Myburgh, Naudé, Niewoudt and others quickly moved into action in the Eastern Cape and in the Midlands. These developments necessitated more blockhouses and still more pursuing columns, supplemented by different units of irregular Cape troops and "Town Guards" who were prepared to wear the British uniform. Milner's admission, on 6 February, 1901, that the British situation had deteriorated in the previous six months, is therefore understandable. Furthermore, the recruiting of irregular troops in Britain and the dominions had virtually come to a standstill in the meantime, and now had to be started again. The decision, in February, 1901 to send an additional 30,000 troops to South Africa, came at a time when the Liberals were once more pleading for peace and the Cape politicians, J. X. Merriman and J. W. Sauer, had made an unsuccessful attempt to obtain permission to address the British House of Commons on the subject of the war.

Milner, however, refused to consider any kind of peace treaty which did not involve the complete military subjugation of the Boers. He arrived in Johannesburg in March, 1901 and gathered around him a group of talented young Oxford graduates, his "Kindergarten", with whom he was immediately to begin the task of reconstruction in the colonies, while Kitchener had the unenviable task of trying to complete the military subjection. Milner intended to drive the

Boers out of the centre of the country towards the periphery and to fill the central area with new British citizens and Boers who had surrendered, all to be protected by the South African Constabulary. British immigrants were to be encouraged to come to the new colonies in sufficient numbers to outweigh the Afrikaner population, and to take the lead in agricultural development. The potentially richer Transvaal with its gold mines would have to subsidise the Orange River Colony.

The arrival of Milner in Johannesburg coincided with the peace conferences being held between Kitchener and Botha. On 28 February, 1901 the two commanders had an amicable meeting at Middelburg and each put forward his conditions for the termination of the war. Kitchener was prepared to accept a negotiated peace; Botha acted by authority of his government, and, apart from the military discussions, he made use of the opportunity to protest against the treatment of the Boer women and children, and the widespread use of Bantu spies and scouts against the Boers.

The final British peace proposals were formulated by Chamberlain after he had consulted Milner and they were couched in such terms that, on 16 March Botha rejected them in the first instance because the whole settlement depended on a recognition of the annexations, and secondly because no provision was made for an amnesty for rebels.

The bitter year of 1901

The failure of the peace negotiations, largely due to Milner, was clearly a disappointment to Kitchener; time would show that after a further £100,000,000 had been spent, during the ensuing fourteen months of fighting and suffering, the terms of the final peace settlement agreed upon, did not differ radically from those offered at Middelburg.

French's futile drive was still in progress during the Middelburg negotiations; he did prevent Botha from invading Natal, but did not achieve much more than that. In April, however, Lieutenant-General Sir Bindon Blood, who had been specially brought from India because of his experience of war in mountainous terrain, was so successful in the Lydenburg district that the Transvaal government had to leave its seat at Tautesberg and join Botha near Ermelo. At the same time Beyers was pushed back northwards from Warmbaths by Brigadier-General H. C. O. Plumer who occupied Pietersburg on 8 April, 1901. Included in Plumer's force were Australian troops, who acquired an unsavoury reputation as a result of their subsequent actions in the Northern Bushveld. In the second winter of the war Kitchener began to hit hard with his 230,000 troops, one-third of whom were mounted. More use was also made of Bantu and renegade "handsuppers" who served the British as drivers, spies and, especially as scouts with units such as Colonel J. W. Colenbrander's "Kitchener's Fighting Scouts" in the Bushveld, and "Steinacker's Horse" in the Lowveld which became notorious from the Boer point of view.

The darkest shadow in the middle of 1901 was the high mortality rate among the women and children in the concentration camps. The terrain upon which the camps were built was badly chosen and too many people had been assembled in too short a time without sufficient preparation. The administrative personnel and medical services were inadequate, the rations were unsatisfactory, there were dishonest contractors, and inefficient officials were unable to cope with the epidemic of measles and pneumonia which broke out among the 80,000 Whites who were living under canvas in May, 1901. By June the death toll among the children had risen to 120 per thousand.

In Britain the condemnatory report which Emily Hobhouse, founder of the South African Women and Children's Distress Fund, had written after a five month visit to the camps, had been released. It caused a political sensation; in the House of Commons Campbell-Bannerman described the British manner of waging war on civilians as "methods of barbarism" and the great supporter of the Boer cause, William T. Stead, used this phrase in a widely distributed, vitriolic pamphlet which focussed attention on the misery caused by the destruction of farms and the concentrations camps.

Even Milner, who had been on leave in England since May, 1901, during which time he was raised to the peerage, had to admit that the camps were a mistake, in principle as well as in practice. Measures were taken to relieve the anguish of the Boer women and children, but only in February, 1902 was the appalling death rate curbed – even so, more than 26,000 men, women and children had died in the camps by the end of the war. On the Highveld, the itinerant Transvaal government established its headquarters on the farm De Emigratie near Ermelo, its sixteenth seat of government. Here, early in May, the Transvaal leaders once again experienced doubts about the wisdom of continuing the war, but President Steyn strongly opposed any proposal to make peace and the resounding victories gained by Kemp at Vlakfontein on 30 May and by General Chris H. Muller at Wilmansrust, added weight to his arguments. Shortly thereafter the Boers obtained permission from Kitchener to send a cable to President Kruger to consult him on the advisability of continuing the struggle. Kruger's reply exhorted them to stand fast.

On 22 June, 1901 the two Boer governments came to a decision at Waterval near Standerton that the war would be actively continued. Another attempt would be made to invade the Cape Colony to relieve the pressure on the Transvaal and the Free State where British drives had been increasing in intensity and, since May, the columns, guided by "handsuppers", had started attacking at night.

While Smuts enthusiastically made preparations in the Gatsrand for his invasion of the Cape Colony and thereafter trekked southwards eluding the British columns in the Free State, Kitchener, with the approval of Milner and Chamberlain, issued a proclamation on 7 August, 1901 which the Boers later called the "paper bomb". The burghers in the field were informed that their resistance was now so insignificant that they could no longer be regarded as conducting regular warfare; they were therefore given until 15 September, 1901 to surrender. Those who did not do so would be punished; if their leaders and officers were captured by the British they would be banished permanently from the country and their property would be sold to pay for the care of their wives and children.

The proclamation, as was the case with the entire British military policy since the annexation of the two republics, failed to take into account the incalculable strength of Boer morale. This threatening proclamation was nowhere regarded in a serious light, probably not even by Kitchener himself. It had the effect instead of leading to a sudden increase in the activities of the commandos at a time when British forces in all the fighting areas were carrying out merciless "drives" between the growing line of blockhouses against Kemp at Zwartruggens, or against Chris Muller and Ben Viljoen in the Eastern Transvaal, against Beyers in the Pietersburg district, against Botha at Ermelo and everywhere in the devastated Eastern Free State, where there were more blockhouses than in any other theatre of war.

Smuts crossed the Orange River on 3 September near Zastron with a few hundred men while General George Brand engaged the British columns which garrisoned the forts between Bloemfontein and Thaba Nchu. The commandos, comprising about 1,500 men in all, which had been operating in the Cape Colony for several months were encouraged anew by the arrival of Smuts. Commandant Lotter who had been captured shortly before was shot on 11 October. On the same day Gideon Scheepers was captured and on 18 January 1902 was shot at Graaff-Reinet, on account of murders allegedly committed by his commando.

Smuts and his commando played an heroic role in the campaign in the Cape Colony; he and his followers led a precarious existence fighting when it suited them and fleeing from the oncoming British columns under French. They trekked first in the direction of Tarkastad and Grahamstown then past Graaff-Reinet in a north-westerly direction until they reached the district of Calvinia where Manie Maritz had been active for some time.

The arrival of Smuts in the Cape resulted in the proclamation of martial law throughout the Cape Colony including the ports on 9 October 1901. It was also announced that the British army command now had to provide troops for a large new field of activities and had to build more blockhouses. Smuts assisted by four generals, Manie Maritz, Wynand Malan, Jaap van Deventer and Hendrik Lategan, was by the end of the war in command of about 2,600 men in the Cape and, to all intents and purposes the Boers were in full control of the whole North-Western Cape. For the remainder of the war Smuts's forces were never in any danger of defeat.

At the same time as Smuts's invasion of the Cape Botha evaded his pursuers at Ermelo and entered Natal and central Zululand. Despite the close watch kept on his movements by the columns commanded by Lyttelton, Bruce Hamilton, Clements and Walter Kitchener, Botha attacked British military installations during the whole of September, being involved in actions at Blood River Poort (17 September) and at the Mount Prospect and Itala forts (23-26 September). After a difficult return journey in which he was ceaselessly harassed by British columns, Botha arrived at Ermelo on 11 October, in time to offer Ben Viljoen some respite from Lieutenant-Colonel G. E. Benson's raids and night attacks. In a brilliantly conceived action near Bakenlaagte, west of Bethal, on 30 October, 1901, Botha destroyed the columns of Benson, who was killed in the battle.

Botha, after the battle of Bakenlaagte, was deeply concerned about the critical conditions prevailing on the Highveld, and he considered initiating negotiations again. Once more, however, Steyn and De Wet tactfully deterred him and Botha decided to continue the struggle: Bruce Hamilton's force of 1,500 men had started a "drive" which was aimed at capturing Botha and the Transvaal government and from 15 November the Transvaal commandant-general opposed and evaded these columns in a series of masterly manoeuvres. These tactics which entailed fighting at times and flight at others, exhausted Botha's force, however, particularly as he had to continue to apply them until March, 1902, when the first peace talks finally brought relief.

In the meantime, on 30 September, De la Rey gained an important victory at Moedwil, in the Western Transvaal when his force, supported by that of Kemp attacked the column commanded by Kekewich, west of Rustenburg. A characteristic of this battle, as of that of Bakenlaagte a month later, was that the Boers fearlessly charged across open country, tactics which they had not previously employed. A few weeks later, on 24 October, De la Rey cut off one of Methuen's columns on the way to Zeerust and the "Lion of the Western Transvaal" was still deeply involved in this struggle against Methuen when De Wet after months of inactivity entered the fray once again.

With fourteen British columns deployed about him, like the spokes of a wheel, De Wet moved into action in the vicinity of Reitz. But owing to the tremendous strength of the force aligned against him, his movements were restricted to the triangle demarcated by Lindley, Reitz and Bethlehem. With his faithful generals, Michiel Prinsloo and Wessel Wessels, he, nevertheless kept the columns of Rundle and Elliott fully occupied and on Christmas morning 1901 dealt a spectacular blow at Groenkop (Tweefontein) by storming the Yeomanry camp before sunrise and overwhelming it. This was De Wet's last opportunity to initiate an attack of this nature, however, for in the last months of the war, he was involved in a series of desperate struggles and manoeuvres between the blockhouse lines, to prevent the British trap closing on him.

The British war machine was now in top gear, but there were still no signs of the Boer resistance cracking. Milner, in Johannesburg, was nevertheless already attempting to implement his policy of reconstruction: energetic attempts were being made to increase the production of the gold mines, the former inhabitants of the city were being allowed to return to their homes, the stock exchange was re-opened, a *modus vivendi* was concluded with the authorities in Portuguese East Africa to recruit labour for mines from that quarter. In addition, he and his efficient staff were hard at work on schemes for future land settlement and repatriation. In the midst of this extremely full programme,

314

Milner had to find the time to end the tragedy of the concentration camps, which, as he said, had been "a sad fiasco". By November, 1901 this matter demanded his full attention.

The horror and indignation about the camps was still increasing, both on the Continent, and in Britain itself where the apalling conditions in the camps were being used as a dangerous political weapon against Kitchener's continuation of the war. Up to October the number of inmates in the forty camps increased still further to 118,000 Whites and 43,000 non-Whites. The death rate was still 344 per thousand among the Whites; at one stage in the Kroonstad camp the death rate among children was reckoned to be 878 per thousand.

From December no new inhabitants were brought into the camps, and by means of stringent measures, in which even Chamberlain became involved, the death rate was brought down to a normal figure by February, 1902. The total loss of life in the concentration camps, including adult male deaths, was eventually 27,927, of whom 4,177 were adult women and 22,074 were children under 16 years of age.

The last months of the war

Kitchener's military task had become overwhelming. The accepted principles of European warfare had long since proved futile in South African conditions; the tactics and strategy presented in the textbooks had become meaningless early in the war already. All that remained was to crush the commandos by using overwhelming military force, and to use mounted troops who could outride the Boers and pin them down; artillery, it had become apparent, only hampered the mobility of the columns.

It was well known that Kitchener liked to handle everything himself on the highest level from Pretoria. At the beginning of December, 1901, however, he accepted the dynamic Lieutenant-General Sir Ian Hamilton as his chief-of-staff. Hamilton was to play a decisive role in the last five months of the war in the massive "drives" which were used against the desperate Boers making a last stand.

At this late stage of the war Kitchener tried a new measure which was to rouse great ill-feeling among Afrikaners, and bitterness which persisted long after the war. On 7 December, 1901 a corps of "National Scouts" was created which incorporated Boers who were prepared to act as paid spies and scouts, in order, as they claimed, quickly to end a hopeless struggle. About 1,000 of them were active in the Transvaal by May, 1902, and 480 in the Free State; among this last group there were also two former Boer generals.

Early in January, 1902 De Wet was preparing between Heilbron and Reitz to break out from the ring of British columns being thrown around him. The British generals in the meantime were beginning to learn from experience that there had been too many loopholes in their lines in the past and this time were sweeping the area with a solid wall of steel between the lines of blockhouses from Heilbron to Vrede in the north and through Kroonstad – Bethlehem –

Harrismith in the south, right up to the railway between Kroonstad and Wol-wehoek. But even when faced by the 9,000 men of Elliott, Rawlinson, Byng and Rimington advancing virtually with hands joined together, De Wet managed to slip through the net on 8 February and waited at Elandskop for the next "hunt" which promised to be even more thorough.

De Wet was pushed eastwards by 30,000 men employed in two simultaneous moves. Accompanied by the Free State government he effected his last escape of the war by slipping past the blockhouses at Langverwacht, to the south of Vrede, trekking through Commando Drift and on 17 March reached De la Rey's laager at Witpoort in the Lichtenburg district.

There he left President Steyn for medical treatment before returning to the Boshoff district where news of the peace negotiations awaited him.

During the first months of 1902 De la Rey with undiminished zeal continued his struggle against the innumerable British columns in the Western Transvaal. At Ysterspruit on 25 February he, with Kemp, Celliers and Liebenberg, captured an enormous convoy near Klerksdorp, and on 7 March, 1902 at Tweebosch, east of the Harts River, he defeated and captured Methuen, who was wounded in the battle. De la Rey's last success was at Boschbult on 31 March when he attacked the column commanded by Cookson. While De la Rey was attending the first peace negotiations during April, General Jan Kemp engaged Ian Hamilton at Roodewal on the Harts River on 11 April. During this battle the Boers made their most heroic charge of the war, and the gallant Comman-dant Ferdinand Potgieter of Wolmaransstad was killed.

From January to April, 1902 the British forces on the Highveld under Bruce Hamilton were conducting numerous "drives" in which night raids played an important part. The crop of prisoners, however, was very small, but on 25 January, 1902 General Ben Viljoen was captured. The Transvaal government was forced to remain on the move, the districts of Ermelo, Bethal and Carolina were practically lost to the Boers, and Botha had eventually to retreat into the mountains at Vryheid. In the face of all odds the commandos at Lydenburg of Generals P. Viljoen, J. Prinsloo, Chris Muller and of Beyers in the north at Louis Trichardt, remained intact to the end of the war while in far-off Namaqualand, Maritz and Smuts occupied the town of Springbok and in April were besieging O'Kiep when the first reports of peace negotiations reached them.

The road to peace

On 25 January, 1902 the Prime Minister of the Netherlands, Dr. Abraham Kuyper, a statesman of note, a scholar and a friend of the Boers for many years, offered the friendly mediation of his government to the British government in an attempt to bring about peace in South Africa. The offer was made without the knowledge of Dr. Leyds, who considered it to be inadvisable at that stage as he judged it to have a detrimental psychological effect on the Boer cause.

The British government turned down the offer of mediation and expressed the opinion that peace negotiations could only be held in South Africa between Kitchener and the Boer leaders. However, the correspondence with Dr. Kuyper was referred to Kitchener who grasped the opportunity of sending it to the Transvaal government in the field, near Balmoral, its sixty-second seat since the battle of Dalmanutha. Without prior discussion with the Free State government, General Schalk Burger, Acting President of the South African Republic, reported to Kitchener that he was prepared to negotiate for peace and asked for permission to make contact with President Steyn. Permission was granted and President Steyn on 27 March, was faced with a *fait accompli* when he received the report that the Transvaal government was on its way to consult him.

From 9 to 11 April, 1902 the two governments conferred at Klerksdorp and it was immediately apparent that opinion was divided on the matter of opening peace negotiations with the British. After a detailed report on the state of the commandos had been made, there was a discussion which revealed that particularly Steyn, Hertzog, De Wet and De la Rey were opposed to peace discussions; nevertheless the meeting decided that discussions with Kitchener should be held in Pretoria. A five-point proposal was drafted in which the first point was that the British annexation of the republics would not be recognized and that they should retain their independence.

While the war continued at a cost of £1,000,000 per week to the British treasury the Boers discussed peace terms in Pretoria, first with Kitchener alone and then with Kitchener and Milner together. The talks from 12 to 17 April were supplemented by cablegrams to and from the British government, and Milner, still demanding the total surrender of the Boers, was given the opportunity of expressing his opinion to the extent that the British government's answer was in effect Milner's.

The British conditions were actually the same as those proposed to Botha by the British government on 7 March, 1901 at Middelburg, with whatever amendments might be agreed on after negotiations with Milner and Kitchener. These proposals were to be conveyed to the burghers in the field who would then choose delegates, thirty from each republic, who were to meet at Vereeniging on 15 May, 1902 to discuss the proposals. Until 15 May the war was to continue but a safe conduct would be given to members of the government who wished to visit their commandos to inform them about what had been decided.

The representatives of the people, as chosen by the commandos, included all the prominent officers, and General J. C. Smuts was summoned from Namaqualand. President Steyn arrived at Vereeniging sick and half paralysed. He was consulted but only attended a few meetings before being taken away to Krugersdorp on 29 May for medical treatment. It was well-known that President Steyn, who had been the personification of Boer perseverance and resistance in the darkest hours of the war, was determined never to sign any document which sacrificed the independence of his state.

The discussions, in dramatic circumstances, took place in a tent at Vereeniging under the chairmanship of General C. F. Beyers and opinion again proved divided as to whether the circumstances in the republics justified terminating hostilities, if this should entail the loss of independence.

On 17 May a commission consisting of five members, Botha, De la Rey, Smuts, De Wet and Hertzog, was elected to negotiate in Pretoria according to the dictates of their conscience and to report back to the meeting. At these negotiations, from 19 to 28 May, Smuts and Hertzog played the most important part on the Boer side as lawyers as well as in drafting the basis of agreement or "acts of peace".

On the British side Milner constantly opposed the soldier Kitchener over possible concessions and insisted on promising or granting as little as possible in the peace agreement. The agreement which the meeting drafted was referred to London and the text, as amended by Chamberlain, was received on 27 May with the condition that the delegates at Vereeniging had to vote merely "yes" or "no" before 31 May. It contained the following ten clauses:

(1) all burghers to lay down their arms and recognise the British monarch as their lawful sovereign;

(2) all burghers and prisoners-of-war outside the borders of the Free State and the Transvaal to be repatriated if they became British subjects;

(3) personal freedom and retention of their property guaranteed to all burghers and repatriates who might return or surrender;

(4) an amnesty to be granted for war damage caused by the Boers in good faith, except for specific exceptions to be mentioned by the British to the Boer generals;

(5) Dutch would be taught in the Free State and the Transvaal schools as a subject if parents wished: it would be used in courts of law if necessary for the effective execution of the law;

(6) licensed arms which were necessary for purposes of protection might be retained;

(7) military administration would be replaced by civil administration; and representative government as soon as possible, which would lead to ultimate self-government, to be granted as soon as circumstances permitted;

(8) the question of granting the franchise to natives would not be settled before the introduction of representative government;

(9) there would be no special tax levied on fixed property which had been owned in the former republics to meet the costs of the war;

(10) in each district a commission would be appointed on which the inhabitants would be represented, to aid the repatriated and the needy, out of a fund of £3,000,000, which the British government would make available, in addition to certain grants and loans, which would be used to meet the claims of certain individuals against the governments of the former republics.

From 29 May the drama at Vereeniging moved to a climax. In the midst of rising tension the delegates had to choose between continuing the war, accepting the British conditions or surrendering unconditionally. The views expressed in the debate which lasted for three days, showed a growing tendency to support

318

the Transvaal leaders' attitude that the continued existence of the Boer nation depended on the cessation of hostilities, even at the cost of surrendering independence.

De la Rey already accepted this on the tacit belief that such a peace treaty implied the right to resume one day the fight for freedom; De Wet, now acting president of the Free State in the absence of Steyn, was adamant, however. He even displayed some hostility towards the advocates of peace. At last, on 31 May even De Wet accepted the terms, but at his suggestion the meeting entrusted to Smuts and Hertzog the drafting of a resolution in which the decision of the meeting to accept the British proposals was expressed in poignant words and in the form of a severe indictment against British policy in South Africa which had brought matters to this bitter end.

When the vote was taken in the conference tent 54 delegates voted in favour of the proposal and six against it. The governments and their advisers, including General Smuts, left for Pretoria. The formal signing of the peace treaty which in future was to be known as the Treaty of Vereeniging, took place in Kitchener's headquarters in Melrose House in Jacob Maré Street at 11 o'clock on the evening of 31 May, 1902 with Kitchener and Milner representing the British government, while S. W. Burger, F. W. Reitz, Louis Botha, J. H. de la Rey, L. J. Meyer and J. C. Krogh represented the South African Republic, and C. R. de Wet, J. B. M. Hertzog, W. J. C. Brebner and C. H. Olivier represented the Orange Free State.

Early in June, the British supervised the laying down of arms by the commandos. Before the end of 1902 most of the surviving women and children had left the camps and most of the prisoners-of-war from overseas had returned to their devastated homeland.

Apart from the immeasurable human suffering, hardship and damage to property and possessions, it had cost the British treasury £191,000,000 to destroy the independence of the two Boer republics. Among the approximately half-a-million persons who participated on the British side, there were 97,477 casualties of whom 7,091 were killed or died of wounds, and 19,143 were wounded; the rest suffered from illnesses, mostly dysentery.

On the Boer side 3,990 burghers were killed and 1,081 died of disease or accident in the field. Boer statistics of wounded burghers were not kept. However, the civilian death rate and that of prisoners-of-war must be added to the Boer losses which brings the total figure up to 34,116. On closer examination of the Boer death rate 12% would appear to have died in battle, 6% died on commando from other causes, 17% were adults in the camps and 65% were children under the age of 16 years.

In the wake of the war Milner was to try to rehabilitate the devastated former republics as crown colonies under the framework of an enlarged British South Africa. Although conquered, the Boers and their fellow Afrikaners of the Cape would remain a political and cultural force to be reckoned with, for they had been purified by fire in the years of struggle.

16. Reconstruction and Unification, 1902-1910

'Milnerism' and reconstruction

The question of the duality of political power in South Africa had apparently been settled by the Anglo-Boer War. The Treaty of Vereeniging had established British supremacy in unequivocal terms and for the first time since 1852 there were no White states in South Africa which were not under the British Crown. From the imperial point of view, however, the war was merely the prelude to the task of consolidating British supremacy in southern Africa: the war had not decided that South Africa would remain a permanent part of the British Empire, it had only made it possible.[1]

Alfred, Lord Milner, the High Commissioner for South Africa and the Governor of the Transvaal and the Orange River Colony, who had played a prominent role in the events leading up to war, was chiefly responsible for framing and implementing British policy in South Africa from the war up to April, 1905. Milner, who called himself "an Imperialist out and out" and a "British Race Patriot", wished to weld South Africa into a permanent and efficient link in the imperial chain. He had already begun to formulate his *modus operandi* shortly after the outbreak of war and in December, 1900, he explained his programme in a comprehensive memorandum. The British population in South Africa was to be increased by immigration until the majority of the White inhabitants of the country were of British stock. An anglicizing educational policy was to be introduced. "Dutch should only be used to teach English, and English to teach everything else. Language is important, but the tone and spirit of the teaching conveyed in it is even more important. . . . I attach especial importance to school history books".[2] The former republics should remain crown colonies until the immigration and anglicizing policies had made British rule secure, and then they would be federated with the other southern African states to form a self-governing British dominion. Milner's views were supported – in most respects – by Joseph Chamberlain and had the unqualified support of Chamberlain's successor at the Colonial Office, Alfred Lyttelton. Milner's programme has justifiably been compared to the methods which Lord Durham had sixty years before unsuccessfully employed in his attempts to eliminate local French nationalism from the Canadian scene.

The magnitude of Milner's task was increased by the nature of the Anglo-Boer War. In 1899 he had hoped that the war which was to destroy Afrikaner

---

1. Milner was well aware of this. See C. Headlam (ed.): *The Milner Papers* (London, 1933), II, p. 550.
2. *The Milner Papers*, II, p. 243.

nationalism would be a short, sharp struggle. This war actually lasted for more than thirty-one months. During the first phase of the war, as Winston Churchill put it, blood flowed freely but from a healthy wound; in the second phase the blood flowed sluggishly from a festering wound. Milner had not approved of farm burning or of concentration camps, but he was powerless to alter those policies as long as Roberts and subsequently Kitchener justified their actions on the grounds of military expediency. From February, 1901, Milner attempted to put into practice what he called "reconstruction under arms" and although he made some progress he was constantly being hampered by military operations, so that the real work of reconstruction could only begin after the Treaty of Vereeniging had been signed.

Within three weeks of the signing of the peace treaty, all the Boer commandos had laid down their arms, Kitchener was able to leave the country and Letters Patent were issued to establish crown colony government in the former republics. In each colony all power was vested in the Governor, the Lieutenant-Governor and the heads of the main departments. The British Crown Colony of the Transvaal was smaller than the South African Republic had been. Towards the end of the war the Natal ministry, under Sir Albert Hime, pressed for the annexation to Natal of 10,971 square miles of territory from the Transvaal and 6,418 square miles from the Orange Free State. In the end Natal obtained between 7,000 and 8,000 square miles of territory in the Utrecht and Vryheid districts, but no Free State territory, and in return Natal had to accept responsibility for £700,000 of the Transvaal war debt.

The Treaty of Vereeniging had not provided for the treatment of the colonial rebels and it was left to the colonial governments to deal with them. In the Cape only office-bearers received prison sentences; the rank and file were disenfranchised for five years.

Although Milner regarded the Transvaal as the key to the Southern African problem, he was also concerned lest the Cape Colony become the centre of future Afrikaner aspirations and the Cape parliament should obstruct his aims. But his suggestion, supported by forty-two Progressive members of the Cape parliament, that the Cape constitution be suspended so that the Cape could revert to crown colony rule was rejected by the British Cabinet. In February, 1904, however, Jameson's Progressives obtained a majority of five in the Cape Assembly, mainly owing to the disenfranchisement of 10,500 Afrikaners, and Milner was assured, temporarily at any rate, of the support of the Cape government.

Milner's first task was to repair the ravages of war in the conquered territories. He received able assistance from the coterie of dedicated young men – Patrick Duncan, Philip Kerr, Geoffrey Robinson, Lionel Curtis, Robert Brand, Richard Feetham and John Buchan, were some of them – whom he had brought to South Africa from Oxford, and who came to be known as the "Kindergarten".

The war had widely dispersed the former inhabitants of the Transvaal and the Orange River Colony and the problems of repatriation and resettlement were enormous. About 31,000 Boer prisoners of war, 24,000 of them in overseas camps, 116,500 Boer civilians[3] and 100,000 Bantu in the concentration camps, and 50,000 Uitlanders, had to be resettled in the war-devastated areas where at least 30,000 farm houses had been destroyed and lands plundered of livestock and crops. By March, 1903, this vast repatriation exercise had been completed; nearly all the Boers had been returned to the former republics and provided with the basic necessities to begin farming again. Article Ten of the Treaty of Vereeniging had stipulated that the sum of £3,000,000 would be available for distribution as free grants to those who were unable to fend for themselves as a result of the war. Actually far more than £3,000,000 was provided for the Boers and non-interest bearing loans were also made available; in addition £2,000,000 was paid out to compensate British subjects, neutral foreign subjects, and Bantu for war losses. In all, the cost of repatriation and resettlement amounted to £16,500,000 and despite delays and inevitable mistakes the programme was on the whole well carried out.

In December 1902 Chamberlain came to South Africa for discussions with Milner. It was decided that a guaranteed loan of £35,000,000 was to be raised by the Transvaal and the Orange River Colony to nationalize the railway systems of the two colonies, to construct new railways, and public works and to purchase land for new settlers. The difficulties of apportioning this sum between the two colonies led to the creation of the Inter-Colonial Council, which acted in an advisory capacity to Milner in matters of common interest to the two Colonies. The Inter-Colonial Council amalgamated the railway systems of the Transvaal and the Orange River Colony to form the Central South African Railways. In March, 1903, Milner convened a conference of all the British colonies and protectorates south of the Zambesi. This conference established a South African Customs Union which abolished all internal tariff barriers and granted an imperial preference to Britain as well as to British possessions which were prepared to concede reciprocal concessions. Milner's administration encouraged scientific farming, a forestry department was formed, an attempt was made to solve the country's irrigation problems and the Rand Water Board was established. New roads and railways were built; many public buildings in the style of Herbert Baker were erected. Lionel Curtis was busy establishing self-governing municipalities.

Despite these very real administrative achievements, prosperity was slow in coming to southern Africa, partly owing to drought, but mainly because the gold mines had not increased their production so that they could provide the "overspill" to boost the entire South African economy. The main factor retarding gold production was the shortage of unskilled labour; in November, 1903 a commission reported that there was a shortage of 129,364 unskilled workers in the gold mining industry. The *modus vivendi*, which Milner had

3. The estimates of the number of Boer inmates in the concentration camps at the conclusion of the war vary from 155,000 (*Milner Papers*, II, p. 370) to 110,000 (*The Times History of the War in South Africa*, VI, p. 43). I have used the figure quoted in the official British history of the war. (M. H. Grant: *History of the War in South Africa 1899 – 1902* (London, 1910), IV, Appendix 12.

concluded with the Portuguese authorities in December, 1901, whereby the mines were permitted to recruit workers in Mozambique in return for favourable rates on the Delagoa Bay railway line, had not proved as effective as had been hoped, for after the war Milner discovered that the agreement was only valid for approximately one-third of Mozambique. The reluctance of non-Whites to come to the mines may also have been evidence of their disillusionment with the new regime, for although some improvements were effected, British rule did not bring any marked social and economic reforms. A factor which would appear to have been of greater significance, however, was that in the immediate post-war period the reconstruction of the new colonies created a demand and opportunities for non-White workers in other spheres, particularly in railway work and road building.[4] An experiment in using white unskilled labour, initiated by F. H. P. Creswell, the manager of the Village Deep Mine, was not successful, nor was Milner's attempt to recruit mineworkers in other parts of Africa and in India. The mines and Milner had to look elsewhere for labour. In February, 1904, the Colonial Office sanctioned the Labour Importation Ordinance which had been passed by the Transvaal Legislative Council, and which provided for the importation of indentured Chinese labourers. In all, 62,200 Chinese labourers came to the Transvaal, and the economic object was achieved, for the value of gold production rose from £12,628,057 in 1903 to £27,400,992 in 1907. Without Chinese labour some mines would probably have had to close down completely, or at best would have had to wait until the Bantu labourers returned to the mines in sufficient numbers, as they eventually did. The introduction of Chinese labour into South Africa caused a vast political agitation. In Britain the position of the Unionists was considerably weakened and Milner was subjected to sharp criticism from the Liberals. In the Transvaal this matter caused dissension among the British and was one of the factors which led to the Boers once more becoming politically organized. The first Chinese left the Transvaal in 1907, the last in 1910.

By 1905 Milner's policy of material reconstruction was beginning to bear fruit, but this success must be viewed against the background of the general progress of his political objectives. He had little success in attracting British settlers to South Africa and the 1904 census revealed that his aim of achieving a permanent preponderance of British was unlikely to be realised. Nor was he very successful with his anglicizing educational policy. E. B. Sargant, who had been appointed Director of Education in the Transvaal and the Orange River Colony in January, 1901, had established schools in the towns and concentration camps and zealous attempts had been made to carry out Milner's instructions. After the war the Education Ordinance of 1903 had stipulated that English was to be the sole medium of instruction in all state schools and that Dutch was to be taught only as a subject. The rejection of the Boer contention that Article Five of the Vereeniging Treaty meant that Dutch could be used as

4. Cf. D. J. Denoon: "The Transvaal Labour Crisis, 1901 – 1906" in *The Journal of African History*, Vol. VIII, No. 3, 1967, pp. 481 – 494.

the medium of instruction, resulted in the Dutch Reformed Churches establishing the C.N.O. (*Christelike Nasionale Onderwys*) schools. These schools, largely
financed by funds from the Netherlands, preserved the Dutch language and
stimulated Afrikaner nationalism. The measure of Milner's distrust of Afrikaners, and also the measure of the failure of his policy, was his introduction of
an espionage service and his use of the South African Constabulary as a virtual
army of occupation after the war.

Milner abolished the harsher provisions of the pass laws, and improved the
working and living conditions of non-White mineworkers. He was also
responsible for the appointment of the South African Native Affairs Commission under Sir Godfrey Lagden in 1903. In 1905 the Commission's Report,
recommended, *inter alia*, the extension of individual Bantu land titles in certain
specified areas and the setting up of Bantu constituencies in each colony. This
was the first attempt to consider the Native question from the point of view of
South Africa as a whole. Despite such attempts to improve the conditions of the
non-Whites, Milner hesitated to take a stand on the non-White question far to
the left of local opinion, and his policy towards the Indians in the Transvaal did
not differ radically from the old republican policy. In May, 1903, he explained
why, in his opinion, White political supremacy should prevail. "One of the
strongest arguments why the White man must rule is because that is the only
possible means of raising the black man, not to our level of civilization – which
it is doubtful whether he would ever attain – but to a much higher level than
that which he at present occupies".[5]

In April, 1905, Milner left South Africa. He was succeeded by Lord Selborne.
Milner's administration had been honest and efficient and his material reconstruction had been an essential prologue to the unification movement. It is,
nevertheless, to be doubted whether he was the right man for the task; his past
record made it impossible for Afrikaners to accept him and his doctrinaire
approach to the South African problem merely complicated it. Few modern
historians would dispute Professor L. M. Thompson's assessment: "On
balance . . . there can be little doubt that Lord Milner and the Unionist Government wrought harm in South Africa. Encouraging unattainable aspirations
among British South Africans, increasing anglophobia amongst Afrikaners and
doing little to improve the prospects of the non-Whites they made it immeasur-
ably more difficult for the people of South Africa to establish for themselves a
stable and humane society".[6]

The Afrikaner revival and the reaction against imperialism

At Vereeniging Milner had been surprised to find that Boer discipline and
organization had not cracked under stress of the war. Events after the war were
to emphasize the resilience of Afrikanerdom. Despite the war's heavy death

5. *Milner Papers*, II, p. 467.
6. L. M. Thompson: *The Unification of South Africa 1902 – 1910* (Oxford, 1960), pp. 16 – 17.

toll and material devastation, and the internal dissensions among Transvaalers, Free Staters and colonial rebels and between "bitter-enders" on the one hand and "hands-uppers" and National Scouts on the other, Afrikaner nationalism had not been broken by the war.

In August, 1902, Botha, De la Rey and De Wet went to Europe to attempt to ameliorate the peace terms and to raise funds for Boer widows and orphans. The British government, however, was not prepared to modify the Vereeniging terms and they were only able to raise the disappointingly small sum of less than £125,000.

Under crown colony rule the Boers in the conquered territories were politically impotent. Their first reaction to "Milnerism" therefore took the form of a cultural revival; the desire to establish and develop their own language was a vital aspect of the Afrikaners' struggle to maintain their identity. The re-establishment in 1903 of the Taalbond in the Cape by J. H. Hofmeyr, the most influential member of the Afrikaner Bond, and the views expressed in their respective northern newspapers by Gustav Preller and Eugene Marais launched the second language movement. Although the movement was weakened by the reluctance of certain Afrikaners to countenance the Dutch language being superseded by Afrikaans in South Africa, the poetry of Eugene Marais, Louis Leipoldt, Totius (J. D. du Toit) and Jan Celliers not only helped to establish the claims of Afrikaans as a literary language, but also heightened Afrikaner national consciousness.

Soon there was also a political revival among the Afrikaners. In February, 1903, Milner decided to reconstitute the Transvaal Legislative Council, which had hitherto consisted entirely of officials, by nominating fourteen local citizens. Botha, Smuts and De la Rey were offered seats on the Council (disparagingly referred to by the Boers as "Milner's debating society"), but they declined, preferring not to be politically compromised in the eyes of their people by being associated with the Milner regime. In their stead nonentities, who certainly did not represent Afrikaner opinion, were nominated. In July, 1903, an Afrikaner meeting at Heidelberg passed resolutions attacking Milner's educational policy, the proposal to import Chinese labourers and Chamberlain's intention of settling a large war debt on the Transvaal. When those resolutions were rejected by Milner and the Colonial Office, the Boers in the Transvaal began to organize themselves politically under the cover of agricultural societies. The resurgence of Afrikaner national feeling was further stimulated by the emotions engendered by the funeral of Paul Kruger in Pretoria on 16 December, 1904. In January, 1905, the first post-war Afrikaner party came into being in the Transvaal when the committee which had been appointed at the Pretoria Congress in May, 1904, completed its work and established *Het Volk* (The People) under the leadership of Louis Botha (Chairman), Schalk Burger, J. H. de la Rey, C. F. Beyers, J. C. Smuts, A. D. W. Wolmarans and Ewald Esselen. In the Orange River Colony there were also signs of a political re-awakening. After meetings at Brandfort in December, 1904, and at Bloemfontein in July, 1905, the *Orangia Unie* was established in

May, 1906, under the leadership of J. B. M. Hertzog, Abraham Fischer and C. R. de Wet. The establishment of these and other parties before self-government was introduced, helped ensure that a fully developed party system would be functioning in the two former republics immediately after the attainment of responsible government.[7]

In July, 1904, the Colonial Secretary, Lyttelton, had announced his intention of introducing a representative constitution in the Transvaal. The so-called Lyttelton Constitution provided for a uni-cameral legislature consisting of between six and nine officials and between thirty and thirty-five elected members; executive power was to remain in the hands of British officials. This constitution was never implemented, however, owing to the declining fortunes of the Unionists. A series of defeats in by-elections caused the Unionist Premier, Balfour, to resign in December, 1905, and in January, 1906, the Liberals under Sir Henry Campbell-Bannerman were returned to power. Campbell-Bannerman believed that the only hope of maintaining British control in South Africa was to grant self-government to the former republics immediately, but some members of his cabinet favoured a more gradual constitutional progress. Smuts, the brains behind *Het Volk*, knew of this hesitation among the Liberals and in December, 1905, went to Britain to urge the British government to grant responsible government without delay to the Transvaal and the Orange River Colony. His mission was successful: the Lyttelton Constitution was revoked and in April, 1906, a committee under the chairmanship of Sir Joseph West Ridgeway was sent to South Africa to investigate the electoral question. Letters Patent were issued promulgating responsible government in the Transvaal in December, 1906, and in the Orange River Colony in June, 1907.

The Transvaal parliament was to consist of an upper house, the Legislative Council, of fifteen members, and a lower house, the Legislative Assembly, of sixty-nine; the Orange River Colony was to have a Legislative Council of eleven and a Legislative Assembly of thirty-eight. In both colonies executive power was to be in the hands of a ministry, responsible to parliament. The first members of the upper house were to be nominated by the Governor, but as vacancies subsequently occurred in this house they would be filled by nominations made by the Governor acting on the advice of the Colonial Cabinet. The lower house was to be elected by all adult male white citizens of the colony. Non-Whites did not receive the vote in either colony. Article Eight of the Vereeniging Treaty[8] prevented the immediate enfranchisement of the Bantu, but there was some difference of opinion as to whether it also necessarily excluded Coloureds and Asiatics from receiving the vote. After Dr. A. Abdurahman, the president of the African Political Organization, had forwarded a petition from Cape Coloureds asking for political rights for Coloureds in the Transvaal, the Liberal government's attitude on this matter was clarified in the Commons

7. See N. G. Garson: " 'Het Volk': The Botha – Smuts Party in the Transvaal, 1904 – 1911", in *The Historical Journal*, Vol. IX, No. 1, 1966, p. 101.

8. Article Eight of the Vereeniging Treaty stated: "The question of granting the franchise to natives will not be decided until after the introduction of self-government".

on 23 July, 1906, by Winston Churchill, Under-Secretary for Colonies: "I believe the precise meaning attached to the word 'native' is native of any country other than a European country".[9] The Liberals feared that they would not obtain the Boers' confidence if the constitutions did not provide for an absolute political colour-bar.

In February, 1907, the general election in the Transvaal resulted in a victory for *Het Volk* and its English-speaking allies, the Nationalists. Botha became Prime Minister and his right-hand man, Smuts, became Colonial Secretary. Even before the grant of self-government, Botha and Smuts had embarked on their policy of conciliation which entailed not only the re-admittance of "hands-uppers" and National Scouts to the Afrikaner fold, but also an attempt to effect a rapprochement between the Afrikaners and the British in South Africa and a full acceptance of the imperial connexion. Their dream of a "Greater South Africa", which would fuse the English and Afrikaner elements, necessarily precluded a separate Afrikaner nationalism. The grant of self-government so soon after the conclusion of the war, which grant was considered by Botha and Smuts to be very magnanimous, strengthened their attitude. To some extent it was an attitude calculated to win constitutional concessions from Britain and, after the grant of self-government, votes from the English-speaking section of the electorate, but Botha and Smuts never deviated from it. Not all Afrikaners in the Transvaal could accept these ideals, but the chief dissident voice, that of C. F. Beyers, was stilled when Botha had him elected as Speaker of the Legislative Assembly. Despite this manoeuvre, Botha in August, 1908, still had cause to complain to the High Commissioner, "that Hollanders, Krugerites and a large section of Predikants were engaged in a desperate intrigue against him and his policy of closer union and conciliation".[10]

In November, 1907, the general election in the Orange River Colony resulted in *Orangia Unie* winning thirty-one seats. Abraham Fischer became Prime Minister, but J. B. M. Hertzog, the Attorney-General and Minister of Education, dominated the cabinet. Even though Fischer's cabinet contained members of both language groups conciliation, as understood by Botha and Smuts, was not the policy of *Orangia Unie*. This was partly owing to the absence of any large English-speaking section in the electorate and partly to the political views of the leaders of the party. The grant of self-government did not evoke the same response from Hertzog as it had from Botha and Smuts. Hertzog considered that since the Treaty of Vereeniging had stipulated that self-government would be granted to the former republics, there was no need for the Boers to feel morally obliged when it was granted. He was also beginning to formulate his own political philosophy which visualized the creation of a white South African nation composed of two separate sections, Afrikaner and British, each maintaining its distinctive culture and identity and co-operating with each other on a basis of equality and mutual respect.

9. Quoted in G. H. L. Le May: *British Supremacy in South Africa 1899 – 1907* (Oxford, 1965), p. 205.
10. Garson, *op. cit.*, p. 117.

The divergence between *Het Volk* and *Orangia Unie* became more apparent after the grant of self-government. Botha's attitude at the Colonial Conference in 1907 and his presentation of the Cullinan diamond to Edward VII in the same year, caused some of his people to accuse him of undue loyalty to Britain. Botha and Smuts played little part in the cultural revival of the Afrikaners and Smuts's education Act of 1907 was criticized by Afrikaners. The act provided for mother-tongue instruction in the early standards, but in and after Standard IV English was to be the sole medium of instruction for all children, except that permission might be granted for not more than two subjects to be taught through the medium of Dutch. Dutch would only be taught as a subject to those children whose parents did not object. Hertzog's education Act of 1908, on the other hand, gave Dutch equality with English. It stated that up to Standard IV instruction would be in the language best understood by the child, and after that all children would be taught at least three subjects through the medium of English and at least three subjects through the medium of Dutch. Hertzog's act caused consternation amongst English-speaking South Africans, while some Afrikaners began to consider that Hertzog rather than Botha should be their leader.

In February, 1908, when J. X. Merriman's South African Party supported by the Afrikaner Bond came into power in the Cape Colony it meant that the governments of three of the four South African colonies depended on the support of Afrikaners. Even in Natal, where the Afrikaners had no prospect of gaining political power, a meeting at Blood River in March, 1906, led to the formation of an Afrikaner association, the *Boerekongres*. Although there were latent schisms in the Afrikaner body politic, there was even less political solidarity among English-speaking South Africans. In the Transvaal 1907 election some English-speaking voters had supported Botha's conciliation policy while others had supported the Progressives led by Sir George Farrar, Sir Percy Fitzpatrick and Drummond Chaplin, and the small Labour Party had won three seats; the opposition party in the Orange River Colony, the Constitutional Party under Sir John Fraser, had the support of most English-speaking voters in that area, but it had fared very badly in the general election; in the Cape Colony English-speaking political support was divided between Merriman's South African Party and Jameson's Unionist (formerly Progressive) Party; in the predominantly English-speaking Natal, political division tended to be founded on personalities rather than on questions of principle. One thing, at any rate, was clear in both Britain and South Africa: the pendulum had swung away from imperialism.

South African problems and the closer union movement

The Anglo-Boer controversy culminating in the war of 1899–1902 had temporarily pushed the vitally important question of the relationship between Whites and non-Whites into the background of South African affairs. Very soon, however, this matter was once more to become the centre of attention.

328

In 1905 the Natal parliament imposed a poll tax of £1 per head on all adult male inhabitants of the Colony, except indentured Indians and married Bantu. The imposition of the tax, coming as it did soon after the census of 1904 which had been regarded with suspicion by tribal Bantu, caused resentment smouldering among the Zulus to erupt into violence. In the early months of 1906 sporadic murders and disturbances in many parts of the Colony led to the proclamation of martial law and the mobilization of the militia. The unrest developed into open rebellion when Bambata, a minor chief of the Greytown district, defied his magistrate and with his followers withdrew across the Tugela to the Nkandhla forest. On 10 June, 1906, he was killed and his men defeated in a battle at Mome Gorge. Altogether some thirty Whites and about 3,000 Zulus were killed in this so-called Bamabata Rebellion, which clearly had been caused not only by the poll tax grievance but also by widespread Zulu discontent at Natal's native policy. Unrest and violence continued after Bambata's death and the Natal government became convinced that Dinuzulu, the head of the Zulu royal house, was behind the disturbances. In December, 1907, Dinuzulu gave himself up and was committed to trial on twenty-three counts of treason before a specially constituted court. Dinuzulu, who was defended by W. P. Schreiner, a former Prime Minister of the Cape Colony, was acquitted on the more serious charges, but was found guilty of harbouring rebels. In March, 1909, he was sentenced to five years imprisonment and a fine of £100. The Colonial government was severely criticized in Britain and South Africa for what ex-President M. T. Steyn called "the hysterical way in which Natal is dealing with the Native question".[11]

The question of relations between Indians and Whites also became prominent after the war. Even before the war Indians from Natal had migrated to the Transvaal and the Republican Volksraad had passed laws denying Asiatics civil and political rights, forbidding them to own fixed property, rendering them liable to registration and confining their residential quarters to special locations. However, on the whole these laws were leniently applied. After the war Indian hopes that these laws would be repealed were dashed, and indeed they found that the laws were being implemented more strictly under the administrations of Milner and Selborne. Meanwhile South African Indians had found their champion in the barrister, M. K. Gandhi, who in September, 1906, was successful in getting the Colonial Secretary, Lord Elgin, to disallow a new registration ordinance passed by the Transvaal Legislative Council. However, one of the first acts of the new Transvaal Parliament was to pass a law which introduced the principle of finger-print registration to control the influx of Indians. The Indians in the Transvaal, inspired by Gandhi's doctrine of *Satyagraha* (the force of non-violence), launched a campaign of passive resistance. Many Indians were imprisoned and although Smuts and Gandhi reached a temporary understanding in January, 1908, the matter was by no means settled.

11. Thompson, *op. cit.*, p. 47.

From the point of view of White South Africans the Zulu troubles in Natal and the Indian problem in the Transvaal, stressed the dangers inherent in the separate states of South Africa having no common non-White policy. Friction between the colonies in the economic sphere also emphasized the disadvantages of disunity. The coastal colonies experienced five lean years between 1903 and 1908. Their two main sources of revenue, customs and railway receipts, decreased rapidly after 1903, largely owing to factors outside the control of the Cape and Natal administrations. After the war there continued to be keen competition between the Cape and Natal ports and Lourenço Marques for the Witwatersrand trade. The British colonies had hoped that the annexation of the Transvaal would lead to their obtaining the lion's share of this traffic. Their expectations were not fulfilled, however, partly owing to the *modus vivendi* of 1901, but largely owing to the geographical fact that Lourenço Marques was the nearest port to the Witwatersrand and also to the fact that 85 per cent of the Johannesburg-Lourenço Marques railway line was controlled by the Central South African Railways. Consequently by 1908 the Lourenço Marques share of the Rand's traffic was 63 per cent, Durban's share was 24 per cent and the share of the Cape ports 13 per cent. After an Intercolonial Conference in February, 1905, Milner tried unsuccessfully to modify the *modus vivendi*. Selborne's attempt to implement the Conference's resolution to unite at least all the through lines was also abortive. A further source of friction between the coastal colonies and the inland colonies was the customs tariff policy which was applied at the ports. It soon became apparent that there was a crucial difference between the high tariff need of the coastal colonies to boost their revenues and the low tariff need of the inland colonies to reduce the cost of living and the working costs of the mines. Natal's threat to withdraw from the Customs Union was followed by an acrimonious Intercolonial Customs and Railway Conference at Pietermaritzburg in March, 1906, and although the differences were temporarily settled, no colony was really satisfied. By 1907 the issue had become further complicated by a rates war between the different railway systems and the statement of the Natal Premier, F. R. Moor, that he had obtained a reduction in the sea freights to Durban. The status quo was maintained with the greatest difficulty, but in July, 1907, the Transvaal government gave notice, with effect from 30 June, 1908, that she intended to withdraw from the Customs Union as it then existed. Clearly the prevalent intercolonial economic arrangements of a Customs Union rather inadequately supported by ephemeral railway agreements were inadequate to the situation. Short of the colonies going their separate economic ways, which would be disastrous for the coastal colonies, the only way out of the dilemma seemed to be political union.

Members of the Kindergarten who had stayed on in South Africa after Milner's departure concluded that unification of the colonies was essential both from imperial and South African points of view. Richard Feetham first expressed this attitude on 4 October, 1906, in a speech to the Fortnightly Club in Johannesburg. Lionel Curtis in the same month resigned from his official appointment to devote all his attention to the closer union movement. After he had toured the four colonies he compiled a draft memorandum which was slightly amended by other members of the Kindergarten and Selborne. It was decided that the memorandum should be issued in the name of the High Commissioner but, to avoid giving the impression that Selborne was interfering in colonial affairs, in November, 1906, Curtis persuaded the Cape Premier, L. S. Jameson, to recommend that the High Commissioner should review the current situation in South Africa; the governments of the other three colonies and Southern Rhodesia agreed. In January, 1907, copies of the memorandum, which was entitled "A Review of the Present Mutual Relations of the British South African Colonies", were sent to the governments of the South African colonies and to Southern Rhodesia. After discussing the historical causes of disunity in South Africa the memorandum stated that closer union was the only solution to the railway and customs problems, that only in a united South Africa could there be a single policy for the non-White and labour questions, and emphasized that South African statesmen should postpone all other matters "until by a great constitutional reform they have secured to her people the means of considering and deciding them as a whole". The advantages for the Empire of unification were not stressed: Selborne's memorandum essentially aimed at underlining the advantages of unification for all White South Africans.

South African statesmen had also been considering the advantages of closer union. Merriman, Smuts and Steyn corresponded with one another at length on this topic.[12] In the Cape, the Bondsman, F. S. Malan, had in August and September, 1906, spoken out in favour of some sort of closer union in a series of articles in *Ons Land*, and translations of these articles subsequently appeared in *The Star*. However, not all South African statesmen were impressed by Selborne's memorandum: Merriman referred to it as "Lord Selborne's windy effusion"[13] and Steyn considered it to be "crude, full of rhetoric and bad history".[14] What Merriman in particular was concerned about was that Selborne might try to push union through from above. "I do not want to see", Merriman wrote to Smuts in January, 1907, "any union hastily patched up with a view of sowing the seeds of Imperialism – that the whole of South Africa may have one neck in order to fit the yoke easier on to it".[15] So it was, then, that Merriman, Smuts and Steyn, although theoretically in favour of unification, did not wish it to be brought about before Afrikaner-supported, anti-imperialist parties had come to power in the colonies; when by February, 1908, this was indeed the case they allowed the unification movement to gather momentum. Kinder-

<hr>

12. Smuts's concern for closer union in South Africa can be seen in the fact that the original statutes of Het Volk of January, 1905, contained a provision empowering the head committee of the organization to call conferences "elsewhere concerning the interests of South Africa". Garson, *op. cit.*, p. 103.

13. W. K. Hancock and J. Van der Poel (eds.): *Selections from the Smuts Papers* (Cambridge, 1966), II, p. 347.

14. Thompson, *op. cit.*, p. 77.

15. *Smuts Papers*, II, p. 313.

garten members were now relegated to the minor, but nevertheless useful, roles of constitutional advisers and public relations officers. Under their guidance Closer Union societies were formed throughout the country and the monthly journal, *The State*, financed by Sir Abe Bailey, became virtually the official organ of the movement.

The Intercolonial Customs Conference, which met in Pretoria from 4 to 9 May, 1908, and in Cape Town on 26 and 27 May, 1908, set in motion the machinery which ultimately brought about unification. The High Commissioner had presided over all customs conferences since the war, but Merriman regarded it as essential that he should be excluded from this one: this principle was accepted by the other governments and Moor, the senior colonial premier, presided over the 1908 conference. Thus was established the important precedent, which was followed by the National Convention, that the imperial factor should play no part in the preliminary formulation of the constitution. The delegates at the Customs Conference, three cabinet ministers from each of the South African colonies, three representatives from Rhodesia and two from Mozambique, unanimously accepted Smuts's six resolutions which read as follows:

(*a*) that the best interests of South Africa could only be secured by an early union, under the British Crown, of the self-governing South African colonies;

(*b*) that at some future date the question of the inclusion of Rhodesia should be considered;

(*c*) that the parliaments of the various colonies should appoint delegates to a National Convention, whose object would be to prepare a draft constitution;

(*d*) that representation at the Convention should be twelve delegates for the Cape, eight for the Transvaal and five each for Natal and the Orange River Colony;

(*e*) that the Convention should publish a draft constitution as soon as possible; and

(*f*) that voting in the Convention should be *per capita* and not by states, and that a chairman, who would have a casting vote, should be elected from the members.

No solution to the economic deadlock was found and with some minor modifications the existing customs convention was extended for another year. When the Conference re-assembled at Cape Town the Natal delegates tried to re-open the question of state representation at the Convention. They had no success but were somewhat consoled by the decision to hold the first session of the National Convention at Durban in October.

Since the Liberals in Britain had hoped that the grant of self-government to the former republics would result in unification, they naturally approved of Smuts's resolutions. They considered that unification would consolidate the imperial tie and that it would ensure the loyalty of South Africa in the event of Britain being involved in a war in Europe. The British government also considered that Louis Botha was the ideal man to lead a united South Africa

332

so it would be desirable for unification to take place while he was still available. To Afrikaners like Steyn and Hertzog bringing all Afrikaners under one government held out the hope of strengthening Afrikaner nationalism. To Botha and Smuts a united South Africa seemed to provide the best opportunity for achieving self-determination within the framework of the Empire and for fully realising the aims of their conciliation policy.

The National Convention and the drafting of a constitution

Both the government and the opposition parties of the four colonies were represented at the National Convention. The Transvaal was represented by Botha, Smuts, S. W. Burger, J. H. de la Rey and H. C. Hull, who were members of *Het Volk*, and Farrar, Fitzpatrick and H. L. Lindsay, who were Progressives. The Orange River Colony was represented by Steyn, Fischer, De Wet and Hertzog, who were members of *Orangia Unie*, and A. Browne, who was a Constitutionalist. The Cape delegates were Sir Henry de Villiers, Chief Justice of the Cape Colony, who was an Independent; Merriman, F. S. Malan, J. W. Sauer, J. H. M. Beck, H. C. van Heerden and G. H. Maasdorp, members of the South African Party; Jameson, T. W. Smartt, E. H. Walton and J. W. Jagger, members of the Unionist Party, and W. E. M. Stanford, who was an Independent. The Natal delegates, F. R. Moor, E. M. Greene, C. J. Smythe, T. Hyslop and W. B. Morcom (replaced by T. Watt in December, 1908), were all either cabinet ministers or had cabinet experience. Three Rhodesian representatives, Sir Lewis Michell and W. H. Milton, representing the Chartered Company, and C. Coghlan, nominated by the elected members of the Rhodesian Legislative Council, attended the Convention as observers without the right to speak or vote. Even before the first meeting it was unanimously agreed that De Villiers would be President and Steyn Vice-President of the Convention. From 12 October to 5 November, 1908, the Convention met in Durban; it resumed its business in Cape Town on 23 November and concluded the Cape Town session on 3 February, 1909; the final session, for considering the amendments proposed by the colonial parliaments, was in Bloemfontein from 3 May to 11 May, 1909.

J. C. Smuts, because of his powers of intellect, his devotion to duty and his assiduous groundwork, was the outstanding delegate of the Convention and to a large extent, the Constitution of the Union of South Africa was his creation. With Smuts to set its tone, the Transvaal delegation, united in purpose and in a commanding position because of their colony's economic strength, was the most efficient delegation. Although all delegates wished to achieve a united South Africa, there were nevertheless formidable obstacles with which they had to contend.

The first matter which had to be settled was whether the constitution would be a unitary or a federal one. In a union the central government dominates all regional authorities and the individual states or provinces virtually lose their identities; in a federation the powers of the central and regional authorities,

333

strictly defined within their respective spheres, are independent of one another and the individual states retain their identities far more than in a union. A federal constitution is necessarily rigid, that is it cannot easily be amended, whereas a unitary constitution can be either rigid or flexible. Merriman stressed the weaknesses of a federal form of government by pointing to the difficulties which had arisen in Australia and attributing the outbreak of the American Civil War to the nature of the United States's constitution. Smuts argued that a rigid federal constitution implied a lack of faith in posterity, that a union could have uniform native and economic policies and that it would avoid the disadvantage of varying judicial interpretations. The Natal delegates, however, favoured a federation because they believed it would enable English-speaking Natal to retain its identity in a predominantly Afrikaner state. W. P. Schreiner, who was a federalist, had originally been nominated as one of the Cape delegates, but he had withdrawn to defend Dinuzulu, and the Natal delegates received no support. Nevertheless the constitution in its final form was not a purely unitary one; there were some federal traits, notably the provincial system, in the South Africa Act.

The divergent attitudes and laws in the various colonies concerning non-white political rights made the franchise question an extremely contentious one. In the Cape Colony all adult male British subjects who could write their names, addresses and occupations and who either earned at least £50 in wages a year or occupied property worth at least £75 were eligible to vote in parliamentary elections. There was also no colour bar as far as membership of the two houses of parliament was concerned. In Natal, in theory, any adult male British subject could become enfranchised if he earned at least £96 in wages a year, or owned immovable property worth at least £10 a year in rent. In practice, however, the law was administered in such a way that non-Whites were, to all intents and purposes, debarred from obtaining the franchise: in 1907 99.1 per cent of the Natal electorate were Whites. No non-Whites had the vote in the Transvaal or the Orange River Colony. Certain Cape delegates favoured the uniform application of a colour-blind franchise; some delegates from the northern colonies and Natal wished to see the colour-bar restrictions on political rights in the Transvaal and the Orange River Colony enforced throughout South Africa. Even before the start of the Convention, Merriman and Smuts had decided that the only way to bridge the gap between the extreme views was to allow the existing franchise laws in each state to remain in force after union. After De Villiers had sounded Selborne and ascertained that the Imperial government would probably agree, albeit reluctantly, to the maintenance of the status quo, a committee drafted a clause to that effect, but it was stipulated that no non-Whites could become members of parliament. It was also agreed, at the insistence of the Cape delegates, that no alteration could be made to the Cape non-white franchise provisions unless two-thirds of the members of both Houses of Parliament sitting together agreed to such a change.

The matter of parliamentary representation presented a two-fold problem. How were the parliamentary seats to be divided among the various provinces

334

and how was the delimitation of constituencies within the provinces to be arranged? These matters were referred to a committee. It was agreed that the total number of White adult males in each province would be the basis for calculating the number of seats each province would have in the lower house of parliament, but that adjustments would be made to meet the claims of the two smaller colonies. So it was decided that the House of Assembly would consist of 121 members: 51 from the Cape, 36 from the Transvaal and 17 from each of the other two provinces. Each province, regardless of its size, would have equal representation in the Senate. The electoral system for the provinces was determined in the following way: the quota, that is, the number of voters in a constituency, would be fixed by dividing the total number of voters in a province by the total number of members of Parliament in that province; the boundaries of the constituencies would be determined by a delimitation commission consisting of one judge from each of the four colonies. It was laid down that these and subsequent Commissioners (three judges) should consider:

(*a*) community or diversity of interests;
(*b*) means of communication;
(*c*) physical features;
(*d*) existing electoral divisions; and
(*e*) sparsity or density of population.

The number of voters in a constituency could be up to 15 per cent more, or up to 15 per cent less, than the quota. In practice this came to mean that rural constituencies contained fewer voters than urban constituencies.

Smuts and Merriman believed that a general statement in the constitution that English and Dutch would be the official languages of the Union of South Africa should satisfy all the delegates. It soon became apparent, however, that Hertzog and Steyn did not consider that such a statement would be sufficiently explicit. Hertzog drafted a motion on this matter which satisfied most Afrikaners, but many English-speaking delegates considered that it included an element of compulsion. When Hertzog had had a private discussion with Fitzpatrick he amended his motion, and after further discussion amongst the delegates the vital part of the clause was phrased as follows: "Both the English and Dutch languages shall be official languages of the Union and shall be treated on a footing of equality, and possess and enjoy equal freedom, rights and privileges . . .[16] It was further agreed that this clause would be entrenched and that it could only be altered by a two-thirds majority of both houses of parliament sitting together.

The railways and harbours question could only be settled after the Transvaal government had negotiated with the Portuguese authorities for a modification of the existing *modus vivendi*. It was then agreed that Lourenço Marques would receive 50 to 55 per cent of the Witwatersrand traffic, Durban 30 per cent and the Cape ports the remaining 15 to 20 per cent. All railways and harbours belonging to the four colonies were to become the property of the Union,

16. Section 137 of the South Africa Act (1909).

and a board was to be established to administer them "on business principles, due regard being had to agricultural and industrial development within the Union".[17]

The Natal delegates, having failed in their bid to establish a federation, tried to increase the powers of the provincial governments so that the constitution would be a federal one in all but name. However, although most delegates favoured the principle of provincial government, they insisted that the provinces should be subordinate to the Central Government.

The question of the High Commission territories, Basutoland, Bechuanaland and Swaziland, was a matter for negotiation between the High Commissioner and the Convention. As it was generally expected that these territories would soon become part of the Union, the British Government demanded certain conditions for their administration after their transfer. After slight modifications these conditions were incorporated in a schedule to the South Africa Act.

Although these many formidable obstacles had been successfully surmounted, the matter of establishing which was to be the capital city of the Union very nearly caused a deadlock. The Cape delegates considered that Cape Town as the mother-city was the only logical choice. The Transvaal delegates maintained that Pretoria, because of its central situation, would be a better choice if Rhodesia were to become incorporated into the Union and that, in any case, the Transvaal deserved to have the capital as compensation for the financial sacrifices she was making. The Natal delegates realized that they had no grounds for claiming the capital for themselves, and so, because of their economic interests, supported the claim of the Transvaal delegation. This meant that the Orange River Colony delegates would decide the issue. They were not averse to delaying their decision for Bloemfontein was the most centrally situated of all the colonial capitals and, as Fischer put it, the longer the big dogs fought, the greater was the chance that the small dog would get the bone. The matter was eventually settled by a judgment of Solomon. Cape Town was to be the legislative capital, Pretoria the administrative capital and Bloemfontein would be the seat of the Appellate Division of the Supreme Court of South Africa.

After all the delegates had signed the draft South Africa Act on 11 May, 1909, the parliaments of the Transvaal and Orange River Colony accepted it unanimously. The Cape Parliament accepted it with two dissentient votes. In Natal a referendum was held. Only 58.2 per cent of the electorate voted, 11,121 in favour of the draft Act and 3,701 against it. White South Africans gave overwhelming support to the Act, but virtually all politically conscious non-Whites objected to the provisions which concerned them. Bantu delegates from all four colonies had attended a "South African Native Convention" which had opened in Bloemfontein on 24 March, 1909. The Cape Coloured Association, the African Political Organization, had held a protest meeting in the Cape Town city hall on 5 March and a conference in Cape Town in April, 1909.

Sect on 127 of the South African Act (1909)

Both the Bantu and Coloured congresses had decided to appeal to the British government to change the non-White franchise provisions of the Act. W. P. Schreiner accordingly led a deputation of Bantu and Coloured leaders to London, but they did not succeed in their purpose.

The draft South Africa Act was taken to Britain by a delegation headed by De Villiers. Although the colour-bar restrictions were criticized in the British parliament, and the Prime Minister, H. H. Asquith, solemnly appealed to South African statesmen to modify the restrictive franchise provisions, no amendments were made. After the bill had been passed by the Lords and the Commons it was signed, as the South Africa Act, by King Edward VII on 20 September, 1909, and it came into force on 31 May, 1910.

The South Africa Act

The four colonies were to become provinces of the Union of South Africa under the names of the Cape of Good Hope, Natal, the Transvaal and the Orange Free State.

Executive power was vested in the King and was to be administered on his behalf by the Governor-General-in-Council consisting of a Governor-General appointed by the Crown for a period of five years and an executive council or cabinet of not more than ten ministers. A cabinet minister who was not a member of either house of parliament had to become one within three months of his appointment. In all matters the Governor-General was to act on the advice of the cabinet.

Legislative power was vested in the Governor-General, the Senate and the House of Assembly. The Governor-General had the power to summon, prorogue and dismiss Parliament, and it was laid down that Parliament had to be summoned to meet not later than six months after the establishment of the Union. The Senate was to consist of forty members: eight senators were to be nominated by the Governor-General-in-Council (four of these were to be selected principally because of their thorough acquaintance, through official experience or otherwise, with the reasonable wants and wishes of the Coloured races in South Africa); eight senators were to be elected on the basis of proportional representation, in each of the four provinces, by the members of the provincial council and members of the House of Assembly for that province. All senators were to hold office for ten years. To be eligible to became a senator, a person had to

(a)   be at least thirty years of age;
(b)   be qualified to be registered as a voter for House of Assembly elections;
(c)   have resided within the boundaries of the Union of South Africa for at least five years;
(d)   be a British subject of European descent; and
(e)   in the case of elected senators, to own immovable property in the Union worth at least £500.

Senators would choose one of their number to be the president of the Senate.

337

The House of Assembly was to consist of 121 members (Cape 51, Transvaal 36, Natal 17, Orange Free State 17) directly elected for five years by the registered voters. Members of the House of Assembly would choose one of their number to be the Speaker of the House. On the basis of quinquennial census returns the number of members of the House of Assembly could be increased until the total of 150 had been reached and that total was not to be further increased "unless and until Parliament otherwise provides". No province was to have its original number of members reduced until the total number of members of the House of Assembly had reached 150. To be eligible to become a member of the House of Assembly a person had to

(a) be qualified to be registered as a voter;
(b) have resided within the boundaries of the Union of South Africa for at least five years; and
(c) be a British subject of European descent.

However, no person was eligible to become a member of either House of Parliament if any one of the following applied:

(a) he had been convicted of any crime or offence for which he had been sentenced to imprisonment without the option of a fine for a term of not less than twelve months, unless he had received a grant of amnesty or a free pardon, or unless such imprisonment shall have expired at least five years before the date of his election;
(b) he was an unrehabilitated insolvent;
(c) he was of unsound mind and had been so declared by a competent court; or
(d) he held any office of profit under the Crown within the Union (this disqualification would not apply to cabinet ministers, pensioners and members of the armed forces on retired or half pay).

Parliament was to have full power to make laws for "the peace, order and good government of the Union". All financial bills had to originate in the Assembly and the Senate had no power to amend such bills. When a bill was presented to the Governor-General he could give assent, withhold assent or reserve the bill for the signification of the King's pleasure.

In each province the chief executive officer, the Administrator, was to be appointed for a period of five years by the Governor-General-in-Council. Provincial councils were to be elected by the people registered as voters for House of Assembly elections. The number of members in a provincial council would be the same as the number of members of the House of Assembly in that province, but there were not to be less than twenty-five members in any provincial council. Any registered voter was eligible to become a member of his provincial council. The administration of provincial affairs was to be carried on by the Administrator and an executive committee of four members elected by the provincial council, not necessarily from among its members. Provincial councils were to have powers to pass ordinances concerning direct taxation within the province; education other than higher education; agriculture, to the extent of and subject to the conditions to be defined by Parliament; hospitals and charitable institutions; municipal institutions, divisional councils and other local institutions of a similar nature; local works and undertakings within the province other than railways and harbours; roads, *outspans*, ponts and bridges other than bridges connecting two provinces; markets and pounds; fish and game preservation; the borrowing of money on the sole credit of the province with the consent of the Governor-General-in-Council and in accordance with regulations to be framed by Parliament; and all other matters delegated to provincial councils by Parliament. Provincial councils were to be subordinate to the central government, for all ordinances had to be ratified by the Governor-General-in-Council and no ordinance would have the force of law if it was repugnant to any Act of Parliament.

There were to be three divisions of the Supreme Court of South Africa: the Appellate Division consisting of the Chief Justice of South Africa and judges of appeal; the Supreme Courts of the Cape of Good Hope, Natal and the Transvaal and the High Court of the Orange River Colony were to become provincial divisions of the Supreme Court of South Africa and were each to be presided over by a judge-president; the court of the eastern districts of the Cape, the High Courts of Griqualand and the Witwatersrand and several circuit courts were to become local divisions of the Supreme Court of South Africa. All judges of the Supreme Courts of the colonies were to become judges of the Supreme Court of South Africa at the establishment of Union. The Chief Justices of the colonies were to become Judge Presidents of the respective provincial divisions. The Chief Justice, the judges of appeal and other judges appointed after the establishment of Union, were to be appointed by the Governor-General-in-Council and could not be removed from office except by the Governor-General-in-Council on grounds of misbehaviour or incapacity.

The entrenched clauses, Section 35, concerning the franchise qualifications for non-Whites in the Cape, and Section 137 concerning the two official languages, could only be amended by a two-thirds majority of both Houses of Parliament at a joint sitting. Any other section of the constitution could be amended by an Act passed in the normal way. The constitution thus was a unitary one with distinct federal traits, as opposed to the tightly knit federal constitution of the Dominion of Canada and the looser federal constitution of the Commonwealth of Australia.

The first Union government

There was considerable speculation in South Africa and Britain as to who would be the first Governor-General of the united South Africa and there were rumours that Sir Wilfrid Laurier, Prime Minister of Canada, Winston Churchill, the President of the Board of Trade, and Sir Henry de Villiers were being considered for the position. There were, however, no grounds for these speculations and in September 1909 Asquith asked Herbert Gladstone, the Home Secretary, and the fourth son of the great Prime Minister, to accept the position. This news did not meet with general approval. Edward VII commented: "Is there nobody better?", and *The Times* considered it a grievous mistake to impose the failures of the Cabinet upon the dominions.[18]

It had been decided that Gladstone would appoint as Prime Minister of the Union that South African politician whom he adjudged to have the widest support; the Prime Minister would then name the other members of his Cabinet, other essential appointments would be made and only then would the general election take place. With Steyn out of the running owing to ill-health, the only two possible candidates for the premiership were Merriman and Botha. The position was further complicated by neither being willing to serve under the other. Gladstone arrived in Cape Town on 17 May and after interviewing Selborne and the leading South African politicians, he asked Botha on 21 May to form a cabinet. There can be little doubt that this was the only decision which could have been made in the circumstances, for although Hertzog and Fischer would have been prepared to serve under Merriman, the Transvaal and Natal would almost certainly not have been prepared to accept him as premier and he would probably not have been able to form a Cabinet. Since Jameson's negotiations with Botha to form a "best men government" had broken down, Botha appointed his ministers from the ruling parties in the former colonies.

Botha offered Merriman a Cabinet post, but he declined. Botha's main problem was whether or not to include Hertzog in his cabinet. If he were included, English-speaking voters would probably be alienated; if he were excluded, the Free Staters would be alienated. Botha tried to solve the dilemma by offering Hertzog a position as judge of the Appellate Division, but this Hertzog refused. He was then offered the portfolio of Justice. The Premier's other problem was in connexion with Natal. After he had filled all the Cabinet posts Natal objected since she had only one representative. As the South Africa Act provided for only ten ministers in charge of departments, Botha then appointed another Natalian as Minister without portfolio. The members of the first Union Cabinet therefore were:

Louis Botha (Transvaal), Prime Minister and Minister of Agriculture;
J. W. Sauer (Cape), Minister of Railways and Harbours;
J. C. Smuts (Transvaal), Minister of the Interior, Mines and Defence;
J. B. M. Hertzog (Orange Free State), Minister of Justice;
F. S. Malan (Cape), Minister of Education;
H. C. Hull (Transvaal), Minister of Finance;
A. Fischer (Orange Free State), Minister of Lands;
H. Burton (Cape), Minister of Native Affairs;
F. R. Moor (Natal), Minister of Commerce and Industries;
D. P. de V. Graaf (Cape), Minister of Public Works; and
C. O'G. Gubbins (Natal), Minister without portfolio.

Sir Henry de Villiers was appointed Chief Justice of the Union and the Administrators of the four provinces were named (N. F. de Waal, Cape Colony; J. F. B.

18. Thompson, *op. cit.*, p. 449.

Rissik, Transvaal; C. J. Smythe, Natal; A. E. W. Ramsbottom, Orange Free State).

The unification of the South African colonies was undoubtedly a most remarkable achievement in view of the recent stormy history of the country and the wide differences of background and outlook among the leading South African politicians. But as M. T. Steyn pointed out, the millenium had not yet arrived. The first Union Government was faced by vast and complex problems and it would have been naive to have supposed that the Convention spirit of compromise was to become a permanent feature of South African politics.

17. The Union of South Africa up to the Statute of Westminster, 1910–1931

The first parliament

When the Union of South Africa came into being on 31 May, 1910, its Prime Minister, General Louis Botha, and his cabinet ministers were able to take over the reins of government immediately, for before the birth of the new state everything had been done to ensure a smooth transition. All that was lacking was a legislative body. The creation of a parliament was therefore one of the first tasks of the government. The election date was set for 15 September, 1910, and soon South Africa was in the throes of an election campaign.

There were three parties, or more accurately two parties and one loosely-knit group, standing for election. There were also many independent candidates, especially in Natal where the electorate was not really organised along party lines. The press referred to the supporters of the government as the South African National Party (Nationalists for short) but in fact no such party yet existed. This "party" was actually three provincial parties which had all been formed before 1910 and had not yet merged: the South African Party of the Cape, the South African National Party of the Transvaal (a merger of *Het Volk* and Hull's group) and the *Orangia Unie* of the Free State. The opposition fell into two newly-formed parties. The Labour Party was formed in January 1910, and in May 1910, a few days before Union, the Transvaal Progressives, the Cape Unionists and the Orange River Colony's Constitutional Party merged on a national basis to become the Unionist Party. The leader of the Unionists was Dr (later Sir) L. S. Jameson and the leader of the Labour Party F. H. P. Creswell. The Labour Party had few supporters at this stage, so that the election was essentially a contest between the government party and Jameson's Unionists.

There were no really significant differences between the parties and indeed the election manifestos of the two leaders are remarkably alike. It is true that the Unionists were more closely linked to Britain and were more capitalistically inclined than Botha's supporters, but it is also true that there were greater differences within the ranks of the government party than between it and the Unionists. There was more diversity between Botha and his Minister of Justice, Hertzog, than between Botha and Jameson. Hertzog's was the voice of oppressed Afrikaner nationalism and on such questions as the relationship between South Africa and Britain, the role of the Afrikaner's language and culture in South Africa, and the attitude of South Africans towards their country, his views were very different from those of his Prime Minister. Jameson knew of the conflict within the government ranks and considered it justified the existence of his party, whose task it would be to counterbalance the reactionary element in the government. To Jameson Hertzog personified the reactionary element, so that the Unionists concentrated their attack on him, while their attitude to the Prime Minister was more sympathetic. Indeed Hertzogism was the crucial issue of the first election and may well have cost the government a number of seats. Botha was convinced that it did. "Hertzogism", he wrote to President Steyn shortly after the election, "is certainly the reason why we lost six seats here."[1] Botha also blamed Hertzogism for his own defeat by Sir Percy Fitzpatrick in Pretoria East. Yet the government easily won this first election. The results were: South African National Party (government parties) 67, Unionists 39, Labour 4 and Independents 11.

The first parliamentary session of the Union of South Africa was formally opened on 4 November, 1910, by the Duke of Connaught, a relation of the King of England. The legislation which was introduced during the life of this first parliament (1910 – 1915) may be divided into two main types. The first type was co-ordinative legislation which completed the unification of the four colonies. For example, the state departments had to be centralized, the existing colonial legislation on matters such as immigration, wills, and marriages had to be made uniform, and matters which had not been touched on at all in the constitution, such as the financial relationship between the provinces and the central government, had to be regulated. Since these laws were not concerned with any major questions of principle but merely ensured the smooth functioning of the country's administration it is not necessary to discuss them in more detail. The second type of legislation reflected Parliament's concern with matters of national importance. Since such matters were not only highly controversial but also sometimes affected the whole structure of South African society they require further attention.

One such law was the *Natives Land Act* of 1913 which embodied the recommendations of the Native Affairs Commission of 1903 – 1905, which had sat under the chairmanship of Sir Godfrey Lagden. This act divided the country into white and native areas and prohibited the sale of land owned by Whites to Natives and vice versa. The idea of territorial segregation was of course no new one in South Africa, but the importance of this act lies in the fact that it was the first legislation since Union to reflect this trend of thought. The bill was introduced into parliament by the Minister of Native Affairs, J. W. Sauer, but the groundwork for it was contained in a bill which his predecessor, Hertzog, prepared in 1912. It is doubtful whether Sauer, who favoured the liberal franchise policy of the Cape and who did not object to admitting Natives into parliament, was particularly enthusiastic about the bill, but the fact remains that during the debate on it he advocated separate residential areas for Whites and Natives. Hertzog and Botha supported this policy while its chief critics were John X. Merriman in the House of Assembly and W. P. Schreiner in the Senate. How did the Natives react to the first embodiment in law of a principle which is branded as "racial discrimination" by its opponents and termed "separate development" by its supporters? Most of them were

1. C. M. van den Heever: *Generaal J. B. M. Hertzog* (2nd ed., 1944), p. 282.

opposed to the act, not because of the principle of segregation, but because it drove many native families from their homes. The African National Congress, which had been founded in the previous year (1912), sent a delegation to the government to demand that the act be repealed. The request was refused, and in 1914 a deputation consisting of John L. Dube (the first chairman of the A.N.C.), S. T. Plaatje, A. Msane, T. M. Mapikela and Dr W. B. Rubusana (the first native M.P.C. in the Cape) was sent to London to urge the British government to annul the act. Again the request was refused. It is noteworthy that, unlike people such as Merriman and Schreiner, the Natives who criticised this act did not express any fundamental objection to the policy of territorial segregation as such. They objected only to the "severe restrictions and subesquent hardships" which stemmed from the act.[2] John Tengo Jabavu, editor of the first native newspaper in South Africa (*Imvo*) and the generally acknowledged leader of the educated Natives of the Cape, actually welcomed the act as a step in the right direction. A meeting of his organisation, the South African Races Congress, also expressed approval of the act.

The area granted to the Natives under the *Natives Land Act* amounted to 10.4 million morgen but this was merely a provisional allocation, for the Act also provided for the appointment of a committee to determine whether the Natives ought to be given more or less land. This commission, which met under the chairmanship of Sir William Beaumont, recommended that the Natives be given a further 8.3 million morgen. But neither Botha nor his successor, Smuts, were eager to pass a measure which would adversely affect their popularity among the Whites. It was only in 1936 that Hertzog, after a struggle which had lasted for many years, was able to add further land to the area which had been demarcated for the Natives in 1913.

Afrikaner strife: Hertzog and Botha

The government supporters, who had kept to the old colonial party divisions during the 1910 general election, finally amalgamated in Bloemfontein in November 1911 when they formed the South African National Party. Virtually all the great South African leaders of the time were present at the foundation congress. From the Transvaal came Botha, Smuts and Koos de la Rey, from the Free State Steyn, Hertzog and Fischer, and from the Cape Merriman. Never before had the Afrikaners been to such an extent united in one political party, nor were they ever to be so again. They were joined by many English-speaking South Africans who had already outgrown their "home" complex.

This new-found unity did not last long however, being broken before the end of 1912 by a dispute between Botha and Hertzog. This was in fact inevitable, for the differences between Botha and his rebellious minister were fundamental. What were these differences?

2. C. M. Tatz: *Shadow and Substance in South Africa; a study in land and franchise policies affecting Africans, 1910 – 1960* (1962), p. 24.

Botha considered it his life's task to bridge the gap between Afrikaans and English-speaking South Africans. He called this "conciliation". He thought his purpose could best be achieved by his steering a middle course, and siding neither with Afrikaners nor English-speaking South Africans. One cannot find fault with Botha's middle course which was indeed the only just policy to adopt; but Hertzog maintained that Botha deviated from the middle course to favour the English-speaking South Africans at the expense of the Afrikaners. To the historian viewing this dispute after more than half a century, it seems that Botha over-estimated the Afrikaners' loyalty to himself and failed sufficiently to consider the Afrikaners' feelings. It was a mere ten years since the Anglo-Boer War and the bitterness it had engendered was slow to die. Botha's admiration of the English-speaking South Africans and of the British Empire offended many Afrikaners; and his gift of the Cullinan diamond to King Edward VII in 1907, his indifference to the Afrikaans language movement, his readiness to give financial support to the British Navy in 1911 and his unveiling of a statue of Cecil Rhodes, the arch-imperialist, on Table Mountain in 1912, further annoyed them. To many Afrikaners Botha's fraternization with the Unionists was incomprehensible. Botha treated Dr L. S. Jameson, the leader of the Unionists, as a colleague and co-operated with him behind the political scenes, while Jameson repeatedly stated in public that it was only the reactionary elements in the cabinet which prevented Botha from following the course advocated by the Unionists. Hertzog was very disturbed by Botha's relationship with his political opponents. On 13 May, 1911, he wrote to President Steyn: "If the old trend of ignoring and sacrificing the peoples' interests in order to gain popularity with the opposition continues, I shall soon have to refuse to be a party to it any longer."[3] To Hertzog it seemed obvious that Botha was not adhering to the middle course but was gravitating towards the English, and this meant that the English language and culture which already dominated in South Africa would be strengthened still further while the Afrikaans language and culture would be threatened with total annihilation, a possibility which Hertzog could not bear to contemplate. The Afrikaners' language and culture had to continue to exist side by side with those of the English-speaking South African. To Hertzog the life of the people of South Africa consisted of two streams, the English-speaking and the Afrikaans-speaking, and each stream had the right to flow unimpeded. This was Hertzog's so-called "two-stream policy" which was sometimes misunderstood because the distinction it drew between culture and nation was not perceived. Hertzog, unlike Botha, wished to keep the two languages and cultures separate, but like Botha he wished to mould the two cultural groups into one South African nation.

Hertzog's attempts to lift the Afrikaners' language and culture from the inferior position they occupied after the Anglo-Boer War were viewed with suspicion and he was regarded as a fanatic stirring up racial hatred. The Free State Education Act in particular was attacked. This act of Hertzog's, seeking to

3. C. M. van den Heever: *Generaal J. B. M. Hertzog* (2nd ed., 1944), p. 290.

conform to the principle of language equality, provided that English children must learn Dutch and Afrikaans children must learn English. The Afrikaners accepted this measure, but many English-speaking people could not understand why their children should learn Dutch. Although it applied in the Free State only, this act and the man responsible for it were attacked from all parts of the country. Shortly after the opening of parliament Sir Charles Crew of the Unionist Party introduced a motion in the House of Assembly censuring the compulsory bilingualism of the Free State Education Act. The Prime Minister, Botha, avoided making a stand by suggesting that a select committee investigate the matter and make recommendations. The committee, of which Hertzog was a member, found that there was no language equality in any of the provinces except the Free State and that English was dominant in the Transvaal, Natal and the Cape Colony. The committee opposed Hertzog's compulsory bilingualism and recommended that parents be permitted to choose the language medium of their children. Hertzog did not conceal his disapproval of this alteration of his principle of compulsory bilingualism but for the sake of peace accepted it and even asked the Free State to bring its act into line with the committee's recommendations.

All this did little to improve the relations between Hertzog and his opponents. The Unionists still regarded him as their chief enemy and pitied Botha for having such a fanatic in his cabinet. Hertzog was not one to suffer their attacks submissively and retaliated viciously. He concentrated on the particular point of his opponents' loyalty to Britain and their disloyalty to South Africa. In a series of speeches during the last months of 1912, starting at Nylstroom on 5 October and reaching a climax at De Wildt on 7 December, Hertzog denounced the "foreign fortune hunters" who were loyal to the British Empire rather than to South Africa. He felt that Sir Thomas Smartt, the new leader of the Unionists was, for example, not inspired by true South African patriotism and therefore had no right to govern the country. Only an Afrikaner ought to lead South Africa, but by Afrikaner, he explained repeatedly, he meant anyone, Afrikaans or English-speaking, whose first loyalty was to South Africa. "Imperialism," declared Hertzog in his speech at De Wildt, "meets with my approval only in so far as it serves South Africa: where it clashes with South Africa's interests, I am decidedly against it."[4] And by this policy of "South Africa first" Hertzog was prepared to stand or fall.

Today, half a century later, Hertzog's arguments seem to be so self-evident that it is difficult to imagine anyone disagreeing with them. But things were different in those days. The leader of the Unionists, Sir Thomas Smartt, openly admitted that he put the British Empire before South Africa, and one of the cabinet ministers, Sir George Leuchars, was so disturbed by Hertzog's speech that he resigned. The Prime Minister, Botha, could not find fault with Hertzog's principles but felt that he should not voice them in public. Supported by the rest of the cabinet, he demanded Hertzog's resignation. But to Hertzog, who

4. C. M. van den Heever: *Generaal J. B. M. Hertzog* (2nd ed., 1944), p. 313.

always valued honesty and outspokenness above tact and diplomacy, it was quite incomprehensible that he should not be allowed openly to express a view with which the Prime Minister in fact agreed, and he refused to resign. Botha then tendered his own resignation on 14 December, 1912, but on the same day was asked by the Governor-General to form a new cabinet. Botha omitted Leuchars and Hertzog from his new cabinet. The omission of Leuchars was of little significance, but that of Hertzog changed the course of history.

All Botha's colleagues in the cabinet, including Hertzog's fellow Free Stater, Abraham Fischer, supported him in his dispute with Hertzog. In parliament Hertzog's position was not much better; only 5 of the 121 members of the House of Assembly supported him. Yet this was far from being a true reflection of public opinion. It very soon became apparent that various prominent Afrikaners, including the influential President Steyn, supported Hertzog's views on South African nationalism. At the Free State party congress in May, 1913, 47 voted in favour of Hertzog and only one against him. At the party congresses in the other provinces Botha certainly gained overwhelming support, but at the national congress which was held in Cape Town in 1913, 90 votes were cast for Hertzog as against 131 for Botha. Hertzog and his followers left the hall and in January, 1914, in Bloemfontein formed the National Party. Ten years later this party was to come to power.

Discontent among mineworkers and Indians

Although the dispute between Botha and Hertzog was by far the most significant political development during the period immediately after Union, there were other sensational happenings which at the time received even more attention than the split in the Afrikaner ranks. Two of these in particular deserve attention. The one was a dispute between workers and capitalists in which the government had to intervene, the other a dispute between the Indians and the government.

The workers' dissatisfaction led to two strikes, the first in June-July 1913 and the second in January 1914. The first strike arose out of a trivial dispute concerning working conditions at the Kleinfontein mine near Benoni. The miners' case was taken up by their trade union and soon developed into a dispute with the mine-owners concerning recognition of the miners' trade union. The miners went on strike, the strike spread throughout the Witwatersrand and riots followed. Since the police could not control the situation, and there was as yet no South African army, Smuts, as the responsible minister, was obliged to call in the help of such British troops as were still in the country. Clashes between strikers and troops occurred, and the strikers vented their resentment by setting fire to the Johannesburg station and the offices of *The Star*, mouthpiece of the mine-owners. When the strike appeared to be getting out of control Botha and Smuts decided to go to Johannesburg to negotiate with the miners. On 5 July, 1913, discussions with the miners took place in the Carlton Hotel, while a turbulent crowd gathered in the street outside. Botha and Smuts realized that they were powerless and were obliged to accede to the miners' demands, which were, first, for a reinstatement of the dismissed miners of Kleinfontein and, secondly, for an investigation of the miners' grievances. This victory made the strikers believe that further strikes would be as profitable. Extremists such as the Hollander H. J. Poutsma began to emerge as leaders in labour circles and in January, 1914, another strike broke out which immediately assumed far worse proportions than the first one. It started among railway workers in Pretoria, spread to other railway centres and then to gold-miners on the Witwatersrand. This time Smuts was determined not to yield to the demands of the strikers. He mobilised units of the new South African Defence Force, which he had created in the second half of 1913, and sent them into Johannesburg under General Koos de la Rey. The strikers, realizing that resistance would be futile, capitulated. But Smuts was not content to let the matter rest there; he took the law into his own hands and deported nine of the ringleaders without trial. This autocratic move evoked much criticism, but it certainly helped to quell the miners' urge to strike. Not until 1922 did friction between workers and capitalists flare up again.

The Indian problem, which caused the government so much concern in the years immediately after Union, had already been acute in the colonies, but it was aggravated by the new government's decision to stop the influx of Indians into South Africa. A bill designed to end the uncontrolled influx of "Indians and other Asiatics" into South Africa was published in 1911 but was withdrawn when the Viceroy of India and the Free Staters objected to it – the former because the bill discriminated against Indians, and the latter because it did not discriminate enough. The government was determined, however, to stem the flow of Indians into South Africa and in 1913 an Immigration Act was passed which did not refer specifically to Indians, but nevertheless made their further immigration impossible. The violent protests which this Act evoked prompted M. K. Gandhi, leader of the Indians in South Africa and the great apostle of passive resistance (*satyagraha*), to demand the repeal of all South African laws which discriminated against Indians. There were many such laws, for colonial legislation concerning Indians had been taken over unchanged by the Union of South Africa. In a five point demand Gandhi asked for the repeal of the Natal law which imposed a £3 tax on Indians, the repeal of the law which prohibited Indians from entering the Free State, the recognition of marriages according to Indian custom, the reform of the land, liquor and immigration laws which discriminated against Indians, and permission for Indians who had been born in the Cape to return there. To add force to his demands Gandhi mustered about two thousand Indians from Natal and at the beginning of December, 1913, he led them across the Transvaal border at Volksrust. This was an infringement of the law prohibiting the entry of Indians into the Transvaal. As Gandhi had expected they were arrested, and as he had hoped his passive resistance movement caused such an uproar that the government appointed a commission to inquire into the Indians' grievances and Smuts even agreed to meet Gandhi personally. This resulted in a compromise measure, namely the *Indian Relief Act*

348

of 1914, which abolished the £3 tax on Indians in Natal, recognised the validity of Indian marriages and facilitated the entry of Indian wives into South Africa. For the moment Gandhi was content with what he had achieved, but he informed Smuts that there were other questions relating to the Indians in South Africa which would have to be attended to at a more opportune time. Others had to continue the struggle for the rights of Indians in South Africa, however, for Gandhi left for India on the eve of the First World War.

The rebellion of 1914

The outbreak of the First World War caused a section of the South African population to take up arms against the government. The main reasons for this revolt or rebellion, in which Afrikaner fought Afrikaner while the English-speaking section looked on in bewilderment, seem to have been the hope of regaining republican independence, disagreement with the government's decision to attack the German colony, South-West Africa, and annoyance at the government's decision to call up civilians for military service. The relative importance of these factors can be determined only by considering the rebellion itself.

On 4 August, 1914, Britain and the entire British Empire declared war on Germany and her allies. Various Afrikaners thought this the opportune moment to throw off their British yoke and declare an independent republic. Among them was the influential General Koos de la Rey of the western Transvaal. Within days of the outbreak of war notices were circulating in his district of Lichtenburg calling on the burghers to arm themselves and assemble at Treurfontein on 15 August, 1914. When the Prime Minister, Botha, heard of this he summoned General de la Rey to Pretoria and warned him earnestly not to incite the Afrikaners to revolt against Britain. De la Rey, who was a supporter of Botha, promised the Prime Minister that he would not act irresponsibly, and in fact at the meeting at Treurfontein a motion of confidence in the government was carried. But at the time of the meeting (15 August, 1914) it was not generally known that on 10 August, 1914, the cabinet had agreed to the British government's request to attack German South-West Africa. Botha convened a special session of parliament to obtain approval for the campaign against South-West Africa. Botha's war policy was vehemently opposed by Hertzog, but approved in the House of Assembly by the overwhelming majority of 92 to 12. Yet this parliamentary majority did not reflect popular opinion. Many Afrikaners, including popular idols such as Generals Christiaan de Wet and Koos de la Rey, and high-ranking army officers such as Commandant-General C. F. Beyers, Lieutenant-Colonel Manie Maritz and Major J. C. G. Kemp, were opposed to a campaign against South-West Africa. De la Rey, after much soul-searching, turned against Botha and encouraged by Beyers, Maritz and Kemp decided to urge Afrikaners to protest against Botha's policy. It is uncertain what kind of protest he had in mind but on the afternoon of 15 September, 1914, the "lion of the western Transvaal" left Pretoria by car for the military camp at Potchefstroom. He was accompanied by Beyers, who had that day resigned as Commandant-General of the Defence Force. At a police checkpoint at Langlaagte their driver, on De la Rey's orders, ignored a police signal to stop. The police opened fire and a ricochet shot killed De la Rey. The whole protest plan, whatever it envisaged, was now thrown into confusion, for none of the other malcontents, Beyers, Maritz or Kemp, had sufficient influence with the Afrikaners to lead such a movement.

Nevertheless, as soon as the government's war plans were known, it became clear that many Afrikaners were strongly opposed to them. Opposition increased when rumours began circulating that the government was going to call up civilians to serve in the campaign against the Germans. It was also rumoured that General de la Rey had been murdered at the instigation of the government. When on 10 October, 1914, the news came that Maritz, commander of the military camp at Upington, had rebelled and gone over to the Germans, tension increased. This incident in the north-western Cape was a strong inducement to the Free State and the Transvaal to revolt. When Smuts allowed the newspapers to publish an ultimatum he had received from Maritz in which Maritz threatened to invade the Cape unless Hertzog, De Wet, Beyers and some others were permitted to confer with him at Kakamas, the situation deteriorated still further, for the ultimatum created the impression that prominent and influential Afrikaners, such as Hertzog and De Wet, supported Maritz. When the government reacted to Maritz's threat by calling up burghers to subdue him, the malcontents in the Free State and the Transvaal began forming their own commandos. On 22 October, 1914, it was decided at Koppies that De Wet and Beyers would lead the rebels in the Free State and the Transvaal respectively. Within a few days the rebels had occupied virtually all the villages in the northern Free State, while in the area north of the Vaal River they were concentrated mainly in the western Transvaal. In the Free State there were about 7,000 rebels, in the Transvaal about 3,000 and in the Cape about 2,000, but their fighting potential was limited not only because they were inadequately armed and poorly disciplined, but also because their leaders had divergent purposes. Both Beyers and De Wet spoke of "armed protest", but whereas the undecided Beyers merely wanted to make a show of force, De Wet, the man of action, intended to obtain arms from Maritz, shoot his way through to Pretoria and there proclaim a republic.

No government worthy of its name can passively allow its subjects to take up arms against it. Thus when Botha had failed in his attempts to end the rebellion by peaceful means he led a vastly superior force against the rebels. On 12 November, 1914, the leader of the Free State rebels, De Wet, who had moved west, was surrounded and defeated at Mushroom Valley, south of Winburg. He then fled with a few of his men to the north-west but on 1 December, 1914, was finally overtaken and arrested near Kuruman. The other rebels fared just as badly. Beyers's force, which had moved from the western Transvaal to the Free State, was attacked repeatedly and was completely dispersed at Bultfontein on 16 November, 1914. Beyers and a few of his men managed to get away, but on

8 December, 1914, he was drowned in the Vaal River while attempting to escape his pursuers. With Beyers dead and De Wet a prisoner the rebellion was virtually ended in the Transvaal and the Free State. It was only near Pretoria that a group led by Jopie Fourie, who had joined the rebels without resigning from the Defence Force, fought on obstinately, causing considerable losses among the government troops. When, after a fierce struggle, Fourie laid down his arms on 16 December he was court-martialled, sentenced to death and executed a few days later. This was the end of the rebellion in the Transvaal and the Free State.

In the far north-western Cape Maritz and Kemp were still fighting on, Kemp having joined Maritz on 28 November after an astonishing ride of four weeks across the Kalahari. But they knew that further resistance would be suicidal, and on 2 February, 1915, Kemp surrendered with his own and Maritz's forces while Maritz, the first rebel, fled to German South-West Africa.

So ended the 1914 rebellion. It had been a struggle entirely between Afrikaners, for Botha, anxious to avoid racial strife, had used only Afrikaans-speaking soldiers to fight the rebels. There had been surprisingly few casualties: 190 among the rebels and 132 among the government forces. Of the nearly 12,000 rebels only 281 were summoned to appear in court. Those convicted were imprisoned, the maximum period being 7 years, or fined, the maximum sum being £2,000. With the exception of the execution of Jopie Fourie, which was completely justified at law but politically a great blunder, the government treated the rebels very leniently. Before the end of 1916 all those imprisoned had been released, but despite this conciliatory gesture on the part of the government much bitterness remained. In fact the chief result of the rebellion was that from that time on Botha and Smuts were branded by a section of the Afrikaners as henchmen of Britain and betrayers of the Afrikaners.

From the conquest of S.W.A. to the Treaty of Versailles

Despite the opposition of some of his people Botha was determined to keep his promise to invade South-West Africa. As soon as the rebellion in his own country had been quelled he mobilized a great force of 43,000 men and prepared to attack the German colony which could muster at most about 9,000 men. Botha himself took command and in mid-February, 1915, he landed at Walvis Bay with part of his force. After various preparations and delays he began to advance on Windhoek in mid-April, 1915. At the same time a three-pronged attack was launched on the Germans from the south. Smuts, who headed the southern forces, marched from Luderitz in the west towards Keetmanshoop, Berrange invaded the German colony from Bechuanaland in the east, and Van Deventer advanced from the Orange River in the south. It was very soon apparent that the Germans were no match for the South Africans, not only because of their inferiority in numbers but also because their leaders were not of the calibre of the Boer generals. By the end of April, 1915, the whole area south of Windhoek had been occupied by Smuts's forces. Shortly afterwards, on 13 May, 1915, Botha entered an undefended Windhoek and then marched north in pursuit of the retreating Germans. The German Governor, Dr Theodor Seitz, and his forces surrendered between Otavi and Tsumeb on 9 July, 1915. Botha's terms were remarkably generous: non-commissioned officers and men were to be interned; officers could settle where they wished; all reservists and volunteers could return to their farms while those with the rank of officers were allowed to retain their weapons. Botha placed the colony under provisional military rule, then returned to Pretoria and appointed Sir Howard Gorges as South-West Africa's first administrator. The campaign against German South-West Africa had been concluded speedily, at small expense and with little loss of life (only 113 South Africans had been killed). It was a military triumph which earned Botha and his able lieutenant, Smuts, the thanks of the British government.

Botha, however, was to pay a considerable price in South African politics for supporting the British war effort. Many of his followers went over to Hertzog as a consequence. In the years after the 1914 rebellion Afrikaner nationalism came strongly to the fore. The first mouthpiece of the National Party, *Die Burger*, started publication in 1915, while the work of poets such as Jan Celliers, Eugene Marais and Louis Leipoldt was proof of the healthy growth of the Afrikaans language movement. But the result of the general election of October 1915 was the clearest indication of the growth of Afrikaner nationalism. In this first election since 1910 the main point at issue was whether South Africa should continue to support Britain's war effort. Hertzog's National Party, formed only the previous year, polled 78,000 votes; the South African Party 94,000. In parliament the distribution of seats was South African party 54, Unionists 40, Nationalists 26, Labour 4 and Independents 6, so that the government now needed the support of either the Unionists or the Nationalists.

During 1916 universities were the subject of important legislation. Of the University of the Cape of Good Hope's eight colleges, two, the Victoria College in Stellenbosch and the South African College in Cape Town, became independent universities. The others became constituent colleges of the University of South Africa which now replaced the University of the Cape of Good Hope. These were the Grey University College in Bloemfontein, the Huguenot University College in Wellington, the Natal University College in Pietermaritzburg, the Rhodes University College in Grahamstown, the Transvaal University College in Pretoria and the South African School of Mines and Technology in Johannesburg. In 1921 the Potchefstroom University College became the seventh member of this group. All these colleges, except the Huguenot University College which closed in 1950, eventually attained the status of independent universities. The University of the Witwatersrand came into being in 1922, the University of Pretoria in 1930, the University of Natal in 1949, the University of the Orange Free State in 1950, Rhodes University and the Potchefstroom University for Christian Higher Education in 1951. In 1946 the University of South Africa, which up to that time had been mainly a supervising and examining body, began to teach through correspondence. Its growth was so rapid that within a few years it became the largest university in South Africa.

When the South-West African campaign was over the question arose whether South Africa should take any further part in the war. The Unionists felt that she should and Smuts and Botha also favoured voluntary aid to Britain. Thus in November 1915, immediately after the election, volunteers were sent to Europe, and shortly afterwards 19,000 South Africans left for Tanganyika to help in the imperial campaign against this German colony.

By the end of 1915 the British forces in Tanganyika, under the command of Major-General Tighe, had achieved little and Smuts was invited to assume command of these forces. He accepted the offer and arrived in Tanganyika in February 1916 to take over command of the imperial forces of 45,000 men, comprising South Africans, Rhodesians, Indians and Natives. In the Tanganyikan, as in the South-West African campaign, Smuts's forces were numerically far superior to those of his opponent but in this case the German commander, Lettow-Vorbeck, was a military strategist equal if not superior to Smuts. Thus when in January 1917 Smuts went to represent South Africa at a war conference in London the Germans in Tanganyika had not yet capitulated. The war in Tanganyika really ended only when Germany herself surrendered.

When the First World War ended in November 1918 Smuts was in London where since March 1917 he had considerably helped the British war effort. As a member of the British war cabinet he had played a key part in the organization and strategy of the entire war, and many important tasks had been entrusted to him. Lloyd George, for example, said that Smuts had the right to be called the father of the British Air Force. When peace had been restored he played an equally important part in the creation of the League of Nations, drawing up a memorandum which formed the basis of the League's Covenant and which earned him the admiration of statesmen and historians. Botha joined Smuts in London in December 1918 and at the beginning of 1919 they went to Versailles to represent South Africa at the peace conference. In the distribution there of former German possessions South-West Africa was awarded to South Africa as a so-called C-mandate, to be administered under the supervision of the League of Nations. Botha and Smuts accepted this reward for their country's war effort, but were unhappy about the unfair treatment meted out to Germany at Versailles. Smuts in particular was bitterly disappointed by his allies' greed and insatiable desire for revenge. He warned insistently and repeatedly that the peace treaty upon which they insisted would merely be the prelude to another war. "It is a terrible document," he wrote to his wife from Versailles, "not a peace treaty but a war treaty, and I am troubled in my conscience about putting my name to such a document."[5] Indeed it was with the greatest reluctance that on 28 July, 1919, he and Botha signed the Treaty of Versailles. The course of history during the next two decades was to prove that Smuts and those who agreed with him were more far-sighted than the statesmen who were responsible for the peace treaty.

Smuts and Botha were South Africa's official delegates at Versailles but two

5. W. K. Hancock: *Smuts I: The sanguine years, 1870 – 1919* (1962), p. 524.

other deputations from South Africa also found their way there. One, led by Hertzog, was inspired by President Wilson's doctrine of the right of self-determination to plead for the restoration of independence to the two former Boer republics. The other deputation, consisting of delegates of the African National Congress, went to Versailles to urge a change in South Africa's native policy. Both deputations were granted interviews by the British Prime Minister, Lloyd George, but this was as far as their efforts got them. Lloyd George listened to them politely but summarily rejected their pleas. He told Hertzog that compliance with his request would mean the dissolution of the Union and was impossible; and his reply to the Native delegates was that the British government could not interfere in the domestic affairs of South Africa.

Smuts in power: fusion of the S.A.P. and the Unionists

On 27 August, 1919, a few weeks after his return to South Africa, Botha died at the age of 56. During his lifetime he had done his best to reconcile Boers and British but unhappily he had also alienated many of his own people. The greatest tragedy of his life was that, although an Afrikaner, he was blind to the strength of Afrikaner nationalism.

Botha's mantle automatically fell on the shoulders of his friend and confidant, Smuts. The new Prime Minister was a man of exceptional intellect who had already made his mark outside the Union but who lacked Botha's personal following in South Africa. It was now his difficult task to lead a party whose popularity was steadily declining. This trend continued after his accession, for in the election of March 1920 the South African Party won 41 seats (as against 54 in the previous election), the Nationalists 44 (previously 26), the Unionists 25 (previously 40), the Labour Party 21 (previously 4) and the Independents 3 (previously 6). The noticeable features of this election were the National Party gains in the rural areas at the expense of the South African Party, and the success of the Labour Party in urban areas at the expense of the Unionists.

These Nationalist and Labour gains made it difficult for Smuts to remain in power. Even with the support of the Unionists he had only a majority of four in the House of Assembly. He immediately started seeking ways and means of strengthening his position and within two weeks was making overtures to the Nationalists. He started to negotiate with Hertzog, but their views on South Africa's relations with Britain differed so radically that they could find no common ground. Some of their followers nevertheless believed that co-operation between Smuts and Hertzog was possible and during 1920 there was a series of congresses where attempts were made to re-unite the two parties. Little progress was made. At a big "reunion congress" held at Bloemfontein on 22 September, 1922, efforts to bridge the gap were finally abandoned. The insurmountable problem was South Africa's right of self-determination. Hertzog wanted South Africa to acquire the right to secede from the British Empire (some of his followers wished to go even further and apply

354

that right in practice), but Smuts wanted to maintain the "British connection", which in effect amounted to South Africa's being subordinate to Britain.

Smuts then turned to the Unionists. Negotiations in this direction led to a merger with the South African Party in November, 1920. This "political blood transfusion"[6] strengthened Smuts's party considerably. In order also to strengthen his position in parliament Smuts went to the polls again on 8 February 1921, eleven months after the previous election. This time there were no three-cornered urban contests involving Unionists, South African Party and Labour, and consequently the South African Party captured many urban seats from Labour. Labour seats were reduced from 21 to 9, the South African Party took 79 and the National Party maintained its total of 45. Smuts was once again firmly in control and rewarded his new colleagues by including three ex-Unionists, Sir Thomas Smartt, J. W. Jagger and Patrick Duncan in his cabinet. The transformation of the South African Party was thus complete: Hertzog, who had been a government minister in 1912, was now leader of the opposition, while Sir Thomas Smartt, opposition leader in 1912, now held a cabinet post. This was the logical outcome of a trend which had been evident since 1910: while the gap between the South African Party and most Afrikaners widened, that between it and the English-speaking section steadily diminished and finally disappeared.

Growing criticism of Smuts

Smuts's government had to face mounting criticism in the early twenties. In 1921 and 1922 revolts occurred in various parts of the country, and the stern measures adopted by the government to quell them made Smuts more unpopular than ever.

In the Queenstown district about 1,000 Natives (men, women and children) members of a religious sect, settled illegally on the farm Bulhoek. They resisted all efforts to remove them and the government therefore decided to use force. In May 1921 the government sent out about 800 policemen and soldiers and in the clash which followed 163 Natives were killed. Smuts as the responsible minister was severely criticised for his handling of the incident.

In 1922 the government had to face its most serious crisis since the 1914 rebellion. This was the great strike or revolt on the Witwatersrand. It began as a strike but degenerated into a large-scale revolt against the government. It must be viewed against the background of the severe economic slump of 1920 which followed the post-war period of expansion and inflation. This depression which lasted from 1920 to 1923, followed the same pattern as other South African depressions, with falling prices, shrinking profits, bankruptcies, budget deficits, unemployment and wage cuts. The gold mines were also seriously affected in three respects: the gold price fell from 130/- in February 1920 to 95/-

6. D. W. Krüger: *The Age of the Generals* (2nd ed., 1961), p. 114.

in December 1921, gold production decreased from 8,332,000 fine ounces in 1919 to 8,129,000 in 1921, and productions costs rose from 22/11d per ton of ore in 1919 to 25/8d in 1921. As a result of these setbacks the Chamber of Mines in October 1921 proposed a wage cut and in November proposed that the *status quo* agreement which regulated the ratio of Whites to Natives in the mines should be adjusted in favour of the Natives. In terms of this agreement, which had been entered into in September 1918 between the Chamber of Mines, representing the mine-owners, and the South African Industrial Federation, representing the miners, no change in the ratio which then existed was permissible. The miners summarily rejected both proposals. The proposal to alter the *status quo* was considered to be particularly dangerous. If it were accepted many White miners might be dismissed, for the Native, with his low standard of living, was prepared to work for £1 a week while a White worker demanded £1 a day. Obviously the mine-owners would prefer the Native if he could do the work as well as the White man. Thus the White worker in South Africa was fighting on two fronts: on the one hand, like his European counterparts, against the capitalists and on the other hand, unlike his European counterparts, against the competing Natives. This situation sometimes created considerable confusion of thought. Thus in 1922 when the strikers marched through Johannesburg one of the banners which they carried read: "Workers of the World fight and unite for a White South Africa". No-one seemed to realise that this adaptation of the Marxist slogan was contradictory.

In December 1921, despite the workers' opposition, the coal-mine owners announced a wage cut of 5/- per shift. The coal-miners refused to accept this cut and on 1 January, 1922, the day on which the new wage scale was to come into effect they went on strike. On 10 January, 1922, the workers on the Rand gold-mines followed their example. The strike of the 20,000 White miners meant that the 180,000 Native miners had no work either. Negotiations between mine-owners and workers continued, but by 27 January, 1922, it was clear that no agreement was in sight. Meanwhile the South African Industrial Federation began to lose control of the strike and the so-called Council of Action, whose five members were all extremists, assumed command. The strikers began forming "commandos" and drilling in military formation. Feelings began to run high against the government, which was regarded as being hand in glove with the mine-owners, so that what had begun as a dispute between workers and capitalists gradually took on a distinctly political flavour. At a mass meeting at the Johannesburg city hall on 5 February, 1922 the strikers even decided to use force to overthrow the government and to declare a republic. The workers asked both the Labour Party and National Party for support, but although their sympathy was clearly with the strikers the shrewd politicians did not favour the use of force.

After the death of some strikers in a clash with the police at Boksburg on 27 February, 1922, the situation deteriorated rapidly. Gangs of miners roamed the streets committing robbery, arson and even murder. Various attacks on Natives caused deaths of both Whites and Natives. At first Smuts had favoured the view that "we should let things develop"[7] but on 10 March, 1922, he declared martial law and entered Johannesburg with detachments of the army, supported by the air force. Fierce street fighting took place at various points and aircraft bombed the strikers. On 14 March, 1922, after heavy bombardment of the market building at Fordsburg which housed the strikers' headquarters, the red flag on the building was lowered and resistance ended. Two of the strikers' leaders, Fisher and Spendiff, who were in the building chose to commit suicide rather than to surrender. This ended the influence of the Council of Action and the strikers returned to work. Those who were charged with the commission of crimes during the rebellion – there had been several cold-blooded murders of Natives, policemen and opponents of the strike – were summonsed to appear in court and 18 of the accused, half of whom were Afrikaners, were sentenced to death. Most of them were reprieved however; only four were executed.

The Rand rebellion of 1922 in which 153 people died (some sources estimate 219 or even 250) ended in total defeat for the miners. The *status quo* agreement was cancelled, more Natives engaged and Whites dismissed, White miners' wages were cut, and the principle that only one particular kind of work be done by one person ("one man one job") was abandoned. For Smuts and his government, who had suppressed the rebellion, the outcome was equally disastrous. Smuts was severely criticized both for his initial apathy and his sudden ruthless quelling of the rebellion. In the House of Assembly Hertzog spoke of Smuts as "the man whose hands dripped with the blood of his own people".[8] The miners, seething with resentment against the government, ranged themselves solidly on the side of the two opposition parties, Labour and the Nationalists. The strike also paved the way for co-operation between these two parties.

The violence on the Witwatersrand had scarcely ended when the government again resorted to force in dealing with another rebellion, this time in South-West Africa. The Bondelzwarts, a Hottentot tribe in the south, refused not only to pay dog tax, but also to deliver five members of their tribe, including the notorious Abraham Morris, to the police. In May 1922 the Administrator of South-West Africa, Gysbert Hofmeyr, then marched against the Bondelzwarts with a force of 370 men, and several aircraft from Pretoria bombed the rebellious Hottentots. Within a matter of days the campaign was over. The government forces had lost two men, but the Bondelzwarts, who had been able to muster only two hundred men, suffered more than a hundred killed in action. The opposition, and in particular the Labour Party, seized on the incident as further proof that Smuts was prone to shed blood unnecessarily. In the House of Assembly R. B. Waterston referred to Smuts as "The Bloody Jeffreys of South Africa".[9]

In 1922, when Rhodesia had to choose between joining the Union and continuing as a self-governing colony under British protection, Smuts did his best

7. Ivan L. Walker and Ben Weinbren: *2,000 Casualties: a history of the Trade Unions and the Labour Movement in the Union of South Africa* (1961), p. 116.
8. Oswald Pirow: *James Barry Munnik Hertzog* (n.d.), p. 94.
9. A. M. Davey: *The Bondelzwarts Affair; a study of the repercussions, 1922 – 1959* (1961), p. 11.

to ensure that this territory would become the fifth province of the Union. This was of course in accordance with his holistic philosophy but he also saw such an incorporation as an opportunity to strengthen his own party (which the Rhodesians, being English-speaking, would support), to extend South Africa's borders considerably and to acquire a rich copper area. But a disappointment was in store for him. When the Rhodesians went to the polls in October 1922 they decided against incorporation by a majority of 2,785 votes, despite the attractive terms Smuts had offered them.

An even heavier blow for Smuts came in April 1923 when the two opposition parties, Labour and Nationalists, agreed to join forces against candidates of the South African Party in the next election. Smuts and his supporters, much disconcerted, tried to ridicule the agreement by dubbing it an "unholy alliance" between Christian Afrikaners and Bolsheviks. In fact it was a firm alliance based on resentment at the government's disregard of the White worker (Afrikaans and English-speaking), and strengthened by the esteem which the leaders of the two parties, Hertzog and Creswell, had for each other. Although Malan, the leader of the Cape Nationalists, at first opposed the agreement and finally consented to it only with reluctance, he and Creswell were eventually on good terms.

Since the previous election in 1921 the South African Party had been steadily losing ground. By-elections had caused an alarming shrinkage in the government's majority in the House of Assembly. When the loss of the Wakkerstroom seat in a by-election in April 1924 reduced the government's majority in the House of Assembly to eight, Smuts announced that a general election would be held as soon as possible. The opposition was delighted, but Smuts's supporters were surprised. The government's term of office still had two years to run and Smuts had decided to go to the polls without consulting his party. In this election, which was held in June 1914, the Nationalist and Labour party alliance easily unseated the South African Party. The voting was as follows: Nationalists 63 (as against 45 in the previous election), Labour 18 (previously 9), South African Party 53 (previously 79) and Independents 1. Smuts, who had been Prime Minister for five years, resigned, and the Governor-General asked Hertzog to form a cabinet.

The pact government: early years

Hertzog's cabinet included Nationalists as well as Labour Party members. His chief assistants were to be his fellow Nationalists and in particular Tielman Roos, leader of the Transvaal branch of the party and Deputy Prime Minister, Dr D. F. Malan, leader of the Cape branch of the party, and N. C. Havenga, who more and more became Hertzog's confidant. But he also included in his cabinet F. H. P. Creswell and T. Boydell, two English-speaking members of the Labour Party. He did so not only to express his gratitude for the support which the Labour Party had given him in the election, but also to strengthen the "pact" or agreement with them. From the outset the two groups co-operated well and respected each other's opinions. During the flag dispute Creswell remained loyal even in the face of a rift in his own party.

One of the first acts of the coalition government was to create a Department of Labour, which, with the Department of Defence, was at first entrusted to Creswell, but when a third member of the Labour Party, W. B. Madeley, was admitted to the cabinet at the end of 1925, Boydell took over the Department of Labour. One of the first laws which Creswell piloted through parliament while Minister of Labour was the *Wages Act* of 1925. It supplemented the *Industrial Conciliation Act* of 1924, that had regulated wages payable to skilled workers, by dealing with unskilled and unorganised labour, excluding agricultural workers and domestic servants. It also created a Wage Board which regulated rates of pay for certain types of work, regardless of race. This does not mean to say that there was no discrimination in the labour field. As we have seen, the policy of both Labour and Nationalists was to protect the white workers from competition from the Natives. For this reason Hertzog's policy of civilized labour, which became effective in 1924, drew a sharp distinction between civilized (white) and uncivilised (native) labour, and definitely gave preference to the former. As early as October 1924 the government requested all state departments to give preference to more "civilized workers", and the South African Railways and Harbours in particular appointed increasing numbers of white workers, of whom approximately 95% were Afrikaners. In 1924 only 4,760 white workers (9.5% of the total) were employed by the S.A.R. & H., but by 1929 the number had grown to 16,248 (28.7% of the total). Thus the government policy assured the poorer section of the white population of considerably higher wages than those paid to Natives for the same work. In 1926 the government further protected the white workers by again passing, with the necessary alterations, the *Mines and Works Act* of 1911, which had been invalidated in 1923. This Act, also known as the *Colour Bar Act*, was of particular interest to the Labour Party for it protected skilled white urban workers against competition from Natives and Indians (but not Coloureds). By stipulating that certificates of competency for skilled work could be issued only to Whites or Coloureds, the Act gave the force of law to the colour bar which was already operating in the labour field. In the grouping of Coloureds with Whites the continuing influence of the liberal Cape tradition is to be seen. Hertzog also favoured the economic and political integration of Coloureds and Whites.

During the twenties a certain non-White political group wielded more influence than any similar body ever had in South Africa. This was the Industrial and Commercial Workers Union of South Africa (the I.C.U.) which in 1919 had begun modestly in Cape Town as a non-White dock workers' trade union, but had soon lost its economic character and developed into a political organisation with half a million members. For many years it quite supplanted the African National Congress. The founder and leader of the I.C.U. was Clements Kadalie, a native from Nyasaland, whose organizing ability, drive and exceptional demagogic talent compensated for his inability to speak the South African native languages. Under Kadalie's leadership the I.C.U. spread to the other provinces, and gained a particularly large following in Natal. At first Kadalie did not object if Whites wished to join the Union, provided they were prepared to associate themselves with the fight for the rights of non-Whites, but in 1926, after he had quarrelled with white communists who had penetrated the I.C.U. and expelled them, the organisation assumed a more racial character. In 1927 the I.C.U. and Kadalie were at the height of their power and Kadalie travelled to Europe to ask trade union leaders to send him an adviser. The adviser who was sent was W. G. Ballinger. After 1927, however, internal friction led to the gradual decline of the I.C.U. and eventually it disappeared.

The Nationalist victory in the 1924 election meant that the Afrikaans language and culture movement now enjoyed full government support. As Minister of the Interior Dr D. F. Malan did much to promote Afrikaans in the civil service where English still predominated. In 1925 he also piloted an act through parliament in terms of which Afrikaans replaced Dutch as one of South Africa's two official languages.

The pact government was fortunate in that a complete economic revival occurred shortly after it assumed office, and continued from 1924 to 1929. In May 1925 South Africa joined Britain, the Netherlands and Australia in reverting to the gold standard after a period of five years. The general prosperity was further reflected in the budget surpluses which the Minister of Finance, Havenga, announced year after year. Gold production also gradually increased and the value of diamond production soared from £6 million in 1923 to £14.5 million in 1927.

This enormous rise in the value of the diamond yield was partly the result of the discovery of rich alluvial diamond deposits at Lichtenburg in the western Transvaal and Alexander Bay at the mouth of the Orange River. Hundreds of fortune seekers, especially poor Whites, streamed to the diggings but very few became rich and most became poorer. The state feared that large scale exploitation of the invaluable diamond deposit at Alexander Bay would completely disrupt the diamond market, so it prohibited all diggings and made exploitation solely a state concern.

The Nationalists' great ideal was to free South Africa from Britain as much as possible. Thus they enthusiastically supported Arthur Barlow, a Labour Party member, when in February 1925 he moved in the House of Assembly that the King of England be requested no longer to confer titles on South Africans because such customs were alien to the South African national character. It was pointed out that outstanding South Africans such as John X. Merriman, General Louis Botha and "Onse Jan" Hofmeyr had refused offers of such honours. In spite of opposition from the South African Party which argued that the conferment of such honorary titles was a mark of appreciation of services rendered to the South African people, the motion was carried. This bitterly dissappointed some imperialists who had expected a liberal bestowal of honours when the Prince of Wales visited South Africa later that year.

Hertzog and the constitutional status of South Africa

The constitutional status of the Union of South Africa was a problem which had occupied Hertzog for many years before he came to power. His deepest desire was to change his country's status from one of subordination to Britain to one of sovereign independence within the Commonwealth. In his election agreement with Creswell in April 1923 he had indeed promised not to alter the "existing constitutional relationship of South Africa to the British Crown",[10] but this did not prevent him from trying to clear up the confusion surrounding this issue, and from insisting on his theoretical right to alter that constitutional relationship if he wished to. The gulf between the actual and the legal status of the dominions was the main reason why the politicians were so confused about the constitutional position of the self-governing states. The legal status had not kept pace with the changes which had taken place in practice. In practice there was a great measure of equality, but not so in law. As Smuts put it in 1917: "Although in practice there is great freedom, yet in actual theory the status of the Dominions is of a subject character. Whatever we may say, and whatever we may think, we are subject Provinces of Great Britain. That is the actual theory of the Constitution and in many ways which I need not specify to-day that theory still permeates practice to some extent."[11] Since some politicians failed to perceive this difference between practice and theory or, like Lloyd George, did not make it clear to what they were referring when they spoke of "complete equality" between Britain and South Africa, there was endless confusion concerning the dominions' constitutional position. Hertzog therefore in October 1926 went to the Imperial Conference in London determined to obtain from the British government an acknowledgement that South Africa's status was on an equal footing with Britain's. At the conference all questions concerning relations within the British Empire were referred to a committee, whose members, besides the chairman Lord Balfour, were the Prime Ministers of South Africa, Canada, Australia, New Zealand and Newfoundland, the Vice-President of Ireland, the Secretary of State for India, and the two British ministers for the Dominions and for Foreign Affairs. In this committee Hertzog made his demand for a clear statement concerning the status of the dominions. At first this move was opposed but in the end the members of the committee agreed to draw up a statement. Its wording presented problems, however, for Hertzog steadfastly resisted the attempts of other members to include such terms as "common citizenship" and "duties and obligations" which, he contended, would create the impression of a sort of superstate and not of a free community of peoples with equal status. Thanks particularly to the support of Lord Birkenhead, Secretary of State for India, Hertzog succeeded in getting his way. The committee made the following statement: "They (Britain and the

---

10. D. W. Krüger (ed.): *South African parties and policies, 1910 – 1960; a select source book* (1960), p. 75.
11. K. C. Wheare: *The Statute of Westminster and Dominion Status* (4th ed., 1949), p. 22.

dominions) are autonomous Communities within the British Empire, equal in status, in no way subordinate one to another in any aspect of their domestic or external affairs, though united by a common allegiance to the Crown, and freely associated as members of the British Commonwealth of Nations". This statement cleared up the uncertainty surrounding the status of the dominions; in theory Britain and the dominions were now on an equal footing.

On his return to South Africa Hertzog was enthusiastically hailed as the father of his country's new found independence. "Yes", said Hertzog, "the outcome of the Imperial Conference is that the old British Empire of the past no longer exists. The old Empire was a dominant state to which we and the other dominions had to submit and to which we did submit for years. Of the old Empire nothing remains. All that remains is a free association."[12] But Smuts was quick to destroy such complacency. He admitted that the 1926 declaration was a step in the right direction but, even after the Statute of Westminster had come into effect in 1931, he denied that South Africa, or any dominion, had the right to remain neutral in any war into which Britain might enter, or to leave the British Commonwealth, for example by declaring a republic. During the negotiations which preceded the fusion of the National Party and South African Party in 1933, the two leaders, Hertzog and Smuts, agreed to differ on these points.

Hertzog, quite satisfied that South Africa was now a free and independent country within the British Commonwealth, next took steps which developed naturally from this new-found independence. In 1927 he created a Department of Foreign Affairs, and in 1929 sent South Africa's first ambassadors abroad.

Disputes over a flag, and a steel industry

For a long time various members of all three political parties, especially the Nationalists, had felt that South Africa ought to have her own flag. In 1925 Dr D. F. Malan, the Minister of the Interior, introduced a bill which provided for a national flag but at Smuts's insistence it was agreed to hold the bill back. It was re-introduced during the 1926 parliamentary session, and almost immediately a bitter dispute arose over the flag's appearance. While at one extreme there were those who were so pro-British that they wanted nothing but the Union Jack, at the other extreme were people like Dr D. F. Malan who wanted a "clean" flag, that is, a flag with no British symbols on it. However, certain politicians, among them Tielman Roos, very soon realized that a compromise was necessary and that some form of recognition would have to be given to the "British connection". Malan, a man of rigid principles, was most unwilling to agree to a compromise, and even those who advocated a compromise could not agree about the place of the Union Jack in a new flag. The dispute caused increasing concern among the various population groups and a split threatened to develop in the Labour Party when the leader, Creswell, supported the Nationa-

12. C. M. van den Heever: *Generaal J. B. M. Hertzog* (2nd ed., 1944), p. 500.

362

lists on this issue. Creswell and Roos then urged the Prime Minister to delay the passing of the bill for another year. He agreed to do so in spite of strong opposition from Malan. During the parliamentary recess Malan's position as the responsible minister was made very difficult by the intrigues of his colleague Roos. Tielman Roos was a political opportunist who changed sides all too easily. Shortly after Hertzog's departure for London he began to advocate the withdrawal of the Flag Bill. But Hertzog was determined to proceed with the measure, and in 1927 the bill was again laid before parliament. In an effort to reach a compromise Hertzog suggested that the Van Riebeeck flag be used (three horizontal stripes of orange, white and blue) and on it a shield incorporating the Union Jack, the Transvaal "Vierkleur" and the Free State flag, while Smuts suggested that the whole flag should consist of a combination of these three historical flags. Hertzog's suggestion received a fair amount of support, but Smuts's flag was such an "atrocity"[13] that even his own supporters wanted nothing to do with it. Yet the Senate, where the South African Party was in the majority, lent its support to Smuts's flag. Tielman Roos then took the extraordinary step of secretly approaching the Governor-General and requesting him to use his influence to make Smuts and Hertzog reach a compromise. The responsible minister, Malan, not being consulted, Hertzog and Smuts did come to an agreement, and after a cabinet crisis, with first Hertzog and then Malan threatening to resign, Malan finally agreed to accept the compromise. The resulting bill gave South Africa two official flags; one was the national flag consisting of three horizontal stripes of orange, white and blue with miniature versions of the Union Jack and the two republican flags on the middle stripe; the other was the Union Jack, which could not be flown alone, but only together with the national flag in certain specified places such as the Houses of Parliament and the more important government buildings. The South African national flag was flown for the first time on 31 May, 1928.

In 1927 the government introduced another controversial bill, providing for the establishment of the South African Iron and Steel Industrial Corporation Limited in which the government was to hold a controlling interest. The pact government was for various reasons very anxious to establish an iron and steel industry in South Africa. First, there was the prospect that an iron and steel industry would stimulate further industrial development in the country. Then, too, South Africa had exceptionally rich deposits of coal and iron ore, the raw materials necessary for this industry. The Nationalists were convinced that an iron and steel industry would advance South Africa's independence, while the Labour Party was pleased that the state was to share in the enterprise so that the much-hated capitalists could not appropriate all the profits. For all these reasons the government thus decided in 1927 to introduce legislation which made provision for the establishment of a South African Iron and Steel Industrial Corporation Limited, in which the government would have a controlling interest. The opposition on the other hand was very much against the state's

13. D. F. Malan: *Afrikaner-Volkseenheid* (3rd ed., 1961), p. 124.

363

sharing in the enterprise, which, it contended, would be a form of state socialism. They also criticised the bill on the grounds that it would harm the British iron and steel industry unnecessarily. Thus the bill was twice blocked in the Senate where the opposition was in the majority. In order to get the measure through parliament the government was obliged to convene a joint sitting of both houses on 29 March, 1928. Shortly afterwards Iscor was founded, and Dr H. J. van der Bijl was appointed its first chairman. According to law the state had to provide only 15% of the total capital (£3½ million), and the public the rest in the form of shares. Public response was so unenthusiastic however, that the government was obliged to purchase the unclaimed shares so that today it possesses 99% of Iscor's shares and has sole authority to appoint directors. Since 1928 the iron and steel industry has grown enormously, and has become of the utmost importance in South Africa's economy.

Although the pact government could now boast of several noteworthy achievements, its chances in the forthcoming election were reduced by a revolt within the Labour Party against Creswell's leadership. Nevertheless the results of the election of 12 June, 1929, were in the government's favour: Nationalists 78 (formerly 63), S.A.P. 61 (formerly 53), Labour Party 8 (formerly 18) and Independents 1. The Labour ranks were thus greatly diminished, but the position of the Nationalists had improved considerably; in fact this party had a clear majority of 8 over all the other parties. Hertzog was thus in a position to dispense with Labour support but he stood by his Labour friends and included both Creswell and H. W. Sampson, who replaced the defeated Boydell, in his cabinet. Oswald Pirow replaced Tielman Roos who had resigned for health reasons, and E. G. Jansen and A. P. J. Fourie were also included in the cabinet.

The Statute of Westminster

The Balfour declaration of 1926, in which Hertzog had played such an important part, had stated unequivocally that the status of the dominions was one of equality with Britain. But was this the position at law? It certainly was not. The following inequalities were still embodied in statutes:–

1. The Governor-General represented the King. Since the King was advised by the British government the Governor-General too was advised by the British government.

2. If advised to do so by the British government the King could reject any dominion legislation, even if the Governor-General had approved it.

3. The Governor-General was at liberty to refuse to sign any act and to ask the advice of the King, who would be advised by the British government. Thus, in theory, the British government could enforce its will on South Africa.

4. South Africa, unlike Britain, could not legislate on extra-territorial matters.

5. The *Colonial Laws Validity Act* of 1865 provided that no colony (and at law the dominions were still colonies) could pass a law which conflicted with a British law.

6. The Appeal Court, the highest South African court, was still subordinate to the Privy Council.

7. South Africa could not pursue an independent foreign policy.

It was generally realised that these inequalities ought to be removed to bring the legal position into line with the 1926 declaration. Conferences in 1929 and 1930 continued the work which the 1926 conference had begun. Inequalities which could not be removed except by legislation were removed by the *Statute of Westminster* in 1931. Thus the nature of the British Empire was radically altered during the years between 1926 and 1931. Who were the architects of this new British Commonwealth? "It was not a British invention, it was, if responsibility can be allocated, a Canadian, South African and Irish invention. Sir Wilfrid Laurier of Canada, Generals Smuts and Hertzog of South Africa and Mr De Valera of Eire have been its chief architects, though they were odd architects who built without a plan. A French-Canadian, two Afrikaners and a Spanish-Irishman share the major part of the credit, if there be credit, because they were concerned essentially with the problems of the Commonwealth from the peculiar angles of their peoples."[14] And, it may be added, the greatest contribution undoubtedly came from Hertzog.

14. Ivor Jennings: *The British Commonwealth of Nations* (4th ed., 1963), p. 188.

18. From the Statute of Westminster to the Republic of South Africa, 1931-1961

The depression of 1930–1932

When at the end of 1931 the Statute of Westminster opened a new period in the constitutional history of South Africa, the country, like the rest of the world, was in the grip of an extremely serious economic depression. This depression started towards the end of 1929 and in South Africa resulted, amongst other things in the price of wool falling sharply from 14d per pound in 1928–1929 to 4d in 1931–1932, the price of maize falling from 15s 4d per bag of yellow mealies in 1929 to 9s 4d in 1932, the number of employees busy on relief works increasing from 4,123 in 1929 to 30,613 in 1933, and the number of bankruptcies rising alarmingly from 1,695 in 1929 to more than 2,500 for each of the years 1930, 1931 and 1932. In almost all spheres of economic activity there were marked recessions. In addition during 1932 and 1933 South Africa was struck by a drought which was one of the longest and worst of this century and which affected the farming community particularly badly. The critical economic situation overshadowed all political matters and demanded the undivided attention of the government.

When on 20 September, 1931, Britain announced that she had left the gold standard and had formed a non-party national government as an emergency measure to pilot the country through the depression, the South African government declined to follow Britain's example and expressed its intention to maintain the gold standard. There were two main motives for this decision: first, the government, after consulting eminent economists, was convinced that such a policy would be to South Africa's advantage and, secondly, South Africa's leaving the gold standard simply because Britain had done so would seem to contradict the arguments of the Prime Minister, General J. B. M. Hertzog, about South Africa's independence.

Many people however doubted South Africa's ability to remain on the gold standard. Convinced that South Africa would follow Britain's example such people sent large sums of money out of the country in the hopes of making a large profit when South Africa left the gold standard and the exchange rates changed. As a result of the outflow of capital the already precarious economic condition deteriorated even further. Measures to control the movement of capital thus became necessary. Parliament was convened on 18 November, 1931, for a short special session and the government passed the necessary legislation to control the outflow of money. These measures were not, however, altogether effective since money continued to leave the country.

As a result of the deterioration in the economic situation the Hertzog government lost some of its support. Enormous pressure from many sides, amongst

366

others from the opposition and the mines, was exerted for the government to leave the gold standard, but the Prime Minister was determined not to deviate from his chosen course. Hertzog and his Minister of Finance, N. C. Havenga, were strengthened in their conviction when a committee, appointed at the beginning of 1932 to investigate matters relating to the gold standard, found that it was in the interests of South Africa to remain on the gold standard. Never before in the history of South Africa had a purely economic matter so overshadowed all other questions on the political scene. In parliament the leader of the opposition, General J. C. Smuts, stated: "We . . . are like a wounded man who feels that he is bleeding to death, who sees his life's blood running away, in just the same way our money continually flows out of this country. We are doomed to inevitable and certain destruction."[1] By the end of 1932 £17.5 million had already been sent out of the country. By this time even some of Hertzog's followers had started complaining about his economic policy. His government was clearly in a precarious position. Against this background of rising tension ex-minister Tielman Roos, who had for health reasons resigned from the Hertzog government in 1929, once more came into prominence.

For some time during 1932 there had been rumours that this genial but opportunistic ex-minister was contemplating a return to politics. The office of appeal judge, which demanded calm and impartial deliberation, was clearly not suited to an intriguer like Roos. The bench soon became torture for him and when many of his admirers began to urge him to return to politics he did not long disregard their suggestions. On 16 December, 1932, he was the main speaker at the Dingaan's Day ceremony at Haakboslaagte (near Lichtenburg), but instead of discussing the past he announced his return to politics, demanded that South Africa immediately leave the gold standard and advocated coalition government on a non-party basis. Into the strained situation then prevalent in South Africa Roos's speech burst like a bombshell. Within three days £2–3 million was withdrawn from South African banks and sent out of the country by people who were convinced that South Africa could no longer remain on the gold standard. Rumours began circulating that many Nationalists had come out in support of Roos and that he and Smuts were busy negotiating. This was a disturbing prospect for the Hertzog government with its slender majority. Furthermore the next parliamentary sitting, with its possibility of a motion of no confidence in the government, was imminent. The government thus had to do something drastic. Within fourteen days after Roos's speech the Minister of Finance, Havenga, announced that South Africa had left the gold standard. The effects of this step were felt immediately. The price of gold and gold mining shares started to climb and money began pouring back into South Africa from overseas.

1. M. P. A. Malan: *Die Nasionale Party van Suid-Afrika* (1964), p. 129.

The idea of a coalition government which had been suggested by Roos had in the meantime caught the imagination of the people. Many felt that a government on a non-party basis was what was needed to help South Africa through the depression. Smuts also supported the idea of a coalition government. When parliament met in 1933 he proposed that the government should resign so that a coalition government could be formed. Hertzog at once rejected the proposal but immediately after his speech he began to doubt the wisdom of his words. The next day he discussed with some members of his cabinet his intention of approaching Smuts with the idea of negotiating the formation of a coalition government. The cabinet was divided concerning the desirability of co-operating with Smuts. Havenga and Oswald Pirow, amongst others, supported Hertzog and declared themselves in favour of a coalition, while others, especially Dr D. F. Malan, were emphatically opposed to a coalition. According to Malan coalition would necessarily result in a dilution of nationalist principles and for this reason he was not prepared to co-operate with the imperialistically orientated South African Party.

Despite the opposition of Malan and other members of the cabinet Hertzog decided to negotiate with Smuts about a coalition and then to ask a congress of the National Party to approve the results of the negotiations. "Whether my friends in the cabinet agree with me or not I will have to do my duty . . .", Hertzog said in the caucus of the National Party.[2] Why did Hertzog consider it his duty to negotiate with Smuts about a coalition? In a speech he made at Smithfield on 5 March, 1933, he mentioned, among others, the following reasons: first, the nation desired coalition; secondly, the economic condition of the country demanded it; and thirdly, the National Party might be defeated at the next election. It appears that the fear of a defeat in the forthcoming election was the decisive factor for Hertzog. In the caucus of the National Party he declared: "If we must rely on our own strength at the next election we will lose . . . We will suffer a defeat and it will be the end of Afrikanerdom."[3]

The negotiations between Hertzog, assisted by N. C. Havenga, and Smuts, assisted by Patrick Duncan, began on 15 February, 1933. Agreement was reached within a few days. Smuts would serve as deputy premier under Hertzog, Hertzog's cabinet would consist of six members of the National Party and six members of the South African Party, and an election would be held as soon as possible to test public opinion. A seven-point plan for co-operation between Hertzog and Smuts was also approved. These seven points were:

(1) the country would be governed in accordance with its independent status;
(2) the unitary basis of the central government would be retained;
(3) there would be equal language rights for English and Afrikaans-speaking citizens;

2. D. F. Malan: *Afrikaner-Volkseenheid* (3rd ed., 1961), p. 155.
3. D. F. Malan: *Afrikaner-Volkseenheid* (3rd ed., 1961), p. 154.

(4) a prosperous farming community would be striven for;
(5) the civilized labour policy would be maintained;
(6) an attempt would be made to solve the racial problem by means of separate political development; and
(7) a sound national economic policy would be adopted.

This seven-point basis for co-operation was subsequently submitted for approval to the various congresses of the two parties. The congresses approved the agreement but there were some anti-coalition groups at each congress. The National Party of the Cape in particular was not enthusiastic about the intended coalition. At its congress on 15 March, 1933, it passed a resolution to accept the agreement between Hertzog and Smuts only under protest.

In the general election of 17 May, 1933, the two coalition parties were returned with an overwhelming majority. The government, i.e. the Hertzog-Smuts coalition, had 144 supporters in parliament while the opposition had only 6 (2 Labour Party, 2 Roosites and 2 Natal Home Rulers).

The coalition between Hertzog and Smuts was not, however, a very strong alliance. There were fundamental matters, such as the divisibility of the Crown, the right of neutrality and the question of secession from the Commonwealth on which the two parties could not agree. The two leaders, however, did not feel compelled to decide on these matters when drawing up a programme of principles. Such matters were considered to be merely academic questions about which the partners legitimately could hold different opinions. The seeds of the dissension which in 1939 would disrupt the partnership were therefore present from the beginning in the coalition between Hertzog and Smuts.

After the election of 17 May, 1933 (and even before) there were nevertheless many people in various parts of South Africa who desired that the coalition should proceed to the fusion or unification of the two parties. This was particularly so in the rural areas of the Transvaal and the Free State where branches of both parties insisted on the complete fusion of the two coalition parties into a new party. In the Transvaal a few branches of the National Party and the South African Party had by the middle of 1933 united on their own initiative. Under these favourable circumstances Hertzog and Smuts both worked to promote fusion during the latter half of 1933. They tried to persuade the extremist wings of their parties that in the projected party there would be room for the views which they represented. Many were not convinced, however.

There were many extremists in Smuts's party who rejected fusion because they did not want to be in the same party as Hertzog. These extremists rallied around Colonel Charles Stallard. Stallard opposed any development towards sovereign independence and regarded fusion as a plot to weaken imperial bonds. He and a number of his supporters broke away from Smuts to join the Natal Home Rule Party. After fusion the party adopted the name Dominion Party.

More serious and more extensive was the threatened split in the National Party between the supporters and opponents of fusion. While Hertzog worked for fusion, Malan, who had already objected to coalition, protested vehemently against a fusion which he considered would be a superficial and artificial union

369

of two incompatibles, nationalism and imperialism. He advocated *hereniging*, by which he meant unification based on common political convictions and principles. While Hertzog and his supporters considered that the time was ripe for co-operation with English-speaking South Africans, Malan and his followers felt quite otherwise. To them the Afrikaner's struggle against English domination was not yet over. Because the Afrikaner under Hertzog's leadership had won one round it did not mean that the struggle was at an end. The Malanites did not consider that the Statute of Westminster had settled everything. As far as they were concerned constitutional questions such as the divisibility of the Crown, the right of secession and the choice of neutrality were not academic matters, but vital matters about which they wanted to hear definite pronouncements. They wanted to move towards the attainment of an independent republic. The many imperial symbols, such as the British flag, the British anthem and the head of the British monarch on South African coins which daily confronted them, bitterly reminded them of the past. They wanted the Afrikaner to find his rightful place. They were deeply antagonistic towards British imperialism which in the past had so often humiliated the Afrikaner. They remembered Slagtersnek, the Great Trek, the annexation of Natal, the annexation of the diamond fields and the Anglo-Boer War. Unlike Hertzog they did not see any improvement in the attitude of the English-speaking South Africans toward South Africa. They regarded Hertzog as a great man seduced by an illusion. How was it possible for the people of South Africa to become one nation if those who spoke English were not yet true South Africans but still gave allegiance to Britain before South Africa?

The conflict in the National Party between the supporters and opponents of fusion (i.e. between the supporters of Hertzog and the supporters of Malan) was bitter but neither Hertzog nor Malan desired to split the Afrikaners. Consequently during the first half of 1934 Hertzog and Malan made several attempts to come to an agreement, but without success. Malan's demands were such that to meet them Hertzog would have had to break with Smuts. On 25 July, 1934, the congress of the Cape National Party at Somerset West decided by a majority of 164 to 18 against fusion and for the continuation of the National Party. The Cape, in contrast to the other provinces, was thus overwhelmingly against fusion. The minorities in the other provinces associated themselves with the Cape majority. This meant that the National Party, although weakened, would continue to exist when the followers of Hertzog fused with the South African Party. Hereafter Malan's supporters referred to their party as the "Purified National Party" although the official name remained the National Party.

In Bloemfontein on 5 December, 1934, the contemplated fusion did occur when the United South African National Party or, as it is known, the United Party, was formed. The new party's principles were based on the same seven points on which the coalition had been based in 1933. When parliament met in 1935 the nineteen members of Malan's Purified National Party therefore sat on the opposition benches.

The United Party administration (1934-1939)

The formation of the coalition government in 1933 and the subsequent fusion of the two coalition parties in 1934 created a political situation favourable to Hertzog's proposed non-White legislation. He had already, in 1926, introduced four bills in parliament affecting the non-Whites. These bills dealt with Native representation in parliament, a Natives Representative Council, the enlargement of the Native reserves and the extension of the Coloured vote to the northern provinces. In 1927 these bills were referred to a committee which reported in 1929. The bill dealing with Native representation was laid before a joint sitting of the Legislative Assembly and the Senate in the same year, 1929, but failed to secure the required two-thirds majority. The three Native bills, were once again referred to a committee while the Coloured bill was referred to a separate committee. The committee for the Native bills did not report until 1935. It reduced Hertzog's three bills to two: a Native Trust and Land Bill and a Native Representation Bill. In 1936 the Prime Minister again laid the two bills before parliament and despite opposition from the liberal wing of his own party he secured the required two-thirds majority. Although the final details differed considerably from the three original bills which had been introduced ten years earlier Hertzog's segregation policy still was the basis of the laws. The *Native Representation Act* removed Cape Natives from the ordinary White voters' roll but gave them the right to elect three White representatives to the Legislative Assembly while the Natives of all four provinces could elect four White representatives to the Senate by means of electoral colleges. Provision was also made in this Act for the creation of a Natives Representative Council which would act in an advisory capacity. The *Native Trust and Land Act* implemented a 1913 promise to enlarge the Native reserves. It provided for a trust fund to buy a further 7.2 million morgen to enlarge the existing reserves from 10.4 million to 17.6 million morgen. This would amount to 12% of South Africa's land area.

Hertzog followed a policy of political, economic and social segregation as far as the Natives were concerned, but he regarded the Coloureds as part of the White community. He was in favour of the Coloureds being absorbed politically and economically, but he wanted to maintain social segregation between the two groups. The Prime Minister's 1926 bill concerning the Coloureds' political representation provided for the extension of the Coloured vote to the three northern provinces, but it never became law. The commission which was appointed in 1934 to investigate the position of the Coloureds supported Hertzog's idea in its 1937 report, but supporters of total segregation between Coloureds and Whites, in both Malan's National Party and Hertzog's own party, made it impossible for the Prime Minister to proceed with legislation concerning the political status of the Coloureds.

The years 1933-1939 during which the Hertzog-Smuts alliance governed South Africa were prosperous ones. Although the prosperity must be largely attributed to the general economic improvement which followed the depression of 1930-1932, it is also true that the coalition government was instrumental in improving South Africa's economy. The years 1933–1939 saw much excellent legislation: in 1935 the construction of tarred roads was begun; the airways improved enormously; a start was made with modernizing Cape Town harbour; the South African Broadcasting Company was founded in 1936; and the Market Act of 1937 ensured a hitherto unknown price stability for agricultural products by introducing control boards.

The United Party faced the general election of 1938 with confidence. It had tackled the Native question spiritedly with Hertzog's 1936 legislation, had helped South Africa further on the road towards sovereign independence and had brought the country material prosperity. But more than anything else it had shown that Afrikaans-speaking and English-speaking South Africans could work together if they were prepared to forget the differences of the past. The 1938 election results were as follows: United Party 111 (previously 117), National Party 27 (previously 20), Dominion Party 8 (previously 5), Labour Party 3 (previously 4), Independents 1 (previously 4). Once again the middle of the road party was strongest with the two extreme wings (nationalists and imperialists) forming the most important opposition parties. The two extremist parties had gained a few seats from the government, but whereas the gains of the insignificant Dominion Party were negligible, the National Party's gains were of greater moment. This party, which polled 247,000 votes as against the 448,000 votes of the United Party, was still growing, and under trying circumstances, because the years after the fusion of the two big parties were difficult ones for the Purified Nationalists. The onus was on Malan to convince the Afrikaners that Hertzog had indeed abandoned their national interests and this was no light task. Hertzog had founded the National Party and had done much for the Afrikaners. But today it is obvious that Hertzog, who since 1914 had led Afrikaner nationalism, had underestimated its strength. If he and his supporters felt that Afrikaner nationalism had reached its goal and should in future be more accommodating toward the English-speaking section of the population there were many others who, like Malan, held different opinions. After 1933 Malan increasingly came to symbolize Afrikaner nationalism.

In 1938 a remarkable revival of Afrikaner patriotism and nationalism accompanied the centenary celebrations of the Great Trek. Afrikaners throughout South Africa paid homage to the Voortrekkers. It was decided to lay the foundation stone of a monument worthy of the Voortrekkers on 16 December, 1938, on a hill outside Pretoria, and the *Taal en Kultuurvereniging van die Suid-Afrikaanse Spoorweë en Hawens* organized a symbolic ox-wagon trek from the four corners of South Africa to Pretoria. A wave of Afrikaner patriotism swept the country. People wore Voortrekker clothes, men grew beards, children were christened in the shadows of ox-wagons and the heroic struggle of the Voortrekkers against British imperialism and Bantu barbarism was re-enacted. This rising nationalism produced in the political sphere a strengthening of the National Party, in the economic sphere the formation of the *Reddingsdaadbond* and in the cultural sphere the formation of the *Ossewa Brandwag* (O.B.) – all bodies to protect and promote the interests of Afrikaners.

372

While Malan's National Party grew steadily it was very apparent by 1939 that the dualism which had been present in the United Party at its inception had not yet disappeared. When at the beginning of 1938 Hertzog announced in the House of Assembly that the *Stem van Suid-Afrika* would in future be the official anthem of South Africa, this news was not well received by those United Party members who wished to retain "God Save the King" as the South African anthem. When shortly after Union Day in 1939 Hertzog announced that the Union flag would henceforth be the national flag of South Africa and that the Union Jack was only to be flown on special occasions, the crack in the United Party was very evident. An announcement in 1938 by General J. C. G. Kemp, a member of the cabinet, that Roberts Heights would in future be known as Voortrekkerhoogte caused an even more serious disagreement in the United Party.

What was to break the Hertzog-Smuts coalition was the question of South Africa's attitude toward the Second World War which broke out on 3 September, 1939. Hertzog maintained that it was a war between European powers which did not affect South Africa and was in favour of remaining neutral. Smuts on the other hand maintained that it was in South Africa's interest to enter the war as an ally of Britain. Of the cabinet members five supported Hertzog and six supported Smuts. The House of Assembly would have to decide the issue. By a strange twist of fate parliament had at this time of crisis been convened for a special sitting in order to prolong the life of the Senate which was due to expire in a few days' time. On 4 September, 1939, the day after the declaration of war, the cabinet could thus refer the difference of opinion within its ranks to the House of Assembly. The debate continued throughout the day in a tense atmosphere. Hertzog was supported by a number of his own followers as well as by those of Malan, while Smuts was supported by his own followers, the members of the Dominion Party, the members of the Labour Party, the Native representatives, and a number of Hertzog's followers. When the vote was taken at 9 o'clock in the evening the count was 80 for Smuts and 67 for Hertzog. The United Party had split in two. The Prime Minister still had one card to play. That same evening he asked the Governor-General to dissolve parliament and announce an election. His request was refused and he resigned as Prime Minister. Thereupon Sir Patrick Duncan, the Governor-General, asked Smuts to form a cabinet. Smuts complied with the request and succeeded Hertzog as Prime Minister.

South Africa and the Second World War

It was therefore a divided South Africa which entered the Second World War on 6 September, 1939. Smuts united all those who wished to enter the war in a coalition government. He included Walter Madeley of the Labour Party and Colonel C. F. Stallard of the Dominion Party in his cabinet and also succeeded in forming it of an equal number of English and Afrikaans-speaking members. As far as administrative ability was concerned the only really outstanding minister besides the Prime Minister himself was the brilliant Jan Hofmeyr.

In the triple capacity of Prime Minister, Minister of Defence and Officer Commanding the South African Forces, Smuts threw all his amazing energy into the South African war effort. He was determined that his country should contribute her share in the struggle against Germany and Italy. Apart from the activities of South Africa's fighting forces, an important aspect of the country's share in the war would be the provision of military supplies for its own soldiers and for those of its allies. Consequently the appointment of a Director-General of War Supplies was announced in a proclamation of 24 November, 1939. Smuts appointed Dr H. J. van der Bijl to this important post. The Director-General of War Supplies had a vast organization under his control. He was granted extensive powers to organize all facilities in South Africa for the local production of war material, and to purchase from other countries whatever could not be locally manufactured. Large industrial state concerns such as the South African Railways and Harbours, the mines, the Mint and Iscor switched over largely to the production of war materials. Various private companies were also encouraged to organize themselves to manufacture military equipment. As a result South Africa was able to provide not only for its own military needs but also for some of its allies. A variety of war materials, including two-pounder anti-tank guns, ammunition (18 million rounds per month), high explosive shells, mortar bombs, howitzers and rifle spares was produced. In a proclamation dated 22 December, 1942, Smuts made the Director-General of War Supplies responsible for supervising civilian requirements as well and gave him the new title of Director-General of Supplies. The purpose of this proclamation was to effect the same balance in the needs of the civilian population as had been ensured for the military forces by the Director-General of War Supplies. This step further extended Dr van der Bijl's powers and next to Smuts, to whom he was responsible, he was the key figure in South Africa's war effort. In addition to the Director-General of Supplies Smuts appointed many other councils, directorates and committees to run the country's war machinery efficiently.

At the outbreak of war in 1939 South Africa's armed forces consisted of an army of 17,038 men, of whom 3,548 were in the permanent force, an air force of 1,837 and a navy of 432. Smuts intended to increase these numbers as quickly as possible. That he succeeded is clear when these figures are contrasted with the total number of people who served in the defence force during the war: 132,194 men in the army, 44,569 in the air force, 9,455 in the navy, as well as 24,975 women and 123,131 non-Whites.

During the Second World War South African soldiers were engaged in four principal theatres of war: East Africa (July 1940–November 1941), North Africa (May 1941–November 1942), Madagascar (June–November 1942), Italy (April 1943–May 1945). The first South African soldiers left for East Africa on 16 July, 1940. They belonged to the First South African Infantry Brigade under the command of Brigadier Dan Pienaar, which was enlarged later in the year to form the First South African Division. The South Africans in East Africa were under the supreme command of the British Lieutenant-General Alan Cunningham. Before the end of 1940 South African soldiers were responsible for one of the first Allied successes when, with the help of a Gold Coast Brigade, they defeated the Italians at El Wak. On 5 April, 1941, South Africans entered Addis Ababa and on 19 May, 1941, the Duke of Aosta with 5,000 men surrendered to Brigadier Pienaar. The war in East Africa continued in a desultory manner until the end of 1941, but its further progress in which South Africans played an important part, was almost throughout in favour of the Allies.

In the meantime the focus of the war in Africa had shifted to North Africa where the Germans, under the command of the brilliant General Erwin Rommel, had at the beginning of 1941 come to the help of the Italians. South Africa had two divisions in the Allied force which was known as the Eighth Army and which was originally under the command of Lieutenant-General Cunningham. The South African soldiers distinguished themselves at the battles of Sidi Rezegh (18–23 November 1941), Taib el Esem (22–26 November 1941), and Bardia and Sollum (16 December 1941–17 January 1942), but the Tobruk catastrophe was a serious blow to their prestige. Leading up to Tobruk was the large-scale offensive which Rommel launched on 26 May, 1942, and which resulted in heavy fighting at Knightsbridge, El Adem and Bir Hacheim. At first it seemed that the Allied forces – the two South African divisions at Gazala and Tobruk were just outside the battle area – had the ascendancy but after an unremitting battle lasting two weeks the better tanks and tactical superiority of the Germans gained them the victory. After the fall of Knightsbridge on 14 June, 1942, the Eighth Army hurriedly retreated. The First South African Division under Major-General Dan Pienaar was also forced to evacuate Gazala and retreat. The Second South African Division under Major-General H. B. Klopper was ordered to defend Tobruk. In Tobruk Klopper commanded combined units which, besides the South Africans, consisted of many British and Indian soldiers. Rommel was chasing the fleeing Eighth Army but he detached part of his force to wheel and attack Tobruk. Klopper's forces were unable to resist the German attack and on 21 June, 1942, he surrendered with approximately 25,000 men, among whom there were 10,722 South Africans. This was a great blow to the Allies in general and to the South African soldier in particular, but South Africa's contribution to the Second World War did not end on this depressing note. South Africans also played a part in the great battle of El Alamein which launched General Bernard Montgomery's offensive against Rommel. The tide had now turned against the Germans and on 13 May, 1943, the entire *Afrika Korps* under the command of Rommel's successor surrendered at Cape Bon.

This was the end of the war in Africa but there was still to be much fighting in Europe. Wishing his compatriots also to take part in the war on the European continent, Smuts now revoked his 1939 promise that South Africans would fight only in Africa and not be sent "overseas". On 27 January, 1943, he asked parliament's approval to send South African soldiers to Europe. The result was that the Sixth South African Armoured Division, under the command of Major-General W. H. Evered Poole, entered the war in Italy in April, 1943. The Sixth Division served in this theatre as a part of the Eighth (British) Army and the Fifth (American) Army for the rest of the war. In Italy 753 South Africans were killed as compared to 152 in East Africa and 2,104 in North Africa.

Afrikaner strife and discord

The most important aspect of South African history during the years of the Second World War was not, however, the country's contribution to the war against Germany and Italy but the violent internal political struggle which was sparked off by the war. Although there was no repetition of the 1914 rebellion the political conflict which erupted over South Africa's entry into the war was extraordinarily bitter. The nation was sharply divided into two large groups, those who supported South Africa's war effort and those who opposed it.

Smuts had to work carefully to prevent a repetition of the 1914 rebellion. His decision to confiscate all privately licensed fire-arms was partly directed at preventing an armed uprising. Hertzog and Malan urged the people to remain calm and repudiated any unconstitutional or violent action. Despite attempts from both sides to prevent violent clashes between the pro and anti-war groups some did occur. There were several clashes between the members of the *Ossewa Brandwag* and soldiers. There were also more extreme elements – *Stormjaers* – in the O.B. who could not be controlled and committed sabotage and treason or, as they viewed it, heroic acts of resistance against the government's war effort. These desperadoes achieved little and were soon confined in internment camps and prisons.

In the beginning it had seemed that parliament's decision for South Africa to enter the war would unite the Afrikaners. Because both Hertzog and Malan were opposed to South Africa's participating in the war they automatically moved closer to each other. Malan pleaded seriously for *hereniging* and Hertzog also favoured "co-operation between the . . . two parts of national-minded Afrikanerdom".[4] The political unification of the Afrikaners seemed to have been accomplished when Hertzog and Malan jointly addressed a large gathering of their followers at Monument Hill outside Pretoria on 9 September, 1939, i.e. only a few days after South Africa's entry into the war. Both leaders mentioned the new unity which had resulted from the disaster into which Smuts and his followers had plunged the country. Afrikaner unity seemed yet further ensured when on 1 November, 1939, at the Cape National Party Congress at Paarl Malan magnanimously proposed that Hertzog should become the leader of the new re-unified party. On 23 November, 1939, the two leaders and representatives of their two groups met in Pretoria to lay the foundation for unity.

4. D. F. Malan: *Afrikaner-Volkseenheid* (3rd ed., 1961), p. 177-182.

Agreement on many points was reached at this two-day conference but there were two points, namely the name of the new party and the republican ideal, on which no agreement was achieved. The name National Party was not acceptable to the supporters of Hertzog, especially N. C. Havenga, because this would amount to the Hertzog supporters being absorbed by the supporters of Malan. Hertzog objected particularly to the republican aim as proposed by the supporters of Malan in accordance with the principles of the National Party. Hertzog wanted the question of a republic to be dealt with in the same way as it had been in the old National Party (before fusion) and the United Party. This meant that individual members of the party would be free to propagate the republican ideal within the party, but that the endorsement of the republican ideal would not be a condition of party membership and that it would not be part of the constitution of the party. Hertzog argued that there were many Afrikaners and English who were opposed to imperialism and Smuts but who were nevertheless not republicans. The new (re-unified) party must also try to include this group. Malan's supporters had a totally different point of view. They insisted that the constitution of the new party should contain a clause which stated explicitly that the party was a republican party. Dr N. J. van der Merwe, one of Malan's followers at the conference, summarized the deadlock over the republican issue as follows: "General Hertzog stated that, just as in 1927, he should have the right to oppose me if I propagated the republican ideal. On this point we were deadlocked."[5] The negotiations of 23 and 24 November, 1939, broke down over the inability to reach agreement concerning the name of the party and the republican ideal.

However, the hope for unity was not abandoned. At the beginning of the 1940 parliamentary session Hertzog and Malan again began negotiating and on 29 January, 1940, they announced that an agreement had been reached between their respective caucuses. It was agreed that the new party should be known by the impossible name of *Herenigde Nasionale Party of Volksparty*, and the clash over the republican ideal was settled by Malan's supporters agreeing to the inclusion of a clause in the constitution which stated that party membership would not be refused to persons who were not convinced of the desirability of a republic. This latter concession was a victory for Hertzog. After this the supporters of Hertzog and Malan sat together in parliament and they also had a common caucus. This agreement seemed to ensure that the political unity of Afrikanerdom had at last been attained. It was, however, nothing more than a makeshift arrangement. There were serious differences between Hertzog and Malan and especially between Hertzog and a number of Malan's more extreme supporters. They were the same differences which had caused the 1933 split. Hertzog thought that he could persuade Malan's supporters to accept his principles. This was clearly a delusion. That Malan had been magnanimous enough to offer Hertzog the leadership of the new party did not mean that all Malan's supporters were satisfied with this arrangement. There were prominent

5. G. D. Scholtz: *Nicolaas Johannes van der Merwe* (1944), p. 404.

members of Malan's National Party who were not content to have Hertzog for a leader. They considered the former Prime Minister to be too moderate, insufficiently enthusiastic as far as Afrikaner nationalism was concerned and without principles. During 1940 they worked continually to undermine his leadership. Against Hertzog's express wishes some of Malan's followers, among them Dr N. J. van der Merwe and C. R. Swart, arranged a national republican gathering for 20 July, 1940, in Bloemfontein to consider ways of establishing a republic. According to Malan the decisions reached at this meeting were "the height of folly" and could not but offend Hertzog.[6] At about the same time as this republican gathering there was a rumour in Bloemfontein that two letters written by Hertzog and Havenga had been found in a Free Mason's suitcase. In these letters they were supposed to have declared themselves willing in the event of Britain losing the war to support Smuts if he declared a "red" (i.e. British orientated) republic in South Africa in which the Afrikaners would be suppressed. This rumour, which was fostered by Dr N. J. van der Merwe and C. R. Swart, spread rapidly through the country. Complaints, clearly aimed at Hertzog, about the lack of leadership for Afrikanerdom began appearing in the nationalist press. Hertzog's prestige as a leader was further undermined by J. G. Strijdom and C. R. Swart with slogans such as "stick to principles not leaders" and warnings against a slavish worship of leaders.[7]

At the Free State foundation congress of the *Herenigde Nasionale Party of Volksparty* it became clear to what extent the congress members were opposed to Hertzog's leadership. When two draft constitutions, one from Hertzog and one from the Acting Federal Council for the new party, were voted on at the congress, Hertzog's draft was rejected by a large majority. Hertzog considered this to be a motion of no confidence in his leadership and resigned as party leader. He was followed by a small number of loyal followers when he left the congress hall. He also resigned as member of parliament, withdrew from public life and settled on his farm near Witbank. He died two years later on 21 November, 1942.

The *Herenigde* Party was no longer re-unified. Afrikanerdom, which was overwhelmingly opposed to the war, was once again split. Besides the *Herenigde* Party led by Malan there were various other parties. Some of Hertzog's followers effected a reconciliation with Malan but the more loyal ones formed the Afrikaner Party under Havenga. Oswald Pirow broke away and founded the *Nuwe Orde* into which he drew all those who were admirers of the Germans and their national socialism. Besides these groups there was the *Ossewa Brandwag* which started out as a cultural movement but gradually became very influential in the political arena.

These opposition parties attacked one another even more vigorously than they attacked the government. A particularly bitter conflict developed between

6. D. F. Malan: *Afrikaner-Volkseenheid* (3rd ed., 1961), p. 192.
7. M. Roberts and A. E. G. Trollip: *The South African Opposition 1939 – 1945* (1947), pp. 45 and 50.

the *Herenigde* Party and the O.B. Briefly, the story behind this feud was this: The so-called Cradock agreement was entered into on 29 October, 1940 (a few days before Hertzog's resignation) between Malan and the O.B., in terms of which the *Herenigde* Party would represent Afrikanerdom in the political sphere while the O.B. would limit its activities to the non-political field. When, however, Dr Hans van Rensburg resigned as Administrator of the Free State and became the Commandant-General of this semi-military organization on 15 January, 1941, this agreement was honoured in the breach. The O.B.'s new leader also entered the political arena and since he advocated a political philosophy which differed little from that of Adolf Hitler and did not disguise his contempt for the party politics of a democracy he soon clashed with Malan and the *Herenigde* Party. As a result Malan came out strongly against the O.B. with its foreign ideology and asked members of his party to resign from it. From the time in the middle of 1941, when Malan began to oppose the O.B., it lost ground.

It was a divided opposition which faced the 1943 election, while Smuts's United Party could approach the contest with self-confidence. In 1943 the war was starting to turn in favour of the Allies and this was to the advantage of the United Party. The governing party won 105 seats and also enjoyed the support of 2 Independents and 3 Native representatives while the opposition shrank from 63 to 43. If Smuts had cause to be satisfied so also had Malan. The leader of the *Herenigde* Party increased his own following in parliament by 2 while the other opposition parties, the Afrikaner Party and the *Nuwe Orde*, were eliminated.

Economic growth (1939–1948)

The economy of South Africa changed little during the first two years of the war but from 1942 the effects of the war began to be felt. Especially remarkable in the economy of South Africa from 1939 to 1945 was that money was plentiful but that commodities and foodstuffs were scarce.

The amount of money in circulation, including money on demand in the banks, rose from £116 million in 1939 to £349 million in 1945. This was owing particularly to increased state expenditure which created income, an increase in the price of gold from £7 8s to £8 8s at the outbreak of the war, a greater increase in exports than imports, higher prices for exports, visiting ships, and a considerable investment in South Africa by foreign governments. As was the case during the First World War prices rose sharply. From 1939 to 1945 the wholesale price index rose from 97.6 to 152.6 and the retail price index from 99.9 to 132.2. In order to counter this inflationary tendency the government introduced price control. A price controller, with wide powers to control price increases, was appointed on 29 August, 1941.

The shortage of commodities was owing to the production capacity being used for war purposes as well as to the limiting of imports. The scarcity of certain articles necessitated the introduction of control measures in 1942. During the first half of 1942 various commodities such as petrol, rubber, paper, motor vehicles, building material, textiles, agricultural implements and wood were declared to be controlled goods. A controller was appointed for each of the above-mentioned commodities. That South Africa experienced a shortage of those goods which before the war had all been imported is easy enough to understand. What, however, is less understandable is that there should have been shortages of foodstuffs such as maize, sugar, wheat and meat. The maize-board appeared to lose all sense of proportion. During the 1941–1942 season they recommended the export of maize when there was already a shortage of this food so important for the non-Whites. Sugar was exported to Britain on a large scale while there was a sugar shortage in South Africa. The wheat shortage assumed such proportions that the baking of white bread was prohibited. The greatest dissatisfaction, however, was that concerning the scarcity of meat in the cities. The government's measures against the increase in the price of meat were such that in the urban areas – controlled areas – meat was unobtainable while in the rural areas – uncontrolled areas – it could easily be obtained. In his attempt to combat the shortage of meat in urban areas the Minister for Agriculture, J. G. N. Strauss, considered it advisable to proclaim one day per week a "meatless day". This measure had no effect on the meat shortage but only on the minister's popularity. The food shortage caused much criticism of the government. The remarkable thing was that South Africa was an agricultural country which was unable to feed itself. The food shortage was so serious in 1946 that Smuts invited two experts from the British Ministry of Food to South Africa. These two experts proposed a scheme for rationing bread, wheat flour, mealie meal and maize products and a registration scheme for the customers of retailers to control the purchase of items such as tea, sugar and soap. However, an improvement in the food position during 1947 made the implementation of this scheme unnecessary.

Despite the irritating shortages of imported commodities and food the war years were a period of economic prosperity in South Africa. Even during the war there were good overseas markets for South Africa's most important exports such as gold, wool and diamonds. The standard of living also improved because the incomes of the poorer classes (especially the poorer Whites) rose spectacularly during the war. By the end of the Second World War South Africa's prosperity, prestige and self-confidence had all increased.

A noteworthy aspect of the South African economy during the years 1939–1948 was the rapid development of industry. To encourage the establishment of industries the government founded the Industrial Development Corporation (I.D.C.) in 1940, and in 1945 the development of industries was further stimulated by the foundation of two more important institutions, the Council for Scientific and Industrial Research (C.S.I.R.) which was to help solve various difficulties encountered frequently by the industries, and the South African Bureau of Standards (S.A.B.S.) which was to test the quality of locally manufactured industrial goods.

With the termination of hostilities in Europe the strife between those who supported and those who opposed South Africa's participation in the war also came to an end. Other questions now became the focus of attention in South African politics and resulted in a reorientation of the political parties. The Smuts-Madeley-Stallard coalition broke up even before the end of 1945 when Madeley of the Labour Party and Stallard of the Dominion Party resigned from the cabinet and with their followers joined the opposition. In the post-war political atmosphere they were more at home among the members of Malan's *Herenigde* Party than among the members of Smuts's United Party. On the racial question, which had become the centre of South African politics, their attitude was closer to Malan's than it was to that of the left-wing (Hofmeyr) of the United Party.

Race relations in South Africa had deteriorated rapidly during Smuts's government. Smuts's act concerning Asiatic Land Tenure and Indian Representation (1946), in terms of which on the one hand the rights of Indians to possess fixed property were curtailed, while on the other they were granted a voice in political matters, satisfied neither the Indians nor the opposition. The *Herenigde* Party, the Dominion Party, and a part of the Labour Party under Madeley were opposed to granting the franchise to the Indians while the Indians considered this legislation to be "a diabolic attempt to strangulate the Indians economically and degrade them socially".[8] India broke off trade relations with South Africa in protest against this act. Relations between the government and the Bantu were also not satisfactory. The Native Representative Council, which had been introduced in 1936, refused to co-operate any more with the government.

In agreement with Hegel's dialectic theory the period of racial discrimination which had characterized Hitler's Germany was after the war followed almost throughout the world by a period in which an attempt was made to remove all barriers and distinctions between races. We are living in the period of anticolonialism, the age of Asia and Africa which is characterized by the abdication of the white man and the rise of the black man. The outside world as well as many Whites and non-Whites in South Africa demanded that South Africa forsake its traditional policy of segregation and fall into step with the rest of the world. In 1946, amidst strong criticism of South Africa's racial policy, Smuts went to Lake Success to obtain U.N.O.'s approval for his plan to incorporate South-West Africa into the Union of South Africa. He was unsuccessful in his endeavours, however, owing to resolute opposition from India, who, supported by other member states, launched a bitter attack on South Africa's racial policy. Even Smuts's great international prestige was unable to counter the attacks on South Africa's racial policy.

In South Africa itself foreign criticism of the country's traditional racial policy had an effect opposite to that intended. The Whites in South Africa

8. D. W. Krüger: *The Age of the Generals* (2nd ed., 1961), p. 218.

viewed the rise of the black man and the elimination of colour bars elsewhere in the world as a threat to their own survival and did not intend to change their traditional policy because of pressure from outside their borders. The race question assumed a central position in politics and it was clear that it would play an important role in the first post-war election.

Few people in South Africa, even among the Nationalists, expected a change of government in 1948. The United Party's prestige had increased because of the war and it was also fortunate in having a leader of world-wide reputation. Although he was Prime Minister of one of the lesser states Smuts had developed into a world figure during the war years. He filled his roles as soldier, statesman, philosopher and prophet with distinction. When he spoke the world listened attentively. In Britain and the United States of America he was highly esteemed and he was repeatedly showered with honours. The King raised him to the rank of Field Marshal in the British Army in 1941; of all the statesmen in the dominions he alone was admitted to the War Cabinet; the preamble to the charter of the U.N.O. was written by him. No other South African had ever risen to such heights of international fame. The world in general regarded Smuts as a great man but there were people in South Africa who thought otherwise. In his own country many of his own Afrikaner compatriots did not admire him. In their eyes he had placed Britain before his own country and was a traitor to Afrikanerdom. These Afrikaner nationalists considered Smuts to be a great Englishman but a bad Afrikaner. They wanted at any cost to prevent Smuts from governing South Africa for another five years.

Because of this determination divided Afrikanerdom succeeded in closing its ranks. In 1947 Malan, the leader of the *Herenigde* Party, and Havenga, the leader of the Afrikaner Party, succeeded in reaching an election agreement despite the opposition of some of the provincial leaders of the *Herenigde* Party.[9] The colour question was the crux of their attack on the Smuts government. In a country where racial integration would inevitably cause the White minority to lose power, the idea of apartheid or separate development which the *Herenigde* Party and its ally the Afrikaner Party now advocated attracted the White electorate. The Malan-Havenga alliance also exploited other weaknesses in the Smuts government, such as the hundred and one war-time irritations which were still fresh in the voters' minds, the government's immigration policy, its inability to solve the housing problem, and its general administrative ineptitude.

On 26 May, 1948, the nation voted. The result was a victory for Afrikaner nationalism: *Herenigde* Party 70 (previously 43), Afrikaner Party 9 (previously 0), United Party 65 (previously 89), Labour Party 6 (previously 9). The Malan-Havenga coalition had a majority of 5 over the combined United Party, the Labour Party and the Native representatives. A bitterly disillusioned Smuts resigned as Prime Minister and Malan formed a cabinet.

9. Dr D. F. Malan mentions in his book *Afrikaner-Volkseenheid* (3rd ed., 1961), pp. 233-234, that both J. G. Strijdom and C. R. Swart were opposed to concluding an alliance with the Afrikaner Party, but according to Swart's biographer, Jannie Kruger, in his book *President C. R. Swart* (1961), pp. 128-129, this assertion is false as far as Swart is concerned.

Although not many years have lapsed since 1948 it is already possible to perceive that that date represents one of the major turning points in the history of South Africa. In that year not only did Afrikaner nationalism experience its greatest triumph but also a decisive choice was made between the two possible solutions to the colour question. When the nation was confronted with a choice between integration and segregation, it chose segregation or apartheid,[10] a term which was destined for world-wide notoriety.

Malan included two members of the Afrikaner Party in his cabinet, one of whom, Havenga, was named as Deputy Prime Minister. The members of Malan's cabinet were all Afrikaans-speaking but were also all fully bilingual. In both these respects it was unique in ways to which no former cabinet could lay claim.

To begin with the government's majority in the Assembly was very small, so small in fact that the *Herenigde* Party was entirely dependent on the support of its ally, the Afrikaner Party. Its position gradually improved, however. In 1949 Vereeniging was won from the United Party in a by-election, and when in 1950 South-West Africa also started electing representatives to parliament – six members for the House of Assembly and four Senators – the *Herenigde* Party's position improved considerably because they gained all six South-West African seats. In 1951 the government was further strengthened, not by an increase in seats, but internally by the fusion of the *Herenigde* and Afrikaner Parties to become what was thereafter known as the National Party.

With the 1953 election the National Party increased its majority in the Assembly from 86 to 94 while the United Party's seats decreased from 64 to 57 and the Labour Party's from 6 to 5.

On 30 November, 1954, Malan, who was already eighty, resigned as Prime Minister owing to his advanced age. Unlike Smuts he did not designate his successor but left it to the party caucus to decide. It was, however, well known that he would have liked Havenga, the leader of the former Afrikaner Party, to succeed him. Both Havenga and Strijdom were nominated by the caucus but when it became clear that Strijdom would obtain a majority vote Havenga withdrew, and retired from politics. Strijdom, the new Prime Minister, was a fiery republican who was well known for his severity towards anti-Afrikaans and anti-apartheid ideas and for whom apartheid was synonymous with "white domination".

Under Strijdom's leadership the National Party moved toward the 1958 election, as towards the previous two, relying on its policy of apartheid. Once again the Nationalists strengthened their position and increased their number of seats from 94 to 103 – almost two-thirds of the House – while the United Party seats decreased from 57 to 53 and the Labour Party lost all five of its seats.

10. For the history of this word see N. J. Rhoodie and H. J. Venter: *Die Apartheidsgedagte* (1959), pp. 174 – 177.

Since the establishment of the Union of South Africa no party had ever succeeded in increasing its parliamentary representation after it had been in office for two terms. The White population of South Africa was apparently in no mood to tolerate any dilution of the policy of apartheid.

Strijdom was not destined to be the Prime Minister of South Africa for long. He died on 24 August, 1958, after having held office for a little more than three years. The National Party caucus nominated three men to succeed Strijdom, C. R. Swart, Dr T. E. Dönges and Dr H. F. Verwoerd, all members of the cabinet. Swart was eliminated in the first ballot, thereafter Verwoerd obtained 98 votes and Dönges 75. Verwoerd thus became the sixth Prime Minister of South Africa. The new Prime Minister had risen rapidly in politics since his election as Senator in 1948. In October, 1950, he had been appointed Minister of Native Affairs and in this function he impressed both his supporters and opponents with his intellect, his dedication and his strong will. More than anyone else he was the architect of and driving force behind the policy of apartheid, and more than anyone else he was responsible for transforming this policy of apartheid from a merely negative policy of domination and suppression (baasskap) into a positive policy of separate development which aimed at "fairness to each and justice to all".[11] His grappling with South Africa's central problem, even should his ideas prove wrong, made him a man of great significance.

Apartheid

Malan's government intended to make a determined attempt to solve the colour question. One law after the other was placed on the statute-book to emphasize the division between the races. In 1949 the *Prohibition of Mixed Marriages Act* made marriages between Whites and non-Whites, of which there had never been more than 100 per year in comparison with 25,000 White marriages, illegal. This was followed in 1950 by the *Immorality Amendment Act* which prohibited extra-marital sexual relations between Whites and all non-Whites (which included Coloureds) and not only between Whites and Natives as was the position in terms of a 1927 act. To clarify the often vague distinction between the races the *Population Registration Act* was enacted in 1950. In terms of this act every South African subject over sixteen had to possess an identification card on which his race (White, Asiatic, Coloured or Bantu) was indicated. The next step was the introduction of residential apartheid through the *Group Areas Act* (1950). Residential apartheid between Whites and Bantu was a long established South African custom but the residential areas of the Coloureds and Indians were not clearly demarcated from the White residential areas. This act, which was considered by Dr T. E. Dönges to be the corner-stone of apartheid, changed this, and demarcated separate residential areas for all the various racial groups. Next to appear on the Statute Book was the *Reservation of Separate Amenities Act* (1953) which made apartheid compulsory in all public places where any, however

11. A. N. Pelzer: *Verwoerd aan die Woord* (2nd ed., 1964), p. XXXVI.

defective, provision was made for separate amenities. This law stated that when the owner or person in charge of any property, whether a park, a train, a swimming bath, offices or anything else, provided separate conveniences for the various races it would be a punishable offence to transgress such separations. Apartheid in public places was naturally not new because there had been separate buses, separate railway coaches, separate benches in public parks and separate bathing facilities and beaches for the different races long before 1948. The innovation was that what had previously been custom had now become a written law. Residential apartheid was further enforced through two laws which were closely related to the previously mentioned *Group Areas Act:* the *Resettlement of Natives Act* of 1954 which resulted in 100,000 Bantus being removed from the squatter camps in the western areas of Johannesburg and resettled in the better residential area of Meadowlands, and the *Natives (Urban Areas) Amendment Act* of 1955 which also became known as the "Locations in the Sky Act" and which ended the large-scale accommodation of non-White servants on the top floors of flat buildings.

The most contentious of all the apartheid measures introduced by the government was not, however, in the sphere of social apartheid but in that of political apartheid. In accordance with its policy of apartheid the government decided to remove the enfranchised Coloured voters, approximately 38,000, from the ordinary (White) voters' roll and place them on a separate (Coloured) voters' roll so that they could return their own representatives to parliament. The government naturally knew that the relevant clauses in the South Africa Act of 1909 were entrenched and could only be changed by a two-thirds' majority. There were, however, eminent constitutional jurists in South Africa and England who considered that, because of later developments such as the Statute of Westminster in 1931 and a 1937 decision of the Appeal Court, these clauses were no longer entrenched and that an ordinary majority would be sufficient to change the relevant clauses. Acting on this legal advice the government in 1951 piloted a bill through parliament with an ordinary majority (that is to say without a two-thirds' majority) to place the Coloureds on a separate voters' roll. The opposition would not accept this and on behalf of a Coloured voter contested the validity of the *Separate Representation of Voters Act* in the Supreme Court. When the Supreme Court, basing its decision on the previously mentioned 1937 Appeal Court decision, declared the law valid, the opposition took the matter to the Appeal Court. On 20 March, 1952, the country's highest court declared the act invalid. The government refused to leave the matter there and piloted a bill through parliament which stipulated that parliament was to be the highest court for constitutional matters. The Appeal Court also declared this law, the *High Court of Parliament Act*, invalid and continued to consider itself the highest court in the country for all matters including constitutional ones. The attempt to place the Coloureds on a separate voters' roll was thus repeatedly obstructed by the Appeal Court. The government, however, had no intention of accepting defeat. When the 1953 election returned the National Party to power with an increased majority the government was strengthened in its resolve to place the Coloureds on a separate voters' roll. The government needed fifteen votes for a two-thirds' majority and when several members of the opposition declared their willingness to support the bill, the government was encouraged to open the matter again. In 1953 the government, calling on the support of the right-wing of the United Party, once again introduced a bill in parliament, but although they came very close to securing a two-thirds' majority their attempt was not successful.

The matter was temporarily shelved but, when at the end of 1954 Malan resigned as Prime Minister, his successor, Strijdom, resumed the struggle. The government's plan was first to increase the number of judges who had to hear constitutional matters and secondly to "pack" the Senate with its own supporters to obtain the necessary two-thirds' majority. In spite of vehement protests, amongst others by the Black Sash, against the means the government was using to achieve its purposes the two bills which were to effect the government's plan were introduced and became law in 1955. The *Appellate Division Quorum Act* stipulated that when constitutional cases were heard the number of Appeal judges would be increased from five to eleven and the *Senate Act* not only increased the number of senators from 48 to 89 but also changed the way in which the Senate was constituted so that the National Party held 77 seats in the new Senate. Thus assured of a two-thirds' majority in parliament the government introduced a bill in 1956 to cancel the entrenchment of the clauses relating to the non-White franchise and at the same time to place the Coloureds on a separate voters' roll. This bill was passed by a two-thirds' majority. The opposition also took this law to the Appeal Court but the enlarged Appeal Court decided with a majority of ten to one that the Coloureds had been legally removed from the common voters' roll. This decision ended the five-year struggle concerning the separate representation of the Coloureds.

In 1959 the government also introduced apartheid in the universities with the *Separate Universities Act*. This law prohibited South Africa's "open" universities, Witwatersrand and Cape Town, from admitting any more non-Whites and provided for separate universities for the non-Whites, at Ngoye in Zululand for the Zulus, at Durban for the Indians, at Turfloop in the Northern Transvaal for the Sothos, at Bellville near Cape Town for the Coloureds and at the existing Fort Hare at Alice near King William's Town for the Xhosas.

All these laws enforced apartheid but did not touch the core of the race problem. These laws did not answer any of the questions concerning the political rights of the non-Whites, the largest part of the South African population. They were negative laws aimed at emphasizing the division between the various races but the policy of apartheid as a policy of separate development also has a positive aspect. The non-Whites would be granted political rights in their own homelands just as the Whites enjoyed political rights in the white areas of South Africa. The first step towards granting self-government to the Bantu was the *Bantu Authorities Act* of 1951. Verwoerd's *Bantu Education Act* of 1953

12. G. M. Carter: *The Politics of Inequality* (3rd ed., 1962), p. 84.

was also a step towards Bantu self-government. This act, which was based on the Eiselen Commission's report on Bantu education, first placed all Bantu education, which formerly had been mainly in the hands of subsidized churches and mission societies, under the control of the state, secondly, it gave the parents more share in determining their children's education and, thirdly, the syllabi were to conform more to the nature and needs of the Bantu. Various churches and mission societies, for example the Anglican church, protested vehemently against this act but Verwoerd was not deterred by this criticism and continued to implement the law. In 1959 the *Promotion of Self-Government Act* was a further step towards self-governing Bantu reserves from which the Whites would be completely withdrawn. This act divided the many Bantu reserves in South Africa into eight territorial units. A Commissioner-General was appointed at the head of each of these eight units and instructed to guide his territory towards self-government. The granting of political rights to the Bantus in their own homelands made the native representatives who had been sitting in parliament since 1936 unnecessary, and *The Promotion of Self-Government Act* therefore also eliminated them.

The opposition: decline and disintegration

What was the history of the opposition from 1948 to 1961 while the National Party was steadily increasing its power and imperturbably carrying out its programme of apartheid? After 1948 the United Party began to decline steadily. Smuts who, at the insistence of his followers, remained on as leader of the United Party, was not only a tired old man but had been dazed by the election defeat which his party had suffered. Furthermore, although a statesman of international repute he was yet unable to offer a constructive solution to South Africa's greatest problem, namely that of race relations. He had always shied away from this problem and now, after 1948, and in his last years, he could offer nothing to counter Malan's apartheid policy. In 1948 Smuts and his party suffered a serious loss with the death of Jan Hofmeyr who next to Smuts was the most brilliant personality in the ranks of the United Party and who was considered by many to be Smuts's successor.[13] Smuts died in September 1950 and in accordance with his wish was succeeded as leader of the United Party by J. G. N. Strauss. From the beginning the new leader encountered opposition in his own party, partly because many doubted his qualities of leadership and partly because he had to combine so many divergent elements in the United Party.

Excepting the non-Whites all opponents of the government belonged to one of two opposition parties, the United Party or the Labour Party, but during the first half of 1951 an organization known as the Torch Commando was established. It was outside the field of party politics and took a strong stand

13. Various members of the United Party were however of the opinion that Hofmeyr's liberal convictions lost them the election. See A. Paton: *Hofmeyr* (1964), pp. 490 – 505.

against the government in general and the policy of separate representation of the Coloureds in particular. It campaigned against the "monstrous act" which aimed at separate representation for the Coloureds with nightly torch processions, protest meetings and petitions. Because of the antipathies they had in common the Torch Commando, the United Party and the Labour Party joined forces in 1952 to form the United Front in an effort to defeat the government at the next election. This effort was in vain, however, and the National Party increased its majority at the 1953 election.

The election defeat suffered by the United Party in 1953 resulted in three groups splitting off to form the Liberal Party, the Union Federal Party and the Conservative Party. After the suppression of the Communist Party the Liberal Party, led by Margaret Ballinger, was the political party in South Africa which was furthest to the left and which propagated general integration and political equality of Whites and non-Whites; the Union Federal Party under the leadership of Senator Heaton Nicolls was a last desperate attempt of some English-speaking people, principally in Natal, to resist the steadily growing influence of Afrikanerdom; Bailey Bekker's Conservative Party consisted of some of the United Party's right wing who were not happy with Strauss's leadership. None of these parties was, however, important in the political history of South Africa. Two of them, the United Federal Party and the Conservative Party, died an early death and although the Liberal Party still exists it has little support. The secession of refractory groups from the United Party did not, however, decrease dissatisfaction in Strauss's leadership and on 21 November, 1956, he was replaced by Sir de Villiers Graaff. This change of leadership could not halt the decline of the United Party and its number of parliamentary seats decreased still further in the 1958 election.

After the 1958 election there was a split between the United Party's right and left wings when, on 13 August, 1959, twelve United Party members of parliament broke away to form the Progressive Party under the leadership of Dr Jan Steytler. This new party, which was fortunate enough to gain the support of Harry Oppenheimer, the biggest financial magnate in South Africa, as well as of several newspapers, advocated a qualified franchise for all races. The supporters of the Progressive Party completely reject the policy of apartheid and differ from the Liberal Party only in that they are more moderate and do not wish to introduce the concept of one-man-one-vote without qualification. For a short while from 1959 to 1961 the Progressive Party had eleven members in parliament (one of the original twelve resigned from the party) but with one exception they were all eliminated in the 1961 election.

Non-Whites: discontent and resistance

There were clear signs, even before 1948, of a growing dissatisfaction among some of the non-Whites in connection with their political impotence and economic backwardness. After this date their dissatisfaction increased steadily and was fanned by communist agitators. The political and economic lag of the non-

Whites was fertile ground for Marxism. The history of the Communist Party in South Africa was closely associated not only with honest attempts to improve the economic position and political strength of the non-Whites but also with non-White strikes, disturbances, anarchy and violence. Sam Kahn, a Native representative in Parliament, and Fred Carneson, a Native representative in the Cape Provincial Council, were both members of the Communist Party. Several of the officials of the African National Congress were also fervent communists. This infiltration of communism into South Africa disturbed the government and in 1950 the *Suppression of Communism Act* was passed to ban the Communist Party, exclude communists from trade unions and other bodies and make the propagation of communism a crime. If this law did control communism in South Africa it could not, however, remove evil influences already at work or mitigate the grievances of the non-Whites.

The African National Congress, which had been founded in 1912 and always considered itself to be the only mouthpiece of the Bantu, adopted a provocative attitude after 1948. To mark its protest against the apartheid laws this body called on all Bantu to stay away from work on 1 May, 1951. When that day arrived and the government tried to protect non-strikers against intimidation, clashes between the police and the strikers resulted in the deaths of eighteen Bantu. The leaders of the African National Congress were not, however, deterred by the consequences of their attempted resistance but decided to adopt an even more provocative attitude towards the government. At a meeting of this organization held at Bloemfontein from 15 to 17 December, 1951, it was decided that unless the government revoked six of its discriminatory laws before 29 February, 1952, protest demonstrations would be held on 6 April, 1952 – to coincide with the Van Riebeeck Festival, and these demonstrations would herald further resistance to the government's unfair laws. The Prime Minister, Malan, was informed of this decision in a letter dated 21 January, 1952, and signed by James S. Moroka (president) and W. M. Sisulu (secretary). This letter referred to "a rising tide of bitterness and tension" amongst the Bantu and protested against "legislation that continues to insult and degrade the African people".[14] In his reply to this letter the Prime Minister rejected the African National Congress's demand and warned them that if their plans encouraged the Bantu to violate law and order they would have to bear the consequences. The African National Congress, however, refused to withdraw their demands. When the government continued to ignore them they held a number of protest meetings on 6 April, 1952. The actual resistance campaign which took the form of large scale offences against the apartheid regulations began on 26 June, 1952. In the months that followed more than 8,000 Bantus, mainly in the large urban areas, started infringing the pass laws, entering railway coaches and waiting rooms for Whites, ignoring curfews, and breaking apartheid regulations. When the offenders were arrested they offered no resistance and pleaded guilty in court.

14. L. E. Neame: *The History of Apartheid* (1962), p. 98; and G. M. Carter, *The Politics of Inequality* (3rd ed., 1962), p. 370.

They refused to pay fines and elected to serve prison sentences. The whole resistance campaign was characterized by strict discipline but undisciplined action followed in its wake. Riots, apparently originating in the tension which accompanied the non-violence resistance movement, broke out in locations in Port Elizabeth, East London and Kimberley, and resulted in murder and arson.

At the beginning of 1953 the government enacted two drastic laws which increased its powers of dealing with passive resistance movements and riots. The *Criminal Law Amendment Act* provided for severe penalties where persons deliberately offended against the laws of the land as a form of protest or resistance to such laws, while the *Public Safety Act* gave the government the necessary authority to declare a state of emergency in a specific area or in the country as a whole.

Although these laws threatened agitators and anarchists they naturally did nothing to dispel the bitterness and urge to resist of some of the non-White leaders. A "Congress of the People" was held at Kliptown near Johannesburg on 26 June, 1955, and was attended by 3,000 delegates of the African National Congress, the Coloured People's Organization, the Indian Congress and the Congress of Democrats, the latter being a White leftist organization. Even before the police could end the meeting on the second day a "Freedom Charter" was adopted which demanded a type of socialist democracy with equal rights for all races in South Africa. In 1956 the government, which considered communist agitators to be the source of all unrest among the non-Whites, ordered the Russian Consulate to be closed since it had evidence that members of the consulate were in contact with anarchist elements in South Africa. In its fight against communist agitators the government went even further. On 5 December, 1956, the police arrested 156 people, White and non-White, all over South Africa on charges of high treason. Among these 156 there were Albert Luthuli (president of the African National Congress), Dr G. M. Naiker (president of the Indian Congress) and L. B. Lee-Warden (Native representative in parliament). The accused were charged with inciting people to violence and preparing for the overthrow of the government by violent revolution. Although most of the accused were discharged after nine months, the case against the remaining twenty-nine dragged on until March, 1961, when they were all found not guilty. The case attracted much interest both locally and abroad. The sympathy of the outside world was clearly with the accused and in Britain £173,000 was collected to pay their legal costs.

But even this high treason case did not deter the revolutionary elements. There were signs of increasing resistance. Some members of the African National Congress considered it to be too moderate and favoured a more aggressive tone and more drastic action. In 1959 this section broke away and formed the Pan African Congress under the leadership of Robert Sobukwe.

During 1959 riots repeatedly broke out in various parts of the country. In Lady Selborne, Pretoria (26 February), in Cato Manor, Durban (19 June), in Pietermaritzburg (15 August), in Paarl (11 November), and in Windhoek (11

December), the police were compelled to fire on insurgents. Numbers of Bantu, in Windhoek as many as twelve, were killed. The riots continued, however, and in 1960 the resistance movement became very serious indeed. The Pan African Congress encouraged Bantus to go to their nearest police stations and ask to be arrested because they refused to carry passes. On 21 March, 1960, the police at Sharpeville, near Vereeniging, fired on a large number of Bantus who were advancing on the police station and killed 69. On the same day riots also broke out in Langa, a Bantu township near Cape Town. There were strikes in a number of cities and in Cape Town a procession of 30,000 Bantus moved right into the centre of the city. This was the most serious crisis of its type that South Africa had yet experienced.

The government reacted by ordering a mass arrest of the instigators, declaring a state of emergency in eighty districts, mobilizing units of the Active Citizen's Force and piloting the *Unlawful Organizations Act* through parliament. This act enabled it to declare the African National Congress and the Pan African Congress unlawful organizations. The Bantu township, Langa, was encircled by heavily armed troops and cut off from the outside world.

A few days later, on 9 April, 1960, South Africa was shocked again when Dr Verwoerd was critically wounded in an attempted assassination by a mentally unbalanced White. The Prime Minister, who was shot twice in the head, miraculously escaped death.

The government's drastic steps against the resistance movement produced the desired effect and within a short while all traces of resistance and violence had disappeared. The state of emergency was ended a few months later on 31 August, 1960.

Opposition to South Africa's policy of apartheid did not occur only within the country's borders. In fact the most severe and hostile criticism of South Africa's racial policy came from outside the country: from numerous small and backward states in Africa, from Asia, from Eastern Europe and also from Western Europe and the United States of America. In particular, South Africa was continuously criticized in the United Nations Organization. Since 1946, even before the National Party came to power in South Africa, various states in the U.N.O. had repeatedly stated that they did not approve of South Africa's discriminatory attitude towards the non-Whites within its borders. Opportunity for criticism of South Africa originally arose when South-West Africa, over which the U.N.O. claimed trusteeship rights, was discussed, and when India protested against South Africa's treatment of the Indians within its borders, but after 1952 South Africa's racial policy was specifically and directly attacked on the grounds that it was a threat to world peace.

Economic growth (1948–1961)

Since 1948 the racial problem has dominated the South African scene to such an extent that other equally important matters tend to escape the notice of the historian. One of these is South Africa's enormous economic progress.

The discovery of the Free State gold-fields, the working of the new gold mines on the West Rand, and the development of deep-level mining, contributed to economic growth in the years immediately after the war. From the beginning of 1947 foreign capital poured into the country. Partly because of the uncertainty which followed the 1948 election the flow of capital diminished towards the middle of 1948. Because imports went on increasing, the country's gold and foreign reserves decreased rapidly. Consequently the Minister of Finance, Havenga, introduced certain measures even before the end of 1948 to stop the outflow of capital and by the middle of 1949 he went even further to introduce stricter import control. In the latter half of 1949 South Africa, like most non-dollar countries, decided to devalue its money and the value of the South African £ decreased from $4.03 to $2.80. After this the economic position gradually improved. In 1960 there was another economic decline when the serious race riots of that year together with racial clashes elsewhere on the African continent resulted in so much uncertainty that £80 million of private capital was withdrawn from South Africa. More foreign capital was withdrawn in 1961 when South Africa decided to discontinue her membership of the Commonwealth. However, confidence in the South African economy was speedily re-established and the upward economic tendency reappeared. In fact, apart from these and a few other minor setbacks, the economic prosperity of the country from immediately after the Second World War has continued uninterruptedly.

South Africa's industrial development which had been so rapid during the war and the first post-war years declined slightly after 1948 but nevertheless maintained an amazing momentum. According to a 1961 survey by the Department of Trade and Industry 85% of the consumer goods bought in South African shops were manufactured in South Africa. Some highlights in primary and secondary industrial developments are the beginning of production in the first two Free State gold mines in 1951; the opening of the first uranium installation in South Africa on the West Rand in 1952; the beginning of phosphate concentrates production at Phalaborwa in 1955; and the beginning of the production of petrol from coal at Sasolburg in 1955. Sasol was a particular milestone in South Africa's industrial development. Not only is it the only successful undertaking of its kind in the world but it also offers great possibilities to South Africa with its almost inexhaustible supply of coal. The world's cheapest coal, 5s per ton, is converted by Sasol into products with a minimum value of £4 10s per ton.

The triumph of Afrikaner nationalism

Another important facet of South African history during the years 1948–1961 is the victory of Afrikaner nationalism over its old enemy, British imperialism. Whereas the Afrikaner had previously been dominated by British imperialism, since 1948 he has not only succeeded in freeing himself completely from its toils, but also has mastered his opponent. Afrikanerdom has now disposed of all signs of its past degradations. In 1949 the old British subject status, which annoyed every true nationalist, was abolished and South Africans were given their own citizenship. Another symbol of subordination was removed in 1950 when the right of appeal to the Privy Council was abolished because this did not agree with South Africa's constitutional position as a sovereign independent state. In 1951 Dr E. G. Jansen was appointed Governor-General – the first time a member of the republican National Party had been appointed to this office. In 1953 the *Royal Name and Titles Act* ended the old controversy concerning the divisibility of the crown by "dividing" it, thus distinguishing between the monarch of Britain and the monarch of South Africa. That the old resistance of imperialist bitter-enders to such developments in the constitutional sphere was not even by 1957 something of the past, is clearly apparent in the opposition's resistance to Arthur Barlow's bill that the Union Jack should no longer be one of South Africa's flags and that the South African flag should be the country's only official flag. After the Union Jack ceased in 1957 to be a South African flag a law was passed in the same year to make *Die Stem* ("Call of South Africa") the only South African national anthem, so that "God Save the Queen" was no longer one of the anthems. In 1957 also, South Africa took over the naval base at Simonstown, thereby ending British control of this South African port. Concurrently with the abolition of the clumsy British monetary system and the introduction of the decimal coinage system in South Africa the head of the ruling British monarch was removed from South African coins and replaced by that of Jan van Riebeeck. This was one of the last British symbols to disappear from the South African scene. This natural and sound policy of bringing all South African symbols which previously had expressed subordination to Britain into line with the country's sovereign status was, however, sometimes taken so far that even generally accepted and respected titles of English origin were replaced by archaic words which had not been used for more than half a century. In this way the Minister of Justice (C. R. Swart) even had *magistraat* replaced by *landdros* (in English *magistrate* remained the official title) and the Minister of Defence (F. C. Erasmus) had the rank of *luitenant* changed to *veldkornet* (in English *lieutenant* remained the official rank).

There was one dream of many South Africans which had still, however, not been realized: a Republic of South Africa. Malan, and after him Strijdom, had worked for a republic during their terms as Prime Minister. They felt that the nation should be educated in this respect until it was ready for a republican form of government. During his period of office Verwoerd decided that the time for a republic had arrived and on 5 October, 1960, the nation went to the polls to decide in a referendum whether South Africa should become a republic or not. The result was that 850,458 (52%) were in favour of a republic while 775,878 (48%) voted to retain the monarchal form of government. The government had thus obtained a mandate from the nation to transform the Union of South Africa, which had just celebrated its fiftieth anniversary, into a republic.

Because of his promise that the republic would remain within the British Commonwealth Verwoerd left for London in March, 1961, to give formal notice to the Commonwealth Premiers Conference that South Africa intended changing its form of government and at the same time applying for continued membership of the Commonwealth. Normally to do this would have been a mere formality but obstructions were placed in Verwoerd's way, not concerning the constitutional changes but concerning South Africa's racial policy. Various Commonwealth countries, especially the non-White states, criticized South Africa's racial policy very severely. Consequently Verwoerd withdrew his country's application for membership of the Commonwealth.

The Republic of South Africa, based on a constitution which differed little from the previous one, came into being on 31 May, 1961. The title of the Governor-General, C. R. Swart, was altered to that of State President but this did not imply any change in his relatively unimportant constitutional position. The Prime Minister remained in charge of affairs.

19. South Africa and the African Continent

The new hinterland

During the Great Trek white men journeyed north as far as the Soutpansberg; to the east were the fever-ridden Lowveld and warlike tribes separating the newcomers from the chain of Portuguese coastal settlements. The hinterland had changed from being the lands between the Orange River and the Limpopo to being the area dominated by the Matabele and stretching westwards across the Kalahari.

Into this "no man's land" ventured elephant hunters and traders, but there are only fragmentary records of their hazardous journeys. Kuruman, Potchefstroom, Rustenburg, Klerksdorp and Pretoria (1855) were the centres from which they set forth to collect tusks and skins and, after 1865, to search for precious minerals. Among these hardy and self-reliant pioneers Afrikaner and British colonial stocks were represented by men such as Jan Viljoen, Piet Jacobs, Jacob Hartley and William Finaughty. The south was the geographical base for the explorers who opened up the interior, Livingstone in his early journeys, Andersson, Baines and Mauch; there they procured the waggons, oxen, supplies and bearers that made their journeys possible. The south also was the point of departure for missionaries such as the Moffats, Helmore, Price, Coillard who worked outside the confines of settled society.

Beyond the Limpopo

In the south of Africa the two imperial colonies and the two republics all had various aspirations concerning the hinterland and each sought to outdo the other. The Cape Colony extended her influence into Damaraland, into Griqualand West along "the missionaries road", and, more reluctantly, into Basutoland (1871 – 1884); in 1868 the South African Republic claimed that its boundaries extended across the Limpopo, westwards to Lake Ngami and eastwards via the Maputa River to the sea; the Orange Free State fought the Basuto periodically for control of the fertile Caledon lands; even Natal, through Shepstone, interested herself in Mzilikazi's successor. But these local rivalries were overshadowed by the ambitions of larger competitors. Between 1884 and 1900 the European powers rapidly partitioned off most of the African continent. Boundaries were no longer fluid and indeterminate. British imperialism particularly gained considerable territory in southern Africa.

As early as 1836 the Voortrekkers had explored parts of modern Southern Rhodesia.[1] From 1853 to 1887 the South African Republic was on fairly friendly

1. P. J. van der Merwe: *Nog Verder Noord* (Cape Town, 1962).

terms with the Matabele rulers, but after 1887 the British were in the ascendant at Lobengula's court. Although Jeppe's 1889 map of the Transvaal shows the trans-Limpopo as "The Hunting Ground of the Boers", by the following year the British South Africa Company had become entrenched in that area in consequence of Imperial control being established over Bechuanaland and "the missionaries road". The South African Republic was thus thwarted to the west and to the north, and also in her bid for an eastern seaport, but in 1894 she did gain control of Swaziland. The Great Trek had carried the rule of the white man to the Limpopo; British imperialism extended it rather more violently to the Zambezi and beyond. Men of South African origin played a prominent part in this stage of Africa's development. Among these men were some of Rhodes's adherents such as "Matabele" Thompson, Hans Sauer and Johan Colenbrander. The Cape Colony was well represented in the Pioneer Column of 1890 and many of the British South Africa Company officials were drawn from the Cape Civil Service. Roman-Dutch law was introduced into Charterland. Sir Robert Coryndon, who secured the protectorate over Barotseland, and Sir Charles Coghlan, the first Prime Minister of Southern Rhodesia, were Cape "colonials" by birth and upbringing.

South Africa and Southern Rhodesia

Two early examples will show how closely the fortunes of South Africa were linked with her northern neighbour, Southern Rhodesia. The Matabele had withdrawn from their conquests in the Transvaal in the face of the Voortrekker advance and established themselves as overlords of the less war-like races in the north until they encountered the force of the second phase of white expansion. The Jameson Raid, harbinger of bad times in the south, had ill effects in the north as well; in 1896 the Matabele grasped the opportunity of rebelling for the second time and the Bechuanaland Protectorate passed from the "Rhodesian" sphere of influence into direct Imperial control. By 1902 Rhodesia and the south were at peace. There were political and economic differences, but on a reduced scale, so that one may perhaps quote as a parallel the tranquillity that exists between the United States and Canada.

The Cape cart and the Zeederberg coach remained the quickest means of transport until "the railway frontier" followed rapidly in the wake of "the mining frontier". In 1897 Bulawayo was connected by rail with Kimberley, the line following the old "missionaries road". The Rhodesian railway network was eventually connected with Beira, Katanga and Benguela and was therefore an extension of the southern system. The north, with its potentialities for enterprising farming and mining, attracted a steady trickle of South Africans. Blood ties made for easy relations; Rhodesians were no strangers to South Africa where many had been educated. The White people of Rhodesia and South Africa led similar lives and faced the same problems, from drought and locusts to intractable racial problems. It seemed that the Customs Union of 1903 would soon be followed by closer bonds between the two countries. In 1909 Rhodesia sent three delegates to the National Convention.

Jealous of their young nationhood, Rhodesians were somewhat chary of being swamped by their richer and more densely populated neighbour. After 1914 they became apprehensive of the growth of Afrikaner nationalism in the south and to counter it tended to emphasize their British affiliations and their loyalty to the Empire. It was their disapproval of republicanism, reluctance to accept bilingualism and fears of economic inferiority that caused Coghlan and his followers to oppose General Smuts's plan for incorporating Southern Rhodesia into South Africa. Southern Rhodesia elected to remain a self-governing colony, but the majority that in the 1922 referendum rejected a union was not large. The South African Party government offered insufficiently flexible conditions and the Nationalist Opposition evinced no enthusiasm for the merger. Both sides let slip a great opportunity to consolidate.

Southern Rhodesia prospered under self-government but her white population remained small. The Copperbelt of Northern Rhodesia was her own hinterland and also attracted many South African miners and artisans. At this time Southern Rhodesia looked to the north rather than to the south in politics and in economics. After 1933, under the leadership of Sir Godfrey Huggins, she began to see herself as the corner-stone of a new British dominion in Central Africa. The dichotomy so familiar in South African politics was also apparent in Southern Rhodesia. On the one hand White Rhodesians had inherited the Cape liberal tradition as interpreted by their founder, Cecil Rhodes, on the other, they were convinced that it was the White man's role to assume responsibility in the lands he occupied and that there were natural social barriers between white and black that should not be breached.

In both World Wars there was close co-operation between Rhodesia and South Africa. Rhodesians shared in the campaigns in German South West Africa and East Africa. After the Second World War Southern Rhodesia, like South Africa and Portugal, was the target for bitter attacks from African nationalists, Communists and other forces committed to the overthrow of "colonialism" and "white supremacy". Both Rhodesia and South Africa were sensitive to the world-wide inroads made by Communism. A Southern Rhodesia contingent assisted in suppressing Communist guerillas in the Malayan jungles and Dr Malan sent the "Cheetah" squadron to participate in the grim Korean struggle.

In 1953 when the Federation of Rhodesia and Nyasaland came into being, many South Africans were sceptical about the outcome of its policy of "partnership" between races, while others thought that this policy might be the prototype of a solution to the problems of race relations more equitable than that of "apartheid". The Federation made steady economic progress for nearly ten years and carried through the mighty Kariba Dam scheme, but it was hampered by limited sovereignty and was not proof against the rising forces of African nationalism or the vacillations of the British government. When in 1963 Northern Rhodesia and Nyasaland withdrew from the Federation, the Federation dissolved. Southern Rhodesia thus soon had as neighbours the independent black states of Zambia and Malawi who were politically antagonistic to her and economically uncertain as far as future markets were concerned. Southern Rhodesia was dangerously isolated and she could count on little support from Britain in her desire to attain complete independence.

Many Rhodesians felt that their loyalty to the Empire in times of war and crisis had been ill-requited. Conservative forces dominated the political scene in Southern Rhodesia and the time was ripe for a reorientation of policy. In 1964 the Southern Rhodesian premier, Mr. Ian Smith, began to establish closer relations with the Republic; one result of his negotiations was a new trade agreement favourable to Southern Rhodesia which was seen as the possible precursor of a "common market". Most White South Africans sympathised with Southern Rhodesia in her determination not to yield to immature and extreme black nationalism or to pressures from outside her borders. Obviously it was also in South Africa's interest thet militant black nationalism should not penetrate the buffer area between the Zambezi and the Limpopo.

Southern Rhodesia's unilateral declaration of independence (UDI) on the 11th November, 1965, confronted the South African Government with a delicate diplomatic situation. The Prime Minister, Dr Verwoerd, declared that the Republic's policy would be one of non-intervention and that it would take no part in boycotts and sanctions. Before and after the rupture between Great Britain and Rhodesia it was the official South African view that the issue was a domestic one which should be settled by negotiation between the parties. As economic sanctions were imposed on Rhodesia by Britain, and later by many other members of the United Nations, it was obvious that Rhodesia's survival might depend on her economic outlet to the south and that pressure would be brought to bear on the Republic to adhere to the punitive policy of the United Nations. Mr. Ian Smith's defiant stand had the sympathy of a wide sector of White South African opinion. Private organisations raised funds to supply Rhodesia with gifts of petrol and other commodities that were in short supply. Whilst the Republican Government was hardly less sympathetic towards its neighbour, it had to seek to avert South Africa's involvement in a wider controversy.

The appearance of bands of well-armed terrorists in Rhodesia, some of them Bantu of South African origins who had received military training abroad, resulted in the Republic undertaking an active commitment outside her own borders. In September, 1967, it was disclosed that detachments of the South African Police had joined the Rhodesian security forces in their operations against the intruders.

Portuguese neighbours

At the time between 1840 and 1890 when the Transvaal and Southern Rhodesia were being opened to white settlement, the Portuguese had been established on the Mozambique coast for more than three hundred years. They were few in numbers and often had scant backing from a poorly endowed motherland; their earlier ambitions to control the interior had been frustrated by disease and the

398

indigenous tribes. Yet the Portuguese had clung to the remnants of their possessions on the west and east coasts with astonishing tenacity. At Luanda, Inhambane, Tete and Delagoa Bay there may have been few signs of material progress, but the Portuguese belief in their civilizing mission in Africa persisted.

The advance of the Boer and British frontiers from the south and the covetous eyes which Britain and Germany turned on Angola and Mozambique after the Berlin Conference of 1884 – 1885 spurred the Portuguese to renewed colonial activity. The Portuguese claims to tracts of the interior had to be made good or else others would challenge their possession by means of "effective occupation". Delagoa Bay, in particular, was a valuable strategic point. The Dutch East India Company had held it briefly from 1721 to 1730; the British had claimed it on several occasions, but Portuguese possession had been confirmed by the MacMahon award of 1875. Also, Cecil Rhodes had unsuccessfully tried to acquire the harbour of Lourenço Marques as a key factor in his grandiose imperial designs.

The South African Republic remained friendly with the Portuguese in Mozambique. In 1895, after twenty years of frustration, Lourenço Marques and Pretoria were linked by rail. Lourenço Marques's consequent prosperity benefited both countries; it was the port on the shortest route to the Witwatersrand goldfields and gave President Kruger the access to the sea, independent of British control, that had been denied him at Kosi Bay. Commerce revived Mozambique's sluggish economy and her native labourers found work on the Transvaal mines.

During the Anglo-Boer War Britain exerted strong pressure on Portugal to stop the flow of munitions through her colonial territory. British troops were landed at Beira to reinforce the Rhodesian garrison. Nevertheless the Portuguese on the whole sympathised with the Republic's cause and sheltered many Boer refugees. In 1900 the British gained control of the Delagoa Bay Railway from Pretoria to Komati Poort, but basic economic relations between Mozambique and the Transvaal remained unchanged. In 1901 Milner, anxious to keep the mines operating, entered into a *modus vivendi* with the Portuguese which ensured the continuation of rail traffic and the supply of mine labourers. This arrangement was confirmed by the Transvaal Mozambique Convention of 1909 and after Union was extended and modified slightly. In terms of the 1934 agreement the Delagoa Bay line was guaranteed 45 % – 50 % of the rail traffic to the Witwatersrand. Mozambique was second only to South Africa as a source of mine labour; statistics for 1960 show that nearly 83,000 labourers from Mozambique were on contract to the mines of South Africa.

During a period when Portugal had been under Spanish domination, the Dutch had temporarily controlled Angola, 1641 – 1648, but contacts with this colony from the south were tenuous until the Thirstland Trekkers from the Transvaal moved from Ovamboland into Southern Angola to settle in 1881 in developed country around Humpata until 1928. As transport riders and as allies in campaigns against recalcitrant tribes they rendered the Portuguese valuable service. Their presence was also an incentive to Portugal to settle peasants on the southern plateau. With the 1915 conquest of South West Africa, South Africans came into friendly contact with the Portuguese authorities north of the Kunene River.

After the Second World War both South Africa and Portugal were subjected to pressures from the Black African states and from the United Nations. Despite widely divergent native policies, there was close co-operation between the two neighbouring states. The fall of Mozambique to African nationalism would have presented a serious threat to South Africa's eastern flank. When terrorist inroads into Mozambique followed the pattern that had already been revealed in Angola, the Republic realised how important the holding actions of the Portuguese were.

The accelerated economic development of Angola, especially of its oil-fields, and of Mozambique, afforded new opportunities for South African industries and for the investment of South African capital. South African airlines had the use of an air-port at Luanda on the route to Europe via the west coast "bulge" of Africa; this was important since by 1963, Kenya, the Sudan and Egypt had refused the Republic landing rights on the more direct routes across the continent.

South Africa and the Protectorates

After 1910 the British protectorates of Basutoland, Swaziland and Bechuanaland, wholly surrounded by South African territory in the first case and partly so in the case of the other two, were curious anomalies. Yet it was only through quirks of history that these territories had not become part of the body politic of the Union in the same way as Zululand or the Transkei. Shrewd native rulers such as Mosheshwe and Khama managed to retain their independence while the main northward advance of the white man passed them by. The Cape Colony acquired control over Basutoland for a short period, 1871 – 1884, before the territory was transferred to Imperial rule. British Bechuanaland, the Vryburg-Mafeking region, was annexed to the Cape Colony in 1895. In Swaziland British influence was strong during the late 19th century; a contingent of Swazi allies assisted Wolseley to overthrow Sekhukune in 1879. The South African Republic also was particularly interested in this territory since it was a winter-grazing area and straddled a possible route to the sea. For a few years after 1894 convention rights gave the South African Republic hegemony over Swaziland, but by 1907 the supreme authority in all three protectorates was vested in the Imperial High Commissioner.

In 1903 the protectorates entered a customs union with the four main colonies of South Africa and with Southern Rhodesia; no closer constitutional ties were achieved. The South Africa Act of 1909 and a schedule to it provided for a later accession of the protectorates to the Union, with the approval of the British government. In the Imperial view the inhabitants had to be consulted. British governments came to interpret consultation as "consent" and all subsequent negotiations foundered on this issue. In 1913 General Botha raised the question of incorporation and from 1913 to 1949 it was again raised at different levels by General Smuts, Mr N. C. Havenga and Dr Malan. The British considered that "the time was not yet ripe" and the question of the protectorates remained an irritant in the relations between Pretoria and Westminster. In 1949 Dr Malan referred to an "intolerable encroachment on the rights of South Africa". South Africa considered the British government's attitude to indicate a lack of confidence in the Union's Native policies.

The South African case for the incorporation of the protectorates into the Union hinged on the following considerations: the protectorates were "economic appendages" of the Union; much of their revenue came from favourable customs union quotas; they were backward areas and before 1935 received little financial support from the United Kingdom; the Union provided employment for many of their people and markets for their agricultural products. After the Second World War considerations of military security loomed large. It was undesirable that Basutoland, in particular, should be allowed to be a breeding-ground of Communism and sedition; moreover in its territory were the sources of the great South African rivers on which large irrigation and hydro-electric schemes were being developed. Finally, the inclusion of the protectorates in South Africa was considered necessary in order to be able fully to implement the "Bantustan" policy.

Meanwhile the British government advanced the protectorates constitutionally towards self-government and eventual independence. They were also given more generous assistance under the Colonial Development Act and from other sources. When under Verwoerd, South Africa's policy of "separate development" became more positive, the South African government ceased actively to consider incorporation of the protectorates into South Africa. In Dr. Verwoerd's opinion the future envisaged by the British for the protectorates did not differ markedly from that foreseen by South Africa for the Transkei and other Bantu areas; at some future date there might emerge a "Commonwealth" of South African states, Black and White, in which the protectorates could be included.

During the 1960's Swaziland, whose White minority was larger than the other two protectorates, made considerable economic progress along the lines of the Republic. The exploiting of the territory's asbestos, iron ore and timber afforded opportunities for South African skill and capital.

There were indications that South Africa would achieve a satisfactory *modus vivendi* with her emergent neighbours. In the winter of 1965 Basutoland was overtaken by a severe food shortage; the South African government donated 100,000 bags of maize and kaffir corn to relieve the situation. On 2 September, 1966, the Prime Minister of Basutoland, Chief Leabua Jonathan, met Dr. Verwoerd in Pretoria and their discussion hinged on good neighbourly relations and mutual non-interference. When the Bechuanaland Protectorate (Botswana) and Basutoland (Lesotho) gained independence on 30 September and 4 October, 1966, respectively, the South African Minister of Foreign Affairs was among the guests at the national festivities. The leaders of both states, Sir Seretse Khama and Chief Jonathan, indicated that they could not support any external measures to impose sanctions on the Republic. The Prime Minister of Lesotho turned to South African constitutional, financial and industrial advisers for guidance in solving the economic and other problems of his country. These were pointers to the possibility of the Republic being able to achieve cordial relations with the more moderately led of the new black states on the continent.

In January, 1967, Mr. Vorster and Chief Jonathan of Lesotho met in Cape Town and agreed that peaceful co-existence and vigilance against Communism were in their common interest.

South West Africa – "The Fifth Province"

White penetration of South West Africa may be said to date from 1760 and is coupled with the name of a great hunter, Jakobus Coetzé. Among the occupants of South West Africa, the Rehoboth (or Baster) community and the Orlams Hottentots, had migrated from the lands south of the Orange River. The vast region between the Kunene and the Orange Rivers, two-thirds the size of the Republic of South Africa, is bounded by an inhospitable coast and the Namib and Kalahari deserts. A few hunters, traders and missionaries traversed its arid tracts and contacted a diversity of races that included small Nama groups in the south, the Herero further north and the more numerous Ovambo on the fringes of the country claimed by Portugal. The nature of the country greatly hindered the spread of civilization.

During the 19th century a steady trickle of Afrikaner farmers from the Cape settled in the southern region of South West Africa whilst the Thirstland Trekkers settled temporarily in Ovamboland before moving on to Angola in 1881. Before 1880 the largest single political influence in the area was that of British imperialism. The guano islands off the coast of South West Africa were annexed by Britain between 1861 and 1866 and Walvis Bay in 1878. Six years later control of the Walvis Bay enclave was transferred to the Cape Colony. At a time when Africa was rapidly being partitioned the Cape Colony was tardy of extending her influence into Damaraland. In 1884 Imperial Germany snatched South West Africa at a time when the British government was unenthusiastic about expansion. The German annexation briefly preceded the establishment of the small Boer settlement of Upingtonia in the north under G. D. P. Prinsloo. Afrikaner immigration into the German colony continued and in 1896 the Boer White minority numbered 782.

In 1914 when the First World War broke out General Louis Botha agreed to the British government's request that South Africa should occupy German South West Africa. His decision was strongly opposed in the Union and was one of the causes of the Rebellion of 1914. The small German garrison in South West Africa was no threat to South Africa. It is doubtful whether Generals Botha and Smuts were prompted only by zeal for the British cause; this was a magnificent opportunity for the Union to expand territorially and the alternative to a South African occupation of South West Africa might well have been a British one.

In conquering South West Africa in 1915 the young South African Union acquired some prestige and her first "colony"; the mandate granted her in 1920 confirmed her control of the former German colony, but it was to be colonial rule with a difference. As a "C" class mandate of the League of Nations, South West Africa was to be governed in trust for the welfare of its inhabitants. The mandatory power was responsible for the administration, but was subject to the supervision and advice of a distant Permanent Mandates Commission at Geneva.

To the Union her acquisition was a mixed blessing. The territory was poor and relied heavily on South Africa for financial support; it was afflicted by droughts and had little diversity in its economy. The Germans, who soon became a white minority group, were disgruntled and not easily reconciled to the new order. German rule had incurred the bitter opposition of the Hereros and Namas. This enmity, much of which sprang from the tribes having been dispossessed of their land, was transferred to the mandatory power. Although the South African administration "made serious and largely successful efforts to grapple with the acute racial problem which it had inherited from the previous regime",[2] it was soon in the unfortunate position of having to account for its actions to the Permanent Mandates Commission. The suppression of the Bondelzwarts uprising in 1922 brought South Africa much dubious publicity and reminded her of her circumscribed sovereignty in South West Africa.

After the Union took over South West Africa the latter's railway system was joined to that of the Union (via Upington) and South African authority firmly established in areas where the German control had been indeterminate, particularly in Ovamboland. There was a considerable influx of South African farmers, businessmen and civil servants into South West Africa. By 1928 many of the Angola Boers had been resettled in the territory. In 1926 the territory was granted a legislative assembly based on white suffrage. It seemed that it would soon evolve into the Union's fifth province, but the League of Nations refused to consider such an incorporation since it held that this would contravene the mandate. After years of economic depression the territory began to show signs of revival. From 1939 onwards copper, lead and diamond mining, karakul farming and a rich fishing industry stabilized the territory's finances and provided lucrative opportunies for the investment of South African capital.

Between 1933 and 1939 the rise of the Third Reich and Hitler's demands for the return of Germany's former colonies created problems for the mandatory power, but these disappeared with the Nazi defeat in the Second World War. The League of Nations was dissolved in 1946 without any special provision having been made for the mandated territories and the time again seemed ripe for the merger of South West Africa with the Union.

After the war the Legislative Assembly at Windhoek unanimously requested to be incorporated into the Union. The South African government fully endorsed this proposal, but the changed post-war world of 1946 constantly opposed these plans. In the new United Nations Organisation in which Asia

2. A. Toynbee: *Survey of International Affairs, 1920 – 1923* (London, 1927).

and certain African countries as well as the Communist bloc, were well-represen-
ted, South Africa and her venerable chief spokesman, General Smuts, no longer
were respected as they had been at Geneva. South Africa's 1946 refusal to place
South West Africa under UNO trusteeship was criticised hotly. South Africa
decided to abandon the matter of incorporation and to continue to administer
South West Africa in the spirit of the mandate. In 1949 Dr Malan's government
again refused to entertain the idea of UNO trusteeship for South West Africa
and declined to submit any further reports on the territory. To the annoyance of
South Africa's official representatives, UNO committees gave hearings to the
Reverend Michael Scott, an itinerant partisan of the Hereros, and other aggrieved "spokesmen" of the non-White races of the territory. Legislation passed
in 1949 gave South West Africa six seats in the Union House of Assembly and
four in the Senate. The few remaining grievances of the German-speaking
minority were settled, particularly concerning their language, and concerning
relations with South Africa there was general unanimity among the white population of South West Africa. The territory's police, railways, customs, defence
and Native policy were administered from Pretoria rather than from Windhoek.
South West Africa's status might be somewhat obscure internationally, but to
all intents and purposes it had become "the fifth province" of South Africa.

The South West Africa issue was debated year after year with increasing
acrimony at UNO. In 1950 the International Court of Justice at the Hague gave
a number of advisory opinions: South Africa was obliged to rule the territory
in terms of the original mandate; she could not legally be compelled to place
South West Africa under UNO trusteeship; South Africa could not change the
status of the territory without UNO consent and she should submit reports to
UNO on her charge. These opinions gave South Africa little respite from criticism. The Republic's declared intention of extending her racial policy of
"separate development" to South West Africa was attacked sharply. The Afro-
Asian bloc saw South West Africa as "the Achilles heel" of White supremacy
in southern Africa. In 1963, Liberia and Ethiopia, members of the Organisation
of African Unity (OAU), asked the International Court to rule that South Africa
should be compelled to place South West Africa under trusteeship because of
South Africa's "violations" of the mandate and her refusal to submit reports.
Should she refuse to comply with such ruling, the case for "sanctions" would be
strengthened and could be referred to the Security Council of UNO.

The Republic showed no signs of yielding to external pressure about South
West Africa. The history of Walvis Bay fortunately excluded it from the mandate
and enabled a reinforced garrison to be stationed there without infringing mandatory clauses. There may be differences of opinion concerning the way in which
the non-Whites of South West Africa have been advanced politically, but few
would credit the extremists' contention that South West Africa constitutes "a
threat to the peace" within the meaning of the Charter of the United Nations.

In March, 1965, the International Court of Justice commenced its hearing of
the charges by Ethiopia and Liberia that South Africa was oppressing and dis-
criminating against the non-White inhabitants of the territory and establishing

404

military bases there contrary to the terms of the mandate. The Republic's delegates presented her case with skill and well-supported evidence. In the course of the proceedings the complainants changed their ground, dropping the charges of repression and militarisation, and centring their argument on racial discrimination. The court's verdict was awaited with some suspense and apprehension. Its decision, given on the 18 July, 1966, created a sensation. The judges of the court were evenly divided in their views and the president, Sir Percy Spender of Australia, registered a decisive casting vote against the complainants; Ethiopia and Liberia were held not to have established any legal right or interest in the matter.

In a mood of relief South Africa hailed the verdict as a great victory whilst her more extreme critics were disgruntled at the dismissal of the case through a legal "technicality". If the court's decision brought temporary relief, it was an over-sanguine view that international pressure over South West Africa would cease. On the 27 October, 1966, the General Assembly of the United Nations resolved by a large majority that the mandate held by South Africa over South West Africa was terminated and that the territory would fall under the United Nations Organisation. An *ad hoc* committee was appointed to consider practical measures for the institution of UNO administration in South West Africa. Mr B. J. Vorster, the new South African premier, rejected the General Assembly's resolution as unconstitutional and contrary to international law.

During 1966 the internal tranquillity of the territory was disturbed by the appearance in Ovamboland of small armed bands of terrorists. Their intrusion was ineffective and successful counter-measures were taken against them. It appeared that these saboteurs had been trained in Tanzania and elsewhere and had made their entry into the territory via Angola.

South Africa and the rest of the African continent

South Africa had little impact other than on her immediate neighbours. Small groups of South Africans, mostly Afrikaners, settled at Eldoret in Kenya and at Arusha in Tanganyika (then German East Africa) after the Anglo-Boer War. In the thirties the Copperbelt of Northern Rhodesia attracted many miners and artisans from the south. In agriculture and mining these communities rendered services to the countries of their adoption quite out of proportion to their numbers.

In the mission field South Africa operated beside societies that were directed from Europe; the Dutch Reformed Church did pioneering work at Morgenster in Southern Rhodesia (1891) and in Nyasaland (1889); the Anglican Church of South Africa laboured in the Lebombo Diocese of Portuguese East Africa and missionaries of various denominations served in Angola and with the Sudan United Mission in Nigeria.

South African banks and mining houses such as De Beers and the Anglo American Corporation have ramifications extending far into Central and East Africa. Before the 1960's, however, there was little surplus capital available in

South Africa for investment outside South Africa, for her own economy was expanding and depended very much on overseas investors.

It was in the scientific sphere that South Africa probably rendered her most service to Africa towards the close of the colonial era, in the years 1940 to 1950. She co-operated freely with other authorities in Africa in eradicating and preventing human and animal disease. The research facilities of the veterinary laboratories at Onderstepoort and the results of the research at the Institute for Medical Research, Johannesburg and the Council for Scientific Investigation and Research, Pretoria, were made available to other African territories. In combating soil erosion, in ridding Zululand of nagana and the Lowveld of malaria, South Africa showed how to rehabilitate large parts of the African continent. In 1950 South Africa was a sponsor and founder member of two important co-ordinating bodies – the Commission for Technical Co-operation in Africa South of the Sahara (CCTA) and the Scientific Council for Africa South of the Sahara (CSA).

Before the Second World War there were few institutions for advanced education in the colonial territories; many young Africans from the north were educated at South African colleges, especially at the Fort Hare University College. South African universities did much research into ethnology and African languages. Archaeologists of the quality of Van Riet Lowe, Broom and Dart opened up new vistas in the pre-history of the African continent.

During and after the First World War, South Africans were enthusiastic aviators. In 1920 Van Ryneveld and Brand made a notable flight from England to the Cape and Major Miller pioneered airways in the south. Air routes supplemented the railways in carrying passengers and mail north across the continent and South African aviation played a considerable part in this new field of transport. Distances began to dwindle.

Between 1920 and 1938 there were signs of renewed interest in African development. The mandate system and Lord Lugard's views on the responsibilities of colonial rulers towards tropical dependencies were partly responsible. General Smuts also helped to increase this interest by a series of lectures delivered at Oxford in 1928. He pleaded for a new approach to, and co-ordinated efforts in dealing with, the problems of Africa. Some fruits of his suggestions were evident in Lord Hailey's *African Survey*, 1938, and in Professor Frankel's standard text on the economy of sub-Saharan Africa. The latter work revealed the great role of mining in the south and showed that South Africa was responsible for one-third of the capital investment in the southern half of the African continent.

During the critical years of the mid-1930's the South African Minister of Defence, Mr. Oswald Pirow and General Smuts prophesied that in any future conflict South Africa would have to be defended beyond her borders. This proved indeed to be the case. The world wars turned many South Africans into soldier travellers. From 1916 to 1918 thousands of South Africans experienced the rigours and tropical diseases of German East Africa. The Second World War carried representatives of the next generation to theatres of war in Kenya,

Somaliland, Ethiopia, Egypt, Libya and Madagascar. Even if fleeting, these impressions did broaden the outlook of such young men. War stimulated South African industries and their products found new markets, particularly in the tropical colonies of Equatorial Africa whose motherlands were temporarily cut off from them by Nazi occupation.

Despite these varied associations and contacts, however, most South Africans remained very insular; they were lulled by the apparent permanence of colonial rule and showed little awareness of the stirrings of African nationalism. To the average South African the continent beyond Lourenço Marques and Ndola was remote and of little importance; South Africa happened to be situated on the African continent, but her main cultural and commercial ties were with Europe. The rapid withdrawal of France, Belgium and Britain from the colonial scene and the appearance of independent black states came as a rude awakening to South Africa. In 1957 Ghana attained independence and membership of "the inner circle" of the Commonwealth. South Africa was powerless to alter the course of events in the former colonial territories and was consequently faced with urgent problems, particularly concerning her own security and her relations with a succession of new Black states in Africa. Feeling insecure in the new states, many former South Africans and colonial Whites abandoned their occupations there to start new lives in the Republic of South Africa.

By 1960, even if only temporarily, Africa was in the forefront of world affairs. In South Africa and elsewhere there was an unprecedented demand for books and information about African affairs. The Africa Institute in Pretoria, founded in 1960, was one recognition of this need. Universities offered new courses in African history and administration, and newspapers featured the swift succession of events in Africa's new epoch.

South Africa was the only industrialized country on the continent of Africa; in deep-level mining, geology, meteorology, cartography, medical research, housing and manufacturing she was in the forefront of progress. She was in a position to be able to help the independent African states with equipment, techniques and skilled personnel. However, the political beliefs of most of the new African leaders made them reject offers of South African assistance. They professed solidarity with the "oppressed" Bantu in the South and proclaimed their desire to end "White supremacy" throughout the African continent. Taking their cue from India they expressed their hostility to South Africa by using their growing representation at UNO to attack South Africa on the Indian minority question, South West Africa and her application of "apartheid" policies.

After the Accra Conference in 1958 and the Sharpeville shooting in 1960 the campaign against South Africa intensified. The Afro-Asian membership of the Commonwealth played a large part in deciding South Africa to withdraw from that association when she became a republic in 1961. Many African states consequently severed trade relations with the Republic and she was ousted from CCTA and CSA. Particularly after the Organisation of African Unity (OAU) was established in 1963, there were widespread attempts to boycott South

African goods, and even to resort to more militant "sanctions". The airfields and ports of several African states were closed to South African planes and ships. A gulf separated the new Africa from the Republic, Southern Rhodesia and the Portuguese territories, and the prospect of bridging it seemed remote. South Africa's former careless isolation on the African continent threatened to become real isolation that was not without menace. South of the Zambezi "western civilization" was on the defensive. The menace came not from the closing of comparatively insignificant markets or from the military strength of the Black African states but from forces in the world, at UNO and elsewhere, whose support the African states sought to obtain.

The Republic responded to this widespread animosity by tightening the bonds among her White population, encouraging immigration from Europe and maintaining an armed vigilance. She was fortunate in that she was enjoying an economic boom. The new African states were in the first flush of independence and possibly "on the morning after" more pacific counsels would prevail among them. Zambia and Malawi both showed that they were unable to relinquish commercial links with the south, and when Bechuanaland and Basutoland achieved independence it was clear that their economic dependence on South Africa had increased.

Of great significance in the Republic's policy of establishing cordial relations with the new Black states was the conclusion of a trade treaty with Malawi in 1967. Dr H. Banda, the President of Malawi, was not prepared to subscribe to the hostile attitude of O.A.U. towards the Republic and in September, 1967, it was decided that the Republic and Malawi would exchange diplomatic representatives.

South Africa attracted hundreds of thousands of Bantu workers from neighbouring territories. The standard of economy and educational facilities among her Bantu peoples was unrivalled in the rest of sub-Saharan Africa, but there was a wide gap between White and Black standards of living. Should the Bantu advance appreciably both economically and politically under the policy of separate development this would obviously assist to create a favourable climate for new relations on the African continent. The degree to which White South Africans would be prepared to revise their traditional attitudes towards less advanced races and sympathetically consider their legitimate aspirations was equally important.

20. The Republic of South Africa, 1961-1968

One of the main streams of Afrikaner political thought had long been concentrated on the establishment of a republic in South Africa and the achievement of that ideal seemed to terminate an era of South African history. Since 1961, however, it has become evident that the inception of the Republic merely intensified and accelerated significant earlier tendencies.

Although South Africa is no longer a member of the Commonwealth her constitution, based on that of Britain, is essentially unaltered. Despite a few modifications South Africa's trade relations with Britain and the joint use by Britain and South Africa of the Simonstown naval base are also as they were before the Republic was established.

In politics the unparalleled growth of the ruling National Party as compared to that of the United Party, which is virtually the only opposition party, has continued unabated since the inception of the Republic. During Dr Verwoerd's term of office English and Afrikaans-speaking South Africans drew closer together. This process was considerably hastened by British policy in Black Africa, which caused thousands of English-speaking Whites from the former British colonies to emigrate to the south.'Since the assassination of Dr Verwoerd in the House of Assembly and the succession of Mr B. J. Vorster as Prime Minister an even more marked tendency towards closer co-operation between the two language groups has become evident. The sitting of Parliament that was so dramatically interrupted, was resumed in an unusually conciliatory atmosphere. In the Provincial and General Elections of 1965 and 1966 respectively, the National Party for the first time captured certain Pietermaritzburg and Durban constituencies. In the 1966 election the National Party was supported by 58% of the electorate (which gave it 126 of the 170 seats in the enlarged Assembly), the United Party by 37% (with 39 seats), the Progressive Party by 3.1% (with 1 seat) and others by 1.9% (with no seats).[1]

In May, 1966, large-scale celebrations of the fifth anniversary of the establishment of the Republic were held throughout South Africa with Pretoria as the venue of the main ceremonies. They were characterized by a new community of outlook among English and Afrikaans-speaking citizens in the face of great international pressure. Since Rhodesia's unilateral declaration of independence in November, 1965, South African diplomacy has been faced by the new problem of how to prevent the last buffer between White South Africa and Black Central Africa from being destroyed by the general trade boycott against Rhodesia without becoming directly involved in the dispute. The U.N. became

1. The four representatives of the Coloureds did not participate in this election.

involved by first imposing an oil embargo on Rhodesia and then mandatory sanctions.

These developments placed South Africa in a difficult position. Not only had her domestic policies since 1961 been constantly criticized by an increasing number of the U.N.'s committees and investigating bodies, but for more than five years she had been defending her administration of South-West Africa as a League of Nations mandatory territory at the International Court at the Hague. K. Highet, the American advocate for Ethiopia and Liberia, stated in March, 1967, that the history of South Africa for the following few years would possibly have been completely different if the verdict of the International Court had gone against South Africa. "It would have been difficult for members of the Security Council to avoid the responsibility for supporting the rule of law had South Africa defied the judgment. It is almost inevitable that the judgment and its implications will have a profound effect on the future of all of Southern Africa, a region where the interlocking destinies of several minority governments have effectively created one 'Southern Africa Problem' which presents cumulative difficulties far greater than the sum of its parts".[2] In July, 1966, when the Court refused on purely legal grounds to accept the pleas of Liberia and Ethiopia it only temporarily removed the pressure at one particularly vulnerable point. After the judgment the U.N. concentrated on South-West African affairs, which were regarded as a threat to world peace. The General Assembly having resolved to terminate the Republic's control of South-West Africa in October, 1966, a special committee unsuccessfully tried for months to find some way of implementing the resolution. During April and June, 1967, a special session of the General Assembly wrestled with the same problem without finding a practical solution and without obtaining the support of the major powers for the Afro-Asian and Latin-American majority decision.

The South African government's policy of separate development for Whites and non-Whites was accelerated in this period. In January, 1962, Dr Verwoerd announced in the Assembly that a measure of Bantu self-government would be introduced in the reserves, and that this heralded their future development as separate states. In 1963 legislation granting partial self-government to the Transkei, with its more than 3 million Xhosa-speaking inhabitants, and the subsequent appointment of Commissioners-General in a number of other Bantu homelands, advanced this policy a step further. By early 1968 of the 2,500 senior established posts in the Transkei Service, only 350 remained in White hands. This is indeed an "irreversible experiment".[3] During this five-year period the gross produce increased by 125 per cent. In 1967 Parliament approved a record R490 million in the second five-year development plan for the Bantu homelands. In 1964 the Odendaal Commission recommended the application of the same

2. "The South West Africa Cases" in *Current History*, 52(307), March, 1967, p. 160. Cf. also M. Hidayatullah: *The South West Africa Case* (London, 1967).
3. Patrick Orr: "The irreversible experiment in the Transkei", *Southern Africa*, 25 March, 1968, p. 192.

system to South-West Africa and early in 1967 it was announced that the system would be extended to Ovamboland. The border industries which were begun at this time coupled political policy with more rapid economic development. In the cities as well as in the tribal areas, the Bantu benefited from the Republic's economic progress and vice versa. As a corollary to the Group Areas legislation large-scale non-White housing schemes were undertaken by the administration. The standard of living of the non-Whites in the Republic was by 1967 the highest of any non-White state in Africa.

Naturally these attempts of the South African government to solve the extremely complex racial problem caused much discussion and considerable differences of opinion on moral and on practical grounds, not only abroad and in all opposition circles, but also among passive and active supporters of the government. There is much divergence of opinion concerning the best ways of implementing government policy. Putting the policy into effect often entails many sacrifices and this further complicates the matter. It is therefore not to be wondered that the already extensive literature on the South African racial question, and the Bantu question in particular, has increased steadily. These publications which approach the question from widely divergent points of view range from blatantly polemical works to serious scientific studies. Increased interest in South African racial affairs has also been promoted by the critical nature of the period which has seen the U.N. decide to impose diplomatic and economic sanctions against the Republic (6 November, 1962). "It is clear", says Professor Vernon McKay, "that the quick rise of African states is one of the major revolutions of the twentieth century, but our understanding of its meaning and ramifications is beclouded by the fact that it is not yet complete. Not only have Africans not yet freed their compatriots in the White redoubt in southern Africa, but in northern and middle Africa the political revolution that brought African leaders to power has understandably failed to satisfy the economic and social needs of the people".[4] The chief contention of the Afro-Asians, that South African racial policy is a major danger to international peace and security, has not been accepted by leading Western powers such as the United States of America, France and Britain. Nevertheless South African racial policy has assumed a central position in world politics, and has attracted so much international attention that the sale of American and British weapons to the Republic has been suspended. International pressure groups are now more frequently asserting that massive economic sanctions or a timely armed intervention by the U.N. in South Africa, although expensive, would be considerably less expensive and entail far less bloodshed than the later race conflagration (with disastrous world-wide repercussions) which they believe will be the inevitable outcome of the Republic's racial policy. "If South Africa wins now", Prof. J. A. Davis, President of the American Society of African Culture,

---

4. *International Conflict Patterns*, Chapter I in *African Diplomacy: studies in the determinants of foreign policy* (Published for the School of Advanced International Studies, the Johns Hopkins University by Pall Mall Press, London, 1966), p. 3.

said in 1965, "the holocaust in Africa will certainly eventually be much greater".[5] The outcome depends not only on events in South Africa or on the African continent, but also on developments in numerous other focal points of international unrest. Indeed, the serious disturbances and chronic tension in regions such as Vietnam and the Middle East tend to refute the arguments of the Afro-Asians that South Africa is a major threat to world peace which merits urgent attention.

The Republic of South Africa has continued to maintain its position of being by far the economically strongest state in Africa. The economic cycle during the years under discussion fluctuated alternatively between consolidation of stability and stimulation of growth. Attempts to raise the price of gold or to demonetize gold has highlighted the significant part which the Republic is in a position to play in international finance.

The flow of overseas capital and immigrants into South Africa began to increase shortly after Sharpeville. Internal capital growth was also aided by the investments of local financial interests. In addition to the increased production of gold and many other minerals industrialization continued at a particularly rapid rate, and the total value of agricultural and pastoral products increased remarkably. Despite the fixed price of gold the Republic, already by far the largest gold-producer in the world, enlarged its production to supply 71.7 per cent of the free world's gold; but in the meantime production costs are rising owing to the rapidly increasing cost of living, while the gold-price is frozen. If this situation continues the life of the gold-mines will be considerably shortened and South African economy will be drastically affected. Rapidly increasing quantities of coal were extracted from rich coal-fields, and the diamond industry, also active in the inhospitable west coast waters, increased its productivity in the five years up to 1964 by nearly 100 per cent. During this same period the fishing industry grew considerably and contributed much to the country's export trade. The Republic is the largest producer of fish products in the southern hemisphere, the eighth largest fishing nation in the world. This industry is exploiting the rich potential of South African waters so heavily that conservation measures have become necessary. It has also proved difficult to prevent Russian, Japanese, Spanish and other large foreign fishing fleets from making enormous catches off the South African coasts. Politically inspired trade boycotts have had little effect on the South African economy. The powerful company, Safmarine, has greatly developed the long lagging South African shipping interests. Towards the end of 1965 this company announced that it had bought, among other purchases, two mailships from the Union Castle Line. By 1968 it was despatching freighters to Japan and the Canadian Great Lakes. The ship-building industry had progressed and in the near future it will be

5. J. A. Davis and J. K. Baker (eds.): *Southern Africa in Transition* (New York, 1966), p. xxvii. Cf. also C. and M. Legum: *South Africa: Crisis for the West* (London and Dunmow, 1964), pp. 1-5, 307-309; and K. Irvine: "Southern Africa: The White Fortress" in *Current History*, 54(318), February, 1968, p. 112.

possible for the largest types of ships to be built in South African shipyards. Ambitious harbour development projects are being planned for Table Bay and Saldanha Bay in order to accommodate giant modern vessels. A projected deep-sea harbour at Richard's Bay will be strategically situated for importing oil.

Towards the end of 1964 a new state department of planning was created to enable the government to co-ordinate and control future development in South Africa. An oil pipe-line has been laid from Durban to the Rand. Sasol and the crude oil refineries are the main components of a vast new complex of profitable chemical industries which have been expanding into various fields. Some subsidiary products provide the raw materials for the manufacture of synthetic rubber, plastics, fertilizers and explosives for mining. No effort or money is being spared in prospecting for petroleum in all promising areas on land and off-shore. A local aeroplane industry has come into being and factories manufacturing motor cars have been erected. A tea industry, guided by expert advisers from central Africa, has been started. The iron and steel industries have expanded tremendously and prospects of further development are excellent. The comprehensively planned, long-term Orange River scheme has been inaugurated and the construction of the enormous Hendrik Verwoerd dam and other large dams has already been started. During times like the drought-ridden sixties when agriculture and stock-breeding suffered heavy losses the urgent need for many more irrigation schemes for the barren interior became apparent. The installation of huge electrical power stations also became necessary to stimulate further development in the vast and largely arid hinterland.

The tempo of South African economic development during the years under discussion has been so rapid that it is possible to talk of a second industrial revolution. The growth between 1963 and the end of 1965 has been described by Dr H. J. van Eck as the greatest recorded in modern times.[6] South Africa, in the late sixties, is by far the largest industrial country on the African continent, and the second most important in the southern hemisphere. The gross national production from 1961 to 1964 showed an average annual rate of increase of $6\frac{1}{2}\%$ – one of the highest in the world. The Republic is already the twelfth largest commercial nation in the world.

Whereas previously South Africa was principally dependent on foreign capital the country has now reached a stage where, to a large extent, it can supply its own capital needs. Since 1961 Afrikaner capital and Afrikaner business acumen have been playing increasingly important parts in most sectors of the South African economy, including mining and industry. Under Dr A. Rupert the Rembrandt Tobacco Company has expanded its operations to practically all continents. By 1968 the total share of Afrikaner enterprise in the national economy of the Republic is close to 20 per cent.

International pressure and particularly the hostile attitude of central and north African countries have compelled the Republic to increase her armaments and

6. Hendrik van der Bijl Lecture, University of Pretoria, 19 May, 1967, as reported in *The Star*, 20 May, 1967.

to introduce an intensive military training scheme. South Africa, although situated on a continent predominantly hostile to her, has become so powerful because of her economic development that only a strong alliance of countries to the north would be a serious military threat to her. Her economic vitality has made it possible for her to establish her own armament factories and to assemble jet aeroplanes. Her military preparedness has enabled her to maintain the *status quo* in South-West Africa and to counter the attacks of well-armed and trained terrorists from the north. The security police have been exceptionally successful in rounding up saboteurs and other subversive elements, trained locally and abroad, and bringing them to court. A series of dramatic events terminated in Advocate Abram Fischer, the head of Communist groups, being sentenced to life imprisonment after a lengthy trial. While a high degree of internal security has been achieved South Africa has become much more isolated in the international sphere. Together with her White controlled neighbours the Republic is alienated from most of the black states to her north, and there seems little immediate prospect of her acquiring any allies overseas. South Africa, by no means a power of the first rank, has been forced by circumstances to adopt the hazardous policy of a great power. Because of her global and regional importance, South Africa is rapidly assuming a more significant position in international affairs. She is one of the most powerful states in the southern hemisphere, and by far the most powerful, the most advanced and the richest country in Africa. It is precisely her favourable southerly geographical situation which has resulted in the growth of her sphere of influence, which stretches from Lesotho to Swaziland through Botswana to Rhodesia (which has been in "rebellion" against Britain since November, 1965) and even to Malawi, in the heart of Africa. Although Zambia considers South Africa to be a hostile country with a repugnant domestic policy, and although she gave notice towards the end of 1964 that her trade agreement with the Republic would be terminated, South Africa has become Zambia's most important supplier of goods. In 1964 Zambia imported goods to the value of R32 million from the Republic. This figure increased to R41.4 million in 1965, R58.4 million in 1966 and R52.2 million in the first nine months of 1967.[7]

Notwithstanding the increasing demands for man-power the white population of South Africa showed only a 6% increase from 3,088,492 in September, 1960, to approximately 3,395,000 in June, 1965. In the same period the coloured population showed a 17% increase to about 1,742,000, the Indians an 11% increase to about 533,000 and the Bantu an 11% increase to about 12,162,000.[8]

7. An anonymous article, "South Africa and emergent Africa", *Bulletin of the Africa Institute*, V, 5, June, 1967, pp. 131-2.
8. In June, 1966, the estimate of the Bureau of Statistics was as follows: Whites 3,481,000; Coloureds 1,805,000; Indians 547,000 and Bantu 12,465,000. (Republic of South Africa, *Bureau of Statistics: Statistical Yearbook 1966*, Pretoria, 1966, p. A-11). A further estimate by the Bureau of Statistics in the middle of 1967 yielded the following figures: Whites 3,563,000, Coloureds 1,859,000, Indians 561,000 and Bantu 12,750,000. This means that in less than seven years the South African population has increased by about 2¾ million.

The slow increase in the white population of South Africa is a tendency which was apparent long before 1961. A systematic state-aided scheme to combat the white labour shortage by importing more white immigrants than in previous years has been in operation since 1962. In this way new blood and new skills have been brought to South Africa, but the immigrants have often found it difficult to adjust themselves to local social, cultural and language patterns. The conservative South Africans have not always found it easy to accept the 200,000 new white skilled workers, whose alien habits and ideas make it difficult, in some cases, for them to be absorbed readily into the English-speaking and, more particularly, the Afrikaans-speaking communities. The historical conflict between the two main white language groups is another factor which complicates the assimilations of new blood into South African society. Afrikaners in particular have doubts about some of the new settlers' lack of colour-conciousness and their religious affiliations. The Afrikaners' traditional aversion to immigrants who could possibly upset the balance between the established white groups is diminishing but it has by no means disappeared. In fact the growing stream of immigrants 37,960 in 1963 (net gain 30,809), 40,865 in 1964 (net gain 32,773), 38,319 in 1965 (net gain 29,113), and 48,048 in 1966 (net gain 38,160), is once again causing increasing dissatisfaction in certain circles. This was also the case in 1947 when there were 28,839 immigrants (net gain 20,922) and in 1948 when there were 35,631 (net gain 28,097). It was only in those two earlier years that a significant rate of increase in immigrant vis-a-vis the natural growth of the white population was discernible. In 1966 more than 13,000 Britons came to the Republic. Immigrants from the Netherlands are fewer than from many other countries: in 1966 less than 1,300 Dutch arrived in South Africa.[9]

There has also been considerable progress in cultural and intellectual spheres since 1961. The new University Colleges for non-Whites have received so much support and have so grown in status and numbers of students that their conversion into autonomous institutions has been decided on. In 1964 a new bilingual white university was established at Port Elizabeth, and in 1968 a second university in Johannesburg, an Afrikaans medium one, opened its doors to almost 800 students. The universities do not yet receive as much state aid as those in Britain, for example, and gifted lecturers and students often succumb to more attractive financial and research prospects overseas. There is also progress in primary and secondary education because of better planning, but here also far more financial support is demanded. The co-ordination of secondary education on a national level is being undertaken. In 1961 a five year plan was announced in terms of which R100 million would be allotted for Bantu educational development. In the four years since 1964, when the Transkei adopted its own Education Act, nearly 1,700 additional teachers and administrative officers have been appointed to nearly 50 new schools. The Transkei's

9. Republic of South Africa, *Bureau of Statistics, Report no. 286, Statistics of Immigrants and Emigrants 1924-1964* (Pretoria, 1965); *Bulletin of Statistics*, Quarter ending June, 1967, (Pretoria, 1967.)

school population increased by nearly 33 per cent to 325,000. By 1967 the Transkei had established its own educational system.

There has been a renewed interest in research, both in intensified work in old established fields and in pioneering work in new fields, such as in Antarctica and in nuclear physics. The first operation to transplant a human heart, which was undertaken in December, 1967, in Cape Town by Prof. C. Barnard and his team (and followed a month later by a second and much more successful one), placed South African cardiac surgery in world class. This not only improved the Republic's image overseas, but led to the allocation of very substantial funds to promote further research and to attract overseas specialists. An increase in state aid and in private initiative had developed many cultural activities. A healthy critical approach which weighs new ideas against old is much in evidence. Book production had increased and, in comparison with previous years, book sales are rising. Despite persistent overseas efforts, initiated by politically hostile groups, to sever South Africa's cultural and intellectual ties with the outside world (as has occurred to some extent in the sporting sphere by for example barring her from two consecutive Olympiads), contact has been maintained in many quarters. External and internal air services have expanded despite the fact that practically all African states have refused to permit South African airlines to fly over their territories.

The real significance of the very many developments in South Africa since the establishment of a republic will only become apparent in the future. Prof. F. G. Butler of Rhodes University has said: "We do not know the road, we have not got the answers. We must learn to dwell in the midst of uncertainties, patiently, sanely".[10] If there is any clear tendency discernible in the eventful seven years under discussion it is that the Republic has begun to assume control in southern Africa whilst Britain under the Labour Government of Wilson has been extricating herself from commitments in the area. This South African control is not political or military, although Britain has withdrawn her ships from the Simonstown naval base, and will also withdraw her last vestige of control from Swaziland in 1968. Nor is South Africa's control an ideological one, for all her neighbouring states reject apartheid. It is in the commercial, technical and cultural spheres that the Republic is exerting considerable influence, and in attempting to further the common interests of her region she is offering her services, skills and accomplishments to her neighbours.

Apart from adjustments made by the Republic in her foreign relations there is also evidence of domestic adjustments, although it is not yet clear whether these will become historically significant. Since the establishment of the Republic the white population increase has been half a million, of which 200,000 were immigrants. The remarkable number of "new" South Africans would seem to indicate that the Republic has been passing through a period of relatively rapid transition. There has also been an influx of foreign concepts: in the

10. *The Republic and the Arts: Lecture 7, The Republic in a changing world* (Johannesburg, 1964) p. 6.

cultural, religious and social spheres, new patterns and structures have become apparent. These tendencies have on occasion been sharply opposed by conservative elements in South Africa. There has been more opportunity for co-operation in the political sphere between English and Afrikaans-speaking South Africans, and the traditional division between the two groups has also become blurred. Attitudes towards the colour question and towards Communism have become crucial factors in deciding affiliations. Despite a sharp division between many university students there are clear indications that a new white nation is being born. In March, 1968, Prof. F. G. Butler sensed that "English and Afrikaans-speaking South Africans are reaching out towards each other with unusual, if fumbling frankness. This is more than fear-inspired mutual back-slapping in our little white laager; it is a recognition of common ground and shared sentiments".[11]

The influence of Western European standards on the non-White population (which expanded by more than two million in the period under discussion) has increased, and these standards are rapidly being accepted at all levels. In the Republic, both in the depopulated rural areas and in the rapidly growing cities, the Bantu still preponderate: consequently there are considerable doubts concerning the practicality of moving most of the Bantu to their own homelands in the foreseeable future, even though some important steps have already been taken in this direction. The future destinies of the Coloureds and Indians are also at stake: without total territorial segregation, some measure of self-government must be granted them. Although the non-Whites are co-operating with the government more than before, South Africa's racial experiment is still at an early stage: many courageous steps will be required in the near and more distant future. Sabotage organized by forces within the Republic has virtually ceased. White and black revolutionary leaders, whether detained in prison or "exiled" abroad, no longer play any significant part. Although the cost of living is rising rapidly, the years 1961 to 1968 have been relatively peaceful as far as racial and labour matters are concerned. Attention has increasingly been focussed, however, on the big gap between white and black wages and salaries.

Owing to the minimal number of constitutional changes and the competence and tact of the last Governor-General, C. R. Swart, who filled the new office as State-President until his retirement on 31 May, 1967, the Republic, under the powerful National Party, was one of the most stable states in an unstable continent. The contrast between South Africa's stability and the many bloody and disruptive revolutions and counter-revolutions in Black Africa and elsewhere have been marked. Scholars are becoming interested in the *malaise* of Black Africa.[12]

Events in Ghana and Nigeria particularly, as well as those in the smouldering

---

11. "The future of English-speaking South Africa", *New Nation*, March, 1968, p. 4. Cf. E. S. Munger: "New White Politics in South Africa" in *Southern Africa and the United States* edited by W. A. Hance, p. 83, Columbia University Press, New York and London, 1968.
12. Cf. R. Dumont: *False start in Africa*, New York and London, 1966.

Congo, strengthened this reaction. As the "progressive" writer, Rita Hinden, in her article, "Ghana's February Revolution", put it in 1967: "The Ghanaian story is probably the most tragic of any of the new African states, just because hopes were highest and were most cruelly dashed".[13] In Nigeria there were no fewer than three coups, two of which succeeded early in 1966. The shock they caused was all the greater for Nigeria's having been considered to be the exemplary "giant of Africa". In March, 1967, W. A. E. Skurnik concluded: "As 1966 was nearing its end, a description of Nigeria as a nation was an exaggeration".[14] Towards the end of May, 1967, the prosperous Eastern Nigeria, now called Biafra, declared its independence, and a bitter, protracted and bloody civil war resulted, which is attracting increasing humanitarian attention especially because of loss of life through hunger and disease. In February, 1968, John D. Chick wrote: "Eventually, by coercion or conciliation, hostilities will be ended, but the welcome return of peace will not end Nigeria's troubles. Territorial integrity may have been preserved, but national unity will be as remote as ever . . . social reconstruction will take generations . . . and the federalist front, relieved of the immediate threat to its principles of action, will begin to reveal its inner contradictions . . . ".[15]

The International Court's verdict on South-West Africa can be regarded as a turning-point in South African history. Coming as it did at the end of a drawn-out debate, at a psychological moment in international affairs, it provided no avenue for the Great Powers to intervene legally on behalf of the U.N. in southern Africa. The U.S.A. does not consider there is sufficient ground for allowing the U.N. to use armed force in South West Africa on the pretext that the situation there is a threat to world peace. America acquired power in the Congo because of the U.N.'s financially disastrous action, and this has caused Russia to maintain that the U.N., as such, should not intervene in South-West Africa: intervention should be left to the African states. This is significant because it means that in this connection the U.N. will not be backed by any Great Power. The U.N. nevertheless appointed a council to take over the administration of South-West Africa from the Republic, but, faced by the refusal of the Republic to admit this body, it was compelled to return to New York. Although confronted by a serious loss of prestige, the U.N. has as yet found no way out of this impasse.

Rapidly developing new international crises seem to have created the situation in which the U.N. in the immediate future will leave the invasion of Ovamboland and the Northern Transvaal to black "freedom fighters". While Angola, Rhodesia and Mozambique still exist as northern buffer states for South Africa this threat is not immediate to the Republic itself. Angola and Mozambique are vast, however, and their frontiers can not easily be indefinitely defended alone by one of the smaller, although determined, states of Europe,

13. *Encounter*, XXVIII, (5), May, 1967, p. 44.
14. "Nigeria in Crisis", in *Current History*, 52(307), March, 1967, p. 142.
15. "Nigeria at War", in *Current History*, 54(318), February, 1968, p. 113.

while Rhodesia is, since 1967, regularly attracting increasing numbers of terrorists. The Republic found it necessary to support more actively efforts to combat the terrorists in her neighbouring territories. Late in 1967 South African police units were already in action in Rhodesia against Bantu terrorists, mainly from the Republic, who were crossing the Zambesi in relatively large groups from Zambia. Britain protested, but the police were not withdrawn. Subsequently Rhodesian and South African forces, having engaged larger groups of well-trained and well-armed terrorists in a series of bitter, protracted engagements in heavy bush, continually wiped out their hard core of determined fighters. The others, who received no appreciable support from the Rhodesian Bantu, fell back into Zambia, where a number of supporting bases are ready to re-equip them. Early in October, 1967, a terrorist group also unsuccessfully penetrated Malawi. In the meantime attacks from Tanzania into northern Mozambique were continuing. When the apparent deadlock in the U.N. on the issue of the whole of southern Africa is taken into consideration, the general stepping up of activities by Russian, Chinese, Algerian and Egyptian trained terrorists is very likely. A regular series of massive invasions from central Africa along a broad belt into the Deep South can therefore be anticipated. K. Irvine predicted in February, 1968, " . . . the guerilla movement in Central Africa, like those in Algeria and Vietnam, is likely to gain in experience with the passage of time and to gain greater African support as well as material support from any outside interests who . . . oppose Southern Africa's White coalition".[16] It is more than likely that the Republic will soon become militarily deeply involved well beyond her northern frontiers. In late July, 1968, the first South African fell on the Zambesi front. This casualty, coupled with a Zambian call for more and better arms to defend their exposed southern Black bastion, focussed attention on an important zone of imminent Black-White confrontation. A severe flare-up here would serve to strengthen the Afro-Asian's contention that White Southern Africa constituted a permanent threat to world peace; and this might precipitate intervention by the U.N.

A new phase in the history of southern Africa has opened in which the Republic as the leader of a White South is adopting an effective defensive attitude against the revolutionary ideology and military aggression of the Black North. Most Black states and all revolutionary organizations agree that White rule in the South must be overthrown, but there is no unanimity as to who or what will replace the old order. The clashes between the ambitious leaders of the multifarious revolutionary organizations and of the African nations, and the conflicting interests of the various Black states have further limited the efficacy of the revolutionary North in opposing the conservative, but changing South. Meanwhile the importance of her trade and her diplomacy and rapidly growing military power all operate in South Africa's favour. Editor W. A. Hance concludes in his Postscript to *Southern Africa and the United States:* "Externally,

16. "Southern Africa: the White fortress" in *Current History*, 54(318), February, 1968, p. 112.

the forces which might bring sufficient weight are weak and divided . . . there is growing frustration among the exiles, the independent states north of the Zambezi lack the military and logistic capability of intervening, the United Nations is not a promising organ for military or even economic measures, and neither the United Kingdom nor the United States wishes to use military force or to assume the burden of effecting a change".[17]

Nevertheless, the situation in the sixties is still very fluid. Events in far off places such as Vietnam, the West Indies, France or Portugal could radically influence the course of events in South Africa. Predictions concerning South Africa's future differ even more radically than do the interpretations of her past. At one extreme is the view that the logical consequence of a tragic history culminating in large-scale white suppression of Blacks in a black continent and in a predominantly coloured world will be a catastrophic, bloody revolution. At the other extreme are the prophecies of a period of peaceful and prosperous co-existence for all South Africa's racial and language groups, with steadily increasing progress in all spheres of life, and a gradual solution of the Republic's complex problems.

17. New York and London, 1968, p. 163. Cf. also V. McKay on pp. 14-15.

21. Conclusion: Factors which Shaped the History of South Africa.

To predict the future is fortunately not one of the historian's functions; indeed it has been difficult enough to analyze one of the most interesting, and certainly one of the most important, problems in the history of southern Africa: "how did it come about that so small a number of Whites, just over 3½ million, came to assume such a position of power, and consequently to play such an important role on the African continent and in international affairs?" From the days of the early voyagers round southern Africa to the present day, factors which promoted South Africa's development into the most powerful state on the African continent should be distinguished from factors which retarded this development.

In order to do this one has to go back almost 500 years to the days when the Portuguese pioneers to the East Indies viewed the dangerous rocky headlands of the Cape chiefly as physical obstacles in far away stormy southern seas. These had to be overcome before sailing northwards to more attractive countries. A century later the English and the Dutch adopted a more positive, but still hesitant, approach to the Cape. Although they sometimes landed for refreshments and repairs they did not always consider it worth the effort or the risk; which explains the long delay in establishing a White settlement. Only after more than a 150 years did the Dutch East India Company adequately respond to the challenge of the stormy Cape's coasts by sending Jan van Riebeeck to establish, at the foot of Table Mountain, a small refreshment and hospital station for sailors and a harbour where ships could be put in for repairs.

For some time after the establishment of this first European settlement the Cape remained an unpretentious and poor outpost of civilization, in marked contrast to the contemporaneous North American colonies. The narrow mercantilist policy of the Dutch Company, which was primarily directed at increasing the profits of its shareholders as rapidly as possible, was a serious deterrent to the development of White South Africa. Free Burghers were introduced to assist the poorly paid and unenthusiastic Company officials to produce cheap fresh food in sufficient quantities to meet their own needs as well as those of the many visiting ships. After the coming of the Huguenots it was not considered necessary to promote further immigration to the Cape. The bitter conflict which developed between the burghers and Governor W. A. van der Stel caused the Company to decide to use black slave labour rather than free white labour at the Cape. This further reduced the small demand for white labour which had existed from early times.

Although mountain ranges blocked the way into the interior, and although the Karoo immediately to the north of the Cape peninsula was unattractive, the Cape Colony nevertheless provided a relatively healthy open country which could have sustained a large population. The Company, desirous of deriving direct profit from diamonds and other mineral riches, searched avidly in the immediate Cape interior and along the immense coastal strip from the later South-West Africa around the Cape to Portuguese East Africa, but in vain. These riches were present in quantities unequalled anywhere on the African continent, but ironically were not to be discovered in exploitable quantities until much later. In consequence of all these factors South Africa in her early formative period received no strong, steady stream of immigrants, which seriously retarded her rate of development.

Company policy, combined with the nature of southern Africa, turned agriculturists into cattle farmers, and cattle farmers into half-nomadic trekboers. These trekboers in the 18th century moved rapidly into the interior where they came into contact with the Hottentots, Bushmen and Xhosa. This small group of individualistic, self-supporting, independent Afrikaners (as they were soon called) became a factor to contend with in southern Africa. In vain the Company endeavoured to restrict the expansion of its colony at the extreme southern tip of Africa, and to regulate the economic activities of the Afrikaner Boers who were still within reach. The Afrikaner Boer emerged as an important new historical factor despite the Company policy and, in many cases, owing to that policy. The Company was not prepared to provide adequate defence or protection for the Afrikaner Boer on the distant, extensive colonial frontiers against the agile Bushman or the more powerful Xhosa. While the Company's policy retarded the further expansion of the Whites in South Africa it at the same time stimulated the Afrikaner Boer's spirit of independence. The latter was compelled to be self-reliant and came to view the Company government as oppressive. This circumstance in no small measure contributed to the development of the Afrikaner national consciousness. Within a few generations all Whites in the interior were completely integrated into Afrikaner Boer society. The common, continual struggle against overwhelming non-white odds helped to eliminate basic differences among the Whites. A good example of this process is that of the well-known Trigardt family, of Swedish descent, of whom the renowned pioneer Louis Trigardt, having penetrated to the south-east coast of Africa, found his last rest in Lourenço Marques. To him we are indebted for a unique diary illuminating South African pioneer life.

The chronic lack of immigrants to South Africa meant that the white population grew almost exclusively by natural increase. Because the original settlement was so small the population of the Cape Colony could not increase as fast as the population of other similar European colonies. A comparison of the Cape with the British North American colonies (later the United States of America) is most revealing. In 1660 there were already 80,000 white colonists in the British American colonies, while at the same time the Cape only had 200. In 1743 there were one million white Americans, but in 1750 there were only 5,000 free burghers at the Cape. By 1820 there were already more than $7\frac{3}{4}$ million white Americans, but on the eve of the Great Trek there were only about 65,000 Whites in the Cape Colony – still less than 1% of the American white population. Although Australia was only colonized in 1788, this same tendency is unmistakable in a comparison between their white population increases. In 1850 the Australian white population in pushing over the 400,000 mark had already out-stripped by far the total white population of the whole of southern Africa, and a decade later the white Australians topped a million.

The Company's policy attempted to restrict the activities not only of the Afrikaner Boer of the interior but also those of the richer and more cultured inhabitants of the Cape Peninsula. Any display of initiative was rigidly opposed. Consequently commercial and maritime activities were, as far as possible, reserved for the Company. Concessions were granted only in those cases where the Company could not or would not act. Entrepreneurs did not easily accumulate capital. All private enterprise, however, was by no means eliminated. Company officials, their families and friends used the Company's monopoly system as a shield to enrich themselves. There was a vast difference between the Company's practice and theory.

The fact that no big capitalists could develop under the conditions prevalent at the Cape had important repercussions on the history of South Africa. At a time when the Industrial Revolution was beginning to take place the strategically important Cape was being offered almost unlimited prospects, given unrestricted commercial activities and backed by enough capital. No particularly significant private commercial enterprises developed along the South African coasts nor, for that matter, along the contiguous shores of the Portuguese territories, nor near the Equator, nor on the islands off the east coast of Africa, nor on the East Indian islands, nor in the South American trading complex. Because of these factors the discovery of minerals and diamonds, which were immediately to attract many more white immigrants to South Africa, was inevitably postponed till much later. This also retarded the opening up of the most fertile parts of southern Africa.

Such settlement as did take place in southern Africa was not a rapid one brought about by maritime activity, but a comparatively slow one of opening up the interior overland. Under the conservative and unimaginative regime of an obsolete Company magnificent opportunities for the Cape's expansion were lost. For example, the logical expansion of the Cape Colony to South-West Africa and Natal did not occur at the time when it would have met with no foreign competition. Later such expansion was to become considerably more difficult and more dangerous. Perhaps the lack of competition from the Portuguese and other European powers made the Dutch politically apathetic in southern Africa. During the third decade of the 18th century they occupied the excellent harbour of Delagoa Bay as a trading post, but abandoned it as an unprofitable death-hole. The whole position in southern Africa was in marked contrast with that of North America where French interest in Louisiana and the Spanish development of California strongly stimulated settlement.

The Company's neglect of its many opportunities in and around South Africa during the century and a half of its rule did have some positive consequences however: it meant that the Afrikaner frontier farmers were unimpeded in developing their self-sufficiency. Ultimately, towards the end of the 18th century they were to agitate against the rule of the Company and of Britain, and finally escape entirely from British authority into the independent Voortrekker states of the third decade of the 19th century. Whatever was not done in the 18th century provided opportunities for the men of the 19th century. The Voortrekkers only temporarily gained access to Port Natal: they soon depended wholly on the ports of Portuguese East Africa for a neutral outlet to the Indian Ocean. The Voortrekkers made their immense effort only in the nick of time. The Bantu were already beginning to exchange their assegais and shields for fire-arms, and if they had had time to complete this tactical revolution it would have been much more difficult for the Voortrekkers to conquer the interior. Only after much blood and tears did the Voortrekkers finally defeat the splendidly disciplined Matabele and Zulu impis who had so successfully used their stabbing assegais to conquer other Bantu tribes.

The achievements and the sufferings of the Voortrekkers developed the nascent national consciousness of the Afrikaner frontier farmers into an enduring national awareness, which was to unite all Afrikaners firmly during the 19th century. In the middle of this century Britain recognized independent Voortrekker republics in the interior, isolated as they were and with no gateways to the outside world. These republics preserved the Afrikaners' language, traditions and aspirations until the end of the 19th century, when the massive onslaught of British imperialism produced a general awakening throughout South Africa of Afrikaner national consciousness. Inspired by a Calvinistic trust in God, the Afrikaners began to believe that they were destined to spread western Christian civilization in Africa. In no small measure is the determination and efficacy of the Afrikaner due to this belief.

In general the Great Trek, in its indirect results, did much to unite the Afrikaners, but also contributed much to the estrangement of the two white groups in South Africa. From the time of the Great Trek until nearly a century and a half later the duality of white power was a feature of South African life. The conflict of 1899-1902 intensified the general bitterness between the two white groups and strengthened a narrow Afrikaner nationalism. The Afrikaners, who already in the 18th century had shown signs of forming a separate national group, were during the 20th century to develop much stronger characteristics. Their bitter War of Independence made them view their separate identity as one of their most precious possessions which they must at all cost maintain. The sacrifice of tens of thousands of South African Whites was the price which had to be paid to end the balkanization of the late 19th century. About 30,000 Boer men, women and children died during this war, as against nearly 22,000 British and colonial soldiers killed and nearly 100,000 wounded or incapacitated by sickness. Many of those who lost their lives on the British side were colonial South Africans. Although this was a catastrophic reduction of South Africa's already sparse white population South Africa at the same time gained many new immigrants. Many British and colonial soldiers, nurses and techni-

424

cians settled permanently in South Africa, and the great interest aroused by the war attracted other immigrants to the country.

The discovery and exploitation of diamonds, gold and other minerals were hastened by the Great Trek. The endemic antagonism and conflict between the Boers and the English which were legacies of the Great Trek made the Boers of the South African Republic highly suspicious of all the foreign Whites who streamed into South Africa to mine, process and market her riches. The extraordinarily rich gold deposits in South Africa was one of the factors which led to the great white civil war in this country, the main purpose of which was to re-establish British supremacy in South Africa. The British annexation of the two Boer republics foreshadowed the restoration of the franchise on democratic principles (as far as the Whites were concerned) and at the same time the British government undertook not to grant the franchise to 'natives' in the former republics before the introduction of self-government. The British government's subsequent interpretation of this clause precluded not only the Bantu but also other non-Whites from receiving the vote in these territories when they were granted responsible government. These concessions to the former republicans were carried a stage further when at the time of Union the British government did not insist on any alteration in the existing franchise provisions in the Transvaal and Orange Free State. This meant that political control remained in the hands of the Whites, who were numerically inferior to the non-Whites, but who were generally superior to them in administration, technology, culture and military power.

An extremely important factor which contributed to the maintenance of White power in South Africa was that the Bantu were divided into so many different tribes, some of whom were traditional enemies. During the White disunity of the last decades of the 19th century and the early decades of the 20th century the various Bantu groups of South Africa were still very isolated geographically and had no generally acknowledged national leaders. Most Bantu were still illiterate and were governed primarily by their tribal structure. There was a decline of Bantu leadership from tribal chiefs such as Moshesh and Khama and, mainly because there were so few literate men among the Bantu, a new type of leadership did not yet emerge.

A further important factor which helped establish White supremacy in southern Africa was the fact that Black Africans in the North had not yet developed any interest in their fellow Africans in the White South. Without radio and air communications it was indeed almost impossible for Black Africa, which had never known unity except in some regions, and was further balanized by the imposition of colonial boundaries and the rivalries of Europe, to acquire any substantial knowledge of southern Africa.

The situation changed only after the Second World War when there was a sharp reaction against all forms of racial discrimination. In the mid-forties there was a marked tendency towards decolonization, first in the East where India gained her independence, then from the late fifties in Africa, after Ghana gained her independence; political developments which inaugurated the emergence of independent Black states which, strongly supported by new Asian states and the Soviet bloc, soon formed a numerically dominant pressure group in the U.N. This group naturally concentrated on freeing the Black majority in the White South from White control.

In the meanwhile a relatively passive racial policy of differentiation and segregation had preserved the White man's position in the Union of South Africa during the first half of the 20th century. The non-Whites were being increasingly integrated into the economy of the Whites, non-White labourers were beginning to become organized on a nation-wide basis and the Whites grew increasingly dependent on non-White, particularly Bantu, labour. A situation was thus being created which would make it more difficult to implement any policy of territorial segregation at a later date. So few non-Whites had, however, as yet acquired the franchise that the possibility of curtailing this privilege, or even eliminating it altogether, could be contemplated in the forties, fifties and sixties. The domestic struggle over non-White suffrage and other legislative measures initiated by the National Party government from 1948 onwards attracted much attention in the international sphere because of universal sensitivity to racial matters. There was increasing foreign condemnation of South Africa's traditional colour policy which, in certain respects, was being carried to its logical conclusion. International opposition to apartheid was so strong that South Africa was beginning to appear in an exceptionally unfavourable light.

After the devastating White civil war of 1899 – 1902 the country recovered amazingly rapidly. The cost of South Africa's subsequent participation in two world wars was considerable. At the same time both wars, and especially the Second World War, stimulated local industries and broadened the South African perspective. For the first time since the Anglo-Boer War South Africa figured in world affairs. A further consequence of the First World War was that South West Africa, which Germany had acquired during the scramble for Africa, fell to South Africa as a League of Nations mandate. Thus the boundaries of the Union were geographically rounded off more neatly than they had been before and the enlarged area commanded a wide variety of natural resources.

By the mid-20th century it was clear that further consolidation of South Africa's frontiers was no longer feasible. Basutoland, an enclave of South Africa in 1966 became the independent state of Lesotho while Bechuanaland, which was largely cut off from the outside world, also in 1966 achieved independence as Botswana. Swaziland was hemmed in by Mozambique and South Africa and earmarked for independence in 1968. These developments seemed to indicate the division of southern Africa into one large white state and a number of black states, both inside and outside the Republic. Within the Republic there are 260 separate Bantu areas curving like a gigantic horseshoe round the Transvaal and the Orange Free State. The new circumstances confronting the Republic together with the Government's blueprint for future development seem to indicate a return to the White-Bantu frontier situation of the 18th and 19th centuries. No exact parallel can be drawn, however, for the Bantu are now largely westernized. Nevertheless typical frontier problems will no doubt again confront South Africa: inherent in this state of affairs is a situation which could become difficult to control, but today the overwhelming opinion among Whites in South Africa is that the present policy of the government in power is the only alternative to racial integration.

Partly because of the extraordinarily rapid progress of the Republic comprehensive schemes to safeguard the position of the White man have been initiated, and with considerable success. Over more than half a century White unity has been slowly, painfully, but steadily built up. South Africa's exceptionally rich resources and strategic situation stood her in good stead against overseas enmity. Without aid from a major power or powers outside Africa it soon became clear that an overland invasion through the difficult Central African terrain would be extremely hazardous for any group of African states. Probably the strongest African state north of the Republic, Egypt, is far removed from the Republic and is situated in the inflammatory Middle East. As a leading Arab state her prime concern is to cope with the growing strength of Israel. Egypt's humiliating defeat in the Six Days' War of June, 1967, has, however, considerably reduced her prestige among African States. Algeria's armed power has clearly emerged in recent years. Nigeria, the giant of West Africa, has for more than a year been waging a bitter, bloody, and devastating civil war. As yet there is no indication who is going to fill the vacuum left by Britain's withdrawal from the Indian Ocean. Neither India, Pakistan, China or, for that matter, Russia is at the moment able to move down to the south-east African coast in sufficient force to bring heavy pressure to bear on the White South. In the meantime the Republic is opening up friendlier relations with major South American powers on the South Atlantic seaboard. The Republic's natural commercial and financial partners, Britain and the United States, are not prepared to sacrifice their flourishing economic connections. With the Suez Canal closed their merchant and naval vessels often want to, and sometimes have to, call at strategic South African ports.

Although the Republic of South Africa is still apparently in a strong position in the sixties of the 20th century, her white population is steadily decreasing in proportion to her non-white population. The position of the White man is by no means assured and more and more Blacks are becoming integrated in the white Republic of South Africa. Both her weaknesses and strength stem from white South Africa's peculiar process of development over nearly five centuries. On the one hand there were factors which limited the Whites' power and on the other hand there were factors which sporadically and gradually developed their authority. The effects of the two groups of factors cannot always be clearly distinguished: at times a particular new opportunity has been created by a "lost chance" of an earlier period. So, for example, the restrictive policy of the Dutch East India Company left certain areas "open" for the Voortrekkers to settle beyond the control of the British when the right moment arrived. This ultimately resulted in the appalling bloodshed of the Anglo-Boer War, which in its turn effected an amalgamation of White forces in a constitutional union and the formulation of a common non-White policy. The present position of the Whites in South Africa can be ascribed to the fact that they seldom experienced long unbroken periods of success. In South Africa fortune was usually closely followed by misfortune: brilliant victories were succeeded by serious set-backs. This is how South Africa has arrived at her present position of relative power and partial security.

What moral, if any, can be drawn from this account of the White man's interest in southern Africa and his activities in the sub-continent? There are so many possible interpretations of South African history that it is doubtful if there are any "lessons" to be learnt. It is also, for the same reason, impossible to determine whether the White man by reacting differently, on occasion, to circumstances in these five centuries could have improved the present-day position of his descendants in South Africa. Whatever particular "lessons" or "mistakes" are sought will undoubtedly be found. In any case the "mistakes" of the past cannot now be remedied, since most situations which gave rise to them have long since disappeared; indeed it is a moot point whether they will still be regarded as "mistakes" in the unknown future, and even more doubtful whether there will still be an urge to "correct" them in the years that lie ahead.

In few lands and times has so much been done by so few, have the activities of such small groups of people attracted so much attention outside their country. It must also be remembered that during its first 400 years South Africa's development was exceedingly slow and that at the beginning of this century a devastating and bitter civil war was in progress. Naturally the unique story of South Africa has been told, is being told and will be told in many different ways; but in whatever way it is told and from whatever point of view it is presented, there are few other historical tales which can surpass it for sheer dramatic intensity. While the inhabitants of the Republic of South Africa, and for that matter the inhabitants of the whole of southern Africa, are living through the crucial tension of the nineteen-sixties, which is one of the results of their past, they are also moving towards the ultimate revelation of the deeper meaning of these events.

There are two extreme possibilities for South Africa's future. The Republic could go the same way as ancient Carthage which disappeared completely after seven hundred years of progress and prosperity. The Republic could also, however, develop into one of Africa's chief spreaders of Western ideas, at a time when Western power had declined in Africa and elsewhere. Between these two extremes there are, of course, countless possibilities and probabilities.

It is not yet clear how modern technology, from a military point of view, will affect the Republic in her isolated position in the southern hemisphere. As in the past it would appear that it will be chiefly the interests and policies of the Great Powers in the northern hemisphere which will again determine South Africa's future. The Republic's success in handling its major domestic and external problems will obviously be of importance. Much will depend on the quality of South Africa's leaders. The nature of the support given by the people of South Africa to her leaders in their efforts to maintain the *status quo* and combat revolutionary tendencies will also be a potent factor in determining

428

South Africa's future. A further important consideration is whether white South Africans – and particularly Afrikaners – will be prepared to augment their scanty numbers by encouraging immigrants to come to South Africa from the over-populated northern hemisphere; and whether they will be prepared to adjust themselves to the possibly radical alterations of the composition of the white population. If they are able to do so the disadvantages of the early crystallization of the Afrikaner people into a too limited numerical structure and a too rigid pattern could be remedied. It is essential that an accelerated rate of population growth should be encouraged in an under-populated land of enormous potential.

Situated in the southern part of an under-developed continent the Republic with its highly developed technology and its stable government has tremendous advantages over the rest of Africa. The intemperate criticism of the Republic is a major factor in forging white unity. Cataclysmic threats in the sixties of the 20th century have sowed fear but they have also reaped white unity. The cardinal problem is what sort of place and status the Whites and non-Whites are prepared to grant to one another in southern Africa. The nature of South Africa's difficult passage to the 21st century will be determined not only by the interaction of domestic and foreign events, but also by the Republic's ability to adapt itself to rapidly changing circumstances. And this applies, in particular, to the Republic's ability to adapt itself to the radically new conditions now obtaining in the whole of southern Africa.

Appendix I: The Natives of South Africa

Introduction

Our knowledge of the early history of the native peoples of South Africa has been acquired primarily by word of mouth. Fortunately the first missionaries and travellers kept some records, and historians such as Theal, Bryant, Ellenberger and Stow made special studies of South African oral history. Later, some Bantu such as Soga, Kama and Ndamase were able to make further contributions. Nevertheless there are still today many untapped sources for an historian who would study what South Africa's indigenous peoples transmit orally from generation to generation. It is no mean task to attempt to analyse oral tradition, compare it with other data and arrange it into a meaningful, reliable history. This chapter aims to give the principal ascertainable events in the history of the most important South African tribes up to the time of their first contact with organized White groups.

The non-White peoples of South Africa are divided into three main groups, namely, the Bushmen, the Hottentots and the Bantu. The Bushmen, who are generally considered to be the oldest living indigenous race of South Africa, were preceded by prehistoric peoples. We do not know whether these peoples were known to the early Bushmen, but we do know that the early Bushmen, like their predecessors, had a stone age culture. There are many indications that successive waves of peoples came down from the north of Africa. We can only surmise how one primitive culture was overrun by the next more advanced one. The culture of prehistoric man is today studied by the archaeologist who probes the nature of the primitive man responsible for producing stone implements, ranging from large hand-axes to the microlithic scraper, still found scattered over large parts of South Africa.

The appearance of the Whites

When the first Portuguese discoverers landed in southern Africa late in the 15th century they met an indigenous race, which was later named the Hottentots. For more than a century and a half European travellers bartered with the Hottentots for provisions, and sometimes were killed in violent clashes with them. Regular contact with this people began only when Van Riebeeck settled permanently at the Cape. As Whites penetrated deeper into the interior of southern Africa they encountered more and more tribes and another race, the Bushmen.

Whites on expeditions to the east had already met the third indigenous race, namely the Bantu, principally when their ships were wrecked on the coast. The

430

first armed clash with a Bantu group was in the last quarter of the 18th century, and heralded a series of wars, the first six of which were confined to the Xhosa frontier. As the Whites moved further into the interior they encountered more and more tribes, some friendly and some not. Contact among the indigenous peoples themselves had already caused upheavals which influenced the subsequent history of southern Africa as much as the contact between White and non-White.

Background of later relations

To view the history of the Bantu in perspective and be able to understand their attitude toward the Whites it is necessary to examine the Bantu's relations with their original neighbours. Before the time of Shaka (Chaka) the Bantu consisted of many small tribes each with its own tribal chief. These tribes were of various sizes. As the tribes migrated southwards from the north of Africa the tribes in the rear of the movement pressed on those in front. The southern part of Africa was comparatively uninhabited; it was, however, the hunting ground of Bushmen bands and Hottentot tribes. The Zulus have a well-known anecdote which recounts that when one suddenly comes upon a Bushman he will immediately ask one "From where did you first see me" to which the diplomatic answer is "I saw you when I was still a long way off"· From this we may deduce not only that the Bushmen felt inferior about their small build but also, and more important from a historical point of view, that the Zulu must have known them for a long time and were probably afraid of them. The Bushmen were nomadic hunters, whereas the Bantu tribes settled in particular places because they were pastoralists and agriculturists. Since the country was relatively uninhabited a tribe could, by moving southwards, relieve the pressure on it of new migrants from the north. The southwards movement was finally checked at the Fish River by contact with the Hottentots.

The Bushmen had particular hunting grounds and unless the Bantu interfered with their hunting habits it was possible in the beginning for the two races to co-exist peacefully. Although we do not hear of stock thefts we can assume that there were some, but large scale thefts were unlikely because game was plentiful and cattle were guarded against wild animals. When the Bantu began to move into the south in large numbers the Bushmen were compelled to withdraw to the mountains and the less habitable regions. By the time the great wars between the Whites and the Blacks started at the beginning of the 19th century the Bushmen had ceased to be a danger to the Bantu.

The Bantu in contacting the Hottentots met a culturally more highly developed people than the Bushmen. The Hottentots were pastoralists and wandered in search of pasture for their stock. If they hunted they did so away from where they lived. Possibly when they crossed paths with the Bantu friction resulted.

Traditionally the Bantu never formally declared war on an enemy. There were many possible causes for clashes among the Bantu. A border dispute, a stock theft, assault and such matters were sufficient reasons for opening hostilities. A

431

messenger would deliver a complaint and if no satisfaction was forthcoming the complainant would attack whenever he felt like it. Such an attack was generally launched shortly before daybreak. The enemy was overrun, his village burnt and the inhabitants speared or clubbed to death. The fighting was on a hand-to-hand basis and cattle were driven off. The victor seldom showed any mercy and the war lasted for a day or two at the most. Sometimes the victors carried off women and children and this resulted in reprisals. When eventually a tribe accepted defeat its chief sued for peace. Usually the peace terms demanded that the loser pay a tribute to the victor or that the vanquished tribe be incorporated into the tribe of the victor. Often the incorporated tribe was given a measure of autonomy. It was in this manner that Shaka expanded his nation, but it was his policy to appoint his own headmen over vanquished tribes.

The Bantu custom of attacking without a formal declaration of war explains the frontier wars of early Cape history and the attacks on the border farmers. The Bantu felt no particular animosity towards the Whites; they were merely acting within their tradition. The frontier farmers, complained of stock-thefts; the Bantu claimed that the farmers did not honour recognized boundaries. In a period when the Bantu regarded violence as a type of pastime the most trifling incident could motivate an attack. The role played by superstition and witchcraft in determing the attitude of the Bantu should also be considered. To the Bantu the bullets of the Whites merely indicated their superior witchcraft. The witch-doctor's own life was never safe since he had to be constantly proving his powers, and if he could find even a trivial reason to initiate a punitive expedition which would be advantageous to his people he would use it to enhance his own prestige. The fearlessness of a warrior was mainly a consequence of his faith in the witch-doctor and his potions because no expedition was ever undertaken without the warriors having been strengthened with potions. Also many tribal chiefs dealt horribly with armies returning home defeated and this was a further incentive to the warriors to conquer or die.

In inter-tribal affairs might was right. Diplomacy was a sign of weakness. The only acceptable diplomacy was that which either convinced the enemy that the defeated had subjected himself to him, or which alternatively presented the enemy who had been defeated but still remained a formidable opponent with a gift to wish him a pleasant journey home. Such diplomacy was characteristic of Moshwêshwê and his time and was adopted in the hope that although it might not permanently settle accounts it might at least defer their presentation.

To the Bantu it was actually ludicrous to consider that land of a tribal chief could be exchanged for cattle as if it were a woman. Land could only be obtained by force with the defeated either being destroyed or incorporated into the victor's tribe. We must view Bantu history against this background. The clashes among the Bantu were the results of causes peculiar to themselves; the clashes between Bantu and Whites were the results of their mutual inability to appreciate each other's point of view because their outlooks were diametrically opposed. From each one's point of view the fault always lay with the enemy.

The Bushmen and Hottentots

We know very little about the migration of the Bushmen to the south of Africa. Microlithic stone implements, bone implements and rock paintings are associated with the Bushmen and are to be found all over South Africa right down to its southern tip, but the Dutch and the sea voyagers before them found only Hottentots on the shores of southern Africa.

When, however, the Dutch farmers started hunting north of the coastal mountains they did meet Bushmen. Presumably by then the Bushmen were already withdrawing into the interior in the face of the Hottentot threat. According to Theal the Hottentots had already taken the springs from the Bushmen.

The Bushmen roamed between their water supply and their hunting grounds. They were organized in family groups and recognized no larger units. All attempts to civilize them failed so that both Hottentots and Whites often regarded them as wild animals. In 1774 the farmers in the north-western districts raised a commando which included Hottentots to drive off the plundering Bushmen. The Bushmen could not assert themselves against the physically stronger and technically more advanced Hottentots and, later, Bantu. With the arrival of the Whites the untenable position of the Bushmen deteriorated even further. They were forced to withdraw deeper and deeper into the interior to avoid clashes with their stronger enemies. The Bushmen of the Cape and of the interior have now virtually disappeared. The remaining Bushmen of South-West Africa, Botswana and Angola were in the vanguard of the great Bushman movement to the south, but never moved further south than these points. In South-West Africa reserves have been established for them. Here attempts are made to teach the Bushmen a more static way of life and to provide school facilities for them.

To the Whites the Hottentots proved to be sharp traders. A head of cattle which on first contact with the Whites was priced in iron was soon priced in copper and one also reads of Whites complaining about the thin cattle which the Hottentots offered for sale.

The Dutch East India Company's policy was that good relations must at all costs be maintained with the Hottentots. Although this policy was adhered to by consecutive governors they sometimes had difficulty in not becoming involved in the internal quarrels of the various tribes around Cape Town, Stellenbosch and Drakenstein.

The Hottentots were organized into tribes. When the Whites arrived at the Cape the Hottentots were occupying the area from the mouth of the Orange along the coast to the Fish River, as the names of various mountain ranges, such as the Outeniqua, remind us today. Their culture was much more advanced than that of the Bushmen and they kept sheep and cattle. It would appear that their cattle were tempting to the Bantu whose stock were probably inferior. Physically the Hottentots were related to the Boskop man and philogically to the North African Hamites. Click sounds were common to both the Hottentot and Bushman languages although in other respects the languages were quite different. The Hottentots probably adopted the click sounds from the Bushmen during their migration to the south.

Some of the Hottentot tribes which originally occupied the coastal area of southern Africa probably withdrew into the interior either because of quarrels with other Hottentots or because of pressure from their neighbours. In the 19th century we find some of them, the Koranas and the Griquas, in the country west of the Vaal River. These two nations were destined to play an important share in the unrest which made the interior chaotic between 1820 and 1840.

Today only a few unidentifiable Hottentot names remain of the many Hottentot tribes which are mentioned in early records of southern Africa. They were largely wiped out by the small-pox epidemics against which they had no resistance. It is chiefly the Nama of South-West Africa who have retained their identity and language. Today we know only the names of the Korana and the Griqua who were once forces to be reckoned with in the western Transvaal. Recently, however, hitherto unknown Hottentot tribes have been discovered in the uninhabitable areas of South-West Africa and Botswana.

The Bantu

At the beginning of the 16th century the Black peoples – the Bushmen and Hottentots had much lighter skins – who later became known as the Bantu began moving towards the south of Africa. (The term Bantu was introduced by the philologist Bleek, derived from the Bantu word for "people", cf. Zulu–Xhosa *abantu*). There were three groups of Bantu which moved down the eastern half of southern Africa and at least three groups which moved down the western half, that is, through the present western Transvaal.

The eastern groups were given the name Nguni although they were not all descendents of Mnguni, the first leader of one of the groups. It is presumed that the first of these groups, sometimes known as the Lala, migrated down the east coast between the Lebombo Mountains (Ubombo in Zulu) and the sea. The second group were Mnguni's followers (also known as Ntungwa (AbaNtungwa) tribes) from which the Xhosa (AmaXhosa), among others, are descended. The third goup were the Mbo (AbaseMbo) from whom the Mpondo (AmaMpondo) are descended. The two latter groups apparently migrated across the eastern Transvaal highveld.

The Nguni today inhabit the eastern littoral from the Crocodile River north of Swaziland to the Ciskei.

On the western side of the Transvaal there are stone ruins which were probably occupied even before the arrival of the Bantu by peoples other than Bushmen or Hottentots. By 1500, if not earlier, the first Bantu migrants from the north entered southern Africa either through the Transvaal or through Botswana. Subsequently there were more waves of migrants. The first group, of whom only the name has remained, were known as the Digôya. The second group were the Rolong (Barolong) of whom the present day Rolong tribes and

434

branches such as the Tlhaping (Batlhaping) are important representatives. Finally came the third group, the Hurutshe (Bahurutshe), and related Kwena (Bakwêna). By 1450 these groups are supposed to have split up into separate tribes, of whom the most important present-day representatives are the Hurutshe, the Tlharo (Batlharo), the Kwena, the Ngwato (Bangwato) and the Ngwaketse (Bangwakêtse). The Fokeng are also important and although regarded by some as a separate group they are probably also a branch of the Hurutshe.

The tribes who share the collective name of Sotho (Basotho) (divided into West Sotho (Tswana), North Sotho and South Sotho) are distinguished from the Nguni in the east not only by their language but also by the large villages with thousands of inhabitants in which they today still live and the fact that they practise totemism (the honouring of an animal or object). The Rolong honour the kudu (*thôlô*) and iron (*tshipi*) while the Kwena honour the crocodile (*kwêna*) and the Hurutshe the eland (*phôfu*).

Another group, the Venda (Vhavenda), settled in the northern Transvaal in about 1700 after supposedly migrating from the great lakes in central Africa.

The last group of Bantu to arrive in southern Africa are the Tsonga (va-Tsonga) better known as the Shangaans. They are migrants from Mozambique and have been in the north-eastern Transvaal for little more than a hundred and fifty years.

THE SOUTHERN NGUNI

The Xhosa[1]

Information obtained from castaways leads us to believe that the southern Nguni tribes already occupied the Transkei coast by the middle of the 17th century. Traditional history at this stage becomes less legendary. When the Bantu contacted the eastern Hottentots the former were already called Xhosa – with the click sound – being named after their second leader, the son of Mnguni.

The name Xhosa is important for it indicates that the Bantu had already at some stage been in contact with the Hottentots and/or the Bushmen for long enough to be influenced by their click sounds or else the Bantu had adopted these sounds earlier – possibly from the Bushmen who inhabited the route along which they had migrated. The fact remains that, if we can accept the philological evidence, the Nguni must have adopted the click sounds even before the arrival of Van Riebeeck. Whether this implies physical contact with the speakers of the click languages has not been established.

Toward the end of the 17th century the Xhosa were led by Tshiwo. Phalo, his successor, was only born after Tshiwo's death and in the interim Gwali, one

---

1. The following symbols and their approximate English pronunciations are to be noted: *c*, *q* and *x* (often accompanied by *n*, *g* or *h*) are click sounds; *ph* = *p* in *pit*; *th* = *t* in *tip*; *kh* = *c* in *cat*; *r* in Xhosa is the *ch* of *loch*; *h* in Zulu represents *ch* in *loch*; *hl* is the Welsh *ll* and *dl* its voiced equivalent.

of Phalo's elder brothers by a different mother, attempted unsuccessfully to assume control of the tribe. After a bloody battle Gwali and his uncle, Ntinde, fled across the uMbashe (Bashee) River and settled near the present Somerset East. These tribes were responsible for the first clashes with the Whites who by this time had reached what was later known as the Eastern Frontier. At this time we also learn for the first time of a split in an important Bantu tribe.

Phalo's uncle, Mdange, a famous warrior who was regent, decided to teach the fugitives, who were under the protection of the Hottentot chief Hintsati, a further lesson. Mdange and Hintsati fought on the western bank of the Fish River and Hintsati fell in battle. The Xhosa captured many Hottentot women, children and cattle. Although defeated the Hottentots continued to harass the Xhosa and even succeeded in recapturing some cattle. By now the 18th century had begun.

It was during the reign of Phalo that the first skirmish with the Whites occurred namely in 1736 with Hübner's hunting party.

Phalo's heir, Gcaleka, feeling that his father had lived long enough rebelled against him. Phalo suppressed the rebellion with the aid of his favourite son Rarabe, and Rarabe and Phalo moved across the Kei River. This was a notable split in a Xhosa tribe, which continues to this day in this tribe. Gcaleka, Hintsa and Sarili (called Kreli by the Whites) were important in the later history of the main section of their tribe. From the house of Rarabe the names of Ngqika (known as Gaika by the Whites) and Sandile are well-known.

The later history of Rarabe records another clash between the Xhosa and the Hottentots. When Rarabe crossed the Kei River he fought a bloody battle with the Hottentots that barred his way. Although the Xhosa pursued the fleeing Hottentots they could not subjugate them. Rarabe made peace with Hoho, the Hottentot queen, and obtained from her land between the Keiskamma and Buffels Rivers.

On one occasion Rarabe protected his in-laws, who were Thembu, against their short-tempered chief Ndaba. When Ndaba offered to pay a mere hundred head of cattle for one of Rarabe's daughters the insult was too much for Rarabe. He was fatally wounded in the ensuing skirmish.

It is maintained that Rarabe attempted to maintain good relations with the frontier farmers. He repeatedly assured them that the people of Gwali and Ntinde who were involved in the first frontier war were not his subjects.

Only one Xhosa tribe, the Gqunukhwebe (AmaGqunukhwebe), is traditionally considered to be a mixture of Xhosa and Hottentots. The name itself is derived from Gqunukwa, the name of a Hottentot tribe which lived on the coast next to the uMzimvubu River. The story is told of how Khwane, King Tshiwo's chief executioner, hid convicted Xhosa among the Hottentots instead of executing them. These Xhosa married Hottentot women, and in this way the Gqunukhwebe tribe came into being. Later they joined Gwali and Ntinde's fugitive tribes and after Mdange's war they fled to the Ciskei with Hintsati's Hottentots. This must have been the beginning of the end of the remaining Hottentots of the Eastern Province.

Interestingly enough Xhosa history does not admit of large-scale inter-marriage between Xhosa and Hottentot. By the end of the 18th century nothing more is heard of the Xhosa's Hottentot neighbours, except that a group of forty Hottentots are supposed to have assisted the Boers in the first frontier war. Apparently most of the organized Hottentot tribes were wiped out by the second smallpox epidemic of 1755. The Xhosa tribes near the Kei River also suffered heavily from this epidemic. However, at the beginning of the nine-teenth century Lichtenstein was still able to study the Hottentot language in the interior and Van der Kemp wrote a catechism in Hottentot.

After the death of Phalo internal strife characterized the Rarabe section. Ndlambe (Slambie), a son of Phalo, acted as regent for the minor Ngqika, a grandson of Phalo. Undoubtedly Ndlambe was a capable ruler but he was constantly trying to make the tribe appoint him ruler in his own right.

Although among the Xhosa the successor to the chief was determined by the Great House and the Right Hand House, intrigues among the sons and grand-sons of a deceased chief were a characteristic of Xhosa history, as indeed of Bantu history in general.

During the Second Frontier War of 1789 Ndlambe, it is said, was asked by the frontier farmers to persuade the plundering tribes to withdraw over the Fish River. He magnanimously expressed the desire that Boer and Xhosa should live together peacefully but omitted to say that he had no authority over the smaller tribes. According to Xhosa legend Ndlambe helped the frontier farmers in the Third Frontier War because he hoped that by so doing he would strengthen his position in the tribe.

In the meantime Ngqika had attained his majority but was rather wild and is said to have even had an affair with one of his uncle Ndlambe's wives. Mean-while there had been a change in the White area of southern Africa. The English had occupied the Cape and Lord Charles Somerset paid a visit to Ngqika. This is the first recorded occasion on which the White authorities interfered in Xhosa affairs. Ngqika was recognized as the "Sovereign of all the Xhosas" (Soga) and when later in 1818 he went to war with Ndlambe and Hintsa the Whites came to his assistance and ended Ndlambe's power and influence.

We now reach a mile-post in the history of the Xhosa. A war which originated in family feuds soon grew to such a size that the White authorities intervened to protect one group against the other. From now on the happenings on the eastern border were matters which concerned both Bantu and Whites.

The history of the Gcaleka branch of the Xhosa is also important. Because of his mother's lack of restraint and his own function as a witch-doctor, Gcaleka was unpopular among his own people. A king who was also a witch-doctor was too much of a danger as a ruler. Gcaleka needed only to point a finger for an unfortunate man to be hurled from a precipice. During the reign of Gcaleka's successor, Khawuta, nothing of importance happened. He was succeeded by Hintsa who, together with Ndlambe, former regent of the Rarabe section, made common cause against Ngqika. In 1835 war also came to Hintsa's country. It was also in his time that disturbances in Natal, a consequence of Shaka's conquests, resulted in the southern tribes of Natal seeking shelter with Hintsa at the end of their wild flight from Shaka. These tribes were named Mfengu (Fingos), of whom most were of Hlubi (AmaHlubi) and Zizi (AmaZizi) origin. Later they caused trouble between the British government and Hintsa when Hintsa was accused of slavery.

The Mpondo (*AmaMpondo*)

The Mpondo, the advance guard of the Mbo tribes, were not of Xhosa origin. They were already settled next to the uMzimvubu river in the 17th century. Related tribes are the Mpondomise (AmaMpondomise) and Xesibe (Ama-Xesibe).

As a result of an argument over a bluebuck which was killed on a hunting expedition Qiya, the son from the Great Hut of his father Cibe, was dethroned and replaced by a younger brother Gangatha. The two Mpondo groups, namely those of the Great Hut (Gangatha) and those from the Right Hand Hut, are today represented by the eastern and western Pondo respectively. Undoubtedly the best known Mpondo chief was Faku. His rule was characterized by Shaka's attacks from the north and infiltration by refugee tribes from Natal. Faku received small thanks from some of the tribes he protected, amongst others the Bhaca. When matters quietened down somewhat Faku courageously stepped forward and claimed the land as far as the uMthatha River as his own, but it was not long before he was dragged into the British politics of the time.

Lesser Nguni tribes

The tribes which today still exist, namely the Mpondomise, the Bomvana (AmaBomvana) and Bhaca (AmaBhaca), the latter refugees from Natal (*ukubhaca* means hide away), were completely over-shadowed in the history of the Eastern Province by the Xhosa and Mpondo. It is enough to say that wars amongst the various tribes continued to flare up at short intervals until the second half of the 19th century.

THE WEST SOTHO (TSWANA)

The Rolong (*Barolong*)

Of the first fourteen Rolong chiefs only the names are known. Tau was the fifteenth ruler and he founded an empire which stretched from the Molôpô[2] River to near the present Klerksdorp. Of Tau it is said that he was equal to

---

2. In Sotho the pronunciation of symbols differ from corresponding Nguni symbols: $ô = o$ in *born; ê = e* in *bet; o = oo* in *boor; e = ee* in *beer; r = r* in *rob; g = ch* in *loch; h* as in *English; ph, th, kh* as in Nguni; *u = oo* in *boot; tsh = ts* in *cats; ng = ng* in *sing; s = sh; tl(h) =* the contracted pronunciation of *ttl* (kettle).

Shaka in cruelty. We also learn that Tau attacked the Taaibos-Korana but that he was no match for their poisoned arrows which killed him on the field of battle.

After Tau's death his tribe moved from Taung in the south to Mosita in the north where it broke up, each son founding his own tribe.

The first Whites to supply information about the Tswana tribes were Hendrik Hop and Brink in 1761/62. It was only after 1801 that other Whites, mainly missionaries and travellers such as Barrow and Burchell, visited the Tswana country. They give us glimpses of conditions at that time. In the years after 1820 the Methodists and the London Missionary Society began their work among the Rolong. In this connection the names of Robert Moffat and David Livingstone are well-known.

In 1824 the Rolong were attacked by invaders, of whom there were quite a number at this time. Moffat describes these attacks well. After the defeat of Mzilikazi the Rolong withdrew to their old area in the south.

It must be remembered that there were various Rolong tribes and that each held a particular seniority in the Rolong complex. Each had its own history and they were all more or less involved in later South African history.

The Rolong are connected with the history of the Great Trek because of the land which the Trekkers bartered from their chief Morôka. This chief's tribe, who were known as the Barolong bôô Seleka, had previously lived north of the Vaal. In the days of Sehunêlô they were involved in various wars with neighbouring tribes, amongst others the Kwena (Bakwêna). They were also attacked by the hordes of Mmanthatisi. When in 1824 Sehunêlô was attacked at his capital near Makwassie by the Taung Tribe he called upon the Griquas and Koranas for help. After this Waterboer, the senior Griqua chief, considered Sehunêlô to be a vassal and made him pay six hundred cattle in tribute. Still more wars followed. When Sehunêlô died he was succeeded by his son Morôka who in 1834, because of droughts and fear of Mzilikazi, moved south-eastwards to where he and his tribe eventually settled at Thaba Nchu. Whether he obtained Moshwêshwê's permission to do so is seriously doubted by some writers. Although a part of this Rolong tribe later returned to the Transvaal the original tribe today still lives at Thaba Nchu. Apart from this tribe most of the Rolong tribes at present live in the Mafeking district.

The Hurutshe (Bahurutshe or Bafurutshe)

This old tribe, of which the most important branches today live in the Marico district, is generally accepted as the senior Tswana tribe. In the past no Tswana tribe could enjoy the crops of the new year before the Hurutshe ruler had performed specific ceremonies and celebrated the first fruits ritual (go loma ngwaga). The beginning of the time of initiation and the harvesting season could only be announced by the Hurutshe. They are supposed to have lived near the present day Brits until the death of their fifth chief, Malope.

After the death of this chief the history of his tribe followed the characteristic

439

pattern of Bantu tribes, that of splitting up into rival sections. The sixth ruler is said to have been a woman, Mohurutshe. The sons of lesser houses of Chief Malope refused to be ruled by a woman and Kwena, Ngwato and Ngwaketse, each with their own followers, formed a new tribe. Mohurutshe and her followers moved westwards towards Modimong near Taung. After her death her sons moved back to the vicinity of Pilansberg.

These events meant that "the Hurutshe continued to take precedence to other tribes in certain ceremonies, but the Bakwena gained the political power". (Breutz).[3]

Of the new tribes the Kwena split into many sections, some of which moved as far as modern Lesotho.

The Hurutshe had built up a great empire by the end of the 17th century. They waged various wars with their neighbours and with related tribes. In 1815 the first White, Conrad Buys, visited Hurutsheland. In 1820 the missionary Campbell also visited the Hurutshe. After this they were attacked by Sebêtwana We once more hear of them when, in 1831, Moffat visited chief Mokgatla. Mzilikazi appeared on the scene and the Hurutshe fled southwards, repulsing a Korana attack. We have once more reached the time of the Whites' appearance; in 1837 chief Moilwa received some land for helping the Boers against Mzilikazi.

The Kwena (Bakwena)

No Tswana tribe suffered so much under the yoke of Mzilikazi as did the Kwena, the other important branch of the Hurutshe. Today this tribe is found from Botswana to Lesotho. In the 17th century the Kwena empire was bounded by the Crocodile, Apies and Pienaars Rivers. In the time of Mzilikazi, their country, like those of their neighbours, was occupied and the Sotho tribes were almost entirely destroyed. By 1820 they were defending themselves against attacks from the east, amongst others, from one of the greatest Sotho armies of the time, namely the Pedi under their commander Malekutu. In this battle More, the Kwena chief, was so old that he had to be carried, but his warriors were still able to inflict heavy losses on the enemy. The last battle of More and his son Segwati was against Mzilikazi. Thereafter, the Kwena became vassals of the Matebele and even had to wear the same dress as their conquerors. They were even ordered to help Mzilikazi against a Zulu invasion. When Hendrik Potgieter and his followers settled at Rustenburg the Kwena were almost starving; the farmers paid them in cattle in exchange for their labour.

The Fokeng (Bafokeng)

Another tribe which is regarded as very old and whose relations with the other tribes has not yet been exactly determined is the Fokeng. We meet them in the Free State where they played a part in forming the South Sotho nation. Origi-

---

3. P. L. Breutz: *The Tribes of the Marico District*, Pretoria, 1953, p. 25.

nally they lived east of the Marico River. In the days of Diale they resisted the control which the Hurutshe wanted to impose on them. In later years they waged various wars with neighbouring tribes, especially the Kgatla. During the reign of Thêthê his brothers revolted against him. He appealed for help to Sekwati the Pedi king who almost exterminated the Fokeng tribes between 1815 and 1822. In 1830 Mzilikazi scattered the tribe and it was only in 1837 that Mokgatle was able to unite it again. He also supported Potgieter against Mzilikazi for which service he was given a farm. The Boers respected his tribe. In after years young men of the tribe were sent to work on the diamond fields to earn money with which the tribe could buy more land. President Kruger even visited the tribe in 1883.

The Kgatla (Bakgatla)

The Kgatla tribes which live in the Hammanskraal, Pretoria and Nylstroom districts are also a branch of the Hurutshe which had broken away very early from the main tribe. Even before the death of Mogale (after whom the Magalies mountains are probably named) at the end of the 17th century, this tribe had already begun breaking up into the various tribes known as Kgatla. Like other tribes they also fought with their neighbours and intrigues were the order of the day. When more than a century later, in 1825, Sebêtwana marched through Kgatlaland he met with little resistance, because internal strife had weakened the Kgatla. Later when Mzilikazi appeared on the scene he also encountered no resistance and was able to exact tribute from them. When the Kgatla sided with the Hottentots of Barend Barends against the despot Mzilikazi they made an error of judgment and were almost exterminated. Only after Mzilikazi had been driven away were the Kgatla of Kgafêla united by Pilane and Molefi. Shortly afterwards they had to repulse an attack by the Matebele in 1842. After Pilane died in approximately 1850 the Boers were not able to agree with his successor, Kgamanyane, and he moved with his tribe to Mochudi in Botswana. Here they clashed with the Kwena of Setšhele who considered them to be a subject tribe. It was only in 1883 when they combined against the Boers that peace was made between these two tribes. In later years the Transvaal section of the Kgatla of Kgafêla kept in personal contact with President Kruger.

THE NORTH SOTHO

The Pedi (Bapedi)

The Pedi who are grouped under the North Sotho are also supposed to have been a branch of the Kgatla. There are few Transvaal tribes whose history is as well known as that of the Pedi, who today live in Sekhukhuneland.

After they broke away from the Kgatla the Pedi moved eastwards and settled between the Olifants and Steelpoort Rivers, in an area already inhabited by groups of Tau (Batau), Matlala (Ba ga Matlala) and Kone (Bakône). Their

Kgatla totem, the velvet monkey (*kgabo*), was now exchanged for the porcupine (*noko*). It is uncertain as to how they got their name but their occupation of the area was apparently peaceful. This initial peace was disturbed in the middle of the 17th century when Mohube the regent, while hunting on the land of the Kone, was killed by them. Further small wars followed upon this until Mampuru subjugated the smaller tribes.

After the death of Moukangwe, who had already outlived two of his sons, his son Mampuru attempted to oust Morwamotshe the legal successor and sparked off a period of internal strife in the tribe. The life of Mampuru, who was a great warrior, was spared but after the death of Morwamotshe the history of the Pedi entered a new phase.

Mampuru now incited Thulare against his brother Dikôtôpê, the legal successor. The latter attempted to re-establish himself with the help of some of the surrounding small tribes but Thulare defeated Dikôtôpê in a surprise attack and became the sole ruler of all the Pedi.

Thulare did not then remain inactive. Soon he had conquered an area stretching from the Olifants River to the Komati River. He was a moderate and respected ruler who eventually brought peace to his people. When in 1824 he died during an eclipse of the sun, he left behind a large and significant nation. It it recounted that before his death he had two Whites brought to him so that he could see what the White man looked like.

He was succeeded by Malekutu, a great warrior who, as already mentioned, led his dreaded army deep into the western Transvaal. He also attacked Mabhoko's (Mapog's) Ndebele (AmaNdebele). His brothers plotted against him and poisoned him. A period of confusion followed as one after the other the sons of Thulare and their followers attacked neighbouring tribes. It was at this time that Mizlikazi's hordes surprised Phêthêdi with his handful of warriors and overwhelmed the Pedi. Only Sekwati, of all of Thulare's sons, now remained.

Sekwati, with a group of warriors, now became a wanderer plundering wherever he went, even as far north as across the Limpopo. When he returned he found that Marangrang, the Kone freebooter, had gained control of the Pedi.

Slowly but surely Sekwati regained and strengthened his power over the Pedi and settled in his mountain stronghold Phiring. Here in 1851 the Swazi attacked him but they were defeated, principally because Sekwati had seven rifles. By this time the Boers had bartered land from the Swazi, land which Sekwati claimed as his. From this time on Sekwati was involved not only with the Swazi but also with the Boers, the Mapoggers and the English.

THE SOUTH SOTHO (BASUTOS)

The first arrivals from the east

The history of the Sotho tribes of the central plateau south of the Vaal River attains its peak in Moshwêshwê's (Moshesh) domination of the area between the Drakensberg and the Vaal River until his death in 1870. The area between the Drakensberg and the Vaal River was occupied comparatively late by the Bantu. When the Bantu arrived in this area the southern parts were already occupied by the Bushmen and the Griquas. By 1600 the smaller Nguni tribes from Nguniland, east of the Drakensberg, had begun crossing the mountains. They are said to have been friendly with the Bushmen and even to have inter-married with them. These tribes settled mainly near the Caledon River. The mother of the famous Chief Moorôsi is reputed to have been a member of one of these tribes, the Mapolane.

Arrivals from the north

By the beginning of the 18th century the Fokeng (see Western Sotho) began filtering southwards from the area north of the Vaal, apparently in a peaceful manner. Other tribes who had a part in the history of the Southern Sotho, such as the Sia (Basia), the Tlokwa (Batlôkwa) and Phuthi (Maphuthing and later Baphuthi), also originated in the Western Tswana tribes. They migrated across the Transvaal highveld and after much wandering eventually joined the Fokeng in the Eastern Free State. Some of the Kwena also migrated southwards. By the end of the 16th century they had reached the Fokeng at Ntswanatsatsi (Tafelkop, between Frankfort and Vrede). Here the various tribes lived peacefully to-gether, many being united by marriages between the royal houses. Later, as times became difficult, their peace was disturbed. A Fokeng chief took a Bush-man woman as his chief wife whereupon his subject tribes revolted. The Fokeng and Kwena consequently separated, and the Kwena gradually became accepted as leaders. Under Monahêng they withdrew from the area around Heidelberg (Transvaal) and settled further south of the Vaal. The remaining Fokeng settled in the neighbourhood of Butha-Buthe. From among them the mother of Moshwêshwê was born.

The (Southern) Kwena

The Kwena who withdrew from the Transvaal consisted of two main groups, under Monahêng and under Tsulo. Monahêng, who settled near the present-day Bethlehem, was a capable leader whose strong personality induced the smaller tribes to accept him as their leader. His grandson Mohlômi was famous far beyond the borders of his own domain as a traveller, doctor and prophet. Moshwêshwê benefited much from the advice of this old philosopher. The death of Monahêng caused strife between his six sons and the tribe disinte-grated. One of the widows of a deceased brother refused to comply with the custom which decreed she should live with one of her brothers-in-law; instead she chose as husband a Hlubiman, who lived among the Fokeng, subjects of Mokôtêdi (one of Monahêng's sons). A son, Motswane, nicknamed Pêête, was born from this union; he attended Mokôtêdi's initiation lodge and chose a Taung wife, but although Pêête was supposed to succeed Mokôtêdi his birth and weak personality made him unacceptable to his fellow tribesmen. His two sons, Dibe and Mokgatjhane, were, however, men of a different calibre and soon were playing an important part in the affairs of their people. Mokgatjhane was braver and more popular than his older brother.

Although Mokgatjhane was not a direct descendent of a ruling family his wife was the daughter of a Fokeng chief and from this marriage was born Lepôqô, better known as Moshwêshwê. After being initiated the young boy was taken to the wise Mohlômi for his blessing. Moshwêshwê was reputed originally to have been cruel but in time became a diplomat rather than a warrior, and gathered strangers and smaller tribes around him. He was highly esteemed by his mother's royal family and his own in-laws. He settled at Butha-Buthe.

Trouble started brewing in the east but Moshwêshwê, who by now apparently controlled, as well as his own family, the families of his mother and wife, believed in diplomacy rather than in clashing with superior forces. His rule was characterized by gifts of cattle to his enemies, and by his carrying off cattle when circumstances warranted it but not destroying other tribes. The defeated were often drawn into Moshwêshwê's tribe as councillors with various responsibilities.

The disturbances from the east resulted in Moshwêshwê being attacked by Matiwane and his Ngwane warriors, and later also by others among whom were the Tlokwa. They were of the tribe of Sekônyêla whose mother Mmanthatisi we have already mentioned. This Sekônyêla was he with whom later the Natal Trekkers clashed. The Tlokwa was surrounded and besieged by Moshwêshwê's headquarters at Butha-Buthe but Moshwêshwê incited the Bushmen to harass Sekônyêla and the latter withdrew. Moshwêshwê quickly made use of the opportunity to entrench himself in his mountain fortress Thaba Bosiu from where he made his authority felt. Although he sent out punitive expeditions he never fought for fighting's sake. In those years of chaos tribes sought the protection of Moshwêshwê because famine and cannibalism were rife. One of the most important of the tribes which Moshwêshwê compelled to join him was the Phuthi of Moorôsi who ruled in the south east as far as Thembuland. Moorôsi had an inexhaustible spirit of adventure and persuaded Moshwêshwê to attack the Cape Nguni.

Although he was one of the less aggressive rulers of his time, Moshwêshwê had to resist not only Sekônyêla but also Matiwane and Mzilikazi; even the Koranas did not leave him in peace. Thaba Bosiu was impregnable, however.

The Tlokwa of Mmanthatisi

We have repeatedly referred to the Tlokwa of Sekônyêla whose wanderings had made them aggressive. When the Tlokwa chief Mokôtjô died his wife Mmanthatisi acted as regent for their minor son Sekônyêla. Motjhôli, a Hlubi, sought shelter with Mmanthatisi but he was murdered by the jealous Sekônyêla, who also stole Motjhôli's royal bead. The Hlubi below the Drakensberg heard of this murder and with the Ngwane tribe attacked and defeated the Tlokwa. With her remaining followers Mmanthatisi began a new career. As a woman

leading warriors she inspired great fear and carried out marauding raids. In
1823 when she was repelled by the Griquas her son Sekônyêla returned to their
old home with his battered remnant of followers. After rebuilding his tribe and
army he began attacking neighbouring tribes and even had the audacity to
attack Moshwêshwê. He eventually met his match in the Boers.

The Fokeng of Sebetwane

The Fokeng of Patsa lived along the Vet River in the early 1820's, until the
Tlokwa attacked them. The remnants of the tribe began raiding under their
new chief Sebêtwane. They attacked one Tswana tribe after the other and fought
their way through to the north as far as the Ngami lake, leaving devastation in
their wake. Sebêtwane was still not satisfied and crossed the Zambezi River to
encounter the attacks of Mzilikazi. Here Sebêtwane died in 1851. The new tribe
which developed there are today known as the Lozi or Kololo.

The Difaqane period

The years immediately before and after 1820 were the most unsettled that southern Africa has ever known. The Sotho refer to this period as the *Difaqane*
(originally a name for bands of plundering soldiers). Because of the devastation
caused by various invaders, commanded by such men as the notorius Matiwane,
Mzilikazi, Sebêtwane and Shaka, and the woman, Mmanthatisi, famine was widespread. Consequently entire tribes resorted to cannibalism.

The *Difaqane* caused decimated and powerless small tribes and groups to seek
the protection of Moshwêshwê. From this conglomeration of tribes Moshwêshwê built up a new nation which consolidated itself against all attacks.

THE NORTHERN NGUNI

The Zulu

We now return to the middle of the 18th century. The migration of Xhosa,
Mpondo and other southern tribes had already come to a halt in the present
Transkei. A small tribe which was later known as the Zulu (AmaZulu) lived
between the headwaters of the uMhlathuzi[4] and uMfolozi Rivers. At the same
time the mighty Dingiswayo, king of the Mthethwa tribe (AbakwaMthethwa),
lived in the area east of the Zulu down to the sea. South of Dingiswayo lived
the Qwabe (AmaQwabe) of Phakathwayo, and to the north of Dingiswayo a still
mightier neighbour, Zwide, king of the Ndwandwe (AbakwaNdwandwe). It
was inevitable that three such strong chiefs would sooner or later cross swords.
Dingiswayo, who some say had had some foreign military training, soon made
it clear that he intended to subjugate the smaller neighbouring tribes.

4. For pronunciation see footnote under the Xhosa.

Senzangakhona was the chief of the Zulu tribe. His premarital relations with Nandi compelled her and her small son to seek refuge with her Mthethwa family. Here the son, who was named Shaka, grew up, eventually to enter Dingiswayo's army. Dingiswayo soon noticed Shaka and invited Senzangakhona to come to meet his lost son. With Dingiswayo's backing it was a matter of course that Shaka should succeed his father. When Shaka became chief of the Zulu he soon built up a small army and made himself secure by eliminating any possible rival.

Dingiswayo, Zwide and Shaka

Meanwhile Dingiswayo had defeated the Qwabe tribe. However, he believed in subjugation, not extermination. His neighbour Zwide, conversely, believed in exterminating a defeated foe. When he and Dingiswayo eventually met Zwide was the victor. Zwide inspired fear far beyond the borders of his domain. Chief Somhlolo of the Ngwane (Swazi) (BakaNgwane; EmaSwati; AmaSwazi in Zulu) who ruled north of the Phongola River considered it advisable to marry a daughter of Zwide. She became the mother of king Mswazi and played an important role in Swazi affairs.

Although Shaka kept out of Zwide's way the inevitable clash could not be permanently deferred. Shaka, however, was a warrior and tactician without equal, as Zwide was to learn to his sorrow. In the words of Bryant: "With all his wonted energy and resource Shaka was pulling the strings of fate to his own advantage. He had invoked or inveigled into his service all the past-masters of knavery in the land".[5] By 1820 Shaka controlled what is today known as Zululand, and had a highly disciplined, invincible and restless army.

Shaka wished to conquer a world. He had already cleared his immediate neighbourhood of all opposition and his eight years of conquest had started a chain reaction which was felt as far as the Limpopo in the north, Xhosaland in the south and Sotholand in the west.

Matiwane

Shaka had attacked Matiwane's mighty Ngwane (AmaNgwane) tribe when he was a warrior under Dingiswayo. This tribe and their neighbours, the Hlubi (AmaHlubi), lived at the eastern foot of the Drakensberg. Matiwane in turn moved southwards and westwards and attacked the Southern Nguni and Sotho tribes on top of the mountains. These attacks heralded the beginning of the *Difaqane*. Mmanthatisi had already begun her raiding and Moshwêshwê was also to suffer.

Mzilikazi

From the Khumalo (AbakwaKhumalo) tribe we learn of Mzilikazi whose mother was reportedly a daughter of Zwide. He was brave and ruthless, a man after

5. A. T. Bryant: *Olden Times in Zululand and Natal*, London, 1929, p. 204.

Shaka's own heart, but when on an occasion Shaka ordered him to seize some cattle his pride got the better of him and he could not resist keeping some of the prize cattle for himself. Once Shaka learnt of this there was only one course open to Mzilikazi and that was to flee. With his tribe and all their possessions he carved himself a way to safety, dragging with him all the able-bodied men, women and children of the tribes he conquered on the way. He halted at the Olifants River where he established his capital eKuphumuleni (at the rest). He rested only a short while before turning his attention to the west, where he began attacking the Sotho tribes. Those who did not succumb to Mzilikazi were simply swept out of his way; entire Sotho villages were razed to the ground. The might of Mzilikazi (whose Sotho name was Moselekatse or Moselakatse, which the Trekkers abbreviated to Silkaats) was eventually broken in the Transvaal by the Trekkers with the help of Hottentots and Tswana. However, for Mzilikazi this was only a temporary set-back while he fled north to where he founded his Matebele empire.

Soshangane and Zwangendaba

Shortly before 1820 two more of Shaka's generals fled. Soshangane settled among the Tsonga in Portuguese territory where he built up an empire. Zwangendaba trekked as far as Lake Malawi where his descendents are today known as the Angoni.

Dingane succeeds Shaka

In the meanwhile Shaka had come into contact with the British traders of Port Natal. Their descriptions provide us with a clear picture of Shaka the despot. In 1828 a plot was hatched against Shaka by the few remaining members of his family and a number of generals. His aunt Mnkabayi organized the plot. Shaka was murdered while his armies were occupied elsewhere and Mnkabayi chose Dingane to succeed him. Dingane consolidated his position by liquidating all possible claimants to the throne excepting his brother Mpande who was expected to die from an eye disease.

The Trekkers crossed the Drakensberg not long after Dingane became chief of the Zulu and he was at the height of his power when he murdered Retief and his burghers.

The Ngwane (Swazi, BakaNgwane)

While Shaka entrenched himself in Natal the Ngwane under Somhlolo were building an empire in what today is known as Swaziland. The Ngwane, a tribe of Tsonga origin, crossed the Lebombo mountains towards the west. In the southern part of the area under discussion lived Nguni tribes and further to the north were Sotho tribes. The Ngwane rulers, the Dlamini, originally followed a policy of peaceful penetration through intermarriage with the leading tribes.

Chief Somhlolo even married a daughter of the mightly Zwide. Gradually the Dlamini began conquering the Sotho tribes and those who did not acknowledge their might were either destroyed or forced to flee to the north.

By 1840 the Ngwane nation was established. They allowed the Zulu to think that they, the Ngwane, were subjects of Dingane, and so were free to cast their covetous eyes northwards and westwards. By 1840 when Mswazi (uMswati) and his mother Lazidze (Zwide's daughter) ascended the throne (it is a Swazi custom for mother and son to rule together) the Swazi had become a powerful nation which could no longer be overlooked, and it continued as such. Mswazi was a conquerer and attacked the Pedi on his northern border to extend his empire to the Kafferspruit west of the present town of Ermelo.

When the Boers arrived in about 1850 a time of intrigue between Boer, Briton and Swazi began. The Swazi well understood that art of running with the hare and hunting with the hounds; this is probably why they are today the only Bantu nation which has not been conquered by either White or Black.

The Ndebele (*AmaNdebele*)

The Ndebele (who must not be confused with the Matebele of Silkaats who were also known as (ama)Ndebele (Matêbêlê in Sotho)), are divided into a southern and a northern group. The southern group are better known as the Mapoggers (after their chief Mabhoko or Mapôgô in Sotho). They are presumed to have migrated from Natal more than three centuries ago. The story of how Ndzundza outwitted his brother Manala is practically identical with the story of Jacob and Esau; nevertheless there is little doubt that this tribe already knew this legend before they came into contact with the missionaries. The southern group then split into the Ndzundza and Manala sections. The tribe of Ndzundza is known in Transvaal history because of the war with Nyabela (also known by the Boers as Mapog). Mapog (Mabhoko) was the father of Nyabela and had repulsed attacks by the Pedi and Swazi. Today the Ndebele live mainly in the Middelburg district of the Transvaal.

The northern Ndebele are the tribe of Makapan or Mugombane, who live near Potgietersrus and Pietersburg. They deny being related to the southern Ndebele and maintain that they migrated from the north through Swaziland and Pretoria to where they live at present. It was in a war with Makapan that Paul Kruger gave proof of his bravery.

The Venda (*VhaVhenda*)

Because this tribe lived in relative isolation and only properly came into contact with the Whites in the second half of the 19th century they had little to do with the main streams of South African history.

Their own history records that they originated in the area around the great lakes of Africa. From there they migrated under the guidance of *Ngoma lungundu*, the drum of their god Mwali, to where they at present live in the Northern Transvaal. Every attempt of rival leaders to break up the tribe was punished by Mwali; the story of the tribe at this time reminds one strongly of that of the Israelites and the ark of the covenant. When, however, the drum mysteriously disappeared the tribe did break up into three sections among whom wars occasionally took place. However, the Venda were not empire builders and even when the Boers founded Schoemansdal the tribe lived comparatively peacefully with the Whites.

Makhado, who is said to have been incited by his uncle Madzhie against the Boers because they made the Venda work for them, attacked the Boers and was repulsed. Makhado then decided to attack Schoemansdal but to his surprise found the town deserted. This disturbance of the peace was followed by a punitive expedition against Makhado.

The Tsonga (VaTsonga)

The Tsonga, better known as the Shangaans, are actually migrants from Portuguese East Africa. When Soshangane fled from Zululand he settled among the Tsonga tribes between the coast and the Transvaal. The greater acumen and systematic military strategy of the Zulu soon compelled the Tsonga to surrender to them. Although the Zulu language and customs were submerged in those of the defeated tribes the Nguni features are apparent in some Shangaans. There must have been some of these people already occupying the north-eastern corner of the Transvaal, since the Trichardt Trek made contact with some tribesmen to whom they referred as "knobnoses". (The name was derived from the fact that the Shangaans tattooed their noses.)

In 1880, during and after the war between Mawele and Mzila, the sons of Manukosi who died in 1858, many Tsonga tribes migrated deep into the Transvaal. The South African Republic later appointed João Albasini as Commissioner over them. Today the most important Tsonga tribes in the Transvaal are the Nkuna and Gwamba in the north and the Nhlanganu to the south at Bushbuckridge.

The area north of the Crocodile River, between the mountains to the east (Sabie and Pilgrim's Rest) and the eastern border of the Transvaal, was a no-man's-land because of its unhealthy climate. In 1873 the travellers Carl Mauch and Cohen found no inhabitants in this area on their expeditions to Delagoa Bay. Subsequently it became a refuge for the tribes known as the Eastern Sotho, namely the Pai, Kutswe and Pulana. Today Sotho, Swazi and Tsonga are found living in this area mixed up with one another.

Before the Whites moved into the interior in organized groups the inhabitants of southern Africa were large and small Bantu tribes who had found the original inhabitants of the interior, the Bushmen and Hottentots, occupying large tracts of country. Both Bushmen and Hottentots were soon greatly reduced in numbers, the Bushmen because of being exterminated by the more powerful Hottentots and Bantu, and the Hottentots mainly because of epidemics.

The movements of the Bantu were checked at an imaginary line running from the Fish River in the east to the Orange River in the west. They had at this stage more or less driven the Bushmen and Hottentots into a corner and would have had to fight these original inhabitants if they had wanted to move further south. There are indications at this time that the most southerly Bantu were indeed preparing for a last assault on the south because other tribes were pressing on them from behind. The Bantu were plagued by internal strife and instead of uniting into large units they broke up into small weak groups who were continually fighting amongst themselves.

At this stage a new factor was introduced into the history of South Africa; the white man arrived in the south. Before the Bantu could move beyond the line where they had paused, the Whites had moved in to face them. Although the Whites were checked at the Fish River they were able to move across the middle of the Orange River and drove a wedge between the eastern Bantu and the western Bantu. This meant that the Whites could be attacked on both flanks. The Whites then curved to the east and divided the Nguni of the coastal area into two. This remained the position until the industrialization of South Africa during the second quarter of the 20th century. The Bantu were drawn into the new developments because of the demand for labour; the barriers which, for three hundred years had held at the Fish River and Orange River, disappeared without fuss. Today the Bantu are to be found all the way to Cape Town, not in tribal units but mainly in leaderless undisciplined masses.

SELECT BIBLIOGRAPHY

A. J. Böeseken: *Simon van der Stel en sy kinders*, Cape Town, 1964; A. T. Bryant: *Olden Times in Zululand and Natal*, London, 1929; J. A. Engelbrecht: *The Korana*, Cape Town, 1936; D. F. Ellenberger and J. C. MacGregor: *A History of the Basotho* ... London, 1912; Department of Bantu Administration and Development: *Ethnological Publications, inter alia* numbers 3, 7, 8, 10-16, 17-22, 25-27, 41, 46, 49; H. C. M. Fourie: *Amandebele van Fene Mahlangu*, Zwolle, 1921; E. M. Ramaila: *Setlogo sa Batau*, Pretoria, undated; J. H. Soga: *The Southern Bantu*, Johannesburg, 1930; G. W. Stow: *Native Races of South Africa* ... London, 1905; Transvaal Native Affairs Department: *Short History of the Native Tribes of the Transvaal*, Pretoria, 1905; E. O. J. Westphal: *The Linguistic Prehistory of Southern Africa*, Africa, vol. XXXIII, No. 3, 1963; D. Ziervogel: *A Grammar of Northern Transvaal Ndebele*, Pretoria, 1959; D. Ziervogel: *The Eastern Sotho*, Pretoria, 1954.

Appendix II: South African Monetary Systems: a Comparative Table with Explanatory Notes

The following Cape monetary values of the seventeenth and eighteenth centuries can be taken as a rough general guide. Obviously the value of money in terms of goods was so different at different times that a direct comparison would be unrealistic.

	Dutch money Value in stuiwers	English money Value in pounds, shillings and pence	South African money Value in rands and cents
stuiwer	1	1d	$\frac{5}{6}$c
dubbeltjie ("double" stuiwer)	2	2d	$1\frac{2}{3}$c
1½ dubbeltjies	3	3d	$2\frac{1}{2}$c
skelling	6	6d	5c
2 skellings	12	1s	10c
Cape guilder (f)	16	1s 4d	$13\frac{1}{3}$c
Dutch guilder	20	1s 8d	$16\frac{2}{3}$c
Cape rix-dollar (rd)	48	4s	40c
Silver ducatoon	72	6s	60c
—	120	10s	1R
—	240	£1	2R

Of course money values fluctuated even during the seventeenth and eighteenth centuries. The second column shows late eighteenth century pound sterling equivalents of Dutch money. In 1825 the value of the Cape rix-dollar, which had depreciated sharply early in the nineteenth century, was fixed at 1s 6d in English money (thus 100 rds = £7 10s). During the Great Trek and afterwards the Dutch and English systems were used side by side in calculations. English money values were used for more than a hundred years during the nineteenth and twentieth centuries before the South African decimal system was introduced in 1961. In the third column the *present-day* South African monetary equivalents of the English sterling system are given.

A few examples will illustrate the reduction of the purchasing power of money over the centuries. From 1690 to 1750 the average price of Cape sheep varied from about 1½ to about 7½ guilders each. In 1700 when Henning Hüsing entered into a contract with the Company to supply it with good mutton and beef for a period of ten years the price was 2½ stuiwers per pound. He also agreed to take over sheep from the Company at 3 guilders each. As a result of the Great Trek and the Sixth Frontier War (1834 – 1835) the price of mutton rose so steeply that Capetonians had to pay up to 4d per pound! In 1834 Saxon stud-rams were imported into the Cape from New South Wales and at a public auction fetched an average of £17 13s 4d which was then considered an exceptionally good price. From 1903 to 1907 the average price of mutton in the Cape Colony dropped from 9½d per pound just after the Anglo-Boer War to 6½d per pound in 1907. During the same period the average price of Cape sheep fell from 26s 2d to 18s 2d each.

The 3 guilders which bought Henning Hüsing a sheep at the beginning of the eighteenth century would have bought him 4 or 5 pounds of mutton at the beginning of the Great Trek, about 2 pounds after the Anglo-Boer War, and in the Republic of South Africa not even half a pound.

We can thus understand why salaries at the Cape were proportionately low in the early days. Jan van Riebeeck started his refreshment post on £75 per month. At the beginning of the Great Trek Field Cornets received £15 per annum for the difficult and time-consuming tasks they performed in their vast wards. At that time First-Class Police Constables at Stellenbosch received a salary of £31 10s per annum, with lodging; and District Surgeons in the Cape country areas received £100 to £150 per annum, with the right to private practice. While the Rev. A. Smith, the Dutch Reformed minister at Uitenhage, was allowed £200 per annum, and a free house, the Voortrekker minister Daniel Lindley received 1,333 rix-dollars, 2 skellings and 4 stuiwers (£100) per annum, with free lodging. The Rev. Erasmus Smit had to be content with a maximum salary of 800 rix-dollars.

In accordance with the prevailing money values and cost of living Lord Macartney, who became Governor of the Cape in 1797, was comparatively speaking one of the highest-paid civil servants in the history of South Africa. His salary was £10,000 per annum, with an entertainment allowance of £2,000.

References: E. H. D. Arndt: *Banking and Currency development in South Africa (1652 – 1927)*, Cape Town etc., 1928; H. B. Thom: *Die Geskiedenis van die Skaapboerdery in Suid-Afrika*, Amsterdam, 1936; J. T. Becklake: *From Real to Rand*, place and date of publication not mentioned; K. M. Jeffreys (ed.): *Kaapse Archiefstukken lopende over het jaar 1779*, Cape Town, 1927.

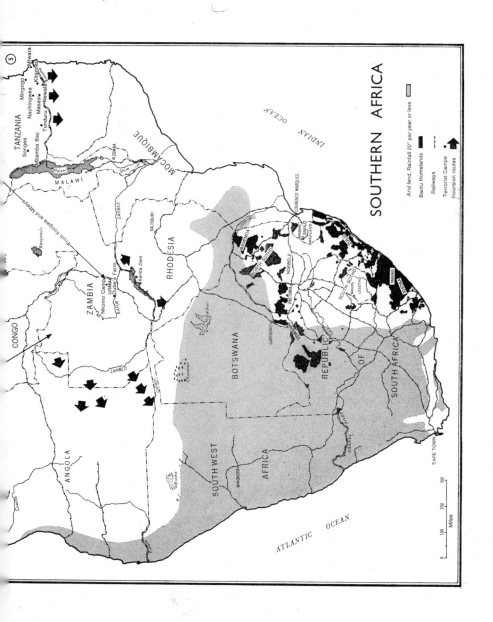

SOUTHERN AFRICA

Arid land, Rainfall 20" per year or less

Bantu Homelands

Railways

Terrorist Camps

Incursion routes

Select Bibliography

GENERAL

1. *General Histories*
Cory, G. E.: *The rise of South Africa*, 5 vols., London, 1910-1930. Facs. reprint (6 vols.), Cape Town, 1965.
De Kiewiet, C. W.: *A history of South Africa; social and economic*, Oxford, 1957.
Scholtz, G. D.: *Suid-Afrika en die wêreldpolitiek*, Johannesburg, 1954.
Theal, G. M.: *History of South Africa*, 11 vols., 1888-1919. Facs. reprint, Cape Town, 1964.
Van der Walt, A. J. H., Wiid, J. A. and Geyer, A. L. (eds.): *Geskiedenis van Suid-Afrika*, 2 vols., Cape Town, 1955. Revised ed. in one volume by D. W. Krüger, Cape Town etc., 1966.
Walker, E. A.: *A history of Southern Africa*, 3rd revised ed., London, 1965.
– (ed.): *The Cambridge history of the British Empire*, vol. VIII, South Africa, 2nd ed., Cambridge, 1963.

2. *Bibliography*
Muller, C. F. J. *et al.*: *A select bibliography of South African history: a guide for historical research*, Pretoria, 1966.

3. *Historical Atlases*
Böeseken, A. J. *et al.*: *Geskiedenis-atlas vir Suid-Afrika*, 4th ed., Cape Town, 1959.
Ploeger, J. and Smith, A. H.: *Pictorial atlas of the history of the Union of South Africa*, Pretoria, 1949.
Stockenström, E.: *Historiese atlas van Suid-Afrika*, Stellenbosch, 1928.
Walker, E. A.: *Historical atlas of South Africa*, Cape Town, 1922.

4. *Books on Historiography*
Van Jaarsveld, F. A.: *Die Afrikaner en sy geskiedenis*, Cape Town, etc., 1959.
–: *Ou en nuwe weë in die Suid-Afrikaanse geskiedskrywing*, Communications of the University of South Africa, A. 16, 1961.
– *et al.*: *Die hervertolking van ons geskiedenis*, Communications of the University of South Africa, B. 19, 1963.

CHAPTER I
Axelson, Eric: *South-East Africa, 1488-1530*, London, 1940.
–: *The Portuguese in South Africa, 1600-1700*, Johannesburg, 1960.
Azurara, Gomes Eannes de: *Conquests and discoveries of Henry the Navigator being the Chronicles of Azurara*, London, 1936. Edited by Virginia de Castro e Almeida and translated by Bernard Miall.
Beazley, Sir C. Raymond: *Prince Henry the Navigator*, 3rd ed., London, 1931.
Bovill, E. W.: *Caravans of the Old Sahara: an introduction to the history of the Western Sudan*, London, 1933.
Boxer, C. R.: *The tragic history of the sea, 1589-1662* (Hakluyt Society, 2nd series, CXII), Cambridge, 1959.
Corrêa, Gaspar: *The three voyages of Vasco da Gama, and his vice-royalty, from the Lendas da India of Gaspar Corrêa*, London, 1869. Translated from Portuguese by H. E. J. Stanley (Lord Stanley of Alderley.)
Cortesão, Armando and Texeira da Mota, Avelino (eds.): *Portugaliae Monumenta Cartographica*, 5 vols., Lisbon, 1960. (Maps, with Portuguese and English text, and bibliographies.)
De Kock, W. J.: *Portugese ontdekkers om die Kaap; die Europese aanraking met Suidelike Afrika, 1415-1600*, Cape Town, 1957.

Hart, Henry H.: *Sea Road to the Indies*, London, 1952.

Hakluyt, Richard: *The principall navigations, voyages, traffiques and discoveries of the English nation made by sea or overland to the remote and farthest quarters of the earth at any time within the compasse of these 1600 yeeres*, 3 vols., London, 1598-1600. Reprint (12 vols.) Glasgow, 1903-1905 and (10 vols.) London, 1927-1928.

Hennig, Richard: *Terrae Incognitae; eine Zusammenstellung und kritische Bewertung der wichtigsten vorkolombischen Entdeckungreisen an Hand der darüber vorliegenden Originalberichte*, 4 vols., Leiden, 1926-1939. Bibliography IV, pp. 430-506.

Houtman, Cornelis de: *De eerste schipvaart der Nederlanders naar Oost-Indië onder Cornelis de Houtman, 1595-1597; journalen, documenten en andere bescheiden, uitgegeven en toegelicht door G. P. Rouffaer en J. W. Ijzerman*, 3 vols., The Hague, 1915, 1925 and 1929.

Jayne, K. G.: *Vasco da Gama and his successors, 1460-1580*, London, 1910.

Linschoten, Jan Huygen van: *Itinerario: Voyage ofte schipvaert van Jan Huygen van Linschoten, naer Oost ofte Portugaels Indien, 1579-1592*, 5 vols., The Hague (I and II) 1910, (III) 1934 and (IV and V) 1939.

Major, R. H.: *The life of Prince Henry of Portugal*, London, 1868.

–: *The Discoveries of Prince Henry the Navigator*, London, 1877.

Mollema, J. C.: *De eerste schipvaart der Hollanders naar Oost-Indie, 1595-1597*, The Hague, 1936.

Oliveira Martins, J. P.: *The golden age of Prince Henry the Navigator*, London, 1914.

Pereira, Duarta Pacheco: *Esmeraldo de Situ Orbis*, London, 1937. Translated and edited by George H. T. Kimble.

Peres, Damiao: *História dos Descobrimentos portugueses*, Oporto, 1943.

Raven-Hart, R.: *Before van Riebeeck: callers at South Africa from 1488-1652*, Cape Town, 1967.

Ravenstein, E. G.: "The voyages of Diogo Cão and Bartholomeu Dias, 1482-1488", *The Geographical Journal*, December, 1900.

Sanceau, Elaine: *D. João II*, Oporto, 1952.

Stapel, F. W. (ed.): *Geschiedenis van Nederlandsch Indië*, vol. II, Amsterdam, 1938.

Theal, G. M.: *Records of South Eastern Africa*, 9 vols., Cape Town, 1898-1903.

–: *Willem Adriaan van der Stel and other historical sketches*, Cape Town, 1913.

Velho, Alvaro: *A journal of the first voyage of Vasco da Gama, 1497-1499*, London, 1898. Edited by E. G. Ravenstein.

Whiteway, R. S.: *The rise of Portuguese power in India 1497-1550*, London, 1899.

CHAPTERS 2-6

Van Houtte, J. A., *et al.* (eds.): *Algemene geschiedenis der Nederlanden*, vols. VII and VIII, Utrecht, 1954 and 1955.

Beyers, C.: *Die Kaapse Patriotte gedurende die laaste kwart van die agtiende eeu en die voortlewing van hul denkbeelde*, 2nd ed., Pretoria, 1967.

Blommaert, W.: *Het invoeren van de slavernij aan de Kaap*, Archives Year Book for S.A. History, 1938, vol. I.

Böeseken, A. J.: *Nederlandsche commissarissen aan de Kaap, 1657-1700*, The Hague, 1938.

–: *Die Nederlandse kommissarisse en die 18de eeuse samelewing*, Archives Year Book for S.A. History, 1944.

–: *Simon van der Stel en sy kinders*, Cape Town, 1964.

– (ed.): *Resolusies van die Politieke Raad*, vols. I-IV, *1651 – 1715*, Cape Town, 1957 – 1962.

– (ed.): *Belangrike Kaapse dokumente*, vol. I: *Memoriën en Instructiën, 1657-1699*, Cape Town, 1966.

Bosman, D. B. (ed.): *Briewe van Johanna Maria van Riebeeck*, Amsterdam, 1952.

– (ed.): *Daghregister gehouden by den oppercoopman Jan Anthonisz van Riebeeck*, 3 vols., Cape Town, 1952, 1955 and 1957.

Burrows, E. H.: *A history of medicine in South Africa*, Cape Town, 1958.

Coolhaas, W. Ph. (ed.): *Generale Missiven*, vols. I and II, The Hague, 1960 and 1964.

Dehérain, H.: *Le Cap de Bonne-Espérance au XVIIe siècle*, Paris, 1909.

De Wet, G. C. (ed.): *Resolusies van die Politieke Raad, 1716-1719*, V Cape Town, 1964.

Engelbrecht, S. P.: *Die Kaapse predikante van die sewentiende en agtiende eeu*, Cape Town, 1952.

Fouché, L. (ed.): *Het dagboek van Adam Tas 1705-1706*, London, 1914.

456

Geyer, A. L.: *Das wirtschaftliche System der niederländischen ostindischen Kompanie am Kap der guten Hoffnung 1785-1795*, München and Berlin, 1923.
Geyl, P.: *De Patriottenbeweging 1780-1787*, Amsterdam, 1947.
Godée Molsbergen, E. C.: *De stichter van Hollands Zuid-Afrika: Jan van Riebeeck 1618-1677*, Amsterdam, 1912.
- (ed.): *Reizen in Zuid-Afrika in de Hollandse tijd*, vols. XI, XII, XX and XXXVI of the Linschoten Society, The Hague, 1916, 1922 and 1932.
Idenburg, P. J.: *The Cape of Good Hope at the turn of the 18th century*, Leiden, 1963.
Jeffreys, M. K. (ed.): *Kaapse Plakkaatboek, 1652-1707*, I Cape Town, 1944.
Karsten, Mia C.: *The Old Company's garden at the Cape and its superintendents*, Cape Town, 1951.
Kloeke, G. G.: *De herkomst en groei van het Afrikaans*, Leiden, 1950.
Marais, J. S.: *Maynier and the first Boer republic*, Cape Town, 1944.
Mees, Mr W. C.: *Maria Quevellerius, huisvrouw van Jan van Riebeeck en haar omgeving*, Assen, 1952.
Moodie, D. (ed.): *The record; or a series of official papers relative to the condition and treatment of the native tribes of South Africa*, Amsterdam and Cape Town, 1960.
Mossop, E. E. (ed.): *Journals of the expeditions of the honourable ensign Olof Bergh (1682 and 1683) and the ensign Isaq Schrijver (1689)*, Cape Town, 1931. (V.R.S., 12.)
-: *Old Cape Highways*, Cape Town, 1928.
Muller, C. F. J.: *Johannes Frederik Kirsten oor die toestand van die Kaapkolonie in 1795*, Pretoria, 1960.
Naudé, S. D. (ed.): *Kaapse argiefstukke: Kaapse plakkaatboek*, vols. II-IV (1707-1795), Cape Town, 1948-1949.
Palmer, R. R.: *The age of the democratic revolution: a political history of Europe and America, 1760-1800*, 2 vols., Princeton, 1959-1964.
Stapel, F. W.: *Geschiedenis van Nederlandsch-Indië*, Amsterdam, 1943.
-: (ed.): *Pieter van Dam: Beschryvinge van de Oostindische Compagnie*, 4 vols., in Rijksgeschied-kundige Publicatiën, vols. 63, 68, 74 and 76.
Theal, G. M.: *Willem Adriaan van der Stel and other historical sketches*, Cape Town, 1913.
- (ed.): *Belangrijke historische dokumenten*, 3 vols., Cape Town, 1896-1911.
Thom, H. B.: *Die Geskiedenis van die skaapboerdery in Suid-Afrika*, Amsterdam, 1936.
Van der Merwe, P. J.: *Die Kafferoorlog van 1793*, Cape Town, 1940.
-: *Die trekboer in die geskiedenis van die Kaapkolonie (1657-1842)*, Cape Town, 1938.
Warnsinck, J. C. M.: *Twaalf doorluchtige zeehelden*, Amsterdam, 1941.
-: *De retourvloot van Pieter de Bitter*, The Hague, 1929.

CHAPTER 7
Barnard, Lady Anne: *South Africa a century ago (1797-1801)*, Cape Town, 1924. (H. J. Anderson ed.)
Fairbridge, D. (ed.): *Lady Anne Barnard at the Cape of Good Hope 1797-1802*, Oxford, 1924.
Gie, S. F. N. (ed.): *The memorandum of commissary J. A. de Mist*, Cape Town, 1920. (V.R.S., 3.)
Lamprecht, F. G.: *Die Bataafse republiek aan die Kaap 1803-1806*, unpublished M. A. thesis, Unisa, 1946.
Lichtenstein, H.: *Travels in Southern Africa in the years 1803-1806*, 2 vols., Cape Town, 1928-1930. (V.R.S., 10 and 11.)
Marais, J. S.: *Maynier and the first Boer republic*, Cape Town, 1944.
Milo, T. H.: *De geheime onderhandelingen tusschen de Bataafsche en Fransche republieken van 1795-1797 in verband met de expeditie van schout bij nacht E. Lucas naar de Kaap de Goede Hoop*, Den Helder, 1942.
Naude, S. D. (ed.): *Kaapse Plakkaatboek, 1795-1806*, 2 vols., Parow, 1950-1951.
Theal, G. M. (ed.): *Records of the Cape Colony, 1793-1806*, vols. 1-6, London, 1897-1900.
Van der Merwe, J. P.: *Die Kaap onder die Bataafse republiek, 1803-1806*, Amsterdam, 1926.
Wieringa, P. A. C.: *De oudste Boeren-republieken*, The Hague, 1921.

CHAPTER 8
Dreyer, A. (ed.): *Boustowwe vir die geskiedenis van die Nederduits-Gereformeerde Kerke in Suid-Afrika*, vol. III: 1804-1836, Cape Town, 1936.

Edwards, I. E.: *Towards emancipation; a study in South African slavery*, Cardiff, 1942.
Franken, J. L. M.: *Piet Retief se lewe in die Kolonie*, Cape Town, 1949.
Giliomee, H. B.: *Die administrasietydperk van Lord Caledon (1807-1811)*, Archives Year Book for S.A. History, 1966, vol. II.
Hockly, H. E.: *The story of the British settlers of 1820 in South Africa*, Cape Town, 1957.
Jooste, J. P.: *Die verhouding tussen Kerk en Staat aan die Kaap tot die tweede helfte van die 19de eeu*, Bloemfontein, 1946.
Kotzé, C. R.: *Die owerheidsbeleid teenoor die Afrikaners (1806-1820)*, unpublished D. Phil. thesis, University of Stellenbosch, 1958.
Leverton, B. J. T.: *Government finance and political development in the Cape (1806-1834)*, Archives Year Book for S.A. History, 1961.
MacMillan, W. M.: *Bantu, Boer and Briton*, London, 1929.
–: *The Cape Colour Question*, London, 1927.
Marais, J. S.: *The Cape Coloured People*, London, 1939.
Millar, A. K.: *Plantagenet in South Africa: Lord Charles Somerset*, London, 1965.
Moorrees, A.: *Die Nederduitse Gereformeerde Kerk in Suid-Afrika, 1652-1873*, Cape Town, 1937.
Scholtz, J. du P.: *Die Afrikaner en sy taal, 1806-1875*, Cape Town, 1939.
Schutte, C. E. G.: *Dr. John Philip's observations regarding the Hottentots of South Africa*, Archives Year Book for S.A. History, 1940, vol. I.
Theal, G. M. (ed.): *Records of the Cape Colony*, vols. V-XXXVI, 1805-1831, London, 1897-1905.
Van Biljon, P.: *Grensbakens tussen blank en swart in Suid-Afrika*, Cape Town, 1947.
Van der Merwe, P. J.: *Die noordwaartse beweging van die Boere voor die Groot Trek (1770-1842)*, The Hague, 1937.
–: *Die Trekboer in die geskiedenis van die Kaapkolonie (1657-1842)*, Cape Town, 1938.
Van der Westhuizen, W. S.: *Onderwys onder die algemene skoolkommissie: die periode 1804-1839*, Archives Year Book for S.A. History, 1953, vol. II.
Van Wyk, A. H. du P.: *Die invloed van die Engelse skoolwese op die Kaapse skoolwese, 1806-1915*, Pretoria, 1947.
Venter, P. J.: *Landdros en heemrade (1682-1827)*, Archives Year Book for S.A. History, 1940, vol. II.

CHAPTER 9
Agar-Hamilton, J. A. I.: *The Native Policy of the Voortrekkers, 1836-1858*, Cape Town, n.d.
Becker, P.: *Path of Blood: The rise and conquests of Mzilikazi, founder of the Matabele tribe of Southern Africa*, London, 1962.
–: *Rule of fear: The life and times of Dingane King of the Zulu*, London, 1964.
Bird, J. (ed.): *The Annals of Natal, 1495-1845*, 2 vols., Cape Town, n.d.
Chase, J. C.: *The Natal Papers, 1498-1843*, 2 vols. Grahamstown, 1843.
Cory, G. E. (ed.): *The diary of the Rev. Francis Owen*, Cape Town, 1926. (V.R.S., 7.)
Cory, Preller and Blommaert: *Die Retief-Dingaan-Ooreenkoms*, Annals of the University of Stellenbosch, serie B, no. 1, May, 1924.
Dreyer, A. (ed.): *Die Kaapse Kerk en die Groot Trek*, Cape Town, 1929.
Du Plessis, A. J.: *Die Republiek Natalia*, Archives Year Book for S.A. History, 1942, vol. II.
Franken, J. L. M.: *Piet Retief se lewe in die Kolonie*, Cape Town, 1949.
Galbraith, J. S.: *Reluctant Empire: British policy on the South African frontier 1834-1854*, Berkeley and Los Angeles, 1963.
Jansen, E. G.: *Die Voortrekkers in Natal*, Cape Town, etc., 1938.
Kotze, D. J.: *Die eerste Amerikaanse sendinge onder die Matabeles*, Archives Year Book for S.A. History, 1950, vol. I.
–: *Die eerste Amerikaanse sendinge onder die Zoeloes, 1835-1838*, Archives Year Book for S.A. History, 1958, vol. I.
Krüger, D. W.: *Die weg na die see*, Archives Year Book for S.A. History, 1938, vol. I.
Le Roux, T. H. (ed.): *Dagboek van Louis Trigardt*, Pretoria, 1964.
Liebenberg, B. J.: *Nederland en die Voortrekkers van Natal*, Communications of the University of South Africa, C. 51, Pretoria, 1964.

458

MacKeurtan, G.: *The cradle days of Natal (1497-1845)*, London, 1930.
Midgley, J. F.: *The Orange River Sovereignty, 1848-1854*, Archives Year Book for S.A. History, 1949, vol. II.
Muller, C. F. J.: *Die Britse owerheid en die Groot Trek*, 2nd ed., Johannesburg, 1963.
Nathan, M.: *The Voortrekkers of South Africa*, London, 1937.
Potgieter, C. S. and Theunissen, N. H.: *Kommandant-generaal Hendrik Potgieter*, Johannesburg, n.d.
Preller, G. S.: *Andries Pretorius*, Johannesburg, 1937.
–: *Piet Retief*, Cape Town, 1930.
– (ed.): *Voortrekkermense*, 6 vols., Cape Town, etc., 1918-1938.
Punt, W. H. J.: *Louis Trichardt se laaste skof*, Pretoria, 1953.
Smith, E. W.: *The life and times of Daniel Lindley (1801-1880)*, London, 1949.
South Africa, State Archives: *Suid-Afrikaanse argiefstukke: Natal no. I: Notule van die Natalse Volksraad (volledig met alle bylaes daarby) 1838-1845*, ed. by J. H. Breytenbach, Parow, 1958.
–: *Suid-Afrikaanse argiefstukke: Transvaal nos. I en 2: Notule van die volksraad van die Suid-Afrikaanse Republiek (volledig met alle bylaes daarby) 1844-1853*, ed. by J. H. Breytenbach, Cape Town and Parow, 1949-1950.
–: *Transvaalse argiefstukke: Staatssekretaris, Inkomende Stukke, 1850-1853;* ed. by D. W. Krynauw and H. S. Pretorius, Pretoria, 1949.
–: *Voortrekkerargiefstukke, 1829-1849;* ed. by H. S. Pretorius, D. W. Krüger and C. Beyers, Pretoria, 1937.
Thom, H. B.: *Die Geloftekerk en ander studies oor die Groot Trek*, Cape Town, 1949.
–: *Die lewe van Gert Maritz*, Cape Town, 1965.
Van der Merwe, P. J.: *Die noordwaartse beweging van die Boere voor die Groot Trek (1770-1842)*, The Hague, 1937.
Van Jaarsveld, F. A.: *Die eenheidstrewe van die republikeinse Afrikaners, I: Pioniershartstogte (1836-1864)*, Johannesburg, 1951.
Van Schoor, M. C. E.: *Die nasionale en politieke bewuswording van die Afrikaner in migrasie en sy ontluiking in Transgariep tot 1854*, Archives Year Book for S.A. History, 1963, vol. II.
Walker, E. A.: *The Great Trek*, London, 1938.

CHAPTER 10

Arndt, E. H. D.: *Banking and currency development in South Africa, 1652-1927*, Cape Town, 1928.
Brookes, E. H.: *The history of Native policy in South Africa from 1830 to the present day*, Cape Town, 1924.
Campbell, W. B.: *The South African frontier 1865-1885: A study in expansion*, Archives Year Book for S.A. History, 1959, vol. I.
Cloete, B.: *Die lewe van senator F. S. Malan: president van die senaat*, Johannesburg, 1946.
Davenport, T. R. H.: *The Afrikaner Bond, 1880-1900*, Cape Town, 1960.
De Kock, W. J.: *Ekstraterritoriale vraagstukke van die Kaapse regering (1872-1885) met besondere verwysing na die Transgariep en Betsjoeanaland*, Archives Year Book for S.A. History, 1948, vol. I.
Du Toit, A. E.: *The Cape frontier: A study of Native policy with special reference to the years 1847-1866*, Archives Year Book for S.A. History, 1954, vol. I.
Du Toit, P. S.: *Onderwys in Kaapland; 'n historiese oorsig*, Pretoria, 1951.
Fryer, A. K.: *The government of the Cape of Good Hope, 1825-1854: The age of imperial reform*, Archives Year Book for S.A. History, 1964, vol. I.
Hofmeyr, J. H. and Reitz, F. W.: *Het leven van Jan Hendrik Hofmeyr (Onze Jan)*, Cape Town, 1913.
Hopkins, H. C.: *Maar een soos hy; die lewe van kommandant C. A. van Niekerk*, Cape Town, 1963.
Hunt, K. S.: *The development of municipal government in the Eastern Province of the Cape of Good Hope, with special reference to Grahamstown, 1827-1862*, Archives Year Book for S.A. History, 1961.
Joelson, A.: *South African yesterdays*, Cape Town, 1940.

Kilpin, R.: *The old Cape House, being passages from the history of a legislative assembly*, Cape Town, 1918.
–: *The romance of a colonial parliament*, London, 1938.
Lawrence, P.: *The life of John Xavier Merriman*, London, 1930.
Lewsen, P.: *The first crisis in responsible government in the Cape Colony*, Archives Year Book for S.A. History, 1942, vol. II.
– (ed.): *Selections from the correspondence of John X. Merriman, 1870-1898*, 2 vols., Cape Town, 1960-1963. (V.R.S., 41 and 44.)
Lockhart, J. G. and Woodhouse, C. M.: *Rhodes*, London, 1963.
Macquarrie, J. W. (ed.): *The reminiscences of Sir Walter Stanford*, Cape Town, 1962. (V.R.S., 43.)
Marais, J. S.: *The Cape coloured people, 1652-1937*, Johannesburg, 1957.
Martinius, M. E.: *A sketch of the development of rural education (European) in the Cape Colony, 1652-1910*, Grahamstown, 1922.
MacCracken, J. L.: *The Cape parliament 1854-1910*, Oxford, 1967.
Millin, S. G.: *Rhodes*, London, 1934.
Murray, M.: *Ships and South Africa*, Oxford, 1933.
–: *Union Castle chronicle, 1853-1953*, London, 1953.
Oberholster, J. J.: *Die anneksasie van Griekwaland-Wes*, Archives Year Book for S.A. History, 1945.
Preller, G. S.: *Scheepers se dagboek en die stryd in Kaapland (1 Okt. 1901-18 Jan. 1902)*, Cape Town, 1938.
Schnell, E. L. G.: *For men must work*, Cape Town, 1954.
Snyman, J. H.: *Rebelle-verhoor in Kaapland gedurende die Tweede Vryheidsoorlog met spesiale verwysing na die militêre howe*, Archives Year Book for S.A. History, 1962.
Strydom, C. J. S.: *Kaapland en die Tweede Vryheidsoorlog*, Cape Town, 1937.
Theal, G. M. (ed.): *Basutoland records, 1833-1868*, 4 vols., Cape Town, 1964.
Thom, H. B.: *Die geskiedenis van die skaapboerdery in Suid-Afrika*, Amsterdam, 1936.
Trapido, S.: "The origins of the Cape franchise qualifications of 1853", *The Journal of African History*, V(1), 1964.
Tylden, G.: *The rise of the Basuto*, Cape Town, 1950.
Van Biljon, P.: *Grensbakens tussen blank en swart in Suid-Afrika*, Cape Town, 1947.
Van der Poel, J.: *Railway and customs policies in South Africa, 1885-1910*, London, 1933.
Vindex: *Cecil Rhodes: his political life and speeches, 1881-1900*, London, 1900.
Walker, E. A.: *Lord de Villiers and his times; South Africa 1842-1914*, London, 1925.
–: *W. P. Schreiner: a South African*, London, 1937.

CHAPTER 11
Barnett, P. A. and Sweeney, G. W.: *Natal: the state and the citizen*, London, 1904.
Binns, C. T.: *The last Zulu king; the life and death of Cetshwayo*, London, 1963.
–: *Dinuzulu*, London, 1968.
Brookes, E. H. and Webb, C. de B.: *A history of Natal*, Pietermaritzburg, 1965.
Bulpin, T. V.: *Shaka's country, a book of Zululand*, Cape Town, 1952.
Campbell, E. D.: *The birth and development of the Natal railways*, Pietermaritzburg, 1951.
Furneaux, R.: *The Zulu war: Isandhlwana and Rorkesdrift*, London, 1963.
Gibson, J. G.: *The story of the Zulus*, London, 1911.
Hattersley, A. F.: *More annals of Natal*, Pietermaritzburg, 1936.
–: *Later annals of Natal*, London, 1938.
–: *The Natalians: further annals of Natal*, Pietermaritzburg, 1940.
–: *Portrait of a colony: the story of Natal*, Cambridge, 1940.
–: *The British settlement of Natal*, Cambridge, 1950.
Holden, W. C.: *The history of the colony of Natal*, London, 1855, reprint 1963.
Ingram, J. F.: *Natalia*, London, 1897.
Lugg, H. C.: *Historic Natal and Zululand*, Pietermaritzburg, 1949.
Morris, D. R.: *The washing of the spears*, London, 1966.
Norris-Newman, C. L.: *In Zululand with the British throughout the war of 1879*, London, 1880.

Robinson, J.: *A life time in South Africa*, London, 1900.
Rosenthal, E.: *Schooners and skyscrapers*, Cape Town, 1963.
Russell, R.: *Natal: the land and its story*, 9th ed., Pietermaritzburg, 1903.
Steenkamp, L.: *Onderwys vir blankes in Natal 1824-1940*, Pretoria, 1941.
South Africa: State Archives: *South African Archival Records, Natal Nos. II-V: Records of the Natal Executive Council 1846-1859*, 4 vols., Cape Town, 1960-1964.
Thompson, L. M.: *Indian immigration into Natal (1860-1872)*, Archives Year Book for S.A. History, 1952, vol. II.
Twentieth century impressions of Natal, London, 1906.
Van Zyl, M. C.: *Luitenant-goewerneur Martin West en die Natalse Voortrekkers, 1845-1849*, Archives Year Book for S.A. History, 1955, vol. II.
–: *Die uitbreiding van Britse gesag oor die Natalse noordgrensgebiede 1879-1897*, Archives Year Book for S.A. History, 1966, vol. I.
Young, L.: *The Native policy of Benjamin Pine in Natal, 1850-1855*, Archives Year Book for S.A. History, 1951, vol. II.

CHAPTER 12
(a) *Published Sources:*
Gouvernements Courant van den Oranje-Vrijstaat, 1857-1900.
Notulen der Verrigtingen van den Hoogedelen Volksraad, 1854-1899. (1854-1858 was published with appendices in the series S.A. Archival Sources as vols. I to III.)
Ordonnantie-boek van den Oranje-Vrijstaat, 1854-1884.
Wetboek van den Oranje-Vrijstaat, 1891.
Newspapers:
The Friend of the Free State and Bloemfontein Gazette, 1854-1900; *De Tijd*, 1862-1863, 1865-1872; *De Express—Vrijstaatsche Advertentieblad*, 1875-1900; *De Burger*, 1894-1897; *The Daily News*, 1882-1900; and *The Daily Friend*, 1896-1900.
Periodicals:
De Fakkel, 1876-1900; *O.F.S. Monthly Magazine*, 1877-1880.
(b) *Literature:*
Arndt, E. H. D.: *Banking and currency development in South Africa*, Cape Town, 1928.
Attree. E. M.: *The Closer union movements between the Orange Free State, South African Republic and Cape Colony (1838 – 1863)*, Archives Year Book for S.A. History, 1949, vol. I.
Bauman, G. en Bright, E.: *The lost republic*, London, 1940.
Beelaerts van Blokland, F. A. G.: *De Oranje-Vrijstaat*, Amsterdam, n.d.
Bester, J. J. H.: *Die ekonomiese ontwikkeling van die Oranje-Vrystaat, 1888-1899*, unpublished M.A.-thesis, U.C.O.F.S., 1946.
Boon, M. J.: *The history of the Orange Free State*, London, 1885.
Bauer, A.: *Der Oranje-Freistaat, 1854-1888*, Emsdetten, 1931.
Collins, J. A.: *The struggles of an infant state*, Cape Town, 1925.
Collins, W. W.: *Free Statia*, Bloemfontein, 1907.
Fraser, J. G.: *Episodes in my life*, Cape Town, 1922.
Gerdener, G. B. A.: *Ons kerk in die Transgariep*, Cape Town, 1934.
Grobbelaar, J. J. G.: *Die Vrystaatse-republiek en die Basoetoe-vraagstuk*, Archives Year Book for S.A. History, 1939, vol. II.
Grobbelaar, P. A.: *Die ontstaan en die ontwikkeling van die O.V.S. tot aan die einde van president Boshof se regering in 1859*, unpublished D. Phil.-thesis, Unisa, 1941.
Hofstede, H. J.: *Geschiedenis van den Oranje-Vrijstaat*, 's-Gravenhage, 1876.
Kieser, A.: *President Steyn in die krisisjare, 1896-1899*, Cape Town, 1939.
Lampbrecht, G. J.: *Ekonomiese ontwikkeling van die Vrystaat, 1870-1899*, unpublished D.Phil.-thesis, University of Stellenbosch, 1954.
Lindley, A. F.: *Adamantia*, London, 1873.
Malan, J. H.: *Die opkoms van 'n republiek*, Bloemfontein, 1929.
Muller, H. P. N.: *Oude tyden in den Oranje-Vrystaat*, Leiden, 1907.

461

Oberholster, J. J.: *Die anneksasie van Griekwaland-Wes*, Archives Year Book for S.A. History, 1945.

Oberholster, J. J. and Van Schoor, M. C. E., *et al.*: *Die Nederduitse Gereformeerde Kerk in die Oranje-Vrystaat*, Bloemfontein, 1964.

–: *President Steyn aan die woord*, Bloemfontein, 1954.

Orpen, J. M.: *Reminiscences of life in South Africa*, 2 vols., Cape Town, 1964.

Rompel, F.: *Marthinus Theunis Steyn*, Amsterdam, 1902.

Scholtz, G. D.: *Die konstitusie en die staatsinstellings van die Oranje-Vrystaat, 1854-1902*, Amsterdam, 1937.

–: *President Johannes Henricus Brand, 1823 – 1888*, Johannesburg, 1957.

Spies, F. J. du T.: *'n Nederlander in diens van die Oranje-Vrystaat*, Amsterdam, 1946.

–: *Hamelberg en die Oranje-Vrystaat*, Amsterdam, 1941.

Theron, J. D.: *Die ekonomiese en finansiele toestand in die Oranje-Vrystaat Republiek, 1854-1880*, unpublished M.A.-thesis, Unisa, 1943.

Van der Merwe, N. J.: *Marthinus Theunis Steyn, 'n lewensbeskrywing*, 2 vols., Cape Town, 1921.

Van Ittersum, W. A.: *De Vrijstaters en hun geschiedenis*, Leiden, 1900.

Van Jaarsveld, F. A.: *Die eenheidstrewe van die republikeinse Afrikaners*, vol. I, Johannesburg, 1951.

Van Oordt, J. F.: *De levensgeschiedenis van President J. H. Brand*, Cape Town, 1914.

Van Schoor, M. C. E.: Contributions to "Die Republikeinse Byvoegsel" of *Die Volksblad*, 23.2.1954.

Van Schoor, M. C. E. and Van Rooyen, J. J.: *Republieke en republikeine*, Cape Town, 1960.

Warden, Chas.: *Reminiscences of the early days of the Orange Free State*, Harrismith, 1899.

CHAPTER 13

Coetzee, D. J.: *Spoorwegontwikkeling in die Suid-Afrikaanse Republiek (1872-1899)*, Cape Town, 1940.

De Kiewiet, C. W.: *British colonial policy and the South African Republics, 1848-1872:* London, 1929.

Du Plessis, J. S.: *Die ontstaan en ontwikkeling van die amp van die staatspresident in die Z.A.R.*, Archives Year Book for S.A. History, 1955, vol. I.

Engelbrecht, S. P.: *Thomas Francois Burgers*, Pretoria, 1933.

Gross, F.: *Rhodes of Africa*, London, 1956.

Hugo, M. J.: *Die stemregvraagstuk in die Z.A. Republiek*, Archives Year Book for S.A. History, 1947.

Kotze, J. G.: *Biographical memoirs and reminiscences*, 2 vols., Cape Town, vol. I, 1934 and vol. II, n.d.

Krüger, D. W.: *Die weg na die see, of die ooskus in die Boerebeleid voor 1877, met besondere verwysing na die Portugese*, Archives Year Book for S.A. History, 1938, vol. I.

–: *Paul Kruger*, 2 vols., Johannesburg, 1961-1963.

Lockhart, J. G. and Woodhouse, C. M.: *Rhodes*, London, 1963.

Marais, J. S.: *The fall of Kruger's republic*, Oxford, 1961.

Mouton, J. A.: *Genl. Joubert in die geskiedenis van Transvaal*, Archives Year Book for S.A. History, 1957, vol. I.

Nathan, M.: *Paul Kruger, his life and times*, Durban, 1941.

Pakenham, E.: *Jameson's Raid*, London, 1960.

Pelzer, A. N.: *Geskiedenis van die Suid-Afrikaanse Republiek*, vol. I: *Wordingsjare*, Cape Town, etc., 1950.

Pieterse, D. J.: *Transvaal en Britse susereiniteit, 1881-1884*, Archives Year Book for S.A. History, 1940, vol. I.

Scholtz, G. D.: *Die oorsake van die Tweede Vryheidsoorlog, 1899 – 1902*, 2 vols., Johannesburg, 1947.

Uys, C. J.: *In the era of Shepstone*, Lovedale, 1933.

Van der Poel, J.: *The Jameson Raid*, London, etc., 1951.

Van Winter, P. J.: *Onder Kruger's Hollanders*, 2 vols., Amsterdam, 1937-1938.

Vulliamy, C. E.: *A study of imperial expansion in South Africa, 1877-1903*, London, 1938.
Wichmann, F. A. F.: *Die wordingsgeskiedenis van die Z.A. Republiek*, Archives Year Book for S.A. History, 1941, vol. II.

CHAPTER 14
Attree, E. M.: *The closer union movements between the Orange Free State, South African Republic and Cape Colony (1838-1863)*, Archives Year Book for S.A. History, 1949, vol. I.
Coetzee, D. J.: *Spoorwegontwikkeling in die Suid-Afrikaanse Republiek (1872-1899)*, Cape Town, 1940.
De Kiewiet, C. W.: *British colonial policy and the South African republics 1848-1872*, London, 1929.
—: *The imperial factor in South Africa*, Cambridge, 1937.
De Kock, W. J.: *Ekstraterritoriale vraagstukke van die Kaapse regering (1872-1885)*, Archives Year Book for S.A. History, 1948, vol. I.
Garson, N. G.: *The Swaziland question and a road to the sea 1887-1895*, Archives Year Book for S.A. History, 1957, vol. II.
Goodfellow, C. F.: *Great Britain and South African Confederation*, London, 1966.
Krüger, D. W.: *Paul Kruger*, 2 vols., Johannesburg, 1961 and 1963.
Lockhart, J. G. and Woodhouse, C. M.: *Rhodes*, London, 1963.
Marais, J. S.: *The fall of Kruger's republic*, Oxford, 1961.
Oberholster, J. J.: *Die anneksasie van Griekwaland-Wes*, Archives Year Book for S.A. History, 1945.
Rademeyer, J. I.: *Die land noord van die Limpopo in die ekspansiebeleid van die Suid-Afrikaanse Republiek*, Cape Town, 1949.
Scholtz, G. D.: *Die oorsake van die Tweede Vryheidsoorlog 1899-1902*, 2 vols., Johannesburg, 1947.
Uys, C. J.: *In the era of Shepstone*, Lovedale, 1933.
Van der Poel, J.: *Railway and customs policies in South Africa 1885-1910*, London, 1933.
Van der Poel, J.: *Basutoland as a factor in South African politics (1858-1870)*, Archives Year Book for S.A. History, 1941, vol. I.
Van Jaarsveld, F. A.: *Die eenheidstrewe van die republikeinse Afrikaners*, vol. I, Johannesburg, 1951.
—: *Die ontwikkeling van die Afrikaanse nasionale bewussyn 1868-1881*, Johannesburg, 1957.
Wilde, R. H.: *Joseph Chamberlain and the South African Republic, 1895-1899* Archives Year Book for S.A. History, 1956, vol. I.

CHAPTER 15
Amery, L. S.: *The Times history of the War in South Africa*, 7 vols., London, 1900-1909.
Anonymous: *A handbook of the Boer War*, London, 1910.
Botha, J. P.: *Die beleg van Mafeking tydens die Anglo-Boereoorlog*, unpublished D.Litt. et Phil. thesis, University of South Africa, 1967.
Breytenbach, J. H.: *Die Tweede Vryheidsoorlog, deel I: Voorspel tot die stryd, deel II: Ontplooiing van die Boere-offensief, Oktober, 1899*, Cape Town, 1948 and 1959.
Davitt, Michael: *The Boer fight for freedom*, New York, 1902.
De Wet, C. R.: *De strijd tusschen Boer en Brit*, Amsterdam and Pretoria, 1902.
Gardner, B.: *Mafeking, a Victorian Legend*, London, 1966.
Waters, W. H. H. and Du Cane, H. (translators): *The German official account of the War in South Africa: prepared in the historical section of the Great General Staff, Berlin*, 2 vols., London, 1905 – 1906.
Haferkorn, H. E.: *The South African War: a bibliography*, Washington, 1924.
Hamilton, Ian: *Listening for the drums*, London, 1944.
Hancock, W. K.: *Smuts: I. The Sanguine Years, 1870-1919*, Cambridge, 1962.
Hancock, W. K. and Van der Poel, J.: *Selections from the Smuts Papers*, vol. I, 1886-1902, Cambridge, 1902.
Headlam, Cecil (ed.): *The Milner Papers*, 2 vols., London, 1931-1933.
Hobhouse, Emily: *The brunt of the war and where it fell*, London, 1902.
Holt, Edgar: *The Boer War*, London, 1958.

Kestell, J. D. and Van Velden, D. E.: *De vredesonderhandelingen tusschen Boer en Brit in Zuid-Afrika*, Pretoria, 1909.
Leyds, W. J. (ed.): *Correspondentie (1899-1902)*, 8 vols., The Hague, 1919-1934.
Maurice, J. Frederick: *History of the war in South Africa 1899-1902; compiled by direction of H. M. Government*, 4 vols. text and 4 vols. maps and sketches, London, 1906-1910.
Nierstrasz, P. A.: *Der Süd-Afrikanische Krieg*, manuscript, State Archives, Pretoria.
Otto, J. C.: *Die konsentrasiekampe*, Cape Town, 1954.
Pemberton, W. B.: *Battles of the Boer War*, London, 1964.
Scholtz, G. D.: *Europa en die Tweede Vryheidsoorlog*, Johannesburg, 1939.
Strydom, C. J.: *Kaapland en die Tweede Vryheidsoorlog*, Cape Town, 1947.
Symons, Julian: *Buller's campaign*, London, 1963.
Van der Merwe, N. J.: *Marthinus Theunis Steyn: 'n lewensbeskrywing*, 2 vols., Cape Town, 1921.
Van Zijl, P. H. S.: *Die helde-album van ons vryheidstryd*, Johannesburg, 1944.

CHAPTER 16
Brand, R. H.: *The Union of South Africa*, Oxford, 1909.
Brookes, E. H. and Webb, C. de B.: *A history of Natal*, Pietermaritzburg, 1965.
Buchan, J.: *Memory hold-the-door*, London, 1940.
Cloete, B.: *Die lewe van senator F. S. Malan: president van die senaat*, Johannesburg, 1946.
Coetzee, J. A.: *Politieke groepering in die wording van die Afrikanernasie*, Johannesburg, 1941.
Colvin, I.: *The life of Jameson*, 2 vols., London, 1922.
Curtis, L.: *With Milner in South Africa*, Oxford, 1951.
Davenport, T. R. H.: *The Afrikaner Bond: the history of a South African political party*, Cape Town, 1966.
Denoon, D. J. N.: "The Transvaal Labour Crisis, 1901-1906", *The Journal of African History*, VIII (3), 1967.
Engelenburg, F. V.: *General Louis Botha*, Pretoria, 1929.
Eybers, G. W., (ed.): *Select constitutional documents illustrating South African History 1795-1910*, London, 1918.
Fitzpatrick, J. P.: *South African memories*, London, 1932.
Garson, N. G.: " 'Het Volk': The Botha-Smuts party in the Transvaal, 1904-1911", *The Historical Journal*, IX (1), 1966.
Halperin, V.: *Lord Milner and the empire: the evolution of British imperialism*, London, 1952.
Hancock, W. K.: *Smuts: I. The sanguine years, 1870-1919*, Cambridge, 1962.
Hancock, W. K. and Van der Poel, J. (eds.): *Selections from the Smuts Papers*, vol. 2, Cambridge, 1966.
Headlam, C. (ed.): *The Milner papers: South Africa 1899-1905*, vol. 2, London, 1933.
Krüger, D. W.: *The age of the generals: a short political history of the Union of South Africa 1910-1948*, Johannesburg, 1961.
Laurence, P.: *The life of John Xavier Merriman*, London, 1930.
Le May, G. H. L.: *British supremacy in South Africa, 1899-1907*, Oxford, 1965.
Mansergh, N.: *South Africa, 1906-1961: the price of magnanimity*, London, 1962.
Millin, S. G.: *General Smuts*, 2 vols., London, 1936.
Newton, A. P.: *Select documents relating to the unification of South Africa*, 2 vols., London, 1924.
Preller, J. F. (ed.): *Die konvensie-dagboek van sy edelagbare Francois Stephanus Malan, 1908-1909*, Cape Town, 1951 (V.R.S., 32.)
Pyrah, G. B.: *Imperial policy and South Africa, 1902-1910*, Oxford, 1955.
Reeves, J. A.: *Chinese labour policy in South Africa, 1901-1910*, unpublished M.A.-thesis, U. W., 1955.
Spoelstra, B.: *Die bewindsaanvaarding van die Botha regering oor Transvaal as selfregerende Britse kolonie in 1907*, Archives Year Book for S.A. History, 1953, vol. II.
Stuart, J.: *A history of the Zulu rebellion and Dinuzulu's arrest, trial and expatriation*, London, 1913.
Thompson, L. M.: *The unification of South Africa, 1902-1910*, Oxford, 1960.
Trollip, A. E. G.: *The first phase of Hertzogism*, unpublished M.A.-thesis, U.W., 1947.
464

Van der Merwe, N. J.: *Marthinus Theunis Steyn: 'n lewensbeskrywing*, 2 vols., Cape Town, 1921.
Vermooten, F.: *Transvaal en die totstandkoming van die Unie van Suid-Afrika, 1906-1910*, Archives Year Book for S.A. History, 1957, vol. II.
Walker, E. A.: *Lord de Villiers and his times: South Africa 1842-1914*, London, 1925.
–: *W. P. Schreiner: a South African*, London, 1937.
Walton, E. H.: *The inner history of the National Convention*, Cape Town, 1912.
Williams, B. (ed.): *The Selborne Memorandum: a review of the mutual relations of the British South African colonies in 1907*, Oxford, 1925.
Worsfold, W. B.: *The reconstruction of the new colonies under Lord Milner*, 2 vols., London, 1913.
Wrench, J. F.: *Alfred Lord Milner: the man of no illusions, 1854-1925*, London, 1958.

CHAPTERS 17-18
Carter, Gwendolen, M.: *The politics of inequality: South Africa since 1948*, 3rd ed., London, 1962.
Cope, John: *South Africa*, London, 1965.
Crafford, F. S.: *Jan Smuts; a biography*, London, 1946.
Creswell, Margaret: *An epoch of the political history of South Africa in the life of Frederic Hugh Page Creswell*, Cape Town, n.d.
Feit, Edward: *African opposition in South Africa; the failure of passive resistance*, Stanford, 1967.
Hancock, W. K.: *Smuts*, 2 vols., Cambridge, 1962 and 1968.
–: *Survey of British commonwealth affairs*, vol. I: *Problems of nationality, 1918-1936*, vol. II, *Problems of economic policy 1918-1939*, London, 1937 and 1942.
Herd, Norman: *1922: the revolt on the Rand*, Johannesburg, 1966.
Krüger, D. W.: *The age of the generals; a short political history of the Union of South Africa, 1910-1948*, 2nd ed., Johannesburg, 1961.
– (ed.): *South African parties and policies 1910-1960; a select source book*, Cape Town, 1960.
Kuper, Leo: *Passive resistance in South Africa*, New Haven, 1960.
Long, B. K.: *In Smuts's camp*, London, 1945.
Louw, Louis (ed.): *Dawie 1946-1964; 'n bloemlesing uit die geskrifte van 'Die Burger' se politieke kommentator*, Cape Town, 1965.
Malan, D. F.: *Afrikaner-volkseenheid en my ervarings op die pad daarheen*, 3rd ed., Cape Town, 1961.
Malan, M. P. A.: *Die Nasionale Party van Suid-Afrika; sy stryd en prestasies 1914-1964*, Elsiesrivier, 1964.
Neame, L. E.: *General Hertzog; prime minister of the Union of South Africa since 1924*, London, 1930.
–: *The history of apartheid; the story of the colour bar in South Africa*, London, 1962.
Official Year Book of the Union of South Africa, No. 23, 1946: Chapter XXIX: "The Second World War".
Pelzer, A. N. (ed.): *Verwoerd speaks; speeches 1948 – 1966*, Johannesburg, 1966.
Pirow, Oswald: *James Barry Munnik Hertzog*, Cape Town, n.d.
Roberts, M. and Trollip, A. E. G.: *The South African opposition 1939-1945; an essay in contemporary history*, Cape Town, 1947.
Roux, Edward: *Time longer than rope: a history of the black man's struggle for freedom in South Africa*, 2nd ed., Madison, 1964.
Sachs, E. S.: *The choice before South Africa*, London, 1952.
Scholtz, G. D.: *Die rebellie, 1914-1915*, Johannesburg, 1942.
–: *Dr. Nicolaas Johannes van der Merwe, 1888-1940*, Johannesburg, 1944.
–: *Die Republiek van Suid-Afrika en die nuwe wereld*, Johannesburg, 1962.
Tatz, C. M.: *Shadow and substance in South Africa; a study in land and franchise policies affecting Africans, 1910-1960*, Pietermaritzburg, 1962.
Van den Heever, C. M.: *General J. B. M. Hertzog*, Johannesburg, 1946.
Walker, Ivan L. and Weinbren, Ben: *2000 casualties; a history of the trade unions and the labour movement in the Union of South Africa*, Johannesburg, 1961.

CHAPTER 19

Axelson, E. A. (ed.): *South African explorers*, London, etc., 1954.
Ballinger, R. B.: *South West Africa: the case against the Union*, Johannesburg, 1961.
Carter, G. M. (ed.): *Five African states responses to diversity*, London, 1964.
Davey, A. M.: *The Bondelzwarts affair: a study of the repercussions, 1922-1959*, Pretoria, 1961.
Duffy, J.: *Portuguese Africa*, Harvard, 1959.
Frankel, S. H.: *Capital investment in Africa: its course and effects*, London, etc., 1938.
Gann, L. H.: *The birth of a plural society*, Manchester, 1958.
Giniewski, P.: *Die stryd om Suidwes-Afrika*, Cape Town, 1966.
Goldblatt, I.: *The conflict between the United Nations Organisation and the Union of South Africa in regard to South West Africa*, Windhoek, 1960.
–: *The mandated territory of South West Africa in relation to the United Nations*, Windhoek, 1961.
Gregory, T. E.: *Ernest Oppenheimer and the economic development of Southern Africa*, Cape Town, etc., 1962.
Hailey, W. M.: *The Republic of South Africa and the high commission territories*, London, etc., 1963.
Henry, J. A.: *The first hundred years of the Standard Bank*, London, etc., 1963.
Oliver, R. and Fage, J.: *A short history of Africa*, London, 1962.
Pelzer, A. N. (ed.): *Verwoerd speaks; speeches 1948-1966*, Johannesburg, 1966.
Perham, M. F. and Curtis, L.: *The protectorates of South Africa; the question of their transfer to the Union*, London, 1935.
Rademeyer, J. I.: *Die land noord van die Limpopo in die ekspansiebeleid van die Suid-Afrikaanse Republiek*, Cape Town, etc., 1949.
Scholtz, G. D.: *Het die Afrikaanse volk 'n toekoms?* Johannesburg, 1954.
–: *Die Republiek van Suid-Afrika in die Nuwe Wêreld*, Johannesburg, 1962.
–: *'n Swart Suid-Afrika?* Cape Town, 1964.
Smuts, J. C.: *Africa and some world problems*, Oxford, 1930.
Tabler, E. C.: *The far interior: chronicles of pioneering in the Matabele and Mashona countries 1847-1879*, Cape Town, etc., 1955.
Trümpelmann, G. P. J.: *Die Boer in Suidwes-Afrika*, Archives Year Book for S.A. History, 1948, vol. II.
Wellington, J. H.: *South West Africa and its human issues*, Oxford, 1967.
Wessels, L. H.: *Die Mandaat vir Suidwes-Afrika*, The Hague, 1938.
Wills, A. J.: *An introduction to the history of Central Africa*, London, 1964.
Worthington, E. B.: *Science in the development of Africa*, London, 1958.
Young, K.: *Rhodesia and Independence*, London, 1967.

CHAPTER 20

Andrews, H. T., *et al.*: *South Africa in the sixties: a socio-economic survey*, Cape Town, 1962.
Anonymous: "Die eerste vyf jaar van die Republiek van Suid-Afrika", *Tegniek*, 18(5), May, 1966, pp. 1 and 4.
–: "Communist-backed Terrorist onslaught (on) Southern Africa", *Africa Institute Bulletin*, VI(5), June, 1968, pp. 130-148.
Austin, D.: *Britain and South Africa*, Oxford, 1966. Royal Institute of International Affairs.
Ballinger, R. B.: *South Africa and the United Nations: myth and reality*, Johannesburg, 1963. (South African Institute of International Affairs, University of the Witwatersrand).
Butler, F. G.: *The republic and the arts*, Johannesburg, 1964. (Lecture 7: The Republic in a changing world.)
Davis, J. A. and Baker, J. K. (eds.): *Southern Africa in transition*, New York, 1966.
Hance, W. A. (ed.) with others: *Southern Africa and the United States*, New York and London, 1968. (Columbia University Press.)
Hancock, Sir K.: *Are there South Africans?* Johannesburg, 1966. (The Alfred and Winifred Hoernle Memorial Lecture, 1966.)
Horwitz, R.: *The political economy of South Africa*, London, 1967.
Houghton, D. Hobart: *The South African economy*, Cape Town, 1964.

Irvine, K.: "Southern Africa: the White fortress" in *Current History*, 54(318), February, 1968, pp. 72-77, 111-112.

Kuschke, G. S. J.: "Die Jong Nywerheidsreus", *Die Huisgenoot*, 20 May, 1966, pp. 98-103.

Lombard, J. A. and Stadler, J. J.: *Die ekonomiese stelsel van Suid-Afrika*, Cape Town, 1967.

Munger, E. S.: *Afrikaner and African nationalism: South African parallels and parameters*, Oxford, 1967. (Institute of Race Relations.)

Norval, A. J.: *A quarter of a century of industrial progress in South Africa*, Cape Town, etc., 1962.

Pelzer, A. N. (ed.): *Verwoerd speaks; speeches 1948-1966*, Johannesburg, 1966.

Republic of South Africa, Bureau of Statistics: *Statistical Year Book* (1965-1966), Pretoria, 1965 and 1966.

Republic of South Africa, Bureau of Statistics: *Report no. 286: Statistics of Immigrants and Emigrants 1924-1964*, Pretoria, 1965.

Sabikhi, V.: "The South African scene", *Africa Quarterly*, VI(3), Oct.-Dec., 1966, pp. 206-217.

Scholtz, J. J. J.: *Die Moord op dr. Verwoerd*, Cape Town, etc., 1967.

Smit, P.: "Bantu homelands in South Africa" in *Africa Institute Bulletin*, IV(11), Nov.-Dec., 1966, pp. 249-255.

South Africa Today, Johannesburg, 1968.

Spence, J. E.: *Republic under pressure: a study of South African foreign policy*, Oxford, 1965.

Stoop, G. (ed.): "Feesuitgawe: Die wetenskap in die Republiek", *Scientiae* 7(5), May, 1966, pp. 1-28.

Suid-Afrikaanse Panorama, II(6), June, 1966, pp. 1-9 and 38-41.

Thompson, L. M.: *Politics in the Republic of South Africa*, Boston, 1966. (The Little Brown Series in Comparative Politics.)

Van der Walt, A. J. H.: "South Africa: Five years after", *Africa Institute Bulletin*, IV(5), May, 1966, pp. 91-98.

Van Heerden, W.: "Die Verwoerd-era – en daarna", in *Standpunte*, XX(3), Feb., 1967 (New Series 69), pp. 1-4.

Van Jaarsveld, F. A. and Scholtz, G. D. (eds.): *Die Republiek van Suid-Afrika: agtergrond, ontstaan en toekoms*, Johannesburg, 1966.

Vermaak C.: *Braam Fischer: the man with two faces*, Johannesburg, 1966.

Index